Strategic Information Management

Today, there are few in senior management positions who can afford to ignore modern information technology, and few individuals who would prefer to be without it. Modern IT is key to organizational performance; yet we often assume the benefits will occur without forethought or effort. As managerial tasks become more complex, so the nature of the required information systems changes – from structured, routine support to ad hoc, unstructured, complex enquiries at the highest levels of management. If taken for granted, serious implications can arise for organizations.

This fifth edition of *Strategic Information Management* has been brought fully up to date with recent developments in the management of information systems, including digital transformation strategy, the issues surrounding big data and algorithmic decision-making. The book provides a rich source of material reflecting recent thinking on the key issues facing executives, drawing from a wide range of contemporary articles written by leading experts in North America, Europe and Australia. Combining theory with practice, each section is fully introduced, includes further reading and questions for further discussion.

Designed for MBA, master's level students, and advanced undergraduate students taking courses in information systems management, it also provides a wealth of information and references for researchers.

Robert D. Galliers is the University Distinguished Professor Emeritus, formerly Provost, at Bentley University, USA; Professor Emeritus, formerly Dean, at Warwick Business School and Honorary Visiting Professor at Loughborough University, UK. Previously, he was a Professor and Research Director at the London School of Economics and Head of the School of Information Systems at Curtin University, Australia.

Dorothy E. Leidner is the Randall W. and Sandra Ferguson Professor of Information Systems at Baylor University, USA; a Senior Research Fellow at Lund University, Sweden, and a Visiting Professor at the University of Mannheim, Germany. Previously she was an Associate Professor at INSEAD, France and held Visiting Professorships at ITESM, Mexico and the University of Caen, France.

Boyka Simeonova is an Assistant Professor at Loughborough University, the Director of the Knowledge and the Digital Economy Network, the Deputy Director of the Centre for Information Management, and a Fellow of the Higher Education Academy, UK.

"This fifth edition of *Strategic Information Management* updates and extends a unique selection of theories and valuable practice insights, established in the previous editions, and offers a roadmap for executives navigating in the digital landscape and coping with the digitization challenges associated with organizational transformation. The book has the right balance of theoretical frameworks and practical insights. Taken together, the book reflects recent thinking regarding many of the key issues facing executives in getting the most out of their investments in information technology and digitalization initiatives, highlighting the complex strategy, organizational and governance issues involved."

– IOANNA CONSTANTIOU, Copenhagen Business School, Denmark

"I'm pleased the editors of *Strategic Information Management* have produced this fifth edition, which represents a major overhaul, including online supporting materials not available with prior editions. Particularly valuable is the amplification of theory in this edition – not theory for theory's sake, but rather practice-guiding theory; the implication being that we are all researchers and that complex matters demand research and unique approaches and solutions. I strongly encourage students and practitioners to assume an evidence-based practice perspective when reading and reflecting on these writings which, combined, provide a much-needed stimulus for critical thinking on these complex matters in what are challenging times."

– GUY GABLE, Queensland University of Technology, Australia

"The fifth edition of *Strategic Information Management* has great value in providing directions for practitioners and scholars towards an understanding of the strategic importance and managerial challenges of digital transformation in today's organizations. With inputs from international scholars, the book offers really useful management frameworks and principles to help in understanding how organizations and industries are transformed by disruptive digital technologies."

– CAROL HSU, Tongji University, China

"This fifth edition of *Strategic Information Management* updates and strengthens what has long served as a vehicle through which current and future executives obtain a foundational understanding as well as pragmatic insights regarding a host of strategic and managerial issues associated with the digital transformation of organizations. As with the earlier editions, the authors refuse to fall into the too-often-taken route of providing readers with a handbook offering 'one-size-fits-all' practices and procedures – solutions which ultimately fail to align with the situations faced by readers. Instead, the editors successfully provide readers with exposures to critical themes and frameworks and to illustrations of how some of our brightest executives are applying these in addressing digitalization initiatives and challenges – providing readers with the capability to formulate workable solutions to many, if not most, of the situations they face in their digital transformation efforts."

– ROBERT W. ZMUD, University of Oklahoma, USA

Strategic Information Management

Theory and Practice

Fifth Edition

Edited by

**Robert D. Galliers, Dorothy E. Leidner and
Boyka Simeonova**

Routledge
Taylor & Francis Group

NEW YORK AND LONDON

Fifth edition published 2020
by Routledge
52 Vanderbilt Avenue, New York, NY 10017

and by Routledge
2 Park Square, Milton Park, Abingdon, Oxon, OX14 4RN

Routledge is an imprint of the Taylor & Francis Group, an informa business

© 2020 selection and editorial matter, Robert D. Galliers, Dorothy E. Leidner
and Boyka Simeonova; individual chapters, the contributors

The right of the Robert D. Galliers, Dorothy E. Leidner and Boyka Simeonova to
be identified as the authors of the editorial material, and of the authors for their
individual chapters, has been asserted in accordance with sections 77 and 78 of
the Copyright, Designs and Patents Act 1988.

First edition published by Butterworth-Heinemann 1994
Fourth edition published by Routledge 2009

Library of Congress Cataloging-in-Publication Data
A catalog record has been requested for this book

ISBN: 978-0-367-25250-2 (hbk)
ISBN: 978-0-367-25251-9 (pbk)
ISBN: 978-0-429-28679-7 (ebk)

Typeset in Perpetua
by Swales & Willis, Exeter, Devon, UK

Contents

Preface

This is the fifth edition of *Strategic Information Management*. First published in 1994, each of the editions deals with the *challenges and strategies in managing information systems*, as indicated by the subtitle of the first four editions. We have changed the title of this edition slightly to *Strategic Information Management: Theory and Practice* to better reflect the content of this edition of the book and to reinforce Kurt Lewin's (1943) maxim that, 'There's nothing as practical as a good theory'. As before, we aim to present the many complex and inter-related issues confronting those in management positions concerned with the management of information systems with their organizations.

As previously, the primary audiences are MBA or other master's level students and senior undergraduate students taking courses in the management, organizational and/or strategic implications of business information systems. Students embarking on research in these areas should also find the book of help in providing a rich source of material that reflects recent thinking regarding many of the key issues facing executives in getting the most out of investments in information technology – whether these issues relate to strategy processes or organizational and governance issues. For research students in particular, prior editions of the book can also be referred to with a view to obtaining a contemporaneous understanding of such issues and concerns over the period of the last quarter century.

In line with this latter point, we have organized this edition of *Strategic Information Management* into four sections; the first of which provides something of an historical foundation to our treatment of information systems strategy, including the processes and practices of information systems strategizing. We then move on to more recent treatments of digital strategy and organizational transformation in Part II, while Part III considers organizational and governance issues associated with an organization's information technology function. We end, in Part IV, with a

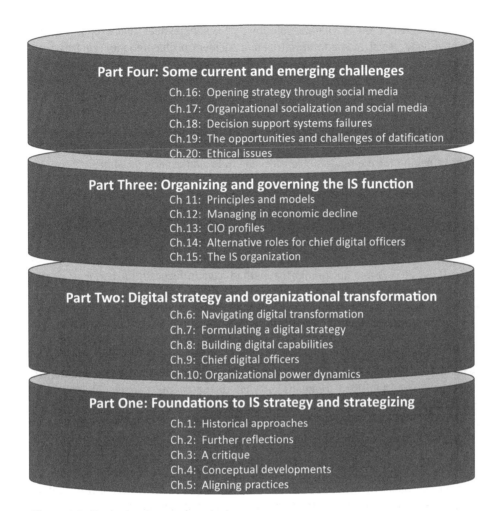

Part Four: Some current and emerging challenges

Ch.16: Opening strategy through social media
Ch.17: Organizational socialization and social media
Ch.18: Decision support systems failures
Ch.19: The opportunities and challenges of datification
Ch.20: Ethical issues

Part Three: Organizing and governing the IS function

Ch 11: Principles and models
Ch.12: Managing in economic decline
Ch.13: CIO profiles
Ch.14: Alternative roles for chief digital officers
Ch.15: The IS organization

Part Two: Digital strategy and organizational transformation

Ch.6: Navigating digital transformation
Ch.7: Formulating a digital strategy
Ch.8: Building digital capabilities
Ch.9: Chief digital officers
Ch.10: Organizational power dynamics

Part One: Foundations to IS strategy and strategizing

Ch.1: Historical approaches
Ch.2: Further reflections
Ch.3: A critique
Ch.4: Conceptual developments
Ch.5: Aligning practices

Figure 0.1 Book structure and contents

consideration of some of the current and emerging challenges. The book's structure and content are summarized in Figure 0.1 above.

As with previous editions of *Strategic Information Management*, the book is structured in such a way as to enable readers *either* to follow each chapter in the sequence in which they are presented *or* to 'dip into' the book as they wish, depending on their needs or interests at the time. Additionally, and this may be of particular interest to those who wish to consider historical developments, readings taken from previous editions of the book are recommended (cf. Galliers and Baker, 1994; Galliers and Leidner, 2003, 2009; Galliers et al., 1999).

In many instances, the approach taken is to challenge taken-for-granted notions that are often to be found in the mainstream or popular literature; you won't find an assumed 'best practice' solution, for example (cf. Swan et al., 1999; Wagner and Newell, 2004; Wagner et al., 2006). The subject matter of strategic information management is too complex for simple 'solutions'. The American columnist H.L. Mencken was one of the most quoted thinkers of the first half of the twentieth century for good reason. One famous quotation of his is apposite in this context: 'For every complex problem, there is a simple solution that is simple, neat, and wrong.' Putting it another way, the strategic information management *problematique*[1] requires critical, reflexive thinking that takes account of the many aspects of the topic, considering them as mutually constituted and very much inter-related. We shall therefore endeavor to refer to related chapters when considering any particular topic.

The individual chapters included in each part of the book will be briefly summarized in the Introduction to each part, with related readings introduced. In preparing to study each chapter, however – and this applies in particular for research students – it might be helpful for the reader to consider the following generic questions:

- The research question: what is the major research question being posed and why is it important?
- The assumptions: what are some of the primary assumptions guiding the study, and are these valid in your context?
- The method: what method was used to investigate the questions (e.g., case study, survey) and how might the method have influenced, for better or worse, the results (cf. Galliers et al., 2006)?
- The results: what were the major findings; what was new, interesting or unexpected, and what are the implications for practice?

In addition, and following each chapter, we offer some questions that could serve as points of departure/debate for classroom discussion or individual reflection. We also recommend additional readings relevant to the chapters in the Introductions to each Part. By doing so, we hope to have covered some of the important aspects of each topic, while at the same time providing references to other important work. Additionally, presentation slides for each chapter are available online.

We hope that, by adding new material in this edition, dealing with theoretical considerations as well as practical implications and examples, we have been able to build on the foundations provided in the first four editions of *Strategic Information Management*. While our understanding – both theoretical and practical – of the topic areas has developed over the years since the first edition was published, there are clearly many complex issues and persistent problems requiring our attention if information systems really are to contribute to organizational success and business value. We trust that this new edition will contribute to enhanced understanding.

Robert D. Galliers, Dorothy E. Leidner and Boyka Simeonova

References

Galliers, R.D., Baker, B.S.H. (eds.) (1994). *Strategic Information Management: Challenges and Strategies in Managing Information Systems*, Oxford: Butterworth-Heinemann.

Galliers, R.D., Leidner, D.E. (eds.) (2003). *Strategic Information Management: Challenges and Strategies in Managing Information Systems*, 3rd edition, Oxford: Butterworth-Heinemann.

Galliers, R.D., Leidner, D.E. (eds.) (2009). *Strategic Information Management: Challenges and Strategies in Managing Information Systems*, 4th edition, New York: Routledge.

Galliers, R.D., Leidner, D.E., Baker, B.S.H. (eds.) (1999). *Strategic Information Management: Challenges and Strategies in Managing Information Systems*, 2nd edition, Oxford: Butterworth-Heinemann.

Galliers, R.D., Markus, M.L., Newell, S. (eds.) (2006). *Exploring Information Systems Research Approaches: Readings and Reflections*, London & New York: Routledge.

Lewin, K. (1943). Psychology and the process of group living. *Journal of Social Psychology*, 17, 113–131.

Swan, J., Newell, S., Robertson, M. (1999). The illusion of 'best practice' in information systems for operations management, *European Journal of Information Systems*, 8(4), 284–293.

Wagner, E.L., Newell, S. (2004). 'Best' for whom? The tension between 'best practice' ERP packages and diverse epistemic cultures in a university context, *The Journal of Strategic Information Systems*, 13(4), 305–328.

Wagner, E.L., Scott, S.V., Galliers, R.D. (2006). The creation of 'best practice' software: myth, reality and ethics, *Information & Organization*, 16(3), 251–275.

Note

1   A nexus of inter-related problems.

Acknowledgments

We gratefully acknowledge all the many contributors to this book, not least the authors of the chapters and the respective publishers who have so willingly given their permission to use their material in this way. Special mention should be made to Alexander Barsi Lopes for his willing support in enabling the use of materials first published in *MIS Quarterly Executive*; to Laura Mesquita and Laura Pritchard of Elsevier in doing likewise for materials first published in *The Journal of Strategic Information Systems* and *Long Range Planning*; to Mary Bergin-Cartwright for materials first published by *Oxford University Press*; and to Jan DeGross for the chapter first published in *MIS Quarterly*.

We also wish to acknowledge Jess Harrison, Sophia Levine and Emmie Shand of Routledge for all their encouragement and support at various times during the book's development in bringing this fifth edition of *Strategic Information Management* to publication.

Bob Galliers, Dorothy Leidner and Boyka Simeonova

The editors and the publisher would like to thank the following for permission to reprint:

- *MIS Quarterly*

Chapter 1: M.J. Earl, 1993. Experiences in information systems planning (17:1), 1–24.

- *Oxford University Press*

Chapter 2: R.D. Galliers, 2004. Reflections on information systems strategizing, in *Social Study of Information and Communication Technology: Innovation, Actors, and Contexts*, C. Avgerou, C. Ciborra & F. Land, eds., 231–262.

Chapter 3: R.D. Galliers, 2007. On confronting some of the common myths of IS strategy discourse, in *Oxford Handbook of Information and Communication Technologies*, R. Mansell, C. Avgerou, S. Quah & R. Silverstone, eds., 225–243.

Chapter 4: R.D. Galliers, 2011. Further developments in information systems strategizing: unpacking the concept, in *Oxford Handbook of Management Information Systems: Critical Perspectives and New Directions*, R.D. Galliers & W. Currie, eds., 329–345.

- *SAGE Publishing*

Chapter 5: A. Karpovsky & R.D. Galliers, 2015. Aligning in Practice: from current cases to a new agenda, *Journal of Information Technology*, (30:2), 136–160.

- *MIS Quarterly Executive*

Chapter 6: I.M. Sebastian, J.W. Ross, C. Beath, M. Mocker, K.G. Moloney & N.O. Fonstad, 2017. How Big Old Companies Navigate Digital Transformation (16:3).

Chapter 7: T. Hess, C. Matt, A. Benlian & F.Wiesböck, 2016. Options for Formulating a Digital Transformation Strategy, (15:2).

- *MIS Quarterly Executive and the LEGO Group*

Chapter 8: O. El Sawy, H. Amsinck, P. Kræmmergaard, & A. L. Vinther, 2016. How LEGO Built the Foundations and Enterprise Capabilities for Digital Leadership (15:2).

The LEGO co-authors of the *MISQE* paper, Henrik Amsinck and Anders Lerbech Vinther, thank the following senior executives at the LEGO Group for their insights and help in writing the article, Jakob Damkilde, Conny Kalcher and Eric Wolfe, and also Charlotte Simonsen of LEGO Corporate Communications for her thoughtful comments on the initial draft.

- *MIS Quarterly Executive*

Chapter 9: A. Singh & T. Hess, 2017. How Chief Digital Officers Promote the Digital Transformation of their Companies (16:1).

- *The authors*

Chapter 10: B. Simeonova, R.D. Galliers, & S. Karanasios, 2020. Strategic Information Systems and Organizational Power Dynamics (unpublished manuscript).

- *MIS Quarterly Executive*

Chapter 11: R.S. Agarwal & V. Sambamurthy, 2002. Principles and Models for Organizing the IT Function (1:1).

Chapter 12: D.E. Leidner, R.C. Beatty & J.M. Mackay, 2003. How CIOs Manage IT During Economic Decline: Surviving and Thriving Amid Uncertainty (2:1).

Chapter 13: D.S. Preston, D.E. Leidner & D. Chen, 2008. CIO Leadership Profiles: Implications of Matching CIO Authority and Leadership Capability on IT Impact (7:2).

Chapter 14: S. Tumbas, N. Berente & J. vom Brocke, 2017. Three Types of Chief Digital Officers and the Reasons Organizations Adopt the Role (16:2).

- *John Wiley and Sons*

Chapter 15: J. Peppard, 2018. Rethinking the concept of the IS organization, *Information Systems Journal* (28:1), 76–103.

- *Elsevier*

Chapter 16: J. Baptista, A. Wilson, R.D. Galliers & S. Bynghall, 2017. Social media and the emergence of *reflexiveness* as a new capability for open strategy, *Long Range Planning*, (50:3), 322–336.

Chapter 17: D.E. Leidner, E. Gonzalez & H. Koch, 2018. An Affordance Perspective of Social Media and Organizational Socialization, *The Journal of Strategic Information Systems* (27:2), 117–138.

Chapter 18: P. Aversa, L. Cabantous & S. Haefliger, 2018. When Decision Support Systems fail: Insights for Strategic Information Systems from Formula 1, *The Journal of Strategic Information Systems*, (27:3), 221–236.

Chapter 19: S. Newell & M. Marabelli, 2015. Strategic opportunities (and challenges) of algorithmic decision-making: a call for action on the long-term societal effects of 'datification', *The Journal of Strategic Information Systems*, (24:1), 2–14.

- *MIS Quarterly Executive*

Chapter 20: K.E. Martin, 2015. Ethical Issues in the Big Data Industry (14:2).

PART I

Foundations to Information Systems Strategy and Strategizing

WE BEGIN OUR DISCUSSION of key aspects of strategic information management by focusing on information systems (IS) planning and strategy making – the bottom layer of Figure P1.1 below. We start with something of an historical focus on IS planning approaches used by organizations and then reflect and provide a critique on some of the popular, taken-for-granted notions before considering in greater depth key conceptual underpinnings that arise from what we have learned on the topic over the years. We end with a chapter with a consideration of the practices concerned with aligning IS considerations within organizational strategies. Thus, as with the remainder of the book, we attempt to combine theory with practice. Additionally, we provide something of a snapshot of our thinking on IS strategizing over two decades and thereby provide a foundation for more recent treatments of the subject matter in subsequent chapters.

In our search for articles that provide the necessary foundations, we decided to retain two of the chapters from the fourth edition of *Strategic Information Management* – Chapters 2 and 3 – while introducing new material that provides both a critical reflection on the past and a useful segue into the current and future. Thus, in Part I of the book, we set out to provide greater clarity to what is a key aspect of strategic information management, as well as to highlight the results of more recent thinking and practice.

As already noted, Chapter 1 is retained from the fourth edition of the book. It is written by Michael Earl and considers different approaches to strategic IS planning that had been developed and used by organizations in the 1990s. Based on a study of a number of companies' actual experiences in IS planning, Earl found five different 'styles' of planning approach, ranging, *inter alia*, from those that were clearly business strategy-driven, to those that were very much focused on technological considerations, to those that focused on the organization

Figure P1.1 The focus of Part I: Foundations to Information Systems Strategy and Strategizing

of IS services. The framework that emerges from his study may be used as a diagnostic tool to analyze and evaluate an organization's experience with, and capability in, IS strategizing (cf. Peppard and Ward, 2004).

Chapter 2, by Bob Galliers, is also retained from the fourth edition. In it, Galliers reflects on developments in IS strategy – or more particularly on the processes of IS strategizing over the years, but also on the almost total disregard for IS in the mainstream strategic management and organizational behavior literature for much of the last decade of the 20th century and the early years of the 21st. This is beginning to change thanks to the efforts of those who are concerned with the *opening* of strategy and the use of IT in this regard (e.g., Morton et al., 2019; Seidl et al., 2019; Whittington, 2014). See also Chapters 16 and 17 for considerations of the role and use of social media in this regard.

As noted in the Chapter 2, the reflections are provided against the backdrop of something of a hiatus in research on the topic in the IS literature at the time. The absence of research in this topic area was somewhat surprising given that IS strategy was becoming increasingly important, with flexible information infrastructures being a requirement for any organization dealing with the kind of turbulent and dynamic competitive environments they are facing. Add to this the emergence of algorithmic decision-making – so-called 'big data' – and the use of artificial intelligence; it is of no surprise that the topic is regaining its preeminent place in the IS universe (cf. Günther et al., 2017). The strategic opportunities and associated challenges concerning algorithmic decision-making are topics covered extensively in Chapter 19.

Chapter 3 is also written by Galliers; as the title of the chapter suggests, the focus is on confronting some of the common myths associated with topics in strategic IS that have been prevalent over the past 30 years or so. The topics considered in this chapter are the competitive advantage that can supposedly be derived from IT; knowledge management systems, and issues associated with business – IT alignment. In line with our treatment of the topic of strategic information management throughout the book, the chapter focuses more on the processes of strategizing than on the outcome of the process – the strategy itself. As noted in the introduction to the chapter, Galliers argues that benefit is to be gained from a more inclusive, exploratory approach to strategizing (cf. Galliers, 1993). This perspective is set against the common view, expressed widely at various times over the period, which is concerned more with the exploitation of IT for organizational transformation. Note, for example, the tenor of Hammer's *HBR* article (Hammer, 1990). The arguments outlined in Chapter 3 are very much in line with the notion of ambidexterity originally brought to prominence by Michael Tushman (e.g., Tushman and O'Reilly, 1996). Implicit in them is the view that it is to be intellectually bankrupt to accept such common myths as 'self-evident truths'. Too often we are subjected to hyperbole in the realm of strategic information management.

These arguments are extended in Chapter 4, which aims to unpack the concepts underlying the IS strategizing framework introduced in Chapter 2 by examining, in considerably greater depth, the literature that has informed our thinking on the topic. As with the preceding chapters, it focuses attention on the term 'strategizing', with a view to giving emphasis to the processes and practices of strategy making. Importantly, the chapter views IS strategizing as an integral aspect of business strategy rather than something apart that may require alignment (see Chapter 5). The aim is to provide a theoretical rationale for the whole framework and its constituent parts. In line with the rationale of the book to apply theory in practice, however, it concludes with a consideration as to how the framework may be put to good practical use in organizations.

Part I is brought to a close by a chapter that arises from a review of the literature on alignment. Written by Anna Karpovsky and Bob Galliers, the chapter makes the point that, despite the extensive literature on IT/IS-business alignment, the topic has tended to be treated in a predominantly static manner. While they argue that the increasing interest in taking a process perspective on alignment may well be a promising avenue to study the phenomenon's dynamic nature, it provides only a partial picture of organizational practice in this regard. The authors point out that we still know very little about what it is that people in organizations actually *do,* on a day-to-day basis, to align IS and related concerns with business imperatives. Thus, in order to address the current gap in our understanding of the *practices* of aligning, there is a need for research that goes beyond the abstract *macro* analysis of alignment processes to that which considers the actual *micro* practices of aligning. This line of argument mirrors the view of 'practice' scholars referred to earlier in this Introduction – see also the special issue of *JSIS* on the topic (Peppard et al., 2014). The authors' analysis of the literature on the topic leads to the identification and classification of aligning activities that are being undertaken in practice. While the classification of aligning activities is partial, based as it is on the extant literature only, it is argued that it may usefully form the basis for further research of the actual practices that are being attempted. The classification can be added to with further research and can be used in practice to compare and contrast with what is being attempted in individual organizations.

Thus, Part I provides a strong foundation for consideration of the other key topics covered in this book as part of the multi-faceted strategic information management *problematique*. It deals with how our thinking and practice have developed over the years, provides examples of the approaches that have been developed and used, and introduces frameworks that can be applied in practice as analytical tools to assess IS capability and promote better management of IT within and across organizations.

References

Galliers, R.D. (1993). IT strategies: Beyond competitive advantage, *The Journal of Strategic Information Systems*, 2(4), 283–291.

Günther, W.A., Rezazade Mehrizi, M.A., Huysman, M., Feldberg, F. (2017). Debating big data: A literature review on realizing value from big data, *The Journal of Strategic Information Systems*, 26(3), 191–209.

Hammer, M. (1990). Reengineering work: Don't automate, obliterate, *Harvard Business Review*, 68(4), 104–113.

Morton, J., Wilson, A., Galliers, R.D., Marabelli, M. (2019). Open strategy and information technology. Chapter 10 in Seidl et al. (eds.) 2019.

Peppard, J., Galliers, R.D., Thorogood, A. (2014). Information systems strategy as practice: Micro strategy and strategizing for IS, *The Journal of Strategic Information Systems*, 23(1), 1–10.

Peppard, J., Ward, J. (2004). Beyond strategic information systems: Towards an IS capability, *The Journal of Strategic Information Systems*, 13(2), 167–194.

Seidl, D., von Krogh, G., Whittington (eds.) (2019). *The Cambridge Handbook of Open Strategy*, Cambridge: Cambridge University Press.

Tushman, M. L., O'Reilly, C.A. (1996). Ambidextrous organizations: Managing evolutionary and revolutionary change, *California Management Review*, 38(4), 8–30.

Whittington, R. (2014). Information systems strategy and strategy-as-practice: A joint agenda, *The Journal of Strategic Information Systems*, 23(1), 87–91.

Chapter 1

Michael Earl

APPROACHES TO INFORMATION SYSTEMS PLANNING: EXPERIENCES IN STRATEGIC INFORMATION SYSTEMS PLANNING

FOR MANY IS EXECUTIVES strategic information systems planning (SISP) continues to be a critical issue.[1] It is also reportedly the top IS concern of chief executives (Moynihan, 1990). At the same time, it is almost axiomatic that information systems management be based on SISP (Synott and Gruber, 1982). Furthermore, as investment in information technology has been promoted to both support business strategy or create strategic options (Earl, 1988; Henderson and Venkatraman, 1989), an 'industry' of SISP has grown as IT manufacturers and management consultants have developed methodologies and techniques. Thus, SISP appears to be a rich and important activity for researchers. So far, researchers have provided surveys of practice and problems, models and frameworks for theory-building, and propositions and methods to put into action.[2]

The literature recommends that SISP target the following areas:

- aligning investment in IS with business goals
- exploiting IT for competitive advantage
- directing efficient and effective management of IS resources
- developing technology policies and architectures.

It has been suggested (Earl, 1989) that the first two areas are concerned with information systems strategy, the third with information management strategy, and the fourth with information technology strategy. In survey-based research to date, it is usually the first two areas that dominate. Indeed, SISP has been defined in this light (Lederer and Sethi, 1988) as 'the process of deciding the objectives for organizational computing and identifying potential computer applications which the organization should implement' (p. 445). This definition was used in our investigation of SISP activity in 27 United Kingdom-based companies.

Calls have been made recently for better understanding of strategic planning in general, including SISP, and especially for studies of actual planning behavior in organizations (Boynton and Zmud, 1987; Henderson and Sifonis, 1988). As doubts continue to be raised about the pay-off of IT, it does seem important to examine the reality of generally accepted IS management practices such as SISP. Thus, in this investigation we used field studies to capture the *experiences* of large companies that had attempted some degree of formal IS planning.[3]

We were also interested as to whether any particular SISP techniques were more effective than others. This question proved difficult to answer, as discussed below, and is perhaps even irrelevant. Techniques were found to be only one element of SISP, with process and implementation being equally important. Therefore, a more descriptive construct embodying these three elements – the SISP *approach* – was examined. Five different approaches were identified; the experience of the organizations studied suggests that one approach may be more effective than the others.

Methodology

In 1988–89, a two-stage survey was conducted to discover the intents, outcomes, and experiences of SISP efforts. First, case studies captured the history of six companies previously studied by the author. These retrospective case histories were based on accounts of the IS director and/or IS strategic planner and on internal documentation of these companies. The cases suggested or confirmed questions to ask in the second stage. Undoubtedly, these cases influenced the perspective of the researcher.

In the second stage, 21 different UK companies were investigated through field studies. All were large companies that were among the leaders in the banking, insurance, transport, retailing, electronics, IT, automobile, aerospace, oil, chemical, services, and food and drink industries. Annual revenues averaged £4.5 billion. They were all headquartered in the UK or had significant national or regional IS functions within multinational companies headquartered elsewhere. Their experience with formal SISP activities ranged from one to 20 years.[4] The scope of SISP could be either at the business unit level, the corporate level, or both. The results from this second stage are reported in this chapter.

Within each firm, the author carried out in-depth interviews, typically lasting two to four hours, with three 'stakeholders'. A total of 63 executives were interviewed. The IS director or IS strategic planner was interviewed first, followed by the CEO or a general manager, and finally a senior line or user manager. Management prescriptions often state that SISP requires a combination or coalition of line managers contributing application ideas or making system requests, general managers setting direction and priorities, and IS professionals suggesting what can be achieved technically. Additionally, interviewing these three stakeholders provides some triangulation, both as a check on the views of the IS function and as a useful, but not perfect, cross-section of corporate memory.

Because the IS director selected the interviewees, there could have been some sample bias. However, parameters were laid down on how to select interviewees, and the responses did not indicate any prior collusion in aligning opinions. Respondents were supposed to be the IS executives most involved with SISP (which may or may not be the CIO), the CEO or general manager most involved in strategic decisions on IS, and a 'typical' user line manager who had contributed to SISP activities.

Interviews were conducted using questionnaires to ensure completeness and replicability, but a mix of unstructured, semi-structured, and structured interrogation was employed.[5] Typically, a simple question was posed in an open manner (often requiring enlargement to overcome differences in organizational language), and raw responses were recorded. The same question was then asked in a closed manner, requesting quantitative responses using scores, ranking, and Likert-type scales. Particular attention was paid to anecdotes, tangents, and 'asides'. In this way, it was hoped to collect data sets for both qualitative and quantitative analysis. Interviews focused on intents, outcomes, and experiences of SISP.

It was also attempted to record experiences with particular SISP methodologies and relate their use to success, benefits, and problems. However, this aim proved to be inappropriate (because firms often had employed a variety of techniques and procedures over time), and later was jettisoned in favor of recording the variety and richness of planning behavior the respondents recalled. This study is therefore exploratory, with a focus on theory development.[6]

Interests, Methods, and Outcomes

Data were collected on the stimuli, aims, benefits, success factors, problems, procedures, and methods of SISP. These data have been statistically examined, but only a minimum of results is presented here as a necessary context to the principal findings of the study.[7]

Respondents were asked to state their firms' current *objectives* for SISP. The dominant objective was alignment of IS with business needs, with 69.8 percent of respondents ranking it as most important and 93.7 percent ranking it in their top five objectives (Table 1.1). Interview comments reinforced the importance of this objective. The search for competitive advantage applications was ranked second, reflecting the increased strategic awareness of IT in the late 1980s. Gaining top management commitment was third. The only difference among the stakeholders was that IS directors placed top management commitment above the competitive advantage goal, perhaps reflecting a desire for functional sponsorship and a clear mandate.

Table 1.1 suggests that companies have more than one objective for SISP; narrative responses usually identified two or three objectives spontaneously. Not surprisingly, the respondents' views on benefits were similar and also indicated a multidimensional picture (Table 1.2). All respondents were able to select confidently from a structured list. Alignment of IS again stood out, with 49 percent ranking it first and 78 percent ranking it in the top five benefits. Top management support, better priority setting, competitive advantage applications, top management involvement, and user-management involvement were the other prime benefits reported.

Respondents also evaluated their firm's *success* with SISP. Success measures have been discussed elsewhere (Raghunathan and King, 1988). Most have relied upon satisfaction scores (Galliers, 1987), absence of problems (Lederer and Sethi, 1988), or audit checklists (King, 1988). Respondents were given no criterion of success but were given scale anchors to help them record a score from 1 (low) to 5 (high), as shown in Appendix B.

Ten percent of all respondents claimed their SISP had been 'highly successful', 59 percent reported it had been 'successful but there was room for improvement', and 69 percent

Table 1.1 Objectives of SISP

Rank order	Objective	Respondents selecting (n = 63)	Primary frequency	Sum of ranks	Mean rank
1	Aligning IS with business needs	59	44	276	4.38
2	Seek competitive advantage from IT	45	8	161	2.55
3	Gain top management commitment	36	6	115	1.83
4	Forecast IS resource requirements	35	1	80	1.27
5	Establish technology path and policies	30	2	77	1.22

rated SISP as worthwhile or better. Thirty-one percent were dissatisfied with their firm's SISP. There were differences between stakeholders; whereas 76 percent of IS directors gave a score above 3, only 67 percent of general managers and 57 percent of user managers were as content. Because the mean score by company was 3.73, and the modal company score was 4, the typical experience can be described as worthwhile but in need of some improvement.

A complementary question revealed a somewhat different picture. Interviewees were asked in what ways SISP had been *unsuccessful*. Sixty-five different types of disappointment were recorded. In such a long list none was dominant. Nevertheless, Table 1.3 summarizes the five most commonly mentioned features contributing to dissatisfaction. We will henceforth refer to these as 'concerns'.

It is apparent that concerns extend beyond technique or methodology, the focus of several researchers, and the horizon of most suppliers. Accordingly we examined the 65 different concerns looking for a pattern. This inductive and subjective clustering produced an interesting classification. The cited concerns could be grouped almost equally into three distinct categories (assuming equal weighting to each concern): method, process, and implementation, as shown in Table 1.4. The full list of concerns is reproduced in Appendix C.

Method concerns centered on the SISP technique, procedure, or methodology employed. Firms commonly had used proprietary methods, such as Method 1, BSP, or Information Engineering, or applied generally available techniques, such as critical success factors or value chain analysis. Others had invented their own methods, often customizing well-known techniques. Among the stated concerns were lack of strategic thinking, excessive internal focus, too much or too little attention to architecture, excessive time and resource requirements, and ineffective resource allocation mechanisms. General managers especially emphasized these concerns, perhaps because they have high expectations but find IS strategy making difficult.

Table 1.2 SISP benefits

Rank order	Benefit	Respondents selecting (n = 63)	Primary frequency	Sum of ranks	Mean rank
1	Aligning IS with business needs	49	31	208	3.30
2	Top management support	27	7	94	1.49
3	Better priority setting	35	3	75	1.19
4	Competitive advantage applications	21	4	67	1.06
5	Top management involvement	19	3	60	0.95
6	User/line management involvement	21	2	58	0.92

Table 1.3 Unsuccessful features of SISP

Rank order	Unsuccessful features
1	Resource constraints
2	Not fully implemented
3	Lack of top management acceptance
4	Length of time involved
5	Poor user-IS relationships

Implementation was a common concern. Even where SISP was judged to have been successful, the resultant strategies or plans were not always followed up or fully implemented. Even though clear directions might be set and commitments made to develop new applications, projects often were not initiated and systems development did not proceed. This discovery supports the findings of earlier work (Lederer and Sethi, 1988). Evidence from the interviews suggests that typically resources were not made available, management was hesitant, technological constraints arose, or organizational resistance emerged. Where plans were implemented, other concerns arose, including technical quality, the time and cost involved, or the lack of benefits realized. Implementation concerns were raised most by IS directors, perhaps because they are charged with delivery or because they hoped SISP would provide hitherto elusive strategic direction of their function. Of course, it can be claimed that a strategy that is not implemented or poorly implemented is no strategy at all – a tendency not unknown in business strategy making (Mintzberg, 1987). Indeed, implementation has been proposed as a measure of success in SISP (Lederer and Sethi, 1988).

Process concerns included lack of line management participation, poor IS-user relationships, inadequate user awareness and education, and low management ownership of the philosophy and practice of SISP. Line managers were particularly vocal about the management and enactment of SISP methods and procedures and whether they fit the organizational context.

Analysis of the reported concerns therefore suggests that method, process, and implementation are all necessary conditions for successful SISP (Figure 1.1). Indeed, when respondents volunteered success factors for SISP based on their organization's experience, they conveyed this multiple perspective (see Table 1.5). The highest ranked factors of 'top management involvement', and 'top management support' can be seen as process factors, while 'business strategy available' and 'study the business before technology' have more to do with method. 'Good IS management' partly relates to implementation. Past research

Table 1.4 SISP concerns by stakeholder

	Total citations %		IS directors (n=21)		General managers (n=21)		User managers (n=21)	
			Citations %		Citations %		Citations %	
Method	45	36	14	36	18	44	13	28
Process	39	31	9	23	11	27	19	41
Implementation	42	33	16	41	12	29	14	31
	126	100	39	100	41	100	46	100

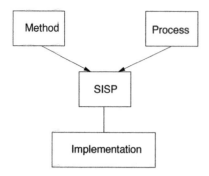

Figure 1.1   Necessary conditions for successful SISP.

has identified similar concerns (Lederer and Mendelow, 1987), and the more prescriptive literature has suggested some of these success factors (Synott and Gruber, 1982). However, the experience of organizations in this study indicates that no single factor is likely to lead to universal success in SISP. Instead, successful SISP is more probable when organizations realize that method, process, and implementation are all necessary issue sets to be managed.

In particular, consultants, managers, and researchers would seem well advised to look beyond method alone in practicing SISP. Furthermore, researchers cannot assume that SISP requires selection and use of just one method or one special planning exercise. Typically, it seems that firms use several methods over time. An average of 2.3 methods (both proprietary and in-house) had been employed by the 21 companies studied. Nine of them had tried three or more. Retrospectively isolating and identifying the effect of a method therefore becomes difficult for researchers. It may also be misleading because, as discovered in these interviews, firms engage in a variety of strategic planning activities and behavior. This became apparent when respondents were asked the open-ended question. 'Please summarize the approach you have adopted in developing your IS strategy (or identifying which IT applications to develop in the long run)'. In reply they usually recounted a rich history of initiatives, events, crises, techniques, organizational changes, successes, and failures all interwoven in a context of how IS resources had been managed.

Prompted both by the list of concerns and narrative histories of planning-related events, the focus of this study therefore shifted. The object of analysis became the SISP *approach*. This we viewed as the interaction of method, process, and implementation, as well as the variety of activities and behaviors upon which the respondents had reflected. The accounts of interviewees, the 'untutored' responses to the semi-structured questions, the documents supplied, and the 'asides' followed up by the interviewer all produced descriptive data on each company's approach. Once the salient features of SISP were compared across the 21 companies, five distinct approaches were identified. These were then used retrospectively to classify the experiences of the six case study firms.

SISP Approaches

An approach is not a technique *per se*. Nor is it necessarily an explicit study or formal, codified routine so often implied in past accounts and studies of SISP. As in most forms of business planning, it cannot often be captured by one event, a single procedure, or a particular technique. An approach may comprise a mix of procedures, techniques, user-IS interactions,

Table 1.5 Success factors in SISP

Rank order	Success factor	Respondents Selecting	Primary frequency	Sum of ranks	Mean rank
1	Top management involvement	42	15	160	2.55
2	Top management support	34	17	140	2.22
3	Business strategy available	26	9	99	1.57
4	Study business before technology	23	9	87	1.38
5	Good IS management	17	1	41	0.65

special analyses, and random discoveries. There are likely to be some formal activities and some informal behavior. Sometimes IS planning is a special endeavor and sometimes it is part of business planning at large. However, when members of the organization describe how decisions on IS strategy are initiated and made, a coherent picture is gradually painted where the underpinning philosophy, emphasis, and influences stand out. These are the principal distinguishing features of an approach. The *elements* of an approach can be seen as the nature and place of method, the attention to and style of process, and the focus on and probability of implementation.

The five approaches are labeled as Business-Led, Method-Driven. Administrative, Technological, and Organizational. They are delineated as ideal types in Table 1.6. Several distinctors are apparent in each approach. Each represents a particular philosophy (either explicit or implicit), displays its own dynamics, and has different strengths and weaknesses. Whereas some factors for success are suggested by each approach, not all approaches seem to be equally effective.

Business-Led Approach

The *Business-Led Approach* was adopted by four companies and two of the case study firms. The underpinning 'assumption' of this approach is that current business direction or plans are the only basis upon which IS plans can be built and that, therefore, business planning should drive SISP. The emphasis is on the business leading IS and not the other way around. Business plans or strategies are analyzed to identify where information systems are most required. Often this linkage is an annual endeavor and is the responsibility of the IS director or IS strategic planner (or team). The IS strategic plan is later presented to the board for questioning, approval, and priority setting.

General managers see this approach as simple, 'business-like', and a matter of common sense. IS executives often see this form of SISP as their most critical task and welcome the long overdue mandate from senior management. However, they soon discover that business strategies are neither clear nor detailed enough to specify IS needs. Thus, interpretation and further analysis become necessary. Documents have to be studied, managers interviewed, meetings convened, working papers written, and tentative proposals on the IS implications of business plans put forward. 'Home-spun' procedures are developed on a trial and error basis to discover and propose the IT implications of business plans. It may be especially difficult to promote the notion that IT itself may offer some new strategic options. The IS planners often feel that they have to 'take the lead' to make any progress or indeed to engage the business in the exercise. They also discover that some top executives may be more forceful in their views and expectations than others.

Users and line managers are likely to be involved very little. The emphasis on top-level input and business plans reduces the potential contribution of users and the visibility of local requirements. Users, perceiving SISP as remote, complain of inadequate involvement. Because the IS strategy becomes the product of the IS function, user support is not guaranteed. Top management, having substantially delegated SISP to the specialists, may be unsure of the recommendations and be hesitant to commit resources, thus impairing implementation.

Nevertheless, some advantages can accrue. Information systems are seen as a strategic resource, and the IS function receives greater legitimacy. Important strategic thrusts that require IT support can be identified, and if the business strategy is clearly and fully presented, the IS strategy can be well-aligned. Indeed, in one of the prior case study companies that adopted this approach, a clear business plan for survival led to IT applications that were admired by many industry watchers. However, despite this achievement, the IS function is still perceived by all three sets of stakeholders as poorly integrated into the business as a whole.

Method-Driven Approach

The *Method-Driven Approach* was present in two companies and two of the case study firms. Adherents of this approach appear to assume that SISP is enhanced by, or depends on, use of a formal technique or method. The IS director may believe that management will not think about IS needs and opportunities without the use of a formal method or the intervention of consultants. Indeed, recognition or anticipation of some of the frustrations typical of the Business-Led Approach may prompt the desire for method. However, any method will not do. There is typically a search for the 'best method', or at least one better than the last method adopted.

Once again, business strategies may be found to be deficient for the purpose of SISP. The introduction of a formal method rarely provides a remedy, however, because it is unlikely to be a strong enough business strategy technique. Also, the method's practitioners are unlikely to be skilled or credible at such work. Furthermore, as formal methods are usually sponsored by the IS department, they may fail to win the support or involvement of the business at large. Thus, a second or third method may be attempted while the IS department tries to elicit or verify the business strategy and to encourage a wider set of stakeholders to participate. Often, a vendor or consultant plays a significant role. As the challenges unfold, stakeholders determine the 'best' method, often as a result of the qualities of the consultants as much as the techniques themselves. The consultants often become the drivers of the SISP exercise and therefore have substantial influence on the recommendations.

Users may judge Method-Driven exercises as 'unreal' and 'high level' and as having excluded the managers who matter, namely themselves. General managers can see the studies as 'business strategy making in disguise' and thus become somewhat resistant and not easily persuaded of the priorities or options suggested by the application of the method. IS strategic plans may then lose their credibility and never be fully initiated. The exercises and recommendations may be forgotten. Often they are labeled the 'xyz' strategy, where 'xyz' is the name of the consulting firm employed; in other words, these strategies are rarely 'owned' by the business.

Formal methods do not always fail completely. Although a succession of methods achieved little in the companies studied, managers judged that each method had been good in some unanticipated way for the business or the IS department.[8] For example, in one firm it showed the need for business strategies, and in another it informed IS management about business imperatives. In the former firm, IS directors were heard to say the experience had been 'good for the company, showing up the gaps in strategic thinking!' Nevertheless, formal strategy studies could leave behind embryonic strategic thrusts, ideas waiting for the right time, or new thinking that could be exploited or built upon later in unforeseen ways.

Table 1.6 SISP approaches

	Business-Led	Method-Driven	Administrative	Technological	Organizational
Emphasis	Business	Technique	Resources	Model	Learning
Basis	Business plans	Best method	Procedure	Rigor	Partnership
Ends	Plan	Strategy	Portfolio	Architecture	Themes
Methods	Ours	Best	None	Engineering	Any way
Nature	Business	Top-down	Bottom-up	Blueprints	Interactive
Influencer	IS planner	Consultants	Committees	Method	Teams
Relation to business strategy	Fix points	Derive	Criteria	Objectives	Look at business
Priority setting	The board	Method recommends	Central committee	Compromise	Emerge
IS role	Driver	Initiator	Bureaucrat	Architect	Team member
Metaphor	It's common sense	It's good for you	Survival of the fittest	We nearly aborted it	Thinking IS all the time

Administrative Approach

The *Administrative Approach* was found in five companies. The emphasis here is on resource planning. The wider management planning and control procedures were expected to achieve the aims of SISP through formal procedures for allocating IS resources. Typically, IS development proposals were submitted by business units or departments to committees who examined project viability, common system possibilities, and resource consequences. In some cases, resource planners did the staff work as proposals ascended the annual hierarchical approval procedure. The Administrative Approach was the parallel of, or could be attached to, the firm's normal financial planning or capital budgeting routine. The outcome of the approach was a one-year or multi-year development portfolio of approved projects. Typically no application is developed until it is on the plan. A planning investment or steering committee makes all decisions and agrees on any changes.

Respondents identified significant down sides to the Administrative Approach. It was seen as not strategic, as being 'bottom-up' rather than 'top-down'. Ideas for radical change were not identified, strategic thinking was absent, inertia and 'business-as-usual' dominated, and enterprise-level applications remained in the background. More emotional were the claims about conflicts, dramas, and game playing – all perhaps inevitable in an essentially resource allocation procedure. The emphasis on resource planning sometimes led to a resource-constrained outcome. For example, spending limits were often applied, and boards and CEOs were accused of applying cuts to the IS budget, assuming that in doing so no damage was being done to the business as a whole.

Some benefits of this approach were identified. Everybody knew about the procedure; it was visible, and all users and units had the opportunity to submit proposals. Indeed, an SISP procedure and timetable for SISP were commonly published as part of the company policy and procedures manual. Users, who were encouraged to make application development requests, did produce some ideas for building competitive advantage. Also, it seemed that radical, transformational IT applications could arise in these companies despite the apparently bottom-up, cautious procedure. The most radical applications emerged when the CEO or finance director broke the administrative rules and informally proposed and sanctioned an IS investment.

By emphasizing viability, project approval, and resource planning, the administrative approach produced application development portfolios that were eventually implemented. Not only financial criteria guided these choices. New strategic guidelines, such as customer service or quality improvement, were also influential. Finally, the Administrative Approach often fitted the planning and control style of the company. IS was managed in congruence with other activities, which permitted complementary resources to be allocated in parallel. Indeed, unless the IS function complied with procedures, no resources were forthcoming.

Technological Approach

The *Technological Approach* was adopted by four companies and two of the case study firms. This approach is based on the assumption that an information systems-oriented model of the business is a necessary outcome of SISP and, therefore, that analytical modeling methods are appropriate. This approach is different from the Method-Driven Approach in two principal characteristics. First, the end product is a business model (or series of models). Second, a formal method is applied based on mapping the activities, processes, and data flows of the business. The emphasis is on deriving architectures or blueprints for IT and IS, and often Information Engineering terminology is used. Architectures for data, computing, communications, and applications might be produced, and computer-aided software engineering

(CASE) might be among the tools employed. A proprietary technology-oriented method might be used or adapted in-house. Both IS directors and general managers tend to emphasize the objectives of rigorous analysis and of building a robust infrastructure.

This approach is demanding in terms of both effort and resource requirements. These also tend to be high-profile activities. Stakeholders commented on the length of time involved in the analysis and/or the implementation. User managers reacted negatively to the complexity of the analysis and the outputs and reported a tendency for technical dependencies to displace business priorities. In one case, management was unsure of the validity and meaning of the blueprints generated and could not determine what proposals mattered most. A second study of the same type, but using a different technological method, was commissioned. This produced a different but equally unconvincing set of blueprints.

These characteristics could lead to declining top management support or even user rebellion. In one firm, the users called for an enterprise modeling exercise to be aborted. In one of the case study firms, development of the blueprint applications was axed by top management three and a half years after initiation. In another, two generations of IS management departed after organizational conflict concerning the validity of the technological model proposed.

Some success was claimed for the Technological Approach. Benefits were salvaged by factoring down the approach into smaller exercises. In one case this produced a database definition, and in another it led to an IT architecture for the finance function. Some IS directors claimed these outcomes were valuable in building better IT infrastructures.

Organizational Approach

The *Organizational Approach* was used in six companies and one of the case study firms. The underpinning assumption here is quite different. It is that SISP is not a special or neat and tidy endeavor but is based on IS decisions being made through continuous integration between the IS function and the organization. The way IT applications are identified and selected is described in much more multidimensional and subtle language. The approach is not without method, but methods are employed as required and to fit a particular purpose. For example, value analysis may be used, workshops arranged, business investigation projects set up, and vendor visits organized. The emphasis, however, is on process, especially management understanding and involvement. For some of these companies, a major SISP method had been applied in the past, but in retrospect it was seen to have been as much a process enabler as an analytical investigation. Executive teamwork and an understanding of how IT might contribute to the business were often left behind by the method rather than specific recommendations for IS investment. Organizational learning was important and evident in at least three ways.

First, IS development concentrated on only one or two themes growing in scope over several years as the organization began to appreciate the potential benefits. Examples of such themes included a food company concentrating on providing high service levels to customers, an insurance company concentrating on low-cost administration, and a chemical company concentrating on product development performance. Second, special studies were important. Often multidisciplinary senior executive project teams or full-time task forces were assigned to tackle a business problem from which a major IS initiative would later emerge. The presence of an IS executive in the multidisciplinary team was felt to be important to the emergence of a strategic theme because this person could suggest why, where, and how IT could help. Teamwork was the principal influence in IS strategy making. Third, there was a focus on implementation. Themes were broken down into identifiable and frequent deliverables. Conversely, occasional project cost and time overruns were acceptable if they allowed evolving ideas to be incorporated. In some ways, IS strategies were discovered through implementation. These three learning characteristics can be seen collectively as a preference for incremental strategy making.

The approach is therefore *organizational* because:

1   Collective learning across the organization is evident.
2   Organizational devices or instruments (teams, task forces, workshops, etc.) are used to tackle business problems or pursue initiatives.
3   The IS function works in close partnership with the rest of the organization, especially through having IS managers on management teams or placing IS executives on task forces.
4   Devolution of some IS capability is common, not only to divisions, but also to functions, factories, and departments.
5   In some companies SISP is neither special nor abnormal. It is part of the normal business planning of the organization.
6   IS strategies often emerge from ongoing organizational activities, such as trial and error changes to business practices, continuous and incremental enhancement of existing applications, and occasional system initiatives and experiments within the business.

In one of the companies, planning was 'counter-cultural'. Nevertheless, in the character described above, planning still happened. In another company there were no IS plans, just business plans. In another, IS was enjoying a year or more of low profile until the company discovered the next theme. In most of these firms, IS decisions were being made all the time and at any time.

Respondents reported some disadvantages of this approach. Some IS directors worried about how the next theme would be generated. Also, because the approach is somewhat fuzzy or soft, they were not always confident that it could be transplanted to another part of the business. Indeed, a new CEO, management team, or management style could erode the process without the effect being apparent for some time. One IS director believed the incrementalism of the Organizational Approach led to creation of inferior infrastructures.

The five approaches appear to be different in scope, character, and outcome. Table 1.7 differentiates them using the three characteristics that seem to help other organizations position themselves. Also, slogans are offered to capture the essence of each approach. Strengths and weaknesses of each approach are contained in Table 1.8.

It is also possible to indicate the apparent differences of each approach in terms of the three factors suggested in Figure 1.1 as necessary for success: method, process, and implementation. Table 1.9 attempts a summary.

In the Business-Led Approach, method scores low because no formal technique is used; process is rated low because the exercise is commonly IS dominated; but implementation is medium because the boards tend to at least approve some projects. In the Method-Driven Approach, method is high by definition, but process is largely ignored and implementation barely or rarely initiated. In the Administrative Approach, only a procedure exists as method. However, its dependence on user inputs suggests a medium rating on process. Because of its resource allocation emphasis, approved projects are generally implemented. The Technological Approach is generally method-intensive and insensitive to process. It can, however, lead to some specific implementation of an infrastructure. The Organizational Approach uses any method or devices that fit the need; it explicitly invests in process and emphasizes implementation.

Table 1.7 Five approaches summarized

	Business-Led	Method-Driven	Administrative	Technological	Organizational
Underpinning assumption	Business plans and needs should drive IS plans	IS strategies will be enhanced by use of a formal SISP method	SISP should follow and conform with the firm's management planning and control procedures	SISP is an exercise in business and information modeling	SISP is a continuous decision-making activity shared by the business and IS
Emphasis of Approach	Business leads IS and not vice versa	Selection of the best method	Identification and allocation of IS resources to meet agreed needs	Production of models and blueprints	Organizational learning about business problems and opportunities and the IT contribution
Major influence of outcomes	IS planners	Practitioners of the method	Resource planning and steering committees	Modeling method Employed	Permanent and *ad hoc* teams of key managers, including IS
Slogan	Business drives IS	Strategy needs method	Follow the rules	IS needs blueprints	Themes with teams

Table 1.8 Strengths and weaknesses of SISP approaches

	Business-Led	Method-Driven	Administrative	Technological	Organizational
Strengths	Simple Business first Raises IS status	Provides a methodology Plugs strategy gaps Raises strategy profile	System viability System synergies Encourages user input	Rigor Focus on infrastructure *Favors integrated tools*	Becomes normal Emphasis on implementation Promotes IS-user partnership
Weaknesses	*Ad hoc* method Lacks management commitment Depends on quality of business strategy	User involvement Too influenced by method Implementation unlikely	Non-strategic Bureaucratic Resource-constrained	Lacks management support Only partial implementation Complexity	Generation of new themes Soft methodology Architecture becomes difficult

Table 1.9 SISP approaches vs. three conditions for success

	Business-Led	Method-Driven	Administrative	Technological	Organizational
Method	Low	High	Low	High	Medium
Process	Low	Low	Medium	Low	High
Implementation	Medium	Low	High	Medium	High

Preliminary Evaluations

The five approaches were identified by comparing the events, experiences, and lessons described by the interviewees. As the investigation proved to be exploratory, the classification of approaches is descriptive and was derived by inductive interpretation of organizational experiences. Table 1.6, therefore, should be seen as an ideal model that caricatures the approaches in order to aid theory development. One way of 'validating' the model is to compare it with prior research in both IS and general management to assess whether the approaches 'ring true'.

Related Theories

Difficulties encountered in the Business-Led Approach have been noted by others. The availability of formal business strategies for SISP cannot be assumed (Bowman et al., 1983; Lederer and Mendelow, 1986). Nor can we assume that business strategies are communicated to the organization at large, are clear and stable, or are valuable in identifying IS needs (Earl, 1989; Lederer and Mendelow, 1989). Indeed, the quality of the process of business planning itself may often be suspect (Lederer and Sethi, 1988) . In other words, while the Business-Led Approach may be especially appealing to general managers, the challenges are likely to be significant.

There is considerable literature on the top-down, more business-strategy-oriented SISP methods implied by the Method-Driven Approach, but most of it is conjectural or normative. Vendors can be very persuasive about the need for a methodology that explicitly connects IS to business thinking (Bowman et al., 1983). Other researchers have argued that sometimes the business strategy must be explicated first (King, 1978; Lederer and Mendelow, 1987). This was a belief of the IS directors in the Method-Driven companies, but one general manager complained that this was 'business strategy making in disguise'. The Administrative Approach reflects the prescriptions and practices of bureaucratic models of planning and control. We must turn to the general management literature for insights into this approach. Quinn (1977) has pointed out the strategy-making limitations of bottom-up planning procedures. He argues that big change rarely originates in this way and that, furthermore, annual planning processes rarely foster innovation. Both the political behavior stimulated by hierarchical resource allocation mechanisms and the business-as-usual inertia of budgetary planning have been well-documented elsewhere (Bowers, 1970; Danziger, 1978).

The Technological Approach may be the extreme case of how the IT industry and its professionals tend to apply computer science thinking to planning. The deficiencies of these methods have been noted in accounts of the more extensive IS planning methods and, in particular, of Information Engineering techniques. For instance, managers are often unhappy with the time and cost involved (Goodhue et al., 1988; Moynihan, 1990). Others note that IS priorities are by definition dependent on the sequence required for architecture building

(Hackathorn and Karimi, 1988; Inmon, 1986). The voluminous data generated by this class of method has also been reported (Bowman et al., 1983; Inmon, 1986).

The Organizational Approach does not fit easily with the technical and prescriptive IS literature, but similar patterns have been observed by the more behavioral studies of business strategy making. It is now known that organizations rarely use the rational-analytical approaches touted in the planning literature when they make significant changes in strategy (Quinn, 1978). Rather, strategies often evolve from fragmented, incremental, and largely intuitive processes. Quinn believed this was the quite natural, proper way to cope with the unknowable – proceeding flexibly and experimentally from broad concepts to specific commitments.

Mintzberg's (1983) view of strategy making is similar. It emphasizes small project-based multiskilled teams, cross-functional liaison devices, and selective decentralization. Indeed, Mintzberg's view succinctly summarizes the Organizational Approach. He argues that often strategy is formed, rather than formulated, as actions converge into patterns and as analysis and implementation merge into a fluid process of learning. Furthermore, Mintzberg sees strategy making in reality as a mixture of the formal and informal and the analytical and emergent. Top managers, he argues, should create a context in which strategic thinking and discovery mingle, and then they should intervene where necessary to shape and support new ways forward.

In IS research, Henderson (1989) may have implicitly argued for the Organizational Approach when he called for an iterative, ongoing IS planning process to build and sustain partnership. He suggested partnership mechanisms such as task forces, cross-functional teams, multi-tiered and cross-functional networks, and collaborative planning without planners. Henderson and Sifonis (1988) identify the importance of learning in SISP, and de Geus (1988) sees all planning as learning and teamwork as central to organizational learning. Goodhue et al. (1988) and Moynihan (1990) argue that SISP needs to deliver good enough applications rather than optimal models. These propositions could be seen as recognition of the need to learn by doing and to deliver benefits. There is therefore a literature to support the Organizational Approach.

Data Assessment

The field data itself can be used to assess the suggested taxonomy of approaches. Questions that arise are: do the approaches actually exist, and is it possible to clearly differentiate between them? Analysis of variance tests on reported success scores indicated that differences between approaches are significant, but differences between stakeholder sets are not.[9] This is one indication that *approach* is a distinct and meaningful way of analyzing SISP in action.

A second obvious question is whether any approaches are more effective than others. It is perhaps premature to ask this question of a taxonomy suggested by the data. Caution would advise further validation of the framework first, followed by carefully designed measurement tests. However, this study provides an opportunity for an early, if tentative, evaluation of this sort.

For example, as shown in Table 1.10, success scores can be correlated with SISP approach. Overall mean scores are shown, as well as scores for each stakeholder set. No approach differed widely from the mean score (3.73) across all companies. However, the most intensive approach in terms of technique (Technological) earned the highest score, perhaps because it represents what respondents thought an IS planning methodology should look like. Conversely, the Business-Led Approach, which lacks formal methodologies, earned the lowest scores. There are, of course, legitimate doubts about the meaning or reliability of these success scores because respondents were so keen to discuss the unsuccessful features.

Table 1.10 Mean success scores by approach

	Business-Led	Method-Driven	Administrative	Technological	Organizational
Total means	3.25	3.83	3.60	4.00	3.94
IS directors	3.50	4.50	3.60	4.25	4.00
General managers	3.00	4.00	3.40	4.00	4.17
Line managers	3.25	3.00	3.80	3.75	3.66
Number of firms	4	2	5	4	6

Note: 5 = high; 1 = low

Accordingly, another available measure is to analyze the frequency of concerns reported by firms, assuming each carries equal weight. Table 1.11 breaks out these data by method, process, and implementation concerns. The Organizational Approach has the least concerns attributed to it in total. The Business-Led Approach was characterized by high dissatisfaction with method and implementation. The Method-Driven Approach was perceived to be unsuccessful on process and, ironically, on method, while opinion was less harsh on implementation, perhaps because implementation experience itself is low. The Administrative Approach, as might be predicted, is not well-regarded on method. These data are not widely divergent from the qualitative analysis in Table 1.9.

Another measure is the potential of each approach for generating competitive advantage applications. Respondents were asked to identify and describe such applications and trace their histories. No attempt was made by the researcher to check the competitive advantage claimed or to assess whether the applications deserved the label. Although only 14 percent of all such applications were reported to have been generated by a formal SISP study, it is interesting to compare achievement rates of the firms in each approach (Table 1.12). Method-Driven and Technological Approaches do not appear promising. Little is ever initiated in the Method-Driven Approach, while competitiveness is rarely the focus of the Technological Approach. The Administrative Approach appears to be more conducive, perhaps because user ideas receive a hearing. Forty-two percent of competitive advantage applications discovered in all the firms originated from user requests. In the Business-Led Approach, some obviously necessary applications are actioned. In the Organizational Approach, most of the themes pursued were perceived to have produced a competitive advantage.

These three qualitative measures can be combined to produce a multidimensional score. Other scholars have suggested that a number of performance measures are required to measure the effectiveness of SISP (Raghunathan and King, 1988). Table 1.13 ranks each approach according to the three measures discussed above (where 1 = top and 5 = bottom). In summing the ranks, the Organizational Approach appears to be substantially superior. Furthermore, all the other approaches score relatively low on this basis.

Table 1.11 SISP concerns per firm

	Business-Led	Method-Driven	Administrative	Technological	Organizational
Method	2.75	2.50	2.80	1.75	1.33
Process	0.75	3.00	1.60	2.50	2.16
Implementation	2.75	1.00	1.60	3.00	1.83
Total	6.25	6.50	6.00	7.25	5.32
Number of Firms	4	2	5	4	6

Table 1.12 Competitive advantage propensity

Approach	Competitive advantage application frequency
Business-Led	4.0 applications per firm
Method-Driven	1.5 applications per firm
Administrative	3.6 applications per firm
Technological	2.5 applications per firm
Organizational	4.8 applications per firm

Thus, both qualitative and quantitative evidence suggest that the Organizational Approach is likely to be the best SISP approach to use and, thus, a candidate for further study. The Organizational Approach is perhaps the least formal and structured. It also differs significantly from conventional prescriptions in the literature and practice.

Implications for Research

Many prior studies of SISP have been based on the views of IS managers alone. A novel aspect of this study was that the attitudes and experiences of general managers and users were also examined. In reporting back the results to the respondents in the survey companies, an interesting reaction occurred. The stakeholders were asked to select which approach best described their experience with SISP. If only IS professionals were present, their conclusions often differed from the final interpretative results. However, when all three stakeholders were present, a lively discussion ensued and, eventually, unprompted, the group's views moved toward an interpretation consistent with both the data presented and the approach attributed to the firm. This is another soft form of validation. More important, it indicates that approach is not only a multidimensional construct but also captures a multi-stakeholder perspective. This suggests that studies of IS management practice can be enriched if they look beyond the boundaries of the IS department.

Another characteristic of prior work on SISP is the assumption that formal methods are used and in principle are appropriate (Lederer and Sethi, 1988, 1991). A systematic linkage to the organization's business planning procedures is also commonly assumed (Boynton and Zmud, 1987; Karimi, 1988). The findings of this study suggest that these may be false assumptions and that, besides studying formal methods, researchers should continue to investigate matters of process while also paying attention to implementation. Indeed, in the field of business strategy, it was studies of the process of strategy making that led to the

Table 1.13 Multidimensional ranking of SISP approaches

	Business-Led	Method-Driven	Administrative	Technological	Organizational
Success score ranking	5	3	4	1	2
Least concerns ranking	2	3	4	5	1
Competitive advantage potential ranking Sum of ranks	2	5	3	4	1
	9	11	11	10	4
Overall ranking	2	4	4	3	1

'alternative' theories of the strategic management of the firm developed by Quinn (1978) and Mintzberg (1987).

The Organizational Approach to SISP suggested by this study might also be seen as an 'alternative' school of thought. This particular approach, therefore, should be investigated further to understand it in more detail, to assess its effectiveness more rigorously, and to discover how to make it work.

Finally, additional studies are required to further validate and then perhaps develop these findings. Some of the parameters suggested here to distinguish the approaches could be taken as variables and investigated on larger samples to verify the classification. Researchers could also explore whether different approaches fit, or work better in, different contexts. Candidate situational factors include information intensity of the sector, environmental uncertainty, the organization's management planning and control style, and the maturity of the organization's IS management experience.

Implications for Practice

For practitioners, this study provides two general lessons. First, SISP requires a holistic or interdependent view. Methods may be necessary, but they could fail if the process factors receive no attention. It is also important to explicitly and positively incorporate implementation plans and decisions in the strategic planning cycle.

Second, successful SISP seems to require users and line managers working in partnership with the IS function. This may not only generate relevant application ideas, but it will tend to create ownership of both process and outcomes. The taxonomy of SISP approaches emerging from this study might be interpreted for practice in at least four different ways. First, it can be used as a diagnostic tool to position a firm's current SISP efforts. The strengths and weaknesses identified in the research then could suggest how the current approach could be improved. We have found that frameworks used in this way are likely to be more helpful if users and general managers as well as IS professionals join together in the diagnosis.

Second, the taxonomy can be used to design a situation-specific (customized) approach on a 'mix-and-match' basis. It may be possible to design a potentially more effective hybrid. The author is aware of one company experimenting at building a combination of the Organizational and Technological Approaches. One of the study companies that had adopted the Organizational Approach to derive its IS strategy also sought some of the espoused benefits of the Technological Approach by continuously formulating a shadow blueprint for IT architecture. This may be one way of reconciling the apparent contradictions of the Organizational and Technological Approaches.

Third, based on our current understanding it appears that the Organizational Approach is more effective than others. Therefore, firms might seriously consider adopting it. This could involve setting up mechanisms and responsibility structures to encourage IS-user partnerships, devolving IS planning and development capability, ensuring IS managers are members of all permanent and ad hoc teams, recognizing IS strategic thinking as a continuous and periodic activity, identifying and pursuing business themes, and accepting 'good enough' solutions and building on them. Above all, firms might encourage any mechanisms that promote organizational learning about the scope of IT.

Another interpretation is that the Organizational Approach describes how most IS strategies actually are developed, despite the more formal and rational endeavors of IS managers or management at large. The reality may be a continuous interaction of formal methods and informal behavior and of intended and unintended strategies. If so, SISP in practice should be eclectic, selecting and trying methods and process initiatives to fit the needs of the time. One consequence of this view might be recognition and acceptance that planning need not always generate plans and that plans may arise without a formal planning process.

Finally, it can be revealing for an organization to recall the period when IS appeared to be contributing most effectively to the business and to describe the SISP approach in use (whether by design or not) at the time. This may then indicate which approach is most likely to succeed for that organization. Often when a particularly successful IS project is recalled, its history is seen to resemble the Organizational Approach.

Conclusions

This study evolved into a broad, behavioral exploration of experiences in large organizations. The breadth of perspective led to the proposition that SISP is more than method or technique alone. In addition, process issues and the question of implementation appear to be important. These interdependent elements combine to form an approach. Five different SISP approaches were identified, and one, the Organizational Approach, appears superior.

For practitioners, the taxonomy of SISP approaches provides a diagnostic tool to use in evaluating the effectiveness of their SISP efforts and in learning from their own experiences. Whether rethinking SISP or introducing it for the first time, firms may want to consider adopting the Organizational Approach. Two reasons led to this recommendation. First, among the companies explored, it seemed the most effective approach. Second, this study casts doubt on several of the by now 'traditional' SISP practices that have been advocated and developed in recent years.

The 'approach' construct presented in this chapter, the taxonomy of SISP approaches derived, and the indication that the least formal and least analytical approach seems to be most effective all offer new directions for SISP research and theory development.

Appendix A: Field study companies

Descriptive statistics for field study companies

Company	Annual revenue (£B)	Annual IS expenditure (£M)	Years of SISP experience
1 Banking	1.7*	450	4
2 Banking	1.9*	275	2
3 Retailing	4.2	80	4
4 Retailing	0.56	8	4
5 Insurance	2.8†	30	11
6 Insurance	0.9†	15	15
7 Travel	0.75	8	4
8 Electronics	1.35	25	3
9 Aerospace	4.1	120	17
10 Aerospace	2.1	54	20
11 IT	3.9	77	21
12 IT	0.6	18	11
13 Telecommunications	0.9	50	6
14 Automobile	0.5	14	9

(continued)

Company	Annual revenue (£B)	Annual IS expenditure (£M)	Years of SISP experience
15 Food	4.5	40	1
16 Oil	55.0	1000	6
17 Chemicals	2.18	5	10
18 Food	1.4	20	8
19 Accountancy/ Consultancy	0.55	1	5
20 Brewing	1.7	23	9
21 Food/Consumer	2.5	27	1

*Operating costs.

†Premium income.

Appendix B: Interview questionnaire

Structured (closed) questions

1	What prompted you to develop an IS/IT strategy?	(RO)
3	What were the objectives in developing an IS/IT strategy?	(RO)
4a	What are the outputs of your IS/IT strategy development?	(MC)
4b	What are the content headings of your IS strategic plan or strategy?	(MC)
5	What methods have you used in developing your IS strategy; when, why?	(MC)
7	What have been the benefits of strategic information systems planning?	(RO)
8	How successful has SISP been?	(LS)
9	What have you found to be key success factors in SISP?	(RO)
10	How is your SISP connected to other business planning processes?	(MC)
11	How do you review your IS strategies?	(MC)
12	What are the major problems you have encountered in SISP?	(RO)

All these questions were asked using multiple-choice lists (MC), Likert-type scale (LS), or rank-order lists (RO).

Example rank-order questions

3   What were the objectives in developing an IS/IT strategy?

Tick		Rank
. . . . . .	Align IS development with business needs	. . . . . .
. . . . . .	Revamp the IS/IT function	. . . . . .
. . . . . .	Seek competitive advantage from IT	. . . . . .
. . . . . .	Establish technology path and policies	. . . . . .
. . . . . .	Forecast IS requirements	. . . . . .
. . . . . .	Gain top management commitment	. . . . . .
. . . . . .	Other (specify)	. . . . . .

Example multiple-choice questions

5   What methods have you used in developing your IS strategy; when, why?

When	Method	Why
. . . . . .	Critical success factors	. . . . . .
. . . . . .	Stages of growth	. . . . . .
. . . . . .	Business systems planning	. . . . . .
. . . . . .	Enterprise modeling	. . . . . .
. . . . . .	Information engineering	. . . . . .
. . . . . .	Method 3	. . . . . .
. . . . . .	Other proprietary (specify)	. . . . . .
. . . . . .	In-house IS strategy	. . . . . .
. . . . . .	In-house business strategy	. . . . . .
. . . . . .	In-house application search techniques	. . . . . .
. . . . . .	Informal	. . . . . .
. . . . . .	Other (specify)	. . . . . .

Example Likert-type scale question

8a How successful has SISP been on the following scale?

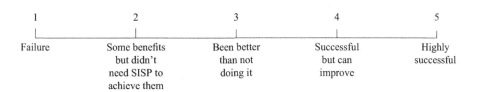

1	2	3	4	5
Failure	Some benefits but didn't need SISP to achieve them	Been better than not doing it	Successful but can improve	Highly successful

Semi-structured (open) questions

2a   Please summarize the approach you have adopted in developing your IS strategy (or in identifying and deciding which IT applications to develop in the long run).

2b   What are the key elements of your IS strategy?

6a   Have you developed any applications that have given competitive advantage in recent years? If so, what?

6b   How was each of these applications identified and developed?

8b   In what ways has SISP been unsuccessful?

13   Can you describe any key turning points in your SISP experience, such as changes in aims, approach, method, benefits, success factors or problems?

Appendix C: Concerns or unsuccessful features of SISP

Method concerns

1   It did not lead to management identifying applications supportable at a cost

2   No regeneration or review

3   Failed to discover our competitors' moves or understand their improvements
4   Not enough planning: too much emphasis on development and projects
5   It was not connected to business planning
6   It was too internally focused
7   Sensibly allocating resources to needs was a problem
8   Business needs were ignored or not identified
9   Not flexible or reactive enough
10   Not coordinated
11   Not enough consideration of architecture
12   Priority setting and resource allocation were questionable
13   The plans were soon out of date
14   Business direction and plans were inadequate
15   Not enough strategic thinking
16   The thinking was too functional and applications-oriented and not process-based
17   It was too technical and not business-based
18   It was overtheoretical and too complicated
19   It could have been done quicker; it took too long
20   It developed a bureaucracy of its own
21   We have not solved identification of corporate-wide needs
22   The architecture was questionable; people were not convinced by it
23   We still don't know how to incorporate and meet short-term needs
24   We did not complete the company-entity model
25   We found it difficult justifying the benefits
26   It was too much about automating today's operations
27   It was too ad hoc; insufficient method
28   Many of the recommendations did not meet user aspirations.

Process concerns

1   Some businesses were less good at, and less committed to, planning than others
2   The exercise was abrogated to the IS department
3   Inadequate understanding across all management
4   Line management involvement was unsatisfactory
5   Lack of senior management involvement
6   No top management buy-in
7   The strategy was not sold or communicated enough
8   We still have poor user-IS relationships
9   Too many IS people have not worked outside of IS
10   Poor IT understanding of customer and business needs
11   Line management buy-in was low
12   Little cross-divisional learning
13   IS management quality was below par
14   Senior executives were not made aware of the scale of change required
15   Users lacked understanding of IT and its methods
16   It was too user-driven in one period
17   We are still learning how to do planning studies
18   Planning almost never works; there are too many 'dramas'
19   The culture has not changed enough
20   We oversold the plan
21   Too much conflict between organizational units.

Implementation concerns

1   We have not broken the resource constraints
2   We have not implemented as much as we should
3   It was not carried through into resource planning
4   The necessary technology planning was not done
5   We have not achieved the system benefits
6   We made technical mistakes
7   Some of the needs are still unsatisfied
8   Appropriate hardware or software was not available
9   Cost and time budget returns
10   We were not good at specifying the detailed requirements
11   Defining staffing needs was a problem
12   We have not gotten anything off the ground yet
13   We had insufficient skilled development resources
14   Regulatory impediments
15   We were overambitious and tried to change too much
16   We still have to catch up technically.

Notes

1   See, for example, surveys by Dickson et al. (1984), Hartog and Herbert (1986), Brancheau and Wetherbe (1987), and Niederman et al. (1991).
2   Propositions and methods include Zani's (1970) early top-down proposal, King's (1978) more sophisticated linkage of the organization's IS strategy set to the business strategy set, and focused techniques such as critical success factors (Bullen and Rockart, 1981) and value chain analysis (Porter and Millar, 1985). These are supplemented by product literature such as Andersen's (1983) Method 1 or IBM's (1975) Business System Planning. The models and frameworks for developing a theory of SISP include Boynton and Zmud (1987), Henderson and Sifonis (1988), and Henderson and Venkatraman (1989). Empirical works include a survey of practice by Galliers (1987), analysis of methods by Sullivan (1985), investigation of problems by Lederer and Sethi (1988), assessment of success by Lederer and Mendelow (1987) and Raghunathan and King (1988), and evaluation of particular techniques such as strategic data planning (Goodhue et al., 1992).
3   Prior work has tended to use mail questionnaires targeted at IS executives. However, researchers have called for broader studies and for surveys of the experiences and perspectives of top managers, corporate planners, and users (Lederer and Mendelow, 1989; Lederer and Sethi, 1988; Raghunathan and King, 1988).
4   Characteristics of the sample companies are summarized in Appendix A.
5   Extracts from the interview questionnaires are shown in Appendix B.
6   This exploration through field studies was in the spirit of 'grounded theory' (Glaser and Strauss, 1967).
7   Fuller descriptive statistics can be seen in an early research report (Earl, 1990).
8   Methods employed included proprietary, generic, and customized techniques.
9   Differences between approaches are significant at the 10 percent level (f = 0.056). Differences between stakeholder sets are not significant (f = 0.126). No interaction was discovered between the two classifications.

References

Arthur Andersen & Co. (1983) *Method/1: Information Systems Methodology: An Introduction*, The Company, Chicago, IL.

Bowers, J. L. (1970) *Managing the Resource Allocation Process: A Study of Corporate Planning and Investment*, Division of Research, Graduate School of Business Administration, Harvard University, Boston, MA.

Bowman, B., Davis, G. and Wetherbe, J. (1983) Three stage model of MIS planning. *Information and Management*, 6(1), August, 11–25.

Boynton, A. C. and Zmud, R. W. (1987) Information technology planning in the 1990s: Directions for practice and research. *MIS Quarterly*, 11(1), March, 59–71.

Brancheau, J. C. and Wetherbe, J. C. (1987) Key issues in information systems management. *MIS Quarterly*, 11(1), March, 23–45.

Bullen, C. V. and Rockart, J. F. (1981) *A Primer on Critical Success Factors*, CISR Working Paper No. 69, Center for Information Systems Research, Massachusetts Institute of Technology, Cambridge, MA, June.

Danziger, J. N. (1978) *Making Budgets: Public Resource Allocation*, Sage Publications, Beverly Hills, CA.

de Geus, A. P. (1988) Planning as learning. *Harvard Business Review*, 66(2), March–April, 70–74.

Dickson, G. W., Leitheiser, R. L., Wetherbe, J. C. and Nechis, M. (1984) Key information systems issues for the 1980s. *MIS Quarterly*, 10(3), September, 135–159.

Earl, M. J. (ed.) (1988) *Information Management: The Strategic Dimension*, Oxford University Press, Oxford.

Earl, M. J. (1989) *Management Strategies for Information Technology*, Prentice Hall, London.

Earl, M. J. (1990) *Strategic Information Systems Planning in UK Companies: Early Results of a Field Study*. Oxford Institute of Information Management Research and Discussion Paper 90/1, Templeton College, Oxford.

Galliers, R. D. (1987) *Information Systems Planning in Britain and Australia in the Mid-1980's: Key Success Factors*, unpublished doctoral dissertation, London School of Economics. University of London.

Glaser, B. G. and Strauss. A. L. (1967) *The Discovery of Grounded Theory: Strategies for Qualitative Research*, Aldine Publishing Company, Chicago, IL.

Goodhue, D. L., Quillard. J. A. and Rockart, J. F. (1988) Managing the data resource: A contingency perspective. *MIS Quarterly*, 12(3), September, 373–391.

Goodhue, D. L., Kirsch, L. J., Quillard, J. A. and Wybo, M. D. (1992) Strategic data planning: Lessons from the field. *MIS Quarterly*, 16(1), March, 11–34.

Hackathorn, R. D. and Karimi, J. (1988) A framework for comparing information engineering methods. *MIS Quarterly*, 12(2), June, 203–220.

Hartog, C. and Herbert, M. (1986) 1985 opinion survey of MIS managers: Key issues. *MIS Quarterly*, 10(4), December, 351–361.

Henderson, J. C. (1989) *Building and Sustaining Partnership between Line and I/S Managers*. CISR Working Paper No. 195. Center for Information Systems Research, Massachusetts Institute of Technology, Cambridge, MA, September.

Henderson, J. C. and Sifonis, J. G. (1988) The value of strategic IS planning: Understanding consistency, validity, and IS markets. *MIS Quarterly*, 12(2), June, 187–200.

Henderson, J. C. and Venkatraman, N. (1989) *Strategic Alignment: A Framework for Strategic Information Technology Management*. CISR Working Paper No. 190. Center for Information Systems Research. Massachusetts Institute of Technology, Cambridge, MA, August.

IBM Corporation (1975) *Business Systems Planning – Information Systems Planning Guide*, Publication #GE20-0527-4, White Plains, NY: White Plains.

Inmon, W. H. (1986) *Information Systems Architecture*, Prentice Hall, Englewood Cliffs, NJ.

Karimi, J. (1988) Strategic planning for information systems: Requirements and information engineering methods. *Journal of Management Information Systems*, 4(4), Spring, 5–24.

King, W. R. (1978) Strategic planning for management information systems. *MIS Quarterly*, 2(1), March, 22–37.

King, W. R. (1988) How effective is your information systems planning? *Long Range Planning*, 1(1), October, 7–12.

Lederer, A. L. and Mendelow, A. L. (1986) Issues in information systems planning. *Information and Management*, 10(5), May, 245–254.

Lederer, A. L. and Mendelow, A. L. (1987) Information resource planning: Overcoming difficulties in identifying top management's objectives. *MIS Quarterly*, 11(3), September, 389–399.

Lederer, A. L. and Mendelow, A. L. (1989) Co-ordination of information systems plans with business plans. *Journal of Management Information Systems*, 6(2), Fall, 5–19.

Lederer, A. L. and Sethi, V. (1988) The implementation of strategic information systems planning methodologies. *MIS Quarterly*, 12(3), September, 445–461.

Lederer, A. L. and Sethi, V. (1991) Critical dimensions of strategic information systems planning. *Decision Sciences*, 22(1), Winter, 104–119.

Mintzberg, H. (1983) *Structure in Fives: Designing Effective Organizations*, Prentice Hall, Englewood Cliffs, NJ.

Mintzberg, H. (1987) Crafting strategy. *Harvard Business Review*, 66(4), July–August, 66–75.

Moynihan, T. (1990) What chief executives and senior managers want from their IT departments. *MIS Quarterly*, 14(1), March, 15–26.

Niederman, F., Brancheau, J. C. and Wetherbe, J. C. (1991) Information systems management issues for the 1990s. *MIS Quarterly*, 15(4), December, 475–500.

Porter, M. E. and Millar, V. E. (1985) How information gives you competitive advantage. *Harvard Business Review*, 66(4), July–August, 149–160.

Quinn, J. B. (1977) Strategic goals: Plans and politics. *Sloan Management Review*, 19(1), Fall, 21–37.

Quinn, J. B. (1978) Strategic change: Logical incrementalism. *Sloan Management Review*, 20(1), Fall, 7–21.

Raghunathan, T. S. and King, W. R. (1988) The impact of information systems planning on the organization. *OMEGA*, 16(2), 85–93.

Sullivan, C. H., Jr. (1985) Systems planning in the information age. *Sloan Management Review*, 26(2), Winter, 3–11.

Synott, W. R. and Gruber, W. H. (1982) *Information Resource Management: Opportunities and Strategies for the 1980s*, John Wiley and Sons, New York.

Zani, W. M. (1970) Blueprint for MIS. *Harvard Business Review*, 48(6), November–December, 95–100.

Questions for Discussion

1   Consider the success factors listed in Table 1.5. Is it worth undertaking SISP without top management involvement and support?

2   Compare the author's concept of SISP with more recent considerations of IS strategizing covered in Chapters 2–4. Does his treatment remain relevant?

3   Debate the strengths and weaknesses of the various SISP approaches introduced in this chapter. Assuming time constraints prevent an 'everything goes' approach, which approach might:
    • help improve IS credibility?
    • do the most to align IT with business strategy?
    • do the most to enable competitive uses of IT?
    • do the most to achieve an organization-wide vision?
    • best deal with management of change issues?

4   The author states that 'successful SISP seems to require users and line managers working in partnership with the IS function'. Who should be involved in SISP and how should those involved be determined according to the approach adopted?

5   How do the approaches that have been introduced in this chapter square with recent developments in the opening of IS strategy?

Further Reading

The "Information systems strategy-as-practice" special issue of *The Journal of Strategic Information Systems*: Peppard, J., Galliers, R.D. Thorogood, A. (eds.), Volume 23, Issue 1, March 2014, pp. 1–92. https://www.sciencedirect.com/journal/the-journal-of-strategic-information-systems/vol/23/issue/1

Chapter 2

Robert D. Galliers

CONCEPTUAL DEVELOPMENTS IN INFORMATION SYSTEMS STRATEGY: FURTHER REFLECTIONS ON INFORMATION SYSTEMS STRATEGY

THIS CHAPTER HAS THE aim of reflecting on developments in the area of information systems strategy and, more particularly, on the process of information systems strategizing. It does so against the background of something of a hiatus in the treatment of the topic in the Information Systems literature, especially since the heightened interest in this area of research up to the early 1990s. A further motivation arises from the relative paucity of serious reflection on Information Systems issues in much of the Strategic Management and Organizational Behavior literatures on strategy and strategizing (Orlikowski 2000 being a notable exception). The chapter also aims to take account of key advances in the early twenty-first century in information and communication technologies, knowledge management, and the rapidly-changing nature of the business environment.

Surely, few would argue that the strategic management of data, information, and knowledge—and associated ICT—represents a major strategic challenge and opportunity for organizations in the twenty-first century. The market for ICT products and services can be measured in tens of billions of dollars/euros. It has been estimated that companies in the developed world spend something in the region of two percent of turnover annually on hardware and software alone (Willcocks 1992, 1999). This figure would no doubt grow considerably if the costs associated with staff development, maintenance, and the management of change associated with the implementation and ongoing operation of ICT-based systems were taken into account. But we still talk glibly of the information age, of the networked society, of globalization, of knowledge management—each in its own way enabled and facilitated by ICT. It is therefore surprising how little we strategize about these issues.

Although attitudes differ, there is little doubt that ICT is here to stay (Land 1996). While some see the advent of this 'brave new world' as being nothing other than a boon, others mutter their discontent at the spiraling costs involved, at 'techies' who fail to understand the subtleties of organizational life, at the disruption created, at the invasion of privacy, and so on (Galliers 1992). Notwithstanding, the impact of ICT is likely to be felt increasingly as its power and reach continue to outstrip even the wildest predictions. This impact is felt by individuals, organizations, national governments, and society as a whole. What more need be said to argue that this is a topic worthy of our attention in any strategy discourse?

Given the above, it would seem strange that information systems strategy barely rates a mention in most business strategy courses. Strange that the topic most often appears as an optional course, at best, in MBA curricula or in master's courses in Management or Organizational Behavior. Strange that many firms rush, lemming-like, to avoid the pain of managing their information resource and the related technologies by outsourcing their ICT or information services departments (Lacity and Willcocks 2000). Strange that we reel from one bandwagon, one fad to the next with apparent abandon, often to rue the consequences later.[1] Strange that we simultaneously revel in, and yet revile, the industry that plies us with one solution after the next—an industry that, nonetheless, appears not to ask what questions its 'solutions' are meant to be answering.

The purpose of this chapter, then, is to counter these cavalier attitudes and provide a serious commentary on some of the key issues associated with strategizing in the context of managing organizational information and knowledge, and the related ICT. This will not be a technologically oriented, nor indeed a technologically deterministic, treatment of the topic although, inevitably, developments in ICT have had a profound effect on the scope and orientation of information systems strategy. Rather, it will deal with developments in our thinking and practice in Information Systems from a strategy—or, rather, strategizing—perspective. Even more important, it will provide a critical commentary on some of the more trite treatments of the topic that tend to appear in the popular media.

The chapter is organized as follows. First, an attempt is made to provide something of a tutorial on developments in the theory and practice of information systems strategy from the early days of commercial data processing (DP) up to the 1990s (e.g. Somogyi and Galliers 1987, 2003). Secondly, it examines some of the key concepts and frameworks that have underpinned much of information systems strategy theory during this period. We then proceed to consider some of the more recent developments and new thinking in the field that have emerged over the last decade or so, with a view to pointing out future directions and current concerns, culminating in a proposed inclusive framework for information systems strategizing.

Background History: From Data Processing to Competitive Advantage

There have, of course, been many developments in ICT since the earliest days of business computing. In parallel with these innovations, and with an increasingly sophisticated understanding of the role of these technologies in organizations, our understanding of information systems strategy has grown too during this period. Figure 2.1 provides a simplified framework within which to situate some of these developments. It suggests that we might usefully view such developments in four phases that have differed in terms of:

(a)   the degree to which the information systems strategy might be viewed as a business-driven, 'top-down' process—as against more technology-driven, 'bottom-up' concerns; and

(b)   the extent to which such strategies have been based on short-term problem-solving as against more long-term strategic goal-setting.

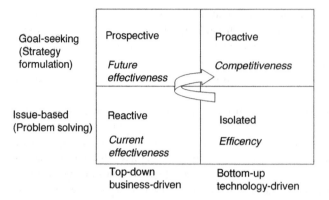

Figure 2.1 Tracing the developments in information systems strategizing.
Adapted from Galliers (1987: 226).

The model in Figure 2.1 suggests that the focus of information systems strategizing may be seen to have gone through four phases, during which it has shifted away from— and back to—ICT, and from matters of efficiency to matters of effectiveness and competitiveness. This is clearly a highly stylized and overly simplistic view of developments, but the framework helps to provide something of an overview of the changes that have taken place since the 1960s. In some respects, we might suggest that current information systems strategizing incorporates aspects of each of these phases. For example, there is evidence of what has come to be been termed 'storage resource planning', characterized by a concern for the efficient storage of data across an enterprise to improve current and future efficiency, effectiveness, and competitiveness.

In the first phase, in the early days of commercial computing, information systems strategy was predominantly concerned with issues of the day and the efficient utilization of the technology for mainly operational purposes. From this perspective, information systems strategy may be viewed as having been fairly *isolated* from the rest of the business. There followed a period where more formal, 'top-down', business-driven strategies were commonplace, with the emphasis being for the most part on *reactive* effectiveness. Such strategies took as read the existing business plans and objectives, and attempted to identify information systems applications to meet those business needs. Over time, information systems strategies became more forward-looking, bearing in mind the need to invest in technology that would stand the test of time despite changing information requirements. Such strategies may be seen as being essentially *prospective* in character. A move towards the *proactive* use of ICT for competitive advantage emerged during the 1980s and 1990s, applying concepts for the most part developed by Michael Porter and his Harvard Business School colleagues such as Warren McFarlan (e.g. McFarlan 1984; Cash and Konsynski 1985; Porter and Millar 1985). This was superseded by Business Process Redesign or Re-engineering (BPR), which aimed to automate streamlined processes in line with customer requirements (e.g. Hammer, 1990). The following subsections provide further detail of such developments, during each of these phases.

Operational Efficiency: The Isolated Phase

In the first phase, during the early days of commercial data processing, hardly any strategic thought was given by senior managers to the uses to which ICT could be put in their organization, other than to think in terms of improving operational efficiency or attempting to cut costs.

Managers would leave it to their information systems colleagues to develop and implement what was thought to be necessary in terms of computing systems. Targets for computerization (automation by another word) were simple production processes and record keeping, such as accounting systems. Little, if any, thought was given to the impact of the 'new' technology to ongoing operations, little concern was expressed over the kinds of skills that might be required to get the best out of the investment, and most developments or acquisitions were undertaken on a piecemeal basis. What little management of information systems there was tended to be considered the province of what we now call the Information Technology function, and its management. In short, there was little planning for information systems, let alone strategizing.

Current Effectiveness: The Reactive Phase

Senior management increasingly became concerned that DP was not delivering the promised efficiency gains, nor focusing on key business concerns and imperatives. From the days when DP was seen as almost entirely the province of the technologist, we gradually saw the emergence of business-driven IS planning approaches. One such was IBM's Business Systems Planning (BSP) methodology (Zachman 1982), a service IBM provided to its customers that was meant to identify not only how the organization could harness ICT to meet business needs but also, of course, to demonstrate the need for more computing. In essence, BSP was developed to identify key business processes and their associated information requirements. A comparison with the data output from existing information systems would then lead to the identification of additional required information systems applications—and additional hardware and software too.

The idea that ICT and business needed to be aligned was first introduced during this 'reactive' era. Alignment is an issue that has remained with us ever since, as discussed later in the chapter. At the time of this era, organizations had to rely on mainframe technology, with so-called 'dumb' terminals on employees' desks usually providing periodic output for control purposes. This was commonly known as 'batch processing', as data were processed in batches rather than on a continuous, real-time basis. For example, weekly or monthly management reports—forming what were called management information systems (MIS)—would be produced on reams of paper. This usually required much additional human analysis to provide anything meaningful.

Future Effectiveness: The Prospective Phase

The advent of database systems in the late 1970s and 1980s not only led to the development of executive information systems (EIS), where managers could ask the database for answers to specific questions, but also to a major rethink of information systems strategy. The thought here was that, rather than identifying particular information systems applications, organizations would simply have to identify the key data entities with which they were dealing (e.g. customer; product) and their attributes (e.g. name, address; product code, size). These could then be mapped to demonstrate their linkages, as a precursor to database design. A champion of this approach was James Martin (1982). Something of a 'garbage can' model (see Cohen et al. 1972) for information systems strategy, with database technology in mind, thus appeared on the scene. It was thought that organizations would no longer have to concern themselves with issues of prioritizing information requirements associated with particular functions, managers, or processes. Rather, the database would enable the delivery of whatever information was required, wherever and whenever it was needed. In some cases, the error in this line of reasoning was not realized until after the invoice had been received for the massively increased computing power necessary to run the resultant database.

In some ways, this era may be seen to have spawned the so-called critical success factor (CSF) approach (Rockart 1979). Under the guise of executives defining for themselves their own critical data needs, the approach was rapidly appropriated by managers and consultants alike, since it enabled prioritization to take place. The approach was also welcomed because it brought an element of control back to harassed executives, who had seen their ICT budgets expanding at a time when they were being promised increased computing power for their limited financial resources—but nonetheless were becoming increasingly concerned with budget overspends. In outline, the approach centered on the identification of key objectives for the organization or strategic business unit (SBU) concerned, followed by the identification of key management processes necessary to enable the achievement of the stated objectives. CSFs associated with these processes were then pinpointed as a means of identifying the data that had to be made available for executives to manage and control the processes within their spheres of responsibility. The CSF concept was utilized by various approaches, such as Process Quality Management (PQM)—another IBM methodology (Ward 1990)—and has continued to be incorporated into management thinking to this day.[2]

Competitiveness: The Proactive Phase

As we moved into the 1980s, the concepts of Porter and colleagues at Harvard had an enormous impact on thinking regarding the competitive advantages to be gained by firms from the astute application of ICT. Utilizing such concepts as the 'Five Forces' and 'Value Chain' models, they demonstrated how ICT, and the information it produces, could: provide added value to good and services; retard competition from both traditional rivals and new entrants; and be used to leverage relationships with suppliers and customers alike (Porter 1980, 1985; McFarlan 1984; Porter and Millar 1985). A considerable amount of consultancy activity was spawned by this kind of thinking, and a great deal of literature was written on the topic throughout the 1980s and into the 1990s.

In line with this style of thinking, there emerged in the 1990s another approach to the strategic utilization of ICT, but this time focusing more on internal processes. The movement was spawned by the likes of Michael Hammer and Tom Davenport and became known as BPR (e.g. Davenport and Short 1990; Hammer 1990; Davenport 1993). A basis for their argument was that the mere computerization of a messy situation will lead to nothing more than a computerized mess. They argued for a clean slate approach that identified and streamlined the key business processes. The trick was then to identify which of these processes could be automated, thereby improving efficiency and cutting costs. In addition, by focusing on customer requirements, the processes would lead to improved effectiveness.

While success rates were reported as being quite low (e.g. Davenport 1996), and advocates of the process were at pains to warn organizations of the risks involved, BPR was big business and was attempted by most major corporations in the English-speaking world. For example, the market for BPR services in 1995 was estimated to be in excess of $50 billion (ibid.). By 1996, however, the bubble had begun to burst when one of the founding fathers of the movement, Tom Davenport, finally recognized the loss of considerable organizational knowledge through the swathes of redundancies brought about by the downsizing strategies that accompanied many BPR efforts. BPR had become, in his words, 'the fad that forgot people' (ibid.: 70).

In some respects, then, we had come full circle. When we first began to think of information systems planning and strategy, the focus was primarily on the technology itself, since managerial concerns regarding the application of computing were mainly about matters of operational efficiency. We then moved into an era during which business-driven approaches were prevalent, with concern shifting to matters of effectiveness, and prioritization. As we entered the 1980s, and then into the 1990s, the focus moved to ICT for competitive advantage, and subsequently to BPR. In this era, attention shifted once more to a concern for how the technology could be harnessed proactively to increase competitiveness, at first through an analysis of the competitive environment and, later, by an analysis of internal processes. Throughout the whole 'competitive' phase, however, approaches to information systems strategy might reasonably be characterized as being based on a rational, deliberate paradigm, rather than the kind of emergence discussed by Mintzberg (e.g. Mintzberg and Waters 1985), among others. Additionally, little attention had been paid to more pluralistic and innovative strategizing.

This characterization of information systems strategy theory and practice as predominantly rational, objective, and unitary is illustrated by Figure 2.2, which is based on Whittington's (1993) framework for mapping the developments in strategic thinking in the latter half of the twentieth century. It soon becomes clear that much information systems strategizing has been of the traditional school, with strategy formulation based on profit maximization as the primary, if not sole, objective. What is more, there has been a tendency, certainly in practice, to assume the equivalence of data, information, and knowledge. Latterly, however, both tendencies have been brought into question, as we shall see later in the chapter. A contrast can be found with the traditional school of information systems strategizing in the soft systems methodology (Checkland 1981; Galliers 1993a; Stowell 1995). Here, the outcome of the analysis is not predetermined and an ICT 'solution' is by no means a foregone conclusion. Additionally, alternative outcomes will be the subject of debate and further iteration. The process of strategizing, with a view to gaining a shared appreciation of the context in which this strategizing is taking place, is just as important, if not more so, than the decisions made as a result. Thus, soft systems methodology might be seen as spanning the two quadrants in the lower portion of Figure 2.2.

From Localized Exploitation to Business Scope Redefinition

A somewhat different framework, but nonetheless one that also provides a perspective on the changes in information systems strategic thinking, arose from a major research program conducted during the late 1980s, coordinated at the Massachusetts Institute of Technology (MIT)

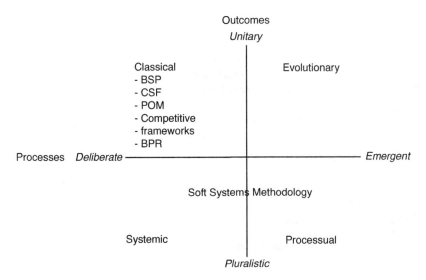

Figure 2.2 Locating common information systems strategy approaches.
Adapted from Whittington (1993: 3).

under the title 'Management in the 1990s' (Scott Morton 1991). Funded by major corporations from both sides of the Atlantic, it sought to uncover the means by which ICT could be harnessed to provide truly significant advances in terms of business performance. The framework is reproduced here as Figure 2.3.

One conclusion drawn by the MIT research team was that many companies were obtaining only relatively low business benefits from their investment in, and application of, ICT. They argued that this was due mainly to the fact that a relatively low level of business transformation had been attempted, with most companies operating at levels 1 and 2 of Figure 2.3. The researchers argued that such evolutionary approaches would not deliver the requisite order-of-magnitude improvements being sought after, which they deemed necessary in highly-competitive markets. This, they argued, could occur only via revolutionary change of the style proposed by the BPR advocates (level 3).

'Don't automate, obliterate' was the uncompromising title of a famous *Harvard Business Review* article by Hammer (1990). But, as we have seen, BPR focused for the most part on internal process redesign. The MIT team extended the focus of BPR, in much the same way as the Porterian school had done with the value-chain concept, to include what they termed 'business network redesign' (level 4). This extended the process analysis to ensure electronic links provided along the value chain included suppliers and customers, in order to form electronically-mediated strategic alliances (Rayport and Sviokla 1995). At one stage, this would have involved utilizing electronic data interchange (EDI) technology. Nowadays, the World Wide Web and the Internet would be used.

The MIT team concluded that truly significant business benefits would emerge only from redefining the very scope of the business through the utilization of the full power of ICT to create new products and services (level 5). Case examples that have entered the mythology of strategic information systems include: the Apollo and Sabre airline reservation systems of United and American Airlines; Thomson Holidays; Frito-Lay; Otis Elevators; American Hospital Supply; and Mrs Field's Cookies (Galliers 1993a). Senn (1992) and Ciborra (1994), among others, have argued that these systems were introduced initially with a view to increasing efficiency, but subsequently underwent various enhancements that—somewhat serendipitously—provided the companies concerned with a competitive advantage.

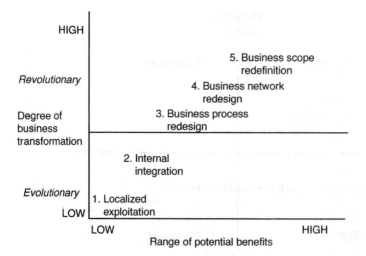

Figure 2.3 The MIT management in the 1990s program: 'IT-based revolutionary change leads to major benefits'.
Adapted from Venkatraman (1991: 127).

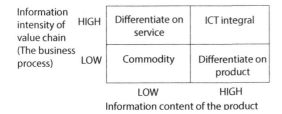

Figure 2.4 Applying the Information Intensity Matrix.
Amended from Porter and Millar (1985).

While Figure 2.3 stresses only the revolutionary potential of ICT when used proactively, it is clear that it is not always sensible to base one's business strategy on such an aggressive use of the technology. Indeed, Figure 2.3's 'range of potential benefits' axis might reasonably be re-labeled 'degree of business risk', given that revolutionary change can bring with it much greater risks than would be the case with a more incremental approach (Galliers 1997). A means of assisting in deciding whether there is a potential strategic advantage by providing added-value services based on information and ICT is provided by the Information Intensity Matrix (Porter and Millar 1985), which is depicted in Figure 2.4.

Figure 2.4 asks us to consider the extent to which information forms a critical part of the value-chain activities and of the product itself. In situations where this 'information intensity' is high, it can be concluded that ICT is integral to the delivery of goods and services. Where it is low, the potential use of ICT is more limited. Competing on the basis of providing additional information in terms of the product itself, or in relation to value-chain processes, can thus be considered by using this framework.

Distinguishing the Components of Information Systems Strategies

Much of the MIT research—and indeed a great deal of mainstream thinking on information systems strategy—suggests that the key issue is to align ICT with the business strategy, as might be supposed from the earlier approaches such as BSP, CSF and PQM.[3] However, there is quite a conceptual gap between a business strategy and the necessary IT infrastructure to support it. As illustrated in Figure 2.5, Earl (1989) makes a distinction between information

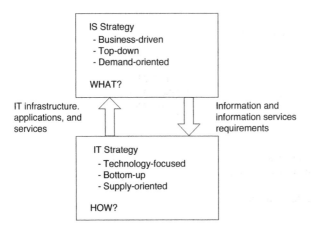

Figure 2.5 Earl's distinction between information systems and information technology strategies.
Amended from Earl (1989: 63).

systems and information *technology* strategy, arguing that the former is essentially concerned with the 'What?' of the information required, while the latter is concerned with the 'How?' questions about the use of ICT to provide that information.

Note that, as indicated in Figure 2.5, Earl proposes that the information systems strategy is essentially business-led and demand-driven: it can be seen as a 'top-down' process, feeding off the business strategy. He further argues that information systems strategy should be the concern of the business executive—not the IT Director. Conversely, the information technology strategy is seen as being driven more by technology and supply, in that it depends to an extent at least on the existing technological infrastructure—on what is feasible from a technological standpoint within the current planning horizon. This is much more within the province of the IT Director.

Earl's distinction also brings with it some implications for the concept of alignment. For example, information systems strategy is viewed here as being about strategizing because it is ongoing and process-based ('processual'). Conversely, the information technology strategy is relatively fixed. This makes alignment difficult, as explored later in the chapter. Earl developed this line of thinking further by adding another component to the information systems and information technology strategy, namely the information management strategy. Having asked the 'What?' and the 'How?' questions, the information management strategy, in Earl's (1989: 64) formulation, asks the question 'Wherefore?'—to find answers to 'Why?' questions such as: 'Why this particular strategy as against any other?'

The field of Information Systems is generally replete with terms that mean different things to different people. For instance, 'information technology' and 'information systems' are often used synonymously. The 'information management' term is another such example. This can sometimes connote a much broader concept than in Earl's amended model by encompassing the general field associated with the management issues concerned with information and ICT. Galliers (1991) noted this terminological confusion when building on the earlier work of Earl to produce a more comprehensive framework for information systems strategizing (see Figure 2.6). This framework included the questions related to 'What?' (in

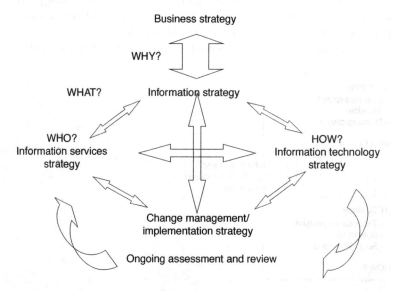

Figure 2.6 Components of information systems strategy.
Amended from Galliers (1991: 60, 1999: 230).

Earl's terms, the *information* strategy) and 'How?' (*information technology* strategy), but added the question 'Who?', relating to the *information services* strategy—the organizational arrangements for the provision of IS-related services. It also included considerations associated with the implementation of the strategy, with all its attendant management-of-change issues.

In terms of the 'Who?' question, the framework emphasizes the importance of developing an integrated information services strategy. This would need to include the kind of information systems staffing and skills needed to facilitate the strategy, including training requirements. In particular, a key question to consider, as an integral aspect of information systems strategizing, would be whether to outsource ICT provision—a topic that was particularly popular in the 1980s and 1990s. IT outsourcing refers to the 'significant contribution by external vendors in the physical and/or human resources associated with the entire or specific components of the ICT infrastructure in the user organization' (Loh and Venkatraman 1992). As Lacity and Willcocks (2000) remind us, however, the appropriate question is not whether to outsource *per se,* but what would be the appropriate sourcing arrangements.

Another additional element in the Figure 2.6 framework is the explicit recognition of the importance of managing the change process associated with the implementation strategy. Galliers had become very much aware from empirical research and consultancy assignments that the outcome of many information systems strategy projects was what might be termed 'shelfware', as plans for such projects often collected dust on the office shelf because such little information systems implementation occurred as a result of such projects.

It also appeared that few lessons had been learned from the mainstream literature on strategizing. From the start, this was particularly the case in relation to the consideration of implementation and change management issues (Wilson 1992). Other issues that required attention included: the emergent quality of strategies and strategizing (Mintzberg and Waters 1985); the unanticipated consequences of any ICT implementation (e.g. Brown and Eisenhardt 1995; Robey and Boudreau 1999), and what Weick (2001) terms interpretative flexibility. As a result—and also drawing on Systems Theory (e.g. Checkland 1981)—the model depicted in Figure 2.6 incorporated features that demonstrated the need to monitor and learn from the emergent features of strategic decisions. It also takes account of the unintended consequences of these decisions, and the various interpretations of, and reactions to, events and innovations expressed by different stakeholders. 'Change management' and 'ongoing review and feedback' were therefore incorporated into the model.

The framework can be used in analyzing information systems strategies in organizations by considering the extent to which each of the components is in place. This may provide an insight into the orientation of any particular organization towards information systems strategy. For example, does the organization emphasize ICT strategy to the detriment of identifying strategic information requirements? Or does the organization consider implementation and change management issues as part of their strategizing?

In addition, however, it suggests that each component of the information systems strategy is mutually dependent on each other component. For example, questions can be asked about whether strategic decisions regarding the organization of information systems services (e.g. whether they should be centralized or distributed; whether to outsource or not) are considered as an integral part of the information systems strategy, or whether—as is often the case—they are considered in isolation. Similarly, questions can be asked not only in relation to the extent to which required information is identified in line with the existing business strategy, but also if information is available that can actually question whether the strategy is appropriate or not, given changing business circumstances and as a consequence of the ongoing assessment and review of outcomes. This is the 'Why?' question that appears in Figure 2.6. The framework therefore envisions information systems strategy to be more all-encompassing than the distinction between IS and IT strategies provided by Earl in Figure 2.5.

Assessing Information Systems Capability

Deciding on an appropriate strategy depends, in part at least, on an organization's ability to carry out that strategy successfully. However, Figure 2.7 shows there are occasions when it may well be advisable to follow a more conservative line, notwithstanding the arguments of those who follow the 'revolutionary change' school of thought. For example, a more evolutionary approach would appear to be called for if an analysis of the information intensity (Figure 2.4) of an organization's business processes and products and/or services found that the opportunities for adding value through information are limited. Nevertheless, if the opportunities are there but the capability is limited, then such an aggressive approach may well present too great a risk without outside assistance, or the development of internal human and technological resources.

The problem is that many organizations find themselves in the 'Catch-22' position of the lower right-hand quadrant of Figure 2.7, where—in a sense—they are damned if they do and they are damned if they don't. In such circumstances, organizations have to beware of the aggressive strategies of a competitor that might well have greater information systems capability than themselves. In response, an organization may well attempt a similar strategy itself, but fail in the attempt due to a lack of internal information systems resources—human as well as technical. Should the organization decide the risk is too great and do little in response, it is likewise open to attack.

How, then, might an organization evaluate its current information systems capability? One approach is to assess its current information systems strategy using the framework illustrated in Figure 2.6. But this provides an overview only. A more detailed positioning framework, which is explained below, is based on the so-called 'Stages of Growth' thesis first enunciated by Nolan (Gibson and Nolan 1974; Nolan 1979) and on the well-known '7-S' framework of McKinsey & Co. (Pascale and Athos 1981). Nolan's Stages model has its roots in Greiner's (1972) earlier work, essentially positing that firms will grow in maturity through recognizable 'stages' in terms of their management and use of ICT.

Nolan first formulated a four-stage model, but later extended this to six stages to take account of the database technology that was becoming available at the time—a technology that enabled firms to integrate their systems across functions and business units in a manner that had previously been impossible (see the second 'internal integration' stage of the MIT

Figure 2.7 When, and when not, to pursue an aggressive business strategy based on information technology.
Amended from McLaughlin et al. (1983).

model in Figure 2.3). His six stages were (using Nolan's numbering system, that I also adopt below for a revised model):

I   Initiation
II   Contagion
III   Control
IV   Integration
V   Data Administration
VI   Maturity.

The story told through these stages unfolds as follows. At first, organizations are relatively unaware of the capabilities and potential uses of new and emerging ICT (Stage I). But once they have a few adherents, a kind of 'me too' mentality sweeps through the organization and demands increases almost exponentially (Stage II). As a result, management becomes increasingly concerned that things—especially budgets—are getting out of control, and they therefore impose tighter controls on ICT expenditure (Stage III). As management becomes increasingly aware that the looked-for business benefits from the ICT investment are escaping them because of lack of compatibility between different systems and a lack of information flow across processes and functions, further investment occurs in technologies that enable greater systems integration (Stage IV). This stage leads into one during which greater efforts are expended in ensuring the consistency of the data being shared across the organization, for example in terms of definition and interpretation (Stage V). The final stage of maturity is reached once integration is complete and compatibility is assured (Stage VI).

As is implied by the above, patterns of expenditure on ICT give a clue to which stage an organization has reached. Expenditure accelerates during Stages II and IV/V and tapers off in Stages III and VI—thus following a kind of double-S curve. While Nolan's (1979) model has been criticized in academic circles for its lack of conceptual underpinnings and its failure to provide an accurate prediction of growth empirically (Benbasat et al. 1984; King and Kraemer 1984), it was nonetheless highly popular and used extensively by many major corporations in the English-speaking world. Indeed, it spawned a consultancy company—Nolan Norton and Co.—which was eventually taken over by KPMG. Despite this popularity, it clearly had its limitations, particularly in relation to its technological focus. An extended Stages model was therefore developed by Galliers and Sutherland (1991), following case study research in Europe and Australia. This model, shown here as Table 2.1, focused on broader information management issues and borrowed the McKinsey 7-S framework that was in widespread circulation at the time (see first column in Table 2.1).

The framework depicted by Table 2.1 may be difficult to take in at first glance, but it essentially parallels the Nolan (1979) model in terms of the six stages of growth, which it renames (keeping the same numbering system):

I   Ad hocracy
II   Starting the foundations
III   Centralized dictatorship
IV   Democratic dialectic and cooperation
V   Entrepreneurial opportunity
VI   Integrated harmonious relationships.

Referring to our account earlier in this chapter of the developments in thinking and practice with respect to information systems strategy, we can trace this development through the six stages of strategy growth. We can see, for example, that information systems strategy

Table 2.1 An extended Stages of Growth model

Stage:	I Ad hocracy	II Starting the foundations	III Centralized dictatorship	IV Democratic dialectic and cooperation	V Entrepreneurial opportunity	VI Integrated harmonious relationships
Element:Strategy	Acquisition of IT (services)	Audit of IT provision	Top-down analysis	Integration, coordination	Competitive advantage	Interactive planning, collaboration
Structure	Informal	Finance controlled	Centralized IS department	Information Center	SBU coalition	Coordinated solutions
Systems	Ad hoc operational, accounting	Gaps/duplication, large backlog, heavy maintenance	Uncontrolled enduser computing versus centralized systems	Decentralized approach, some Executive Information Systems	Coordinated centralized and decentralized IS, some strategic IS	Inter-organizational systems, IS/IT-based products and services
Staff	Programmers, contractors	Systems analysts, data manager	IS planners, IS manager, database specialists	Business analysts, information resource manager	Business and IS planners integrated	IS/IT Director (Board level)
Style	Unaware	'Don't bother me, I'm too busy'	Abrogation, delegation	Partnership, benefits management	Individualistic (product champions)	Multi-disciplinary teams (key themes)
Skills	Individual, technical, low-level	Systems development methodology, costbenefit analysis	IS awareness, project management	IS/business awareness	Entrepreneurial marketing	Lateral thinking (IT/IS potential)
Shared values	Obfuscation	Confusion	Senior management concern, IS defense	Cooperation	Opportunistic	Strategy making and implementation

Amended from Galliers and Sutherland (1991: 111), with elements from Pascale and Athos (1981).

develops from what is little more than the acquisition of IS products and services on more or less an ad hoc basis, through to top-down, business-led planning (see Earl's model, Figure 2.5)—and on to competitive advantage. The sixth stage is characterized by a strategy that integrates information systems considerations into the business strategy itself. Similarly, we can trace developments in the kind of staff and skills that are available to the organization (whether in-house or through a sourcing arrangement).

Managerial attitudes towards the strategic aspects of information systems can also be traced. From the bewilderment and confusion of the early stages of growth (Stages I and II), there has been a tendency for management to adopt the somewhat negative and adversarial stance associated with Stage III. This has tended to be as a result of past disappointments and concerns over spiraling ICT expenditure—with sometimes little in the way of perceived business benefits in return. The latter stages are characterized by a more positive, but informed, perspective. More specifically, with growing cooperation and a realization that greater integration across functions and SBUs is called for, a more concerted approach towards integration is evident in Stage IV. A more outward-facing perspective characterizes Stages V and VI, with an entrepreneurial and opportunistic stance being in evidence. A number of lessons emerged from the application of the Table 2.1 Stages of Growth framework, including the following.

First, it should be noted that the model is no more than a model—it is a positioning framework only. The foregoing discussion might unwittingly give the sense that all this development is preordained and is followed in every instance. This is far from being the case. The model has been found to be useful as a means of facilitating shared understanding as a result of posing a series of questions in relation to aspects of information systems management, based on the 7-S list. It certainly does not provide any answers. And shared understanding does not necessarily mean consensus. It is a subjective measure, and opinions will sometimes diverge, but it at least provides a kind of benchmark against which to assess matters, and to begin to understand why certain views are held by some, but not others. The model is an aid to sensemaking (Weick 1990); used judiciously, it can be of assistance in gaining a shared appreciation of key information systems management issues on the part of management teams.

Second, there is no intrinsic right for organizations to move inexorably through the stages towards Stage VI. Indeed, some companies have realized that they have occasionally moved 'backwards'. A series of discussions as to why movement has or has not occurred may provide further insight. Third, different parts of the organization may each present a different profile. As a result, assessments can be made as to whether these differences are harmful and need to be dealt with—or that the company can live with them, or indeed, that they are entirely appropriate. Fourth, organizations will not find themselves at a particular stage with respect to all the elements, but will find that some of these will lag 'behind' while others will be further 'ahead'. Again, assessments can be made as to what these differences mean in terms of strategic directions and imperatives. Further, it will seldom be the case that an organization's profile will fit neatly into the stages, as there will be elements that exhibit characteristics of more than one stage. This is an imprecise 'science'.

Fifth, it may prove useful to map the implied profile of a proposed strategy and contrast this with the existing situation. If there is considerable distance between the two, an assessment of the risks involved in attempting the proposed strategy can be made. Sixth, as a result of these kinds of deliberations, the shared understanding reached should lead to the identification of change projects designed to move the organization to a desired position. Finally, what constitutes 'maturity' (as referred to in the earlier Nolan models) will be changing and contextual, so Stage VI should not be viewed as an end in itself. Other elements to the model could also be incorporated; for example, an eighth 'S' might usefully be concerned with security issues.

Information Systems Strategic Thinking in the 1990s[4]

As we have seen, the field of information systems strategy had come some distance in the latter part of the twentieth century. From a relatively isolated, narrow, and technologically oriented activity, it had become much more business-oriented and competitively minded. There had been increasing realization, too, that the management of change and people issues are a significant—perhaps the key—aspect of what is required.

In some respects, though, IS strategy had not come very far at all. It had reached a point at which current thinking might reasonably be summarized by another framework from the MIT Management in the 1990s Program (see Figure 2.8). For example, we had learnt our lessons from the many BPR failures: IS strategy and change was more, much more, than focusing on business processes and technology alone. People mattered, and their capabilities and knowledge had to be nurtured. Information systems needed to be seen as social systems, admittedly with an increasingly technological component—but not as technological systems *per se*. While this model moves us well beyond the technological focus of earlier information systems strategy approaches, it is also similar to Leavitt's (1965) 'diamond' of the mid-1960s. Leavitt argued that organizations could be viewed as complex systems, consisting of four interacting variables: objectives, structure, technology, and people. These variables clearly bear a remarkable resemblance to those identified in Figure 2.8.

Despite this, information systems strategy had indeed come a long way, but it also had a very long way to go to catch up with other strategy discourses. This emphasizes the point already made with regard to Figure 2.2, that builds on the framework developed by Whittington (1993) for identifying different schools of thought relating to strategy and strategizing. That point is also illustrated in the next section, which questions some prevailing myths about the strategic potential of ICT.

Uncovering the Myths of Strategic ICT

There have, of course, been many developments in ICT in recent years. In this section, a number of these recent developments will be considered in relation to the various strategy issues. Specifically, it will be argued that—despite the developments in thinking about information systems strategy discussed earlier—many myths about ICT continue to be promulgated: myths about how to develop ICT strategically, how to use ICT to support knowledge management, and about ICT and competitive advantage.

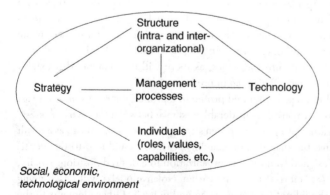

Figure 2.8 The MIT model of strategic change and fit.
Adapted from Scott Morton (1991: 20) and Sauer, Yetton, and Associates (1997: 281).

Myths about How to Develop ICT Strategically

There are essentially two related elements to the myth about ICT strategic developments. The first is that ICT systems should align with the business strategy and the second is that ICT systems should be rationally planned. As noted earlier, a central tenet of much of the theory and practice of information systems strategy has been the concept of alignment. The notion of alignment suggests that information systems strategy is a rational and deliberate activity. Intuitively appealing, alignment has been a taken-for-granted concept that remained largely unchallenged for many years. Earl's (1989) distinction between information systems and information technology (or ICT) strategies (Figure 2.5) is very helpful in terms of demarcating the two terms, as we have seen. However, it can too easily hide a key issue with respect to alignment, concerning the fact that the information needs for the great majority of organizations are in constant flux. Of course, there is a subset of information requirements that remains reasonably constant over time but, with fast-changing competitive environments, that subset is by no means representative of the totality.

Conversely, organizations are investing in ICT that will remain with them for quite some time, and will have to serve the test of time. Additionally, the view we have put forward here is that information systems strategy is ongoing and processual. ICT decisions, while they may be cumulative, are nevertheless one-off. The question of alignment is therefore a vexed one, as it is about changing requirements and (relatively) unchanging technology. There is often a dynamic involved, with strategies falling in and out of alignment over time (Sabherwal et al. 2001). The introduction of Internet technology internally, in the form of 'intranets', has assisted considerably in providing the requisite flexibility. However, most firms are having to deal with significant problems in upgrading their so-called legacy systems—both in terms of meeting changed information needs and of integrating them with new systems and technology. Enterprise Resource Planning (ERP) systems are sold partly on the basis of the need to replace such legacy systems (CACM 2000). Presumably, however, in time, ERP systems will themselves become legacy systems. Increasingly, too, alignment is required along the 'virtual' value chain—with electronic links to suppliers and customers alike (Rayport and Sviokla 1995). The open nature of the Internet, with new customers and sources emerging constantly, can complicate matters enormously. 'Alignment with whom?' becomes a more significant and increasingly difficult question to answer.

The second ICT strategic development myth, as we have seen, is that most of the approaches to information systems strategy suggest a rational analysis of ICT needs. For example, the radical approach championed by the MIT Management in the 1990s team (Scott Morton 1991), or as articulated by the advocates of the BPR approach, both start from the premise that a rational analysis of business needs should be undertaken. Indeed, as we have seen, the very notion of alignment suggests that information systems strategy is a rational and deliberate activity. However, following Mintzberg (e.g. Mintzberg and Waters 1985), there is an increasingly strong school of thought that talks of the 'emergent' nature of information systems strategy and of strategic information systems (e.g. Ciborra 1994). Neither should we forget the essentially political nature of most technological appropriations (Swan and Clark 1992). Moreover, as mentioned previously, many of the successful ICT systems that have been developed, and lauded as being 'strategic'—for example, the Apollo and Sabre airline reservation systems—have emerged though a process of gradual enhancement (Senn 1992) and improvisation (e.g. Ciborra 1994, Chapter 1 this volume; Galliers 1991, 1993b). Ciborra uses terms like 'bricolage' and 'tinkering' to signify the bubbling up of innovative ideas within organizations. This is in stark contrast to the kind of radical approach championed by the MIT team, or as articulated by the advocates of BPR (e.g. Davenport and Short Hammer 1990, 1990).[5]

This analysis suggests that no amount of rational planning can ever hope to create an ICT system that aligns with the business strategy, even in the short term. ICT system development is thus best considered as an interactive process, constantly ongoing and emergent as new information needs arise and new opportunities are identified. This conclusion is somewhat in line with the analysis of alignment conducted by Sabherwal et al. (2001), when they talk of 'punctuated equilibrium'.

Myths about How ICT Can Support and Enable Knowledge Management

Knowledge management is one of the latest fads to be adopted by management (e.g. Abrahamson 1991). The emergence of this concept followed the recognition that knowledge is perhaps *the* key resource of organizations, allowing them to innovate and compete. Ironically, perhaps, this recognition occurred at about the same time as the BPR revolution, when much valuable knowledge was lost through companies' back doors, along with the legions of middle-ranking executives made redundant in the name of efficiency—often as a direct result of BPR initiatives. The ERP systems subsequently developed were claimed to be more in tune with the recognition of the importance of capturing organizational knowledge. Such systems have been diffused and adopted widely during the late 1990s and early 2000s, sold on the premise that they will assist to improve efficiency by integrating knowledge about business processes that cut across functions in SBUs and locations.

Efficiency and Innovation

> Importantly, ERP is promoted as a means of helping to transfer 'best practice' knowledge. Thus, a key feature of an ERP system is that it has built-in processes which force an organization using it to adapt itself and its processes to the exigencies of the ERP software. These inbuilt processes are, supposedly, based on 'best practice' industry models. In this instance, then, ICT can be seen as a force for standardization, and therefore for speeding competitive convergence, given that the models remain more or less constant irrespective of the organization implementing the system. The myth is thus created that the adoption of an ERP system will enable an organization to transfer to itself the 'best practice' industry knowledge of how best to organize various processes.

Further, it is interesting to consider such systems in relation to the earlier discussion on alignment which explained how ERP systems are implemented partly to replace legacy systems—but themselves eventually become a legacy. Moreover, by advocating the copying of 'best practices' to improve efficiency, organizations are, potentially at least, running the risk of reducing their capacity to create the new knowledge that is needed to innovate and creatively respond to their ever-changing environment—a key concern of business strategy, surely. Another way of putting this might be to think of the issue in terms of the long-standing dilemma between efficiency and innovation, or between exploitation and exploration (Clark and Staunton 1989; March 1991; McElroy 2000).

The above distinction between efficiency and innovation is important in attempting to understand the role ICT can play in an information systems strategy that seeks to harness the increasing power of the technology, while facilitating innovation and knowledge creation in organizations—especially those that operate on a global basis. Information systems strategy, as we have seen, attempts to square the circle between efficiency, effectiveness, and competitiveness. The latter increasingly relies on constant innovation for it to be sustained. If the Internet, ERP systems, and other ICT have been a force for competitive convergence, as Porter (2001) argues, then how can we claim that ICT such as this provides firms with new means of competing?

These problems and myths surrounding ERP systems can be related to more general myths that have emerged about knowledge management and, more particularly, knowledge management systems (KMS). Most importantly, the myth has been created that suggests KMS can store and transfer knowledge, thus supporting and facilitating knowledge exploitation (the reuse of knowledge across time and space, for example by the transfer of 'best practices') and knowledge creation. The software solutions that were peddled as EIS or mere database systems at the end of the last century have been metamorphosed by marketing executives into the KMS of the twenty-first century. Such systems are based on the view that knowledge is 'out there', ready and available to be harvested or mined. A contrary perspective is provided here.

Data, Information, and Knowledge

> To comprehend the argument here more fully, it is perhaps useful to go back to basics and understand the distinction between data, information, and knowledge—terms that tend to be used synonymously in everyday parlance. Data become informative for a particular purpose to human beings by the way people interpret the world about them through their own individual lenses, and by applying their memory and personal knowledge to each new situation they confront. This is how we innovate and adapt. Data are contextfree and can be interpreted in many different ways for different purposes. For example, the results of a government election in any country in the world will doubtless be interpreted in different ways by the victor and the vanquished. So-called *information* technology therefore processes data, not information. We should, as a result, revert to the original name used for information systems in the 1960s and 1970s: *data* processing systems.
>
> (Galliers and Newell 2003b)

Individuals inform themselves in order to undertake some particular task or make a particular decision. Information is therefore context dependent, and information systems have to include human beings and the act of interpretation for the term to be at all meaningful. Knowledge, on the other hand, is tacit and embedded. It resides within our brains, and enables us to make sense of the data we capture. Knowledge is individuals' 'justified belief'—a belief that allows them to interpret and take purposive action in the world around them.[6] The distinction between the terms is made clearer in Table 2.2, although the latter should be interpreted with some care—given that the characteristics are provided merely to assist in sense-making (see Weick 1990).

The above characterization of knowledge, or rather, 'knowing' (Blackler 1995) suggests that knowledge sharing is facilitated through discourse and dialogue (von Krogh et al. 2000). Thus, the emphasis is on developing communities of practice (Brown and Duguid 1991; Lave and Wenger 1991) and project teams where individuals interact over time to develop shared understandings that can lead to innovation and creativity. ICT systems can support this dialogue, at least partially, but they cannot store or communicate knowledge as such. ICT systems store and transfer *data* that can be interpreted in each context by individuals who make sense of these data, for a particular purpose, based on their personal knowledge, experiences, and predilections.[7]

Table 2.2 Key characteristics of data, information, and knowledge

Data	Information	Knowledge
Explicit	Interpreted	Tacit/embedded
Exploit	Explore	Create
Use	Build/construct	Rebuild/reconstruct
Accept	Confirm	'Disconfirm'
Follow old recipes	Amend old recipes	Develop new recipes
No learning	Single-loop learning	Double-loop learning
Direction	Communication	Sense-making
Prescriptive	Adaptive	Seminal
Efficiency	Effectiveness	Innovation/redundancy
Predetermined	Constrained	Flexible
Technical systems/networks	Socio-technical systems/networks	Social networks
Context-free	Outer context	Inner context

Reproduced from Galliers and Newell (2003a: 189, 2003b: 11).

Myths about ICT and Competitive Advantage

Undoubtedly, the growth and impact of the Internet has been the most noticeable ICT development around the turn of the century, spawning the so-called dotcom companies and a considerable degree of hyperbole concerning e-business. In a *Harvard Business Review* article, Michael Porter (2001) argues that firms should view the Internet as a complement to, rather than something that cannibalizes, more traditional forms of organization and organizational ICT. He claimed that while some have argued that 'the Internet renders strategy obsolete … the opposite is true … it is more important than ever for companies to distinguish themselves through strategy' (Porter 2001: 63). His argument echoes what he was saying twenty years before: it is not the technology itself (in this case, the Internet) that will create competitive advantage, but the uses to which it is put that may do so. As ever, he sees the two fundamental factors that will ultimately determine profitability as being industry structure and sustainable competitive advantage. The former determines the profitability of the average competitor. The latter allows a firm to outperform the average competitor.

Porter goes on to argue that, although the Internet has created new companies and even industries (e.g. online auctions and financial institutions), its impact will be felt most in enabling 'the reconfiguration of existing industries that had been constrained by high costs for communicating, gathering information, or accomplishing transactions' (ibid.: 66). He gives, as examples, distance-learning programs, catalog retailers, and automated fulfillment centers, and contends that the Internet 'only changes the front end of the process' (ibid.: 66).

Porter maintained his belief in his Five Forces analysis (Porter and Millar 1985), stating that these 'still determine profitability even if suppliers, channels, substitutes, or competitors change' (ibid.: 66). However, because the impact of each force varies from industry to industry, he argues that it would not be appropriate to attempt to draw any general conclusions regarding the Internet's impact on long-term profitability. He does point to some general trends, though. For instance, he notes that ICT tends to: bolster buyer bargaining power by providing easier access to information on products and services; reduce barriers to entry by circumventing existing channels; and create substitute products and services. Rivalry intensifies because of the open nature of the Internet and the resultant difficulties that firms confront in retaining proprietary offerings. Rivalry also intensifies because of the global reach of the new technology. Finally, he argues that the Internet's tendency to reduce variable costs leads to pressure to engage in price competition. He observes:

> The great paradox of the Internet is that its very benefits—making information
> widely available; reducing the difficulty of purchasing, marketing, and distribu-
> tion; allowing buyers and sellers to find and attract business with one another
> more easily—also make it more difficult for companies to capture those benefits
> as profits.
>
> (ibid: 66)

This analysis leads Porter to foresee greater competition due to increased numbers of competitors and pressure on prices, exacerbated by growing customer power. With the average profitability of most industries falling, the need for individual firms 'to set them-selves apart from the pack' grows considerably. This leads to the conclusion that advantages must be gained in terms of cost and price, through improved operational efficiency and effec-tiveness, strategic positioning, and by doing things differently from the competition. He notes (ibid.: 70): 'The Internet affects operational effectiveness and strategic positioning in very different ways. It makes it harder for companies to sustain competitive advantages, but it opens new opportunities for achieving or strengthening a distinctive strategic positioning.'

It should be clear from the foregoing why Porter (ibid.: 78) argues that the Internet has not altered the basic principles of competitive advantage:

> In our quest to see how the Internet is different, we have failed to see how the
> Internet is the same. While a new means of conducting business has become
> available, the fundamentals of competition remain unchanged. The next stage of
> the Internet's evolution will involve a shift in thinking from e-business to busi-
> ness, from e-strategy to strategy. Only by integrating the Internet into overall
> strategy will this powerful new technology become an equally powerful force
> for competitive advantage.

Porter sees competitive advantage as being gained by those companies that can integrate uses of the Internet with traditional means of doing business. He contends that it is easier for 'traditional' companies to do this than for dotcoms to adopt and integrate traditional approaches. But the traditional strengths of any company remain the same, with or without the Internet, such as unique products, superior knowledge of products and customers, strong personal service, and effective relationships.

Thus, we can raise serious concerns about ICT's impact on firms' long-term competitive business strategy. In essence, perhaps, the problem is that in each instance companies are utilizing new developments in ICT to promote efficiency. But, as already noted, in doing this they are—potentially at least—running the risk of reducing the capacity to innovate and to respond creatively to their ever-changing environment. Again, then, we return to the dilemma between efficiency and innovation (e.g. Clark and Staunton 1989; March 1991; McElroy 2000).

Synthesis: Towards an Inclusive Framework for Information Systems Strategizing

Where is the argument followed in this chapter leading in terms of our reflections on the concept of information systems strategy? One would hesitate to propose an all-encompassing framework that captures the essence of the above—and, indeed, the very concept of such a framework might well seem antithetical to the arguments immediately preceding this.

Having said that, and as Weick (1990) might argue, frameworks do help with respect to sense-making, and do provide something of a benchmark against which informed debate and communication might take place. It is in this spirit that the following is presented for consideration.

Figure 2.9 builds on Figure 2.6, but is an attempt to incorporate some of the more recent thinking that we have just introduced. For example, the concept of an information infrastructure strategy—or what might be termed an information 'architecture'—is adopted and incorporated in an attempt to connote an enabling socio-technical environment for both the exploitation of knowledge (efficiency) and the exploration of knowledge (innovation). The debate was previously often couched in terms of exploration *versus* exploitation. Increasingly, however, we see different ICT initiatives, such as ERP and KMS, being implemented in tandem in an attempt to foster the simultaneous development of organizational efficiency and flexibility (Newell et al. 2003).

The concept of an information infrastructure (or architecture) has developed in response to the need for greater flexibility, given changing information requirements (Ciborra 2000). In the 1980s and 1990s, the term information infrastructure usually connoted the standardization of corporate ICT, systems, and data, with a view to reconciling centralized processing and distributed applications. Increasingly, however, Figure 2.9 depicts how the concept has come to relate not just to data and ICT systems, but also to the human infrastructure (roles, skills, capabilities, viewpoints, etc.)—and this is where knowledge creation, and sharing and innovation, play a crucial role. Star and Ruhleder (1996) unbundled the concept still further by talking of infrastructures in terms of, for example, their embeddedness, transparency, reach, links with conventions of practice, and installed base. Infrastructures are thus seen as being heterogeneous and socio-technical in nature.

As depicted here, then, information systems strategy, incorporating an information architecture strategy, is meant to be interpreted as being a part, albeit an increasingly important part, of collaborative business strategizing. It is collaborative because the focus will not be related just

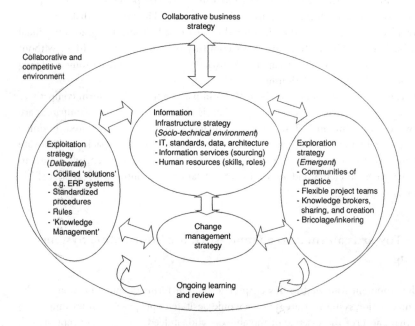

Figure 2.9 Towards a more inclusive framework for information systems strategizing. Reproduced in Galliers and Newell (2003a: 193).

to internal matters but will also, crucially, involve partner organizations, such as customers, suppliers, and other organizations, for example those with whom sourcing arrangements are in place. The implication here is that the very boundary of an organization will become increasingly porous, debatable, and changing. Therefore, strategy needs to take this into account, especially information systems strategizing, given the virtual nature of many collaborative arrangements. This means that information systems strategizing has both a location and temporal dimension (Adam 1990)—the latter, in particular, being as yet under-researched.

Information systems strategy should also be seen as being ongoing and processual, crucially dependent on learning from 'below', from tinkering and improvisation, and from the emergent and unintended consequences of strategic decisions, as well as from the more deliberate, designed, and codified ICT 'solutions' that have been implemented. Figure 2.9 attempts to incorporate the embedded, socio-technical characteristics of information architectures—architectures that provide the kind of environment in which knowledge sharing and knowledge creation may be fostered, in tandem. Strategic information, therefore, not only supports existing strategic processes, but also questions the kind of taken-for-granted assumptions on which existing information systems strategies may be based. ICT is there too: not as *the* answer, not as a 'solution', but as a means of capturing data that may be interpreted in a purposeful manner, with which to make sense of phenomena in unique circumstances.

Conclusions

This chapter has attempted to reflect on developments in the thinking and practice associated with information systems strategy and the process of strategizing. In so doing, and in drawing on a fairly broad literature base, we have been able also to question some of the more taken-for-granted concepts found in mainstream accounts of IS, and reflect on the appropriate role of ICT in modern-day organizations. Concepts such as the alignment of business and ICT strategies, ICT and competitive advantage, 'best practice', knowledge management, and—more particularly—KMS have all been called into question in what Robey and Boudreau (1999) term a 'logic of opposition'. Indeed, the very nature of information and knowledge have been examined in a fresh light. In addition, Information Systems, as a field of study, may be seen to suffer from an element of faddishness, similar to the world of practice and ICT-based 'solutions'. By providing something of a historical account, an attempt has been made to draw together lessons from the past into the kind of cumulative account that has often continued to be missing from Information Systems discourse (Keen 1990). It is hoped that such reflection may prove useful to those interested in the social study of ICT, and not just those who share an interest in information systems strategy itself.

Notes

1   Examples of recent fads include business process redesign and re-engineering, enterprise resource planning, and knowledge management systems—concepts that will be introduced and discussed later in the chapter.
2   PQM was a further refinement of the BSP and CSF approaches. Again, essential business processes were identified in line with business objectives. These processes were assessed in terms of the number of CSFs impacting on them, and the quality and cost of IT-based systems in place to support them. Further developments deemed to be necessary were identified on the basis of criticality (in business terms) and performance (both business and technological, current and future).

3   A more considered approach to the question of alignment is provided in Sabherwal et al. (2001), where they consider how ICT and business strategies move into, and out of, alignment over time.

4   A taxonomy of approaches to strategic information systems planning prevalent in the early 1990s is provided by Earl (1993).

5   For critiques of the BPR approach, see for example: Davenport (1996); Sauer and Yetton (1997); Galliers (1998); and Galliers and Swan (1999).

6   Nonaka and Takeuchi (1995), after Plato, talk of knowledge as 'justified true belief '. Given the emphasis here on the process of applying knowledge to data in order to make informed judgements about the world in which we live, the word 'true' has been dropped from the definition.

7   The contrast provided here is similar to the personalization—codification distinction of Hansen et al. (1999), and the community-codification distinction made by Scarbrough et al. (1999).

References

Abrahamson, E. (1991). 'Managerial Fads and Fashions: The Diffusion and Rejection of Innovations'. *Academy of Management Review*, 16/3: 586–612.

Adam, B. (1990). *Time and Social Theory*. Oxford, UK: Polity Press.

Benbasat, I., Dexter, A., Drury, D., and Goldstein, R. (1984). 'A Critique of the Stage Hypothesis: Theory and Empirical Evidence'. *Communications of the ACM*, 27/5: 476–85.

Blackler, F. (1995). 'Knowledge, Knowledge Work and Organizations: An Overview and Interpretation'. *Organization Studies*, 16/6: 1021–46.

Brown, J., and Duguid, P. (1991). 'Organizational Learning and Communities of Practice: Toward a Unified View of Working, Learning, and Innovation'. *Organization Science*, 2/1: 40–56.

Brown, S., and Eisenhardt, K. (1995). 'Product Development: Past Research, Present Findings, and Future Directions'. *Academy of Management Review*, 20/2: 343–78.

CACM. (2000). 'Communications of the ACM. Special issue on Enterprise Resource Planning (ERP) Systems'. *Communications of the ACM*, 43/4.

Cash, J. I., and Konsynski, B. R. (1985). 'IS Redraws Competitive Boundaries'. *Harvard Business Review*, 63/2: 134–42.

Checkland, P. B. (1981). *Systems Thinking. Systems Practice*. Chichester, UK: John Wiley.

Ciborra, C. U. (1994). 'From Thinking to Tinkering. The Grassroots of IT and Strategy', in C. U. Ciborra and T. Jelassi (eds.), *Strategic Information Systems: A European Perspective*. Chichester, UK: John Wiley, 3–24.

——. (2000). *From Control to Drift: The Dynamics of Corporate Information Infrastructures*. Oxford, UK: Oxford University Press.

Clark, P. A., and Staunton, N. (1989). *Innovation in Technology and Organization*. London, UK: Routledge.

Cohen, M. D., March, J. G., and Olsen, J. P. (1972). 'A Garbage Can Model of Organizational Choice'. *Administrative Science Quarterly*, 35/1: 1–25.

Davenport, T. H. (1993). *Process Innovation: Re-engineering Work through Information Technology*. Boston, MA: Harvard Business School Press.

——. (1996). 'Why Re-engineering Failed. The Fad that Forgot People', *Fast Company*. Premier Issue: 70–4.

——. and Short, J. E.) (1990). 'The New Industrial Engineering: Information Technology and Business Process Redesign'. *Sloan Management Review*, 31/4: 11–27.

Earl, M. J. (1989). *Management Strategies for Information Technology*. London, UK: Prentice Hall.

——. (1993). 'Experiences in Strategic Information Systems Planning'. *MIS Quarterly*, 17/1: 1–24.

Galliers, R. D. (1987). 'Information Systems Planning in the United Kingdom and Australia—A Comparison of Current Practice', in P. I. Zorkoczy (ed.), *Oxford Surveys in Information Technology*, vol. 4. Oxford, UK: Oxford University Press, 223–55.

——. (1991). 'Strategic Information Systems Planning: Myths, Reality and Guidelines for Successful Implementation'. *European Journal of Information Systems*, 1/1: 55–64.

——. (1992). 'Information Technology: Management's Boon or Bane?'. *Journal of Strategic Information Systems*, 1/2: 50–56.

——. (1993a). 'Towards a Flexible Information Architecture: Integrating Business Strategies, Information Systems Strategies and Business Process Redesign'. *Journal of Information Systems*, 3/3: 199–213.

——. (1993b). 'IT Strategies: Beyond Competitive Advantage'. *Journal of Strategic Information Systems*, 3/4: 283–91.

——. (1997). 'Against Obliteration: Reducing Risk in Business Process Change', in C. Sauer and P. W. Yetton, and Associates (eds.), *Steps to the Future: Fresh Thinking on the Management of IT-based Organizational Transformation*. San Francisco, CA: Jossey-Bass, 169–86.

——. (1998). 'Reflections on BPR, IT and Organizational Change', in R. D. Galliers and W. R. J. Baets (eds.), *Information Technology and Organizational Transformation: Innovation for the 21st Century Organization*. Chichester, UK: John Wiley, 225–43.

——. (1999a). 'Towards the Integration of e-Business, Knowledge Management and Policy Considerations within an Information Systems Strategy Framework'. *Journal of Strategic Information Systems*, 8/3: 229–34.

——. (2001a). 'Rethinking Information Systems Strategy: Towards an Inclusive Framework for Business Information Systems Management?'. Paper presented at EGOS Conference, Lyon, France, July.

——. Newell, S. (2003a). 'Strategy as Data + Sense Making', in S. Cummings and D. C. Wilson (eds.), *Images of Strategy*. Oxford, UK: Blackwell, 164–96.

——. (2003b). 'Back to the Future: From Knowledge Management to Data Management'. *Information Systems and e-Business Management*, 1/1: 5–13.

——. (Sutherland, A. R.). (1991). 'Information Systems Management and Strategy Formulation: The 'Stages of Growth' Model Revisited'. *Journal of Information Systems*, 1/2: 89–114.

——. Swan, J. A. (1999). 'Information Systems and Strategic Change: A Critical Review of Business Process Re-engineering', in W. L. Currie and R. D. Galliers (eds.), *Rethinking Management Information Systems: An Interdisciplinary Perspective*. Oxford, UK: Oxford University Press, 361–87.

Gibson, C. F., and Nolan, R. L. (1974). 'Managing the Four Stages of EDP Growth'. *Harvard Business Review*, 52/1: 76–88.

Greiner, L. E. (1972). 'Evolution and Revolution as Organizations Grow'. *Harvard Business Review*, 50/4: 37–46.

Hammer, M. (1990). 'Don't Automate, Obliterate'. *Harvard Business Review*, 68/4: 104–12.

Hansen, M., Nohria, N., and Tierney, T. (1999). 'What's your Strategy for Managing Knowledge?'. *Harvard Business Review*, 77/2: 106–16.

Keen, P. G. W. (1990). 'MIS Research: Reference Disciplines and a Cumulative Tradition', in E. R. McLean (ed.), *Proceedings: 1st International Conference on Information Systems, Philadelphia, PA*. Atlanta, GA: Association for Information Systems, 9–18.

King, J., and Kraemer, K. (1984). 'Evolution and Organizational Information Systems: An Assessment of Nolan's Stage Model'. *Communications of the ACM*, 27/5: 466–476.

Lacity, M. C., and Willcocks, L. (2000). *Global Information Technology Outsourcing: In Search of Business Advantage*. Chichester, UK: Wiley.

Land, F. (1996). 'The New Alchemist: Or How to Transmute Base Organisations into Corporations of Gleaming Gold'. *Journal of Strategic Information Systems*, 5/1: 5–17.

Lave, J., and Wenger, E. (1991). *Situated Learning: Legitimate Peripheral Participation*. Cambridge, UK: Cambridge University Press.

Leavitt, H. J. (1965). 'Applying Organizational Change in Industry: Structural, Technological and Humanistic Approaches', in J. G. March (ed.), *Handbook of Organizations*. Chicago, IL: Rand McNally, 264–291.

Loh, L., and Venkatraman, N. (1992). 'Information Technology Outsourcing: A Cross-sectional Analysis'. *Journal of Management Information Systems*, 9/1: 7–24.

March, J. (1991). 'Exploration and Exploitation in Organizational Learning'. *Organization Science*, 2/1: 71–86.

Martin, J. (1982). *Strategic Data Planning Methodologies*. Englewood Cliffs, NJ: Prentice Hall.

McElroy, M. (2000). 'Integrating Complexity Theory, Knowledge Management and Organizational Learning'. *Journal of Knowledge Management*, 4/3: 195–203.

McFarlan, F. W. (1984). 'Information Technology Changes the Way You Compete'. *Harvard Business Review*, 62/3: 98–102.

McLaughlin, M., Howe, R., and Cash, J. I. (1983). 'Changing Competitive Ground Rules—The Impact of Computers and Communications in the 1980s'. Unpublished Working Paper. Boston: Graduate School of Business Administration, Harvard University.

Mintzberg, H., and Waters, J. A. (1985). 'Of Strategies, Deliberate and Emergent'. *Strategic Management Journal*, 6/3: 257–72.

Newell, S., Huang, J. C., Galliers, R. D., and Pan, S. L. (2003). 'Implementing Enterprise Resource Planning and Knowledge Management Systems in Tandem: Fostering Efficiency and Innovation Complementarity'. *Information & Organization*, 13: 25–52.

Nolan, R. L. (1979). 'Managing the Crises in Data Processing'. *Harvard Business Review*, 57/2: 115–26.

Nonaka, I., and Takeuchi, H. (1995). *The Knowledge-creating Company: How Japanese Companies Create the Dynamics of Innovation*. Oxford, UK: Oxford University Press.

Orlikowski, W. (2000). 'Using Technology and Constituting Structure: A Practice Lens for Studying Technology in Organizations'. *Organization Science*, 12/4: 404–28.

Pascale, R. T., and Athos, A. G. (1981). *The Art of Japanese Management*. London, UK: Penguin.

Porter, M. E. (1980). *Competitive Strategy: Techniques for Analyzing Industries and Competitors*. New York: The Free Press.

——. (1985). *Competitive Advantage: Creating and Sustaining Superior Performance*. New York: The Free Press.

——. (2001). 'Strategy and the Internet'. *Harvard Business Review*, 79/3: 63–78.

——. and Millar, V. E. (1985). 'How Information Gives You Competitive Advantage'. *Harvard Business Review*, 63/4: 149–60.

Rayport, J. F., and Sviokla, J. J. (1995). 'Exploiting the Virtual Value Chain'. *Harvard Business Review*, 73/6: 75–85.

Robey, D., and Boudreau, M. C. (1999). 'Accounting for the Contradictory Organizational Consequences of Information Technology: Theoretical Directions and Methodological Implications'. *Information Systems Research*, 10/2: 167–85.

Rockart, J. F. (1979). 'Chief Executives Define Their Own Data Needs'. *Harvard Business Review*, 57/2: 81–93.

Sabherwal, R., Hirschheim, R., and Goles, T. (2001). 'The Dynamics of Alignment: Insights from a Punctuated Equilibrium Model'. *Organization Science*, 12/2: 179–97.

Sauer, C., and Yetton, P. W., and Associates. (1997). *Steps to the Future: Fresh Thinking on the Management of IT-based Organizational Transformation*. San Francisco, CA: Jossey-Bass.

Scarbrough, H., Swan, J., and Preston, J. (1999). *Knowledge Management and the Learning Organization*. London, UK: IPD.

Scott Morton, M. S. (ed.). (1991). *The Corporation of the 1990s: IT and Organizational Transformation*. Oxford, UK: Oxford University Press.

Senn, J. A. (1992). 'The Myths of Strategic Systems: What Defines True Competitive Advantage?'. *Journal of Information Systems Management*, 9/3: 7–12.

Somogyi, E. K., and Galliers, R. D. (1987). 'Applied Information Technology: From Data Processing to Strategic Information Systems'. *Journal of Information Technology*, 2/1: 30–41.

——. (2003). 'Information Technology in Business: From Data Processing to Strategic Information Systems', in R. D. Galliers and D. E. Leidner (eds.), *Strategic Information Management: Challenges and Strategies in Managing Information Systems*. Oxford, UK: ButterworthHeinemann, 3–26.

Star, S. L., and Ruhleder, K. (1996). 'Steps Towards an Ecology of Infrastructure: Design and Access to Large Information Spaces'. *Information Systems Research*, 7/1: 111–34.

Stowell, F. (1995). *Information Systems Provision: The Contribution of Soft Systems Methodology*. London, UK: McGraw-Hill.

Swan, J. A., and Clark, P. A. (1992). 'Organisation Decision-making in the Appropriation of Technological Innovation: Cognitive and Political Dimensions'. *European Work and Organisational Psychologist*, 2/2: 102–27.

Venkatraman, N. (1991). 'IT-induced Business Reconfiguration', in M. Scott Morton (ed.), *The Corporation of the 1990s: IT and Organizational Transformation*. Oxford, UK: Oxford University Press, 122–58.

von Krogh, G., Ichijo, K., and Nonaka, I. (2000). *Enabling Knowledge Creation: How to Unlock the Mystery of Tacit Knowledge and Release the Power of Innovation*. Oxford, UK: Oxford University Press.

Ward, J. (1990). 'Planning for Profit', in T. Lincoln (ed.), *Managing Information Systems for Profit*. Chichester, UK: John Wiley, 103–46.

Ward, J., and Peppard, J. (2002). *Strategic Planning for Information Systems*. Chichester, UK: Wiley.

Weick, K. E. (1990). 'Technology as an Equivoque: Sensemaking in New Technologies', in P. Goodman and L. Sproull (eds.), *Technology and Organizations*. San Francisco, CA: Jossey-Bass, 789–819.

——. (2001c). *Making Sense of the Organization*. Oxford: Blackwell.

Whittington, R. (1993). *What is Strategy?—And Does it Matter?*. London, UK: Routledge.

Willcocks, L. (1992). 'IT Evaluation: Managing the Catch 22'. *European Management Journal*, 10/2: 220–29.

——. (1999). 'Managing Information Technology Evaluation: Techniques and Processes', in R. D. Galliers, D. E. Leidner and B. S. H. Baker (eds.), *Strategic Information Management: Challenges and Strategies in Managing Information Systems*. Oxford, UK: Butterworth-Heinemann, 271–90.

Wilson, D. C. (1992). *A Strategy of Change: Concepts and Controversies in the Management of Change*. London, UK: Routledge.

Zachman, J. A. (1982). 'Business Systems Planning and Business Information Control Study: A Comparison'. *IBM Systems Journal*, 21/1: 31–54.

Questions for Discussion

1   This chapter suggests that there have been four phases in the development of the thinking and practice of IS strategizing (ISS): isolated; reactive; prospective, and proactive. Do you agree with this analysis? If so, explain why and describe the approaches to ISS that might fit in each phase. If not, then explain why not.

2   Do the four phases account for recent developments in ISS? How would you amend or extend the framework?

3   Attempt to apply the components of the ISS framework to an organization with which you are familiar. Is each component in place? Are the components linked in a coherent manner? What does this tell you about the organization's approach to ISS?

4   A number of myths are identified (see also Chapter 3) including those associated with alignment, strategic IT, knowledge management and competitive advantage. Do you agree with identifying these as myths? Why? Why not?

Further Reading

Picolli, G., Ives, B. (2005). IT-dependent strategic initiatives and sustained competitive advantage: A review and synthesis of the literature. *MIS Quarterly*, 29(4), 747–776.

Zheng, W., Yang, B., McLean, G. N. (2010). Linking organizational culture, structure, strategy, and organizational effectiveness: Mediating role of knowledge management, *Journal of Business Research*, 63(7), 763–771.

Chapter 3

Robert D. Galliers

ON CONFRONTING SOME OF THE COMMON MYTHS OF INFORMATION SYSTEMS STRATEGY DISCOURSE

> I wonder if we could contrive ... some magnificent myth that would in itself carry conviction to our whole community
>
> Plato: Republic, Bk 3; 414

IN THE ABOVE QUOTATION from Plato's *Republic,* the word 'myth' is sometimes translated as 'the noble lie'. Whether the myths – or – lies common in the mainstream treatment of Information Systems (IS) strategy are noble or not, deliberate or not, I am uncertain. Irrespective, these myths – let us call them misconceptions certainly – need to be confronted. This is the purpose of my contribution to this collection.

Over the relatively short history of IS planning and strategy,[1] a number of general principles have arisen that are often taken as being axiomatic. Three such principles that have appeared in the mainstream literature include:

- *alignment:* information and communication technology (ICT) systems should align with the business strategy;
- *competitive advantage:* ICT systems can provide a firm with an advantage over its competitors; and
- *knowledge management:* ICT systems can and should be a repository of an organization's knowledge resources.

As with other management fields,[2] IS has been subject to a faddishness that fails to answer Keen's (1981) challenge for a more cumulative tradition. The 'holy grail' of IS has taken a number of different forms over the years. One can reasonably argue that the database was the IS 'solution' of the 1970s, soon to be followed, later in the decade and into the 1980s, by decision support systems. The competitive advantage to be gained from information technology (IT) took root as a key topic in the mid 1980s. The advent of the business process re-engineering (BPR) movement in the early 1990s presaged a feeding frenzy in the mainstream academic and popular literature. Later in the decade, perhaps as a result of the loss of organizational knowledge that occurred as a result of the more extreme applications of BPR, the concept of knowledge management and knowledge management systems appeared on the scene. Since then, we have been subjected to enterprise systems and, latterly, the offshoring phenomenon.

Given the strategic focus of this contribution, I shall focus in this chapter on two key considerations – one more prevalent in the 1980s, the other a focus of attention in the 1990s and into the 21st century – namely, competitive advantage and knowledge management. The third consideration – alignment – has been a major focus, and a source of some contention, and I shall therefore incorporate this into my treatment of the subject matter.

Another admission before we begin: I am a self-confessed adherent to the transdisciplinary school of thought in the field of IS. There are some who argue for disciplinary purity, preferring our sole focus of attention to be on the IT artefact (for example, Benbasat and Zmud 2003) and the design of IT-based IS. I do not; indeed, I go further. I do not perceive IS as a discipline at all. I see it – like all organizational subjects – as a transdisciplinary field of interest, possibly even a meta-discipline (for example, Galliers 2003c). And our focus of attention – I argue – should be not simply the artefact 'IT', but the complex and mutually constituted nature of IT use by human beings in and between organizations, and in society.

Taking each in turn – alignment, competitive advantage and knowledge management – I shall question these 'self evident truths' with a view to developing an alternative perspective on IS strategy. This perspective focuses more on the process of *strategizing* than on the outcome of the process – the strategy itself. I argue that benefit is to be gained from a more inclusive, exploratory approach to the strategy process. This perspective is set against the common view, which is concerned more with exploiting the potential of ICT systems for business gain. Implicit in my arguments is the view that is intellectually bankrupt to accept these myths as 'self evident truths'; that it is actually a dangerous game we play were we to do so. Too often, our IT solutions are peddled without attention being paid to the questions they are meant to 'solve', and certainly without an appreciation of their unintended consequences (Robey and Boudreau 1999).

Having provided a critique of each of the myths, an attempt will be made at synthesizing the arguments, utilizing concepts of, inter alia, architecture and infrastructure (for example, Star and Ruhleder 1996) and of 'ambidextrousness' (Tushman and O'Reilly 1996), with a view to refining a revised framework of IS strategizing, introduced in Galliers (2004). The aim is to provide a more balanced perspective, a sense-making device (Weick 1995), that will have an impact in both theory and practice.

Alignment

A central plank on which much of IS strategy theory and practice has been built is the concept of alignment. For example, almost 30 years ago, McLean and Soden (1977) compared the theoretical need for a 'strong link' between the business plan and the IS plan with the then current practice. They found that in less than 50 per cent of cases in their US study was there this strong link. A similar figure was reported by Earl (1983) in the UK. In later work, Earl (1989) makes the important distinction between an information *systems* strategy and an information *technology* strategy. He notes that the IS strategy should be concerned with identifying what information is needed to support the business, and what information services need to be provided. In other words, the IS strategy is demand-oriented. Conversely, he sees the IT strategy as being supply-oriented. It demarcates what is and will be available in terms of IT infrastructure, applications, and services. His argument is that these two aspects of IS/IT strategy should be aligned. Other proponents of alignment include, for example, Parker et al. (1988), MacDonald (1991), Baets (1992), Henderson and Venkatraman (1992,1999), and Peppard and Ward (2004). These different perspectives on alignment make a telling point: what is being aligned with what? The examples given here refer to alignment between the business and IT strategies; between IS and IT strategies, between business performance and IT acquisitions; between the internal and external environments, and between IS capability and organizational performance.

While the alignment concept may be intuitively appealing, an issue that has remained relatively unchallenged and unquestioned is how to align ICT that is relatively fixed, once implemented in an organization, with a business strategy and associated information requirements that are constantly in need of adjustment, in line with the dynamic nature of the organization's business imperatives.[3] Despite the useful distinction made between IS and IT strategies, Earl's (1983) model, for example, is relatively static and does not account adequately for the *changing* information requirements of organizations, in line with a *changing* business strategy. While a subset of those requirements will doubtless remain relatively constant over time, the dynamic nature of the competitive, collaborative, and regulatory environments in which organizations conduct their business dictates that constant and careful attention should be paid to the ever-changing nature of information need. In addition, and as I have pointed out elsewhere (Galliers 1993, 1999), information is needed to *question* whether an existing strategy continues to remain appropriate, given the changing environmental context – *external* considerations in other words – and lessons learned from the unintended consequences of actions taken and IT systems implemented (Robey and Boudreau 1999) – the *internal* considerations.

This issue leads us to the conclusion that information itself is a medium through which alignment might take place, and that this might usefully be perceived to be – at the very least – a two-way process: 'top-down' and 'bottom-up'. Indeed, this is implied by Earl's (1983) model. I say at the very least a two-way process because, as indicated above, alignment between the internal and external environments is an additional dimension to be incorporated into the alignment debate. Note, however, that from the perspective that information is the alignment medium, the focus is on such artifacts as technology, the strategic plan, and bottom-line business benefit. There are, however, those whose approach is more focused on exploration rather than exploitation (cf. March 1991). The former approach is otherwise known as coming from the processual school (for example, Whittington 1993), being more concerned with the process of strategizing than with the strategy itself.

This brings us to the issue of emergence – a topic of debate in the business strategy literature for the past 20 years or so (for example, Mintzberg and Waters 1985). In practice, IS strategy approaches tend to be based on a rational analysis of need – either in response to an extant business strategy, and/or an analysis of current ICT capability – or in a proactive manner, based on a 'clean slate' approach. With respect to the latter, the argument was essentially that revolutionary change would lead to 'order-of-magnitude' business benefits (Davenport and Short 1990; Hammer 1990; Venkatraman 1991; Davenport 1993). The approach was based on identifying and streamlining key business processes and key customer requirements, and then on identifying how ICT might support (and often automate) these processes and requirements, with a view to improving efficiency and effectiveness, and cutting costs. The approach involved quite some risk (Galliers 1997) and often led to what was euphemistically called 'downsizing', with many middle managers being required to leave the company. This had a consequent, unintended (cf. Robey and Boudreau 1999) deleterious effect on organizational memory and available expertise (Davenport 1996; Galliers and Swan 1999).

But what of innovation and serendipity? As indicated above, there is a school of thought that argues for the emergent nature of strategic processes. In the field of IS, Ciborra used terms such as bricolage (after Levi-Strauss 1966), drift, and tinkering (Ciborra 1992, 2000, 2002) to propose a more incremental, ad hoc approach to strategizing. He argued that even in situations where strategic advantage had been gained from the astute application of ICT, the resultant gain was by no means always expected and in no way pre-ordained. Rather, the organizations concerned had benefited from creating an environment – or infrastructure – in which innovation might emerge. The approach he advocated smacks of playfulness. Others see benefit in combining incremental and radical change. Tushman and O'Reilly (1996), for example, speak of 'ambidextrous' organizations, while He and Wong (2004) confirm this hypothesis in a study of more than 200 manufacturing firms (see also Gibson and Birkinshaw 2004).

All in all then, the question of alignment is a vexed one. I posed the question 'alignment with what?' earlier. There is the question of 'alignment with whom?' in addition. Given the advent of inter-organizational systems, and more so, of the Internet, alignment is also presumably required along the virtual value chain, with relationships with suppliers and customers, for example, needing to be taken into account. It is in such circumstances that we note the need for human interaction, rather than an almost total reliance on rational analysis of organizational need or on ICT per se. As will be argued in the context of knowledge management, there is a need for 'boundary spanning' (Tushman and Scanlan, 1981) activity, for understanding, and trust (Newell and Swan 2000), and the natural development of 'communities of practice' (Brown and Duguid 1991; Lave and Wenger 1991) – both within organizations and externally – in order for new knowledge to emerge.

But let me conclude this discussion regarding the contentious issue of alignment, as a means of providing something of a link between this discussion and the discussion that follows on ICT and competitive advantage. We have seen that alignment has been considered from different perspectives – alignment between 'what' and 'whom' are key questions. There is a more basic point to consider here though, and that is the conceptual link that appears to be missing between what is after all a conceptual business strategy and a physical, technological artifact. I earlier pondered whether the missing ingredient might be information, and there is certainly a reasonable argument here. In addition, however, it should be remembered that organizations often comprise many technologies and many – often dispersed – individuals.[4] Increasingly, these individuals are 'organized' on a project-by-project basis, thereby adding increased dynamism to the mix, and compounding the issue of alignment still further. Hansen talks of the need for weak ties across organizational sub-units. Gheradi and Nicolini (2000) call for the establishment of safety for individuals to form communities of practice for sharing understanding and knowledge. The processes of developing weak ties and safe communities are learned – and these learning processes are as important as the content knowledge itself (Newell et al. 2003).

Competitive Advantage

Considerable attention was paid in the 1980s and 1990s to what became something of a Holy Grail of IS – the gaining and retention of competitive advantage from the astute and proactive use of ICT in and by organizations. ICT 'changes the way you compete' noted one venerable proponent of the cause (McFarlan 1984). Later, during the 1990s, and as indicated above, radical business transformation on the back of business process change –

and enabled by ICT – was all the rage (Davenport and Short 1990; Hammer 1990; Venkatraman 1991; Davenport 1993). But rage of a different kind soon ensued and the bubble burst as the millennium dawned. Why was that? There are many answers to this question of course, but let me highlight two of them. One relates to the purchase of so-called 'best practice' solutions, such as enterprise systems, off-the-shelf. The other relates the question of sustainability.

It was always the case that ICT in and of itself would not provide a firm with competitive advantage, despite the more popular press claiming this to be the case. And this is certainly even more the case these days with the commoditization of ICT. The advent of the Internet and enterprise systems has seen to that. What is perhaps surprising is that we are still treated to claims of 'best practice' solutions (sic.) as if there were no contradiction between an advantage to be gained over others by the purchase of a 'solution' that could be obtained just as easily by those same competitors, from the same vendors! Thus, vendors of off-the shelf 'best practice' enterprise systems make the implausible claim that advantage will ensue with the purchase of a technology and services that are equally available to one's competitors.[5] But there is more: this so-called 'best practice' technology – this readily implementable solution – also turns out to require on-going support and consultancy.[6]

Even in the 1980s, it became clear that there was an issue of sustainability that had to be addressed. While there *may* have been first mover advantage from the purchase of new technology, the lead gained needed to be sustained over time (for example, Porter 1985; Ghemawat 1986; Hall 1993; Suarez and Lanzolla 2005). And it was Porter who provided something of an answer to those who proclaimed advantage from the technology alone (Porter and Millar 1985). The important point he raised at that time was that it was the *use* made of the technology that mattered – it was information that could provide the advantage, not the technology. Later, others joined the fray. Senn (1992), for example, echoed the later thoughts of Ciborra and others in criticizing the very concept of strategic IS, and later still, Land (1996) questioned the basic premises on which the BPR movement was built.

What is perhaps both surprising and disappointing about the faddishness of much of the literature on IS strategy is that many key lessons were soon forgotten as a new technology or movement emerged. Thus, for example, Leavitt's (1965) argument that organizations could usefully be viewed as complex socio-technical systems, comprising four elements – objectives, structure, technology and people – seems to have become lost in the excitement, the *Zeitgeist,* if you will. The focus in the age of BPR was primarily on ICT and processes, and in the age of enterprise systems, it appears to be primarily on a technological architecture that actually dictates how processes should be undertaken. Even one of the founding fathers of the BPR movement proclaimed that it had become 'the fad that forgot people' (Davenport 1996) – of which more in the section on knowledge management.

With the emergence of the Internet and e-business, again we are confronted with considerable hyperbole, notwithstanding the bursting of the dotcom bubble. Again, we have been treated to many arguments that another new technology would fundamentally change the basis of competition. In his compelling *Harvard Business Review* article, Porter (2001) refutes any such suggestion. Porter sees the Internet as something that complements rather than cannibalizes organizations and organizational ICT as we have come to know them. As I have noted previously (Galliers 2004: 254), 'while some have argued that "the Internet renders strategy obsolete" ... the opposite is true ... it is more important than ever for companies to distinguish themselves through strategy' (Porter 2001: 63). While Porter sees the Internet as just another means of doing business, opening up a new channel, he makes the point that it is likely to increase competition and make it *more* difficult for companies to sustain their competitive advantage. Thus, in his view, ICT in and of itself, rather than being a force *for* competitive advantage, becomes a force *against* competitive advantage. He goes on to argue that 'only by integrating the Internet into overall strategy will this powerful new technology become an equally powerful force for competitive advantage' (Porter 2001: 78).

To develop this argument further, competitive advantage may be gained by those companies that can integrate uses of the Internet with their core competences (Prahalad and Hamel 1990). Porter's contention is that it may well be easier for 'traditional' companies to do this than for dotcoms to adopt, develop, and integrate such competencies themselves. He argues that these core competencies and traditional strengths are likely to remain the same, with or without the Internet, and it is these that will provide competitive advantage, not the technology.

Thus, we might argue that ICT's impact on competitiveness may well be negative rather than the positive view most often expounded in the mainstream literature. In addition, we have seen companies attempting to utilize ICT in an attempt to increase efficiency and reduce costs. Having said that, and as noted in the discussion on BPR and enterprise systems, in adopting this approach, companies run the risk of reducing their effectiveness, dexterity and innovative capacity. Unless they can develop the ambidextrousness of which Tushman and O'Reilly (1996) speak, they face the common dilemma of gaining efficiency at the expense of innovation (Clark and Staunton 1989; March 1991; McElroy 2000). And they also run the risk of losing their capacity for organizational learning – and knowing – as discussed in the section that follows.

Knowledge Management

Knowledge is considered by many to be a key organizational resource, and the knowledge management movement that followed the BPR era has encouraged organizations to attempt to exploit more strategically their knowledge assets (for example, Kogut and Zander 1992; Grant 1996).[7] Companies are thus lured by the suggestion that they can gain competitive advantage – that expression again! – by managing their knowledge assets more astutely, and in particular, by transferring knowledge across individuals, groups, and organizational units, using ICT to achieve this end. There is a knowledge management aspect to the enterprise systems phenomenon, and I shall introduce this section by attacking these myths before progressing to a consideration of knowledge management systems (KMS) themselves. Incorporating knowledge management considerations into a discourse on IS strategizing will be left to the final section of this chapter, but it is perhaps worth noting the current relative lack of such considerations in mainstream IS strategy discourse. This is somewhat surprising given the common view that knowledge is a strategic organizational resource, and that ICT systems are means by which such knowledge can be transferred across time and space.

As already discussed, enterprise systems are often promoted as a means of transferring 'best practice' knowledge. An enterprise system's built-in processes require the adopting organization to adapt its existing processes to the exigencies of the software. The argument is that, since these inbuilt processes are based on 'best practice' industry standards, the organization concerned will automatically benefit as a result.

But, as we have seen, vendors of enterprise systems make much of the consultancy services they offer during and after implementation. Presumably, these services are provided in order for the 'best practice' solution to become 'better', and the off-the-shelf 'solution' to be customized. Research undertaken by Wagner (Scott and Wagner 2003; Wagner and Newell 2006) demonstrates how these so-called best practices have to be molded and adapted to the realpolitik of organizations, to some extent at least, despite the services of the vendor. In addition, and in relation to the earlier discussion on alignment, enterprise systems are often implemented to replace legacy systems, which presumably have drifted out of alignment – presumably, too, to become legacy systems in their own right over time.

Moreover, by advocating copying best practices to improve efficiency, organizations are, potentially at least, running the risk of actually reducing their ability to create the new knowledge needed to innovate and respond creatively to changing imperatives. Given that this is a key concern of business strategy, and that KMS are meant to support and inform the process of strategizing, it appears we may have another problem here. ICT such as enterprise systems and the Internet can be thus seen to be a force for standardization, thus speeding competitive convergence, given that the technology is more or less common – and increasingly commoditized – irrespective of the organization implementing it. But there is more to this enigma, as presaged by the earlier comments on knowing as opposed to knowledge.

The myth of KMS emerged in the 1990s. That is, ICT-based KMS can store and transfer knowledge. Thus, existing knowledge can be collected and re-used, utilizing ICT. From this perspective, knowledge is 'out there', ready to be mined, harvested. We thus return to the mythology of 'best practice' that underpins much of this kind of thinking. Presumably, for such knowledge to be worth re-using, knowledge of what is best practice is required.[8] But, let us consider some basic principles here. Checkland (1981) reminds us that, while ICT can be exceptionally powerful and proficient in processing data, it is human beings who apply meaning (their knowledge) to selected data in order to make sense (cf., Weick 1990) of these data, for a specific purpose. Data may therefore be context-free, while information can only be informative within a particular context. ICT systems are therefore data processing systems – nothing more, nothing less. IS require the presence of human beings who apply their knowledge to turn data into information. Knowledge is therefore tacit (cf. Polanyi 1966) and embedded. 'It resides within our brains, and enables us to make sense of the data we [choose to] capture' (Galliers 2004: 253). It is also 'sticky' (Szulanski 1996; Szulanski and Jensen; 2004) in that its contextual nature means that it is less easily transferred than the KMS perspective might otherwise suggest.

Responsibility for the myth of codified knowledge that can be captured in ICT systems can, partially at least, be laid at the doorstep of Nonaka (for example, Nonaka and Takeushi 1995). Their model depicts the transformation of tacit knowledge into codified knowledge and is widely known and frequently cited in this context. An alternative perspective has also appeared on the scene, however, one that is much more in line with the perspective adopted in this essay. Blackler (1995), Boland and Tenkasi (1995), Tsoukas (1996), and Cook and Brown (1999), among others, raise issues of knowledge transfer and *knowing* rather than knowledge capture and codification. Individuals working with colleagues in organizations learn (for example, Bogenreider and Nooteboom 2004) from their interactions with each other and their interactions with formal (and informal) data processing systems (cf. Land 1982). Similarly, Wenger (1998) talks of situated learning in the context of communities of practice, while Sole and Edmondson (2002) develop the concept further in relation to geographically dispersed teams. The contrast between these perspectives on knowledge and knowing, on capture and creation, and on explicit and tacit knowledge is similar to the personalization-codification distinction of Hansen et al. (1999), and the community-codification distinction made by Swan and Preston (1999). In taking the more processual perspective, I would argue that there is potentially considerably more to be gained from the process of knowing, of knowledge creation, of learning and human interaction – in the context of this essay, the process of strategizing[9] – than the mere transfer of 'knowledge' per se.

Synthesis: Towards a Revised Framework for IS Strategizing

An attempt is made in this final section to bring together aspects of the foregoing arguments as a basis for the development of a revised framework for IS strategizing. Thus far, we have considered the issues of alignment, competitive advantage, and knowledge management, as they each relate to the development and use of ICT systems in and between organizations. An attempt has been made to raise serious doubts about some of the mythology that has surrounded these concepts in the more popular, mainstream literature. With regard to the topic of alignment, we have noted, inter alia, that there are vexed issues associated with aligning dynamic information needs with a relatively static technology. Alignment with what and with whom were issues that were also raised. Competitive advantage on the back of an increasingly commoditized technology also presents us with something of a conundrum, with the importance of ICT use and capability, core competence, and the key role of information each being highlighted. In relation to knowledge management and KMS, questions were raised as to whether ICT systems could in fact capture and transfer knowledge and, just as importantly, the process of knowing and knowledge creation was privileged over knowledge capture and transfer.

In attempting to synthesize these arguments, with a view to developing a revised, integrated framework for IS strategizing, the socio-technical concept of an information architecture or infrastructure is a useful building block (for example, Star and Ruhleder 1996; Monteiro 1998; Ciborra 2000; Hanseth 2004;), as argued in Galliers (2004). In introducing this framework, it was argued that organizations could be ambidextrous (cf. the arguments introduced earlier, based on the work of Tushman and O'Reilly 1996) in combining an ability both to exploit current capability and to explore new possibilities. Modes of exploitation and exploration, I argue, may be facilitated by an environment – an information infrastructure or architecture – that provides a supportive context for learning and interaction. I shall take each of these components of the proposed framework in turn, as a means of refining the framework and describing how it might be used as a sense-making (cf. Weick 1995) device in organizations.

The process of exploitation adopted in the revised framework bears many of the hallmarks of mainstream thinking on IS strategy. This is the deliberate – as compared to the emergent – strategy of which Mintzberg speaks (Mintzberg and Waters 1985). A deliberate attempt is made to identify and develop ICT applications that both support and question the organization's strategic vision, and current need for information and expertise. Here, we find both the IS and IT strategies that Earl (1989) proposes. It is likely that enterprise systems and so-called KMS, and standardized procedures for adopting ICT products, hiring ICT personnel, and developing customized applications will each contribute to this exploitation strategy. And, in line with the models introduced in Galliers (1991, 1999), an aspect of this strategy will relate to the organizational arrangements for IS/IT services, including sourcing considerations (cf. Lacity and Willcocks 2000, for example). Policies on such issues as risk, security, and confidentiality will also need to be considered in this context (for example, Backhouse et al. 2005).

With respect to the exploration aspects of strategizing, here the emphasis is much more on issues associated with situated learning, communities of practice, and cross-project learning. Ciborra and colleagues (Ciborra 2000) talk of drift in this context – as against control – but there is nonetheless a sense of direction and purpose associated with this activity. I therefore prefer the term emergence in this regard, but there is certainly a sense of bricolage (cf. Levi-Strauss 1966) and tinkering at play here, to return to terms favored by Ciborra (1992). As noted, organizations are increasingly reliant on project teams whose membership may well be in flux and distributed. Considerations of trust (Sambamurphy and Jarvenpaa 2002) and learning from one project to another (for example, Scarbrough et al. 2004) are key features at play here. The role of communities of practice (for example, Wenger 1998) is crucial in knowledge creation as we have seen, as is the role of boundary spanning individuals (Tushman and Scanlan 1981), or what we might term knowledge brokers (see also, Lave and Wenger 1991; Hansen 1999).

While the concept of the ambidextrous organization has been postulated (Tushman and O'Reilly 1996), and some empirical research has been conducted to test the thesis (for example, He and Wong 2004), there remains little in the literature that might be of assistance to organizations in providing an enabling, supportive environment that might foster this sought-after 'ambidexterity'. Relating concepts of infrastructure introduced earlier to the concept of ambidexterity would appear to hold some promise in this regard.

> In the 1980s and 1990s, the term information infrastructure usually connoted the standardization of corporate ICT, systems, and data, with a view to reconciling centralized processing and distributed applications. Increasingly, however … the concept has come to relate not just to data and ICT systems, but also the human infrastructure.
>
> (Galliers 2004: 256)

Thus, the kind of socio-technical environment proposed by Star and Ruhleder (1996), Ciborra (2000), and Hanseth (2004), for example, would combine information and knowledge sharing services – both electronic and human – that would facilitate both exploration and exploitation of knowledge, and the kind of flexibility necessary to enable appropriate responses to changing business imperatives. In some ways, this kind of infrastructure would help circumvent the alignment issue that was introduced at the beginning of this chapter.

I have also stressed the importance of on-going learning and review, given the processual view adopted here, the unintended consequences arising not only from ICT implementations (Robey and Boudreau 1999) and the dynamic nature of alignment (Sabherwal et al. 2001), but also the emergent nature of strategizing (Mintzberg and Waters 1985). The whole process of strategizing is one of visioning, planning, taking action, and assessing outcomes, all with an eye to changing circumstance and imperatives, *and* the actions of individuals and groups outside, and notwithstanding, any formal strategy process. There are countless books on breakthrough change management focusing on the role of ICT (for example, Lientz and Rea 2004) and on so-called transformational leaders (for example, Anderson and Anderson 2001). The major features of this genre include prescriptive, deliberate approaches that suggest guaranteed, order-of-magnitude gains. Organizational realities suggest an alternative, incremental approach more akin to 'muddling through' (Lindblom 1959), however. The incremental exploration of possibilities – the tinkering (Ciborra 1992) and bricolage (Levi-Strauss 1966) – along with the more deliberate, analytical approaches that incorporate oversight of implementations and review of outcomes (for example, Willcocks 1999) is what is envisaged here.

Bearing all this in mind, the following framework is an attempt to further refine the IS strategizing framework introduced in Galliers (2004: 256). The framework is not meant to be a prescriptive tool, nor a solution. It is a sense-making (cf. Weick 1995) device, meant more as an aide memoir, to be used to raise questions and facilitate discussion concerning the strategizing elements and connections that may or may not be in place in any particular organization.

One final point in closing: the fact that I continue to refer to the strategizing framework as one concerned with IS (as opposed to either ICT at one pole or knowledge sharing and creation at the other) is deliberate. There are two primary reasons for this. The first

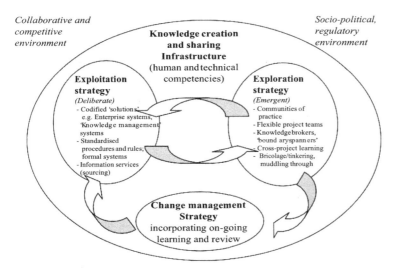

Figure 3.1 A revised IS strategizing framework

relates to the above discussion of the nature of data, information, and knowledge. The socio-technical infrastructure depicted in Figure 3.1 comprises human beings who can make sense of data provided by both formal and informal systems via the application of their (situated) knowledge. In doing so, they turn data into purposeful information. The second reason is to provide an otherwise missing link between the literatures on IS/IT strategy, on knowledge management, and on organizational strategies for change – the transdisciplinary perspective mentioned in the introduction. Too often viewed as discrete, an underlying argument in this essay is that the concepts emerging from these literatures should be viewed as complimentary and synergistic. If I may be permitted to misquote Porter (2001: 78), the next stage of strategy evolution will involve a shift in thinking from business strategy and knowledge strategy, to IS strategizing. By integrating IS considerations into the discourse on business and knowledge strategy, the resultant thinking and practice will become mutually constituted and significantly more robust. In saying this, I realize that I may have unintentionally constructed a new myth. Please accept though that my intentions – my 'lies' if you will – are 'noble'.

Notes

1   Early academic literature on these topics dates back to the work, e.g., of Young (1967); Kriebel (1968); McFarlan (1971), and Lincoln (1975).
2   I take an organizational/managerial perspective in this chapter in providing a critique of the mainstream literature, rather than a social science perspective.
3   Sabherwal et al. (2001) being an exception – these authors refer to the concept of punctuated equilibrium in noting the natural tendency of organizations' IS strategies and business strategies to fall in and out of alignment over time.
4   Indeed, it is instructive in this context to recall that the Department of Organisation, Work and Technology in the Lancaster University Management School was known formerly as the Department of Behaviour *in* Organisations (my emphasis), rather than by the more usual term, Organisational Behaviour.
5   For example: (i) 'Oracle ROI Series studies document the quantifiable values and strategic benefits of Oracle-enabled business transformations', http://www.oracle.com/customers/index.html; (ii)

'You've stretched every budget and trimmed every expense. Or have you? SAP solutions give you real-time visibility across your entire enterprise, so you can streamline your supply chain, bring products to market faster, get more out of procurement, and eliminate duplication of effort. SAP is a world leader in business solutions, offering comprehensive software and services that can address your unique needs', http://www.sap.com/solutions/index.epx.

6   For example: (i) 'Oracle Consulting builds creative solutions for modern businesses. Drawing on industry best practices and specialized software expertise, Oracle consultants help you assess your current infrastructure, create your enterprise computing strategy, and deploy new technology. With Oracle's flexible and innovative global blended delivery approach, we assemble the optimal team for your organization by matching the right expertise, at the right time for the right cost in every phase of your project. Whether you have a new Oracle implementation or a system upgrade, Oracle Consulting helps you face today's most complex technology challenges and increase the financial return on your Oracle investment', http://www.oracle.com/consulting/index.html; (ii) 'Ensuring the value of your SAP investment takes more than software. It takes SAP Consulting – and the expertise and skill we've gained from 69,000 implementations over 30 years. With more than 9,000 consultants, plus a global network of 180,000 certified partners, SAP Consulting can provide the depth and breadth of coverage your business demands' (http://www.sap.com/services/consulting/index.epx).

7   A special issue of the *Journal of Strategic Information Systems* is devoted to the issue of knowledge management and KMS (Leidner 2000).

8   Nonaka and Takeuchi (1995) define knowledge as 'justified true belief', following Plato. Given adherence to the social construction of reality (cf., Berger and Luckman 1966), knowledge here might better be interpreted as 'justified belief'.

9   Building on the concept of alternative interpretations of the same data, and thus alternative futures, or scenarios (cf., Galliers, 1993, 1995), Cummings and Angwin (2004) use the metaphor of the chimera to discuss potential future developments in strategic thinking.

References

Anderson, D. and Anderson, L. A. (2001). *Beyond Change Management: Advanced Strategies for Today's Transformational Leaders*. San Francisco, CA: Joessey-Bass/Pfieffer.

Backhouse, J., Bener, A., Chauvidul, N., Wamala, F., and Willison, R. (2005). 'Risk Management in Cyberspace', in R. Mansell and B. Collins (eds.), *Trust and Crime in Information Societies*. Cheltenham: Edward Elgar, 349–379.

Baets, W. (1992). 'Aligning Information Systems with Business Strategy'. *Journal of Strategic Information Systems*, 1(4): 205–213.

Benbasat, I. and Zmud, R. (2003). 'The Identity Crisis within the IS Discipline: Defining and Communicating the Core's Properties'. *MIS Quarterly*, 27(2): 183–194.

Berger, P. L. and Luckman, T. (1966). *The Social Construction of Reality*. Garden City, NY: Double Day and Co.

Blackler, R. (1995). 'Knowledge, Knowledge Work and Organizations: An Overview and Interpretation'. *Organization Studies*, 16(6): 1021–1046.

Bogenrieder, I. and Nooteboom, B. (2004). 'Learning Groups: What Types are There? A Theoretical Analysis and an Empiricial Study in a Consultancy Firm'. *Organization Studies*, 25(2): 287–313.

Boland, R. J. and Tenkasi, R. V. (1995). 'Perspective Making and Perspective Taking in Communities of Knowing'. *Organization Science*, 6(4): 350–372.

Brown, J. S. and Duguid, P. (1991). 'Organizational Learning and Communities of Practice: Toward a Unified View of Working, Learning, and Innovation'. *Organization Science*, 2(1): 40–56.

Checkland, P. B. (1981). *Systems Thinking. Systems Practice*. Chichester: Wiley.

Ciborra, C. U. (1992). 'From Thinking to Tinkering: The Grassroots of IT and Strategy'. *The Information Society*, 8(4): 297–309.

——. (ed.). (2000). *From Control to Drift: The Dynamics of Corporate Information Infrastructures*. Oxford: Oxford University Press.

——. (2002). *The Labyrinths of Information: Challenging the Wisdom of Systems*. Oxford: Oxford University Press.

Clark, P. A. and Staunton, N. (1989). *Innovation in Technology and Organization*. London: Routledge.

Cook S. D. and Brown J. S. (1999). 'Bridging Epistemologies: The Generative Dance between Organizational Knowledge and Organisational Knowing'. *Organization Science*, 10(4): 381–400.

Cummings, S. and Angwin, D. (2004). 'The Future Shape of Strategy: Lemmings or Chimeras?'. *The Academy of Management Executive*, 18(2): 21–36.

——. (1993). *Process Innovation: Re-engineering Work through Information Technology*. Boston: Harvard Business School Press.

——. (1996a). 'Why Re-engineering Failed. The Fad that Forgot People'. *Fast Company*, Premier Issue, 70–74.

Davenport, T. H. and Short, J. E. (1990). 'The New Industrial Engineering: Information Technology and Business Process Redesign'. *Sloan Management Review*, 3(4): 11–27.

Earl, M. J. (1983). 'Emerging Trends in Managing New Information Technologies', in N. Piercey (ed.), (1986) *The Management Implications of New Information Technology*. London: Croom Helm, 189–215.

——. (1989). *Management Strategies for Information Technology*. London: Prentice Hall.

Galliers, R. D. (1991). 'Strategic Information Systems Planning: Myths, Reality and Guidelines for Successful Implementation'. *European Journal of Information Systems*, 1(1): 55–64.

——. (1993). 'Towards a Flexible Information Architecture: Integrating Business Strategies, Information Systems Strategies and Business Process Redesign'. *Journal of Information Systems*, 3(3): 199–213.

——. (1995). 'Reorienting Information Systems Strategy: Integrating Information Systems into the Business', in F. A. Stowell (ed.), *Information Systems Provision: The Contribution of Soft Systems Methodology*. London: McGraw-Hill, 51–74.

——. (1997). 'Against Obliteration: Reducing Risk in Business Process Change', in C. Sauer, P. W. Yetton and Associates (eds.), *Steps to the Future: Fresh Thinking on the Management of IT-based Organizational Transformation*. San Francisco, CA: Jossey-Bass, 169–186.

——. (1999). 'Towards the Integration of e-Business, Knowledge Management and Policy Considerations within an Information Systems Strategy Framework'. *Journal of Strategic Information Systems*, 8(3): 229–234.

——. (2004). 'Reflections on Information Systems Strategizing', in C. Avgerou, C. Ciborra, and F. Land (eds.), *The Social Study of Information and Communication Technology: Innovation, Actors, and Contexts*. Oxford: Oxford University Press, 231–262.

——. and Swan, J. A. (1999). 'Information Systems and Strategic Change: A Critical Review of Business Process Re-engineering', in W. L. Currie and R. D. Galliers (eds.), *Rethinking Management Information Systems: An Interdisciplinary Perspective*. Oxford: Oxford University Press, 361–387.

——. and Newell, S. (2003b). 'Back to the Future: From Knowledge Management to the Management of Information and Data'. *Information Systems and e-Business Management*, 1(1): 5–13.

——. (2003c). 'Change as Crisis or Growth? Toward a Trans-disciplinary View of Information Systems as a Field of Study – A Response to Benbasat and Zmud's Call for Returning to the IT Artifact'. *Journal of the Association for Information Systems*, 4(6): 337–351.

Ghemawat, P. (1986). 'Sustainable Advantage'. *Harvard Business Review*, 64(5): 53–58.

Gherardi, S. and Nicolini, D. (2000). 'The Organizational Learning of Safety in Communities of Practice'. *Journal of Management Inquiry*, 9(1): 7–18.

Gibson, C. B. and Birkinshaw, J. (2004). 'The Antecedents, Consequences, and Mediating Role of Organizational Ambidexterity'. *The Academy of Management Journal*, 47(2): 209–226.

Grant, R. (1996). 'Prospering in Dynamically-competitive Environment: Organizational Capability as Knowledge Integration'. *Organization Science*, 7(4): 375–387.

Hall, R. (1993). 'A Framework Linking Intangible Resources and Capabilities to Sustainable Competitive Advantage'. *Strategic Management Journal*, 14(8): 607–618.

Hammer, M. (1990). 'Don't Automate, Obliterate'. *Harvard Business Review*, 68(4): 104–112.

Hansen, M., Nohria, N., and Tierney, T. (1999). 'What's your Strategy for Managing Knowledge?.' *Harvard Business Review*, 77(2): 106–116.

Hansen, M. T. (1999). 'The Search Transfer Problem: The Role of Weak Ties in Sharing Knowledge across Organizational Sub-units'. *Administrative Science Quarterly*, 44(1): 82–111.

Hanseth, O. (2004). 'Knowledge as Architecture', in C. Avgerou, C. Ciborra, and F. Land (eds.), *The Social Study of Information and Communication Technology: Innovation, Actors, and Contexts*. Oxford: Oxford University Press, 103–118.

He, Z.-L. and Wong, P.-K. (2004). 'Exploration vs. Exploitation: An Empirical Test of the Ambidexterity Hypothesis'. *Organization Science*, 15(4): 481–494.

Henderson, J. and Venkatraman, N. (1992). 'Strategic Alignment: A model for organizational transformation through information technology', in T. A. Kochan and M. Useem (eds.), *Transforming Organizations*. New York: Oxford University Press, 97–117.

———. (1999b). 'Strategic Alignment: Leveraging Information Technology for Transforming Organizations'. *IBM Systems Journal*, 38(2–3): 472–484.

Keen, P. G. W. (1981). 'MIS Research: Reference Disciplines and a Cumulative Tradition', in *Proceedings of the 1st International Conference on Information Systems*. Philadelphia, PA, 8–10 December, 9–18.

Kogut, B., and Zander, U. (1992). 'Knowledge of the firm, combinative capabilities, and the replication of technology'. *Organization Science*, 381–397.

Kriebel, C. H. (1968). 'The Strategic Dimension of Computer Systems Planning'. *Long Range Planning*, 1(1): 7–12.

Lacity, M. C. and Willcocks, L. (2000). *Global Information Technology Outsourcing: In Search of Business Advantage*. Chichester: Wiley.

Land, F. (1982). 'Adapting to Changing User Requirements'. *Information and Management*, 5(2): 59–75.

———. (1996b). 'The New Alchemist: Or How to Transmute Base Organisations into Corporations of Gleaming Gold'. *Journal of Strategic Information Systems*, 5(1): 5–17.

Lave, J. and Wenger, E. (1991). *Situated Learning: Legitimate Peripheral Participation*. Cambridge: Cambridge University Press.

Leavitt, H. J. (1965). 'Applying Organizational Change in Industry: Structural, Technological and Humanistic Approaches', in J. G. March (ed.), *Handbook of Organizations*. Chicago, IL: Rand McNally, 264–291.

Leidner, D. E. (ed.) (2000). *Journal of Strategic Information Systems*. Special Issue on Knowledge Management and Knowledge Management Systems, 9(2–3): 101–261.

Levi-Strauss, C. (1966). *The Savage Mind*. London: Weidenfeld and Nicolson.

Lientz, B. P. and Rea, K. P. (2004). *Breakthrough IT Change Management: How to Get Enduring Change Results*. Oxford: Elsevier Butterworth-Heinemann.

Lincoln, T. J. (1975). 'A Strategy for Information Systems Development'. *Management Datamatics*, 4(4): 121–128.

Lindblom, C. (1959). 'The Science of Muddling Through'. *Public Administration Review*, 19(2): 79–88.

MacDonald, H. (1991). 'Business Strategy Development, Alignment and Redesign', in M. Scott Morton (ed.), *The Corporation of the 1990s*. New York: Oxford University Press, 159–186.

March, J. (1991). 'Exploration and Exploitation in Organizational Learning'. *Organization Science*, 2(1): 71–86.

McElroy, M. (2000). 'Integrating Complexity Theory, Knowledge Management and Organizational Learning'. *Journal of Knowledge Management*, 4(3): 195–203.

McFarlan, F. W. (1971). 'Problems in Planning the Information System'. *Harvard Business Review*, 49(2): 75–89.

McFarlan, F. W. (1984). 'Information Technology Changes the Way You Compete'. *Harvard Business Review*, 62(3): 98–102.

McLean, E. R. and Soden, J. V. (1977). *Strategic Planning for MIS*. New York: Wiley.

Mintzberg, H. and Waters, J. A. (1985). 'Of Strategies, Deliberate and Emergent'. *Strategic Management Journal*, 6(3): 257–272.

Monteiro, E. (1998). 'Scaling Information Infrastructure: The Case of the Next Generation IP in Internet'. *The Information Society*, 14(3): 229–245.

Newell, S. and Swan, J. (2000). 'Trust and Inter-organizational Networking'. *Human Relations*, 53(10): 1287–1328.

Nonaka, I. and Takeuchi, H. (1995). *The KnowledgeCreating Company: How Japanese Companies Create the Dynamics of Innovation*. New York: Oxford University Press.

Parker, M., Benson, R., and Trainor, E. (1988). *Information Economics: Linking Business Performance to Information Technology*. Englewood Cliffs, NJ: Prentice Hall.

Peppard, J. and Ward, J. (2004). 'Beyond Strategic Information Systems: Towards and IS Capability'. *Journal of Strategic Information Systems*, 13(2): 167–194.

Polanyi, M. (1966). *The Tacit Dimension*. Garden City, NY: Doubleday and Co.

Porter, M. E. (1985). *Competitive Advantage: Creating and Sustaining Superior Performance*. New York: The Free Press.

———. (2001b). 'Strategy and the Internet'. *Harvard Business Review*, 79(3): 63–78.

———. and Millar, V. E. (1985). 'How Information Gives You Competitive Advantage'. *Harvard Business Review*, 63(4): 149–160.

Prahalad, C.K. and Hamel, G. (1990). 'The Core Competence of the Corporation'. *Harvard Business Review*, 68(3): 79–91.

———. Edelman, L., Scarbrough, H., Swan, J. A., and Bresnen, M. (2003). '"Best Practice" Development and Transfer in the NHS: The Importance of Process as well as Product Knowledge'. *Journal of Health Services Management*, 16: 1–12.

Robey, D. and Boudreau, M. C. (1999). 'Accounting for the Contradictory Organizational Consequences of Information Technology: Theoretical Directions and Methodological Implications'. *Information Systems Research*, 10(2): 167–85.

Sabherwal, R., Hirschheim, R. and Goles, T. (2001). 'The Dynamics of Alignment: Insights from a Punctuated Equilibrium Model'. *Organization Science*, 12(2): 179–197.

Sambamurthy, V. and Jarvenpaa, S.. (eds) (2002). *Journal of Strategic Information Systems*. Special Issue on Trust in the Digital Economy, 11(3–4): 183–346.

Scarbrough, H., Bresnen, M., Edelman, L. F., Laurent, S., Newell, S., and Swan, J. (2004). 'The Processes of Project-based Learning: An Exploratory Study'. *Management Learning*, 35(4): 491–506.

Scarbrough, H., Bresnen, M., Edelman, L. F., Laurent, S., Newell, S., Swan, J., and Preston, J. (1999). *Knowledge Management and the Learning Organization*. London: IPD.

Scott, S. V. and Wagner, E. L. (2003). 'Networks, Negotiations and New Times: The Implementation of Enterprise Resource Planning into an Academic Administration'. *Information and Organization*, 13(4): 285–313.

Senn, J. A. (1992). 'The Myths of Strategic Systems: What Defines True Competitive Advantage?'. *Journal of Information Systems Management*, 9(3): 7–12.

Sole, D. and Edmondson, A. (2002). 'Situated Knowledge and Learning in Dispersed Teams'. *British Journal of Management*, 13: S17–S34.

Star, S. L. and Ruhleder, K. (1996). 'Steps Towards an Ecology of Infrastructure: Design and Access to Large Information Spaces'. *Information Systems Research*, 7(1): 111–134.

Suarez, F. F. and Lanzolla, G. (2005). 'The Half-Truth of First-Mover Advantage'. *Harvard Business Review*, 83(4): 121–127.

Szulanski, G. (1996). 'Exploring Internal Stickiness: Impediments to the Transfer of Best Practice within the Firm'. *Strategic Management Journal*, 17(1): 27–44.

———. and Jensen, R. J. (2004). 'Overcoming Stickiness: An Empirical Investigation of the Role of the Template in the Replication of Organizational Routines'. *Managerial and Decision Economics*, 25(6–7): 347–363.

Tsoukas, H. (1996). 'The Firm as a Distributed Knowledge System: A Constructionist Approach'. *Strategic Management Journal*, 17(Winter Special Issue): 11–25.

Tushman, M. L. and Scanlan, T. (1981). 'Boundary Spanning Individuals: Their Role in Information Transfer and their Antecedents'. *Academy of Management Journal*, 24(2): 289–305.

———. and O'Reilly, C. (1996). 'Ambidextrous Organizations: Managing Evolutionary and Revolutionary Change'. *California Management Review*, 38(1): 8–30.

Venkatraman, N. (1991). 'IT-induced Business Reconfiguration', in M. Scott Morton (ed.), *The Corporation of the 1990s: IT and Organizational Transformation*. New York: Oxford University Press, 122–158.

Wagner, E. and Newell, S. (2006). 'Repairing ERP: Producing Social Order to Create a Working Information System'. *Journal of Applied Behavioral Research*, 42(1): 40–57.

Weick, K. E. (1990). 'Technology as an Equivoque: Sensemaking in New Technologies', in P. S. Goodman and L. Sproull (eds.), *Technology and Organizations*. San Francisco, CA: Jossey-Bass, 1–44.

———. (1995b). *Sensemaking in Organizations*. Thousand Oaks, CA: Sage.

Wenger, E. (1998). *Communities of Practice: Learning, Meaning, and Identity*. Cambridge: Cambridge University Press.

Whittington, R. (1993). *What is Strategy? And Does it Matter?* London: Routledge.

Willcocks, L. (1999). 'Managing Information Technology Evaluation: Techniques and Processes', in R. D. Galliers, D. E. Leidner, and B. S. H. Baker (eds.), *Strategic Information Management: Challenges and Strategies in Managing Information Systems*, 2nd ed. Oxford: Butterworth-Heinemann, 271–290.

Young, R. C. (1967). 'Systems and Data Processing Departments Need Long-Range Planning', *Computers and Automation*, May, 30–33, 45.

Questions for Discussion

1   A number of myths are identified (see also Chapter 2) including those associated with alignment, strategic IT, knowledge management and competitive advantage. Do you agree with identifying these as myths? Why? Why not?

2   What more recent fads and fashions can you identify in the world of strategic information management? What are the implications of a failure to treat new technologies and innovations more reflexively bearing in mind the arguments raised in this and preceding chapters?

3   Is there such a thing as best practice? Why? Why not? What are the implications of accepting the notion in the context of strategic information management?

4   Consider the concepts of aligning versus alignment and knowing versus knowledge. What distinguishes one from the other? Are the distinctions helpful when considering the applications of these concepts in organizations. Why? Why not?

5   Consider an organization with which you are familiar. To what extent does the concept of ambidexterity apply? What is the relative emphasis placed on exploitation versus exploration? What do you infer from this in terms of revised strategic considerations?

Further Reading

Bloodgood, J. M., Salisbury, W. D. (2001). 'Understanding the influence of organizational change strategies on information technology and knowledge management strategies'. *Decision Support Systems*, 31(1), 55–69.

Henderson, J. C., Venkatraman, N. (1993). 'Strategic alignment: Leveraging information technology for transforming organizations'. *IBM Systems Journal*, 32(1), 472–484.

Chapter 4

Robert D. Galliers

CONCEPTUAL DEVELOPMENTS IN INFORMATION SYSTEMS STRATEGIZING: UNPACKING THE CONCEPT

Prologue: Towards a Revised Framework for Information Systems Strategizing

In previous work (in particular, Galliers, 2004, 2007), an attempt was made to collect together aspects of recent thinking in organizational and information systems (IS) strategic thinking to develop a framework that would aid the process of IS strategizing. The problematic nature of key tenets of much of the mainstream IS strategy literature (i.e., issues of alignment, competitive advantage, and so-called knowledge management systems or 'best practice' solutions) was considered in the context of the development and strategic impact and use of information and communication technology (ICT) systems in and between organizations. *Inter alia*, it was noted that there are vexed issues associated with aligning dynamic information needs with a relatively static technology (see also, Desouza, 2006), and harnessing an increasingly commoditized technology to provide competitive advantage. This is at the heart of Carr's (2003, 2005) argument that 'IT Doesn't Matter'. But Carr misses the point. Crucially, it is the *use* to which ICT is put by organizations, and their capability and competencies in this regard, that are crucial, as is the key role that information can play in questioning, supporting and informing the strategizing process. In relation to knowledge management and knowledge management systems in particular, questions were raised as to whether ICT systems could in fact capture and transfer knowledge, with the *process* of knowing and knowledge creation (e.g., Boland & Tenkasi, 1995; Nonaka & Takeuchi, 1995; Cook & Brown, 1999; von Krogh et al., 2000) being highlighted. This orientation was set against the capture and transfer knowledge that is the focus of much of the mainstream literature on the topic, and the knowledge-based theory of the firm (Grant, 1996; Spender, 1996).

In attempting to synthesize these arguments with a view to developing a more holistic framework for IS strategizing, the socio-technical concept of an information architecture or infrastructure (e.g., Star & Ruhleder, 1996; Monteiro, 1998; Ciborra, 2000; Hanseth, 2004) provided a useful building block. In addition, it was argued that organizations should be 'ambidextrous' (Tushman & O'Reilly, 1996) in that they should combine an ability to *explore* new opportunities as well as *exploit* current capabilities and technology. I argued that this ambidexterity can be facilitated by an environment an information infrastructure or architecture that provides a supportive context for learning and interaction. I introduced each of these components in the context of a framework that is meant to be used as a sense-making (cf. Weick, 1995) device, rather than a prescriptive tool.

Before proceeding to unpack the framework in greater detail than previously, I should first clarify how the term information systems (IS) is used here. As I have argued elsewhere (see, for example, Galliers, 2003, 2006b), I view IS as neither being focused on the IT artefact (a technological perspective common in much of the literature) at one pole nor on knowledge sharing and creation at the other. I view IS as incorporating both aspects as a socio-technical construct in other words, mutually constituted. There are two primary reasons for this. The first relates to the nature of data, information and knowledge (Galliers & Newell, 2003a, 2003b). The socio-technical infrastructure (e.g., Star & Ruhleder, 1996; Ciborra, 2000) depicted in Figure 4.1 comprises human beings who can make sense of data provided by both formal and informal systems via the application of their (situated) knowledge. In doing so, they turn data into purposeful information (see also Chapter 19). The second reason is to provide an otherwise missing link between the literatures on IS/IT strategy, on knowledge management, and on organizational strategies for change. Too often viewed as discrete, an underlying argument in this chapter is that the concepts emerging from these literatures should be viewed as complimentary and synergistic, as argued by Porter (2001), for example

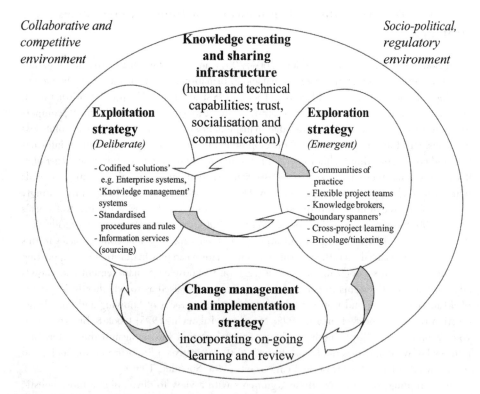

Figure 4.1 A Revised Information Systems Strategizing Framework

(see also Galliers et al., 1997). I shall refer to these other literatures in the course of this chapter in addition to providing a critical treatment of much of the IS strategy and planning literature.

I should also note that aspects of the IS, IT and information management (IM) strategies first articulated by Michael Earl (1989), and developed further in Galliers (1991, 1999) as information, IT and information services strategies the combination forming the IS strategy as a whole are incorporated into both the exploration and exploitation strategies of Figure 4.1. The *exploration* strategy takes more of an informal approach Ciborra (1992); Ciborra (1994), after Levi-Strauss, 1966) would call this tinkering or bricolage as against the formal approaches of the kind identified by Earl (1993). These include what Earl terms business-led, method-driven, administrative (i.e., resource-focused) and technological approaches. His study led to the conclusion that an organizational approach held most promise given its emphasis on process, integration and, crucially, stakeholder involvement (see also, Codoba, 2009). The exploration strategy also takes into account the learning or knowledge that can emerge from communities of practice, boundary spanning individuals and flexible project teams (e.g., Tushman & Scanlan, 1981; Lave & Wenger, 1991; Wenger, 1998; Hansen et al., 1999; Scheepers et al., 2004; Erden et al., 2008), including learning across projects (e.g., Newell & Edelman, 2008). The *exploitation* strategy, as noted, is more formal in its approach and focuses more on codified 'solutions', standardized procedures and standards. It also incorporates issues of how the information services function should be organized, including key sourcing issues (e.g., Lacity & Willcocks, 2000).

In this chapter, then, I shall attempt to unpack the concept of the IS strategizing framework still further, by articulating, in greater depth, the literature that has informed its development. The aim is to ground the framework in the extant literature, provide a rationale for the whole and the component parts, and articulate what is meant by each aspect of the framework. The framework, slightly revised from the 2007 version, is illustrated in Figure 4.1 below. Each aspect will be considered in turn, commencing with the environment internal and external in which the strategizing process is taking place. The chapter ends with a consideration as to how the framework may be put to good use in organizations.

The Strategizing Environment

As indicated above, my treatment of the strategizing environment considers this aspect of IS strategizing from two perspectives: internal as well as external. From the *internal* perspective the focus is on a balance between the formal and the informal; the technological and the organizational; codified and tacit knowledge; the deliberate and the emergent, and implementation and innovation, all with the aim of *exploiting* resources while *exploring* new opportunities. Information transfer and sharing is at its core, very much in line with the arguments of Michael Tushman and colleagues (e.g., Tushman & Nadler, 1978; Tushman & Scanlan, 1981; Tushman & O'Reilly, 1996). In addition, and as argued by Newkirk et al. (2003), a balance has also to be struck between too much planning and too little. Too much planning may lead to delay and may impede implementation, while too little may lead to implementation plans with insufficient detail (see also, Earl, 1993; Ward & Griffiths, 1996; Ward & Peppard, 2002). Room has to made for innovation and improvisation (Vera & Crossan, 2005; Crossan & Sorrenti, 1997), as well as building the necessary capacity and capability for change (Teece et al., 1997; Peppard & Ward, 2004) organizational characteristics that 'enable an organization to conceive, choose and implement strategies' (Barney, 1991). This, too, is where the knowledge creating and sharing infrastructure plays a significant role, as detailed below.

The *external* environment should take account of the institutional context (see Chapter 4) in which the organization operates including the socio-political and regulatory environment, and cultural nuances in different parts of the organization, especially in multinational arrangements, for example (Finnegan & Longaigh, 2002; Mohdzain & Ward, 2007; David et al., 2008). In relation to the latter, there has been increasing focus in the literature on subsidiaries (e.g., Gupta & Govindarajan, 2000; O'Donnell, 2000), for example, given growing globalization (e.g., Walsham, 2001; Sheth & Sisodia, 2007; Galliers, 2007b; Oshri et al., 2008), with Finnegan and colleagues (2003) noting the impact of different cultures and power relationships of external stakeholders, and Ives and colleagues (1993) highlighting the potential of resistance from foreign subsidiaries and the disparity in the IT infrastructure and available products in different parts of the world. The effects of trust in virtual communities may also be significant (Jarvenpaa & Leidner, 1999; Ridings et al., 2002). Depending on particular circumstances, these are the kind of considerations that need to be taken into account. Also of potential relevance is the work on issues associated with integrating IS after mergers and acquisitions (McKiernan & Merali, 1993, 1995; Brown & Renwick, 1996; Giacomazzi et al., 1997), with Wijnhoven and colleagues (2006) developing a variant of Henderson and Venkatraman's (1999) alignment model to take account of the extent of integration: from complete integration to mere co-existence. All this is in addition to the analysis of the competitive forces (e.g., Porter, 2001) and the cooperative or conflictual arrangements (e.g., Webster, 1995) at play.

One final point: in earlier work (Galliers, 1991, 1993, 1999 in particular), and as noted above, I proposed an IS strategizing framework that was closely linked to a business strategy. The business strategy was considered to exist outside the boundary of the IS strategy that is, in its internal environment. The link, it was argued, should be a strong one, with the information strategy feeding off, and feeding into, the business strategy.

The information strategy, in my terms, was concerned with the information needed not only to *support* but also to *question* the business strategy. For example, are assumptions that underpin the strategy being borne out? It should be noted that the business strategy is absent from Figure 4.1, however. This is not an oversight. In line with Porter's (2001: 78) argument, the revised IS strategy is a significant aspect of the overall business strategy, it is integrated into it. In an earlier reflection on the subject (Galliers, 2007a; 238, emphasis added), I re-interpreted a passage from Porter's article, as follows:

> The next stage of strategy evolution will involve a shift in thinking from business strategy and knowledge strategy, to Information Systems strategising. By *integrating* Information Systems considerations into the discourse on business and knowledge strategy, the resultant thinking and practice will become mutually constituted and significantly more robust.

It is with this in mind that the IS strategizing framework is presented without explicit mention of the business strategy, and with which the knowledge creating and sharing infrastructure is introduced to provide the oxygen needed for what should be seen as a dynamic, on-going and iterative process.

The Knowledge Creating and Sharing Infrastructure

In a previous work, I described the knowledge creating and sharing infrastructure in terms of an information architecture (Galliers, 2004; 255–6). This was meant to connote an enabling socio-technical environment for both the *exploitation* of knowledge (efficiency) and the *exploration* of knowledge (innovation) in line with Tushman's concept of ambidexterity (Tushman & O'Reilly, 1996). There are elements here, too, of what Boland and Tenkasi (1995) term communities of knowing. I shall unpack the exploitation and exploration strategies that play an important role in the IS strategizing concept in the sections that follow, but it is important to note at this stage that this socio-technical environment is meant to enable and facilitate the strategizing process by ensuring that the necessary human and technical capabilities are in place (cf., Peppard & Ward, 2004), not only within the organization but with key partners, such as in sourcing arrangements (Beulen et al., 2005).

As noted previously (Galliers, 2004), the concept of an information infrastructure has developed over time.

In the 1980s and 1990s, the term information infrastructure usually connoted the standardization of corporate ICT, systems and data, with a view to reconciling centralized processing and distributed applications. So, the question would need to be asked whether the necessary technologies are in place to support the enterprise moving forward. Increasingly, however, the concept has come to relate to the human infrastructure in addition. For example, what roles and skills are required, not just in terms of developing and delivering information systems increasingly in a distributed environment (Kotlarsky & Oshri, 2005) but also in their management (Galliers & Leidner, 2009)? Weill and Ross (2004) talk in terms of IT governance in commenting on some of these issues. As already noted, trust plays an important role here too (Kanawattanachai & Yoo, 2002; Sambamurthy & Jarvenpaa, 2002), with a team atmosphere needing to be in place (Zarraga & Bonache, 2005). Additionally, the means by which alternative stakeholder concerns are taken into account (Codoba, 2009) is an important consideration, bearing in mind that implicit in many of the more formal approaches to strategizing is the assumption that individuals can make stated organizational objectives their own (Willmott, 1993), with questions of power (Foucault, 1984) often being left unconsidered. As noted earlier, Star and Ruhleder (1996) talk of infrastructures in terms of their embeddedness, transparency, reach, links with conventions of practice, and installed base. An information infrastructure should thus be viewed as heterogeneous in nature.

The concept is further refined here by introducing ideas related to knowledge creating and sharing, building on earlier work by Nonaka, von Krogh and colleagues (e.g., Nonaka, 1991, 1994; Nonaka et al., 1994, 2006; von Krogh et al., 2000; Nonaka & Toyama, 2003; Nonaka & von Krogh, 2007; Erden et al., 2008), and to project learning (Kotnour, 1999; Salas et al., 2000; Schindler & Epplerm, 2003; Scarbrough, et al., 2004) and cross-project learning capability (Newell & Edelman, 2008), bearing in mind the 'stickiness' of knowledge (von Hippel, 1994; Szulanski, 1996; Szulanski & Jensen, 2004), and the resultant need for boundary spanning activity (Tushman & Scanlan, 1981). The creation of a dynamic capability (Zollo & Winter, 2002; Winter, 2003) in this regard is key. According to Zollo and Winter (2002: 340), dynamic capabilities are 'a learned and stable pattern of collective activity through which the organization systematically generates and modifies its operating routines in pursuit of effectiveness'.

Previously, issues of exploration and exploitation have tended to be considered as being in opposition to each other (March, 1991). Increasingly, however, we see different ICT initiatives such as ERP and KM systems being implemented in tandem in an attempt foster the simultaneous development of organizational efficiency and flexibility (Newell et al., 2003) hence the need to view the exploration and exploitation strategies as being mutually constituted and reinforcing (cf., Cook & Brown, 1999). Formal 'organization memory' IS (Nevo & Wand, 2005) will certainly have their place, but so will means by which knowing is facilitated and by which knowledge can flow, even in distributed teams (Carmel, 1999; Desouza & Evaristo, 2004) or in multinational locations (Gupta & Govindarajan, 2000; Oshri et al., 2008).

The Exploitation Strategy

The process of exploitation bears many of the hallmarks of mainstream and earlier thinking on IS strategy. For example, much of earlier and even recent practice follows what might be termed a deterministic path of technology exploitation (cf., Earl, 1993). Thus, Lederer and Sethi (1988), for example, speak of strategic information systems planning as 'the process whereby an organization determines a portfolio of computerbased applications to help it achieve its business objectives'. In a later work, Lederer and colleagues (Newkirk et al., 2003) build on the work of Mentzas (1997) in detailing such planning phases as strategic awareness; situation analysis; strategy conception; strategy formulation, and strategy implementation. This is the deliberate as compared to the emergent strategy of which Mintzberg speaks (Mintzberg & Waters, 1985). A deliberate attempt is made to identify and develop ICT applications that both support and question the organization's strategic vision, and current need for information and expertise (Segars & Grover, 1999). Here, we find both the IS and IT strategies that Earl (1989) proposes. It is likely that Enterprise Systems (e.g., Howcroft, et al., 2004a) and so-called KMS (e.g., Leidner, 2000), and standardized procedures for adopting ICT products, hiring ICT personnel, and developing customized applications will each contribute to this exploitation strategy. Indeed, organizational routines can be a source of connections and improved understandings according to Feldman and Rafaeli (2002). And in line with the models introduced in Galliers (1991, 1999), an aspect of this strategy will relate to the organizational arrangements for IS/IT services, including sourcing considerations (cf. Lacity & Willcocks, 2000; Carmel & Agarwal, 2002, for example). Policies on such issues as risk, security and confidentiality will also need to be considered in this context (e.g., Backhouse, et al., 2005).

The Exploration Strategy

With respect to the exploration aspects of IS strategizing, here the emphasis is much more on issues associated with situated learning (Lave & Wenger, 1991), communities of practice (Wenger, 1998) and of knowing (Boland & Tenkasi, 1995), and cross-project learning (Newell & Edelman, 2008), as noted in the above discussion on infrastructure. Ciborra and colleagues (Ciborra, 2000) talk of drift in this context as against control but there is nonetheless a sense of direction and purpose associated with this activity. I therefore prefer the term emergence in this regard, but there is certainly a sense of bricolage (cf. Levi-Strauss, 1966) and tinkering at play here, to return to terms favored by Ciborra (1992). Elements of what Lindblom (1959) termed 'muddling through' and of improvisation (Crossan & Sorrenti, 1997; Vera & Crossan, 2005) and innovation (Van der Gerben et al., 2002) play an important part in addition. As noted, organizations are increasingly reliant on project teams whose membership may well be in flux and distributed. Considerations of trust (Sambamurphy & Jarvenpaa, 2002), socialization (Ahuja & Galvin, 2003), and learning from one project to another (e.g., Scarbrough et al., 2004) are key features at play here. The role of communities of practice (e.g., Wenger, 1998) is crucial in knowledge creation as we have seen, as is the role of boundary spanning individuals (Tushman & Scanlan, 1981), or what we might term knowledge brokers (see also, Lave & Wenger, 1991; Hansen et al., 1999).

While the concept of the ambidextrous organization has been postulated (Tushman & O'Reilly, 1996), and some empirical research has been conducted to test the thesis (e.g., He & Wong, 2004), there remains little in the literature that might be of assistance to organizations in providing an enabling, supportive environment that might foster this sought-after 'ambidexterity'. Relating concepts of infrastructure introduced earlier in this chapter to the concept of ambidexterity would appear to hold some promise in this regard. Thus, the kind of socio-technical environment proposed by Star and Ruhleder (1996), Ciborra (2000) and Hanseth (2004), among others, would combine information and knowledge sharing services both electronic and human that would facilitate both exploitation *and* exploration of knowledge, together with the kind of flexibility necessary to enable appropriate responses to changing business imperatives. The development of different scenarios can be helpful in exploring alternative futures in this context (Galliers, 1993, 2006a).

The Change Management Strategy

As previously (Galliers, 2007; 236–7), I have attempted to stress the importance of on-going learning and review in the strategizing process. Improved understanding can lead to informed judgments being taken, with a view to further developments taking place in terms of improved systems and processes (formal as well as informal) that may assist individual and collective activity and decision-making, and organizational performance. On-going learning and review are central to the processual view of IS strategizing adopted here, given the unintended as well as the intended consequences arising from ICT implementations (Robey & Boudreau, 1999); the dynamic nature of alignment (Sabherwal et al., 2001) the need for agility therefore (Desouza, 2006), and the emergent nature of strategizing (Mintzberg & Waters, 1985). Thus, the process of strategizing is one of visioning, planning, taking action and assessing outcomes, all with an eye to changing circumstance and imperatives, *and* the actions of individuals and groups outside of, or irrespective of, any formal strategy process. Some means of measuring the impact on firm performance is key in this regard (Rivard et al., 2006).

I noted in the earlier work (Galliers, 2007a) that there are a number of popular books on breakthrough change management focusing on the role of ICT (e.g., Lientz & Rea, 2004) and on so-called transformational leaders (e.g., Anderson & Anderson, 2001). The major features of this genre include prescriptive, deliberate approaches that suggest guaranteed, order-of-magnitude gains. Organizational realities suggest an alternative, incremental approach more akin to 'muddling through' (Lindblom, 1959), however, as has been argued here. The incremental exploration of possibilities the tinkering (Ciborra, 1992) and bricolage (Levi-Strauss, 1966) along with the more deliberate, analytical approaches that incorporate oversight of implementations and review of outcomes (e.g., Willcocks, 2009) are what is envisaged here, with improvements in organizational performance in mind (Rivard et al., 2006). Exploration *and* exploitation (March, 1991; Tushman & O'Reilly, 1996) are therefore the name of the game, as is providing the appropriate organizational architecture for change (Nadler et al., 1992) to revert to terminology introduced earlier in this chapter.

There is not an insignificant literature on the review process. For example, Venkatraman and Ramanujam (1987), Segars and Grover (1998), and Doherty and colleagues (1999) are among those who have considered means by which IS strategy success may be measured. Venkatraman and Ramanujam, for example, stress the need for success measures in on-going evaluation as a means to improve planning capability. Seddon and colleagues (2002) consider this in terms of organizational effectiveness, while Kearns (2004) proposes a multi-objective, multi-criteria approach. Others, such as Kumar (1990) and Norris (1996), focus their attention on system evaluation, and others still call for emancipation as a key design principle (Wilson, 1997). Whatever the focus, it should not be assumed that evaluation is an entirely objective issue. For example, Gwillim and colleagues (2005) consider the politics of post-implementation reviews, noting that few organizations undertake ex-post evaluation. As Walsham (1997) notes, without a formal evaluation policy, IT and business executives alike will act perfectly rationally in their own interests. The pre-eminence of individual interests in organizations is a point made clear by the likes of Handy (1995) and Schein (1997). Thus, Wagner and Newell (2007) emphasize the importance of participation in making further refinements (in this case with respect to enterprise systems) during the post-implementation period. Indeed, Matta and Ashkenas (2003) remind us that even good projects fail, particularly with respect to cross-functional projects. There is a danger in organizations failing to learn from different project experiences and reinventing the wheel (Lyttinen & Robey, 1999; Kearns, 2004). This, in part, stems from formal project reviews that are documented for others to consider at some future point in time (Schindler and Epplerm (2003), or at predetermined milestones (Kotnour, 1999). Drawing on this, Scarbrough and Swan (2001) make the point that the emphasis has tended to be on the supply rather than the demand for knowledge, and this is why Newell and Edelman (2008) emphasize the need to encourage teams to reflect and tell stories about their learning experiences (cf., Boland & Tenkasi, 1995) in a way that comes alive and helps nurture a learning capability by providing context.

Applying the Framework

As I hope has been made abundantly clear, the framework presented in Figure 4.1 is not meant to be a prescriptive tool: it does not and is not meant to provide some kind of solution. It is presented as a sense-making (cf. Weick, 1995) devise, meant more as an *aide memoir*, to be used to raise questions and facilitate discussion concerning the strategizing elements and connections that may or may not be in place in any particular organization. As already mentioned, the IS strategizing process envisaged here is a dynamic and iterative one based on learning and questioning. Assumptions need to be tested and a range of viewpoints sought both from within and outside the organization. The framework can be used to help in this process of enquiry.

Thus, questions can be posed that may surface the presence or absence of key features that make up the framework. For example, is a knowledge creating and sharing infrastructure in place? How supportive is it in terms of both the human as well as the technical capabilities required to implement the strategy? Is there a greater emphasis on exploitation as against exploration? And if so, what impact does this appear to have on organizational performance? Do sourcing considerations form an integral part of the exploitation strategy process? Similarly, does cross-project learning form an integral part of the exploration aspects of strategizing? How does communication and understanding materialize in and between virtual teams? To what extent does on-going learning and review take place as part of the change management and implementation strategy? Are performance measures in place?

All these questions are merely illustrative of how the framework may be used in organizations. Certain of them, and certain aspects of the framework itself, may be more or less relevant and/or important depending on the differing circumstances in which different organizations in different locations in the world, at different stages of growth (Penrose, 1959; Galliers & Sutherland, 1991), and different sectors of the economy find themselves. An aspect of the framework's application that should be consistent, no matter what the circumstances, is its on-going deployment as a learning tool. As already noted, the process of strategizing is an iterative one. While there may be a defined planning horizon, with particular targets being set for that particular time period, the questioning based on the framework and its various components should continue, at least periodically. The framework itself, and its component parts, may be adapted and developed in line with the particular and changing nature of the context in which it is being applied, but its use as a sense-making devise should continue with a view to improving organizational performance, exploiting organizational and technological capabilities, exploring new opportunities, with a view to continuous innovation.

References

Ahuja, M. K. & Galvin, J. E. (2003). Socialization in virtual groups, *Journal of Management*, 29, 161–185.

Anderson, D. & Anderson, L. A. (2001). *Beyond Change Management: Advanced Strategies for Today's Transformational Leaders*. San Francisco, CA: Joessey-Bass/Pfieffer.

Backhouse, J., Bener, A., Chauvidul, N., Wamala, F. & Willison, R. (2005). Risk management in cyberspace. In R. Mansell & B. Collins (Eds.), *Trust and Crime in Information Societies*, Cheltenham: Edward Elgar, 349–379.

Barney, J. B. (1991). Firm resources and sustained competitive advantage, *Journal of Management*, 17(1), 99–120.

Beulen, E., van Fenema, P. C. & Currie, W. (2005). From application outsourcing to infrastructure management: Extending the offshore outsourcing portfolio, *European Management Journal*, 25, 133–144.

Boland, R. J. & Tenkasi, R. (1995). Perspective making and perspective taking in communities of knowing, *Organization Science*, 13, 442–455.

Brown, C. & Renwick, J. (1996). Alignment of the IS organization: The special case of corporate acquisitions, *The DATABASE for Advances in Information Systems*, 27(4), 2533.

Carmel, E. (1999). *Global Software Teams: Collaborating across Borders and Time Zones*. Saddle River, NJ: Prentice Hall PTR.

Carmel, E. & Agarwal, R. (2002). The maturation of off-shore sourcing of information technology work, *MISQE*, 1, 65–77.

Carr, N. G. (2003). IT doesn't matter, *Harvard Business Review*, 81(5), 41–49.

Carr, N. G. (2005). The end of corporate computing, *MIT Sloan Management Review*, 46(3), 67–73.

Ciborra, C. U. (1992). From thinking to tinkering: The grassroots of IT and strategy, *Information Society*, 8, 297–309.

Ciborra, C. U. (1994). The grassroots of IT and strategy. In C. Ciborra & T. Jelassi (Eds.), *Strategic Information Systems A European Perspective*, Chichester: Wiley, 3–24.

Ciborra, C. U. (ed.) (2000) *From Control to Drift: The Dynamics of Corporate Information Infrastructures*. Oxford: Oxford University Press.

Codoba, J.-R. (2009). Critical reflection in planning information systems: A contribution from critical thinking, *Information Systems Journal*, 19(2), 123–147.

Cook, S. D. N. & Brown, J. S. (1999). Bridging epistemologies: The generative dance between organizational knowledge and organizational knowing, *Organization Science*, 10(4), 381–400.

Crossan, M. & Sorrenti, M. (1997). Making sense of improvisation, *Advances in Strategic Management*, 14, 155–180.

David, G., Chand, D., Newell, S. & Resende-Santos, J. (2008). Integrated collaboration across distributed sites: The perils of process and the promise of practice, *Journal of Information Technology*, 23, 44–54.

Desouza, K. C. (ed.) (2006). *Agile Information Systems. Conceptualization, Construction, and Management*, Oxford: Butterworth-Heinemann.

Desouza, K. C. & Evaristo, J. R. (2004). Managing knowledge in distributed projects, *Communications of the ACM*, 47, 87–91.

Doherty, N. F., Marples, C. G. & Suhaimi, A. (1999). The relative success of alternative approaches to strategic information systems planning: An empirical analysis, *Journal of Strategic Information Systems*, 8(3), 263–283.

Earl, M. J. (1989). *Management Strategies for Information Technology*. London: Prentice Hall.

Earl, M. J. (1993). Experiences in strategic information systems planning, *MIS Quarterly*, 17(1), 1–24.

Erden, Z., von Krogh, G. & Nonaka, I. (2008). The quality of group tacit knowledge, *Journal of Strategic Information Systems*, 17(1), 4–18.

Feldman, M. S. & Rafaeli, A. (2002). Organizational routines as sources of connections and understandings, *Journal of Management Studies*, 39, 3.

Finnegan, P., Galliers, R. D. & Powell, P. (2003). Applying triple loop learning to planning electronic trading systems, *Information Technology & People*, 16(4), 461–483.

Finnegan, P. & Longaigh, S. N. (2002). Examining the effects of information technology on control and coordination relationships: An exploratory study in subsidiaries of pannational companies, *Journal of Information Technology*, 17(3), 149–163.

Foucault, M. (1984). The ethics of the concern of self as a practice of freedom. In P. Rabinow (Ed.), *Michel Foucault: Ethics, Subjectivity and Truth: Essential Works of Foucault 1954-1984*, London: Penguin, 281–301.

Galliers, R. D. (1991). Strategic information systems planning: Myths, reality and guidelines for successful implementation, *European Journal of Information Systems*, 1(1), 55–64.

Galliers, R. D. (1993). Towards a flexible information architecture: Integrating business strategies, information systems strategies and business process redesign, *Journal of Information Systems*, 3(3), 199–213.

Galliers, R. D. (1999). Towards the integration of e-business, knowledge management and policy considerations within an information systems strategy framework, *Journal of Strategic Information Systems*, 8(3), 229–234.

Galliers, R. D. (2003). Change as crisis or growth? Toward a trans-disciplinary view of information systems as a field of study a response to Benbasat and Zmud's call for returning to the IT artifact, *Journal of the Association for Information Systems*, 4(6), 337351.

Galliers, R. D. (2004). Reflections on information systems strategizing. In C. Avgerou, C. Ciborra & F. Land (Eds.), *The Social Study of Information and Communication Technology: Innovation, actors, and Contexts*, Oxford: Oxford University Press, 231–262.

Galliers, R. D. (2006a). Strategizing for agility: Confronting information systems inflexibility in dynamic environments. In K. De Souza (Ed.), *Agile Information Systems*, Oxford: Butterworth-Heinemann, 1–15.

Galliers, R. D. (2006b). 'Don't worry, be happy.' A post-modernist perspective on the information systems domain. In J. King & K. Lyytinen (Eds..), *Information Systems: The Need for a Discipline?* Chichester: Wiley, 324–331.

Galliers, R. D. (2007a). On confronting some of the common myths of information systems strategy discourse. In R. Mansell, C. Avgerou, D. Quah & R. Silverstone (Eds.), *The Oxford Handbook of Information and Communication Technology*, Oxford: Oxford University Press, 225–243.

Galliers, R. D. (2007b). IT and globalization: Knowledge creation and sharing across frontiers. In S. Dayal & M. Murphy (Eds.), Global Babel. *Questions of Discourse and Communication in a Time of Globalization*, Newcastle: Cambridge Scholars Publishing, 161–188.

Galliers, R. D., Jackson, M. C. & Mingers, J. (1997). Organization theory and systems thinking: The benefits of partnership, *Organization*, 4(2), 269–278.

Galliers, R. D. & Leidner, D. E. (2009). *Strategic Information Management. Challenges and Strategies in Managing Information systems, 4th Edition*, New York: Routledge.

Galliers, R. D. & Newell, S. (2003a). Strategy as data plus sense-making. In S. Cummings & D. C. Wilson (Eds.), *Images of Strategy*, Oxford: Blackwell, 164–196.

Galliers, R. D. & Newell, S. (2003b). Back to the future: From knowledge management to the management of information and data, *Information Systems and e-Business Management*, 1(1), 5–13.

Galliers, R. D. & Sutherland, A. R. (1991). Information systems management and strategy formulation: The 'Stages of Growth' model revisited, *Journal of Information Systems*, 1(2), 89–114.

Giacomazzi, F., Panella, C., Pernicci, B. & Sansomi, M. (1997). Information systems integration in mergers and acquisitions: A normative model, *Information & Management*, 32(6), 289–302.

Grant, R. M. (1996). Toward a knowledge-based theory of the firm, *Strategic Management Journal*, 17, 109–122.

Gupta, A. K. & Govindarajan, V. (2000). Knowledge flows within multinational corporations, *Strategic Management Journal*, 21(4), 473–496.

Gwillim, D., Dovey, K. & Wieder, B. (2005). The politics of post-implementation reviews, *Information Systems Journal*, 15(4), 307–319.

Handy, C. (1995). *Gods of Management, 2nd ed.*, London: Arrow Books.

Hansen, M. T., Nohria, N. & Tierney, T. (1999). What's your strategy for managing knowledge? *Harvard Business Review*, 77(2), 106–116.

Hanseth, O. (2004). Knowledge as architecture. In C. Avgerou, C. Ciborra & F. Land (Eds.), *The Social Study of Information and Communication Technology: Innovation, actors, and Contexts*, Oxford: Oxford University Press, 103–118.

He, Z.-L. & Wong, P.-K. (2004). Exploration vs. Exploitation: An empirical test of the ambidexterity hypothesis, *Organization Science*, 15(4), July-August, 481–494.

Henderson, J. C. & Venkatraman, N. (1999). Strategic alignment: Leveraging information technology for transforming organizations, *IBM Systems Journal*, 38(2/3), 472–484.

Howcroft, D., Newell, S. & Wagner, E. (eds.) (2004a). Special issue: Understanding the contextual influences on enterprise system design, implementation, use and evaluation, *Journal of Strategic Information Systems*, 13(4), 271–419.

Howcroft, D., Newell, S. & Wagner, E. (eds.) (2004b). Special issue: Understanding the contextual influences on enterprise system design, implementation, use and evaluation, Part II, *Journal of Strategic Information Systems*, 14(2), 91–242.

Ives, B., Jarvenpaa, S. L. & Mason, R. O. (1993). Global business drivers: Aligning information technology to global business strategy, *IBM Systems Journal*, 32(1), 143161.

Jarvenpaa, S. L. & Leidner, D. E. (1999). Communication and trust in global virtual teams, *Organization Science*, 10, 791–815.

Kanawattanachai, P. & Yoo, Y. (2002). Dynamic nature of trust in virtual teams, *Journal of Strategic Information Systems*, 11, 187–213.

Kearns, G. S. (2004). A multi-objective, multi criteria approach for evaluating IT investments: Results from two case studies, *Information Resources Management Journal*, 17(1), 37–62.

Kotlarsky, J. & Oshri, I. (2005). Social ties, knowledge sharing and successful collaboration in globally distributed system development projects, *European Journal of Information Systems*, 14, 37–48.

Kotnour, T. (1999). A learning framework for project management, *Project Management Journal*, 30(1), 32–38.

Kumar, K. (1990). Post implementation evaluation of computer based information systems: Current practices, *Communications of the ACM*, 33, 203–212.

Lacity, M. C. & Willcocks, L. (2000). *Global Information Technology Outsourcing: In Search of Business Advantage*. Chichester: Wiley.

Lave, J. & Wenger, E. (1991). *Situated Learning: Legitimate Peripheral Participation*. Cambridge: Cambridge University Press.

Lederer, A. L. & Sethi, V. (1988). The implementation of strategic information systems planning methodologies, *MIS Quarterly*, 12(3), 445–461.

Leidner, D. E. (ed.) (2000). Special issue: Knowledge management and knowledge management systems, *Journal of Strategic Information Systems*, 9(2-3), 101–261.

Levi-Strauss, C. (1966). *The Savage Mind*. London: Weidenfeld & Nicolson.

Lientz, B. P. & Rea, K. P. (2004). *Breakthrough IT Change Management: How to Get Enduring Change Results*. Oxford: Elsevier Butterworth-Heinemann.

Lindblom, C. (1959). The science of muddling through, *Public Administration Review*, 19(2), 79–88.

Lyttinen, K. & Robey, D. (1999). Leanring failure in information systems development, *Information Systems Journal*, 9(2), 85–101.

March, J. (1991). Exploration and exploitation in organizational learning, *Organization Science*, 2(1), 71–86.

Matta, N. & Ashkenas, R. (2003). Why good projects fail anyway, *Harvard Business Review*, 81, 109–115.

McKiernan, P. & Merali, Y. (1993). The strategic positioning of information systems in post-acquisition management, *Journal of Strategic Information Systems*, 2(2), 105–124.

McKiernan, P. & Merali, Y. (1995). Integrating information systems after a merger, *Long Range Planning*, 28(4), 54–62.

Mentzas, (1997).

Mintzberg, H. & Waters, J. A. (1985). Of strategies, deliberate and emergent, *Strategic Management Journal*, 6(3), 257–272.

Mohdzain, M. B. & Ward, J. M. (2007). A study of subsidiaries' views of information systems planning in multinational organizations, *Journal of Strategic Information Systems*, 16(4), 324–352.

Monteiro, E. (1998). Scaling information infrastructure: The case of the next generation IP in internet, *The Information Society*, 14(3), 229–245.

Nadler, D., Gerstein, M. & Shaw, R. (1992). *Organizational Architectures: Designs for Changing Organizations*. San Francisco, CA: Jossey-Bass.

Nevo, D. & Wand, Y. (2005). Organizational memory information systems: A transactive memory approach, *DSS*, 39, 549–562.

Newell, S. & Edelman, L. F. (2008). Developing a dynamic project-learning and crossproject learning capability: Synthesizing two perspectives, *Information Systems Journal*, 18(6), 567–590.

Newell, S., Huang, J. C., Galliers, R. D. & Pan, S. L. (2003). Implementing enterprise resource planning and knowledge management systems in tandem: Fostering efficiency and innovation complementarity, *Information & Organization*, 13(1), 25–52.

Newkirk, H. E., Lederer, A. L. & Srinavasan, C. (2003). Strategic information systems planning: Too little or too much? *Journal of Strategic Information Systems*, 12(3), 201228.

Nonaka, I. (1991). The knowledge-creating company, *Harvard Business Review*, 69(6), 96–104.

Nonaka, I. (1994). A dynamic theory of organizational knowledge creation, *Organization Science*, 5(1), 14–37.

Nonaka, I., Byosiere, P., Borucki, C. C. & Konno, N. (1994). Organizational knowledge creation theory: A first comprehensive test, *International Business Review*, 3, 337–351.

Nonaka, I. & Takeuchi, H. (1995). *The Knowledge-Creating Company: How Japanese Companies Create the Dynamics of Innovation*. Oxford: Oxford University Press.

Nonaka, I. & Toyama, R. (2003). The knowledge creating theory revisited: Knowledge creation as a synthesizing process, *Knowledge Management Research & Practice*, 1(1), 2–10.

Nonaka, I. & von Krogh, G. (2007). Tacit knowledge, knowledge conversations, and leadership: From critique to advancement of organizational knowledge theory. Working paper, ETH Zurich, Switzerland.

Nonaka, I., von Krogh, G. & Voepel, S. (2006). Organizational knowledge creation theory: Evolutionary paths and future advances, *Organization Studies*, 27(8), 1179–1208.

Norris, G. (1996). Post-investment appraisal. In L. Willcocks (Ed.), *Investing in Information Systems*, London: Chapman & Hall, 193–223.

O'Donnell, S. W. (2000). Managing foreign subsidiaries: Agents of headquarters, or an interdependent network? *Strategic Management Journal*, 21(5), 525–548.

Oshri, I., van Fenema, P. & Kotlarsky, J. (2008). Knowledge transfer in globally distributed teams: The role of transactive memory, *Information Systems Journal*, 18(6), 567–590.

Penrose, E. T. (1959). *The Theory of the Growth of the Firm*. New York: Wiley.

Peppard, J. & Ward, J. (2004). Beyond strategic information systems: Towards an IS capability, *Journal of Strategic Information Systems*, 13(2), 167–194.

Porter, M. E. (2001). Strategy and the internet, *Harvard Business Review*, 79(3), 63–78.

Ridings, C., Gelen, D. & Arinze, B. (2002). Some antecedents and effects of trust in virtual communities, *Journal of Strategic Information Systems*, 11, 271–295.

Rivard, S., Raymond, L. & Verreault, D. (2006). Resource-based view and competitive strategy: An integrated model of the contribution of information technology to firm performance, *Journal of Strategic Information Systems*, 15(1), 29–50.

Robey, D. & Boudreau, M. C. (1999). Accounting for the contradictory organizational consequences of information technology: Theoretical directions and methodological implications, *Information Systems Research*, 10(2), 167–185.

Sabherwal, R., Hirschheim, R. & Goles, T. (2001). The dynamics of alignment: Insights from a punctuated equilibrium model, *Organization Science*, 12(2), 179–197.

Salas, E., Burke, C. S. & Cannon-Bowers, J. A. (2000). Teamwork: Emerging principles, *International Journal of Management Review*, 2, 339–356.

Sambamurthy, V. & Jarvenpaa, S. (eds.) (2002). *Special Issue of Journal of Strategic Information Systems on Trust in the Digital Economy*, 11(3-4), December, 183–346.

Scarbrough, H., Bresnen, M., Edelman, L. F., Laurent, S., Newell, S. & Swan, J. (2004). The processes of project-based learning: An exploratory study, *Management Learning*, 35(4), 491–506.

Scarbrough, H. & Swan, J. (2001). Explaining the diffusion of knowledge management: The role of fashion, *British Journal of Management*, 12(1), 3–12.

Scheepers, R., Venkitachalam, K. & Gibbs, M. R. (2004). Knowledge strategy in organizations: Refining the model of Hansen, Nohria and Tierney, *Journal of Strategic Information Systems*, 13(3), 201–222.

Schein, E. (1997). *Organizational Culture and Leadership*. San Francisco, CA: JosseyBass.

Schindler, M. & Epplerm, M. (2003). Harvesting project knowledge: A review of project learning methods and success factors, *International Journal of Project Management*, 21, 219–229.

Seddon, P., Graeser, V. & Willcocks, L. (2002). Measuring organizational effectiveness: An overview and update of senior management perspectives, *Data Base for Advances in Information Systems*, 33, 11–27.

Segars, A. H. & Grover, V. (1998). Strategic information planning success: An investigation of the construct and its measurements, *MIS Quarterly*, 22(2), 139 163.

Segars, A. H. & Grover, V. (1999). Profiles of strategic information planning, *Information Systems Research*, 10(1), 87–97.

Sheth, J. N. & Sisodia, R. S. (2007). The regional face of globalization. In S. Dayal & M. Murphy (Eds.), *Global Babel. Questions of Discourse and Communication in a Time of Globalization*, Newcastle: Cambridge Scholars Publishing, 144–160.

Spender, J. C. (1996). Making knowledge the basis of a dynamic theory of the firm, *Strategic Management Journal*, 17, 45–62.

Star, S. L. & Ruhleder, K. (1996). Steps towards an ecology of infrastructure: Design and access to large information spaces, *Information Systems Research*, 7(1), 111–134.

Szulanski, G. (1996). Exploring internal stickiness: Impediments to the transfer of best practice within the firm, *Strategic Management Journal*, 17(1), 27–43.

Szulanski, G. & Jensen, (2004).

Teece, D. J., Pisano, G. & Shuen, A. (1997). Dynamic capabilities and strategic management, *Strategic Management Journal*, 18(7), 509–533.

Tushman, M. L. & Nadler, D. A. (1978). Information processing as an integrating concept in organizational design, *Academy of Management Review*, 3(3), 613–624.

Tushman, M. L. & O'Reilly, C. (1996). Ambidextrous organizations: Managing evolutionary and revolutionary change, *California Management Review*, 38(1), 8–30.

Tushman, M. L. & Scanlan, T. (1981). Boundary spanning individuals: Their role in information transfer and their Antecedents, *Academy of Management Journal*, 24(2), 289–305.

Van der Gerben, P., van Beers, C. & Kleinknecht, A. (2002). Success and failure of innovation: A literature review, *International Journal of Innovation Management*, 7, 309338.

Venkatraman, N. & Ramanujam, V. (1987). Planning system success: A conceptualization and operational model, *Management Science*, 33(6), 687–705.

Vera, D. & Crossan, M. (2005). Improvisation and innovative performance in teams, *Organization Science*, 16(3), 203–224.

von Hippel, E. (1994). Sticky information and the locus of problem solving, *Implications for Innovation Science*, 40, 429–439.

von Krogh, G., Ichijo, K. & Nonaka, I. (2000). *Enabling Knowledge Creation: How to Unlock the Mystery of Tacit Knowledge and Release the Power of Innovation*. New York: Oxford University Press.

Wagner, E. & Newell, S. (2007). Exploring the importance of participation in the postimplementation period of an enterprise system project: A neglected area, *Journal of the Association of Information Systems*, 8(10), 508–524.

Walsham, G. (1997). *Interpreting Information Systems in Organizations*. Chichester: Wiley.

Walsham, G. (2001). *Making a World of Difference. IT in a Global Context*. Chichester: Wiley.

Ward, J. & Griffiths, P. (1996). *Strategic Planning for Information systems, 2nd Edition*. Chichester: Wiley.

Ward, J. & Peppard, J. (2002). *Strategic Planning for Information systems, 3rd Edition*. Chichester: Wiley.

Webster, J. (1995). Networks of collaboration or conflict? Electronic data interchange and power in the supply chain, *Journal of Strategic Information Systems*, 4(1), 31–42.

Weick, K. E. (1995). *Sensemaking in Organizations*. Thousand Oaks, CA: Sage.

Weill, P. & Ross, J. (2004). *IT Governance. How Top Performers Manage IT Decision Rights for Superior Results*. Boston, MA: Harvard Business School Press.

Wenger, E. (1998). *Communities of Practice: Learning, meaning, and Identity*. Cambridge: Cambridge University Press.

Wijnhoven, T., Spil, T., Stegwee, R. & Fa, R. T. A. (2006). Post-merger IT integration strategies: An IT alignment perspective, *Journal of Strategic Information Systems*, 15(1), 5–28.

Willcocks, L. (2009). Evaluating the outcomes of information systems plans. Managing information technology evaluation: Techniques and processes. In R. D. Galliers & D. E. Leidner (Eds.), *Strategic Information Management: Challenges and Strategies in Managing Information systems, 4th ed.*, New York: Routledge, 209–226.

Willmott, H. (1993). Strength is ignorance; slavery is freedom: Managing culture in modern organizations, *Journal of Management Studies*, 30, 515–562.

Wilson, F. (1997). The truth is out there: The search for emancipator principles in information systems design, *Information Technology & People*, 10, 187–204.

Winter, S. (2003). Understanding dynamic capabilities, *Strategic Management Journal*, 24, 991–995.

Zarraga, C. & Bonache, J. (2005). The impact of team atmosphere on knowledge outcomes in self-managed teams, *Organization Studies*, 26(5), 661–681.

Zollo, M. & Winter, S. (2002). Deliberate learning and the evolution of dynamic capabilities, *Organization Science*, 13, 339–351.

Questions for Discussion

1   Compare and contrast IS strategizing with IS strategy. What is the distinction? Do you think that the distinction is important? Why? Why not?
2   Does IT matter strategically? Consider Carr's *Harvard Business Review* and *MIT Sloan Management Review* articles (Carr, 2003, 2005) and discuss the arguments pro and con.
3   In Chapter 3, you were asked to consider the concept of ambidexterity in the context of an organization with which you are familiar. Given the additional ideas raised in Chapter 4, go back to your answer and reflect further on the concept. Chapter 4 suggests the ways in which the IS strategizing framework may be applied. What else is uncovered when applying the framework in these ways?
4   Consider the strategizing environment notion. How might you combine analytical approaches and exploitation with learning and exploration? You may wish to use the example of the same organization as in the above when answering this question.
5   Strategies need to be feasible as well as desirable. When considering the change management and implementation aspects of the framework, how might you decide what is feasible?

Further Reading

The "Digital business strategy" special issue of *MIS Quarterly*: Bharadwaj, A., El Sawy, O.A., Venkatraman, N. (eds.), Volume 37, Issue 2, June 2013, pp. 471–633.

Chapter 5

Anna Karpovsky and Robert D. Galliers

ALIGNING IN PRACTICE: FROM CURRENT CASES TO A NEW AGENDA

I T/IS–BUSINESS ALIGNMENT[1] has been a topic of considerable attention in the academic and practitioner literature for over three decades (e.g., McLean and Soden, 1977; Henderson and Venkatraman, 1992; Chan and Reich, 2007). This is unsurprising given that alignment has been consistently rated as a top 10 IT management concern throughout this time (e.g., Brancheau and Wetherbe, 1987; Luftman et al., 2013). Conceptually, alignment has been defined variously as the degree of fit and integration between an organization's business strategy; IS strategy (ISS), business structure (and/or business processes) and IT infrastructure (Henderson and Venkatraman, 1993; Galliers, 2006a; Chan and Reich, 2007). A common theme has been the argument that alignment leads to a more focused and strategic use of IT (Chan et al., 2006) and that those organizations that are able to successfully align their business and IS/IT strategies tend to perform better than their counterparts (e.g., Chan et al., 1997; Kearns and Lederer, 2003).

More nuanced accounts of alignment have appeared in addition to the prominent literature on the topic. It has been argued that alignment is infeasible if the business strategy is unclear, and the difficulty of matching a relatively fixed set of IT assets to constantly changing business imperatives has also been noted (Galliers, 2004), with calls for increased agility arising (Galliers, 2006b; Tallon and Pinsonneault, 2011). Others argue that IT should challenge and transform the business, not simply align with it (e.g., Chan and Reich, 2007). The alignment literature is also criticized for being too conceptual and not reflecting actual practice (Ciborra, 1997). The more critical literature points to models that are infeasible to apply, that are developed conceptually and that do not derive from real world experience. Normative approaches are argued to not account for organizations as organic, dynamic and ambiguous aggregates, with relationships that are parallel and simultaneous (e.g., Tsoukas, 1994), requiring a refocusing on the practices and activities of *aligning* as opposed to alignment *per se* (Wilson et al., 2013). Further, empirical results are argued to be lacking in precision, with the resultant models being prone to subjectivity (Avison et al., 2004).

Given the claimed significance (for both research and practice) of alignment to organizational performance, we embarked on a detailed study of the extant literature. We aimed to determine what we currently know about aligning practice with a view to developing a framework that goes some way to describe the universe of actions that constitute aligning with a future research agenda emerging from this foundation. Thus, and in line with calls for research into the actual practices of strategizing (e.g., Jarzabkowski, 2005; Whittington, 2006), and especially with IS strategizing in mind (Peppard et al., 2014; Whittington, 2014), we argue that alignment research requires greater focus on organizational actors' day-to-day aligning activities. To provide a foundation for further empirical research on alignment practices, we focused on published empirical cases with the aim to identify and classify aligning activities. A contribution of this paper is thus a delineation of a set of aligning activities that could serve as a base for future research, for researchers and practitioners, about the mechanisms organizational actors use to align IS with ongoing processes and strategic imperatives.

The paper is structured to provide context for our study before discussing the research method adopted and our findings. In the next section, we present a brief review of the extant literature that views alignment as a dynamic process of aligning. In the subsequent section, we provide a discussion of the method we employed in our analysis of those cases that report on the actual activities associated with alignment. We go on to report on our findings and conclude with a discussion of next steps, including a future research agenda.

An Overview of the Literature on Alignment as a Dynamic Process

In line with some earlier studies,[2] we conceptualize alignment not as a static end-state but as a continuous, ongoing process of *aligning* involving a series of activities resulting in adjustments in various dimensions and across various organizational levels. Some of this prior research suggests that the alignment process represents a continuous synchronization (Smaczny, 2001) or integration by the organization of various technological, organizational and relational dimensions (Fuchs et al., 2000). Rondinelli et al. (2001). suggest that organizations should continuously readjust and realign four sets of strategic components: business strategy, market penetration decisions, management processes and structures. For others (e.g., Sabherwal et al., 2001), although the alignment process retains its dynamic nature, it is effectuated on an *ad hoc* or punctuated rather than continuous basis, depending upon the evolutionary phases experienced by the organization concerned as well as the evolution of its business environment: organizations may experience relatively long periods of minor, evolutionary strategic change and relatively short periods of sweeping, revolutionary strategic change.

A number of process models of alignment have arisen from this line of research. For example, the 'Strategic Alignment Maturity Model' (SAMM) (Luftman, 2000) posits that, as organizations pursue the goal of strategic alignment, alignment moves through the following process stages: (1) initial, *ad hoc;* (2) committed; (3) established, focused; (4) improved, managed; and finally, (5) optimized. Luftman argues that the greatest benefit to an organization is found when strategic alignment is an optimized process. Thus, the SAMM explores the 'maturity' of strategic alignment and focuses not on the *goal of* alignment, but on developing processes that will enable *ongoing* alignment.[3] Peppard and Breu (2003) propose a coevolutionary model to describe how IS strategies 'co-adapt' with business strategies, where each is considered distinct yet mutually influencing. In addition, Hirschheim and Sabherwal (2001) suggest that organizations seek alignment through incrementalism – changing one or more components of alignment, then changing some other, and occasionally reversing earlier changes. They identify three trajectories that can occur as a result: paradoxical decisions (i.e., change of some components in one direction while changing other components in the opposite direction), excessive transformations (i.e., going too far in changing one or more components) and uncertain turnarounds (i.e., reversing a change to go back to the original configuration).

Several specific steps and sub-processes have been suggested to foster movement toward alignment. These include evaluating the performance of senior executives, in part by noting their innovative use of IT; allowing IT to provide innovative ideas that will shape the business; embedding IT in multiple departments and business processes; using IT to provide strategic flexibility to the business; giving the CIO visibility among the senior executives; and encouraging IT executives to collaborate with business unit and regional managers to develop new capabilities (Agarwal and Sambamurthy, 2002). In addition, Kearns and Lederer (2003) propose two specific processes associated with key actors that contribute to strategic alignment: the CEO participating in IS/IT planning and the CIO participating in business planning. Although the identification of these processes provides insight into means of achieving alignment, it appears that while these processes are a necessary condition they may not be sufficient. A comprehensive, multifaceted conceptualization of strategic alignment appears still to be missing.

From Macro Processes to Micro Practices

While we, thus, have a better understanding of alignment processes as a result of this line of research, we nonetheless know little about what managers and other organizational actors actually *do* in their day-to-day activities to achieve alignment (Campbell, 2005). In order to fill this gap, we extend the conceptualization of alignment from not only something that an organization *attains* to something that an organization *does:* as 'a pattern in a stream of goal-oriented activity over time' (Jarzabkowski, 2005: 40). From this perspective, we differentiate ourselves from the (macro) process perspective on alignment by focusing on micro processes and practices (cf. Peppard et al., 2014; Whittington, 2014).[4]

While the process stream of research considers alignment at various levels of an organization, it tends to focus primarily on the organizational level, with the associated unit of analysis being the sequence of 'high level' organizational events that take place within a period of adjustment. In contrast, we take an activity-based view of aligning practice where activity is the unit of analysis and is associated with the actions of organizational actors. Our use of the term 'practice' refers most closely to its meaning as action or execution, as opposed to theory (Orlikowski, 2010). We make no assumptions concerning how common or established aligning practice is, nor the extent to which it is habitually performed. That is, we are not referring exclusively to praxis.[5] Our definition of alignment further suggests that we should not make theoretically informed *a priori* exclusions of certain classes of activities (Law, 1994). Consequently, we view aligning practice broadly as *all* activities that may contribute to tightening links between IT and business across an organization.

The perspective we adopt addresses 'the detailed processes and practices which constitute the day-to-day activities of organizational life' (Johnson et al., 2003: 3). A broad definition of these activities is, 'the day to day stuff of management. It is what managers do and what they manage. It is also what organizational actors engage in more widely' (ibid.: 15). From an epistemological standpoint, our approach sees practice as providing greater realism than formal theories populated by multivariate analyses of firm or industry-level factors (Whittington, 1999). This perspective emphasizes the study of 'alignment-in-the-making,' rather than alignment as 'readymade.' For example, the implementation of any IT initiative is dependent on making alliances with a range of actors and the cultivation of the social capital needed for action (e.g., Waema and Walsham, 1990), not solely or so much on intended plans or prescribed actions. We argue that, as a consequence, the consideration of aligning practice allows for the identification of previously obscured enablers and inhibitors of alignment. Taking this extended conceptualization of aligning practice, we reviewed the alignment literature to derive a set of activities based on published cases. Before presenting our findings, we discuss the research method employed.

Research Method

Alignment is a key consideration within the broader area of ISS.[6] ISS is, in turn, a mature research topic within the wider IS domain that focuses on strategic issues and methods concerned with IT infrastructure, IT organization and personnel (Merali et al., 2012; Karpovsky et al., 2014). An extensive body of research has contributed to the development of our thinking and practice in this topic area. To capture all the alignment articles that might not explicitly state alignment as a focus of the study but, nonetheless, do consider aligning activities, we embarked on reviewing the ISS literature in its entirety. Searching solely on the basis of such keywords as 'IT/business alignment' would potentially lead us to miss relevant articles since other terminology might be used. In addition, searching using the keyword 'alignment' is problematic as other fields use the term to refer to issues and topics that would be irrelevant for the purposes of our review.

Using a structured methodology (Webster and Watson, 2002), we reviewed over 9000 articles from the IS, strategic management and management literatures concerned with ISS and related topics (Karpovsky et al., 2014). We targeted articles that had been published in peer-reviewed, English language journals. The journals initially selected were those that make up the AIS senior scholar's 'basket' of eight journals (http://ais.site-ym. com/?SeniorScholarBasket) and those used in three recent related literature reviews: Chan and Reich (2007) on IT alignment; Lacity et al. (2009) on IT outsourcing; and Chen et al. (2010) on ISS. In addition, *Information & Organization* and *Long Range Planning* were included following informal evaluation of other possible source journals. Naturally, there were also articles relevant to our search published elsewhere. In order to identify these, a forward and backward search was conducted (cf. Webster and Watson, 2002). While acknowledging the importance of books and conference proceedings (cf. Galliers and Whitley, 2007), our sources were limited to scientific journals, together with major practitioner journals, such as *Harvard Business Review, MIT Sloan Management Review* and *Communications of the ACM*. The resulting set of selected journals is presented in Appendix A.

Screening Articles

To narrow our search, we conducted screening of articles in three rounds. First, the article titles (and the abstract if the title was not sufficiently descriptive) were read and a decision was made whether or not the article in question appeared to bear some relation to ISS. In unclear cases, the article was retained for the next round. This screening reduced the number of articles by about 70%, leaving us with 2690 articles in the data set and was conducted by one or other of the first two authors of Karpovsky et al. (2014), with advice being provided by the third when in any doubt. In Round 2, the article title, abstract, and keywords were read, and a decision was made as to whether the article was out of scope or relevant on a scale from 1 to 3 (where 1 was considered out of scope and 3 denoted articles clearly addressing ISS). This eliminated another 60% of the articles, with approximately 1000 articles that we believed to have at least some relevance remaining (see Appendix B). This round and subsequent rounds were conducted by each of the researchers individually, followed by group discussion to gain consensus.

In Round 3, each of the remaining articles was read and their relevance was further assessed on a scale of 1 to 5 (where 1 was considered out of scope and 5 denoted the most cited core ISS articles). The most cited articles were screened by all three researchers, first individually and then as a group, to ensure that the categories and parameters against which these articles were being evaluated were similarly understood by all. After this 'synchronization of thoughts,' and apart from the 200 most cited articles (which were screened together), Round 3 was again conducted by each researcher alone. We used the following criteria to code the alignment articles: (1) the word 'alignment' appears in the title or keywords, or (2) the body of the article discusses or mentions alignment related themes (e.g., alignment level and types; alignment models and approaches; expressions such as link, fit, synchronization, congruence between business and IT; such business considerations as roles, organization structure and culture, and alignment maturity).

Having identified those ISS-related articles concerned with alignment, we then had the task of identifying those that provided some account of the aligning activities involved. Our selection process followed the inclusion and exclusion criteria recommendations of Yin and Heald (1975) to ensure the academic quality of the material selected and to allow for in-depth analysis of each case. The inclusion criteria were that: (1) the case reported an instance of alignment; (2) it reported organizational actions and organizational actors' activities; and (3) the narrative provided a rich description of the events. A case was excluded even when an alignment methodology was discussed but the activities involved in implementing that methodology were omitted. In addition, while our initial literature of ISS included articles from 1962 to 2010 (Karpovsky et al., 2014), for the purposes of this paper, we extended the review to include articles published subsequently. Two articles published in 2011 were added as a result of this extended search.

Findings

General Patterns of Alignment Case Research

In total, 142 articles on alignment were identified, with alignment being revealed as the dominant ISS-related theme, having been discussed in over 15% of all the ISS articles reviewed (see Appendix B). Of the 142 alignment articles, we identified 37 that discussed alignment activities in some detail. As an article might provide descriptions of multiple case studies and practices, in total these articles reported on 57 aligning episodes. Appendix C lists all the case sources. The reviewed articles were published between 1992 and 2011; the peak year was 2003, with five such publications. In fact, the period 2003–2007 accounted for approximately half these publications,[7] suggesting an increased interest in aligning practice, paralleling similar research interest around the same time in the organization studies and strategy fields more generally (e.g., Jarzabkowski, 2005; Whittington, 2006). The cases were widely distributed amongst a range of journals although *Journal of Information Systems Management, Journal of Information Technology* and *The Journal of Strategic Information Systems* published ten articles (27%) of the total (11%, 8% and 8%, respectively). Table 5.1 lists the number of articles appearing in each journal.

The cases show variation in terms of the sectors in which the organizations studied operate; however, the public sector (22%) and manufacturing (24%) were the most dominant (see Figure 5.1). In addition, six types of actor were identified: top management, middle management, IS management, politicians, consultants and the researchers themselves – the latter in cases adopting an action research approach (e.g., Salmela and Ruohonen, 1992).

Table 5.1 List of journals

Journal name	Number of articles
Journal of Information Systems Management	4
Journal of Information Technology	3
The Journal of Strategic Information Systems	3
Communications of the Association for Information Systems	2
European Journal of Information Systems	2
European Journal of Operational Research	2
European Management Journal	2
IBM Systems Journal	2
International Journal of Information Management	2
MIS Quarterly	2
California Management Review	1
Communications of the ACM	1
Engineering Management Journal	1
Information Systems Research	1
Information Technology & People	1
Journal of the Association for Information Systems	1
Journal of Cases of Information Technology	1
Journal of Information Technology and Application Research	1
MIS Quarterly Executive	1
Organization Science	1
Scandinavian Journal of Information Systems	1
Sloan Management Review	1
Journal of Computer Information Systems	1

Aligning Activities

An iterative analytical technique was used to develop the categorization of aligning activities. First, preliminary working themes were constructed through a process of abstracting and generalizing from the specific case by means of constant comparison, coding and memoing procedures (Strauss, 1987). Coding took the form of a thematic content analysis of the case materials (cf. Mostyn, 1985), which is a systematic and manual procedure carried out in three steps: (1) specifying the unit of analysis – typically ranging from a few words to an entire paragraph to which codes were attached; (2) attaching code – labeling 'chunks' of data, which represent the theme or primary message of the section of text; and (3) categorizing themes – grouping the individual themes to produce the broad categories to which these

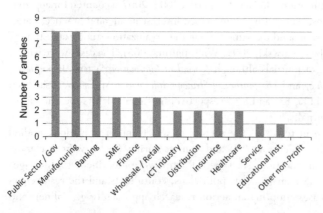

Figure 5.1 Sectors covered by research cases on aligning.

themes relate to and can be reported on collectively. These categories were then interpreted and reconstructed in light of existing alignment themes (e.g., De Haes and Van Grembergen, 2009; Valorinta, 2011). This coding methodology generally follows the logic of Burawoy's (1991) extended case method, in which a single, detailed case study is used to reconstruct and extend existing theory. To summarize, the methodological strategy used in the study aims at developing a descriptive framework of aligning that is useful in analyzing a broad range of alignment activities by reinterpreting existing cases in light of our extended conceptualization of aligning practice.

We consider aligning activity to be any action that any particular organizational actor takes in the process of finding and/or implementing IS that would potentially support business needs. The only differences among the cases studied were the depth of the description of a particular activity and the terms used to refer to these activities. For example, one case might talk about centralization and decentralization of the IT function, while another might describe a decrease in the number of IT employees, and changes in the reporting structure within the IT organization. In either case, we coded these activities as 'restructuring IT organization' as both examples refer to changes in the way IT function is organized.

As noted above, the coding process was iterative, using both the initial coding scheme and open codes. We remained open to new codes and categories where appropriate, as recommended by Miles and Huberman (1994). The final coding reports were recorded in a repository database that was used in the data analysis. The final list of 32 coded aligning activities and the eight categories are presented in Table 5.2. Illustrative quotes from the analyzed cases are provided, as are metaphors, which result from our attempt to merge these activities into a meaningful and parsimonious classification.

We found that two basic conceptual distinctions helped us to organize how the different aspects of aligning have been considered in previous research – the *focus* and the *purpose* of the aligning activity. In terms of *focus,* the alignment literature has widely acknowledged a distinction between two dimensions of alignment: social and intellectual (Chan and Reich, 2007). The social dimension of alignment has been defined as 'the state in which business and IT executives within an organizational unit understand and are committed to the business and IT mission, objectives, and plans' (Reich and Benbasat, 2000: 82). The social dimension refers to factors such as the choice of actors, their degree of involvement and the methods and modes of communication and decision-making (ibid.). The focus is on the actors and their actions and cognitions. The term *actor* refers to organizational members as well as individuals outside the organization involved in the practices of aligning, such as: top/middle/IS management, politicians, consultants and researchers. Conversely, intellectual alignment refers to the degree to which the business strategy and plans, and the IS/IT strategy and plans, are congruent (Kearns and Lederer, 2000; Preston and Karahanna, 2009). Intellectual alignment suggests that activities are focused on methodologies, techniques, configurations, infrastructures, technology, strategies, plans, documents and data used in the form(ul)ation of alignment (Horovitz, 1984). The focus is mainly on these objects and the activity involves a set of tools. The term *tool,* as suggested in the discussion above, is a generic label for frameworks, concepts, models, technologies or methods (Jarzabkowski and Kaplan, 2014). To summarize, while the social dimension of alignment concentrates on the perceptions and actions of organizational *actors involved in* alignment, the intellectual dimension emphasizes the content of plans and planning methodologies, thus focusing on the *tools of* alignment.

In terms of *purpose,* aligning actions can be both ends in themselves *(emerged* actions) and means to some further ends *(intended* actions). Combining these two dimensions yields a 2x2 matrix that locates the four metaphors that can be used to describe aligning as: *experience,*

Table 5.2 Aligning activities: coding and categorization

Aligning activity code	Aligning activity category	Illustration	Metaphor
New governance structure Transformation Turnaround Restructuring IT organization Outsourcing Reward system Integration	RECONFIGURING	The Board interpreted events as raising a new contingency, requiring a structure that would enable Aligning as managers to use the information the system now provided, and so in 1992 they gave those managing the translation five geographical division greater autonomy (Boddy and Paton, 2005: 147).	Aligning as translation
		To support the new direction for Information Systems, Johnson created three new organizational structures. First, a group of senior executives and two independent external consultants met bimonthly as the Information Services Executive Committee. Although the CEO sponsored this meeting, McKean chaired it. The Information Services Executive Committee's purpose was to focus on business issues and ensure that the top team was committed to and satisfied with the projects delivered on their behalf (Thorogood et al., 2004: 131). SDMC applied IT applications to production scheduling and mold designing, intending to reduce operational costs and improve new product development capabilities (Wang et al., 2011: 424).	
New system development Business-focused IT	DEVELOPING	An analysis of RED transactions of a department yielded missing applications and application features … The BIOS committee, made up of the departmental directors and account managers, now had objective information with which to prioritize the portfolio (Ramnath and Landsbergen, 2005: 62).	
User/IT relationship IT-business communication Top management involvement CIO/ CEO relationship IS/business partnership Culture change IT training Human resource management/training Strengthening New position New appointment IT location	STRENGTHENING	Management interpreted key contingencies in the context as requiring them to plan and implement a Aligning as system which would implement the founder's strategic vision for an EPOS system. This closely matched Integration the manual procedures, and staff interpreted the change as reinforcing the existing (effective) alignment between them and their work. It enabled centralization and allowed depot managers to concentrate on customers (Boddy and Paton, 2005: 146). Johnston brought in Chris James to develop relationships with strategic business partners and to act as the account manager, representing IS to the business. James was responsible for managing relationships with strategic partners, primarily Aspect Computing, and for managing relationships with other business units such as the laboratory and Water Services (Thorogood et al., 2004: 131). Key personnel were sent to training seminars to learn and master the essence of the balanced scorecard theory and techniques (Huang and Hu, 2007: 176).	Aligning as Integration

Process	Keywords	Quote	Alignment
SIGNALING		*A few years before the project, the former president had retired, and a new one was employed with the task of organizational and managerial restructuring and modernization of the entire organization (Simonsen, 1999: 10).* *The physical location of the IT division in isolation from the Retail division was symbolic of the general estrangement in working relationships. The image that the business had of IT was that 'IT people don't move around, they just sit in X' (Managing Director, Retail Finance) and they have different agendas and 'just want to be told what needs to be done' (Manager, Group Development) (Coughlan et al., 2005: 311).*	**Aligning as Adaptation**
EVALUATING	*Success measures Reactive response Separation of information/technology management Clarifying objectives Scanning emerging technologies External factors*	*... many private firms and large international logistics firms entered the business area where AMY operated after China's accession into the WTO, which led to a more competitive environment. The oversupply of mechanical and electrical products strengthened the bargaining power of customers and altered the industrial structure. In this environment, AMY's inefficient traditional sales management led to excessive overstock. In 1999, AMY lost over 40 million RMB because of overstock (Wang et al., 2011: 423).* *Following a consulting firm's report in 1993, the CEO and the other senior managers began recognizing the need for major changes to respond to several international companies' entry into Australia (Hirschheim and Sabherwal, 2001: 95).*	
NEGOTIATING	*Review Prioritization Resistance to change Meetings*	*Many customers placed orders without fulfilling their promise to make the payment, creating lots of unpaid accounts receivable (Wang et al., 2011: 426).* *One library visited was one of their largest single customers. They had only one or two booking requests per day. In this situation, they viewed the telephone as the relevant technology for ordering films and videos.* *They would resist paying for equipment for an online connection and for the training of their staff to use the booking system that the Film Board had in mind (Simonsen, 1999: 13).*	**Aligning as Experience**
LEARNING	*Politics Learning the business*	*In the past few years, our sales income and profit went down sharply. We should find some ways to stop this. We realized that we need good integrated computer systems, and we couldn't follow the way we walked along before (Wang et al., 2011: 424).*	
DECISION-MAKING	*Organizational learning Decision-making*	*... the value of IT was questioned by many academics and executives at that time. Some consultants and IT professionals suggested this B2B project be delayed because they thought the investment was too high, while the chance of success was rather slim (Wang et al., 2011: 426).*	

	Focus	
	Tools	Actors
Intended	**ALIGNING AS TRANSLATION** (developing; reconfiguring)	**ALIGNING AS INTEGRATION** (strengthening; signaling)
Emergent	**ALIGNING AS ADAPTATION** (evaluating)	**ALIGNING AS EXPERIENCE** (negotiating; decision-making; learning)

Figure 5.2 Aligning: an analytical framework.

integration, translation and *adaptation* (see Figure 5.2). Aligning as experience and aligning as integration represent a set of activities primarily involving human dynamics: actions, interactions and cognitions. However, while integration activities are characterized as deliberate and instrumental in nature, aligning as experience suggests a set of evolving activities that emerge from unplanned or unintended situations. Similarly, both aligning as translation and aligning as adaptation suggest activities that involve generation and execution of plans, goals, and other intellectual imperatives, but the purpose of these activities differs. While translation is anticipated action, adaptation is more unpredicted and evolving. The sections that follow further expand on each of these types of activity and provide illustrative examples from the analyzed case studies.

Aligning as Adaptation

We identified a number of activities as aspects of adaptation – of adjusting and attempting to fit into a given (sometimes changed) environment. The process is *emergent* and evolves over time – sometimes gradually, sometimes discontinuously – in response to interruptions (Tyre and Orlikowski, 1994). Aligning becomes a practice where the role of organizational actors is to monitor the changes in the organizational environment and to evaluate the conditions as being favorable or threatening, assessing whether any changes need to be made due to the new circumstances. These activities are mainly focused on *tools* as it necessary to determine whether a new system needs to be implemented, or enhanced. Consequently, these actions emerge as a result of the advent of new conditions that are not necessarily foreseeable or can be easily planned for. Some form of improvisation might be evident here. The nature of these activities is, therefore, *emergent* with a main focus on *tools*.

Given the need to be aware of the new conditions, such tools are applied in continuously EVALUATING the environment and ascertaining how technology can support or enable future operations. About half of the 37 articles in our final set report on some form of evaluation of the internal and/or external environment. Evaluating practices are usually reported as something that happens before aligning processes are themselves enacted. Examples include when an organization evaluates its context or seeks to clarify its objectives or business focus (e.g., Sillince and Frost, 1995; Simonsen, 1999), scans emerging technologies (e.g., Tarafdar and Qrunfleh, 2009) or prioritizes applications and application features (e.g., Dutta, 1996; Ramnath and Landsbergen, 2005) before any change process taking place. Further, evaluation of the strategic focus might reveal contradictions in the overall organizational strategy and might indicate new system needs (Simonsen, 1999).

Aligning as Translation

Achieving alignment has traditionally been seen as a part of a CIO's duties, typically involving communication and strategy translation at executive levels (Sabherwal et al., 2001). A number of studies suggest that business and IT 'speak' a different language (e.g., Bassellier and Benbasat, 2004; Rosenkranz et al., 2013) and aligning would thus need to involve IT personnel understanding business needs and rendering these into an IT solutions. These translations involve *intentionality*: clarifying existing strategies; prioritizing projects; formulating and implement plans; applying a set of planning methodologies; and consequently, capturing, though the use of *tools*, the intellectual dimension of alignment.

DEVELOPING a new system or an entirely new IT infrastructure is a common organizational activity that aims to find new IS solutions to align with what may often be a new strategic imperative. Developing is classified as a translating activity because it is tools-focused and is based on *intended* approaches to system implementation. In certain cases, developing entails the consolidation or rebuilding of systems or services rather than implementing a completely new technology (e.g., Sauer and Willcocks, 2003). More than half of the final articles describe the development of a new system. For example, Vayghan et al. (2007) report that IBM developed and deployed data solutions for its customers as well within IBM itself as part of their transformation. The case provides a thorough description of the technical architecture for the IBM internal enterprise data architecture program designed to bring service-oriented, information and event-driven architecture principles together to provide information on demand. Further examples include Dutta (1996) and Ives et al. (1993). Dutta reports on the creation of NovaRede – a new distribution network, with small branches enabled by new IT infrastructure in a Portuguese bank, while Ives et al. describe challenges of development of a worldwide financial reporting system, an inventory management system and a new customer profitability analysis system in a multinational company.

While these studies point to the development of new systems, the activities involved in actually translating the business plans, objectives and ideas into IS developments are not well described. Precisely how such developments arose – or were translated – from business strategy to IS often remains unclear; they are presumed. For example, Wang et al. (2011) indicate that the company received 'financial support ... from the local government and a CIO was hired to oversee the system implementation' (426). However, it is not clear what role the newly hired CIO played in making sure the system aligned with the business's new strategy of low cost and growth. Neither is it clear what the level of involvement of the local government was and what and how these actors contributed to the process. Similarly, Weiss and Thorogood (2011) report on the use of business liaison personnel in IS development, but the level of their involvement and their associated actions are not reported.

RECONFIGURING activities also classify as translation-related actions as they also focus on *intellectual* aspects of aligning such as structures and arrangements and support the changes needed to link business and IS strategies. Reconfiguring refers to activities related to such organizational restructuring actions as a change in the governance and management of IT including outsourcing. Such activities as these accounted for 27% of all the aligning activities referred to in our literature set, and 70% of the articles mention at least one of the reconfiguring activities identified (see Table D1 in Appendix D). Restructuring governance and the IT function is the most commonly observed organizational action as pertaining to aligning activities. For example, Sauer and Willcocks (2003) report on Oracle changing country managing directors' performance measures so that they would be more cost conscious, with the IT function becoming centralized – as a corporate entity – rather than being country-based as was the case previously. Similarly, Boddy and Paton (2005) describe the introduction of divisions with profit responsibilities in a chain of roadside vehicle repair depots. This restructuring resulted in managers' gaining a new appreciation of their organization's IS capabilities. Outsourcing is also a major organizational action when it comes to aligning.[8] Dutta (1996) describes approaches adopted by two banks in their attempts to align IT with the business. Outsourcing results in new management structures internally. The organization that had outsourced its IT had to create a technical oversight group and a 20-person team to coordinate with the vendors. Such reconfiguring activities as these are dynamic, and an organization might go through a number of iterations of reconfiguring. Hirschheim and Sabherwal (2001) describe a number of 'trajectories' of strategic alignment, one being a reversal of structural changes and a move back toward the original structural position.

Aligning as Integration

The alignment literature recognizes that open and effective exchanges and interactions help IT and business work well together (Brown and Ross, 1996). We found a number of planned and *intended* activities that focused on integrating IT/business planning by bringing IT and business functions or tasks closer together to strengthen the communication, understanding and perspectives between them. These activities revolve around *actors* and the necessary steps needed to develop a unified entity in an effort to enable alignment to take place.

We classified STRENGTHENING activities in terms of aligning as integration because, similar to aligning as translation, these are actions stimulated by *deliberate* procedures. Unlike aligning as translation, these activities are focused on bringing IT and business *people* together and enabling a smoother process of mutual understanding and appreciation, invoking the social dimension of alignment discussed earlier. Activities associated with strengthening aligning form another common practice with around 60% of the reviewed articles describing such activities. Primarily, these involve the strengthening of relationships between various organizational groups. To illustrate, some studies consider 'joint' language – to improve the quality of communication between business and IS (e.g., Powell and Powell, 2004). Sauer and Willcocks (2003) suggest advocacy on the part of CIOs in helping their senior business management colleagues to become more sensitive to the challenges associated with designing and managing technology platforms that are scalable; responsive to business change, flexible of cost structure and fast to deploy. User participation has also been reported as a means of strengthening aligning processes. Dutta (1996) describes how users submitted new software development proposals to business groups who then channeled these proposals to user committees. In general terms, Dutta concludes that a high level of participation and involvement on the part of the business operatives and their management, from the board down to front-line staff, contributed to improve alignment. Training, with respect to both IT for non-IT personnel, and with respect to business issues for IT personnel, has also been reported as a practice that might strengthen alignment – both in terms of the process and the outcome. For example, Chan (2002) reports on information sessions and technology demonstrations. Coughlan et al. (2005) consider the acquisition of 'hybrid skills' (cf. Earl and Skyrme, 1992) and Martinez (1995) highlights the skills necessary for large project management.

Another set of activities classified as integration is SIGNALING. Signaling changes in the role of IS in an organization through various organizational practices has been noted. These activities are *people-focused* since they might affect and reshape organizational actors' views or attitudes and might involve changes in roles. For example, a number of cases highlight the establishment of a new position (e.g., Grant, 2003; Thorogood et al., 2004; Chen et al., 2008) or, more commonly (refer to Appendix D), a new appointment to an existing position (e.g., Johnston and Yetton, 1996; Thorogood et al., 2004). To illustrate, Sabherwal et al. (2001) report on the establishment of a new IS director position at an equipment sales company. The position was created to signal the strategic role of IS, however, was discontinued later as the perceived importance of IS diminished a – further signal. The location of the IT division has also been found to be symbolic of working relationships and, ultimately, (mis) alignment between IT and organizational priorities. Coughlan et al. (2005) report on the physical isolation of an IT division, which impacted the image that the business had of IT, and that had an impact on the IT division's (un)willingness to align IT functions with the rest of the business.

Aligning as Experience

A number of reported activities focused specifically on *individuals* and their actions. These actions are indicative of the *emergent* nature of organizing practice. NEGOTIATING – political activities in general – are commonplace in organizational life, and aligning is no different in this regard. A number of studies touch on the issue of organizational politics and external political pressures. For example, Sillince and Frost (1995) describe the evolution of business strategies and IS strategies in the UK public services sector. IS-related reforms in primary care were pushed through to head off political opposition by the medical profession, and to show that something could be done within a short timeframe. However, the IS element was poorly developed and poorly supported – leading to poor alignment. This case was contrasted with another concerned with the work of the national police force. Here, Sillince and Frost note that politicians did not want to be 'saddled' with a reputation for having shaped the police force – not wanting 'to be remembered as having reinforced European federalism' (ibid.: 113). They make the point that, in a different political situation, different organizational practices would likely be apparent. The reduced – or absent – pressure impacted aligning practice as the police force was able to be more flexible in making IS-related decisions and thus – potentially at least – to be in a better position to align its practices.

Illustrations of negotiating can also be found in the private sector. For example, Dutta (1996) reports on an instance of negotiating when a list of proposed IS projects for the year was assembled from a number of user groups. Conflicts arose as the IT users' committee had to determine relative priorities of, and whether any redundancies would arise from, the proposals. Interestingly, the case reports that these conflicts were resolved as a result of *informal* meetings held between members of the IT users' committee and concerned users.

Given the dynamic perspective we take, a process of LEARNING is inherent in aligning practices: by gaining understanding from past experiences and from the practices associated with familiarization with the current environment. We considered those learning activities that are organizational *actor-focused* and address the process of intuiting and interpreting. This process is *emergent* and distinctive from the strengthening activities associated with training, which are intended and instrumental in nature. Learning concerns, for example, the creation of novel insights; building actions based on experience, and developing business awareness (Bontis et al., 2002), which are evolving. Around 20% of the articles reviewed (Appendix D) refer to some form of ongoing learning practice. Salmela and Ruohonen (1992) present an action research study concerned with the alignment of decision support system (DSS) and ongoing business developments. They observed learning to be the single most important aspect of aligning, where organizational members continuously learn to focus on IS as an opportunity for organizational change. Conversely, it has been reported that IT personnel should learn more about the business *per se* to facilitate alignment. Chen et al. (2008) provide the example of IT staff expending considerable effort to understand the manufacturing process of a semiconductor company. Ramnath and Landsbergen (2005), in their account of a city government's strategic planning process, suggest using a short and interleaved planning approach and delivery cycles in aligning, since immediate customer feedback might be used to identify new or additional requirements in readiness for the next planning next cycle.

Aligning will ultimately involve decisions that organizational *actors* must make concerning IS/IT and business functions. DECISION-MAKING is a social activity undertaken by individuals within organizations. Such activities are also *emergent* in nature and occur throughout aligning practice as decisions need to be made on issues such as resource allocation and commitments as and when they arise. Only about 10% of the articles in our final set consider decision-making, however (refer to Appendix D). Of the limited examples in the literature, one is provided by Hirschheim and Sabherwal (2001). They observed decisions being made in three different companies. In one, they describe how a new CEO makes a decision to shift centralized IS to a more distributed form in a company that changed its strategy to one focusing more on efficiency. This apparently paradoxical decision was highlighted since a decentralized structure might be thought more likely to improve IS service quality but not efficiency. Mehta and Hirschheim (2007) consider a merger and acquisition and report on the absence of the CIOs in pre-merger discussions. This decision-making dynamic resulted in the enforcement of the acquirer's systems on the acquired organization – something that was justified by considerations of alignment.

A number of studies report specifically on decisions made by the CEO, with or without discussion or agreement with those responsible for IT (e.g., Dutta, 1996; Sabherwal et al., 2001; Sauer and Willcocks, 2003). Wang et al. (2011) describe the decision-making related to investment in a new system, providing some understanding of the decision-making dynamic – the parties involved and the type of decisions made. The key role played by top management in deciding to pursue an IT project is highlighted given their belief in IT's potential and their innovative and risk tolerant disposition. Wang and colleagues show how conservatism and culture can have an impact on the decisions made. Similarly, Weiss and Thorogood (2011) point to the decision to spin off a company that solely focused on a new initiative as part of its aligning process in light of the existing organizational culture. Overall and as previously noted, we found few cases of decision-making practices.

In Summary

Our findings suggest that aligning happens in practice through a set of activities, which we have classified into 32 categories and four metaphors. There is a clear distinction in terms of how researchers have focused on aligning activities with these activities falling into two main categories: a consideration of tools (aligning as translation and adaptation) and actors (aligning as integration and experience).

A consideration of the *tools* of aligning has been the main focus of the research to date. One set of activities revolving around tools is concerned with *translating* business plans and strategies into IS/IT plans and strategies (and in rare cases, the other way around). Such translation involves some form of reconfiguring, with the emergence of new governance structures or processes, changes in reward systems or a formation of a new IT organization, occasionally resulting in outsourcing. Translation also happens in a form of a system development, where incorporating a new technology into existing operations has been the main aligning activity. The focus on tools is also apparent in activities that aim to evaluate the external and internal environment so as to anticipate and react to the changes. This *adaptation* happens through evaluating activities where emerging technologies might be continuously or occasionally scanned and reviewed; objectives clarified, prioritized or adjusted; and business performance measured.

In terms of *actors*, aligning can be seen as *integration* among units within an organization. Here, aligning involves activities concerned with the notion of strengthening ties among organizational actors through building relationships among users, top management, IT and business personnel, and often specifically, the CEO and the CIO. Building such relationships might be a product of top management involvement, improved communication, culture change or training. Managerial changes are also commonly reported, with new appointments or the creation of new positions (e.g., CIO), signaling an organization's commitment to change that embraces IT. Other cases focus on individual actors describing aligning as *experience*. Examples include negotiating between actors, learning that happens on a more individual cognitive level then actual training and decision-making processes where activities revolve around actual actors making decisions.

Limitations

The 32 aligning practices identified from our review, clustered under the four metaphors – aligning as: adaptation, translation, integration and experience – provide an anthology of how aligning happens in practice, at least in terms of the manner in which practice has been reported. We should note, however, that the activities associated with aligning as experience have received the least attention to date. We should also note that the categories of aligning practices arise from the authors' *interpretation* of the relevant case material and can by no means be seen as being exhaustive or fully representative of all possible practices. In addition, the 32 aligning practices identified arise from *our* analysis of the cases found in the review of the ISS literature; other relevant fields, such as project management (e.g., Jenkin and Chan, 2010), might well provide another relevant source. Further, our review considered peer-reviewed journals alone; however, dissertations and conference papers can also offer a wealth of cases (Galliers and Whitley, 2007). Notwithstanding, we believe that our categorization can be a useful aid to researchers and practitioners. Its purpose is to provide a foundation for further developing our understanding of aligning practices and, thus, provides a steppingstone for future work in this important research arena. We suggest that future research could usefully develop the current categorization further, thereby expanding our understanding of aligning practices – amending and adding to the categories as we learn more about what actually takes place in aligning practice. We consider this future agenda in greater detail in the following.

Discussion: A Research Agenda for Aligning in Practice

Our extension of prior conceptualizations of alignment as aligning practice, comprising aligning activities, allows for a more holistic treatment of alignment: at multiple organizational levels and across multiple dimensions, as called for by Chan and Reich (2007). Such a conceptualization allows alignment research to move away from studies that focus solely on the antecedents, enablers and inhibitors of alignment, to research that focuses on the activities of aligning where actors *do* 'aligning.' Our findings suggest that there is a set of common activities that form aligning practice. Such a refocusing facilitates the study of a broad set of organizational micro processes that go beyond operational-level processes (e.g., Tallon, 2007). It enables the consideration of organizational actors as they do 'aligning work' rather than focusing attention at the level of the organization and its state of alignment. When alignment is thought of primarily as an outcome or a macro-level process, consisting of phases and stages, knowledge of the rich and complex ways in which actors translate, adapt, integrate, experience and thus 'make' alignment happen, is limited.

A contribution of this paper has been the development of a framework (Figure 5.2), which shifts alignment discourse away from characterizations of alignment or misalignment toward an understanding of how organizational actors are engaged in the practice of aligning and what types of activities are involved in that practice. The categorization of activities that emerges is a resource to guide future empirical research. We do not claim that our list of aligning activities is exhaustive; rather, it represents an illustration of what is known or what can be inferred from current research. We anticipate that future research will reveal and explicate other relevant activities.

Suggestions for Future Research

As noted, alignment has been studied extensively over the years, and researchers have produced a significant body of literature on the topic. However, we conclude that the majority of the literature considers the alignment process as following prescribed methodologies, assuming rational decision-making and is often sequential in nature. A focus on activities suggests instead that organizational practice is more organic in nature, being subject to political and interpretive influences (Jarzabkowski, 2005). One implication of this view is that studying processes and actors independently may be less analytically useful than has been assumed. While aligning as adaptation and translation presumes intellectual-level activities materializing at the level of plans, strategies, goals and objectives, it is through the individual use and creation of these tools, and amidst individual actions of actors that aligning happens. Conversely, while aligning as integration and experience both involve the social practice of individual actions and interactions, it is the actions and interactions that also occur in relation to the usage of tools that constrain and/or enable these actions. As such, aligning activities are interrelated and inseparable in practice. If one considers activities inherent in the practices of aligning around strategies and plans, one needs to acknowledge the role of social actors and their actions. Thus, in order to understand and facilitate aligning, examination is needed not only of specific tools or actors, but also the rich interactions within which people and things are engaged in doing 'alignment work.'

Taking a practice perspective allows us to unite the social and intellectual dimensions of alignment. In particular, a consideration of the recursive loops between the social and the intellectual provides an integrated understanding of how organizational actors mobilize tools and how tools can assemble actors to attain alignment outcomes. One such avenue of research might be to study the use of alignment tools in practice. While we know about the tools available in aligning practice – the methodologies and approaches used in 'translations' – we do not yet know the precise nature of the 'tools' the practitioners actually use, nor how they use them. For example, while such tools as balanced scorecards (Huang and Hu, 2007); Andersen Consulting's Method-1 (Lederer and Gardiner, 1992); IBM's Business Systems Planning (Zachman, 1982); Information Engineering (Martin and Leben, 1989) and Total Information Systems Management (Osterle et al., 1993) have been introduced, studies suggest that practitioners ignore or modify them, or develop their own methodologies (e.g., Teubner, 2007). Potential research questions would relate to, for example: (1) How are alignment tools applied in practice? (2) Which tools are utilized and in which context? (3) Are they used in ways in which they were intended? (4) Are the plans and strategies followed mechanistically or used as a guideline in practice? (5) Do tools evolve over the period of aligning and, if so, how do they evolve?

In addition, the strategy-as-practice literature uncovers various impacts of common-or-garden tools such as PowerPoint presentations (e.g., Kaplan, 2011) and social media (e.g., Huang et al., 2013) on strategy formation. Can the use of such tools also be observed in aligning practice? Do aligning practices differ from other organizational practices previously studied? From the literature we have analyzed, it becomes clear that, while we are starting to understand something of the activities involved in the process and practices of aligning, what is still missing are studies on this 'internal life of a process' (Brown and Duguid, 2000: 94).

The lack of focus on micro processes is evident from the relative scarcity of literature on, for example, negotiating, learning and decision-making practices (see Table D1 in Appendix D). Organizational actors make various decisions in relation to business processes and associated IS, and therefore, decision-making becomes central to aligning. Decisional factors such as the motivating reason(s) behind the drive toward achieving strategic alignment can shape the process of its achievement (Negoita et al., 2013). Decision-making plays such a central part in managerial work that some authors consider it almost synonymous with management. Drucker (1955: 115), for example, argues that, 'Whatever a manager does he does it through … making decisions.' Over the following five decades, others have subscribed to this view of decision-making as being the central focus of management (e.g., Simon, 1979; Koontz, 1980). However, there is little discussion of decision-making in the practices associated with aligning. Understanding these practices is crucial in helping practitioners deal with the challenges associated with aligning. The extant alignment literature usually considers the decisions made 'in terms of actions taken, the resources committed, or precedents set' (Mintzberg et al., 1976: 246) but not how these decisions emerge or what the implications might be. Further, we know from prior research that decision-making is infused with politics (Eisenhardt and Bourgeois, 1988); however, the alignment literature rarely considers the contestation and dialog involved. It goes without saying that negotiating is part of organizational life – and this includes aligning activity, given that it involves multiple organizational members with a variety of personal as well as collective agendas.

The framework that emerges from our literature review may prove to be a useful starting point on which to base such investigations, with new sets of organizational activities emerging as a result. We argue for going beyond simply explaining organizational activities that are considered to be part of aligning by also focusing simultaneously on activities at multiple levels beyond the level of the organization. As can be observed from Table D2 in Appendix D, which lists all the articles considered in order of the number of categories of activities observed, only a few studies have captured the full set of proposed categories. We argue that it is through the focus on day-to-day activities that we will better be able to present a more comprehensive picture of aligning practice. Once we have this better understanding of aligning activities, and the actors involved, we would be in a better position to consider micro processes of aligning, the tools used in aligning and the unconscious actions[9] that are performed by 'alignment actors.' In other words, we could begin to unpack aligning practice and reveal 'the social, material and embodied ways of doing' alignment (Jarzabkowski and Spee, 2009).

Therefore, another suggestion for future research is to direct attention away from a focus on whether alignment is achieved or not, or on factors that enable successful alignment toward the study of outcomes related to the micro processes of aligning such as settlement on a decision, learning experience and contestation in aligning. These micro processes can play an unexpected role in aligning activity and, potentially, might have an impact on the extent and characteristics of alignment that is achieved. The introduction of an aligning-as-practice view does not replace the existing views of alignment: it expands its conceptualization by adding the dimension of practice, allowing for the study of routines and day-to-day activities of organizational actors.

An expanded range of research methods is necessary to pursue this research agenda.[10] Our view of aligning-as-practice suggests different units of analysis for research. That is, alignment scholars would not only center on the organization as a uniform whole, but also consider decisions, individuals, groups, projects and tools. To undertake this program of research, a wider range of research methods may need to be employed. Current work in the strategy-as-practice domain is dominated by observational field studies (e.g., Kaplan and Orlikowski, 2013). If our intention is to comprehend practices, there is little or no substitute for spending time in the field observing organizational actors engaged in their daily work-related activities (Jarzabkowski and Kaplan, 2014). A difficulty in undertaking such research, however, is that it is challenging to determine, *a priori*, which of the activities and interactions are related to aligning practice (Bechky, 2008). Consequently, going into the field to observe how organizational actors 'do' aligning work requires being in the right context and at the right time (Jarzabkowski and Kaplan, 2014). To capture aligning as it unfolds doubtless requires longitudinal study (e.g., Pettigrew, 1990). In addition, combining approaches might be valuable to alignment research. Different approaches focus attention on different aspects of the object of study, thereby providing a richer, more complete picture (Mingers, 2003). Interviews and surveys are valuable supplements (Jarzabkowski and Kaplan, 2014).

In sum, we posit that the proposed categories of aligning practices can provide a foundation for researchers in studying a greater number of units of analysis, using a broader range of research methods than has been typically the case in alignment research heretofore. The utilization of a wider range of approaches is, we contend, likely to produce a more dynamic and nuanced understanding of how aligning happens – in practice.

There are a number of potential extensions to our findings that could be explored in future research in addition. These include examining the different implications of other aligning activities that may be surfaced and studying a broader range of contexts, actors and their aligning activities.

Our focus in this study has been on those aligning activities that have been reported in existing, published cases in the academic literature. We might suppose, however, that there are activities and actors that have not thus far been reported upon that might well reflect additional aligning practices. For example, while Grant (2003) reports on such aligning activities as restructuring, hiring and outsourcing, who was involved and how they went about these tasks remains unclear. Similarly, Roepke et al. (2000) present an account of 3M's alignment initiatives, and in particular, their IT management development programs. However, the case fails to account for the manner in which employees' attitudes changed over time. Such cases as these provide some insight into what organizations do in their attempts to align IS with the business; however, they fail to describe the day-to-day practices of the organizational members involved. In many cases, we are yet to know who are the 'alignment practitioners' and what they actually do to align organizational processes, structures and functions. It should be clear from our analysis that organizational actors appear to be involved in all four types of aligning practice, at least to some degree. However, most alignment research to date has focused on aggregate classes of actors (e.g., 'top management'; 'IS management'; 'middle management'), and has attributed specific activities to these archetypes. Consequently, the description of activities performed by these aggregate actor classes becomes abstracted, and somewhat distant from the everyday activities of any individual actor. We suggest a research agenda that focuses on a wider range of individual actors and their everyday work practices in interaction with others. We further suggest that 'external' actors (i.e., those outside of the organization concerned), with whom 'internal' alignment practitioners interact, should also be studied in ongoing studies of aligning practice. We found only a very few external groups to have been considered thus far. For example and as noted, Sillince and Frost (1995) incorporate the role of politicians with respect to the organizational aligning practices of public sector organizations. Consultants and researchers – the latter partially playing the role of consultants as well in action research studies – have been considered in certain studies (e.g., Salmela and Ruohonen, 1992; Powell and Powell, 2004). In addition, the strategy literature indicates that 'strategy gurus' and business media actors play important roles in organizational activities (e.g., Clark and Greatbatch, 2002).

Future research could also usefully consider a wider range of contexts (cf. Figure 5.1). For example, not-for-profit organizations (charity or service organizations) might have a different set of approaches to goal specification and assessment (Newman and Wallender, 1978), methods of performance measurement (Kanter and Summers, 1987) and marketing and competitive practices (Rangan et al., 1996). Consequently, this sector could provide a fruitful setting for comparing the set of aligning activities taking place. Studying these and other related settings and novel sets of actor groups might hold promise.

Implications for Managers

While it may be premature to draw implications for managers from this preliminary (literature) review of aligning practice, in the spirit of establishing an agenda for research and practice, we offer the following. Alignment research has provided managers with a number of methodologies (e.g., Zachman, 1982; Lederer and Gardiner, 1992; Huang and Hu, 2007) to help in achieving and sustaining competitive advantage on the back of IT. However, it has been argued that such tools should not be mechanistically applied in practice, but rather used as means for surfacing assumptions, questioning and aligning interests across the organization (e.g., Galliers and Sutherland, 1991; Galliers, 2011). Methods are often talked of in terms of the 'instrumental mode' (Astley and Zammuto, 1992: 453) of contributing managerial techniques, often associated with the notion of 'best practices' (cf. Wagner and Newell, 2004 for a critique). Yet, in practice, methods are not operationalized precisely as they are designed. For example, IS/IT plans do not typically describe how IT and business personnel have to interact to put these plans into action, and formal conventions often play only a minor part in the interactions between business and IT (Chan, 2002). Recognizing the range of aligning activities involved in practice, such as the ones identified in our study, should allow managers to realize and prepare themselves for unforeseen challenges in alignment.

Concluding Remarks

The intention of this review has been to serve as a catalyst for a broader and richer agenda for alignment research. We believe, as do others (Henderson and Venkatraman, 1993; Queiroz et al., 2012), that this is an important research topic, as it goes to the very essence of the strategic value of IT in organizations and develops a link between business and IT-related issues. The categories of aligning activities that have been described here are somewhat nuanced, but introduce a new departure for research in this domain. Specifically, we propose a subtle shift of focus from the alignment process to aligning practice, with emphasis being placed on day-to-day activities rather than abstract phases. As a result, we propose an agenda that evolves from a (macro) focus on organizations and methodologies that has been common to date, to micro-process research that focuses on organizational actors and their day-to-day interactions and activities that shape aligning practice. While appreciating the contributions of prior research, we argue for a new point of departure that can help alignment research to become more relevant to practice, as called for by Avison and Malaurent (2014) and to practitioners – the people who 'do' aligning. The research agenda we outline recognizes trends in other fields, such as in strategic management (cf. Whittington, 2014), and encourages IS researchers to respond by increasing their theoretical and empirical efforts with respect to aligning *practice*.

Appendix A

Table A1 Journals included in the review of the ISS literature

Journals	Senior scholars 'basket'	Lacity et al: (2009)	Chan and Reich (2007)	Chen et al: (2010)	Added by authors	Backward/forward search	Initial keywords search results	Final set of relevant targeted articles
Academy of Management Executive	x	x					18	0
Academy of Management Journal	x	x					67	2
Academy of Management Review	x	x	x				58	1
American Review of Public Administration				x			1	1
Annals of Cases on Information Technology						x	0	0
Behaviour and Information Technology				x			17	7
BT Technology Journal		x					124	0
California Management Review		x	x				173	6
Communications of the ACM		x					234	15
Communications of the AIS		x	x				164	23
Computers and Automation						x	0	0
Computer & Operations Research		x					650	2
Database for Advances in Information Systems (ACM SIGMIS)		x					78	9
Datamation						x	0	0
Decision Sciences		x	x				73	23
Decision Support Systems		x					396	7
Engineering Management Journal		x					23	0
Engineering Management, IEEE Transactions			x				0	0
European Journal of Information Systems	x	x	x				173	39

Journal								
European Journal of Operational Research					X			49	6
European Management Journal					X	X		30	11
Foreign Affairs			X			X		4	0
Global Journal of Flexible Systems Management								0	0
Harvard Business Review					X	X		127	32
IBM Systems Journal						X		193	21
IEEE Computer					X			0	0
IEEE Transactions on Engineering Management					X	X		0	0
Industrial Management + Data Systems					X	X		569	14
Industry & Innovation					X			21	2
INFOR					X	X		10	4
Information & Management			X		X	X		247	74
Information and Organization					X			20	2
Information and Software Technology					X			209	7
Information Management								0	0
Information Management & Computer Security					X	X		127	6
Information Resources Management Journal					X			109	17
Information Systems Frontiers		X			X			78	5
Information Systems Journal					X			82	18
Information Systems Management					X			289	39
Information Systems Research		X			X	X		123	20
Information Technology & People					X	X		79	5
Information Technology and Management					X			66	4
International Journal of Computer Applications in Technology			X					0	0
International Journal of E-Business Research					X			26	2

(continued)

Table A1 (Continued)

Journals	Senior scholars' 'basket'	Lacity et al. (2009)	Chan and Reich (2007)	Chen et al. (2010)	Added by authors	Backward/forward search	Initial keywords search results	Final set of relevant targeted articles
International Journal of Healthcare Management and Technology			x				13	3
International Journal of Information Management		x	x				407	51
International Journal of Logistics Management		x					9	0
International Journal of Management		x					22	2
International Journal of Management Science			x				4	0
International Journal of Organizational Analysis		x					0	0
International Journal of Technology Management			x				0	0
International Journal of Value-Based Management			x				2	1
International Review of Law, Computers & Technology				x			6	1
Ivey Business Journal			x				6	2
Journal of AIS	x	x					69	1
Journal of Applied Behavioral Science		x					4	0
Journal of Applied Business Research		x					21	1
Journal of Cases on Information Technology			x				70	5
Journal of Computer Information Systems		x					188	8
Journal of Electronic Commerce in Organizations		x					26	1
Journal of End User Computing						x	0	0

Journal						
Journal of Enterprise Information Management				x	346	8
Journal of Global Information Management		x			76	5
Journal of Global Information Technology Management		x			63	4
Journal of High Technology Management Research		x		x	133	3
Journal of Information Science		x			0	0
Journal of Information Systems		x			88	3
Journal of Information Systems Management		x			618	50
Journal of Information Technology	x	x		x	175	46
Journal of Information Technology Case and Application Research		x			71	12
Journal of Information Technology Theory and Applications				x	0	0
Journal of International Management Studies		x			9	0
Journal of Management		x			4	0
Journal of Management Development		x			19	0
Journal of Management Information Systems	x	x		x	203	46
Journal of the Operational Research Society				x	0	0
Journal of Operations Management		x			24	0
Journal of Purchasing & Supply Management		x			2	0
Journal of Services Research				x	0	0
Journal of Small Business and Entrepreneurship			x		1	0
Journal of Strategic Information Systems	x	x		x	182	86

(continued)

Table A1 (Continued)

Journals	Senior scholars 'basket'	Lacity et al: (2009)	Chan and Reich (2007)	Chen et al: (2010)	Added by authors	Backward/forward search	Initial keywords search results	Final set of relevant targeted articles
Journal of Systems and Software			x				253	5
Journal of Systems Management		x					256	27
Long Range Planning					x	x	67	28
Management Datamatics							0	0
Management Decision				x			60	4
Management Science			x				46	2
MIS Quarterly		x	x	x			350	82
MIS Quarterly Executive		x	x	x			44	18
Model, Strategy & Leadership			x	x			0	0
Omega		x	x				63	17
Organization Science		x	x	x			19	3
Organization Studies							0	0
Organizational Behavior and Human Decision Processes				x			0	0
Organization Development Journal						x	0	0
Public Personnel Management		x					8	0
S.A.M. Advanced Management Journal		x					14	2
Scandinavian Journal of Information Systems			x	x			8	5
Sloan Management Review		x					380	53
South African Computer Journal							0	0
Strategic Management Journal			x				22	1
Strategic Outsourcing: An International Journal		x	x				38	5
Strategy & Leadership				x			71	3
Technology Analysis & Strategic Management		x					25	5
Technovation		x					44	3
Total							9336	1020

Appendix B

Table B1 ISS literature review: number of articles in each category

Category description		Number of articles	Percentage
Core IS strategizing articles	Alignment	506	53%
Remaining articles (IS strategizing-related articles)	Competitive advantage	142	47%
	Sourcing	69	
	Capability	64	
	Change management	55	
	Investment	27	
	Governance	28	
	Inter-organizational collaboration	21	
	Knowledge management	20	
		13	
Total		945	100%

Appendix C

Table C1 Case sources

Author(s)	Journal	Year	Title
Salmela, H Finland Ruohonen, M Finland	European Journal of Operational Research	1992	Aligning DSS development with organization development
Ives, B USA Jarvenpaa, SL USA Mason, RO USA	IBM Systems Journal	1993	Global business drivers: Aligning information technology to global business strategy
Sillince, JAA UK Frost, CEB UK	European Journal of Information Systems	1995	Operational, environmental and managerial factors in non-alignment of business strategies and IS strategies for the police service in England and Wales
Martinez, EV USA	Sloan Management Review	1995	Successful reengineering demands IS/Business partnerships
Dutta, S France	European Management Journal	1996	Linking IT and business strategy: The role and responsibility of senior management
Johnston, KD Australia Yetton, PW Australia	The Journal of Strategic Information Systems	1996	Integrating information technology divisions in a bank merger: Fit, compatibility and models of change
Brown, CV USA	Information Systems Research	1997	Examining the emergence of hybrid IS governance solutions: Evidence from a single case site
McKenney, JL USA Mason, RO USA Copeland, DG USA	MIS Quarterly	1997	Bank of America: The crest and trough of technological leadership
Hackney, R UK Little, S UK	European Journal of Information Systems	1999	Opportunistic strategy formulation for IS/IT planning
Simonsen, J Denmark	Scandinavian Journal of Information Systems	1999	How do we take care of strategic alignment? Constructing a design approach

Authors	Year	Journal	Title
Roepke, R. USA Agarwal, R. US Ferratt, TW US	2000	MIS Quarterly	Aligning the IT human resources with business vision: The leadership initiative at 3M
Feurer, R UK Chaharbaghi, K UK Weber, M Germany Wargin, J Germany	2000	Information Systems Management	Aligning strategies, processes, and IT: A case study
Hirschheim, R USA Sabherwal, R US	2001	California Management Review	Detours in the path toward strategic information systems alignment
Sabherwal, R USA Hirscheim, R. USA Goles, T USA	2001	Organization Science	The dynamics of alignment: Insights from a punctuated equilibrium model
Chan, YE Canada	2002	MIS Quarterly Executive	Why haven't we mastered alignment?
Sauer, C UK Willcocks, LP UK	2003	European Management Journal	Establishing the business of the future: The role of organizational architecture and information technologies

(continued)

Table C1 (Continued)

Author(s)	Year	Title	Journal
Grant, GG Canada	2003	Strategic alignment and enterprise systems implementation: The case of Metalco	Journal of Information Technology
Van Grembergen, W Belgium Saull, R Belgium De Haes, S Belgium	2003	Linking the IT balanced scorecard to the business objectives at a major Canadian financial group: Research note	Journal of Information Technology and Application Research
Peak, D USA Guynes, SC USA	2003a	The IT alignment planning process	The Journal of Computer Information Systems
Peak, D USA Guynes, SC USA	2003b	Improving information quality through IT alignment planning: A case study	The Journal of Information Systems Management
Avison, D France Jones, J Australia Powell, P UK Wilson, D Australia	2004	Using and validating the strategic alignment model	The Journal of Strategic Information Systems

Author / Country	Journal	Year	Title
Powell, J UK	European Journal of Operational Research	2004	Scenario networks to align and specify strategic information systems: A case-based study
Powell, P UK Thorogood, A Australia Yetton, PW Australia Vlasic, A Australia	Journal of Information Technology	2004	Raise your glasses — the water's magic! Strategic IT at SA Water: A case study in alignment, outsourcing and governance
Ramnath, R USA Landsbergen, D USA	Communications of the ACM	2005	IT-enabled sense-and-respond strategies in complex public organizations
Sledgianowski, D USA Luftman, J USA	Journal of Cases of Information Technology	2005	IT-Business strategic alignment maturity: A case study
Boddy, D UK Paton, R UK	Journal of Information Technology	2005	Maintaining alignment over the long-term: Lessons from the evolution of an electronic point of sale system
Coughlan, J UK Lycett, M UK Macredie, RD UK	International Journal of Information Management	2005	Understanding the business-IT relationship

(continued)

Table C1 (Continued)

Author(s)	Year	Journal	Title
Hu, Q US Huang, D USA	2006	Communications of the Association for Information Systems	Using the balanced scorecard to achieve sustained IT-business alignment: A case study
Wijnhoven, F The Netherlands Spil, T The Netherlands Tegwee, R The Netherlands Fa, R; Tjang A The Netherlands	2006	The Journal of Strategic Information Systems	Post-merger IT integration strategies: An IT alignment perspective
Vayghan, J USA Gar3nkle, S USA Walenta, C USA Healy, D USA	2007	IBM Systems Journal	The internal information transformation of IBM
Valentin, Z USA Gregor, S	2007	Information Technology & People	Enterprise architectures: Enablers of business strategy and IS/IT alignment in government

Authors	Year	Journal	Title
Australia Hart, D Australia Martin, N Australia Mehta, M Australia Hirschheim, R USA	2007	Journal of AIS	Strategic alignment in mergers and acquisitions: Theorizing IS integration decision making
Huang, DC USA Hu, Q USA	2007	The Journal of Information Systems Management	Achieving IT-Business strategic alignment via enterprise-wide implementation of balanced scorecards
Chen, R Taiwan Sun, C Taiwan Helms, MM USA Wen-Jang USA	2008	International Journal of Information Management	Aligning information technology and business strategy with a dynamic capabilities perspective: A longitudinal study of a Taiwanese Semiconductor Company
Tarafdar, M USA Qrun3eh, S USA	2009	The Journal of Information Systems Management	IT-business alignment: A two-level analysis

(continued)

Table C1 (Continued)

Author(s)	Journal	Year	Title
Weiss, JW USA Thorogood, A Australia	Engineering Management Journal	2011	Information Technology (IT)/Business alignment as a strategic weapon: A diagnostic tool
Wang, N China Xue, Y USA Liang, H USA Ge, S China	Communications of the Association for Information Systems	2011	The road to business-IT alignment: A case study of two Chinese companies

Appendix D

Table D1 List of aligning activities[3]

Aligning activity category	Number of articles	Aligning activity subcategory (%)	Number of occurrences[a]	Frequency of occurrence (%)
RECONFIGURING	26(70%)	New governance structure	20	9.7
		Transformation	1	0.5
		Turnaround	1	0.5
		Restructuring IT organization	17	8.6
		Outsourcing	8	3.8
		Reward system	1	0.5
		Integration	6	3.2
DEVELOPING	25(68%)	New system development	21	9.7
		Business-focused IT	8	3.8
STRENGTHENING	22(60%)	User/IT relationship (user participation)	5	2.7
		IT-business communication	5	2.2
		Top management involvement	12	4.9
		CIO/CEO relationship	1	0.5
		IS/business partnership	5	2.7
		Culture change	11	4.3
		IT training	8	3.8
		Human resource management/training	4	2.2
		Reinforcing	2	1.1
		Strengthening	1	0.5

(continued)

Table D1 (Continued)

Aligning activity category	Number of articles Aligning activity subcategory (%)		Number of occurrences[a]	Frequency of occurrence (%)
EVALUATING	21(57%)	Success measures	2	1.1
		Reactive response	1	0.5
		Separation of information/technology	3	1.6
		management	10	4.9
		Clarifying objectives	1	0.5
		Scanning emerging technologies	2	0.5
		External factors	7	2.7
		Review	6	2.2
		Prioritization		
SIGNALING	15(41%)	New position	6	3.2
		New appointment	13	5.9
		IT location	1	0.5
NEGOTIATING	8(22%)	Resistance to change	2	0.5
		Meetings	1	0.5
		Politics	8	4.3
LEARNING	8(22%)	Learning the business	5	2.7
		Organizational learning	4	1.6
DECISION-MAKING	3(8%)	Decision-making	3	1.1

[a] The numbers appearing in this table are indicative of our findings and do not represent any precise measure of occurrence of these activities in practice. The numbers give us some sense of gaps and relative proportions of the themes covered by researchers in their analysis of the cases.

Table D2 Topic coverage in the cases

Article	reconfiguring	decision – making	negotiating	signaling	evaluating	strengthening	learning	developing	topics covered
McKenney et al. (1997)	x	x	x	x	x	x	x	x	8
Coughlan et al. (2005)	x		x	x	x	x	x	x	7
Wang et al. (2011)	x		x	x	x	x	x	x	7
Dutta (1996)	x		x	x	x	x		x	6
Mehta and Hirschheim (2007)	x	x	x	x		x		x	6
Sillince and Frost (1995)	x		x		x		x	x	5
Chen et al. (2008)	x			x		x	x	x	5
Martinez (1995)	x		x	x		x		x	5
Johnston and Yetton (1996)	x		x	x	x			x	5
Weiss and Thorogood (2011)	x			x	x	x		x	5
Ramnath and Landsbergen (2005)	x				x		x	x	4
Salmela and Ruohonen (1992)			x		x		x	x	4
Gregor et al. (2007)	x				x	x		x	4
Thorogood et al. (2004)	x			x		x		x	4
Chan (2002)	x			x		x	x	x	4
Simonsen (1999)	x		x	x	x			x	4
Tarafdar and Qrumfleh (2009)	x				x	x		x	4
Hirschheim and Sabherwal (2001)	x	x		x					3
Huang and Hu (2007)					x	x		x	3
Powell and Powell (2004)					x	x		x	3
Sauer and Willcocks (2003)	x	x						x	3
Vayghan et al. (2007)	x					x		x	3
Ives et al. (1993)				x	x			x	3
Sledgianowski and Luftman (2005)	x			x		x		x	3

(continued)

Table D2 (Continued)

Article	reconfiguring	decision-making	negotiating	signaling	evaluating	strengthening	learning	developing	topics covered
Van Grembergen et al. (2003)	x				x			x	3
Sabherwal et al. (2001)	x			x		x			3
Huang and Hu (2007)	x				x	x			3
Peak and Guynes (2003b)					x	x	x		3
Avison et al. (2004)					x			x	2
Boddy and Paton (2005)	x					x			2
Grant (2003)	x			x					2
Roepke et al. (2000)	x					x			2
Peak and Guynes (2003a)					x			x	2
Feurer et al. (2000)					x	x			2
Hackney and Little (1999)								x	1
Brown (1997)	x								1
Wijnhoven et al. (2006)					x				1

Notes

1   Herein after, we shall use the simple term 'alignment'.
2   Examples of prior process-oriented studies include: MacDonald (1991); Baets (1996); Broadbent and Weill (1993); Henderson and Venkatraman (1993); Galliers and Baets (1998); Papp (1999); Rondinelli et al. (2001); Hirschheim and Sabherwal (2001); Sabherwal et al. (2001); Kearns and Lederer (2003); Peppard and Ward (2004); Benbya and McKelvey (2006).
3   The SAMM echoes earlier research that presents various forms of maturity model. See, for example, Galliers and Sutherland (1991) for an early review, and more recently, Paulk (2002) for an overview of the Software Engineering Institute's Capability Maturity Model (CMM). Latterly, the Innovation Value Institute has developed a more broadly based IT Capability Maturity Framework (http://ivi.nuim.ie/it-cmf).
4   See also, for example, Arvidsson et al. (2014) and Huang et al. (2014) for illustrations of practice-based studies in IS.
5   We do not limit our use of the term to activities linked to established professions, clearly defined roles, or social contexts, as seems to be the standard definition employed in the communities-of-practice tradition. For instance, Cook and Brown (1999: 386–387) define practice as 'the coordinated activities of individuals and groups in doing their "real work" as it is informed by a particular organizational or group context'. Similarly, Brown and Duguid (2001: 203) define practice as 'undertaking or engaging fully in a task, job, or profession'.
6   Strategic Information Systems Planning and MIS planning are common terms in use, especially in the earlier years.
7   Eighteen articles out of the total of 37 identified.
8   For a review of the sourcing literature as it relates to practice, see Lacity et al. (2009).
9   Unconscious actions are defined as 'something that is constitutive of acting within the world' according to Jarzabkowski and Spee (2009: 82).
10   cf. Galliers and Land (1987) for a taxonomy of IS research approaches and Mingers (2003) for mixed method research.

References

Agarwal, R. and Sambamurthy, V. (2002). Principles and Models for Organizing the IT Function, *MIS Quarterly Executive* 1(1): 1–16.
Arvidsson, V., Holmstrom, J. and Lyytinen, K. (2014). Information Systems Use as Strategy Practice: A Multi-dimensional View of Strategic Information System Implementation and Use, *The Journal of Strategic Information Systems* 23(1): 45–61.
Astley, W.G. and Zammuto, R.F. (1992). Organization Science, Managers, and Language Games, *Organization Science* 3(4): 443–460.
Avison, D., Jones, J., Powell, P. and Wilson, D. (2004). Using and Validating the Strategic Alignment Model, *The Journal of Strategic Information Systems* 13(3): 223–246.
Avison, D. and Malaurent, J. (2014). Is Theory King? Questioning the Theory Fetish in Information Systems, *Journal of Information Technology* 29: 327–336.
Baets, W.R.J. (1996). Some Empirical Evidence on IS Strategy: Alignment in Banking, *Information & Management* 30(4): 155–177.
Bassellier, G. and Benbasat, I. (2004). Business Competence of Information Technology Professionals: Conceptual Development and Influence on IT-business Partnerships, *MIS Quarterly* 28(4): 673–694.
Bechky, B.A. (2008). Analyzing Artifacts: Material Methods for Understanding Identity, Status, and Knowledge in Organizational Life, in D. Barry and H. Hansen (eds.) *The Sage Handbook of New Approaches in Management and Organization*, Thousand Oaks, CA: Sage Publications, pp. 98–110.
Benbya, H. and McKelvey, B. (2006). Using Coevolutionary and Complexity Theories to Improve IS Alignment: A Multi-level Approach, *Journal of Information Technology* 21(4): 284–298.
Boddy, D. and Paton, R. (2005). Maintaining Alignment over the Long-Term: Lessons from the Evolution of an Electronic Point of Sale System, *Journal of Information Technology* 20(3): 141–151.
Bontis, N., Crossan, M.M. and Hulland, J. (2002). Managing an Organizational Learning System by Aligning Stocks and Flows, *Journal of Management Studies* 39(4): 437–469.

Brancheau, J.C. and Wetherbe, J.C. (1987). Key Issues in Information Systems Management, *MIS Quarterly* 11(1): 23–45.

Broadbent, M. and Weill, P. (1993). Improving Business and Information Strategy Alignment: Learning from the Banking Industry, *IBM Systems Journal* 32(1): 162–179.

Brown, C.V. (1997). Examining the Emergence of Hybrid IS Governance Solutions: Evidence from a Single Case Site, *Information Systems Research* 8(1): 69–94.

Brown, C.V. and Ross, J.W. (1996). The Information Systems Balancing Act: Building Partnerships and Infrastructure, *Information Technology and People* 9(1): 49–62.

Brown, J.S. and Duguid, P. (2000). *The Social Life of Information*, Boston: Harvard Business School Press.

Brown, J.S. and Duguid, P. (2001). Knowledge and Organization: A Socialpractice Perspective, *Organization Science* 12(2): 198–213.

Burawoy, M. (1991). *Ethnography Unbound*, Berkeley and Los Angeles, CA: University of California Press.

Campbell, B. (2005). Alignment: Resolving Ambiguity within Bounded Choices, in *PACIS 2005 Proceedings*, Bangkok, Thailand, pp. 1–14.

Chan, Y.E. (2002). Why Haven't We Mastered Alignment? the Importance of the Informal Organization Structure, *MIS Quarterly Executive* 1(2): 97–112.

Chan, Y.E., Huff, S.L., Barclay, D.W. and Copeland, D.G. (1997). Business Strategic Orientation, Information Systems Strategic Orientation, and Strategic Alignment, *Information Systems Research* 8(2): 125–150.

Chan, Y.E. and Reich, B. (2007). IT Alignment: What Have We Learned?, *Journal of Information Technology* 22(4): 297–315.

Chan, Y.E., Sabherwal, R. and Thatcher, J. (2006). Antecedents and Outcomes of Strategic IS Alignment: An Empirical Investigation, *IEEE Transactions on Engineering Management* 53(1): 27–47.

Chen, D., Mocker, M., Preston, D. and Teubner, A. (2010). Information Systems Strategy: Reconceptualization, Measurement, and Implications, *MIS Quarterly* 34(2): 233–259.

Chen, R.S., Sun, C.M., Helms, M.M. and Jih, W.J. (2008). Aligning Information Technology and Business Strategy with A Dynamic Capabilities Perspective: A Longitudinal Study of A Taiwanese Semiconductor Company, *International Journal of Information Management* 28(5): 366–378.

Ciborra, C.U. (1997). De Profundis? Deconstructing the Concept of Strategic Alignment, *Scandinavian Journal of Information Systems* 9(1): 67–82.

Clark, T. and Greatbatch, D. (2002). Collaborative Relationships in the Creation and Fashioning of Management Ideas: Gurus, Editors and Managers, in M. Kipping and L. Engwall (eds.) *Management Consulting: Emergence and Dynamics of a KnowledgeIndustry*, Oxford: Oxford University Press, pp. pp. 127–145.

Cook, S.D. and Brown, J.S. (1999). Bridging Epistemologies: The Generative Dance between Organizational Knowledge and Organizational Knowing, *Organization Science* 10(4): 381–400.

Coughlan, H., Lycett, M. and Macredie, R.D. (2005). Understanding the Business-IT Relationship, *International Journal of Information Management* 25(4): 303–319.

De Haes, S. and Van Grembergen, W. (2009). An Exploratory Study into IT Governance Implementations and Its Impact on Business/IT Alignment, *Information Systems Management* 26(2): 123–137.

Drucker, P.F. (1955). 'Management Science' and the Manager, *Management Science* 1(2): 115–126.

Dutta, S. (1996). Linking IT and Business Strategy: The Role and Responsibility of Senior Management, *European Management Journal* 14(3): 255–268.

Earl, M. and Skyrme, D.J. (1992). Hybrid Managers – What Do We Know about Them?, *Information Systems Journal* 2(3): 169–187.

Eisenhardt, K.M. and Bourgeois, L.J. (1988). Politics of Strategic Decision Making in High-Velocity Environments: Toward a Midrange Theory, *Academy of Management Journal* 31(4): 737–770.

Feurer, R., Chaharbaghi, K., Weber, M. and Wargin, J. (2000). Aligning Strategies, Processes, and IT: A Case Study: Aligning IT and Business Strategy, *Information Systems Management* 17(1): 23–34.

Fuchs, P.H., Mifflin, K.E., Miller, D. and Whitney, J.O. (2000). Strategic Integration, *California Management Review* 42(3): 118–129.

Galliers, R.D. (2004). Reflections on Information Systems Strategizing, in C. Avgerou, C. Ciborra and F. Land (eds.) *The Social Study of Information and Communication Technology*, Oxford: Oxford University Press, pp. 231–262.

Galliers, R.D. (2006a). On Confronting Some of the Common Myths of Information Systems Strategy Discourse, in R. Mansell, C. Avgerou, D. Quah and R. Silverstone (eds.) *The Oxford Handbook of Information and Communication Technologies*, Oxford: Oxford University Press, pp. 225–243.

Galliers, R.D. (2006b). Strategizing for Agility: Confronting Information Systems Inflexibility in Dynamic Environments, in K.C. Desouza (ed.) *Agile Information Systems: Conceptualization, construction, and Management*, Oxford: Butterworth-Heinemann, pp. 1–15.

Galliers, R.D. (2011). Further Developments in Information Systems Strategising: Unpacking the Concept, in R.D. Galliers and W.L. Currie (eds.) *The Oxford Handbook of Management Information Systems: Critical Perspectives and New Directions*, Oxford: Oxford University Press, pp. 329–345.

Galliers, R.D. and Baets, W.R.J. (eds.) (1998). *Information Technology and Organizational Transformation*, New York: John Wiley and Sons.

Galliers, R.D. and Land, F.F. (1987). Viewpoint: Choosing Appropriate Information Systems Research Methodologies, *Communications of the ACM* 30(11): 901–902.

Galliers, R.D. and Sutherland, A.R. (1991). Information Systems Management and Strategy Formulation: The 'Stages of Growth' Model Revisited, *Journal of Information Systems* 1(2): 89–114.

Galliers, R.D. and Whitley, E.A. (2007). *Vive Les Differences?* Developing a Profile of European Information Systems Research as a Basis for International Comparisons, *European Journal of Information Systems* 16(1): 20–35.

Grant, G.G. (2003). Strategic Alignment and Enterprise Systems Implementation: The Case of Metalco, *Journal of Information Technology* 18(3): 159–175.

Gregor, S., Hart, D. and Martin, N. (2007). Enterprise Architectures: Enablers of Business Strategy and IS/IT Alignment in Government, *Information Technology & People* 20(2): 96–120.

Hackney, R. and Little, S. (1999). Opportunistic Strategy Formulation for IS/IT Planning, *European Journal of Information Systems* 8(2): 119–126.

Henderson, J.C. and Venkatraman, N. (1992). *Strategic Alignment: A Model for Organizational Transformation through Information Technology*, New York: Oxford University Press.

Henderson, J.C. and Venkatraman, N. (1993). Strategic Alignment: Leveraging Information Technology for Transforming Organizations, *IBM Systems Journal* 32(1): 4–16.

Hirschheim, R. and Sabherwal, R. (2001). Detours in the Path toward Strategic Information Systems Alignment, *California Management Review* 44(1): 87–108.

Horovitz, J. (1984). New Perspectives on Strategic Management, *Journal of Business Strategy* 4(3): 19–33.

Hu, Q. and Huang, C.D. (2006). Using the balanced scorecard to achieve sustained IT-business alignment: A case study. *Communications of the Association for Information Systems*, 17(1): 8.

Huang, C.D. and Hu, Q. (2007). Achieving IT-Business Strategic Alignment via Enterprise-wide Implementation of Balanced Scorecards, *Information Systems Management* 24(2): 173–184.

Huang, J., Baptista, J. and Galliers, R.D. (2013). Reconceptualizing Rhetorical Practices in Organizations: The Impact of Social Media on Internal Communications, *Information & Management* 50(2–3): 112–124.

Huang, J., Newell, S., Huang, J. and Pan, S. (2014). Site-Shifting as the Source of Ambidexterity: Empirical Insights from the Field of Ticketing, *The Journal of Strategic Information Systems* 23(1): 29–44.

Ives, B., Jarvenpaa, S.L. and Mason, R.O. (1993). Global Business Drivers: Aligning Information Technology to Global Business Strategy, *IBM Systems Journal* 32(1): 143–161.

Jarzabkowski, P. (2005). *Strategy as Practice: An Activity Based Approach*, London SAGE Publications Limited.

Jarzabkowski, P. and Kaplan, S. (2014). Strategy Tools-in-Use: A Framework for Understanding 'Technologies of Rationality' in Practice, *Strategic Management Journal*, advanced online publication 8 May, 10.1002/smj.2270

Jarzabkowski, P. and Spee, A. (2009). Strategy-as-practice: A Review and Future Directions for the Field, *International Journal of Management Reviews* 11(1): 69–95.

Jenkin, T.A. and Chan, Y.E. (2010). IS Project Alignment – A Process Perspective, *Journal of Information Technology* 25(1): 35–55.

Johnson, G., Melin, L. and Whittington, R. (2003). Guest Editors' Introduction, *Journal of Management Studies* 40(1): 3–22.

Johnston, K.D. and Yetton, P.W. (1996). Integrating Information Technology Divisions in a Bank Merger fit, Compatibility and Models of Change, *The Journal of Strategic Information Systems* 5(3): 189–211.

Kanter, R.M. and Summers, D.V. (1987). Doing Well while Doing Good: Dilemmas of Performance Measurement in Nonprofit Organizations and the Need for a Multiple-constituency Approach, in W.W. Powell (ed.) *The Nonprofit Sector*, New Haven, CT: Yale University Press, 220–236.

Kaplan, S. (2011). Strategy and PowerPoint: An Inquiry into the Epistemic Culture and Machinery of Strategy Making, *Organization Science* 22(2): 320–346.

Kaplan, S. and Orlikowski, W.J. (2013). Temporal Work in Strategy Making, *Organization Science* 24(4): 965–995.

Karpovsky, A., Hallanoro, M., and Galliers, R.D. (2014). The Process of Information Systems Strategizing: Review and Synthesis, in H. Topi, and A. Tucker (eds.) *The CRC Handbook of computing, 3rd ed. Vol. II: Information Systems and Information Technology*, London: Chapman & Hall/CRC, pp. 66-1–66-28.

Kearns, G.S. and Lederer, A.L. (2000). The Effect of Strategic Alignment on the Use of IS-Based Resources for Competitive Advantage, *The Journal of Strategic Information Systems* 9(4): 265–293.

Kearns, G.S. and Lederer, A.L. (2003). A Resource-based View of Strategic IT Alignment: How Knowledge Sharing Creates Competitive Advantage, *Decision Sciences* 34(1): 1–29.

Koontz, H. (1980). The Management Theory Jungle Revisited, *Academy of Management Review* 5(2): 175–188.

Lacity, M.C., Khan, S.A., and Willcocks, L.P. (2009). A Review of the IT Outsourcing Literature: Insights for Practice, *The Journal of Strategic Information Systems* 18(3): 130–146.

Law, J. (1994). *Organizing Modernity*, Oxford: Blackwell Publishers.

Lederer, A.L. and Gardiner, V. (1992). The Process of Strategic Information Planning, *The Journal of Strategic Information Systems* 1(2): 76–83.

Luftman, J. (2000). Assessing Business-IT Alignment Maturity, *Communications of the Association for Information Systems* 4(14): 1–50.

Luftman, J., Zadeh, H.S., Derksen, B., Santana, M., Rigoni, E.H., and Huang, D. (2013). Key Information Technology and Management Issues 2012–2013: An International Study, *Journal of Information Technology* 28(4): 354–366.

MacDonald, H. (1991). The Strategic Alignment Process, in M.S. Morton (ed.) *The Corporation of the 1990s: Information Technology and Organizational Transformation*, London: Oxford Press, pp. pp. 310–322.

Martin, J. and Leben, J. (1989). *Strategic Information Planning Methodologies*, Upper Saddle River, NJ: Prentice-Hall, Inc.

Martinez, E.V. (1995). Successful Reengineering Demands IS/Business Partnerships, *Sloan Management Review* 36(4): 51–60.

McKenney, J.L., Mason, R.O., and Copeland, D.G. (1997). Bank of America: The Crest and Trough of Technological Leadership, *MIS Quarterly* 21(3): 321–353.

McLean, E. and Soden, J. (1977). *Strategic Planning for MIS*, New York: John Wiley & Sons Inc.

Mehta, M. and Hirschheim, R. (2007). Strategic Alignment in Mergers and Acquisitions: Theorizing IS Integration Decision Making, *Journal of the Association for Information Systems* 8(3): 144–174.

Merali, Y., Papadopoulos, T., and Nadkarni, T. (2012). Information Systems Strategy: Past, present, Future?, *The Journal of Strategic Information Systems* 21(2): 125–153.

Miles, M.B. and Huberman, A.M. (1994). *Qualitative Data Analysis: An Expanded Sourcebook. Beverly Hills*, CA: Sage.

Mingers, J. (2003). The Paucity of Multimethod Research: A Review of the Information Systems Literature, *Information Systems Journal* 13(3): 233–249.

Mintzberg, H., Raisinghani, D., and Theoret, A. (1976). The Structure of 'Unstructured' Decision Processes, *Administrative Science Quarterly* 21(2): 246–275.

Mostyn, B. (1985). The Content Analysis of Qualitative Research Data: A Dynamic Approach, in M. Brenner, J. Brown, and D. Cauter (eds.) *The Research Interview*, London: Academic Press, pp. 115–145.

Negoita, B., Lapointe, L., and Pinsonneault, A. (2013). Achieving Strategic Alignment: A Decision-making Perspective, in *34th International Conference on Information Systems* (Milan, Italy).

Newman, W.H. and Wallender, H.W. (1978). Managing Not-for-Profit Enterprises, *Academy of Management Review* 3(1): 24–31.

Orlikowski, W.J. (2010). Engaging Practice in Research: Phenomenon, Perspective, and Philosophy, in D. Golsorkhi, L. Rouleau, D. Seidl, and E. Vaara (eds.) *The Cambridge Handbook on Strategy as Practice*, Cambridge: Cambridge University Press, pp. 23–33.

Osterle, H., Brenner, W., and Hilbers, K. (1993). *Total Information Systems Management: A European Approach*, Chichester: John Wiley & Sons Ltd.

Papp, R. (1999). Business-IT Alignment: Productivity Paradox Payoff?, *Industrial Management & Data Systems* 99(8): 367–373.

Paulk, M. (2002). Capability Maturity Model for Software, *Encyclopedia of Software Engineering*, 1–58.

Peak, D. and Guynes, C.S. (2003a). The IT Alignment Planning Process, *Journal of Computer Information Systems* 44(1): 9–15.

Peak, D. and Guynes, C.S. (2003b). Improving Information Quality through IT Alignment Planning: A Case Study, *Information Systems Management* 20(4): 22–29.

Peppard, J. and Breu, K. (2003). Beyond Alignment: A Coevolutionary View of the Information Systems Strategy Process, in Twenty-Fourth International Conference on Information Systems (Seattle, USA). 743–750.

Peppard, J., Galliers, R.D., and Thorogood, A. (2014). Information Systems Strategy as Practice: Micro Strategy and Strategizing for IS, *The Journal of Strategic Information Systems* 23(1): 1–10.

Peppard, J. and Ward, J. (2004). Beyond Strategic Information Systems: *Towards an IS Capability*, *The Journal of Strategic Information Systems*, 13(2):167–194.

Pettigrew, A.M. (1990). Longitudinal Field Research on Change: Theory and Practice, *Organization Science* 1(3): 267–292.

Powell, J. and Powell, P. (2004). Scenario Networks to Align and Specify Strategic Information Systems: A Case-based Study, *European Journal of Operational Research* 158(1): 146–172.

Preston, D.S. and Karahanna, E. (2009). Antecedents of IS Strategic Alignment: A Nomological Network, *Information Systems Research* 20(2): 159–179.

Queiroz, M., Coltman, T., Sharma, R., Tallon, P., and Reynolds, P. (2012). Strategic IT Alignment: An Evaluation and Process-level Reconceptualization of the Construct, in Academy of Management Annual Meeting: The Informal Economy (Boston, MA, USA). 1–32.

Ramnath, R. and Landsbergen, D. (2005). IT-Enabled Sense-and-Respond Strategies in Complex Public Organizations, *Communications of the ACM* 48(5): 58–64.

Rangan, V.K., Karim, S., and Sandberg, S.K. (1996). Doing Better at Doing Good, *Harvard Business Review* 74(3): 42–51.

Reich, B. and Benbasat, I. (2000). Factors that Influence the Social Dimension of Alignment between Business and Information Technology Objectives, *MIS Quarterly* 24(1): 81–113.

Roepke, R., Agarwal, R., and Ferratt, T.W. (2000). Aligning the IT Human Resource with Business Vision: The Leadership Initiative at 3M, *MIS Quarterly* 24(2): 327–353.

Rondinelli, D., Rosen, B., and Drori, I. (2001). The Struggle for Strategic Alignment in Multinational Corporations: Managing Readjustment during Global Expansion, *European Management Journal* 19(4): 404–416.

Rosenkranz, C., Charaf, M.C., and Holten, R. (2013). Language Quality in Requirements Development: Tracing Communication in the Process of Information Systems Development, *Journal of Information Technology* 28(3): 198–223.

Sabherwal, R., Hirschheim, R., and Goles, T. (2001). The Dynamics of Alignment: Insights from a Punctuated Equilibrium Model, *Organization Science* 12(2): 179–197.

Salmela, H. and Ruohonen, M. (1992). Aligning DSS Development with Organization Development, *European Journal of Operational Research* 61(1–2): 57–71.

Sauer, C. and Willcocks, L. (2003). Establishing the Business of the Future: The Role of Organizational Architecture and Information Technologies, *European Management Journal* 21(4): 497–508.

Sillince, J.A.A. and Frost, C.E.B. (1995). operational, Environmental and Managerial Factors in Non-Alignment of Business Strategies and IS Strategies for the Police Service in England and Wales, *European Journal of Information Systems* 4(2): 103–115.

Simon, H.A. (1979). Rational Decision Making in Business Organizations, *The American Economic Review* 69(4): 493–513.

Simonsen, J. (1999). How Do We Take Care of Strategic Alignment? Constructing a Design Approach, *Scandinavian Journal of Information Systems* 11(2): 51–72.

Sledgianowski, D. and Luftman, J. (2005). IT-business Strategic Alignment Maturity: A Case Study, *Journal of Cases on Information Technology* 7(2): 102–120.

Smaczny, T. (2001). Is an Alignment between Business and Information Technology the Appropriate Paradigm to Manage IT in Today's Organisations?, *Management Decision* 39(10): 797–802.

Strauss, A.L. (1987). *Qualitative Analysis for Social Scientists*, Cambridge: Cambridge University Press.

Tallon, P.P. (2007). A Process-Oriented Perspective on the Alignment of Information Technology and Business Strategy, *Journal of Management Information Systems* 24(3): 227–268.

Tallon, P.P. and Pinsonneault, A. (2011). Competing Perspectives on the Link between Strategic Information Technology Alignment and Organizational Agility: Insights from a Mediation Model, *MIS Quarterly* 35(2): 463–486.

Tarafdar, M. and Qrunfleh, S. (2009). IT-Business Alignment: A Two-level Analysis, *Information Systems Management* 26(4): 338–349.

Teubner, R.A. (2007). Strategic Information Systems Planning: A Case Study from the Financial Services Industry, *The Journal of Strategic Information Systems* 16(1): 105–125.

Thorogood, A., Yetton, P., Vlasic, A., and Spiller, J. (2004). Raise Your Glasses – The Water's Magic! Strategic IT at SA Water: A Case Study in alignment, Outsourcing and Governance, *Journal of Information Technology* 19(2): 130.

Tsoukas, H. (1994). *New Thinking in Organizational Behavior*, Oxford: Butterworth-Heinemann.

Tyre, M.J. and Orlikowski, W.J. (1994). Windows of Opportunity: Temporal Patterns of Technological Adaptation in Organizations, *Organization Science* 5(1): 98–118.

Valorinta, M. (2011). IT Alignment and the Boundaries of the IT Function, *Journal of Information Technology* 26(1): 46–59.

Van Grembergen, W., Saull, R., and De Haes, S. (2003). Linking the IT Balanced Scorecard to the Business Objectives at a Major Canadian Financial Group, *Journal of Information Technology Cases & Applications* 5(1): 23–50.

Vayghan, J., Garfinkle, C., Walenta, D., Healy, D., and Valentin, Z. (2007). The Internal Information Transformation of IBM, *IBM Systems Journal* 46(4): 669–683.

Waema, T. and Walsham, G. (1990). Information Systems Strategy Formulation, *Information & Management* 18(1): 29–39.

Wagner, E.L. and Newell, S. (2004). 'Best' for Whom? The Tension between 'Best Practice' ERP Packages and Diverse Epistemic Cultures in a University Context, *The Journal of Strategic Information Systems* 13(4): 305–328.

Wang, N., Xue, Y., Liang, H., and Ge, S. (2011). The Road to Business-IT Alignment: A Case Study of Two Chinese Companies, *Communications of the Association for Information Systems* 28(1): 415–436.

Webster, J. and Watson, R. (2002). Analyzing the past to Prepare for the Future: Writing a Literature Review, *MIS Quarterly* 26(2): 13–23.

Weiss, J.W. and Thorogood, A. (2011). Information Technology (IT)/business Alignment as A Strategic Weapon: A Diagnostic Tool, *Engineering Management Journal* 23(2): 30–41.

Whittington, R. (1999). Strategy as Practice, *Long Range Planning* 29(3): 731–735.

Whittington, R. (2006). Completing the Practice Turn in Strategy Research, *Organization Studies* 27(5): 613–634.

Whittington, R. (2014). Information Systems Strategy and Strategy-as-Practice: A Joint agenda, *The Journal of Strategic Information Systems*, 23(1): 87–91.

Wijnhoven, F., Spil, T., Stegwee, R., and Fa, R.T.A. (2006). Post-merger IT Integration Strategies: An IT Alignment Perspective, *The Journal of Strategic Information Systems* 15(1): 5–28.

Wilson, A., Baptista, J., and Galliers, R.D. (2013). Performing Strategy: Aligning Processes in Strategic IT, in 34th International Conference on Information Systems (Milan, Italy), 15–18.

Yin, R.K. and Heald, K.A. (1975). Using the Case Survey Method to Analyze Policy Studies, *Administrative Science Quarterly* 20(3): 371–381.

Zachman, J.A. (1982). Business Systems Planning and Business Information Control Study: A Comparison, *IBM Systems Journal* 21(1): 31–53.

Questions for Discussion

1   It is suggested that aligning practices can be grouped under the headings, aligning as:
    • translation
    • adaptation
    • integration
    • experience.

2   Consider each and discuss how helpful these headings are in explaining aligning practices. How might you amend or extend this typology?

3   Apply each of the headings to an organization with which you are familiar. What practices can you identify and how do these compare with those listed in the chapter?

4   Consider the findings from this review in light of the subject matter of the previous
strategies. How does the concept of aligning fit with the information systems planning
approaches identified in Chapter 1 and the reflections on information systems strategizing in Chapters 2–4? What do you conclude from this?

The chapter is based on a review of the literature at the time of publication in 2015. How
have things changed since then? Consider in particular the advent of digital strategy.

Further Reading

Chan, Y. E., Reich, B. (2007). IT alignment: What have we learned? *Journal of Information Technology*,
    22(4), 297–315.
Horner Reich, B., Benbasat, I. (2000). Factors that influence the social dimension of alignment between
    business and information technology objectives. *MIS Quarterly*, *24*(1), 81–113.

PART II

Digital Strategy and Organizational Transformation

WE BEGAN OUR DISCUSSION with the foundation of information systems (IS), Strategy and Strategizing in Part I by focusing on IS planning, IS strategy and strategizing, aligning and further developments of IS strategizing. In Part II we focus on current aspects and issues of digital strategy and transformation, digital leadership and capabilities, chief digital officers and issues of power dynamics, IS, and strategy. The contents of Part II are listed in the second-from-bottom layer of Figure P2.1.

The current digital economy is affecting the workplace and society with the use of social media; cloud computing; big data, and artificial intelligence. Navigating through this digital transformation might be considered a daunting experience, where *people's roles* require adjustment (Sandeep and Ravishankar, 2018; Wagg et al., 2019) and *organizations* require clear strategies (Bharadwaj et al., 2013). New forms of capabilities and leadership such as Chief Digital Officers (Weill and Woerner, 2013) emerge and understanding the issues of power and strategy (Marabelli and Galliers, 2017), and power and IS (Simeonova, 2018; Simeonova et al., 2018) gain further significance. Indeed, the importance of power dynamics has recently been recognized and emphasized in a Special Issue on Power Dynamics of the *Information Systems Journal* (Simeonova et al., 2017).

Part II examines the "what", the "how" and the "who" of digital transformation and digital transformation strategy. The "what" of digital transformation and digital transformation strategy are considered in Chapters 6 and 7, while the role of power, and how it affects IS and strategy, is considered in Chapter 10. The "how"—in terms of how to navigate digital transformation and formulate digital transformation strategy—is also dealt with in Chapters 6 and 7, while the "who" is considered in Chapters 8 and 9, in terms of the role of leadership and CDOs in promoting digital transformation.

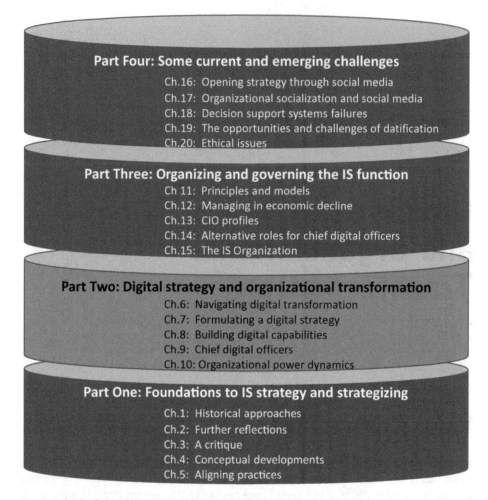

Figure P2.1 The focus of Part II: Digital strategy and organizational transformation

In Chapter 6, Ina Sebastian, Jeanne Ross, Cynthia Beath, Martin Mocker, Kate Moloney and Nils Fonstad outline the elements of successful digital transformation through sampling the practices of twenty-five "big old" companies. The authors explain that the elements of successful digital transformation include a digital strategy that defines the SMACIT (social, mobile, analytics, cloud, and internet of things) inspired value proposition; an operational backbone that facilitates operational excellence, and a digital services platform that enables rapid innovation and responsiveness to new market opportunities. The chapter differentiates between two business strategies: a customer engagement strategy and a digitized solutions strategy. The authors outline two technology-enabled assets for the successful execution of digital strategies. These are an operational backbone and a digital services platform. These assets, they argue, enable business capabilities, which in turn lead to digital business success. How to formulate a digital transformation strategy is examined in Chapter 7.

In Chapter 7, Thomas Hess, Christian Matt, Alexander Benlian, and Florian Wiesböck outline guidelines to help managers formulate business transformation strategies, emphasizing the balance between exploitation and exploration of resources to achieve organizational agility and competitive advantage. The chapter outlines four key dimensions of digital transformation: use of technologies; changes in value creation; structural changes, and financial aspects. The authors develop guidelines for managers regarding how to approach and implement digital transformation strategies and they illustrate this through three case studies. The chapter formulates strategic questions managers need to tackle when embarking on digital transformation. The authors' conclusions outline why it is essential for managers to know what questions to ask for successful digital transformation.

In Chapter 8, Omar El Sawy, Pernille Kræmmergaard, Henrik Amsinck and Anders Lerbech Vinther outline the need for defining and enhancing enterprise capabilities in digital leadership for successful digitalization. The authors illustrate that, for a successful digitalization strategy, six aspects require consideration and change. These are: business strategy; business models; enterprise platform integration; the mindset and skill set; the corporate IT function, and the workplace. Their research was undertaken at the LEGO Group where leveraging digitalization has been a core strategic pillar. To do so, the LEGO Group have used three lenses: products, marketing and enterprise in order to build the foundations of digital leadership. Based on LEGO's success, the authors formulate lessons learned for digital leadership to help companies achieve strategic success of digitalization and digital leadership. The lessons focus on aspects of enterprise digitalization, platforms and the digital workforce and are designed to help other companies in other contexts to develop their digital leadership capabilities.

In Chapter 9, Anna Singh and Thomas Hess examine the roles of CDOs in establishing themselves as top managers in organizations embarking digital transformation. The task of CDOs is to orchestrate digital transformation in their organizations, help formulate and execute the digital transformation strategy, and help to digitize resources and gain value from these digital assets. The authors outline the emerging role of CDOs through six cases. Notwithstanding, the authors are able to summarize three roles for CDOs arising from their research, that of: the entrepreneur, the digital evangelist, and the coordinator. Key skills and competencies associated with each of these roles are identified. Entrepreneurial CDOs require digital pioneering skills, digital evangelists require skills that inspire, as well as resilience and IT competency, and coordinator CDOs require change management skills.

In Chapter 10, Boyka Simeonova, Bob Galliers and Stan Karanasios outline the importance of power dynamics considerations in organizations, IS and strategy. The chapter outlines a new analytical framework on power—the Power Matrix. The framework differentiates between episodic and systemic forms of power, the role of actors and the role of IS and their links to strategy. The matrix includes four quadrants: *power as possession; power as control; power as practice,* and *power as facilitation. Power as possession* is viewed in terms of being hierarchical, authoritative and often legitimate, based on knowledge, resource access and often self-interest, linking to a strategy of exploitation, direction/goal setting, and imposition of change. *Power as control* is more concerned with rules; norms; monitoring; surveillance; discipline; compliance, and digitalization, with strategy being linked to exploitation, performance measurement, and *routinizing* change. *Power as practice* is described more in terms of shared goals/interests; communities of practice; social capital; trust; collaboration; networks; empowerment, and knowing, with strategy being linked to exploration; experimentation; innovation, and *instilling* change. *Power as facilitation* features transparency; autonomy; multivocality; empowerment; discourse; decision-making, and an organizational culture linking to strategy built on exploration and innovation, *institutionalizing* change). The framework outlines the importance of power dynamics in organizations and paves the way for studying different forms of power, IS and strategy.

References

Bharadwaj, A., El Sawy, O. A., Pavlou, P. A., Venkatraman, N. (2013). Digital business strategy: Toward a next generation of insights. *MIS Quarterly*, 37(2), 471–482.

Marabelli, M., Galliers, R. D. (2017). A Reflection on information systems strategizing: The role of power and everyday practices. *Information Systems Journal*, 27(3), 347–366.

Sandeep, M. S., Ravishankar, M. N. (2018). Sociocultural transitions and developmental impacts in the digital economy of impact sourcing. *Information Systems Journal*, 28(3), 563–586.

Simeonova, B. (2018). Transactive memory systems and Web 2.0 in knowledge sharing: A conceptual model based on activity theory and critical realism. *Information Systems Journal*, 28(4), 592–611.

Simeonova, B., Galliers, R. D., Karanasios, S. (2017). Power dynamics in organisations and the role of information systems. *Information Systems Journal*.

Simeonova, B., Karanasios, S., Galliers, R. D., Kelly, P. R., Mishra, J. (2018). Where is power in information systems research? towards a framework. *International Conference on Information Systems*, San Francisco. https://aisel.aisnet.org/icis2018/.

Wagg, S., Cooke, L., Simeonova, B. (2019). Digital inclusion and Women's Health and Well-Being in Rural Communities, In Yates, S. and Rice, R. (Eds) *The Oxford Handbook of Digital Technology and Society*, Oxford: Oxford University Press.

Weill, P., Woerner, S. L. (2013). The future of the CIO in a digital economy. *MIS Quarterly Executive*, 12(2), 65–75.

Chapter 6

Ina M. Sebastian, Jeanne W. Ross, Cynthia Beath, Martin Mocker, Kate G. Moloney and Nils O. Fonstad

HOW BIG OLD COMPANIES NAVIGATE DIGITAL TRANSFORMATION

Elements of Successful Digital Transformation

NEW DIGITAL TECHNOLOGIES, particularly what we refer to as SMACIT[1] (social, mobile, analytics, cloud and Internet of things [IoT]) technologies, present both game-changing opportunities and existential threats to big old companies. GE's "industrial internet" and Philips' digital platform for personalized healthcare information represent bets made by big old companies attempting to cash in on opportunities offered by digital technologies.[2] LEGO is developing an engagement platform to supplement its enterprise systems with the ability to interact with customers and innovate rapidly.[3] These big old companies are rethinking how they will compete in the digital economy, and they are investing in new technologies and new capabilities to reposition themselves as digital leaders.

In recent years, "born digital" pioneers (such as Amazon, Facebook and Google) have grown into powerful behemoths, while companies that had long dominated their industries found their traditional value propositions under threat. Most leaders of big old companies believe their companies can retain leadership positions by taking advantage of both their existing strengths and the capabilities offered by digital technologies. But what must they do to succeed? That is the question we set out to answer in a study of 25 large, successful companies initiating digital transformations. Most of these companies were "big" (with a mean size of 82,297 employees), and most were "old" (with a mean age of 104 years). Our research method and sample are described in the Appendix.

Most big old companies' digital transformations are at an early stage—in most industries, the vast majority of established companies' revenues still come from traditional products and services.[4] Thus. research on successful digital transformation is currently limited to identifying trends that signal improved capabilities to apply SMACIT and related technologies, and to the growing accessibility of electronic data to enrich products, services and customer relationships.

Our study revealed three essential elements for a successful digital transformation:

1   A digital strategy that defines a SMACITinspired value proposition
2   An operational backbone that facilitates operational excellence
3   A digital services platform that enables rapid innovation and responsiveness to new market opportunities.

In this article, we explain how these three elements position big old companies for success in the digital era. We describe the digital initiatives of several companies in our study and offer evidence that shows how these efforts will contribute to long-term digital success.[5] We conclude with recommendations for leaders of companies that are ready to embark—or have already embarked—on their digital transformation journeys.

Two Digital Strategies

As leaders in big old companies recognize the opportunities created by new digital technologies to integrate their existing business capabilities with new capabilities made possible by SMACIT technologies, they are defining their companies' digital strategies.[6] These are not merely technology strategies. Rather, they are business strategies that incorporate the opportunities that the digital economy presents.[7] We define a digital strategy as: *A business strategy, inspired by the capabilities of powerful, readily accessible technologies (like SMACIT), intent on delivering unique, integrated business capabilities in ways that are responsive to constantly changing market conditions.* A digital strategy guides leaders' efforts to create new value propositions by combining their companies' existing capabilities with capabilities enabled by SMACIT and other digital technologies.

We found that company leaders who recognize the opportunities presented by new digital technologies articulate one of two types of digital strategy: *customer engagement* or *digitized solutions*. In our sample of 25 companies, eight were pursuing a customer engagement strategy, and 13 were pursuing a digitized solutions strategy. The remaining four were experimenting with applications of digital technologies but had not yet formulated a clear digital strategy and thus had not embarked on a transformation journey.

Customer Engagement Strategy

Just as Amazon's introduction of customer recommendations and user-friendly online interactions created a passionate base of loyal customers, a company pursuing a customer engagement digital strategy seeks to build customer loyalty and trust by providing superior, innovative, personalized and integrated customer experiences. A customer engagement strategy typically aims to create a seamless, omnichannel experience that makes it easy for customers to order, inquire, pay and receive support in a consistent way from any channel at any time. Such a strategy relies on analytics applied to a growing repository of customer data, to better understand and anticipate varying customer demands. In addition, this type of digital strategy facilitates ongoing communications between a company and its customers and, where appropriate, with a larger community.

An example of a company pursuing a customer engagement strategy is Kaiser Permanente, a U.S. non-profit integrated healthcare organization. Healthcare in the United States is shifting from volume-based to value-based care, with a focus on increasing access while also cutting costs. Kaiser Permanente is attempting to reduce costs and improve individual patient health by facilitating both preventive and traditional care. This involves shifting from a hospital-centric view of healthcare to a patient-centric view. EVP and CIO Richard Daniels explains:

> We need to make it easy for people to get access to care anytime and anywhere, preferably from any device, so that they can reach us. They can have access to their care team, and we want to provide them [with] leading-edge technology, like video [consultation] with your doctor from your smartphone.

Kaiser Permanente is capitalizing on opportunities created by SMACIT technologies in at least three ways:

1   Offering increased opportunities for patient interaction with care delivery teams by supplementing visits and calls with channels like video, text and email
2   Investing in data analytics to identify needs for—and most effective approaches to—personalized outreach, particularly when it encourages patient adherence to medical regimens
3   Leveraging social media to develop communities of patients who have similar interests and to create care circles that engage patients and their families with care providers.

Ten years ago Kaiser Permanente was criticized for inconsistent customer service.[8] As it delivers on its customer engagement strategy, it is earning the healthcare industry's highest "net promoter" scores.[9] Seventy percent of Kaiser Permanente's members are actively engaged online, and studies conducted by the company reveal that actively engaged members are healthier, adhere more to prescribed medications, are more satisfied and are twice as likely to stay with the organization. Like other big old companies pursuing customer engagement digital strategies, Kaiser Permanente is leveraging digital technology to build customer loyalty, which, in turn, is building competitive advantage.

Digitized Solutions Strategy

A digitized solutions strategy aims to reformulate a company's value proposition by integrating a combination of products, services and data. This type of digital strategy is driven by R&D efforts that seek to anticipate—rather than respond to—customer needs. Just as Steve Jobs trusted his instincts (rather than customer input) to guide product innovation at Apple, a company pursuing a digitized solutions strategy tries to imagine what it could do for customers by combining existing competencies with the capabilities offered by digital technologies. An effective digitized solutions strategy invariably involves collecting and using additional data—often gathered through sensors. In many cases, digitized solutions may shift company revenues from the sale of products to recurring revenue from ongoing services.[10] An example of such a shift is GE's expectation of subscription revenue from its asset performance management offering, delivered via its Predix platform-as-a-service (PaaS).

One company in our study that is pursuing a digitized solutions strategy is the Schindler Group, a global provider of elevators, escalators and related services. The elevator and escalator industry is highly competitive, which severely constrains profit margins. Schindler has set out to create digitized solutions with the aim of establishing a unique space in the industry. Its products move one billion people a day—all within buildings in urban areas. Management thought that Schindler's competency in moving people, combined with digital technologies, would position it to provide mobility solutions beyond buildings. Schindler has therefore embraced a strategy called "urban mobility solutions" for experimenting with a much wider range of products and services. The first innovation that went into production involved using its PORT technology[11] and sensor equipped elevators to grant access to registered guests at a building and direct them to their hosts.

> When you have our PORT technology on your phone, the building will recognize you and know where you want to go, so you don t need your badge. If you're a visitor, we send you a message on your smartphone, and then you can flow into the building without signing in at the reception desk.
>
> *Michael Nilles, Chief Digital Officer, Schindler Group*

As part of its digitized solutions strategy, Schindler applies analytics to enhanced sensor data to develop both predictive maintenance models and smart algorithms that optimize routes to any destination in buildings and assign elevators. Like other big old companies pursuing a digitized solutions strategy, Schindler is leveraging digital technologies to offer integrated products and services that distinguish it from competitors.

Choosing a Digital Strategy

A digital strategy is valuable only if it drives resource allocation and capital investments. Many business leaders are reluctant to commit to one digital strategy, in part because they believe that digital success involves both customer engagement and digitized solutions. But our research found that the best strategies guided both strategic choices and operational decisions, and that committing to one strategy paid off. Companies like Kaiser Permanente, LEGO and USAA (a U.S. financial services company) that were pursuing a customer engagement strategy achieved greater customer satisfaction and loyalty. Companies like Schindler and Schneider Electric that were pursuing a digitized solutions strategy gained new sources of revenue. The value of strategic focus is well established, but the more noteworthy finding from our study may be that success with the chosen strategy eventually also led to outcomes associated with the other strategy.

At USAA, for example, seamless channel integration not only generated member delight and loyalty (at USAA customers are referred to as members), but led to increased product integration. USAA's responsiveness to members' needs led it to change its website so that its financial products were listed according to a member's life events. This new arrangement was helpful, but it quickly became clear that members would find it even more helpful if those products were actually integrated. That led USAA to create integrated solutions like AutoCircle—a one-stop shop for buying, insuring and financing an automobile.

Similarly, Schindler's pursuit of digitized solutions meant the company had to engage with customers to convince them of the benefits of those solutions. This led Schindler to design customer engagement tools that communicate the status of Schindler's (and some partners') equipment to customers (usually facility managers).

In short, our study reveals that there is a natural synergy between the two digital strategies. Despite this synergy, however, our research suggests that it is essential to commit to one digital strategy or the other. Committing to one strategy helps leaders make tough choices related to resource allocation. Moreover, digital technologies present so many opportunities that, without clear investment criteria, leaders will find themselves reacting to immediate one-off opportunities rather than proactively designing their business for digital success. In particular, they will find it difficult—or even impossible—to develop and use two technology-enabled assets that our research found are essential for executing a company's digital strategy.

Two Technology-enabled Assets are Essential to Executing a Digital Strategy

The companies we studied found it easier to articulate a digital strategy than to execute it. In fact, all the companies we studied (and we specifically sought out proactive companies for this research) are still at early stages of their digital transformations. (Indeed, we cannot declare that any of the companies we studied have successfully completed a digital transformation.)

We observed enormous variation in companies' abilities to deliver new digital services, such as a seamless omnichannel customer experience or a well-integrated IoT-based service. To consistently deliver new digital services, our research revealed, a company needs two technology-enabled assets: an *operational backbone* and a *digital services platform*.

The operational backbone supports efficiency and operational excellence, while the digital services platform supports business agility and rapid innovation. Both the operational backbone and digital services platform depend on a base of technology, but what makes them powerful is the *business* capabilities that the technology enables. Our research on business transformation initiatives suggests that these capabilities are *the* critical enablers of digital business success.

An Operational Backbone Enables Operational Excellence

To compete in the digital economy, companies must, at a minimum, be able to flawlessly execute transactions and provide access to critical operational data. To accomplish this, they need a strong and scalable operational backbone (also referred to as a digitized process platform).[12] We define an operational backbone as *the technology and business capabilities that ensure the efficiency, scalability, reliability, quality and predictability of core operations.*

Companies have been building operational backbones since the late 1990s, when implementations of ERP and customer relationship management (CRM) systems targeted the benefits of standardized and integrated systems and processes.[13] Each company's operational backbone is focused on its own unique strategic requirements, but the most common elements include:

- A "single source of truth" for critical data (e.g., customer, order and product data)
- Seamless and transparent transaction processing
- Standardized back office shared services.

Although many businesses have been building operational backbones for many years, only 15 companies in our sample had operational backbones that supported their digital strategies. The other ten had managed to survive without wiring in operational excellence.[14] Without an operational backbone, however, they lacked seamless operations. As a result, they did not have the basic competencies needed to execute a digital strategy.

Companies with operational backbones were increasingly able to automate repetitive processes, thus enhancing speed and accuracy. Moreover, the reliability provided by the operational backbone allowed management to focus on strategic issues rather than fighting fires. LEGO and Kaiser Permanente offer examples of how powerful operational backbones give companies the operational excellence critical to executing their digital strategies.

LEGO's Operational Backbone. In 2004, LEGO (renowned for construction kits using the iconic LEGO brick) could not reliably and cost-effectively deliver its products to retailers. Its supply chain problems were so severe at the time that LEGO was facing bankruptcy.[15] Jørgen Vig Knudstorp, LEGO's CEO, recognized that fixing the supply chain was essential to business success:

> One of the things that dawned on me when I arrived at the LEGO Group was that basically you have an allocation problem. You are producing 100,000 components every minute, 24 hours a day, 365 days a year. And you have to allocate them in optimal quantities at different sites, so that you can deliver a set of finished products at Walmart in Arkansas on Tuesday at 5:00 p. m. (and not 5:00 a. m.) in optimal order quantity, optimal transportation quantity, optimal manufacturing batches and so on.

LEGO addressed its crisis by leveraging an under-used ERP system to get its supply chain processes under control. That effort was sufficient to turn the company around, but leadership recognized that other processes were still creating costly inefficiencies. To address these problems, LEGO followed its supply chain management initiative with programs that standardized processes related to HR management, manufacturing and product lifecycle management. By 2012, these efforts had provided efficient, reliable core processes and transparent master data, and had improved customer satisfaction. With the operational backbone in place, management could now focus on defining and pursuing a digital strategy—one that focused on developing the builders of tomorrow.

Kaiser Permanente's Operational Backbone. The operational backbone at Kaiser Permanente is built around the electronic health record (EHR). U.S. healthcare providers generate a great deal of data about patients, but as patients interact with multiple caregivers, the data relating to an individual tends to be poorly integrated. Poorly integrated systems and data lead to frustrated patients and clinicians, who must cope with incomplete information, delays in follow-up actions, inaccurate billing and even medical errors. By taking a disciplined approach to managing its EHR processes and patient data, Kaiser Permanente introduced an extraordinary level of operational excellence. In turn, operational excellence positions the company to pursue a digital strategy centered on enhanced collaboration between healthcare providers, patients and their families.

Challenges and Benefits of Operational Backbones. For big old companies, developing an operational backbone is a long, expensive and transformative journey. Our study revealed that even companies with powerful operational backbones need to continuously invest in improvements and extensions. Many leaders told us that their operational backbones provided a slew of operational and strategic benefits, including cost savings, reliability that generated profits and customer satisfaction, scalability following the launch of new products and markets, and the ability to integrate new acquisitions. These types of benefit have helped companies compete for many years. The new—and critically important—benefit of an operational backbone is that it also establishes a strong and stable foundation for introducing new digital products and features. It frees up management attention to pursue digital innovations and ensures that existing business capabilities can be integrated, as needed, with new digitally enabled capabilities.

In our study, we also learned that while an operational backbone is necessary, it is not sufficient for successfully executing a digital strategy. A digital services platform is also needed.

A Digital Services Platform Enables Rapid Innovation

Because an operational backbone is designed for reliability and efficiency, it does not offer the speed and flexibility that companies need for rapid digital innovation. Thus, in addition to an operational backbone, companies also need a digital services platform, which we define as *the technology and business capabilities that facilitate rapid development and implementation of digital innovations.*

The architecture of a digital services platform must facilitate experimentation and provide reusable technology and digital services. Common characteristics of digital services platforms include:

- Digital components that enable a variety of technical and business services (e.g., biometric authentication, customer alerts)
- Platform-as-a-service (PaaS)—a cloud-based hosting environment for storing and accessing loosely connected services
- Repositories for massive amounts of data, whether from public sources (e.g., from social media), purchased or derived from sensors
- Analytics engines for converting data into meaningful insights
- Connections to data and processes that reside in the company's operational backbone.

Recognizing that their operational backbones were not designed for rapid digital innovation, leaders in our study were beginning to design and build digital services platforms.

Kaiser Permanente's Digital Services Platform. Kaiser Permanente launched its "Generation 2 Platform" in June 2014. This platform supports technology components for developing clinical and operational services that can be assembled via a cloud-based self-service portal (21 services at the time of our study, with many more planned). As of 2016, the portal had delivered more than 1,000 systems—all within one day of a request. New systems enable Kaiser Permanente to create new opportunities for caregivers and patients to share data, consult, commiserate and learn. The Generation 2 platform, along with the IT services management model, has greatly improved Kaiser Permanente's capacity to produce digital innovations across clinical and operational departments.

> Our vision is really simple: it's to be as easy as Amazon. You can go to their website; you get recommendations, you know what you can order—you don't need training to use their website. You can click on how much it's going to cost, you can have a payment transaction, and then there's almost perfection in their logistics. Your package is tracked. You get alerts. It's all self-service, self-enabled.
>
> *Mike Sutten, Senior Vice President and Chief Technology Officer, Kaiser Permanente*

LEGO's Digital Services Platform. LEGO is building an "engagement platform" that supports experimentation and rapid introduction (and, as necessary, elimination) of functionality. The engagement platform will allow the company to continuously adapt its digital interface according to the preferences of individual customers, thus providing a personalized digital experience. For LEGO toys with digital capabilities, the platform will facilitate rapid software updates, so that even older kits will provide new experiences. Finally, the platform will provide an environment for working with digital partners on joint product development and for giving approved partners access to LEGO functionality.

Risks of Not Having a Digital Services Platform. A company that fails to design and build a well-defined digital services platform risks falling behind competitors that can rapidly act on digital opportunities. Developers can build digital functionality without a digital services platform but will likely generate a messy collection of individual services (i.e., APIs) that create new risks and hinder reuse. If instead they choose to build digital services on their operational backbone, development will be slow and expensive. Because operational backbones are built to ensure the integrity of transactions and master data, companies carefully manage releases for maintenance, upgrades and enhancements. However, when applied to digital services, this approach will severely limit innovation and, ultimately, competitiveness.

How Big Old Companies Accommodate Both an Operational Backbone and a Digital Services Platform

Regardless of whether a big old company chooses a customer engagement or digitized solutions digital strategy, the most proactive companies in our research needed both an operational backbone and a digital services platform to deliver the efficiency. reliability, speed and agility that the competitive environment demands. Although these two assets support very different business capabilities, they are complementary. Digital services invariably have to link up with the operational backbone. Consider, for example, a company that collects IoT sensor data to help its customers manage the performance of their assets (such as GE's aircraft engines or Schneider Electric's connected energy management products). The digital service will rely on an operational backbone to provide customer data, invoicing and related transaction processing services. Similarly, operational backbones will be of limited value in a digital economy if they prevent companies from bringing innovative new services to market rapidly. Thus, big old companies that successfully transform will be those that can build and leverage both of these technology-enabled assets.

Given the history of technology, one might expect that an important distinction between an operational backbone and a digital services platform would be the technology on which each is built. However, we found that the important distinction is not technological. All 12 companies in our research that had implemented a digital services platform were relying on the cloud—most often a public cloud. And, although most of the 15 companies with an operational backbone had built it on mainframe technologies, these backbones increasingly ran, at least in part, on some form of cloud services.

For example, Ferrovial (a Spanish multinational that builds, manages and operates infrastructure projects and related services) found it could accelerate development of its operational backbone by using software as a service (SaaS) offerings. With this shift to the cloud, Ferrovial's 70,000 employees adopted new standardized HR and purchasing processes in six months. Similarly, Schneider Electric installed a cloud-based CRM system to facilitate cross-selling in its diverse businesses.[16] In 18 months, this system was adopted by 25,000 employees in 100-plus countries, and cross-selling increased by 20%. We expect that many more companies will turn to SaaS to accelerate development of their operational backbones.

Thus, technology differences between operational backbones and digital services platforms are beginning to disappear. Nevertheless, we found that the different characteristics of these two assets give rise to two very different sets of management practices. Table 6.1 summarizes these contrasting requirements.

Companies have different objectives for the two technology-enabled assets. Reliability and efficiency are essential requirements for an operational backbone. Henrik Amsinck, LEGO's CIO, explains that his enterprise platform runs "beneath the human interaction" and is "the IT below all the business processes that run the LEGO Group end to end—all the software and hardware and wiring."

In contrast, Jørgen Vig Knudstorp, LEGO's CEO. highlighted that a digital services platform must facilitate rapid innovation:

> There are new spaces where software development is still at the edge and revolutionary—areas like consumer interaction and new products. What is the next

Table 6.1 Operational Backbones and Digital Services Platforms Require Fundamentally Different Management Practices

	Operational Backbone	*Digital Services Platform*
Management Objective	Business efficiency and technology reliability	Business agility and rapid innovation
Architecture Principles	Standardized end-to-end business processes; transparency into systems; data access	Plug-and-play business and technology components
Data	Single source of truth for transactional data	Massive repositories of sensor/social media/purchased data
Key Processes	Roadmaps; architecture reviews	Cross-functional development; user-centered design
Delivery Method	Fast waterfall/regular software releases/SaaS adoption	Agile and DevOps;[17] use of MVP (minimum viable product) concepts and constant enhancements
Funding	Major project/program investments	Continuous funding by business owners

> upcoming disruptive gaming or consumer-engaging technology that could really impact our business and our business model? That evolution is unlikely to take place anywhere near our [enterprise platform] development center.

Companies pursue these two different objectives by applying different architectural principles to the two technology-enabled assets. Roadmaps and traditional architecture reviews guide the development of an operational backbone's standardized business processes and controlled access to enterprise data. In contrast, a digital services platform relies on cross-functional development teams that apply user-centered design techniques to develop and assemble reusable plug-and-play business and technology components.

In turn, the different goals and design principles lead to two different approaches to development.

Most companies still use traditional development methods to build their operational backbones—although some interviewees mentioned that their traditional waterfall approach is evolving to a more collaborative, scaled-down "fast waterfall." Even using SaaS to build an operational backbone requires each new enterprise process to be deliberately developed and implemented.

In contrast, companies rely on agile development to deliver new services via their digital services platforms. Small cross-functional teams use iterative, agile methods to build and test new services with minimum viable products. Kaiser Permanente has implemented a DevOps model, which requires near-continuous deployment of new code to dramatically reduce cycle times for launching innovations. Amazon introduces new code onto its digital services platform every 11 seconds.[18] It appears that, over time, DevOps capabilities will become a competitive necessity.

The objectives for digital services platforms are also causing traditional funding models to be disrupted. Traditional project funding approval is just too slow for continuous delivery of digital services—hence the rising popularity of pay-for-use models (similar to cloud and vendor servicing models). In several of the companies in our study, funding is shifting to discrete purchases by business units, on an as-needed basis. Kaiser Permanente allows clinical and administrative departments to purchase technology services on its Generation 2 platform directly from the IT organization. Departments are billed monthly and can acquire or discard services depending on their needs and budgets. Most established companies have been building, enhancing and leveraging their operational backbones for many years, so most participants in our research were experienced with the management practices in the left-hand column of Table 6.1. Practices in the right-hand column were newer, however. In general, the business and IT leaders we interviewed were just starting to recognize the need for—and then to adopt—these new practices.

The Impact of Digital Transformation on the IT Unit

As companies build new technology-enabled business capabilities, they introduce fundamental business changes. At most of the companies we studied, these changes had first—and most profoundly—affected the IT unit.

Kaiser Permanente transformed its IT organization by adopting a service-centric operating model. It now designs standard assemblies for IT services chosen by its business users. As part of Schindler's IT transformation, the company created Schindler Digital Business AG, which comprises teams focused on the operational backbone and teams specifically charged with digital innovation by building and maintaining digital services.

> We have put them together as a new organization, fully focusing on this digital innovation part of the company. We need to have these people understanding that this is [their primary role], so when waking up in the morning they should think about digital business and not something else. That was super important: having this clear commitment.
>
> *Michael Nilles, Chief Digital Officer, Schindler Group*

To enable new requirements for integration across vertical business units, some IT units are serving as integrators. At Schneider Electric, for example, the CIO deployed two architects just to facilitate changes involving multiple parts of the company so that the company could implement its digitized solutions strategy:

> I needed to work more as an orchestrator. The business leaders need to design their operating models, but we need some central thinking about how the design of all those businesses would impact Schneider on the whole and how we could purposefully create commonalities across the business to gain more scale.
>
> *Herve Coureil, CIO, Schneider Electric*

As companies create integrated customer experiences and digitized solutions, many are reorganizing their IT units around services. Kaiser Permanente's Chief Technology Officer described the IT services management model as a great shift—from allocating funds to a few high-value projects to funding many small transactions:

> It [the IT services management model] reduces the barrier to entry, so the risk of failure—of it not being successful—is greatly minimized, and the cost to enter is also much lower. You can scale it very, very quickly for huge success. By doing that, we enable a lot more creativity and innovation, and we enable medium-sized projects to go ahead ... In the past you'd have to consult with

everybody because if it didn't work, then your department just blew $50,000, and someone else's pet project didn't get funded.

Mike Sutten, Senior Vice President and Chief Technology Officer, Kaiser Permanente

Although the IT unit was usually the first part of a company to transform, participants in our research also anticipated that changes in the IT unit would eventually be reflected throughout the entire company. At Kaiser Permanente, for example, new digital services enabled more rapid innovations in delivering healthcare. Initially, the company incrementally introduced these changes, but redesign of the larger organization was expected to facilitate more dramatic—and important—changes to healthcare delivery over time. We anticipate that many of the changes our interviewees described will cascade across the entire enterprise. At some companies, that transformation is already underway.

Recommendations for Digital Transformation at Big Old Companies

SMACIT and other digital technologies have created a moment of truth for big old companies: they bring new customer expectations, younger, more nimble competitors and revolutionary managerial approaches. Since past success does not ensure future success, older companies will need to transform to take advantage of digital era opportunities.

Figure 6.1 summarizes our research findings on the digital transformation journeys big old companies will have to undertake. They must choose either a customer engagement or digitized solutions strategy, and this choice will shape priorities for building two essential technology-enabled assets: an operational backbone and a digital services platform. The operational backbone will ensure efficiencies of scale for critical transactional and decision-making capabilities. The digital services platform will ensure rapid innovation of critical digital offerings for customers. These two assets allow a company to execute its chosen digital strategy and, ultimately, to deliver both customer engagement and digitized solutions.

It is not easy for big old companies to let go of legacy systems, processes and cultures. To transform themselves to digital businesses, they must embark on a protracted journey. From our research, we provide five recommendations for mapping a successful journey.

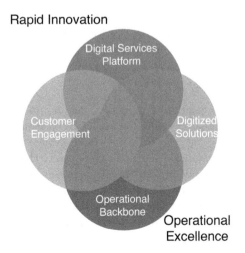

Figure 6.1 Elements of Digital Transformation at a Big Old Company

Define a Digital Strategy

By articulating a digital strategy (whether customer engagement or digitized solutions) a company's leaders can focus employees on clear objectives. With clear direction, a company can start building integrated, difficult-to-replicate capabilities to deliver on that strategy.

Act Now to Invest in an Operational Backbone

Today, investing in an operational backbone is a necessary prerequisite for success in the digital economy. Without such a backbone, a company will lack the foundational capabilities that are needed to enable its digital services platform to provide transaction transparency (e.g., the supply chain) and access to customer data, and to support standardized business processes (e.g., customer account opening, secure access, orders, payments). Just reaching agreement on which operational capabilities are most critical is an extraordinary leadership challenge. To get started in a meaningful way, senior managers should focus on building just one capability critical to the company's digital strategy, such as a well-designed customer database or a supply chain management system. A company without an operational backbone should seek help from cloud providers, vendors, business process outsourcers—anyone who can accelerate the delivery of reusable, efficient and reliable operational capabilities.

Architect a Digital Services Platform

IT leaders can begin to define the architecture for a digital services platform by focusing on a small set of digital innovations they believe will be critical to business success. Once a company has established the data requirements for a small set of critical business components and has set up APIs for accessing the needed data, it can then build (or technology partners can help it build) the infrastructure needed to protect, connect, analyze and support innovative digital services.

Design the Digital Services Platform with Partners in Mind

Our study suggests that effective leaders recognize that customers, suppliers and other stakeholders will want to develop innovative business services or front-end apps that also become integrated capabilities (or common business services). The digital services platform should therefore be designed with those extensions in mind.

Adopt a Services Culture

Business and IT teams will jointly define, design, deliver, price, prioritize, implement, enhance and discard new business services. Companies are beginning to structure themselves around the services they provide. They are empowering service owners to deliver the innovations and efficiency that customers and employees expect. This transition is difficult, so it is prudent for the IT organization to start learning how to manage services—i.e., how to define and deliver IT services to business and IT partners. Organizations that have adopted the ITIL framework (a set of practices for IT service management that focuses on aligning IT services with the needs of business) have long embraced this approach to IT management. Over time, we believe, designing around business services will become the way most companies do business.

Concluding Comments

In an old-school divide-and-conquer approach, managers focused on optimizing the performance of their business unit or function. However, a divide-and-conquer mindset is not well suited to digital transformation. The most exciting SMACIT opportunities integrate products and services across functional, organizational and geographic boundaries. To succeed digitally, big old companies need to embrace new organizational structures and processes that empower their people to collaboratively experiment with technologies and deliver integrated products and services to their customers.

Companies that fail to adopt new technologies and fail to heed the need for digital transformation are likely to be left trailing behind in the dust.

Appendix: Research Methodology

We solicited participants for our study by approaching CIOs in the 85 companies that sponsor the MIT Sloan Center for Information Systems Research (CISR), as well as CIOs in another four companies that we knew were becoming more digital. Boston Consulting Group also invited CIOs from companies that its consultants knew were in the midst of digital transformations.

We asked prospective study participants if they would like to participate in research on how companies were redesigning for the digital economy. While many responded that they were too early in their transformation journeys to participate in the study, and a few were concerned about the confidentiality of their digital initiatives, 25 companies agreed to participate. As shown in the table below, the companies came from a variety of industries. Most were big companies (thousands of employees) and old (only one was less than 25 years old).[19]

Between June 2014 and October 2016, we interviewed three senior executives at each of the 25 participating companies—at least one from the IT organization and at least one from a business function. The interviews were semi-structured and conducted by video or phone, with each taking about an hour. The interviews explored:

1   How the company assesses digital technology opportunities and how its industry is changing
2   The business strategies that the company's leaders were formulating to address digital opportunities
3   Organizational design changes (if any) that the company was implementing to execute its digital strategy.

Research Sample Company Demographics

Company	Industry	Number of Employees	Year Founded
1	Heavy Manufacturing	50,000 99,999	Before 1900
2	Heavy Manufacturing	> 300,000	Before 1900
3	Heavy Manufacturing	50,000 99,999	Before 1900
4	Heavy Manufacturing	10,000 49,999	Before 1900
5	Heavy Manufacturing	10,000 49,999	1950 1999
6	Other Manufacturing	> 300,000	1900 1949
7	Other Manufacturing	100,000 300,000	Before 1900

(continued)

Company	Industry	Number of Employees	Year Founded
8	Other Manufacturing	100,000 300,000	Before 1900
9	Other Manufacturing	100,000 300,000	Before 1900
10	Other Manufacturing	10,000 49,999	1900 1949
11	Other Manufacturing	10,000 49,999	1900 1949
12	Pharmaceuticals	10,000 49,999	1950 1999
13	Civil Engineering	50,000 99,999	1950 1999
14	Financial Services	100,000 300,000	Before 1900
15	Financial Services	10,000 49,999	1900 1949
16	Financial Services	10,000 49,999	Before 1900
17	Life and Health Insurance	< 10,000	Before 1900
18	Software/IT Services	100,000 300,000	1950 1999
19	Software/IT Services	< 10,000	1950 1999
20	Software/IT Services	10,000 49,999	1950 1999
21	Information Services	< 10,000	1950 1999
22	Information Services	< 10,000	Before 1900
23	Healthcare	100,000 300,000	1900 1949
24	Department Stores	< 10,000	1900 1949
25	Government	10,000 49,999	1900 1949

We recorded and transcribed each interview. After coding the transcripts (manually or using the NVivo qualitative data analysis software), we prepared cases or shorter vignettes. For two companies, we conducted additional interviews and wrote full case studies. For the other companies, we summarized the interviews in vignettes written using a standard template (background, strategic context, business model changes, design changes).

We asked each company for permission to publish the case study or vignette. In addition to the two full case studies, nine companies approved their vignettes for publication. The following case studies and vignettes can be downloaded from CISR's website (http://cisr. mit.edu/publications-and-tools/publication-search/five-ways-to-face-digital-disruption/):

- Andersen, P. and Ross, J. W *Transforming the LEGO Group for the Digital Economy*, MIT Sloan CISR Working Paper No. 407, March 2016.
- Beath, C. M., Moloney, K. G. and Ross, J. W. *The Principal: Benefiting from a ServiceOriented Architecture, MIT Sloan CISR Working Paper No. 413, April 2016.*
- Beath, C. M. and Ross, J. W. *USAA: Defining a Digital Experience*, MIT Sloan CISR Working Paper No. 410, April 2016.
- Betancourt, P., Mooney, J. and Ross, J. W. *Digital Innovation at Toyota Motor North America: Revamping the Role of IT*, MIT Sloan CISR Working Paper No. 403, September 2015.
- Fonstad, N. O. and Ross, J. W. *Ferrovial: Leveraging Internal and External Resources to Innovate Competitively, MIT Sloan CISR Working Paper No. 409, April 2016.*
- Kagan, M. H., Sebastian, I. M. and Ross, J. W. *Kaiser Permanente: Executing a Consumer Digital Strategy*, MIT Sloan CISR Working Paper No. 408, March 2016.
- Scantlebury, S. and Ross, J. W. *Schneider Electric: Redesigning Schneider Electric's Operating Model*, MIT Sloan CISR Working Paper No. 412, April 2016.
- Sebastian, I. M., and Ross, J. W. *The Schindler Group: Driving Innovative Services and Integration with Schindler Digital Business AG,* MIT Sloan CISR Working Paper No. 411, April 2016.

After preparing the cases and vignettes, we conducted a cross-case analysis. We recorded the qualitative codes about business model changes, design changes and various other themes in an Excel spreadsheet.

The following table details the status of the companies in our study, in terms of their digital strategy and whether they were building an operational backbone and/or a digital services platform. Companies fall into four groups: 1) Those that had built both an operational backbone and a digital services platform, 2) Those that have an operational backbone, but have not yet started to define a digital services platform, 3) Those that only have a digital services platform and 4) Those with neither (not included in the table). Differential shading in the table highlights differences according to each company's digital strategy (customer engagement, digitized solutions or no digital strategy articulated).

Most digital services platforms are still under construction or in the design phase. In our study, 12 of the 25 companies had created, or were in the process of designing, a digital services platform. In most cases (the ten companies in Group 1), the operational backbone was developed before the digital services platform. The two digital strategy types were equally represented in Group 1 (five companies per strategy type), suggesting that both technology-enabled assets (an operational backbone and a digital services platform) are essential, regardless of whether the digital strategy focuses on digitized solutions or customer engagement.

Group 4, comprising eight companies (4, 8, 14, 17, 18, 21, 22 and 25), had neither an operational backbone nor a digital services platform. This group is not included in the table.

Digital Strategies and Characteristics of the Technology-enabled Assets

Company	Strategy	Operational Backbone Characteristics	Digital Services Platform Characteristics
		Group 1	
1	DS	Global standardized operational processes (packaged software)	Proactive and predictive monitoring with sensor data
3	DS	Global standardized operational processes (packaged software)	Telematics and performance management with sensor data
7	DS	Standardized shared customer relationship management (cloud)	Proactive and predictive monitoring with sensor data
9	DS	Enterprise-wide standardized operational processes—mostly cloud	Aggregation and analysis of health, lifestyle, clinical data from sensors, devices, EHRs
13	DS	Standardized shared CRM; business process outsourcing (cloud)	Digital platform for innovation (in progress)
6	CE	Standardized operational processes; central customer database (mostly cloud)	Customer experience platform with telematics and analytics
11	CE	Global standardized operational processes (mostly packaged)	Customer engagement platform focused on real-time community (in progress)
15	CE	Centralized customer database (home grown)	Personalized, flexible customer experience within a topic area (in progress)
16	CE	Centralized customer database and reusable SOA components (home grown)	Continually adjusted customer experience with analytics and behavioral economics (in progress)

(continued)

Company	Strategy	Operational Backbone Characteristics	Digital Services Platform Characteristics
24	CE	Enterprise-wide EHR system (packaged software)	Same-day delivery of technology services to clinical and operational departments
		Group 2	
20	DS	Standardized key business processes and organizational management system (home grown)	N/A
26	CE	Enterprise-wide standardized operational processes (home grown)	N/A
5	N/A	Global standardized operational processes (packaged software)	N/A
10	N/A	Global standardized operational processes (packaged software)	N/A
12	N/A	Global standardized operational processes (home grown)	N/A
		Group 3	
2	DS	N/A	Performance management with sensor data
19	DS	N/A	Knowledge, data, real-time community services with analytics, facilitation of interactions

DS = digitized solutions strategy CE = customer engagement strategy

N/A indicates that the company did not articulate a digital strategy during our interviews

The five companies in Group 2 had built their operational backbone but had not yet defined a digital services platform, although we believe they were close to doing so. Three of these companies were likely held back by difficulties they were experiencing in choosing a digital strategy. In the other two, opportunities arising from new digital technologies were only beginning to come into focus in their industries; customer expectations had not yet begun to change, so pressure to change was low.

The two companies in Group 3, both with digitized solutions strategies, were each building a digital services platform but had not developed a strong operational backbone. One of these companies, in the software/IT services field, and comparatively young and small in terms of our sample, can be classified as "born digital." Born digital companies invariably build digital services platforms before they build operational backbones because they don't need to manage the scale of a large company. The other company, a manufacturing business, was developing new, innovative solutions that focused on collecting, analyzing and providing insights about equipment. It had decided to move more aggressively on building a digital services platform, which is key to its new business model, than on building an operational backbone. In a way, this company was taking a start-up approach to its new digital solutions.

Seven of the eight companies in Group 4 with neither an operational backbone nor a digital services platform had selected a digital strategy but were struggling to execute on it and to start their digital transformation. Leaders in Group 4 were only beginning to articulate the characteristics of the two technology-enabled assets they would need. Most of these businesses were constrained by their silo structures both in business operations and IT management.

Questions for Discussion

1   What opportunities and threats are presented by digital technologies? How might companies navigate digital transformation?

2   How would you characterize the need for digital transformation in the digital economy? What is the role of digital innovation for competitive advantage? How might companies achieve and leverage digital innovation?

3   What are the implications of digital transformation to organizations? Consider small businesses; large organizations; MNCs; public sector; 'old' companies, and emerging businesses?

4   How could big old companies compete in the digital economy and establish themselves as market and digital leaders?

5   What companies would consider a customer engagement strategy or a digital solutions strategy for their digital transformation? Should companies follow one strategy or a combination of strategies? Could success in one strategy lead to success in other strategies?

6   What is required for a smooth execution of digital strategy and transformation? How might companies develop the needed capabilities?

Notes

1   This acronym is pronounced "smack it"—as in, score a digital strategy home run when you SMACIT out of the baseball park. There are more digital technologies than implied by this acronym, including artificial intelligence, blockchain, robotics and virtual reality. SMACIT is intended as shorthand for the entire set of powerful, readily accessible digital technologies.

2   For more information about these companies' digital innovations and their leaders' expectations, see https://www.ge.com/digital/indus-trial-internet and http://www.usa.philips.com/healthcare/innovation/about-health-suite.

3   El Sawy, O. A., Kræmmergaard, P., Amsinck, H. and Vinther, A. L. "How LEGO Built the Foundation and Enterprise Capabilities for Digital Leadership," *MIS Quarterly Executive* (15:2), June 2016, pp. 143-166.

4   The annual reports of successful, well-established companies like BNY Mellon, Kaiser Permanente, Aetna, GE, Schneider Electric, Philips and the Schindler Group highlight their continued dependence on traditional sources of revenue even as they make significant investments in digital initiatives.

5   In this article, we reference initiatives at Kaiser Permanente, Schindler Group, LEGO Group, Schneider Electric, Ferrovial and USAA. The Appendix includes links to our published case studies and shorter vignettes for these and other companies included in our study.

6   For more on developing digital strategies, see Ross, J. W., Sebastian, I. M. and Beath, C. M. "How to Develop a Great Digital Strategy," *MIT Sloan Management Review*, November 8, 2016, available at http://sloanreview.mit.edu/article/how-to-develop-a-great-digital-strategy/.

7   We distinguish digital strategies from more traditional IT strategies—a digital strategy being the company's high-level business strategy, while an IT strategy is set to enable a business strategy. This distinction is also made in Bharadwaj, A., El Sawy, O. A., Pavlou, P. A. and Venkatraman, A. "Digital Business Strategy: Towards a Next Generation of Insights," *MIS Quarterly* (37:2), June 2013, pp. 471482. IT strategies are thoroughly reviewed in Peppard, J. and Ward, J. "Beyond Strategic Information Systems: Towards an IS Capability," *Journal of Strategic Information Systems* (13:2), July 2004, pp. 167194. For a broad review of different types of technology-related strategies, see Chen, D. Q., Mocker, M., Preston, D. S. and Teubner, A. "Information Systems Strategy: Reconceptualization, Measurement, and Implications," *MIS Quarterly* (34:2), June 2010, pp. 233-259.

8   See Goldsmith, J. "An Interview with George Halvorson. The Kaiser Permanente Renaissance, and Health Reform's Unfinished Business," *Health Affairs*, September 30, 2014, available at http://www.healthaffairs.org/blog/2014/09/30/an-interview-with-georgehalvorson-the-kaiser-permanente-renaissance-and-health-reformsunfinished-business/.

9   At many companies we studied, net promoter score (NPS) is the key metric used to track customer satisfaction. Information on Kaiser Permanente's 2016 NPS can be found in "Kaiser Permanente Again Ranks No. 1 in Customer Loyalty", *Kaiser Permanente Feature Story*, June 29, 2016, available at https://share.kaiserpermanente.org/article/kaiser-permanente-ranks-no-1-customer-loyalty/

10 For more on how digital technologies are transforming companies and competition, see Porter, M. E. and Heppelmann, J. E. "How Smart, Connected Products are Transforming Companies," *Harvard Business Review* (93:10), October 2015, pp. 96-114; and Porter, M. E. and Heppelmann, J. E. "How Smart, Connected Products are Transforming Competition," *Harvard Business Review* (92:11), November 2014, pp. 64-88.

11 For more information, see http://www.schindlerportna.com/

12 For more information on digitized process platforms, see Ross, *J.W.,Weill, P. and Robertson, D.* Enterprise Architecture as Strategy: Creating a Foundation for Business Execution, *Harvard Business Press, 2006.*

13 For more on how standardization and integration of processes has paid off, see Bradley, R., Pratt, R., Byrd, T. A. and Simmons, L. "The Role of Enterprise Architecture in the Quest for IT Value," *MIS Quarterly Executive* (10:2), June 2011 pp. 19-27; Tamm, T., Seddon, P. B., Shanks, G., Reynolds, R. and Frampton, K. "How an Australian Retailer Enabled Business Transformation Through Enterprise Architecture," *MIS Quarterly Executive* (14:4), December 2015, pp. 181-193; and Venkatesh, V., Bala, H., Venkatraman, S. and Bates, J. "Enterprise Architecture Maturity: The Story of the Veterans Health Administration," *MIS Quarterly Executive* (6:2), June 2007, pp. 79-90.

14 The fact that 60% of the companies in our sample have a value-adding operational backbone suggests that we were successful in recruiting technologically mature companies for our study. Our recent survey of 171 senior IT leaders found that only 28% of established companies have value-adding operational backbones. See Ross, J. W., Sebastian, I. M and Jha, L., and the Technology Advantage Practice of The Boston Consulting Group, *Designing Digital Organizations—Summary of Survey Findings*, MIT CISR Working Paper No. 415, February 2017, available at http://cisr.mit.edu/blog/documents/2017/02/28/mitcisrwp415ddosurveyreportrosssebastianbeathjhabcg.pdf/.

15 For details on LEGO's business turnaround, see Robertson, D. C. *Brick by Brick*, Crown Business Books, 2013.

16 *See* Karunakaran, A., Mooney, J. and Ross, J. W. *Accelerating Global Digital Platform Deployment Using the Cloud: A Case Study of Schneider Electric's "Bridge Front Office" Program*, MIT Sloan CISR Working Paper No. 399, January 2015.

17 DevOps, a compound of "development" and "operations," is a software development and delivery approach designed for high velocity. One company's overview of DevOps can be reviewed at https://aws.amazon.com/devops/what-is-devops/.

18 This number was reported in Bort, J. "Former EMC exec: Google's cloud efforts against Amazon are like 'a Microsoft phone'—too little too late," *Business Insider*, August 11, 2016, available at http://www.businessinsider.com/google-vs-amazon-in-cloud-is-like-a-microsoft-phone-tech-exec-says-2016-8. It may be more frequent by now.

19 We have used broad ranges in the table to protect company confidentiality. Most companies in our sample were old. The mean and median ages were 104 years and 107 years, respectively. Only one company was founded after 1990. The youngest was 18 years old; the oldest was 184 years old. Most of them were big companies, with mean and median number of employees of 82,297 and 27,900 respectively. Only four had less than 10,000 employees. The smallest had over 7,500 employees, and the largest had over 344,000.

Further Reading

Chanias, S., Myers, M. D., Hess, T. (2019). Digital transformation strategy making in pre-digital organizations: The case of a financial services provider. *The Journal of Strategic Information Systems, 28*(1), 17–33.

Vial, G. (2019). Understanding digital transformation: A review and a research agenda. *The Journal of Strategic Information Systems, 28*(1), 118–144.

Chapter 7

Thomas Hess, Christian Matt, Alexander Benlian and Florian Wiesböck

OPTIONS FOR FORMULATING A DIGITAL TRANSFORMATION STRATEGY

Digital Transformation Is a High-Priority Management Challenge

INTEGRATING AND EXPLOITING new digital technologies is one of the biggest challenges that companies currently face. No sector or organization is immune to the effects of digital transformation. The market-changing potential of digital technologies is often wider than products, business processes, sales channels or supply chains—entire business models are being reshaped and frequently overturned.[1]

As a result, digital transformation has become a high priority on leadership agendas, with nearly 90% of business leaders in the U.S. and U.K. expecting IT and digital technologies to make an increasing strategic contribution to their overall business in the coming decade.[2] The question is no longer when companies need to make digital transformation a strategic priority—this tipping point has passed—but how to embrace it and use it as a competitive advantage.

Faced with the digital transformation challenge and the need to remain competitive in their industries, business leaders must formulate and execute strategies that embrace the implications of digital transformation and drive better operational performance. Unfortunately, there are many recent examples of organizations that have been unable to keep pace with the new digital reality. Prominent examples include the bankruptcy of the movie-rental company Blockbuster and the sale of the Washington Post to Jeff Bezos, founder of Amazon— largely resulting from those firms' inability to rapidly develop and implement new digitally based business models.

Digital transformation is concerned with the changes digital technologies can bring about in a company's business model, which result in changed products or organizational structures or in the automation of processes. These changes can be observed in the rising demand for

Internet-based media, which has led to changes of entire business models (for example in the music industry).

Digital transformation is a complex issue that affects many or all segments within a company. Managers have to simultaneously balance the exploration and exploitation of their firms' resources to achieve organizational agility[3]—a necessary condition for the successful transformation of their businesses. At present, managers often lack clarity about the different options and elements they need to consider in their digital transformation endeavors. As a consequence, they risk failing to consider important elements of digital transformation or disregarding solutions that are more favorable to their firms' specific situations, which could have unintended adverse consequences.

Recent work in academia has been largely concerned with providing guidance on certain aspects of digital transformation; it has not addressed a holistic approach to the development of a company-wide digital transformation strategy.[4] However, the Digital Transformation Framework (DTF) represents a first step in this direction.[5] This conceptual framework for formulating a digital transformation strategy identifies the four key dimensions of every digital transformation endeavor:

1   The use of technologies reflects a firm's approach and capability to explore and exploit new digital technologies.
2   Changes in value creation reflects the influence of digital transformation on a firm's value creation.
3   Structural changes refer to the modifications in organizational structures, processes and skill sets that are necessary to cope with and exploit new technologies.
4   The financial aspects dimension relates to both a firm's need for action in response to a struggling core business as well as its ability to finance a digital transformation endeavor.

While the building blocks of a digital transformation strategy are known, clearly specified guidelines for managers on how to approach digital transformation and implement a well-defined digital transformation strategy are lacking. The purpose of this article is to provide those guidelines. Based on insights from three case studies of firms that have recently undergone successful digital transformation endeavors, we have derived 11 strategic questions that CIOs and other managers responsible for the digital transformation of their businesses must ask themselves. We have grouped these questions along the four dimensions of the DTF and provide possible answers for each of them through descriptions of the case study firms' actions and their reasoning for adopting a particular option.

The guidance offered in this article seeks to prevent managers from missing any critical decision and to assist them in selecting the most effective options to successfully conduct digital transformation and prepare their firms for the digital future.

The Distinctive Nature of Digital Transformation Strategy

The purpose of the journey toward digital transformation is to reap the benefits of digital technologies, such as productivity improvements, cost reductions and innovation. A clear strategy for deploying and exploiting digital technologies is crucial for future business success. There is, however, disagreement on the relationship between digital strategy and business and IT strategies. Some argue that a digital strategy should be formulated and implemented as a part of a firm's IT strategy. In the context of digital transformation, the argument is that a firm's IT strategy can evolve from a functional strategy (which traditionally has been subordinate to business strategy) to an organizational strategy that leverages a firm's digital resources to create differential value.[6]

Others take the view that such an important and challenging strategic issue as digital transformation demands a standalone strategy that is not part of another organizational or functional strategy. For them, a digitally enriched IT strategy is not the right answer to the problem:

> Everyone thinks they have a digital strategy these days. But while your company may have a business or IT strategy that incorporates digital technology, an IT strategy does not equal a digital strategy. Why? Because most IT strategies treat technology in isolation[7]

IT strategies typically concentrate on the efficient management of IT infrastructure and application systems. What they often lack is the transformational, business-centric orientation that is needed to realize the potential within a company's business model, products, processes and organizational structures made possible by the advent of new digital technologies.

The necessary coordination and alignment of a firm's many strategies in the light of digital transformation has led some researchers to argue for a *digital business strategy* that combines IT and business strategy.[8] However, while a digital business strategy may indicate a firm's vision for future digital business models, it typically does not provide guidelines on the actual transformational steps. On the other hand, a *digital transformation strategy* signposts the way toward digital transformation and guides managers through the transformation process resulting from the integration and use of digital technologies. A digital transformation strategy impacts a company more comprehensively than an IT strategy and addresses potential effects on interactions across company borders with clients, competitors and suppliers. Thus, we argue that firms need a standalone digital transformation strategy. Unfortunately, the accumulated knowledge from previous research and best practice on IT strategies cannot be simply transferred to digital transformation strategies.

To ensure they capture the business value of digital transformation, companies should carefully formulate a digital transformation strategy that coordinates the many independent threads of digital transformation and helps them navigate the complexity and ambiguity of identifying their own digital "sweet spots." Such a digital agenda has to be aligned with other operational or functional strategies and can act as a unifying concept for integrating all coordination, prioritization and implementation efforts of a firm's digital transformation efforts.

To illustrate the concepts of formulating and executing a digital transformation strategy, we describe how three German media companies have approached digital transformation. (See the Appendix for an overview of the research methodology and the interviews conducted.)

The Three Case Companies

The three German media companies we chose for the case studies of digital transformation are:

- ProSiebenSat.1 Media SE (referred to as "P7S1"), a large TV broadcaster with a turnover of €2.6 billion in 2014 ($2.95 billion)[9] and more than 3,500 employees. It is one of the leading TV enterprises in Europe. Munich-based P7S1 operates in 12 countries and owns 15 TV stations, which reach more than 42 million households. P7S1 was founded in 2000 and originated from the former Kirch Group, which established itself as one of two large TV companies in Germany after regulators opened up the market to private TV stations.

- Mittelbayerische Verlag AG (Mittelbayerische) is a small print publisher based in Regensburg, Germany. Its main product is the regional daily newspaper *Mittelbayerische Zeitung*, which has a strong focus on regional content and offerings. Mittelbayerische was founded in 1945 and currently employs about 500 people. With an average daily circulation in 2014 of approximately 110,000, *Mittelbayerische Zeitung* is the most popular newspaper in the area surrounding Regensburg.
- Ravensburger AG, which was founded in 1883, is a mid-sized games publisher that is headquartered in Ravensburg, Germany. Ravensburger remains a family-owned business with about 1,600 employees and a turnover of approximately €359 million in 2013. In addition to the "leisure and promotion service" division and a fairly new "digital products" division, the company has two main divisions: "games, puzzles and arts/crafts" (€286 million turnover) and "children's and youth books" (€9 million turnover). Brand awareness of Ravensburger is high in the Western European games and puzzles market.

Each of these companies has, within the last decade, systematically approached digital transformation and has achieved success in its efforts. At present, over 20% of P7S1's revenues derive from digital business models. At Ravensburger, hybrid products that enrich traditional analog or physical products with digital content have successfully stabilized its core businesses: board games and print publishing. The CEO of Mittelbayerische claims that it owes its leading market position to the decision to actively embrace digital technologies. However, digital transformation in each company is ongoing and will likely occupy them over the next few years. Table 7.1 provides an overview of the three case companies.

Table 7.1 Overview of the Three Cases

	P7S1	*Mittelbayerische*	*Ravensburger*
Core business	TV broadcaster	News publisher	Board games and print publisher
Size	4,200 employees $2.9 billion (2014)	500 employees 110,000 units per day (2014)	1,600 employees €359 million (2013)
Headquarters	Munich (Germany)	Regensburg (Germany)	Ravensburg (Germany)
Founded	2000[10]	1945	1883
Market focus	Europe	Regional	Europe, U.S.
Digital transformation overview	From linear TV broadcasting to video-on-demand and online gaming, and mergers & acquisitions	From print to digital publishing	From analog to digitally enhanced products (books, puzzles and games)
Start of digital transformation	2011	2010	2009
Digital transformation success	20% of revenues through digital business	Defense of market leadership through digital enrichment of analog core product	Digitally enriched products successfully stabilized core business
Organizational scope of digital transformation	Company-wide	Mostly products	Products and processes

The selection of these three companies reflects our aim to cover a wide portion of the media industry in terms of size (a large international corporation vs. mid-cap vs. small) and value focus (print and broadcasting representing two of the media industry's classic major business segments and gaming representing a specialist field). We regard size and value focus as crucial dimensions when investigating digital transformation. Size affects every type of transformation. Moreover, a firm's main product line will most likely play a crucial role in its digital transformation, because the integration of digital technologies into products is one of the key aspects of digital transformation. Although the chosen case companies differ significantly in, for example, how capital requirements or how digital technologies can alter their core products, their breadth allows us to explore a more comprehensive set of options and requirements for digital transformation.

We chose to study media companies because this industry has been a bellwether of the digital revolution and one of the pioneering industries that has undergone dramatic—if not existence-threatening—changes caused by the advent of digital technologies. Further, we decided to focus on media companies with an emphasis on content aggregation, which is one of the classic functions of media companies.

Digital Transformation Strategy at P7S1

Business Drivers for Digital Transformation

P7S1's roots lie in the TV business. When the company's managers first considered the opportunities and threats arising from new digital technologies, the core business was thriving and highly profitable. Thus, the need for immediate action was not as strong as in other branches of the media industry. Nevertheless, managers recognized the potential of digital technologies—both for P7S1's current activities and for new business opportunities. This led to the decision to pursue a two-pronged approach to exploring and exploiting new technologies. One was to digitally enrich the company's TV portfolio. The other was to actively seek out new digitally enabled business models to diversify its business.

Digital Transformation Outcome: Developing New Business Areas

Ten years ago, digital technologies primarily had a supporting function at P7S1 and were mainly used to optimize business processes and provide an efficient infrastructure. Now, however, P7S1 perceives digital technologies as enablers of innovative products and services. To foster the transformation of ideas into new products and services, a dedicated innovation lab was established in 2012. Thus far, though, P7S1 has not sought to be a technology leader but has focused its digital activities on branding and customer interaction via established technologies.

The impact of digital technologies has been mainly on P7S1's products and services, especially its TV business, where digital transformation has led to, for example, video-on-demand or gaming content related to TV content. Production processes have also become increasingly digital. In 2013, P7S1 earned €484 million from digital products and services, approximately 19% of its total turnover. In addition to digitally enhanced broadcast offerings, P7S1 is also active in business segments that are not directly related to content, such as e-commerce. These activities include websites that supplement linear TV programing (from online text to mobile offerings), content platforms ("video-on-demand") such as maxdome and MyVideo, and online games portals such as SevenGames.de. Another area of digital investments is in online travel services. In this area, P7S1 generates earnings through revenue sharing and advertising.

P7S1 generates revenues from its digital products and services both indirectly via advertising and directly via paid content, the sales of virtual goods within online games, or through "freemium" models (providing a free version with a basic functional scope and a paid version that creates additional value; an example is the music video streaming platform AMPYA). Synergies between digital and traditional offerings are actively fostered. For instance, content from traditional TV channels is reused in digital offerings, users are referred from traditional to digital products and vice versa, and cross-media advertising campaigns are conducted. The latter, for example, has been used for the casting format of "Germany's Next Topmodel," a reality TV show, which is complemented by content platforms, web services and corresponding events.

P7S1's main focus, however, remains on content creation, aggregation and distribution (via its TV business). Additionally, though, it strives to expand its revenues from the management of content platforms and e-commerce. Digital activities are expected to become the second pillar of P7S1 in addition to its traditional TV business.

P7S1's pure digital business unit is led by a board member and is supported strongly by the CEO. Most of P7S1's digital activities are organized within a separate business unit called "Digital & Adjacent." P7S1 establishes a new business internally (if necessary, in the form of a joint venture) or takes over startups at an early stage. For the latter, the company has launched a dedicated incubator ("ProSiebenSat.1 Accelerator"), which offers incentives to startups, often in the form of free advertising time on P7S1's TV channels in exchange for equity participation ("media-for-equity-program").

Because P7S1 sees its digital activities becoming a second pillar, complementing its TV business, a large share of corporate investments is made within the digital area. These investments are financed internally. The primary focus of the investments has been and remains on mergers and acquisitions activities where P7S1 acquires and develops digital businesses that complement P7S1's traditional TV business.

Digital Transformation Strategy at Mittelbayerische

Business Drivers for Digital Transformation

According to Mittelbayerische's CEO, decreasing newspaper sales and the resulting financial pressure forced the entire management team to recognize the threats and opportunities from the ongoing digital revolution and the need for action. As a consequence, management decided to follow a careful, deliberate path into the digital world. In addition to introducing of an e-paper and an app, and including digital topics among the newspaper's leading themes, the company developed an Internet-based map service (following the idea of Google Maps) centered around Regensburg, where it is based. The map includes location-specific information such as kindergartens, gas stations, playgrounds and Wi-Fi hot spots.

Digital Transformation Outcome: Exploiting Selected Digital Opportunities

Mittelbayerische's underlying motivation in its approach to digital transformation was to defend its position as the region's No. 1 provider of local news and information. Hence, it decided to maintain its business focus on content creation, accompanied by selected digital add-ons. In general, this newspaper publisher has taken a pragmatic approach to digital technologies. It does not have a department focused on innovation; instead, it introduces established technologies that complement its existing product portfolio. Management regards the role of digital technologies as supporting existing products and services or as a resource to reengineer processes.

To date, Mittelbayerische's digitally enabled diversifications have been rather limited. After introducing online sales channels for its print products, its only diversification into the digital world was to make its classic analog products available via digital channels. These digital activities were fully integrated into the firm's core business and affect mostly production processes and, to some extent, product and service offerings. To date, Mittelbayerische's digital offerings comprise an e-paper and app version of the newspaper and a device-adaptive website. At present, between 10% and 20% of revenues come from digital products and services. Revenues from digital products complement revenues from the print business. Mittelbayerische continues to target traditional publishing revenues from advertising and paid content, with revenue from advertising strongly driven by local offerings.

Mittelbayerische believes that the competencies needed for digital transformation should come from within the company and has established a thorough personal development program that helps foster the necessary digital mindset and skill set among existing staff. The company has also established trainee programs and an integrated university degree program in various business units to attract graduates, young professionals and, above all, "digital natives."

Mittelbayerische's CEO made selective digital transformation a strategic priority and is responsible for the publisher's digital transformation strategy. However, the company has very limited ability to allocate financial resources to the program. Traditionally low margins in the print business constrain the firm's options in this dimension of the Digital Transformation Framework.

Digital Transformation Strategy at Ravensburger

Business Drivers for Digital Transformation

Two decades ago, Ravensburger had already made its first, and admittedly very early, attempt to digitally transform its business. Ravensburger Interactive was launched in the 1990s to develop new digital products and services across all of Ravensburger's business segments. However, it was shut down after ten years because its activities in this area were too early and were unsuccessful. However, since the 1990s, consumer digital technologies in general and mobile technologies in particular have become ubiquitous, especially among Ravensburger's main target group: children.

At present, Ravensburger's core business (analog games and books) is still profitable and appears to be stable. Nevertheless, the company has begun to follow its customers, who are moving toward digital offerings. In addition to introducing electronic sales channels for its products, Ravensburger has entered the e-book and online gaming markets. Additionally, the publisher has begun to develop complementary digital products that enrich its existing analog products.

Digital Transformation Outcome: Smartly Enriching the Core Business

Ravensburger displays a differentiated view on digital technologies. Although IT remains a support function for its core business activities, IT is regarded as a main driver of innovation within the company's digital business unit. This unit has specialists in digital gaming and digital books whose role is to ensure the business remains at the forefront of technological development by identifying emerging digital technologies at an early stage of development that are relevant to the company's core business. These specialists then discuss the opportunities and risks posed by these technologies with the relevant managers in regular workshops.

Thus far, Ravensburger has largely refrained from deploying digital technologies on non-content related business segments and instead has focused on enriching analog products with digital content. The most popular innovation is "tiptoi®," a digital pen that offers additional audio information when touching selected areas of a book or educational game. This pen was developed as a proprietary solution by Ravensburger and exemplifies the liberal attitude of the company toward new technologies and IT development. Ravensburger also offers some digital content, such as online gaming. It has also digitized its production processes for books and offers e-books.

In the future, Ravensburger plans to create, aggregate and publish content (primarily books and games). At the core of Ravensburger's current efforts to generate revenues from digital technologies are online "hybrid products," such as the tiptoi pen, which provide digital content for the firm's most important analog products (books and games). Approximately 20% of Ravensburger's digital revenues are generated by these products. As well as developing hybrid products, Ravensburger focuses its digital transformation activities on providing broader support for business processes in the gaming and books segments. The implementation of ERP and CRM systems has been followed by the introduction of a modern content-management system.

Organizationally, Ravensburger's hybrid products are located in the two core business units: books and games. New digital products and services that are less closely related to the core business are organized in a dedicated subsidiary called "Ravensburger Digital." This business unit was established in 2009, employs 20 to 25 people and has a yearly turnover of approximately €1 million. Ravensburger Digital has been deliberately separated from the core business and is physically separated from the headquarters to make it more appealing to applicants with different skill sets and to foster innovation. Ravensburger Digital largely develops online games that are not related to any of the company's traditional games. The CEOs of Ravensburger Digital and the core business orchestrate all digital activities. The top priority in managing Ravensburger's cash flow is to stabilize its core business. A substantial proportion of any internal surplus is invested in the company's digital initiatives.

Guidelines for Formulating a Digital Transformation Strategy

Each of the three German media companies have chosen a different approach to digital transformation, depending on their individual business models and strategic visions for digital technologies. Together, these three cases provide a rich picture of the different options for formulating a digital transformation strategy.

Based on insights from these cases, we have derived guidelines for managers in the form of the strategic questions they have to address when embarking on digital transformation. We have grouped the questions along the four dimensions of the Digital Transformation Framework described earlier: *use of technologies*, *changes in value creation*, *structural changes* and *financial aspects*. For each dimension, we list the strategic questions about digital transformation that management must address and provide a set of strategic options from which management can choose as they answer the questions.[11] In combination, these questions cover all relevant aspects of a digital transformation strategy.

Use of Technologies Dimension

Digital transformation is driven by the advent of digital technologies. Thus, a company's approach to using new digital technologies is an essential dimension of a digital transformation strategy. This dimension requires that managers assess the role of their IT departments

Table 7.2 Strategic Questions about the Use of New Technologies

Strategic Question	Strategic Options	Description	P7S1	MB	RB	Impetus for the Digital Transformation Outcome
How significant is your firm's IT to achieving strategic goals?	Enabler	IT is an enabler of strategic goals	x		x	• P7S1 regards IT as a core function and understands the potential of digital technologies for business success. • Ravensburger actively follows its customers into the digital world and generates new customer experiences through the combination of analog and digital content.
	Supporter	IT is seen as a support function to reach strategic goals		x		• Mittelbayerische's core business focus remains on the production and distribution of local news. Technology is merely a means for efficient processes.
	Innovator	The firm is at the forefront of innovating new technologies				
How ambitious is your firm's approach to new digital technologies?	Early adopter	The firm actively looks for opportunities to implement new technologies	(x)		x	• Through its mergers and acquisitions activities, P7S1 engages with early-stage technologies. • Ravensburger introduces early-stage technologies to foster the development of innovative, digitally enriched content.
	Follower	The firm relies on well-established solutions	x	x		• P7S1 and Mittelbayerische emphasize process stability and seek to minimize risks following the implementation of new technologies.

and how proactive and innovative they are in their approach toward new technologies. Table 7.2 summarizes the options available when answering these questions and describes how and why the three media companies have chosen the options.

Question 1: How Significant is Your Firm's IT to Achieving Strategic Goals? Emerging digital technologies can create new opportunities for firms and may be crucial for securing a competitive advantage. Nevertheless, the significance of IT and its strategic role varies substantially across companies.

The cases reveal that some firms regard IT as an enabler of new business opportunities. Others, however, use IT to support and fulfill defined business requirements and improvements. Thus, in some firms the initial driver of change is a new digital technology, whereas in others business issues drive the change process, and a suitable technology must be identified to support the change.

An example of the use of IT as an enabler of new opportunities is a cutting-edge content-management system that provides media companies with the ability to easily deliver content via different channels and across countries. Companies with an enabling perspective of IT must carefully monitor digital technologies and identify their potential to boost current business operations or enable the creation of new products and services. In companies with a supporting perspective, digital technologies could assist in functional business operations or in ensuring compliance with regulatory requirements. For instance, determining and verifying a user's location is necessary to ensure that content is available only in licensed regions.

Question 2: How Ambitious is Your Firm's Approach to New Digital Technologies? Regardless of the strategic role of IT, companies can take different approaches to the process of diffusing new digital technologies. More conservative firms may adopt established and widely used technology solutions, while others may deploy new technology solutions at the early stages of their development. A more aggressive approach is to act as an innovator and create and introduce new technology solutions into markets.

The cases suggest that a firm's digital technology ambition is largely determined by its unique context. However, when assessing where they should ideally be in the technology ambition spectrum, firms should consider their existing technological competence, the extent of their technology spending and their size.

Many media companies have traditionally been followers in terms of their technology ambitions, but new Internet-based technologies have created opportunities, and likewise the need for them to act more rapidly to remain ahead of the curve. For example, creating content platforms can reveal new market potential across countries. Similarly, new digital technologies can be used to build strong business ecosystems and to develop proprietary standards, which can be a means of restricting competitors' access to customers. Acting too late may make it difficult to catch up with competitors and establish a company's own standards. However, not all media companies have the technological competencies required to become leaders in technology development or use—nor do they need to do so. Instead, they should carefully assess their technological ambitions and align them with IT investment decisions.

Changes in Value Creation Dimension

Changes in value creation derive from the way in which digital technologies alter a firm's business model. At media companies, changes in value creation relate mainly to the degree to which a company has already diversified its business into the digital world, how it plans to generate revenues from digital technologies and to its main business focus after a digital transformation. Table 7.3 summarizes the three strategic questions that managers must ask about the changes in value creation dimension and the strategic options available when answering these questions, and describes how and why the three media companies have chosen a particular option.

Table 7.3 Strategic Questions about Changes in Value Creation

Strategic Question	Strategic Options	Description	P7S1	MB	RB	Impetus for the Digital Transformation Outcome
How "digital" is your interface to the customer?	Electronic sales channels	Distribution of analog products over digital channels		x	x	• Both Mittelbayerische and Ravensburger have recognized the importance of e-commerce for the sales of their analog products (e.g., print newspapers or analog games).
	Cross-media	Extension of the classic product to digital channels	x	x	x	• While the extension to digital channels at P7S1 and Ravensburger represented a step toward even more digital business models, Mittelbayerische's intention to keep its focus on print content demanded only a limited extension into digital business models (i.e., cross-media offerings).
	Enriched media	Digital enrichment of the classic product	x		x	• Both Ravensburger and P7S1 have understood the opportunities of digital technologies to create new business areas through complementary products based on the enrichment of their classic products (TV and board games, and print, respectively).
	Content platforms	New content-based offerings	x			• P7S1 has decided to benefit from its know-how in content creation, aggregation and distribution and to engage in the management of content platforms.
	Extended business	New offerings without direct relation to content (analog/digital)	x			• Given the opportunities provided by digital technologies, P7S1 has decided to further leverage its competencies and enter adjacent markets.
	Paid content	Revenues from the user for access to or the use of content	x	x	x	• All three companies have decided to keep their existing (i.e., pre-digital transformation) revenue streams through paid content.

Strategic Question	Strategic Options	Description	P7S1	MB	RB	Impetus for the Digital Transformation Outcome
How will you create revenue from future business operations?	Freemium	Revenues from add-ons based on a free basic product	x			• Through its mergers and acquisitions activities, P7S1 engages in the management of content platforms.
	Advertising	Selling of attention	x	x		• P7S1 and Mittelbayerische have decided to sustain existing (i.e., pre-digital-transformation) revenue streams through advertising.
	Selling complementary products	Revenues from products complementary to the core business	x		x	• P7S1 selectively uses complementary digital products to increase the attractiveness of its core business (sales of merchandise complementing TV shows). • Ravensburger has decided to introduce digital products that are complementary to the core business to meet customer demand for digital products and, simultaneously, strengthen analog products.
What will your future business scope be?	Content creation	Creation of content (analog or digital)	x	x	x	• All three companies have decided to continue to create, aggregate and distribute content (i.e., continue their "pre-digital transformation" activities).
	Content aggregation	Aggregation of content (analog or digital)	x	x	x	
	Content distribution	Distribution of content (analog or digital)	x	x	x	
	Content platforms	Management of content platforms	x			• P7S1's management has decided to leverage the firm's core competency (the management of content) and engage in the emerging market for content platforms.
	Other	Other business models	x			• P7S1 engages in strategic mergers & acquisitions (both as financial investments and to obtain access to new technologies/competencies).

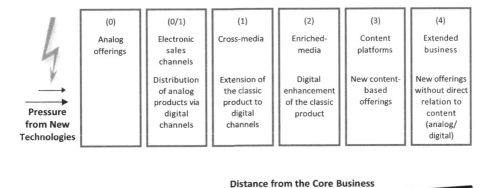

	(0) Analog offerings	(0/1) Electronic sales channels Distribution of analog products via digital channels	(1) Cross-media Extension of the classic product to digital channels	(2) Enriched-media Digital enhancement of the classic product	(3) Content platforms New content-based offerings	(4) Extended business New offerings without direct relation to content (analog/digital)

Pressure from New Technologies

Distance from the Core Business

Figure 7.1 Levels of Digital Diversification at Media Companies

Question 3: How "Digital" is Your Interface to the Customer? Instead of simply transforming previously analog products and services into the digital world, many firms want or need to exploit the possibilities of digital technologies and enter new business areas. Managers have to consider the extent to which their firm should diversify its business into the digital world. For a media company, this means considering how far away it should operate from its traditional core business (see Figure 7.1). The levels of diversification shown in Figure 7.1 allow a media company to assess both its current level of digital transformation and the levels for possible future digital transformation endeavors. The optimal level of diversification is determined by a company's financial background and size.

In the three cases, P7S1 shows the highest level of diversification (having reached Level 4—"Extended business"). Ravensburger's and Mittelbayerische's diversification ends at "Enrichedmedia" (Level 2) and "Cross-media" (Level 1), respectively.

Hence, the cases imply that company size is a major determinate of the level of digital diversification that can be achieved. P7S1, a large corporation, has diversified its traditional business and actively leverages the many possibilities offered by digital technologies in a consumer-centric market. Smaller and medium-sized firms such as Ravensburger or Mittelbayerische have emphasized the stability of their core businesses in their digital transformation efforts.

Question 4: How Will You Create Revenue from Future Business Operations? Finding new sources of revenue is crucial for future business success and therefore an indispensable element of a digital transformation strategy. When designing new digital products and services, companies must consider how they can create value and therefore generate revenue. In the media industry, for example, even if a company's physical and digital products or services are not significantly different, new revenue models may be needed to remain competitive in the online world. For instance, when newspapers were made available in a digital format, most publishers found they could not charge customers similar amounts to those charged for the print versions.

All three cases (as well as many other companies in the media industry) generate revenues from digital business models primarily through advertising and paid content. However, the characteristics of advertising are different in the online world, where advertising is currently dominated by powerful Internet search engines. In addition, the widespread adoption of mobile devices with small screens places additional pressure on advertising revenues.

Some media companies have tried to overcome these constraints by extending their value-chain activities and generating transaction revenues. These companies not only seek to provide paid content but also encourage product purchases linked to their content. Every time a product is sold, the media company receives a commission. In addition, digital technologies have further simplified the differentiation between pricing tariffs, with the "freemium" revenue model being increasingly adopted by media companies.

Question 5: What Will Your Future Business Scope Be? Media companies' business activities traditionally center on content creation, aggregation and distribution. But digital technologies have affected the media industry much more severely than many other industries. Recent examples, such as customers' reluctance to pay for online news or digitally distributed music, demonstrate that digital technologies may require media companies to rethink the scope of their businesses.

The cases demonstrate that media companies generally maintain their focus on content creation and aggregation while they attempt to exploit the opportunities offered by digital transformation and engage in the management of content platforms. Content platforms are a technology-enabled option for media companies to establish new services. But despite their dominant business focus on content, most traditional media companies have thus far missed the opportunity to establish and operate their content platforms in a way that creates valuable assets, as social media platforms do. The major assets of social media platforms derive from establishing connections between users and profiting from users' content to keep the platforms interesting.

In contrast, there are media companies that deliberately shift their product and service portfolios to business areas that are less fundamentally affected by ongoing digital transformation.

Structural Changes Dimension

Digital transformation, as any other type of business transformation, impacts a company's organizational structures. The structural dimension of the Digital Transformation Framework is concerned with who will be in charge of the transformation endeavor. Additionally, management has to decide whether new digitally enabled operations should be integrated into existing structures or be located in independent entities that are separated from the company's core business. The company may also have to acquire specialized know-how or new competencies. Finally, managers must consider what types of operational changes to expect as they explore and exploit digital technologies. Table 7.4 summarizes the four strategic questions that managers must ask about the structural changes dimension and the strategic options available when answering these questions, and describes how and why the three media companies have chosen a particular option.

Question 6: Who is in Charge of the Digital Transformation Endeavor? In many organizations, the success of a digital transformation strategy depends on two factors: top management support and the commitment of the necessary people to the strategy.

The three cases imply that, ideally, the CEO is fully responsible for and adds authority to the digital transformation strategy. The execution of such a strategy is often delegated to a senior manager who could either be the manager of the business unit that is responsible for large portions of the digital business or of the business unit that is most affected by the digital transformation. The CIO may also manage the transformation, which is typically the case if the focus is on business processes. However, companies whose digital focus is on the interface with customers often appoint a chief digital officer (CDO) to work alongside the CIO.[12] The CIO typically focuses on the IT infrastructure and the internal business processes, whereas the CDO primarily addresses digital technologies that involve digital products and services

Table 7.4 Strategic Questions about Structural Changes

Strategic Question	Strategic Options	Description	Description	MB	RB	Impetus for the Digital Transformation Outcome
Who is in charge of the digital transformation endeavor?	Group CEO	The group's chief executive officer	x	x	x	• All three companies have recognized the complexity of digital transformation and made it a top strategic priority of the group CEO.
	CEO of business unit	The CEO of the business unit that tackles the digital transformation endeavor	x		x	• Once a firm's size moves beyond a certain threshold, it is important to involve senior managers other than the group CEO in the digital transformation program. This applies for P7S1 and Ravensburger.
	Group CDO	The group's chief digital officer				
	Group CIO	The group's chief information officer				
Do you plan to integrate new operations into existing structures or create separate entities?	Integrated	Digital operations are fully integrated into an organization's current structures		x	x	• Mittelbayerische wants the digital transformation to happen in close
	Separated	Digital operations are implemented separately from the core business	x			• P7S1 does not want digital initiatives to be influenced by the existing business.
						• Ravensburger separates its activities that go beyond mere complementary products (e.g., online games).
						• All three companies have decided to use digital technologies to generate new customer experiences through digital products and services (e.g., P7S1's maxdome video-on-demand platform or Ravensburger's tiptoi pen).

Strategic Question	Strategic Options	Description	P7S1	MB	RB	Impetus for the Digital Transformation Outcome
What types of operational changes do you expect?	Products and services	Changed products and services	x	x	x	• All three companies have decided to use digital technologies to optimize their business processes (e.g., big data support in TV program planning).
	Business processes	Improvement of business processes	x	x	x	
	Skills	A new set of skills based on digital technologies	x	x	x	• Through its mergers and acquisitions activities, P7S1 automatically acquires new skill sets. • Ravensburger wants to attract and develop a new set of skills to make its separate digital business unit a success.
Do you need to acquire new competencies? If so, how do you plan to acquire them?	Internally Partnerships	Rely on the resources that already exist Foster partnerships	x	x	x	• All three companies believe that they need to develop their current workforce in new, digital technologies.
	Takeovers External sourcing	Accumulate know-how via takeovers Source additional know-how from outside	x	(x)		• Mergers and acquisitions activities give P7S1 an alternative channel to accumulate digital competencies. • Mittelbayerische has realized that it needs to attract "digital natives" for a successful digital transformation.

at the customer interface. Needless to say, the CIO and CDO should actively communicate with one another and closely coordinate their strategies and initiatives.

Question 7: Do You Plan to Integrate New Operations into Existing Structures or Create Separate Entities? Because digital transformation can redefine a firm's business model, one key concern for companies is where to position new digital business activities in the organizational structure. They must decide whether to integrate new operations into their current operations or to organize them as distinct, separate units (perhaps as a newly formed subsidiary).

The three cases illustrate both approaches, each of which has advantages and disadvantages. Integration into the existing corporate structure typically requires less extensive restructuring efforts. The integration approach may be preferred if close coordination between traditional and new digital businesses will be necessary. In this situation, it is important to examine whether synergies between traditional areas and new digital activities can be exploited.

In contrast, organizing new digital activities in separate structures makes it easier for firms to explicitly separate (physically and ideologically) their old and new operations. They can also develop from scratch appropriate structures for new digital activities, which typically are more innovative and provide an increased level of flexibility.

Thus far, it has not been clear whether separation or integration is the preferred approach. However, theory and practice suggest that the greater the distance between digital transformation efforts and a firm's current core activities, the stronger the boundary between new and old operations should be. Thus, for gradual, core-business-related transformations, integration into existing structures should be preferred, but only if the change processes are strongly supported by top management. But digital transformation initiatives often involve significant innovation and change efforts, as well as a willingness to take risks, all of which may be difficult to accommodate within existing organizational structures.

Question 8: What Types of Operational Changes Do You Expect? Depending on the scope of the organization's business and the specific future digital transformation plans, a digital transformation strategy can require different types of operational changes. First, new technologies can significantly change the current products and services delivered to customers. Second, digital technologies can enable changes to business processes. Business processes can be classified as operational, support and management, but the typical focus of digital transformation initiatives is on operational processes. For instance, digital technologies can accelerate the execution of business processes, involve different staff, require different resources or fully automate certain steps.

Reengineering business processes can be complex because they often span divisions or even companies. A company must therefore fully define their processes and assess which of them will be affected by digital transformation initiatives and what the potential impacts will be. The three cases show that digital transformation at media companies can occur internally (through business processes) or at the customer interface (through products and services).

Question 9: Do You Need to Acquire New Competencies? If so, How Do You Plan to Acquire Them? The necessary changes in products, services and business processes to digitally transform an organization, and the maintenance of ongoing operations, will likely require new skills. Managers must carefully assess the firm's existing technology capabilities and identify the new competencies that will be needed.

These three cases indicate that competencies can be acquired in different ways. The best option will largely be determined by the existing capabilities and financial resources of the firm and the scheduled timescale for the digital initiatives. The first option is for firms to build on their current capabilities and acquire the required competencies themselves (e.g., by either training current staff or hiring new employees). However, this approach typically takes time. Another option, therefore, is to partner with other companies that may already have the specific knowledge to facilitate integration processes. This approach reduces the risk of failure. If the jointly shared activities are of high strategic importance, acquiring the partner company may be an option for ensuring that the common resources and knowledge will be retained in-house.

If the technological processes required for digital transformation are well structured and not overly complex, outsourcing these processes is another option. Compared to creating the required competencies internally, both the partnership and outsourcing options can have advantages in terms of lower initial investments and of distributing the risks more widely. The disadvantage of these two options, however, is that they increase the risk both of losing a required competency and of becoming dependent on a third party. Retaining the processes and knowledge required for digital transformation in-house means a company can be better positioned to gain a competitive advantage from future digital transformation initiatives.

Financial Aspects Dimension

The financial dimension of the Digital Transformation Framework is also a significant aspect of digital transformation endeavors. Increasing financial pressure on the current core business might be the trigger that convinces management of the need for action. And financial resources will be necessary to carry out transformational initiatives. Table 7.5 summarizes the two strategic questions that managers must ask about the financial dimension and the strategic options available when answering these questions, and describes how and why the three media companies have chosen the options.

Question 10. How Strong is the Financial Pressure on Your Current Core Business? The willingness of top management to undertake the necessary efforts for, and accept the ensuing risks of, digital transformation endeavors often depends on the competitiveness of the current core business. If the core business continues to create sufficient profits, managers may not see the urgency for embarking on digital transformation efforts or be willing to take the risks.

History, however, has shown that markets can change quickly and that acting too late can be fatal for companies. Several well-known retailers that once dominated domestic markets missed the opportunity to react to e-commerce-driven changes in a timely manner, resulting ultimately in business failure. We urge all companies to take digital transformation seriously and address its potential effects and take necessary measures immediately rather than waiting for the anticipated tectonic shifts to occur in the way profits are generated in their industries.

Question 11. How Will You Finance the Digital Transformation Endeavor? Digital transformation strategies seek to maximize value creation and, thus, future revenues and profits. To finance their digital transformation endeavors, firms can choose either internal or external financing options. Successfully financing a transformation endeavor depends on a firm's current well-being and its future prospects. Investors of any kind must have faith that the digital transformation is beneficial to the firm and that their investments will therefore pay off. Thus, if a company is already financially struggling, its options for financing digital transformations will be severely limited.

Key Decisions in Formulating a Digital Transformation Strategy

Managers can use the 11 questions identified above and their respective answers as guidelines for formulating their digital transformation strategy. Table 7.6 summarizes these 11 questions and provides an overview of the possible management options. Again, we have structured the questions along the four dimensions of the Digital Transformation Framework. Together, these questions and answers cover the most important decisions that have to be made when formulating a digital transformation strategy.

Table 7.5 Strategic Questions about the Financial Dimension of Digital Transformation

Strategic Question	Strategic Options	Description	P7S1	MB	RB	Impetus for the Digital Transformation Outcome
How strong is	Low	Margins in the core business remain mostly unaffected by digital technologies	x		x	• At P7S1 (TV) and Ravensburger (board games and books), margins from the core business remain strong.
the financial pressure on your current core business?	Medium	Digital technologies affect core business margins, but the core business remains profitable		x		• Mittelbayerische's print publishing market suffers from market share losses to digital substitutes.
	High	Digital technologies erode margins				
How will you finance the digital transformation endeavor?	Internal	Finance digital transformation through internal funds	x	x	x	• At all three companies, cash flow is sufficient to finance the digital transformation program.
	External	External financing necessary to finance digital transformation				

Table 7.6 Key Decisions for a Digital Transformation Strategy

Use of technologies

1. Strategic role of IT?	Enabler			Supporter	
2. Technological ambition?	Innovator	Early adopter		Follower	

Changes in value creation

3. Degree of digital diversification?	Electronic sales channels	Cross-media	Enriched media	Content platforms	Extended business
4. Revenue creation?	Paid content	Freemium		Advertising	Complementary products
5. Future main business scope?	Content creation	Content aggregation	Content distribution	Management of content platforms	Other

Structural changes

6. Responsibility for digital transformation strategy?	Group CEO	CEO of business unit		Group CDO	Group CIO
7. Organizational positioning of new activities?	Integrated			Separated	
8. Focus of operational changes?	Products and services	Business processes			
9. Building of competencies?	Internally	Partnerships		Company takeovers	External sourcing

Financial aspects

10. Financial pressure on current core business?	Low	Medium			High
11. Financing of new activities?	Internal			External	

Although this analysis is based on the media industry, we believe that, apart from the questions directly related to a firm's value creation, the findings can be transferred to other customer-oriented industries. The value creation dimension usually varies significantly across industries and business models.

For the media industry, we found that digital transformation can lead to new sources of revenue or even to new business models (e.g., the management of content platforms). Many other industries have also embraced the business opportunities offered through digital technologies. For example, the automotive industry has introduced digitally enriched products (such as the "connected car") and new business models (such as free-floating car sharing). Even so, a major benefit of digital transformation within the automotive industry is in the ongoing automation of product development and production processes (e.g., 3D-modeling). Another example is the insurance industry, where many firms have already implemented digital sales channels and started to adopt digital business models (e.g., online direct insurance). But a fundamental change of an insurer's business model seems unlikely in the near future.

Hence, when applying the Digital Transformation Framework and using the set of 11 strategic questions and answers we offered to formulate a digital transformation strategy, managers will likely need to customize the value creation dimension so it corresponds to the specific requirements of their industries or business models.

Concluding Comments

Digital transformation is a highly complex, company-wide endeavor. A systematic approach to formulating a digital transformation strategy is crucial for success. Moreover, a firm's first steps toward digital business models are characterized by a high level of uncertainty. To help managers address the challenge more systematically, we have extended previous work on digital transformation strategies through the lessons learned from three companies in the German media industry.

Our research has identified a set of strategic questions that managers responsible for digital transformation have to consider. Unfortunately, there are no universal, definitive answers to these questions. Nevertheless, for each question we have offered a set of possible answers and describe how and why the three case firms chose a particular option.

We believe that the most important thing for managers charged with formulating their firms' digital transformation strategies is to know the right questions to ask. By drawing on the successful approaches adopted by the three case firms, answering these questions within their own business contexts will provide managers with a comprehensive and structured approach to digital transformation that will enable them to cut through the complexity of digital transformation strategies.

Notes

1   An article that calls for a new view of disruptive technologies and presents strategic principles for addressing the challenges stemming from disruptive technologies is Downes, L. and Nunes, P. F. "Big Bang Disruption," *Harvard Business Review* (91:3), 2013, pp. 44–56.

2   Bonnet, D., Ferraris, P., Westerman, G. and McAfee, A. "Talking 'bout a Revolution," *Digital Transformation Review* (2:1), 2012, pp. 17–33.

3   See Lee, O. K., Sambamurthy, V., Lim, K. H. and Wei, K. K. "How does IT Ambidexterity Impact Organizational Agility?," *Information Systems Research* (26:2), 2015, pp. 398–417; and Gregory R. W., Keil, M., Muntermann, J. and Mahring, M. "Paradoxes and the Nature of Ambidexterity in IT Transformation Programs," *Information Systems Research* (26:1), 2015, pp. 57–80.

4   An example that concentrates on the digital transformation of a firm's retail channels is Hansen, R. and Sia, S. K. "Hummel's Digital Transformation Toward Omnichannel Retailing: Key Lessons Learned," *MIS Quarterly Executive* (14:2), 2015, pp. 51–66.

5   Matt, C., Hess, T. and Benlian, A. "Digital Transformation Strategies," *Business and Information Systems Engineering* (57:5), 2015, pp. 339–343.

6   Bharadwaj, A., El Sawy, O. A., Pavlou, P. A. and Venkatraman, N. "Digital Business Strategy: Toward a Next Generation of Insights," *MIS Quarterly* (37:2), 2013, pp. 471–482.

7   McDonald, M. P "Digital Strategy Does Not Equal IT Strategy," *HBR Blog Network*, November 2012, available at https://hbr.org/2012/11/digital-strategy-does-not-equa.

8   Academic groundwork that argues for the fusion of IT and business strategy in light of digital transformation is Bharadwaj, A., El Sawy, O. A., Pavlou, P. A., and Venkatraman, N., op. cit., 2013.

9   As of April 2016, €1 = $1.13

10 P7S1 originated from the former Kirch Group, which was founded in 1955.

11 In addition to the three firms' specific digital transformation journeys, the interviewees provided other possible answers to the strategic questions that they considered viable options when designing their digital transformation strategies.

12 Horlacher, A. and Hess, T "What Does A Chief Digital Officer Do? Managerial Tasks and Roles of a new C-Level Position in the Context of Digital Transformation," *Proceedings of the 49th Hawaii International Conference on System Sciences* (HICSS 2016), Hawaii, 2016.

Appendix: Research Methodology

We conducted two rounds of interviews with industry experts and representatives of each of the three case companies. When analyzing the interviews, we carefully scanned for commonalities and differences in these firms' strategies. To verify the statements from the interviews, we also used secondary data sources (e.g., financial statements, company presentations and data from general and professional media).

The first round of interviews was conducted in May and June 2013. It included seven interviews with senior industry experts and decision makers who were responsible for recent digital transformation programs at the German media companies. These interviews included open questions on the firms' motivations for their transformation efforts, their visions and goals and their current capabilities and challenges. The first round interviewees are listed below.

First Round Interviewees

Interviewee Function	Industry Segment	Date
Industry Expert	Consulting	May 2013
Industry Expert	Consulting	May 2013
Head of Business Development	Publishing	May 2013
Chief Operating Officer	Publishing	May 2013
Chief Executive Officer	Publishing	May 2013
Head of Advisory Board	Publishing	May 2013
Chief Executive Officer	Publishing	June 2013

In the second round, we conducted two interviews in July 2013 and one in May 2015. The interviewees in this round—one from each of the case companies—are listed below. These interviews formed the basis for our case analysis.

Second Round Interviewees

Interviewee Function	Industry Segment	Date
Executive Vice President, Strategy and Operations	ProSiebenSat.1 Media SE	July 2013
CEO Ravensburger Digital	Ravensburger AG	July 2013
Group CEO	Mittelbayerische Verlag AG	May 2015

Questions for Discussion

1   How can companies deal with challenges posed by digital technologies? How do you envision the development of digital technologies and their effects on organizations?

2   What would you recommend to companies struggling to embark on digital transformation?

3   How could digital transformation help balance exploitation and exploration? What resources and capabilities might organizations require?

4   Using the digital transformation strategies outlined in Chapter 6, analyze the three case studies presented. What strategies have these organizations utilized? What are the similarities and the differences? How might you advise these companies on their strategies using the terminology of Chapter 6?

5   Using the Digital Transformation Framework outlined in the chapter, analyze the examples of the digital transformation companies presented in Chapter 6.

6   Referring to Part I of the book, discuss IS strategy and digital strategy. Are these distinct strategies?

Further Reading

Sia, S. K., Soh, C., Weill, P. (2016). How DBS bank pursued a digital business strategy. *MIS Quarterly Executive*, *15*(2), 106–121.

Yeow, A., Soh, C., Hansen, R. (2018). Aligning with new digital strategy: A dynamic capabilities approach. *The Journal of Strategic Information Systems*, *27*(1), 43–58.

Chapter 8

Omar A. El Sawy, Pernille Kræmmergaard, Henrik Amsinck and Anders Lerbech Vinther

HOW LEGO BUILT THE FOUNDATIONS AND ENTERPRISE CAPABILITIES FOR DIGITAL LEADERSHIP

DEFINING DIGITAL LEADERSHIP

Mc**KINSEY & COMPANY** has observed that while companies are rushing headlong to become more digital, executives have very diverse perspectives as what "going digital" really means.[1] These perspectives range from a focus on technology, to digital customer engagement, to new digital business models and more. The lack of clarity often results in piecemeal initiatives, missed opportunities and false starts in the digitalization of the enterprise.

The term digitalization goes beyond an organization taking advantage of digital platforms, but rather reflects the way that digital media and platforms influence the restructuring of the economy, society and culture.[2] In a corporate context, Gartner uses the term to describe the process of moving to a digital business and the use of digital technologies to change business models and value-producing opportunities. Gartner also sees digitalization as a new era for enterprise IT, in which business innovation and IT innovation are more integrated and where corporate IT switches from a legacy perspective to a digital perspective – suggesting that there is a critical need for digital leadership.[3]

Similarly, a 2015 survey of 4,800 U.S. management professionals confirmed that the keys to successful digital transformation (the North American term for digitalization) are concerned more with strategy, culture and talent development than with technology issues.[4] That survey also showed that respondents were apprehensive about whether business leaders had the capabilities to lead their organizations in a digital environment.

Clearly, there is a need for clarity on what is meant by effective digital leadership, what enterprise capabilities it requires and how the foundations of digital leadership can be built and reinforced. We define digital leadership as "Doing the right things for the strategic success of digitalization for the enterprise and its business ecosystem."[5] This definition reflects the difference between leadership and management highlighted by leadership scholar Warren Bennis: "Leadership is about *doing the right thing* for the success of the organization, while management is about *doing the thing right.*"[6] We have included "business ecosystem" in the definition because in today's connected world it is not possible to achieve strategic success independently of the business ecosystem.[7]

There is, as yet, no common consensus on the operational aspects of digital leadership. However, there are six foundational building blocks of strategy and organization that will have to change when implementing a successful digitalization strategy:

1   *A different kind of business strategy*: Digital technologies are becoming fused into the very fabric of the business,[8] which means the concept of business strategy should be enlarged to include digitalization. The prevailing view of a functional-level IT strategy aligned to an enterprise's chosen business strategy but always subordinate to it needs to be replaced with an enterprise-wide digital view that reflects the fusion between digital strategy with business strategy. This view is sometimes termed "digital business strategy."[9] Furthermore, business development often occurs in collaboration with partners that leverage ecosystem platforms to co-create value around products and services.[10]

2   *Different kinds of business models:* An integrated digital business strategy and collaborative ecosystem platforms enable new digital business models for creating business value. These models often have different value propositions and different revenue sharing modes. They often also bring together both physical and digital features of products and services.[11]

3   *A different kind of enterprise platform integration*: Intensive interactive digital connectivity to the outside requires integration between the outside and inside of the enterprise that goes beyond the traditional ERP and supply chain management integration paradigm. The upcoming era of adaptive and dynamically responsive digital platforms[12] and accompanying organizational arrangements requires a new kind of platform integration.

4   *A different kind of people mindset and skill set*: All the above will require a different mindset at all levels of the organization. Top management and all employees will need to be more adaptive and willing to experiment and innovate while occasionally failing.[13] Everyone throughout the enterprise will need to have an appropriate adaptive skill set and digital know-how.

5   A different kind of corporate IT function: The organizational changes required for digital leadership and a digital business strategy will require rethinking the roles of the corporate IT function and the CIO.

6   *A different kind of workplace*: As more "born digital" younger employees enter the workforce with different values, they will have different expectations of the workplace in terms of flexibility of location and working hours, sophistication of mobile online access, and the extent to which the workplace environment is "humanized."[14] Creating such a workplace as digitalization increases is especially a key priority in Scandinavia.

To illustrate the kinds of changes that a digitalization strategy entails, this article describes the LEGO Group's decade-long digitalization journey.

LEGO Group Background

Founded in 1932 by Ole Kirk Kristiansen, a carpenter who made wooden toys, the LEGO Group (referred to as LEGO in the rest of the article) is a private company (still owned by the Kristiansen family) with headquarters in Billund, Denmark, and main offices in the U.S., U.K., China and Singapore. Renowned for the iconic LEGO brick, LEGO products are sold in more than 140 countries. It has more than 17,000 employees worldwide and factories in Billund, Hungary, the Czech Republic, Mexico and China. 2015 revenues were 35.8 billion Danish krone (over $5 billion). Net profit was 9.2 billion krone (over $1 billion). To date, more than 760 billion LEGO elements have been manufactured. In 2014, about two thirds of revenues were from new products that did not exist the year before.

The company is committed to the development of children and aims to inspire and develop the "builders of tomorrow" through creative play and learning. The company's main goal is to "inspire and develop children to think creatively, reason systematically and exploit their potential to create their own future and thus exploit man's infinite possibilities."

Organizational Structure

LEGO depicts its organizational structure as a "wheel" (see Figure 8.1). This structure reduces silos and emphasizes communication and sharing of knowledge and insights as well as making decisions in plenary groups. In addition to an external Board of Directors, top management consists of a Management Board of the CEO and four Executive VPs, and a Corporate Management team of 21 people at Senior VP level.[15] The four core business areas—Operations, Market Management and Development, Product and Marketing Development, and Business Enabling—are represented in the Management Board. The CIO, who is the Senior VP for Corporate IT, is part of the Business Enabling area covering group/corporate functions. As Figure 8.1 depicts, members of the Management Board and the Corporate Management team comprising the wheel run the company, and they often communicate across areas as part of the transparent communication culture. They also all meet together regularly.

Values and Culture

The LEGO culture is based on openness and trust, and core values are creativity, imagination, fun, learning, quality and care.[16] Since the company was founded, LEGO's top managers have consistently expressed concern for maintaining the values and beliefs for which the brand stands. The founder's motto of "only the best is good enough" is still applied in all aspects of LEGO's operations. Playfulness is an important element of LEGO's business and management. As LEGO CEO Jørgen Vig Knudstorp likes to say: "We don't stop playing because we grow old. We grow old because we stop playing."

Near-Death Experience and the Start of the Transformation Journey

Although LEGO is now a thriving business, in the early 2000s it verged on defaulting on its debt.[17] Manufacturing was in Europe and the U.S., while competitors were manufacturing in Asia at much lower cost. The toy market had become more fickle with the advent of new electronic games. LEGO had diversified too quickly into adjacent markets: amusement parks, video games, toys for infants, clothing and others that it had little experience in. It almost seemed like the company "lost faith in the brick" and its identity as a company

As LEGO's press officer articulated in 2014:

> We were a little bit complacent, thinking that we knew what we were doing as a company and we knew best. Second, we were not focusing much on our customers. And thirdly, there was a lack of flow of information inside the company.

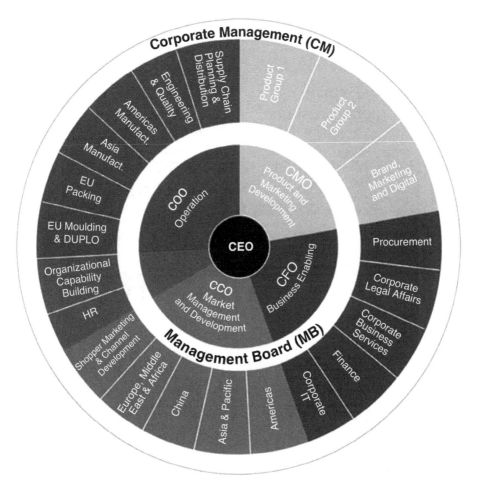

Figure 8.1 The LEGO Group Organizational Wheel
© The LEGO Group

A major organizational transformation and a new business strategy were needed to save what some had called a "burning platform." The starting point for the transformation was the replacement of the CEO in October 2004 when 35-year-old Jørgen Vig Knudstorp, who had initially joined LEGO as a business strategist in 2001 from McKinsey & Company, became CEO. Since 2004, LEGO has enjoyed almost a decade of consecutive growth.

The new CEO's initial focus was on survival, and he instigated a two-pronged strategy based on reducing production costs and closing nonprofitable product lines, and on a clearer focus on the core brand and identity.

The emphasis in 2005–2007 was on creating a defensible core of products. Product lines that were neither profitable nor core were shut down, and the capital structure was rebalanced. LEGOLAND parks were sold to Merlin entertainment. The company downsized from 8,500 to 5,000 employees. Open communication about problems was encouraged and practiced. Refocusing on the LEGO core (the brick) was key, while also pursuing complementary digital opportunities that reinforced that focus and did not wander into adjacent markets.

In 2008, the strategy shifted from stability to growth and the focus was on building sustainable platforms for growth while continuing to improve the core business. Although the

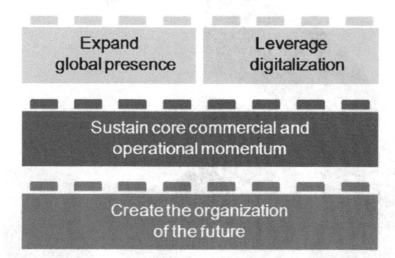

Figure 8.2 The LEGO Strategy
© The LEGO Group

Corporate IT department had been supporting the recovery, stability and growth of the company through enterprise systems, there was a realization of the growing importance of digital platforms for the LEGO Group.

LEGO Group Strategy

The LEGO Group has a long-term corporate strategy toward 2032 consisting of four strategic priorities—one of them being "leverage digitalization" (see Figure 8.2). When it was establishing the strategy, LEGO decided that it would look to respond to the external adaptive challenge of digitalization by purposefully "evolving" its existing business model to integrate digital into everything it does. LEGO consciously decided that it would not have a separate digital products business unit.

Jørgen Vig Knudstorp has an often repeated quote: "You do not think your way into new ways of acting—you act your way into new ways of thinking." It is in that spirit that LEGO has developed the capabilities for digital leadership by attempting multiple (but focused) digitalization moves and learning through the experience. We describe some of these moves below.

Digitalization at the LEGO Group

LEGO used three lenses for leveraging digitalization: a "Products" lens, which centered around product innovation and the product ecosystem; a "Marketing" lens for digital marketing; and an "Enterprise" lens, which centered around enterprise platforms and integration of the outside and the inside of the enterprise. Since 2009, LEGO has undertaken several product and marketing digitalization moves, which have necessitated associated digitalization moves in the enterprise IT platforms. We describe a representative selection of all three types of moves below.

Product Digitalization Moves

The first hybrid digital/physical LEGO experience was LEGO MINDSTORMS®, launched in 1998. MINDSTORMS is a robotics platform created in collaboration with MIT's Media Lab and was targeted at an older segment. A month after its launch, LEGO discovered that the proprietary operating system had been hacked. This was a major surprise to the company, which traditionally was tightly closed, with a culture of close control over every aspect of the LEGO experience. However, LEGO realized that opening up could create a much stronger community of users and become a source of additional value. Instead of prosecuting the hackers, it talked to them and found they were LEGO fans who wanted to build their own creations. As a result, LEGO developed a process-based solution that addressed the real needs of the company and its customers, and the first platform for community interaction was launched.

Since then, LEGO has launched numerous digital platforms to strengthen its connections to the large communities of LEGO fans and strengthen the collaboration and involvement of passionate builders in the development and design process of new models. Additionally, after LEGO MINDSTORMS, numerous product lines combining physical and digital play have been launched, and LEGO now operates an R&D Future Lab to study, improve and nurture those experiences. For example, LEGO Fusion was launched in 2013 and combined real builds with bricks with virtual games: users build something with the bricks and scan the shape with a downloadable app into a smartphone or tablet and watch their creation become part of a virtual game. LEGO Dimensions was launched in late September 2015. This is an action-adventure video game for popular consoles (Sony PlayStation, Nintendo Wii, Microsoft Xbox) that includes many characters from 14 different LEGO franchises. It combines the physical and digital in that the player has LEGO figures and a gateway built with bricks that can be played within the game.

Another product digitalization move involved crowdsourcing innovation and developing LEGO community platforms. LEGO has always designed its products together with children to try to ensure that they are loveable products, and the advent of digital platforms has strengthened this.[18] In 2008, the company launched LEGO Ideas (https://ideas.lego.com), a website where amateur designers share their ideas for new LEGO sets, and fans vote on them and give them "likes." This website has about half a million visits per month and over 100,000 registered users. Any project proposal with more than 10,000 votes goes to a LEGO review board. A chosen project will be developed in collaboration with the project creator, who receives 1% of net sales if the product is launched. Crowdsourced LEGO sets (for example, The Big Bang Theory Apartment set) do as well in the market as standard sets. Crowdsourcing product ideas in this way has added thousands of designers to the 200 in-house product designers.

The LEGO Ideas website can monitor trends and changing interests among LEGO set builders and fans. It also mobilizes communities for user-designed projects as well as deepening the connection between users and the company.

The LEGO Group has also created several community platforms for children. LEGO® Club has five million registered users and offers content and tools to stimulate the creativity of children aged four to 13. My LEGO Network (www.mln.lego.com) is a safe social networking site for children, where they can share their LEGO creations. ReBrick (www.rebrick.lego.com) is a sharing platform designed for users aged 13+, known as Teen Fans of LEGO (TFOL). Projects are created outside of brand-implemented tools and published on independent platforms such as blogs or Flickr. There is also a growing number of Adult LEGO User Communities (AFOLs, or Adult Fans of LEGO) that have their own websites, blogs and discussion forums. The 220+ LEGO user community groups each have a representative who is part of the LEGO Ambassador Network, which serves to nurture the relationship with the LEGO Group. All of these initiatives further the digitalization of the company around product design and community building for the future.

Marketing Digitalization Moves

There is a lot of overlap between marketing and managing the product experience in a digital environment, because the digital experience is part of the product. Furthermore, in an age of social media, chatter, public critique of products, website interaction and customer communities, marketing has become a pull activity and is more about engagement and interaction with customer communities than a push activity for product information. LEGO divides its market constituencies into *customers* (retailers such as Target, Walmart and Amazon), *shoppers* (adults such as parents and grandparents who buy LEGO products for children), *consumers* (those who play and learn with LEGO products, mostly children) and *fans* (adult and teenage fans who are both shoppers and consumers). The marketing digitalization moves have addressed all four constituencies in different ways. We highlight three of the moves below.

1. The Omnichannel Marketing Move. Reaching out to customers in a digital environment requires omnichannel marketing—i.e., using different kinds of digital channels as well as physical channels. LEGO products have physical presence in the company's own stores and retail stores, and brand presence created by several LEGOLAND parks and LEGOLAND Discovery Centers, and very active "Brick" conventions around the world (the conventions are often arranged by AFOLs, not by the LEGO Group.).

In its marketing digitalization efforts, LEGO increased the use of various digital channels, such as social media, the main LEGO website and websites specially designed for fan groups. It has also started using interactive story telling within "trailer" online games to engage with children around new characters in LEGO sets. The company has also created an augmented reality product catalog. A product box can be scanned with a downloadable mobile app, and an animation of the construction set being assembled is instantly displayed. LEGO has also realized that cycle times are very fast for producing interactive digital content for marketing. Although it has an internal ad agency, it has partnered with external digital ad agencies to speed up marketing digitalization efforts.

In addition, LEGO has partnered with Warner Animation, which released The LEGO Movie® (www.thelegomovie.com) in 2014. This is an animated adventure comedy film based on LEGO construction toys and became a $486 million global blockbuster The company received royalties for the use of its brand and the film's intellectual property rights, but most importantly, the construction sets launched in conjunction with the movie were extremely successful both in terms of revenue and of greatly increasing brand affinity with families. Two sequels have been announced, for 2017 and 2018.

2. Increased Digital Engagement with LEGO Communities. Increased engagement with a customer community drives innovation and revenue growth, and LEGO has committed considerable resources to maintaining a culture of engagement around its community platforms. The affinity pyramid (see Figure 8.3) suggests that the more digitally and directly connected members of a community are with an organization and other community members, the more likely they are to engage in providing information, in having two-way dialogues, in collaborating with each other and in co-creating products. Moreover, the more customers move up the affinity pyramid through digital engagement, the more effective

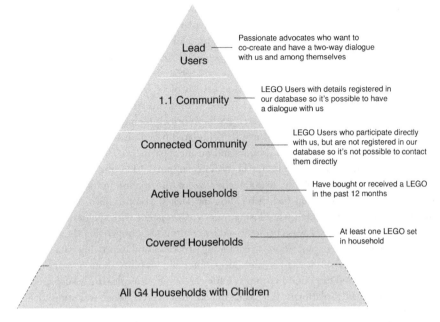

Figure 8.3 The Affinity Pyramid Engagement Map
© The LEGO Group

personalized micromarketing becomes. LEGO has used micromarketing data to better understand the path to purchase for its digitally connected customers and fans.

The company also continuously measures customer experience through a Net Promoter Score, a program that asks customers to rate their experience in real time on the web.

3. Globalizing Digital Assets. LEGO has continuously increased its intellectual property for new characters and franchises that have been hits, such as Chima and Ninjago, balancing its own IP with externally licensed IP rather than resorting to licensing deals. Furthermore, as combined physical and digital play has increased, the number of digital assets that the company has created to promote its products has also increased. For example, "trailer" online games mentioned above may need to be deployed to multiple major markets around the world, with multiple languages. The LEGO Group has sought to globalize these digital assets and to take advantage of economies of scale and scope. This has presented challenges in global governance and has highlighted a new dimension of marketing digitalization that the LEGO Group is learning about through the global deployment of its digital assets.

Enterprise Platform Digitalization Moves

The product and marketing digitalization moves have involved ecosystem partners and have put new demands on enterprise systems and platforms and on LEGO's Corporate IT function. The moves have created requests for applications and IT functionality that have grown from 5% to 30% of the IT portfolio, and that growth is expected to continue. Digitalization moves have also prompted the Corporate IT function to rethink the architecture of its enterprise platforms to meet the new business demands from customers and partners who want more responsive digital engagement. New features and capabilities have been continuously added to the enterprise platform to make it more responsive to digitalization, and its complexity has grown, prompting the need for two different enterprise platforms: a traditional one for transactions and a second-generation one for interactions and customer engagement. We describe five of the most significant enterprise platform digitalization moves.

1. Bolstering the Enterprise IT Platform. Developing and bolstering the existing LEGO enterprise IT platform began as long ago as 1999, when the company wanted to consolidate and increase the efficiency of business processes and formulated a "one company, one system" mission. A company-wide ERP project was launched with four principles: simple, global, consistent and standardized work processes. In late 2001, LEGO had a global enterprise-wide ERP system based on these principles and that supported the basic core processes. In 2002, a new IT plan was formulated based on the company's corporate strategy and the needs of the business units and business partners. The plan identified areas for providing business units with better IT systems support.[19] Despite the implementation of standardized processes globally, in 2004, the flow of information inside the company was inadequate. The LEGO Group had many silos and lacked visibility into which areas were running inefficiently and which were losing money. Consistent with the new CEO's action plan, the period 2004–2007 was characterized by continuously improving the enterprise IT platform, stabilizing the organization, streamlining processes and improving data sharing and business intelligence capabilities to create transparency and visibility about operations. When Henrik Amsinck joined the LEGO Group as CIO in 2007, he was pleasantly surprised by the robust state of the ERP platform. But, as he quickly discovered, there was still much work to be done in the ensuing years as the company's digitalization moves started to have major impacts on enterprise IT platform requirements.

From 2007, there were continual efforts to bolster the enterprise platform in many ways to support operational excellence, including knowledge sharing, collaboration and supply chain management. LEGO continued to enhance its business process management capabilities and its capabilities for sharing knowledge about processes "the LEGO way."

However, there were other factors that influenced the evolution of LEGO's enterprise platform, driven by changing employee expectations as digitalization progressed. The "consumerization" of enterprise IT started to take hold as the experiences of employees as consumers influenced their expectations of ease of use of applications, friendly intuitive graphical user interfaces and simplicity. Just about everyone had a smartphone and was downloading apps, and employees wanted more than the standard cluttered ERP interfaces. As a consequence, LEGO's Corporate IT function augmented the enterprise platform with personalized end-to-end app experiences for employees, with simple graphical interfaces. Employees only got the apps they needed for their work tasks. In this way, Corporate IT managed to deliver personalized ERP functionality on employees' smartphones. Its philosophy was "what you see is what you need" rather than "what you see is what you get," and each app served its own individualized use.

To meet these employee demands, LEGO changed its application development process to have 100% user involvement before development, using collaborative prototyping tools with visualization, such as iRise. The benefits of involving users are shown in Figure 8.4.

Increased connectivity with customers, whether through the LEGO website, online shops, community groups, LEGO fan clubs or social media, has also put many new demands on the enterprise platform. Similarly, product and marketing digitalization moves have placed further demands on both the IT organization and the enterprise platform. The enterprise platform was growing in multiple directions and now had started to become like a gigantic aircraft carrier that housed all applications, whether they related to operations and transactions or to consumer digital engagement and interaction.

As time went on, there was a growing realization that developing digitalization applications was very different from traditional enterprise applications development. The business priorities with traditional enterprise platforms are first cost, then quality, then reliability

Figure 8.4 Benefits of Involving Users in Augmenting the Enterprise Platform through App
Development
© The LEGO Group

and then time. With digitalization platforms the business priorities are different. Time is the
highest priority because the ability to release new business functionality becomes a competitive advantage. Reliability is a close second because in a digitalization environment (such as
an online store) a technology failure cannot be compensated for by manual workarounds of
processes (as in a physical store). The third priority is quality, which is still a key requirement
in areas such as security but becomes less important in the presentation layer as users become
part of the testing and prototyping process. Cost is the lowest priority.

Furthermore, development practices for digitalization platforms are much more fluid,
and there are fewer established industrial-strength development practices than there are for
enterprise platforms. Moreover, the required delivery model and characteristics are also
very different. Eventually, it became clear to LEGO that it needed a separate enterprise
engagement platform.

2. Designing a Complementary Engagement Platform. LEGO identified the need
for an engagement platform that would complement the enterprise platform, with the two
co-existing. By 2015, API (application programming interface) technology was sufficiently
advanced to enable the two platforms to be loosely and dynamically connected, even though
the engagement platform would change rapidly.

LEGO's enterprise platform is rock solid, carefully designed and thoroughly tested.
Its purpose is to handle transactions and records, and its architecture is tightly integrated.
Platform requirements are carefully specified ahead of time. It is not easy to add functionality
quickly and in an ad hoc manner, and its integrity is guarded like the crown jewels because
all enterprise operations depend on it.

However, new customer and partner demands from digitalization moves have a very different set of platform requirements: digital interaction, 24/7 availability even as changes are
made, user-driven experience, experimentation, quickly added functionality that is "good
enough" and a two-way real-time dialogue with users through a simple intuitive interface. It
was clear to LEGO that it needed a different engagement platform and that the two platforms
could not be tightly coupled but had to co-exist. It was also clear that open architecture,

OUTSIDE FOCUS

Digital Consumer / Shopper / Customers

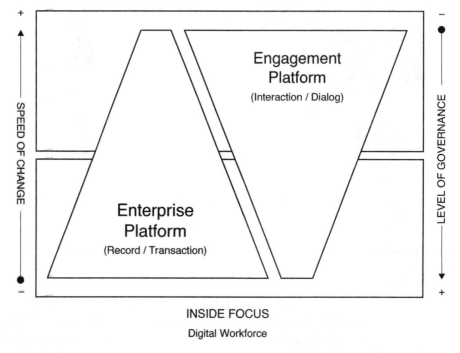

Figure 8.5 Enterprise and Engagement Platforms
©The LEGO Group

micro-services and APIs would drive the architecture of the engagement platform and that it would have loose-tight connectivity to the enterprise platform. At the time of writing (August 2015), the engagement platform and its governance mechanisms were at an advanced stage of design. The conceptual idea behind the engagement platform is shown in Figure 8.5 and contrasted with the enterprise platform.

The key dimensions in the figure are the extent of architecture governance exercised and the speed of platform change. LEGO's expectation is that this new design will result in a 75% decrease in time for delivering functionality and a three-fold increase in development staff productivity (based on function point calculations using scrum/agile development methods). The engagement platform is designed to handle customers' digital interactions and is essential if digitalization is to be effective.

3. Restructuring the Corporate IT Organization for Business Responsiveness. LEGO's rapid revenue growth and the strategic need for increased digitalization has resulted in the Corporate IT organization expanding its staff base by close to 20% year on year for the last three to now approximately 600 full-time regulars. Historically, most IT employees have been located at LEGO headquarters in Billund and at the Enfield hub in the U.S.[20] However, now that LEGO has established new major office hubs in London, Singapore and Shanghai, IT employees are also being located at these locations. This transition started in January 2015, and Corporate IT (CIT) expects there to be more than 50 new colleagues at these three new hubs before the end of 2016.

CIT will keep the competencies for developing the core enterprise platform components in-house at Billund and Enfield. But locating other IT people alongside the rest of the

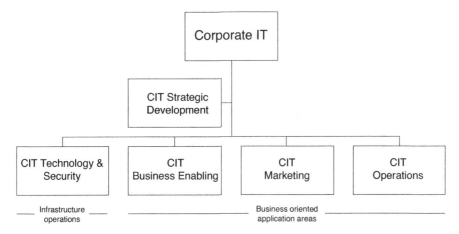

Figure 8.6 Configuring Corporate IT for Business Responsiveness
© The LEGO Group

organization helps them appreciate, understand and share their colleagues' business challenges. Even their office space reinforces that they are LEGO employees first and IT employees second—they are surrounded by assembled LEGO products that range from Ninjago Master Wu Dragon sets to Star Wars Millennium Falcon displays to LEGO brick model replicas of the Sydney Opera House. They may be working on digital platforms, but they should never forget the core focus of the company—LEGO bricks.

With rapidly increasing digitalization, and changing needs from customers and the lines of business, CIT is under constant pressure to be agile and responsive to the business. CIT has therefore been restructured to mesh more closely with the business (see Figure 8.6). It is now organized into five functions, three of which work directly and very closely with the business: CIT Business Enabling, CIT Marketing and CIT Operations. CIT Technology & Security is more internally oriented and manages infrastructure and operations. The fifth function, CIT Strategic Business Development, was established on January 1, 2015, in the Office of the CIO to drive IT business planning and to create the ideas driving the need for new architectures for enterprise platforms and the development of the digital workforce.

Each of the three business-oriented functions has its own business CIO, and the technology-oriented Technology & Security function has a chief technology officer (CTO). This allows CIT to be led by one Executive CIO who can then spend more time focusing on long-term strategy and digitalization, together with the Director of CIT Strategic Business Development.

As well as delivering IT solutions, CIT Business Enabling's responsibilities include internal user experience management, business intelligence solutions, data warehousing, business process management, vendor management and portfolio management. CIT Marketing, which supports the product development, marketing and sales arms of the business, is responsible for CRM, e-commerce, digital marketing and customer front-end management. CIT Operations supports manufacturing, engineering and supply chain management. CIT Technology & Security is focused on the security of the enterprise architecture, core systems, infrastructure and hosting, and is also responsible for the global service desk and local end-user support.

There is a high degree of cross-functional collaboration within CIT and between it and the business. CIT has made a conscious effort to move from the traditional "plan-build-run" requirements-focused model of systems development to a joint collaboration model for finding solutions together with the business units. It has also realized that a very rapid and agile response is typically needed. CIT has also increased collaboration with external partners that bring special expertise, especially for products that have a digital component and for digital games.

4. Orchestrating Distributed Digital Innovation with Multiple Digital Officers. As more businesses offer products and services through digital platforms, they are appointing chief digital officers (CDOs) in addition to CIOs.[21] The CDO is typically closer to the business' customer offerings than the CIO and manages the customer engagement part of the platform as well as the generation of value from the digital product platform. For example, a digital entertainment company might have a CIO to manage its enterprise platform and a CDO to manage the content platform, creating value from it and managing how customers search for and consume digital entertainment content. The CDO will also monitor and manage the introduction of new technology innovations relating to the content platform.

LEGO, however, has taken a different approach to managing digital innovation: it has appointed a digital officer for each business area. LEGO's CIO and his team realized that digital innovation and technological advances that impacted the different business areas were becoming too numerous and overwhelming for CIT to manage by itself. Thus, LEGO is creating digital officers in a growing number of business areas (see Figure 8.7). For example, it has a Digital Games Officer in the marketing area who monitors and manages digital innovations and solutions for digital (online) games, then works with CIT to implement platform solutions for digital games. Having function-specific digital officers increases the digital savvy and proactive digitalization moves of the business units and their ownership of the resultant digital solutions.

The appointment of multiple digital officers is also changing the way that digital innovation occurs at LEGO because the innovation process is now distributed and is closer to the point of business expertise (see Figure 8.8). As a result, the innovation process is now more effective. In the past, the CIO and CIT managers were order-takers; a business unit brought its requirements for a system to CIT, and CIT provided the solution, the platform and technology innovation. Now, the business unit proactively discovers a digital innovation in its area, picks a solution and then discusses it with CIT as a partner. CIT then helps to integrate the solution into the existing enterprise platform (and in the future into the engagement platform as appropriate). The CIO and CIT are now solution-takers, partners and platform-integrators. Distributed digital innovation is a more effective approach in the dynamic and hectic environment of digitalization in the midst of organizational transformation.

Figure 8.7 The Rise of Multiple Digital Officers across the LEGO Group
© The LEGO Group

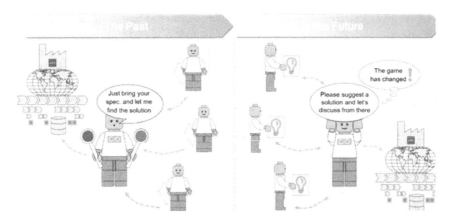

Figure 8.8 Multiple Digital Officers Enable the Digital Innovation Process to be Distributed between Corporate IT and Business Units
© The LEGO Group

5. Building up the Digital Workforce and the Work Environment in Corporate IT. An effective digitalization initiative requires a conscious effort to build up the skill set and change mindsets in both the corporate IT workforce and the entire workforce. Achieving this is especially challenging for a legacy bricks-and-mortar company like LEGO, where there are both traditional long-term employees and born digital younger employees who are continually joining the company.

The dynamic demand for new product and marketing digitalization moves (which resulted in the need for an engagement platform) is changing the mix of work for LEGO's CIT employees. They now spend more time with the business units, devising IT solutions, preparing specifications and prototyping, rather than on traditional development and programming. Not only is the work itself changing, but the mindset within CIT is now one of being more willing to experiment, learn and take risks, and of having an external orientation. There has been a conscious effort to create a mindset that fits with dynamic digitalization. Together with coaching from CIT managers, the new mindset has started to change the work culture.

There has also been a conscious effort to encourage CIT employees in particular and LEGO employees in general to collaborate with the many external partners that provide complementary expertise. In 2015, informal "chatter" from partners was suggesting that collaborating with LEGO is a pleasant experience because of the "playfulness" of the LEGO culture.

CIT has changed its hiring policies so it can develop the flexibility needed for dynamic digitalization. Previously, CIT hired for narrowly specified positions and often recruited highly specialized people. Since 2011, new recruits have been hired for a career at LEGO rather than for a specialized job in CIT. There has been a preference for people who can adapt to task and position changes, whether in CIT or other parts of the enterprise. Every year, about 50 CIT employees are redeployed within the company. This has resulted in CIT people getting greater exposure in the wider organization, their knowledge and expertise being spread more broadly and the internal hiring process having access to a supply of digital talent.

CIT has also put a lot of effort into creating a motivating and exciting workplace. It has taken various initiatives to blend CIT employee development with workplace excitement. In 2013, for example, it ran a two-day digitalization boot camp for young and recently hired graduates, with participation from CIT management and some mid-level CIT employees. The boot camp was facilitated by a prominent consulting firm and covered new digital trends as well as the organizational, cultural, ecosystem, partnering and customer challenges of digitalization.

CIT's efforts to build up the digital workforce and the work environment have paid off. In 2014, LEGO ranked second to Google as being the most popular IT workplace in Denmark among IT graduates.[22] Three years before, LEGO was not even in the top 100. Among IT people with five years' experience, LEGO CIT now ranks in the top five in Denmark.

Business Impacts of Digitalization at LEGO

As described above, the LEGO ecosystem of customers, partners and employees has been transformed through its digitalization moves, resulting in innovative products, new processes and new types of relationships. In combination, the moves have helped LEGO in its multi-year transformation. The pain and critical problems that plagued the group in 2004 after its near-death experience were complacency, excessive diversification into areas in which the company had little experience, losing focus on the bricks, not focusing enough on the customer, lack of flow of information and knowledge silos. LEGO and its ecosystem are better off thanks to digitalization. The group is now on a healthy growth path of increasing revenues and profits.

Focus on the customer has soared during the multi-year transformation. In 2015, LEGO was rated as the most powerful global brand. That cannot be attributed solely to digitalization, but many of the product and marketing moves described above have helped to build brand affinity and enormously enriched digital engagement and interaction with the customer ecosystem in numerous ways. The company, its partners—and most importantly its customers, consumers, shoppers and fans—are all appreciating and enjoying the enhancements that digitalization has brought about.

LEGO's Journey Toward Digital Leadership

Figure 8.9 shows how LEGO depicts its progression toward enterprise digital leadership. Digitalization is primarily a process (and a continual one), but it is also a state, and there can be different levels of digitalization. At first, digitalization efforts are typically ad hoc and disjointed. Next, some enterprises will execute increasingly enterprise-wide digitalization and become committed to it. This is an inflection point at which it is possible to accelerate up the curve. Businesses become more successful at building the foundations and capabilities for enterprise digital leadership. LEGO's digitalization moves and the new ways of thinking about enterprise-wide digitalization indicate that the company is beyond the inflection point and has been building those capabilities, and is climbing the curve to increasingly higher levels of enterprise digital leadership.

The LEGO case shows that it is favorably poised for digital leadership. It is clear that the company, from the CEO and top management team downwards, has a deep commitment to enterprise-wide digitalization, and there are many examples that indicate its capabilities for digital leadership have been enhanced. One is the development of the new separate (but coupled) engagement platform. The design of this platform would not have been possible without the platform capabilities built over the years that allow LEGO to simultaneously take advantage of software-as-a-service (SaaS) applications and APIs in a well-structured open three-layered architecture, while also solidly operating core enterprise platform components such as Oracle ATG and SAP. It would not have been possible to design a full-governance framework and operating model for dynamic adaptive development of applications and new functionalities for the engagement platform without CIT's workforce capabilities that have

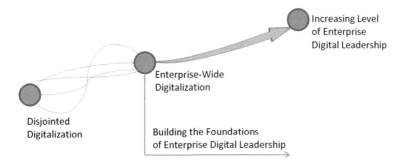

Figure 8.9 The Path to Enterprise Digital Leadership

been developed for digitalization applications over the years. The user experience focus of the engagement platform would not have been possible without the enterprise-wide digitalization capabilities that have developed over the years.

Some of LEGO's early digitalization moves were painful and only partly successful, which caused the company to rethink the approach to building platforms for digitalization and led to the twin platform model. All the learning that was gained from multiple aspects of enterprise-wide digitalization through the years is being built into the new engagement platform so it can serve the digitalization needs of LEGO's business ecosystem of customers, partners and employees in a more agile and resilient way.

LEGO has enhanced its enterprise capabilities through digitalization and has moved further along the path toward digital leadership. It is poised to continue this journey and is much better equipped to handle future digital leadership challenges.

To assist other organizations in their digital leadership journeys, we have constructed Tables 8.1–8.6, one for each of the six foundational building blocks of digital leadership—business strategy, business models, enterprise platforms, people mindset and skill set, the corporate IT function and a humanized workplace. Each table describes the characteristics of the particular building block and the enterprise capabilities needed for that building block. Based on LEGO's journey toward digital leadership, the right-hand column of each table lists *some* of the possible mechanisms for enhancing enterprise capability for a particular characteristic. These tables are not comprehensive because, to avoid overloading readers, we have selected only three distinctive characteristics for each foundational building block.

Lessons for Digital Leadership

LEGO's various digitalization moves have resulted in learning throughout the company. The lessons have resulted in new ways of thinking about the strategic success of digitalization and the requirements for digital leadership and will be of value for other organizations. We describe these lessons under three headings: new ways of thinking about enterprise digitalization, new ways of thinking about platforms and new ways of thinking about the digital workforce. In each of these areas, the lessons have changed both the lens through which LEGO views digitalization, and the vocabulary and culture relating to digitalization. In combination, these lessons and the new ways of thinking have had a transformational impact at LEGO in terms of building better foundations for digital leadership and enhancing its capabilities for digital leadership.

Table 8.1 Distinctive Characteristics of Business Strategy for Digital Leadership

Characteristic	Description	Enterprise Capability	Mechanisms for Enhancing Enterprise Capability
A Fused Business Strategy that is Executed Digitally	The strategy is executed through enterprise-wide digitalization, rather than through a business strategy that has an extra digital layer, with deep top management commitment to digitalization.	Top management team has the organizational capability to devise and implement business strategy through a digitalization mindset.	• Get the CEO to disseminate the digitalization vision to all employees • Ensure top management articulates its commitment to leveraging digitalization as a critical priority for the enterprise • Base the organizational structure on visibility and transparency • Organize the corporate IT function so it is close (proximate) to business units
A Business Strategy that Boosts Core Distinctive Competences through Digitalization	The strategy recognizes that digital platforms and digital media can pull companies into too many adjacent markets or areas where they do not have distinctive competences.	Top management recognizes the need to closely integrate digitalization into strategy rather than loosely couple it.	• Understand and focus on the enterprise's core distinctive competence • Learn how to partner with other companies that bring complementary skills in the digital and media space
A Business Strategy that Leverages the Ecosystem of Partners for Complementary Digitalization Competences	The strategy is based on collaboration with partners rather than viewing them as vendors or going it alone.	The enterprise has the capability to work well with different types of partners across enterprise boundaries and in different types of markets.	• Manage visibility and transparency across porous boundaries • Embed partners in enterprise teams • Work with dynamic partners that can scale up and down quickly in digitalization projects • Work with partners with niche digital expertise when needed

Table 8.2 Distinctive Characteristics of Business Models for Digital Leadership

Characteristic	Description	Enterprise Capability	Mechanisms for Enhancing Enterprise Capability
Business Models for Products and Services that Take Advantage of both the Physical and Digital World as Appropriate	Self-explanatory.	Business unit teams and partners have the organizational and digital platform capability to design, modify and assess digital business models and hybrid business models on all their dimensions (value proposition, interface, platform, partnering processes, revenue sharing).	• Launch new products and services with both physical and digital components • Launch initiatives with partners that bring special technology or media expertise
Business Models for Products and Services that Co-Create Value with Customers and Communities	The business model recognizes the strategic value of leveraging partners and customers in digital business ecosystems with high connectivity.	The enterprise has the capability to manage porous boundaries with customers and partners.	• Use crowdsourcing for new product or service design ideas • Launch online community groups • Move customers up the affinity pyramid to increase engagement • Launch omnichannel marketing initiatives • Launch new products and services with ecosystem partners
Business Models that Assess SMAC Technologies through a Digitalization Value Lens	The business model encourages the use of social media for business discovery, mobile apps for consumer enterprise applications, analytics for insight and cloud services for reducing complexity.	The enterprise and corporate IT has the capability to harness consumer-grade technologies within enterprise applications and business units.	• Use social media for business applications • Launch mobile apps for enterprise functions consistent with "what you see is what you need" • Develop analytics competency centers within business units for micromarketing • Experiment with multiple cloud providers and SaaS applications

Table 8.3 Distinctive Characteristics of Enterprise Platforms for Digital Leadership

Characteristic	Description	Enterprise Capability	Mechanisms for Enhancing Enterprise Capability
A Rock Solid Enterprise Platform that is Consumer-grade-friendly to Employees	A carefully specified, designed and tested enterprise platform, often based on ERP systems. Digitalization, however, requires consumer-grade applications that help make the enterprise more efficient and spread digitalization more easily.	Capability of corporate IT to develop: • Applications using the plan-build-run paradigm. • Consumer-grade apps within the enterprise platform environment.	• Enhance core enterprise platform team capabilities and keep them in-house • Launch mobile apps in enterprise platform environment • Work with external partners only on non-essential enterprise tasks
An Engagement Platform that Responds Very Quickly to Dynamic Demands for New Functionalities	A platform that enables dynamic digital interaction with customers and partners in the ecosystem and that allows rapidly changing functionalities to be added quickly. With such a platform the order of business priorities changes to time, reliability, quality and cost.	Capability of corporate IT to: • Undertake agile development. • Deliver "good enough" solutions and iterate. • Maintain 24/7 availability even when changes are made. • Operate continuously in beta mode.	• Use digitalization requests from customers, partners and business units to enhance the ability to deliver • Develop orientation programs (inspired, for example, by SMAC technologies) to progress the engagement platform concept
A Loose-Tight Coupling of Enterprise and Engagement Platforms that Place a High Priority on User Experience	The enterprise and engagement platforms are architected so they can be simultaneously managed yet give high priority for the user experience needed for digitalization.	Capability of corporate IT to: • Be ambidextrous and have the dual mindset needed to manage both platforms simultaneously. Create strong governance frameworks and operating models for both platforms.	• Use social media for business applications • Launch mobile apps for enterprise functions consistent with "what you see is what you need" • Develop analytics competency centers within business units for micromarketing • Experiment with multiple cloud providers and SaaS applications

Table 8.4 Distinctive Characteristics of People Mindset and Skill Set for Digital Leadership

Characteristic	Description	Enterprise Capability	Mechanisms for Enhancing Enterprise Capability
An Experimenting and Iterating-to-Success Mindset	Propensity of individuals and groups to "act their way into new ways of thinking" and to iterate to success through experimenting, failing and trying again.	Capability to manage transparently and accept failures. Capability to take risks on new initiatives. Capability to operate continuously in beta mode.	• Carry out experiments and prototypes • Train employees to accept failures and have mechanisms for sharing and learning from them • Encourage a culture of collaboration and experimentation • Encourage and deploy flat hierarchies, where decision authority is delegated
Digital Generalist and Collaboration Skill Sets that can Be Deployed across Porous Boundaries	People with the skillset to move between tasks and jobs across business units rather than rigid technical specialists who just want to work in corporate IT.	Ability to move people between business units. Ability of the HR department to have fluid job specifications.	• Rotate people through business units and jobs • Integrate diverse employees, and partners, through shared purpose and meaning • Provide opportunities for employees to constantly develop new skills and seek new opportunities
The Mindset and Skills that Make People Comfortable with Changing Tasks and Assignments Quickly and Flexibly	People with the flexibility to meet challenges and opportunities as they arise, and with an external focus.	Same as above.	• Be prepared to "give up" a good employee in your business unit when there is a critical need elsewhere in the enterprise

New Ways of Thinking about Enterprise Digitalization

Lesson 1. Execute Business Strategy Digitally. In late June 2015, a few days before most Danes go on their annual July summer holiday, Jørgen Vig Knudstorp, LEGO's CEO, posted an internal company blog to all employees wishing them a great summer, with the subject line "No more digital strategy—executing strategy digitally." What he meant was that there was no longer a separate digital strategy that was aligned with business strategy, but that the corporate business strategy, itself was executed through digitalization. He used several examples to illustrate LEGO's new way of thinking. He likened it to the difference between an established taxi company's cab-hailing app and Uber, where digitalization has transformed the entire business model and the corporate strategy. He also likened it to designing an e-book with interactivity and personalization and other unique digitally enabled features that cannot be compared to anything that was available in hard copy form. His words from the blog say it best: "We need to bring the digital technology to bear in a very

Table 8.5 Distinctive Characteristics of the Corporate IT Function for Digital Leadership

Characteristic	Description	Enterprise Capability	Mechanisms for Enhancing Enterprise Capability
A Corporate IT Function that is Meshed Closely with Business Units and Partners, and is Close to the Business on Multiple Proximity Dimensions	The IT organization is a solution-taker, partner and platform integrator. It needs to mesh well with business units and external partners from the ecosystem. It needs to understand the multiple dimensions of proximity and operationalize them for its own cultural context.	Corporate IT function has the capability to collaborate closely with multiple functional areas and different business units. It also has the capability to collaborate closely and work with many changing agile partners that are comfortable with not having clearly defined work packages.	• Restructure the IT organization to improve its proximity to business units and the enterprise at all levels to increase the level of collaboration, mutual understanding and visibility of the IT function • Assign a CTO to manage the plan-build-run way of organizing IT • Promote an "Enterprise first, IT Second" mentality • Embed partners in corporate IT teams
A Corporate IT Function that Distributes the Ownership of Digital Innovation throughout the Enterprise	Digital officers in business units work closely with corporate IT. Responsibility for digital innovation is thus distributed, not centralized with a chief digital officer.	Same as above.	• Appoint digital officers in the business units • Emphasize communication and knowledge sharing about digital solutions • Practice shared-solution finding while realizing that a very rapid and agile response is needed
A CIO Who is Equally Comfortable Running Corporate IT and Overseeing Digitalization in the Enterprise	The CIO spends time focusing on enterprise-wide digitalization and inspires the corporate IT workforce to have an outside-in mentality. He or she will also need to drive ideas for new enterprise platforms.	The enterprise has the capability for transparency and information sharing at the top management level. It also has the capability to build a corporate IT platform that takes an enterprise-wide view.	• Interact and collaborate frequently with top management team • Evangelize the digitalization message and philosophy to the CEO and board • Educate corporate IT employees on digitalization philosophies • Create a strategic business development function within corporate IT

Table 8.6 Distinctive Characteristics of a Humanized Workplace for Digital Leadership

Characteristic	Description	Enterprise Capability	Mechanisms for Enhancing Enterprise Capability
A Workplace that Offers Easy and Accessible Digital Experiences	The workplace provides employees with personalized, mobile and consumer-grade digital experiences (including on the enterprise platform). These experiences provide consistency in private and business use of technology and user interfaces.	Ability of corporate IT to work with employees to co-create (develop, test and build) personalized consumer-grade mobile apps.	• Provide user-friendly enterprise applications/ apps for the workplace • Develop applications/ apps that are personalized for employee tasks • Implement a "bring your own device" policy
A Workplace that Encourages and Prioritizes Ubiquitous Learning and Knowledge Sharing	The workplace provides digital savvy employees, who require a higher purpose for their work, with continual opportunities to develop themselves and learn.	Same as above.	• Launch platforms for collaboration and knowledge sharing • Practice knowledge sharing and open information exchange • Engage employees in enterprise-wide digitalization events
A Workplace that Thrives on Location and Time Flexibility	The workplace accommodates employees' different needs and priorities for working hours and where to work. The born digital generation's desired mode is "working in the moment of need" rather than "working when requested."	Capability of HR and the enterprise to empathize with employees' lives, families and personal preferences while still preserving productivity.	• Allow employees to decide how and when to work • Invest in digital platform capabilities for remote work • Provided 24/7 technology support services • Make information available wherever employees are, via multiple and mobile devices

fundamental and business model changing way, it is not a layer or a way of distributing content—it is the thing itself." In that summer send-off message, the CEO was telling the entire company what was now the new way of thinking about digitalization at the top management level. LEGO has recognized that digital leadership entails communicating a clear vision from the top and a true commitment to execution.

Lesson 2. Use Digitalization to Bolster Business Strategy around Your Core Distinctive Competence. Digitalization has been one LEGO's four strategic priorities since 2009, resulting in a continuously increasing percentage of hybrid products that combine physical and digital play, and many partnerships with companies in the media and digital industries. However, despite all the digitalization moves, LEGO has stayed focused on bricks—its core distinctive competence. LEGO has learned the lessons from its early forays into too many adjacent markets and has learned to keep the core business strategy focused on the brick while leveraging digitalization. Organization's should not be seduced by Apple's success in moving into adjacent markets through digital platforms as it moved from computers to music to mobile phones and more. In all these moves, Apple has transferred its distinctive competencies in software development, hardware design, user-friendly interfaces and supply chain management. For most organizations that is not the case, and they need to be very careful that digitalization neither deflects nor diffuses their core business strategy away from their core distinctive competencies. All C-level executives (including CIOs) need to be acutely aware of that as they co-drive digitalization demands from their companies and their business ecosystems.

Lesson 3. Position the Corporate IT Function Close to the Business to Enable Responsive Digitalization. The LEGO Group restructured its CIT organization for business responsiveness, with more IT people located in the major business hubs. However, it learned that co-location is one of many proximity dimensions. There is also a collaboration proximity dimension, and CIT learned that joint collaboration for solution finding with the business units is much more effective than the "plan-build-run" requirements-focused systems development model used for enterprise platforms. Then there is the business area proximity, where each business area has an associated CIT unit with a CIO who directly engages with and intimately understands that area's issues. There is also cultural proximity; at LEGO, the strong corporate culture precedes and trumps the IT culture. To achieve responsive digitalization in a dynamic business environment, organizations need to understand the multiple dimensions of proximity and how best to operationalize them in their own context. Effective digitalization requires positioning corporate IT close to the business on all these proximity dimensions.

Lesson 4. Create Multiple Digital Officers to Distribute Digital Innovation across the Enterprise. LEGO's CIT learned that creating digital officers in each business area is a much more effective way of orchestrating digital innovation. This arrangement has resulted in more effective digitalization because the business areas are more proactive solution-providers, and the role of the IT function is more of a solution-taker, partner and global platform integrator LEGO's approach is quite different from the emerging wisdom of having a CDO in addition to the CIO and very different from the idea that increased digitalization and the rise of CDOs will mean there is less need for CIOs. In the case of LEGO, there is one Executive CIO and multiple digital officers throughout the business areas. We believe that creating multiple DOs is applicable to all industries and is a prerequisite for effective digital leadership.

Lesson 5. Leverage the Ecosystem of Partners for Complementary Digitalization Competencies. LEGO learned that it is best to leverage the ecosystem of partners for complementary digitalization competencies rather than get involved in an area that deflects from the company's core skills and competencies. In a dynamic digitalization context, leveraging partners with complementary competencies is not only helpful—it is crucial. It is also an effective way of minimizing organizational complexity because it can be hard to establish a critical mass of competencies within some narrow areas of functional expertise.

Lesson 6. Iterate to Success in Digitalization. In a company-wide blog, LEGO's CEO emphasized that effective digitalization and digital leadership require a different mind-set that nurtures the capability to experiment, learn and iterate:

> Working digitally is also a learning curve for us. It takes an ability to focus on getting the minimum loveable experience out there. To live in beta mode, to involve users in making it better. To constantly be behind in upgrading platforms and systems because they move so fast …

This new way of thinking comes from the learning gained from the many iterations of LEGO's digitalization moves—where there have been failures as well as successes. Digital leadership means embedding this way of thinking across the enterprise. Experimenting and iterating is the new normal for designing processes and platform developments.

New Ways of Thinking about Digital Platforms

Lesson 7. Recognize that User Experience Drives IT Architecture, Not Vice Versa. This lesson derives from the efforts LEGO made in bolstering the enterprise platform to accommodate the significantly growing demands for new applications and functionalities arising from the company's product and marketing digitalization moves. It also results from LEGO's realization that there was a need for a complementary engagement platform whose architecture was more suited to digital interaction and that would provide a more "wow" user experience and allow functionality to be added quickly. Through its enterprise platform, LEGO CIT had for years provided employees with classic SAP ERP interfaces but realized it could increase end-user and process efficiency by offering consumer-grade applications. User experience is a fundamental part of IT solutions.

Because the engagement platform will focus on the external digital audience, user experience is a fundamental part of IT solutions on this platform. In the past, LEGO first designed the enterprise IT architecture for integrity and then added the user interface and user experience on top of that—living with whatever constraints that provided for user experience. For dynamic digitalization where the user experience is critical and key, that approach no longer works. Now, LEGO needs to first think through what the user experience requirements are and then build an IT architecture that is suited to that.

Lesson 8. Recognize that Dynamic Engagement Platforms for Digitalization Invert Business Priorities and Generate a New Level of Complexity. LEGO's CIT organization learned that digitalization moves invert the typical business priorities for traditional enterprise platforms (cost then quality then reliability then time). Digitalization requires a dynamic engagement platform where the priorities are time then reliability then quality then cost. This change in priorities requires IT organizations to adopt an "ambidextrous" mindset where they can simultaneously manage both types of platforms, which generates a new level of technical and managerial complexity for corporate IT departments. They must provide a flexible and open engagement platform while also reducing complexity and maintaining security in the enterprise platform. The explosion of demand for new functionalities resulting from increased digitalization will further increase complexity in terms of scale and scope. Managing the ambidextrous nature of IT requirements and the growing complexity is a top priority for corporate IT leaders when designing and managing dynamic digital platforms.

Lesson 9. Collaborate with Technology Vendor Partners to Create Dynamic Digital Platforms. LEGO's CIT organization has had to collaborate and partner with many new technology vendors to deal with all the requirements of the various product and marketing digitalization moves and with the dynamic changes needed in platform function-alities. It has learned that there is a need for technology vendors that work as partners, are agile and are comfortable working without clearly defined work packages. CIT moved from working with a few big partners to working with many diverse partners, some of which are niche players in their specific areas, and it learned how to manage the relationship with those types as well. CIT also realized that as vendors become true partners, they are increasingly embedded in CIT teams, and boundaries become more blurred. Thus, any company that is embarking on digitalization in dynamic business environments will need to think through how to manage its relationships and boundaries with new types of vendor partners.

Lesson 10. View SMAC Technologies Through a Digitalization Value Lens. The term SMAC (social, mobile, analytics, cloud) has been used to concisely express the four key technologies that are driving digital innovation—i.e., digitalization. LEGO learned from its digitalization moves the importance of social media in business and their value in discover-ing customers' concerns and needs. It learned from changing employee expectations and the consumerization of enterprise IT that people expect the same type of user experience in their enterprise applications as they get from mobile apps. It learned the importance of analytics/big data in generating valuable insights from micromarketing and increased digital engage-ment. It learned the value of the cloud in delivering new applications easily from using SaaS technologies for many corporate applications and that cloud computing creates much value as a "complexity reliever" rather than just as a cost saver. Thus, viewing SMAC technologies through a digitalization value lens provides a different perspective: social media in business creates value from discovering things; mobile technologies create value through using con-venient apps; analytics creates value through real-time insights and personalization of mar-keting and products; and cloud services create value through reducing complexity. Assessing SMAC technologies through a value lens will lead to more astute use of the technologies for effective digitalization.

New Ways of Thinking about the Digital Workforce

Lesson 11. Hire Digital Generalists Rather than Just Technical Specialists. An often repeated mantra is "Hire for a Career not a Job." LEGO's CIT organization has recruited more technical staff to meet the company's new digitalization needs and learned that it is best to hire flexible, dynamic and adaptable employees who can cope with task and position changes and can work on digitalization anywhere in the enterprise. Any company seeking to develop digital leadership capabilities and trying to boost its digital workforce should hire technical people for a digitalization career in the company rather than for a spe-cialized job in IT. To augment their enterprises' capabilities for digital leadership, CIOs need to rethink their hiring criteria for corporate IT.

Lesson 12. Create an Attractive Workplace for Digitally Savvy People. LEGO's culture has always nurtured playfulness at work and creating a fun, collaborative environment. It has also realized that the new born digital generation has different work-place expectations in terms of flexible working hours and mobility, information sharing and consumer-grade technology capabilities and access. LEGO's CIT organization has therefore deliberately set out to create a more humanized workplace with more interesting and mean-ingful work. As the extent of digitalization increases and more born digital employees enter the workforce, the need to provide an attractive workplace will become more critical.

Lesson 13. Improve and Monitor the Digital Quotient[23] of the Workforce. As a legacy bricks-and-mortar company, LEGO has a mix of longstanding traditional employees and an increasing number of born digital millennials. As well as digital savvy employees, the digitalization culture requires adaptable and resilient people with the ability to thrive in a fast-changing environment. With such a heterogeneous workforce, LEGO has realized that not everyone can be at the same level of digitalization readiness and has accepted that some employees will never achieve a high level of readiness. Even so, these employees can still have valuable roles in digitalization moves. Companies seeking to develop their workforce for digitalization should measure their digital quotient, seek ways to improve it and monitor it over time. There are various emerging methods and instruments for measuring an organization's digital quotient. These tools have culture and workforce components.

Concluding Comments

This article has described key aspects of LEGO's digitalization experiences and the lessons learned. The LEGO case indicates that digitalization and digital leadership will require six foundational building blocks: a different kind of business strategy, different kinds of business models, a different kind of humanized digital workplace, a different kind of enterprise platform integration, a different kind of people mindset and skill set, and a different kind of corporate IT function. The case has provided a better understanding of the distinctive characteristics of each of these foundations of digital leadership and how enterprise capabilities for digital leadership can be developed.

We believe that digital leadership is a critical issue for organizations around the world in both developed and emerging economies, and in all industries, and for traditional bricks-and-mortar companies as well as born digital companies. The insights from the LEGO case will help CIOs and CXOs in other organizations aspiring to become digital leaders. Our aim has been to present the foundations and capabilities required for digital leadership in way that makes it simpler for others to operationalize them and take advantage of them. Achieving digital leadership will, however, require stamina to stay the course because effective digitalization is a long-term effort and involves deep organizational change.

We believe that LEGO's digitalization experiences and learning helps to advance understanding of how to more effectively lay the foundations and build the capabilities needed for digital leadership. We also hope that this article will stimulate more researchers to develop theories of digital leadership—theories that can be applied in practice so that digitalization can make significant business impacts.

Finally, in the spirit of the LEGO experiential learning philosophy, the collaboration we used in writing this article has enabled us to act our way into a new way of thinking. In particular, we found the collaboration between academics and practitioners both energizing and useful for us all. We believe this collaboration has helped us to develop a better understanding of digital leadership. The energizing song lyric from the LEGO movie continues to play in our heads: "Everything is awesome. Everything is cool when you're part of a team!"[24]

Notes

1   Dorner, K. and Edelman, D. "What 'digital' really means," McKinsey & Company, July 2015, available at http://www.mckinsey. com/industries/high-tech/our-insights/what-digital-really-means.

2   Castells, M. "The Rise of the Network Society," Wiley-Blackwell, 2009.

3   http://www.gartner.com/technology/cio/cioagenda.jsp.

4   Kane, G. C., Palmer, D., Phillips, A. N. and Kiron, D. "Is Your Business Ready for a Digital Future," *MIT Sloan Management Review,* Summer 2015.

5   There are different levels of ambition in defining digitalization. Most commonly, it is viewed as the process of transforming the structure, processes, people skills and culture of the entire organization so it can use digital technologies to create and offer products, services and experiences that

customers, employees and partners find valuable. At LEGO, the definition is more ambitious and goes beyond enhancing current processes and services, and is about doing new things through digitalization that could not be done before.

6   Bennis, W. *On Becoming a Leader,* Addison-Wesley, 1989.

7   Iansiti, M. and Levien, R. "Strategy as Ecology," *Harvard Business Review,* March 2004.

8   El Sawy, O. A. "The 3 Faces of IS Identity: Connection, Immersion, and Fusion," *Communications of the AIS* (12), November 2003.

9   Bharadwaj, A., El Sawy, O. A., Pavlou, P. and Venkatraman, N. "Digital Business Strategy: Towards a Next Generation of Insights," *MIS Quarterly, June 2013.*

10   *Keen, P. G.W. and Williams, R. O.* The Value Path: Embedding Innovation in Everyday Business When the Customer Makes the Rules," *Business Futures Press, 2012.*

11   El Sawy, O. A. and Pereira, F. *Business Modeling in the Dynamic Digital Space*, Springer Books, 2012.

12   Simons, P. *The Age of the Platform,* Motion Publishing, 2011.

13   Vitalari, N. and Shaughnessy, H. *The Elastic Enterprise,* Telemachus Press, 2012.

14   For information on the "humanized" workplace, see "How to Humanize your Workplace™" on http://www.lynntaylorconsulting.com/blog/?p=32

15   http://www.lego.com/en-us/aboutus/lego-group/management.

16   http://www.lego.com/da-dk/careers/our-culture.

17   See, for example, "LEGO CEO Jørgen Vig Knudstorp on leading through survival and growth," *Harvard Business Review*, January 2009; Robertson, D. and Breen, B. *Brick by Brick: How LEGO Rewrote the Rules of Innovation and Conquered the Global Toy Industry,* Crown Business Books, 2013; and We Lost the Focus on the Bricks, available at http://www.internationaltradenews.com/interviews/we-lost-the-focus-on-the-bricks

18   Antorini, Y., Muniz, A. and Askildsen, T. "Collaborating With Customer Communities: Lessons from the LEGO Group, *MIT Sloan Management Review,* Spring 2012.

19   Some of this history up to 2004 is in Rikhardsson, P., Møller, C. and Kræmmergaard, P. *ERP: Danish Experiences with Implementation and Use,* in Danish, Børsens Forlag, 2004.

20   LEGO has outsourced application maintenance for less business-facing tasks to HCL in India. As a strategic partner to LEGO, HCL operates the LEGO-specific Offshore Delivery Center with approximately 200 full-time external consultants.

21   See, for example, Barr, S. *What it takes to build your Digital Quotient*, McKinsey & Company, June 2015, available at www.mckinsey.com/insights/organization/what-it-takes-to-build-your-digital-quotient.

22   "LEGO overhaler Microsoft: Sadan indfanger vi Danmarks bedste it-folk [LEGO overtakes Microsoft: How we capture Denmark's best IT people]," *ComputerworldDenmark*, available at http://www.computerworld.dk/art/231176/lego-overhaler-microsoft-saadan-indfanger-vi-danmarks-bedste-it-folk#Re0jq1AFYWqlwwas.99.

23   A company's digital quotient is a simple metric for its digital maturity. For more information, see Catlin, T., Scanlan, J. and Wilmott, P. "Raising Your Digital Quotient," *McKinsey Quarterly*, June 2015.

24   https://www.youtube.com/watch?v=StTqXEQ2l-Y; this rendering has been viewed over 45 million times.

Questions for Discussion

1   Have companies go designated digital leadership? Who manages organizations' digital transformation?

2   How do companies take culture, economy and society and talent development into account in their digital transformation? Are these considered important?

3   Is digital leadership a new form of leadership requiring new capabilities and foundations? How would these skills and capabilities get acquired?

4   What is the importance of a business ecosystem?

5   Evaluate the role of CDOs in digital transformation. Does the success of digital transformation depend on the CDO?

6   The LEGO Group example outlines three strands of digital transformation: product, marketing and enterprise. Are these equally important? Suggest other important strands for digitalization. Explain and provide examples.

Further Reading

Leidner, D. E., Mackay, J. M. (2007). How incoming CIOs transition into their new jobs. *MIS Quarterly Executive*, 6(1): 17–28.
Preston, D. S., Leidner, D. E., Chen, D. (2008). CIO leadership profiles: Implications of matching CIO authority and leadership capability on IT impact. *MIS Quarterly Executive*, 7(2): 57–68.

Chapter 9

Anna Singh and Thomas Hess

HOW CHIEF DIGITAL OFFICERS PROMOTE THE DIGITAL TRANSFORMATION OF THEIR COMPANIES

THE EMERGENCE OF CHIEF DIGITAL OFFICERS

EMBRACING THE OPPORTUNITIES PRESENTED by new digital technologies is one of the most urgent challenges companies face today. Yet, 63% of executives and managers find that "*the pace of technology change in their organization is too slow.*"[1] Companies obviously need to address this issue.

Until recently, chief information officers (CIOs) were mainly held responsible for digital innovation. For several years, companies have expected their CIOs to extend their roles from pure technologists to business strategists. This means they need "*to spend less time managing IT services and more time delivering broader business value. If they don't, CEOs may appoint other executives to drive that value.*"[2] These new responsibilities have been placing pressures on CIOs, and many have had difficulties in embracing them.[3]

To identify the reasons for these difficulties, it's necessary to examine the nature and purpose of digital transformation. A company undergoing a digital transformation uses new digital technologies such as social media, mobile access, analytics or embedded devices to enable major business improvements like enhancing customer experience, streamlining operations or creating new business models.[4] The term "transformation" (as opposed to "change," for instance) expresses the comprehensiveness of the actions that need to be taken when organizations are faced with these new technologies. Thus, a digital transformation typically involves a company-wide digital (transformation) strategy,[5] which goes beyond functional thinking and holistically addresses the opportunities and risks that originate from digital technologies. A digital transformation strategy guides the organization in its journey toward being digitally transformed.[6]

The responsibilities associated with digital transformation have such a high level of complexity that it is immensely challenging for the CEO or just one senior executive to manage them in addition to his or her original responsibilities. For example, the original responsibilities of a CIO are to manage the operation of the IT infrastructure and the evolution of platforms. Digital transformation, however, goes beyond merely digitizing resources and results in value and revenues being created from digital assets.[7] Moreover, new digital technologies "*demand different mindsets and skill sets than previous waves of transformative technology*,"[8] which might be another reason why CIOs are often not necessarily best equipped to take charge of digital transformation.

Increasingly, companies are establishing an additional position at top management level: the chief digital officer (CDO). The CDO role can be centralized at the group level or decentralized at the subsidiary level. Regardless of positioning, CDOs are employed to make digital transformation a strategic priority in their companies. MTV Networks was the first to hire a CDO, back in 2005. Since then, the number of CDOs has roughly doubled each year. The CDO is one of the fastest-growing C-level positions, and although 88% of CDOs have been hired in the U.S., the role is a global phenomenon.[9]

But what exactly do CDOs do, and how do they differ from their CxO colleagues? And is the CDO a temporary role that will disappear in the future? Although many CDO positions have already been established, there is still confusion about what exactly CDOs are expected to achieve and what their main responsibilities are. The purpose of this article is to provide answers to these questions. Companies need to understand the roles a CDO can play and the skills they should look for in a CDO. Based on six in-depth case studies,[10] we identify the skills and characteristics a CDO should have and offer insights into how the CDO role is performed.

What Chief Digital Officers Are and What They Are Not

To understand the nature and role of CDO positions, it is necessary to distinguish the CDO from adjacent C-level executive positions that might at first glance have similar responsibilities—i.e., the CIO, chief data officer, chief innovation officer and chief strategy officer.

The most important distinction is between CDOs and CIOs. Unlike CIOs, who are the most senior IT executives in an organization,[11] CDOs have no functional IT responsibility. Most often, they have no profit and loss responsibility, and their overall corporate perspective is broader than CIOs'. Even if a firm's CIO does deliver digital business innovation and broader strategic business value, the CDO additionally focuses on fostering cross-functional collaboration, mobilizing the whole company across hierarchy levels and stimulating corporate action to digitally transform the whole company. While the CIO takes the role of the *strategic IT specialist*, the CDO is the company's *digital transformation specialist*. This is the distinguishing factor between CDOs and CIOs: transformation is at the core of the CDO's role, not a responsibility in addition to others.

CDOs also differ from chief data officers, who are their organizations' *data specialists*, focusing on data management and data analytics. Chief data officers put data on the business agenda and, instead of treating data merely as a by-product of running the business, they devise strategies for exploiting the business's data.[12] Chief data officers thus focus on just one organizational capability within the digital realm: big data. Although big data obviously also plays a role in the work of CDOs, the scope of the CDO role is much broader and not confined to this one specific area of digital transformation.

Even though CDOs' responsibilities include digital innovation, they do not replace chief innovation officers, who are the *corporate innovation specialists* and who lead an organization's broader innovation efforts.[13] Chief innovation officers create an environment that fosters innovation and provides the organizational structure to support the development of new products and services. Their role involves exploiting ideas from both internal and external sources, for instance in the form of crowdsourcing and cross-company collaboration. As such, the underlying goals of CDOs and chief innovation officers are different. The latter redefine technologies, company structures and day-to-day practices, without having a dedicated digital focus, while CDOs focus on the digital overhaul of the whole company.

Obviously, digital transformation has strategic importance for a company. Typically, a company's chief strategy officer (CSO)[14] focuses on strategic issues and acts as the *corporate strategist*. But the CSO doesn't have a specific focus on digital transformation. A CSO typically lacks both the specialized knowledge about digital business models and the experience to handle projects in this field. These tasks are the responsibility of the CDO.

Definition of the CDO Role

To clearly distinguish CDOs from these other C-level executives, we offer the following description of the CDO role: The CDO orchestrates the digital transformation of a company. The CDO role thus includes supporting top management in formulating and executing a dedicated digital transformation strategy.[15] By stimulating and leading corporate action, the CDO embraces the full spectrum of opportunities presented by new digital technologies and thus aims to bring the company to the forefront of the digital evolution taking place. Internally, the CDO fosters cross-functional collaboration and mobilizes the whole company across hierarchy levels. It is important to recognize that CDOs have a wider role than heads of individual digital business units; CDOs assume cross-department authority for digital initiatives and aim to transform the company as a whole.

Table 9.1 summarizes the key responsibilities, strategic perspectives and strategic roles of CDOs and the related C-level positions. Keeping the differences in mind is important for a full understanding of what the CDO role entails.

Table 9.1 Comparison of CDO and Other CxO Positions

	Chief Digital Officer	Chief Information Officer	Chief Data Officer	Chief Innovation Officer	Chief Strategy Officer
Key Responsibilities	• Digital mobilization of whole company • Initiation of digital initiatives • Companywide collaboration	• Strategic IT deployment • IT support	• Data management • Data analytics	• Structured corporate innovation • No specific focus on digital initiatives	• Management of strategy process • Strategy execution
Strategic Perspective	Digital Transformation Strategy	IT Strategy	Data Strategy	Innovation Strategy	Corporate Strategy
Specialist Role	Digital Transformation Specialist	Strategic IT Specialist	Data Specialist	Corporate Innovation Specialist	Corporate Strategist

Table 9.2 Overview of the Six Case Organizations

Case Industry	Annual Revenues(€) per Year(a)	Employees	Positioning of the CDO	Most Senior IT Executive	Chief Strategy Officer
1 Retail	20–30bn.	60–70K	Group	CIO	• Oct. 2015 (CDO) • Nov. 2015 (CIO)
2 Tourism	1–5bn.	1–5K	Subsidiary	CIO	• March 2014 (CDO)
3 Education	500mn–1bn	1–5K	Subsidiary	CIO	• April 2014 (CDO)
4 Market Research	100–250mn	500–1,000	Subsidiary	CIO	• Nov. 2015 (CDO) Dec. 2015 (CTO) Jan. 2016 (Managing Director)
5 Financial Services	100–250mn	500–1,000	Subsidiary	Head of IT	• Dec. 2015 (CDO) Dec. 2015 (Head of IT)
6 Publishing	1–100mn	100–500	Group	CDO (b)	• Jan. 2016 (CDO)

(a) The wide range of annual revenues and employees is deliberate to preserve the anonymity of the case organizations.

(b) In case 6, the same person holds both the CDO and CIO positions.

Six Cases Illustrating the CDO Role

In the following sections, we describe the experiences of six companies that employ a CDO to illustrate how CDOs perform their roles in a range of industries (retail, tourism, education, market research, financial services and publishing). Table 9.2 provides an overview of the six cases.

Case 1: A CDO in the Retail Industry

With turnover in the range of €20 to €30 billion[16], with 60,000 to 70,000 employees, Case 1 is the largest retailer in Europe within its business sector. The company operates in 15 countries, and the CDO, along with the CIO, is employed at corporate group level.

Scope of the Digital Transformation. The digital transformation has three major components:

1. *Customer experience enhancement:* An omni-channel strategy that involves the creation of a seamless customer experience across all touch points.
2. *Business operations:* Focusing on (in the CDO's words) "efficiency through automation" to gain more time for enhancing the customer experience.
3. *New business opportunities:* Monitoring potential business opportunities created through the use of digital technologies.

Reason for Creating the CDO Role. According to the CDO, he was employed to transform the company toward a "*digitally empowered and customer driven*" organization. His mandate is to use state-of-the-art technologies to make the company more efficient and to offer customers personalized experiences.

Positioning of the CDO and CIO. Both the CDO and CIO report directly to the CEO, who is also personally involved in the digital transformation efforts. The CDO and CIO participate in the fortnightly strategic board meetings, thus demonstrating the close working relationships between the CDO, CIO and CEO.

CDO Tasks. The CDO defines the digital strategy and is responsible for digital innovation across the group. He uses new digital technologies to enhance the customer experience across all customer touch points and fully integrate the offline and online points of sale. Examples include cross-device online shopping carts and smartphone apps with integrated state-of-the-art technology, such as location-based services and augmented reality. By equipping the retail stores with tablet PCs, he enables the sales employees to quickly retrieve data and respond better to customers' needs.

To continuously keep track of emerging opportunities, the CDO constantly monitors digital trends and digitally savvy start-up companies. His trial-and-error culture means that he can try out new developments to see if they are appropriate for adoption. Although the CDO has a dedicated budget, he has no profit responsibility; such responsibility might hinder his ability to innovate.

The CDO works closely with operational colleagues, develops ideas in cooperation with the company's subsidiaries and conducts pilot projects. If proof-of-concepts are successful, they are rolled out across other subsidiaries. As part of his role in fostering company-wide collaboration and the exchange of ideas, the CDO initiated an annual Digital Campus for the group and all its subsidiaries. At these events, successful digital initiatives are presented to participants and they can experience new technologies hands-on.

Cooperation with the CIO. The CDO and CIO work closely together. In our interviews, both confirmed that the CDO is mainly responsible for the conception and planning of the digital transformation, whereas the CIO is mainly responsible for implementing the corresponding IT solutions.

Case 2: A CDO in the Tourism Industry

This company is a national subsidiary of one of the largest global travel companies. The subsidiary has a turnover in the range of €1 to €5 billion, with 1,000 to 5,000 employees, and has its own CIO. The CDO we interviewed has counterparts in other group subsidiaries.

Scope of the Digital Transformation. Originally, the company had a very traditional business model: it assembled travel packages, which were then sold via travel agencies. It did not have any direct interaction with customers. Today, however, growth in the travel business is driven by pure-play online platforms. When the company decided to employ a CDO, its online market share was only 4%. Although it had a subsidiary that was responsible for all of its digital business, the digital activities were characterized by a marked silo mentality because they were decoupled from the core business. The digital transformation now underway will remove the organizational silos by bundling all digital activities together and transforming the whole organization to become a more customer-centric, digitally savvy enterprise.

Reason for Creating the CDO Role. A dedicated CDO position was created to proactively drive the company's digital transformation and be the driving force behind the new digital initiatives.

Positioning of the CDO and CIO. The CDO and CIO report directly to the subsidiary's CEO. As the CDO noted, it is critical to her success that the CEO supports her digital initiatives and that she can collaborate with the CIO, who implements the digital initiatives.

CDO Tasks. The CDO is tasked with creating a "360 degree" customer experience across all customer touch points and with massively growing the company's online and mobile business. The CDO's main focus is therefore on customer relationship, social media and multichannel management. Overall, her job is split 50/50 into digital strategy implementation and management of ongoing business operations. Initially, the CDO's job consisted mainly of project-based work. After creating a digital growth strategy, she held many workshops, developed a business plan and a road map, and presented her concepts to the decision makers at the corporate holding company. When implementing the projects and programs, the CDO needed to mobilize the whole company [the subsidiary], particularly the project managers who were put in place. A corporate program was created to interlink all stakeholders, particularly decision makers involved in social media, customer relationship management, marketing and multichannel projects.

At the time we interviewed the CDO, a new sub-unit responsible specifically for digital media had already been created. However, the CDO told us that to achieve "*one single view of a customer*" and optimize the customer experience, customer data needed to be organized. Hence, the CDO initiated the creation of a master data management platform. This platform pools the various data sources and uses insights gained from the pooled data at the various customer touch points.

Cooperation with the CIO. The subsidiary's CEO created the CDO and CIO positions at the same time, recognizing that both are needed to progress the digital transformation. The CDO develops IT requirements iteratively and in close collaboration with the CIO. But the CIO has full responsibility for implementing what has been defined.

Case 3: A CDO in the Education Industry

Case 3 is the global operating company of what was originally a traditional publishing house. It provides students, teachers and institutions with educational content, and has revenues in the range of €500 million to €1 billion, with 1,000 to 5,000 employees. The company is currently transforming itself from a pure print publisher to a "*modern education company*" that offers sophisticated e-learning courses. The CDO is employed at subsidiary level, while a CTO is employed at group level.

Scope of the Digital Transformation. While the company's traditional business model was based on educational text books, the digital transformation will offer new opportunities in three areas:

1   *Adaptive learning:* Without a teacher who delivers course material, personalized online courses focus on each student's individual weaknesses in an automated way.
2   *Efficacy management:* The effectiveness of an online course can be systematically evaluated because each student's learning outcomes can be tracked and measured. Moreover, the company's marketing and sales executives can use this information to promote the successes of their users.
3   *Data-driven publishing:* Because the efficacy of the online courses is directly measured, the need to rely on improvement suggestions from teachers becomes obsolete. Instead, decision making is informed purely by data analytics. Should most students of a cohort fail at certain sections of an online course, product developers can promptly publish an improved version.

Reason for Creating the CDO Role. The CDO told us that his position was created to transition the business from a "*pure print publisher to a modern education company.*" The primary role of the CDO is therefore to conceive new digital products and drive their implementation.

Positioning of the CDO and Chief Technology Officer (CTO). The CDO reports directly to the subsidiary's CEO, while the CTO role is centralized at the group level.

CDO Tasks. Initially, the company had no plan for life after printed educational text books. The CDO therefore created a digital vision for the company, defined a cross-functional digital strategy and conceived new digital products.

The CDO sees himself as a strategist rather than a technologist because he focuses primarily on digital product development that is based on current customer needs. He collaborates closely with development partners, who are potential customers, to better identify current customer needs and adjust product development accordingly.

However, highly interactive digital products like online courses cannot simply be created directly from traditional text books, because the interactions and activities involved with online courses need to be modelled on an IT platform. The CDO therefore initiated the implementation of the Learning Management System. Teachers are supposed to log on to this platform, assign tasks to students and track their progress. At the core of this company's digital strategy is the combination of digital content and data analytics. Data analytics techniques are used to measure the performance of students and teachers individually and, at an aggregated level, across classes.

The digital transformation is replacing printed books with sophisticated online courses as the company's core offering. The transformation requires product development to be redefined and expanded because the company now requires employees with completely new skills and capabilities. Many business functions have been affected by the process of creating online courses, which is why the CDO became involved in activities across business units and needed to spread information across the company to convince all decision makers of the need for digital transformation.

Cooperation with the CTO. Technology platforms are essential for the production and distribution of the online courses. The CDO collaborates with the corporate group's CTO on issues concerning the technology infrastructure, but it is the CTO who is responsible for implementing the digital initiatives. However, the CDO works closely with software developers during product implementation.

Case 4: A CDO in the Market Research Industry

Case 4 is a renowned market research and marketing consultancy with revenues in the range of €100 to €250 million, with 500 to 1,000 employees. The company offers business-to-business (B2B) services across industries, and its main customers are corporate market researchers and marketers. It has both a CDO and a CTO, and is a national subsidiary of one of the largest research agencies worldwide. Each national subsidiary has its own CDO.

Scope of the Digital Transformation. The digital transformation has two primary components:

1   *Technology-enabled research*, which focuses on optimizing customer solutions through integrating digital technologies. Traditionally, the company focused on the collection of primary data when conducting its market research, and its main capability was statistical analyses. With the emergence of data from social media and search engines, the company is increasingly supplementing, or even replacing, its primary data collection with data from these new sources. This new kind of data also enables the company to provide predictive modelling and generate early warning indicators.

2   *Integrated marketing*, which is based on new digital touch points, such as social media, that have been changing the marketing activities of its customers. The company is also adjusting its marketing consultancy services to take account of these new touch points.

Reason for Creating the CDO Role. The CDO was appointed to support and drive the above-mentioned digital transformation projects throughout the subsidiary and to consult the customer-facing managers.

Positioning of the CDO and CTO. The CDO and CTO both report directly to the CEO. They are also members of the company's highest level strategy board, which focuses on digital transformation and is the forum where the CDO brings forward his ideas for discussion and decision taking.

CDO Tasks. To progress the company's digital journey and to raise awareness, the CDO regularly informs employees and managers about his current digital initiatives. At the employee level, he speaks at staff meetings; at the management level, he is involved in leadership town-hall meetings. The CDO initiates new ideas and projects and gives fresh impetus to the company's digital transformation journey on an ongoing basis. For instance, he recently conducted a multinational study with a special focus on marketing and e-commerce to investigate customers' perspectives of digital transformation. The insights from this study serve as a decision making tool and support the company in its consultancy activities.

In the area of technology-enabled research, the CDO addresses strategic questions concerning the use of data from social media and search engines—i.e., how the data can be incorporated into market research studies to offer true added value for customers. According to the CDO, "*this is a cultural shift, which is at least such a daunting task as the technological shift*" because customers often do not immediately understand the added value of the new solutions.

Cooperation with the CTO. Throughout the digital transformation journey, the CDO collaborates closely with the company's CTO. While, according to the CTO, the CDO "*listens in to customer needs and takes these insights into the company*," the CTO is responsible for implementing the digital projects.

Case 5: A CDO in the Financial Services Industry

Case 5 is the private banking subsidiary of the national branch of a European financial institution. The subsidiary generates revenues in the range of €100 to €250 million, with 500 to 1,000 employees. This company is at the very early stages of digital transformation and has appointed a CDO who leads the digital transformation unit jointly with the Head of IT.

Scope of the Digital Transformation. The private banking industry is highly conservative, with security and confidentiality being major concerns. The digital transformation is therefore proceeding with great caution and the company is, according to the CDO, "*carefully innovative.*" As a consequence, the scope of the digital transformation currently focuses just on changing the internal mindset and introducing basic digital tools and devices.

Reason for Creating the CDO Role. The CDO position was initiated bottom-up by the now-CDO herself, who has been with the company for several years as an online communication specialist. When she had introduced the company's first online channels, she had collaborated closely with the Head of IT. Jointly, they put forward the idea of creating a Digital Office to take the business in a new direction and proactively drive digital initiatives throughout the business. Due to this bottom-up approach, however, no specific targets for digital transformation have, as yet, been set by top management.

Positioning of the CDO and Head of IT. The digital transformation is not yet on the agenda of the top management team. The Digital Office reports to the communication department, which, in turn, reports to the CEO. Thus, so far there has been no direct input from the top management team on the purpose and aims of digital transformation. As a consequence, it is the CDO and the Head of IT who play a focal role in progressing any digital initiatives brought forward.

CDO Tasks. The CDO's current priority is on changing the mindset within the top management team and among employees before being able to proceed with specific digital initiatives. In her own words, she tries "*to offer new perspectives*" and to establish a more proactive attitude within the company by illustrating the up-coming changes in the market and putting forward innovative solutions. To get a feel for the opportunities presented by digital transformation, the CDO conducted interviews with representatives of firms from different industries that were already at an advanced stage of their digital transformations. She then collated the insights gained from the survey into a digital strategy for her own company.

Although operating in a separate unit, the CDO works closely with different stakeholders, particularly with the internal communication department and the customer consultants. Since the CDO's main goal is to offer customers a better service through the use of digital tools, the customer consultants have already been equipped with tablet computers. She also advises other company subsidiaries on their respective digital strategies.

Cooperation with the Head of IT. The CDO and the Head of IT work closely together to enable digital transformation. Having expertise in complementary fields, they distribute their responsibilities accordingly: the Head of IT takes charge of technology, while the CDO is responsible for communicating the technology benefits across the company.

Case 6: A CDO in the Publishing Industry

This company is an international publishing group with 100 to 500 employees and a focus on specialist psychological books and trade journals. It also provides testing systems for psychological diagnostics. The company has revenues in the range of €1 million to €100 million. The CDO, who is also the CIO, is employed at corporate group level.

Scope of the Digital Transformation. The digital transformation comprises four strategic initiatives:

1   *E-assessment*, which focuses on digitizing the company's psychological testing diagnostics
2   *One portal*, which bundles together content, databases and interactive products, and tailors the bundles to customer needs
3   *One web*, which is aimed at increasing the volume and efficiency of the company's e-commerce business
4   *One IT*, which deals with infrastructure and workplace IT and focuses on a common group infrastructure and common tools for communicating and cooperating more efficiently.

Reason for Creating the CDO Role. The CDO position was created to increase revenues from digital products. The CDO is also the CIO and is therefore also responsible for the IT infrastructure and for implementing IT-enabled business processes and applications aimed at enhancing process efficiency. It is important to note, however, that the CDO in this company clearly distanced himself from the "typical CDO." He stated that usually the CDO and CIO coexist, with the CIO servicing infrastructure and applications, and the CDO contributing to a strong customer perspective of the digital transformation.

Positioning of CDO. Because the digital transformation is on the strategic agenda of the top management team, the CDO reports directly to the group CEO. The CDO has the explicit task of informing and consulting the top management team, so he has a close relationship with the CEO. He is part of the group's strategic board, which involves regular meetings with the top management team and fosters close collaboration.

CDO Tasks. The CDO defines and implements the company's overall e-business strategy. His tasks involve advising the top management team, managing the digital business models and digital product development, and supporting and coordinating the organizational units in specific digital initiatives. His tasks are cross-functional, encompassing the product, e-commerce, IT and online marketing units. Hence, disseminating information and mobilizing employees are high on his agenda.

At the top management level, the CDO disseminates business-critical information across the publishing group and informs top management on current trends and developments in the market. He says his role here is to *"show and make plausible how fundamental the digital transformation is and how much the company's current business models are threatened if no actions are taken."* At the employee level, the CDO organizes workshops and training sessions to inform about the digital strategy and the progress of its implementation, and to train employees.

The CDO works at both the operational and strategic levels. He spends one-third of his time on communicating and exchanging ideas with the company's subsidiaries. He incorporates good ideas into the group strategy and manages the strategy implementation programs. He spends the rest of his time in steering committees or working on specific projects as a project sponsor.

Summary of the Six Cases

Table 9.3 summarizes the six cases in terms of the focus of the digital transformation, the task focus of the CDO and the relationship between the CDO and the most senior IT executive.

The Three Role Types of CDOs

Although the CDOs in the six case companies operate in diverse industries and companies, we were able to identify three main types of roles they play—the *Entrepreneur*, the *Digital Evangelist* and the cross-functional *Coordinator*.

The Entrepreneur Role

We observed a lot of entrepreneurial spirit in the CDOs across the cases. As the CIO in Case 1 put it: *"Our CDO is kind of an innovator, thought leader and consultant for our top management,"* Entrepreneur CDOs explore IT-enabled innovations, establish a digital transformation strategy and help their companies innovate through the use of new digital technologies. They initiate and design the controlled shift of their companies toward becoming digitally empowered organizations that strategically exploit the opportunities presented by new digital technologies. These CDOs point the way for their companies in a fast-paced technological environment and sometimes even adapt whole business models. Their responsiveness to the market is of particular importance in this context, which is why Entrepreneur CDOs have a strong customer focus.

The Digital Evangelist Role

The managing director in Case 4 described his CDO as *"the supreme evangelist. It is his task to inspire the people in the organization and to get them enthusiastic about digital topics."* To successfully inspire people, a corporate culture shift is usually needed because the traditional way of doing business is deeply entrenched in managers and employees. A crucial part of the Digital Evangelist's job is therefore to convince the workforce across all departments and hierarchy

Table 9.3 Overview of the Case Study Findings

	Case 1: Retail	Case 2: Tourism	Case 3: Education	Case 4: Market Research	Case 5: Financial Services	Case 6: Publishing
Focus of Digital Transformation	Enhancing customer experience	Growing the online and mobile business	Introducing sophisticated e-learning courses	Optimizing customer solutions	Enhancing customer service	Fostering
Task Focus of CDO	Digital innovation	Integration of online and traditional business	Development of digital business model and digital products	Support of market managers	Introduction of digital tools and devices	Increasing digital revenues
Relationship Between CDO and Most Senior IT Executive	Close collaboration: • CDO takes charge of strategy • CIO takes charge of IT implementation	Close collaboration and iterative requirements definition: • CDO takes business perspective CIO takes IT perspective	• CDO delegates technical aspects to the CTO at group level • CDO has additional software developers	Close collaboration: • CDO takes customer perspective • CIO delivers corresponding IT	Close collaboration: • CDO focuses on communication tasks • CIO takes on technology perspective	CDO assumes both roles

levels to pull together. In the words of the CDO in Case 5, "*CDOs need to offer new perspectives ... and educate people to look and think ahead.*"

As Digital Evangelists, CDOs communicate their digital strategies across their companies and across departmental boundaries to ensure the whole company is "signed up" to the digital journey. Employee training is an important part of the Digital Evangelist role because employees need to cope with many challenges and corporate changes in the process of digital transformation. In all of the cases we found that, although IT is an important part in CDOs roles, is not the primary challenge they face. According to the managing director in Case 4, "*Changing a whole organization is the true challenge.*"

The Coordinator Role

As well as inspiring all stakeholders, CDOs are responsible for actively stimulating the immense changes that are necessary to successfully execute their companies' digital transformation strategies. As a consequence, CDOs initiate and design the controlled organizational shift from decoupled silo functions to cross-functional cooperation. The CDOs in the case companies emphasized that digital transformation is not an isolated process, but affects many parts and stakeholders of the company, including IT, product development, HR, marketing and sales. It's clear that digital transformation requires strong coordination of different functional areas, leaving no space for previous silo approaches and mentalities. However, functional managers, with their focus on their own departments, are often unwilling to pull together. CDOs therefore need to work across organizational silos because digital transformation requires the alignment of executives across functions. The CDO in Case 2 emphasized that "*digital transformation cannot take place in a single subsidiary.*" CDOs are responsible for interlinking the whole company and acting as coordinators of the digital transformation.

Determinants of the Primary CDO Role

We found that all three CDO roles are important in the work of each CDO in the case companies but that the primary role played by a CDO depends on many factors. (Table 9.4 lists the primary role played by each of the six CDOs in our study.) These factors include the digital transformation maturity of the company, the digital mindset of the workforce, company size and the reporting relationships of the CDO (and thus the CDO's influence within the company). The expectations of the CDO role, both from the perspective of the top management team and the CDO, is also an important determinant of the primary role.

In Case 5, for instance, the company does not yet have a digital transformation strategy, and the digital mindset of the top management team is not yet sufficiently developed. Moreover, the CDO has no direct reporting relationship to the CEO. As a consequence, the CDO does not yet have enough influence to implement any profound changes and focuses primarily on the *Digital Evangelist* role.

Table 9.4 Primary CDO Role Type by Case Company

Entrepreneur	*Digital Evangelist*	*Coordinator*
• Case 1 (Retail)	• Case 4 (Market Research)	• Case 2 (Tourism)
• Case 3 (Education)	• Case 5 (Financial Services)	• Case 6 (Publishing)

The CDO in Case 2 had the very specific assignment to massively grow the company's online and mobile business. First and foremost, this required her to manage and coordinate all digital activities, which is why she primarily acts as a *Coordinator*. The CDO in Case 1, however, has a high level of freedom from the top management team to innovate, enhance the customer experience and look out for new business opportunities. As a result, he acts primarily as an *Entrepreneur*.

Key CDO Skills and Competencies

From our analysis of the CDO roles in the six case companies, we have identified five skills and competencies companies should look for in a CDO.

IT Competency

First and foremost, CDOs need IT competency, as emphasized by the CDO in Case 1: "*It is absolutely necessary that the CDO position is filled by someone who completely feels at ease in the digital world.*" New digital products and services are based on IT, so CDOs need to have an understanding of IT applications and the underlying infrastructures, as well as knowledge on how they can be upgraded and modified. Moreover, most CDOs collaborate closely with CIOs, who are responsible for the implementation of infrastructures and the evolution of platforms and IT systems. Thus, CDOs need a degree of IT competency in order to formulate IT requirements and iteratively develop new digital products and services in collaboration with CIOs. If CDOs do not have IT expertise, they will not be able to define and communicate the IT requirements for new digital-product and service ideas. As the CDO in Case 3 put it, "*If a CDO does not have a basic understanding of IT, then she or he is the wrong person for this job.*"

Change Management Skills

As well as IT competency, CDOs need business acumen. Profound and specific know-how on strategy, transformation and change management are crucial in this context. While the main focus of CIOs is on IT, CDOs need to understand what new digital technologies mean for their businesses and their customers. Not only do they need to understand the nuts and bolts of the business, such as business models, business processes and customer needs, but also the workings of different business functions, such as finance, marketing, sales, HR and others. Having an understanding of all these different aspects of the business enables CDOs to analyze and understand their companies' businesses comprehensively. As the CDO in Case 3 put it, "*I need to be able to take part in conversations of all kinds and in all areas.*" Thus, the CDO's job is both highly cross-functional and interdisciplinary, and requires highly developed change management skills.

Inspiration Skills

The successful execution of a digital transformation requires the ability to inspire others. As the driver of digital transformation, the CDO needs to transmit business-critical information company-wide and across all organizational hierarchy levels. He or she also needs to be able to convince all internal decision makers and employees of the need to digitally transform and to demonstrate the benefits that will come from the transformation. In this context, CDOs need the ability to successfully overcome the resistance and barriers that often stem from traditional corporate cultures. Accordingly, as emphasized by the CDO in Case 6, CDOs need to "*have a profound knowledge of the corporate culture and the handling of employees who find themselves in the middle of transformational processes.*" CDOs should be able to readily recognize the needs of employees and help them overcome barriers that arise during digital transformation. With the skill to inspire others, CDOs not only act as consultants to the top management team, but also act as effective motivators of the whole workforce and thus enable the digital transformation in the first place.

Digital Pioneering Skills

A significant aspect of inspiring and motivating an organization to embark on a digital transformation is that the CDO needs to create a cohesive digital vision for the company. CDOs thus need to act as digital pioneers, which requires them to have a high level of visionary thinking capabilities. Accordingly, CDOs need the ability to look beyond existing strategies and previous procedures and envision the digital future of their companies. Being a successful digital pioneer and conceiving an appropriate digital vision requires CDOs to look at the current and prospective business situations from many different perspectives. As the CDO in Case 4 put it, CDOs need to be "*both outward and inward looking.*"

Resilience

Another key characteristic of a successful CDO is resilience, which will be needed to complete the digital transformation journey. Resilience is even more important in "traditional" companies because digital transformation will require substantial changes. In such companies, colleagues of CDOs, both at managerial and at staff levels, won't always embrace the profound changes required for digital transformation.

Case 3 provides a good example of the importance of resilience. This company's transformation was particularly challenging for the CDO, as it moved from a pure print publisher to a modern online education company. The CDO faced internal resistance from many skeptical stakeholders. But, two years after devising a new digital strategy and developing new digital products and services, the development partners (who were also key customers of the company) were highly satisfied with the results. The resilience of the CDO had more than paid off.

The CDO in Case 1 highlighted another essential aspect of resilience: "*[CDOs need] to acknowledge failures and to learn from them.*" Setbacks are common when companies fundamentally transform their businesses and processes.

CDO Skills and Competencies by Role Type

Although all of the above skills and competencies are needed by any CDO, different CDO role types will need some of them more than others (see Table 9.5). Based on our analysis of the case studies, *Digital Evangelists* need particularly well developed inspiration and digital pioneering skills to enable them to effectively advocate the need for digital transformation. Change management skills are valuable for *Coordinators*, who need to understand all of the many and diverse aspects of a business to effectively coordinate the digital transformation across functions. Finally, the *Entrepreneur* role is easier to fulfill if CDOs have profound digital pioneering skills that help them explore IT-enabled innovation and create a cohesive digital vision for their companies.

All CDOs require IT competency to accomplish their tasks, and this competency is therefore not specific to any CDO role type. While the importance of resilience depends very much on the mindset of the workforce and willingness to transform, CDOs in any role type can strongly benefit from this characteristic.

Table 9.5 Most Important Skills and Competencies by CDO Role Type

Entrepreneur	Digital Evangelist	Coordinator
Digital Pioneering Skills	• Inspiration Skills • Digital Pioneering Skills *IT Competency* *Resilience*	Change Management Skills

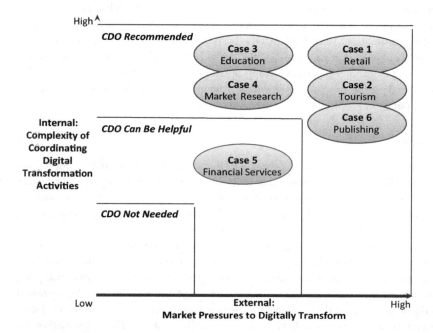

Figure 9.1 Relevance of Chief Digital Officers

When and Why to Establish a CDO Position

Our analysis of the cases shows that companies have established CDO positions to drive their digital transformations in a comprehensive way. We found that CDOs devise and execute digital strategies as *Entrepreneurs*, serve as catalysts for change by mobilizing the whole company in their roles as *Digital Evangelists* and coordinate digital transformation efforts as *Coordinators*. We have also identified the five essential skills and competencies needed by a successful CDO. But does every organization need a CDO to drive its digital transformation?

Across the six case companies, there were two main factors that drove the establishment of CDO positions: (1) there were high levels of external market pressures to digitally transform and (2) there was great internal complexity in the task of coordinating transformation activities across the company. Figure 9.1 positions the six case companies vis-a-vis these two factors.

The CDO is the only position in a company that is exclusively dedicated to digital transformation. Hence, the higher the pressure for digital transformation is, the greater the benefits, from having a CDO. For instance, the CDO in Case 6 confirmed how important it is in his job to "*show and make plausible how fundamental the digital* transformation is and how much the company's current business models are threatened if no actions are taken." *Each of the six case companies faced some level of market pressures to digitally transform. For instance, the CDO in Case 2 told us he had been given "very ambitious goals … to generate a massive growth in the online business, which the company wasn't able to achieve so far."*

It is no coincidence that the very first CDO was installed in a media group, MTV Networks. The media industry was the first to be disrupted by new digital technologies. For media companies, employing a CDO creates a dedicated position to mobilize the whole company and make clear to everybody what kinds of challenges new digital technologies pose and what opportunities they offer CDOs can help transform an organization by motivating employees and demonstrating why the status quo cannot continue. As the CDO in Case 4 put it, "*I do believe that it makes sense to have this role so that somebody can really push this topic, mobilize everybody and continuously give new impulses.*"

A CDO position is also beneficial if there is not an ingrained culture of cross-functional collaboration, which means the company faces an urgent need to better coordinate its digital transformation activities. In the words of the managing director in Case 4, the CDO is "*the conductor of the concert*" and coordinates the controlled transformation of the whole company. For instance, the CDO in Case 1 told us: "*I believe that due to the high velocity in which these changes take place, a CDO is needed: someone who has horizontal responsibility, who coordinates and drives these changes. Otherwise, many parts of the company might drop the changes again.*" The CDO in Case 2 confirmed this view by suggesting that "*a digital transformation does not take place in a single department*" in her company, "*many silos need to be removed*" and "*a dedicated position was necessary to serve as a driving force and bundle all digital activities.*" Thus, in the words of the CDO in Case 3, a CDO should be able "to rethink the whole company in all areas" and "join in any kinds of conversions in each single department."

In particular, we recommend that a business in which the coordination of digital transformation activities across the organization is very complex should create a CDO position. Coordination complexity will be greater in larger companies and in companies with a decentralized structure or a large amount of organizational dependencies between products, processes and IT systems.

Lessons Learned

We have derived four key lessons from the analysis of the six cases. The first lesson addresses and informs organizations, the second is relevant to CDOs, the third applies to CIOs, and the fourth relates to whether CIO positions are a temporary phenomenon.

Top Management Should Ensure CDOs Have Sufficient Authority

Our analysis shows that CDOs assume cross-company authority for digital initiatives to overcome the slow pace of digital transformation in organizations. For far too long, inertia has held back digital transformation initiatives in many industries and companies. These industries and companies now need to adjust rapidly to modified market conditions and customer demands. Organizational dependencies may also have delayed a timely adjustment. Five of the six CDOs in our study have successfully conceived digital transformation strategies and implemented the associated digital initiatives in a timely manner. The striking exception is the CDO in Case 5, who was the only one not reporting directly to the CEO and who did not have a seat at the top management team meetings. This CDO is positioned at business unit level (as part of the communication department) and seems to lack the authority needed to effectively pursue company-wide digital initiatives. This situation results primarily from insufficient top management commitment to digital transformation, which, however, seems to be a critical success factor for the business.

CDOs Should Hone the Skills Required for Their Primary CDO Role(s) and Address the Challenges Caused by Internal Resistance

While all the skills and competencies we identified are highly beneficial for any CDO, CDOs should specifically hone the skills most required by their current primary role type (see Table 9.5). While any CDO role type needs IT competency, *Digital Evangelists* benefit particularly from highly developed inspiration and digital pioneering skills. Change management skills are especially valuable for *Coordinators*, while *Entrepreneurs* benefit most from well-developed digital pioneering skills. Awareness of the relationships between roles types and skills will enable CDOs to hone and employ the skills they require.

Regardless of how skillfully CDOs perform their primary role type during digital transformation, they will inevitably face internal resistance to the transformation process. CDOs therefore also need high levels of resilience and perseverance. They must be aware of potential resistance from colleagues and the organization as a whole and must not shy away from the associated challenges that lie ahead in the digital transformation journey.

Appointment of a CDO Offers Opportunities for the CIO

Some CIOs may fear that they might be replaced by a newly appointed CDO or relegated to a secondary position in the digital transformation journey. At first glance, this fear might be justified, but we believe the contrary is true. CDOs not only act as *Digital Evangelists* for the digital transformation of their companies, but also as advocates for the IT function itself. Many CIOs still struggle to get a seat at the top management table, but there is evidence that appointing a CDO strengthens the authority and reputation of the CIO. In each of the cases where the CDO reported directly to the CEO, the CIO was also a direct report of the CEO. While we do not know if there is a causal link behind this observation, we can certainly say that the CIOs in these cases had a high reputation and that their CEOs and top management teams regarded them as valuable for the digital transformation. CIOs should therefore embrace the opportunities that the appointment of a CDO offers them and make the most of the visibility they can gain through collaborating extensively with CDOs.

CDO Positions May Be a Temporary Phenomenon

Many commentators and researchers on IT management practices regard the CDO position as a temporary phenomenon. Indeed, many of our interviewees held this view. As the CDO in Case 4 put it, "*At the end of the day, this is a position that will disappear as soon as the company has become digital.*" Others, however, propose that CDOs might become the next CEOs. We cannot, as yet, take a final position on this issue because CDOs are still a fairly recent phenomenon. It will be interesting to monitor the future development of the CDO position.

Concluding Comments

To help managers understand why CDO positions have been established and how CDOs can be successfully installed to guide organizations through their digital transformation journeys, this article has presented six case studies of CDOs and described how they fulfill their positions. Based on these cases, we have identified two main factors that drive the creation of CDO positions: high market pressures to digitally transform, and the complexity of coordinating digital transformation activities across a company. We have also identified three role types that CDOs can play (the *Entrepreneur*, the *Digital Evangelist* and the *Coordinator)* and five types of skills and competencies CDOs should have. While each CDO should possess IT competency and resilience, the significance of change management skills, inspiration skills and digital pioneering skills depends on each CDO's primary role type. From our analysis of the case companies, we have derived four key lessons that will ensure businesses equip their CDOs with the skills to successfully navigate them through their digital transformation journeys.

Notes

1   From the 2013 digital transformation global executive study and research project in Fitzgerald, M., Kruschwitz, N., Bonnet, D. and Welch, M. "Embracing Digital Technology. A New Strategic Imperative," *MIT Sloan Management Review* (55:2), 2013, pp. 1–12.

2   Weill, P. and Woerner, S. L. "The Future of the CIO in a Digital Economy," *MIS Quarterly Executive* (12:2), 2013, pp. 65–75.

3   See Peppard, J., Edwards, C. and Lambert, R. "Clarifying the Ambiguous Role of the CIO," *MIS Quarterly Executive* (10:1), 2011, pp. 31–44; and Westerman, W. and Weill, P. "What Makes an Effective CIO? The Perspective of Non-IT Executives," Center for Information Systems Research, *MIT Sloan Management Review* (4:3C), 2005.

4   Fitzgerald, M., Kruschwitz, N., Bonnet, D. and Welch, M., 2013, op. cit.

5   We use the terms "digital transformation strategy" and "digital strategy" synonymously in this article.

6   For an extensive account of digital transformation strategies and how companies can formulate them, see, e.g., Hess, T., Matt, C., Benlian, A. and Wiesböck, F. "Options for Formulating a Digital Transformation Strategy," *MIS Quarterly Executive* (15:2), 2016, pp. 103–119.

7   See McDonald, M.P. and Rowsell-Jones, A. *The Digital Edge: Exploiting Information & Technology for Business Advantage*, Gartner, Inc., 2012.

8   Fitzgerald, M., Kruschwitz, N., Bonnet, D. and Welch, M., 2013, op. cit.

9   For the latest updates on CDO numbers, see http://cdoclub.com.

10   The Appendix describes the research methodology and the interviews conducted.

11   In some companies, the most senior IT position might be labelled differently, e.g., Chief Technology Officer or Head of IT. We use the term "CIO" to cover all these titles.

12   For a comprehensive description of the chief data officer role, see Lee, Y., Madnick, S., Wang, R., Wang, F. and Zhang, H. "A Cubic Framework for the Chief Data Officer: Succeeding in a World of Big Data," *MIS Quarterly Executive* (13:1), 2014, pp. 1–13.

13   For a comprehensive account on chief innovation officers, see Di Fiore, A. "A Chief Innovation Officer's Actual Responsibilities" *Harvard Business Review*, 2014, available at https://hbr.org/2014/11/a-chief-innovation-officers-actual-responsibilities.

14   For more information on the role of the chief strategy officer, refer to Menz, M. and Scheef, C. "Chief strategy officers: Contingency analysis of their presence in top management teams," *Strategic Management Journal* (35:3), 2014, pp. 461–471.

15   For more information on digital transformation strategies, see Matt, C., Hess, T. and Benlian, A. "Digital Transformation Strategies," *Business & Information Systems Engineering* (57:5), 2015, pp. 339–343.

16   As of January 2017, €1 = $1.05.

Appendix: Research Methodology

To explore the CDO role in detail, we investigated six companies and conducted at least one interview in each organization. In total, we conducted ten interviews. These interviews were semi-structured and comprised open-ended questions on topics such as the companies' motivations to install a CDO, the CDOs' tasks and the challenges CDOs face. If necessary, we further probed the interviewees via e-mail to seek clarification. All interviews were audio taped and subsequently transcribed. When analyzing the interviews, we carefully scanned for similarities and differences in the companies' digital transformations and the CDOs' tasks. To verify the statements from the interviews, we used secondary data sources (e.g., company presentations, internal documents and publicly available press).

Questions for Discussion

1   CDOs are considered business strategists. How do CDOs align with the business strategy and the other c-level roles? Do you perceive any conflicts or other issues?
2   Analyzing the six cases presented, would argue for the role of CDOs? What seniority level do you think CDOs need to have? Does the level of seniority affect the success of digital transformation? Consider power dynamics as presented in Chapter 10.
3   The cases in the chapter outline a clear distinction between role type and each case assumes only one role. Could CDOs assume multiple types of roles as part of the organizations' digital transformation?
4   How might CDOs transition between the different roles depending on the needs of the organization? Link your discussion to Chapters 13 and 14.

Further Reading

Leidner, D. E., Beatty, R. C., Mackay, J. M. (2008). How CIOs manage IT during economic decline: Surviving and thriving amid uncertainty. *MIS Quarterly Executive*, 2(1): 1–14.
Tumbas, S., Berente, N., vom Brocke, J. (2017). Three Types of Chief Digital Officers and the Reasons Organizations Adopt the Role. *MIS Quarterly Executive*, 16(2), 121–134.

Chapter 10

Boyka Simeonova, Robert D. Galliers and Stan Karanasios

STRATEGIC INFORMATION SYSTEMS AND ORGANIZATIONAL POWER DYNAMICS

THIS CHAPTER EXAMINES power dynamics in organizations and their implications for the study of strategic Information Systems (IS). While power can be manifest in various forms and has a multitude of connotations and definitions (Jasperson et al. 2002; Lawrence et al. 2012) the definition[1] of power followed here is, "*the dimension of relationships through which the behaviors, attitudes, or opportunities of an actor are affected by another actor, system, or technology*" (Lawrence et al. 2012, p. 105). Within IS research, such issues are typically accounted for in studies of conflicts, politics, surveillance and resistance (e.g., Doolin 2004; Hussain and Cornelius 2009; Markus 1983; Zuboff 1988). However, as noted by several scholars, power dynamics are mostly relegated to the periphery of research on IS (e.g., Willcocks 2004; Willcocks and Lioliou 2011). Introna (2003) observed how power/knowledge issues in IS are often perceived as "nuisances", arguing that such nuisances actually constitute the very community and field of IS. As a result, power dynamics are largely under-theorized or avoided within IS research (Blackler 2011; Marabelli and Galliers 2017; McBride 2013; Silva 2007; Willcocks and Lioliou 2011). This is particularly evident within the literature on strategic IS studies, even though power dynamics are likely to be prominent in strategic management decisions. For example, the digital transformation of an organization and strategizing more generally are likely to be infused with conflicts and tensions. To highlight these issues as important concerns for strategic IS, this chapter explores the links between power, IS and IS strategy and develops a new analytical framework of power.

Scholars have noted that the field of IS endures epistemological and theoretical challenges which can obstruct how power may be studied (Silva 2007). In his review of dominant theories used to study IS namely Phenomenology, Critical Theory and Structuration Theory Silva (2007) identified several limitations to unraveling power. Others have made similar arguments concerning other "grand" theories applied in IS (e.g., Simeonova et al. 2018a, 2018b). Silva (2007, p. 166) argues that, *"given the hidden nature of power and politics … an epistemological approach that emphasizes the interpretations of meanings, intentions and actions would be most suitable for making sense of such a complex phenomenon"*. The need for up-to-date theoretical foundation for studying power is recognized by Fleming and Spicer (2014, p. 38) explaining that, *"as with any analytical concept, the swiftly changing world of organizational life requires theories of power that are up-to-date and current with the emerging trends shaping business and society"*.

In addition to the theoretical challenges of investigating power, studies examining power often follow a one-dimensional (Dhillon et al. 2011) and functionalist (Cendon and Jarvenpaa 2001; Fleming and Spicer 2014) view of power. Most commonly, such examples represent a negative view of power (Ravishankar et al. 2013; Fleming and Spicer 2014). Fleming and Spicer (2014, p. 38) explain that, *"while it is widely recognized that power is a central part of organizations, there is no doubt that it still has rather negative connotations, something that is perhaps derived from popular perceptions about its nature and effects of power"*.

To expand on this narrow view of power we use the notion of "episodic" and "systemic" power following Lawrence and colleagues' (2012) conceptualization. We use this framing because of its emphasis on individual and collective actors, behaviors, attuites, relationship, social systems and technologies. Such a view expands the framing of power dynamics in organizations and permits scholars to tease out different types of power.

The remainder of this chapter outlines existing frameworks on power and how these have been utilized in IS and IS strategy research. Importantly, the chapter emphasizes the multitude of connotations of power and examines the interplay between the different types of power (i.e., episodic and systemic power), and their effect on IS and IS strategy. The chapter outlines a new analytical framework of power examining the interplay of different types of power (episodic and systemic), the role of actors and the role of IS. The framework is presented as a matrix differentiating between "power as possession", "power as practice", "power as control" and "power as facilitation". The framework is designed to help explicate power dynamics in organizations and its interlinkages with IS and strategy and lead to the development of a research agenda on power, IS and strategy.

Perspectives on Power Used in IS

In recognition of the difficulty of accounting for power, scholars have adopted a range of theories and frameworks. Within IS studies four dominant[2] perspectives have been utilized; these are outlined and discussed below. Following a discussion and summary of these views, we theorize the episodic and systemic perspective as useful in teasing out different types of power and we conceptualize the existing literature using this perspective.

Foucauldian Perspective

Perhaps the most popular perspective adopted by scholars is the Foucauldian perspective (e.g., Young et al. 2012; Doolin 2004; Heizmann 2011). Foucault (1977) outlines power as constitutive and exercised through micro-strategies, maneuvers and dispositions. Foucault (1979, 1980) makes the point that power should be considered as something produced and evolving through social relationships as opposed to as a resource, and that power and knowledge are mutually constituted. Hence, power is not understood as a resource that an actor possesses and uses to influence another actor; rather, it is understood as something constituted through the interactions among these actors and is visible through its effects (Clegg et al. 2006). Such conceptualizations of power have been considered in studies of knowledge processes (e.g., Heizmann 2011; Heizmann and Olsson 2015; Marshall and Rollinson 2004; Sewell 2005), IS and strategy (e.g., Ezzamel and Willmott 2008; Hardy and Thomas 2014; McCabe 2010; Webster 1995; Zuboff 1988). The Foucauldian conceptualization of power has dominated IS studies emphasizing the use of IS for surveillance or forms of an electronic "panopticon" (e.g., Doolin 2004; Orlikowski 1991; Webster 1995; Zuboff 1988). Doolin (2004) utilized the Foucauldian perspective to examine disciplinary power exercised by surveillance. Allen et al. (2013) refer to a "panoptic gaze" for using a tele-medicine system to defer decisions. Walsham (2001) acknowledges the importance of Foucault's work on understanding the inseparability of power/knowledge. In particular he argues that its techniques and procedures specify legitimate accounts of truth via "regimes of truth" (Foucault 1980), and the importance of surveillance as a form of control (Foucault 1977; Knights et al. 1993) for example, in organizational monitoring processes (Lyon 1993).

Scholars have argued that the Foucauldian perspective underestimates domination, legitimation, authority, historic structures, and power struggles which are explained as being essential to society and as forming different interests (Clegg et al. 2006). It has also been argued that a Foucauldian analysis privileges a negative view of power, where power is shown as a restrictive and oppressing force (Habermas 1990), as opposed to a productive force (Deleuze 1988). Along these lines Fairclough (1992) has argued that Foucault's conceptualization of power fails to present practical examples of power relations in action, thereby making it difficult to study power.

Circuits of Power

Clegg (1989) introduced the circuits of power framework to represent modalities through which power flows in an organizational context accounting for organizational structure, legitimate power, agency and resistance. The circuits of power framework integrates interrelated concepts: episodic circuits of power, social integration and system integration (Backhouse et al. 2006; Clegg 1989; Silva and Backhouse 2003). The episodic circuit of power is described as causal power, when one actor gets another actor to do something the latter would otherwise not do. Episodic power circuits are defined by agency and the interests of these agencies (Clegg et al. 2006). Power relations are configured by these agents so that they achieve preferential outcomes. These outcomes could subsequently affect the social and system integration circuits (Clegg et al. 2006). The social integration circuit is described as dispositional power linked to the rules of meaning and membership, and conditions of exercising power, providing the conditions for one actor to exercise power over another actor (Backhouse et al. 2006; Clegg 1989). Hence the episodic outcomes lead to changes in rules, social relationships at the social circuit. Subsequently, the changes in rules and social relationships at the social circuit could lead to restriction or facilitation of disciplinary and productive power, which subsequently empowers/disempowers social relations. The system integration circuit, described as techniques of production and discipline, is linked to dominance, electronic panopticon, facilitating the compliance of actors and discipline, following the Foucauldian perspective (Backhouse et al. 2006; Clegg 1989; Silva and Backhouse 2003). Therefore, IS could be regarded as an instrument for control, compliance and discipline, which seem to retain negative connotations of power. Adopting this framing of power has helped scholars to understand the setting, institutionalization of IS (Silva and Backhouse 2003), institutionalization of standards and resistance to standards compliance (Backhouse et al. 2006; Smith et al. 2010).

Silva and Backhouse (2003) utilize the episodic circuit of power to identify and understand the positions occupied by actors, their strategies, the resources they have access to, their actions in implementing the system and the struggles in resisting the using of the system. Hence, the episodic circuit of power concentrates on causal power and helps to identify who the champions of implementing and advocating for the system are and who the resistors are. The social circuit concentrates on dispositional power linked to rules, meaning capacity and position of actors to exercise power. Dispositional power is explained to be a type of power where actors influence the behavior of other actors that might be against the interests of the latter. In the context of institutionalization of IS, the social circuit of power helps identify what the rules and norms are, what the capacity and the positions of the actors are, how the system affects these rules, norms, positions and capacities, and how the new systems are interpreted (Silva and Backhouse 2003). The systemic circuit considers power as facilitative in the achievement of goals. Whilst a positive notion is implied, the circuit is linked to subordination of actors to achieve goals that are achieved through compliance, surveillance, control over employees and disciplining actors. As Clegg (1989, p. 191) has explained, disciplinary practices exist in different forms of control over employees: "*supervision, routinization, formalization, mechanization and legislation, which seek to effect increasing control of employees' behavior, dispositions and embodiment, precisely because they are organizational members*". Regarding the institutionalization of IS, the system circuit of power tackles questions around monitoring actors' compliance and instilling discipline (Silva and Backhouse 2003). Hence, the circuits of power imply negative connotations of power. Similar connotations of the circuits of power are displayed in the institutionalization of standards compliance (Backhouse et al. 2006; Smith et al. 2010).

Power and Empowerment

A number of studies have utilized the framework on power by Hardy and Leiba-O'Sullivan (1998) (e.g., Dhillon et al. 2011; Hekkala and Urquhart 2013). Hardy and Leiba-O'Sullivan's (1998) framework outlines four dimensions of power: (i) power as a resource/power over resources where a dominant actor prevails over subordinate actors through resource dependencies in influencing decision-making; (ii) controlling decision-making processes through limited access and the exclusion of the less powerful; (iii) managing meaning and preventing conflict through the hierarchy and respecting the status quo; (iv) disciplinary action for those non-conforming, which is borrowed from Foucault. Hardy and Leiba-O'Sullivan (1998) examine the probability of empowerment of the subordinate actor and explain that the latter loses out to the dominant actor in all dimensions. For the empowerment of the subordinate actor, the following are required: acquisition of resources and the capacity for mobilizing these, access to and influence in the decision-making process, understanding of political actions and creation of will to resist, radical metamorphosis of the system, or otherwise freedom from power effects is not possible. Hence, similarly to the circuits of power framework and the Foucauldian perspective, the connotations of power appear negative. In their study, Dhillon et al. (2011) examine the interaction of intentionality and power in IS implementation utilizing Hardy and Leiba-O'Sullivan (1998) framework and conclude that intentions affect power, which in turn affects IS implementation, which consequently affects intentions. Dhillon et al. (2011) demonstrate complex relationships between power, intentions and IS implementation; however, they have not differentiated between different types of power. Hekkala and Urquhart (2013) utilized Hardy and Leiba-O'Sullivan's (1998) framework to investigate power in inter-organizational IS projects. A key finding from their study is the role of legitimate/authority power to implement IS projects when informal links between organizations are absent.

Episodic (Power Over) and Systemic (Power To) Perspective on Power

Episodic power is defined as the acts of self-interested actors, where one actor influences or forces another actor to do something which they might otherwise not do (Lawrence et al. 2012); thus the term "power over". The episodic view of power considers power as a capacity as well as something that is exercised in relationships. From the episodic perspective, power is considered as unevenly distributed within organizations and is regarded as a personal or positional resource used to serve self-interest (Kärreman 2010; Lawrence et al. 2012). Therefore, power can be perceived as authority, legitimacy, control, coercion, and resource dependency (Clegg 1989; Gohler 2009). The episodic perspective represents power over, which is characterized by domination, control and self-interest (Clegg et al. 2006; Gohler 2009).

Systemic forms of power are described as *"vested in social and cultural systems, rather than in individual actors"* (Lawrence et al. 2012, p. 106). From this perspective, power can be seen as systemic in that it is embedded in social relations as well as in technical, cultural and bureaucratic systems and practices (Lawrence et al. 2012). The systemic perspective represents "power to", which is characterized as capacity, property, ability and empowerment (Gohler 2009). Therefore, systemic power can be identified through *"situations in which the behaviours, beliefs, or opportunities of actors shift in response to changes in the rules (formal or informal) of meaning and membership, or changes in the technologies of discipline and production (including social and material technologies)"* (Lawrence et al. 2012, p. 106).

However, the effects of power over/episodic and power to/systemic are contingent: *"one person's 'power to' may involve asserting 'power over' many other people; the effects of power as productive or negative are strictly contingent, so for some people the effect may be positive while for others it will be negative"* (Clegg et al. 2006, p. 191). Power "over" or "to" depends on the situation and position of the agents. Power exists in the complex contingent tension of extending or restricting the freedom of others (Clegg et al. 2006). Hence, to understand the interplay between episodic/power over and systemic/power to it is necessary to understand power in organizations and how it is inscribed in strategic IS. As outlined earlier, studies tend to adopt a one-dimensional view (Dhillon et al. 2011) and few studies in IS examine power from different perspectives and even fewer have demonstrated the interlinks between these different forms of power (Jasperson et al. 2002). The following examples present attempts to investigate power from the episodic and systemic perspective.

Utilizing the episodic and systemic power conceptualization, Lawrence et al. (2012) identify mechanisms to trigger and institutionalize radical change, where this is viewed as *"transformations in professional service firms from traditional professional partnerships into managed professional businesses"* (p. 102). The authors find that radical change is initiated through episodic power based on authority and interested actors, and systemic power is needed to institutionalize the triggered radical change through embedding systems and structures as part of practices, identities and rules.

In a study of configurable technologies, Pozzebon and Pinsonneault (2012) provide an alternate framework for examining the interlinkages of different types of knowledge and power. Their framework differentiates between the possession and practice views of knowledge and power. From the possession view (Cook and Brown 1999), knowledge is considered as a codified entity that can be possessed and transferred. Hence, "*knowledge can thus be captured, codified and digitalized*" (Pozzebon and Pinsonneault 2012, p. 38). Power from a possession view is outlined as a resource that can be possessed, a capacity and property of individuals (i.e., episodic power). From a practice perspective knowledge is conceptualized as a dynamic, negotiated, provisional, and socially situated (Cook and Brown 1999; Pozzebon and Pinsonneault 2012) and hence it is referred as "knowing" (Carlile 2002; Orlikowski 2002). From the practice perspective knowledge and power are considered as being intertwined in action outlined as dynamic, invested in practice, relations and maneuvers, and hence power could be considered systemic (Pozzebon and Pinsonneault 2012). Their findings show that the possession view of knowledge and power is key at the IS project launch phase where the objectives and initial decisions are set and resources allocated. These might get negotiated, reinforced, transformed through combination of possession and practice views, which may lead to emergent or planned knowing/powering mechanisms when implementing configurable technology (Pozzebon and Pinsonneault 2012).

In a study of strategizing and IS, Marabelli and Galliers (2017) explore the interplay between different forms of power and differentiate between a "diffusion" and "translation" model of power. The diffusion model is linked to hierarchical power and exploitation, where the exercising of hierarchical power involves the exploitation of a dominant position. The translation model is linked to exploration and performative power, where the systems are molded and appropriated through the practices of the users. Similar to Lawrence et al. (2012), the effects of the different forms of power on IS strategizing show that hierarchical power (i.e., episodic power) helps launch the strategizing initiative, and performance power (i.e., systemic power) leads to the institutionalization of these strategic changes (Marabelli and Galliers 2017). However, it was also found that resistance to these changes exists which leads to emerging practices and workarounds. Hence, Marabelli and Galliers (2017) conclude that (i) hierarchical power/diffusion model/exploitation has limited effects in instilling change but is necessary to define the strategic objectives; (ii) performative power/translation model/exploration is needed to instill change through practices and co-production of outcomes. Thus, it is important to examine different types of power and their interplay as these could lead to different outcomes.

A summary of these four perspectives on power along with their assumptions and applications in the literature is presented in Table 10.1.

The summary of the four perspectives of power demonstrates a predominant negative connotation of power in Foucault, circuits of power, and power and empowerment frameworks.

The summary suggests that diverse perspectives on power are required where positive and negative effects are accounted for. Hence, we adopt the *episodic and systemic perspective on power* and we utilize the framework to understand the effects and interplay of different forms of power.

Episodic and Systemic Power and Implications for Strategic IS

Having established episodic and systemic power as useful lens to study power in IS, here we review and discuss this view further to demonstrate how it may help to uncover hidden effects of power in IS and organizations. We draw on studies from IS, IS Strategy, Organization Studies, General Management, and Knowledge Management to support our argument. While drawing on these fields, the studies are focused on the use of IS, what

Table 10.1 Summary of the four perspectives of power

Perspective on power	Assumptions	Examples	References	Implications for studying strategic IS
Foucauldian perspective	Power considered as produced and evolving through social relationships; Power and knowledge are mutually constituted.	The use of IS for surveillance or forms of electronic "panopticon"	Orlikowski 1991; Webster 1995; Zuboff 1988; Doolin 2004	Emphasis on surveillance, one-dimensional predominantly negative view. Diverse perspectives required.
Circuits of Power (Clegg 1989)	Episodic circuit causal power; Social circuit dispositional power; Systemic circuit techniques of production and discipline.	Institutionalization of IS Institutionalization of standards and resistance to standards compliance	Silva and Backhouse 2003 Backhouse et al. 2006; Smith et al. 2010	IS regarded as an instrument for control, compliance, discipline. Predominantly negative connotations of power. Diverse perspectives required.
Hardy and Leiba-O'Sullivan (1998)	Power as a resource; Controlling decision-making; Managing meaning and preventing conflict; Disciplinary action for the non-conforming.	Intentionality and power in IS implementation Power in inter-organizational IS projects	Dhillon et al. 2011 Hekkala and Urquhart 2013	Limited possibility for empowerment of subordinate actors, mainly negative connotation of power. Diverse perspectives required.
Episodic/power over and systemic/power to perspective	Episodic power possession, resource used to serve self-interest, authority, control, domination, legitimacy, coercion, resource allocation Systemic power practice, relational, empowerment, capacity.	Organizational radical change Knowledge and power IS strategizing Knowledge sharing	Lawrence et al. 2012 Pozzebon and Pinsonneault 2012 Marabelli and Galliers 2017 Simeonova 2018, 2015	Allows for the understanding of different forms of power, their interplay and their effects in organizations, IS and strategy.

IS allow people to do; how IS are used to share information and knowledge; how power distribution affects the use of IS; how IS are used from different hierarchical levels, and how they empower these (i.e., the consequences of the implementation of IS and change in practices and their reflection in terms of power dynamics; how power dynamics affect IS strategy). The effects of the different forms of power in organizations (following the episodic and systemic power perspective) and links to IS and IS strategy are summarized in Table 10.2.

Table 10.2 presents the different manifestations of power following the episodic and systemic conceptualization. The episodic manifestations of power (i.e., hierarchical, authoritative, legitimate, knowledge as power, resource dependence, power asymmetries, surveillance, resistance, self-interest, etc.) appear to be the predominant forms of power, exhibiting negative effects on use of IS, strategy, knowledge processes, organizational relationships, and inter-organizational collaborations. Some systemic traits of power have also been observed in shared goals, empowerment, organizational culture, transparency, autonomy, trust,

Table 10.2 Power in Organizations

Forms of power	Perceived effects of power	Example references
Episodic: hierarchical, authoritative, legitimate power.	Negative effect as people occupying higher hierarchical levels have access to more resources and have the freedom to act as they deem appropriate.	Galinsky et al. 2008;
	Management ban the use of Web 2.0 technologies for communication and knowledge sharing.	Simeonova 2018
	The self-interest of these authoritative higher-power people dominates over the interests of the lower-power people and over the organizational interests.	Raman and Bharadwaj 2012;
	Use of knowledge management systems to increase managers' control and reduce employees' power.	Michailova and Husted 2003 Gray 2001
	Possessors of high power and status influence others as well as policy and IS strategy.	Avison et al. 1999
Episodic: knowledge as power	Perception that by sharing knowledge people give away their power, or lose their competitive position and advantage in the organization.	Lawrence et al. 2005
	Losing ownership of knowledge when sharing using technology.	Wang and Noe 2010
Episodic: equal consideration	Limited opportunity for people from lower levels have to voice their opinions; not giving consideration to ideas stemming from the lower levels.	Bunderson and Reagans 2011; Heizmann 2011

Forms of power	Perceived effects of power	Example references
Episodic: resource dependence	Organizations depending on key employees.	Muthusamy and White 2005
	Dependency between organizational branches; between alliance members; between subsidiaries based in different countries.	
	Power, ascribed in hidden political agendas, self-interests, conflicts, insufficient resource allocation, affects the strategic benefits of business intelligence.	Audzeyeva and Hudson 2016
Episodic: resistance	IS as power instruments in eliciting clashes with existing power structures which leads to resistance.	McBride 2013 Markus 1983 Hussain and Cornelius 2009 Doolin 2004
	Resistance to power affected by the powerful individuals	
Episodic: procedural Systemic: OC	Procedures, governing rules, prescribed norms of behavior. Organizational culture (OC), "unobtrusive" norms and ways of representing, talking or working.	Blackler 2011
Systemic: goals, social aspects	Shared goals, alignment with organizational goals, transparency, communities of practice, social capital.	Contu 2013; Willem and Scarbrough 2006
Systemic: empowerment	Removing resource constraints, participating in decision-making, reduced administrative obstacles.	Chuang et al. 2016
	IS to neutralize power asymmetries through exchange of ideas.	Habermas 1990
Systemic: transparency, multiple voices, communication	Technology provides the opportunity to avow multiple voices without privileging one's opinions and expressions over others.	Leonardi et al. 2013; McAfee 2006
	Providing transparency and facilitating communication and interaction between people from different hierarchical levels. Knowledge management systems to facilitate knowledge management processes.	Alavi and Leidner 2001
Episodic power: power residing in the system	IS implementation shapes power relations, power relations shape how IS gets implemented. Power has an impact on individual intensions which shape IS implementation.	Dhillon et al. 2011
	The introduction of IS could lead to redistribution to power such that power is concentrated in the higher authorities which may be a cause for resistance to change.	Silva and Hirschheim 2007

Forms of power	Perceived effects of power	Example references
Episodic power: self-interest	Gain power over others to the disdain of others and gain access to different resources.	Constantinides and Barrett 2006 Azad and Faraj 2011
	Inscribing interests using power and politics. Power as a manifestation of strategy and interests through IS.	
Systemic power: discourse	Power shapes strategy through discourse and material practices.	Hardy and Thomas 2014
Episodic power: Network Systemic power: network	Controlling resources, centralized decision-making, controlling strategic assets.	Busquets 2010
	Building structural holes, building trust, actors' autonomy and self-control and the capacity of the network to recombine resources, commitment, co-creation.	Busquets 2010
	Building trust, overcoming structural power deficit (i.e. authority, resources).	Ngwenyama and Nielsen 2014
	Learning through a network: evening out power imbalances.	Moe et al. 2017
Episodic power: structural Systemic power: structural	Power and IT governance: power of top management to control strategy.	Bradley et al. 2012
	Inter-organizational structural power: source of influence of powerful organizations over less powerful ones, dependency. Cooperative power, willingness to cooperate, communicate, focus on the community interests, empowerment.	Son et al. 2005 Cendon and Jarvenpaa 2001
Episodic power: behavioral Systemic power: behavioral	Negative behavioral tactics: coercion, manipulation, resistance, self-interests.	Cendon and Jarvenpaa 2001
	Positive behavioral tactics: obtaining external resources, creating alliances and partnerships, help build an infrastructure.	
Episodic power: network of activities and context Systemic power: network of activities and context	Tools: surveillance, monitoring, control, resistance (episodic power); transparency, autonomy, multiple voices (systemic power).	Simeonova et al. 2018a Simeonova et al. 2018b
	Rules: procedures, rules and norms (episodic power); organizational culture (episodic/systemic power). Community: social relationships, trust, social capital, networks (systemic power).	
	Division of labor: hierarchy, position, control, coercion (episodic power); empowerment (systemic power).	

Forms of power	Perceived effects of power	Example references
Episodic power: asymmetries of power	Power imbalances between vendor and client in offshore relationships.	Ravishankar et al. 2013; Ravishankar 2015
	Power imbalances between Eastern and Western countries and cultures.	Levina and Vaast 2008
	Offshore managers' lack of seniority and access to information.	
	Supply-chain domination of large and powerful organizations over less powerful ones.	Webster 1995
	Power imbalance between large organizations and SMEs where the latter lack power, resources and planned IS strategy.	Power and Gruner 2017

networks, cooperation. These systemic manifestations of power have productive effects on knowledge processes, use of IS, strategy, organizational and inter-organizational relationships and collaborations. The review also displays the limited research on the interlinks between episodic and systemic power.

Hence, in order to explicate the different forms of power and their interlinks as well as to account for these in research, we develop an analytical framework of power The Power Matrix which is presented as Figure 10.1. The Power Matrix outlines the interplay of different types of power, actors, and IS. It presents the manifestations of power in organizations along two axes: power (episodic power, systemic power) and locus (role of actors, role of IS).

The Power Matrix outlines four quadrants of different types of power differentiating between episodic and systemic power, the role of actors and the role of IS. Power from the episodic and actor perspective is defined as **power as possession.** The manifestations of power as possession in organizations are: *hierarchical, authoritative, legitimate, knowledge, resource access, self-interest*. Power from the episodic and IS perspective is described as **power as control**. The manifestations of power as control in organizations are: *rules, norms, monitoring, surveillance, discipline, compliance, digitalization*. Power from the systemic and actor perspective is outlined as **power as practice**. The manifestations of power as practice in organizations are: *shared goals/interests, communities of practice, social capital, trust, collaboration, network, empowerment, knowing*. Power from systemic and IS perspective is characterized as **power as facilitation**. The manifestations of power as facilitation in organizations are: *transparency, autonomy, multi-vocality, empowerment, discourse, decision-making, organizational culture*.

The literature typically outlines examples of uni-directional effects (e.g., power as possession leads to the use of IS as power as control), while power as practice leads to the enabling of IS as facilitation. However, the interactions between the four quadrants have been subject to limited research. Therefore, the Power Matrix allows to go beyond the uni-directional effects and demonstrate complex interlinkages of power as possession, practice, control and facilitation.

We posit that power in organizations is dynamic and contingent; hence, power as possession could lead to instances of power as practice, power as facilitation and power as

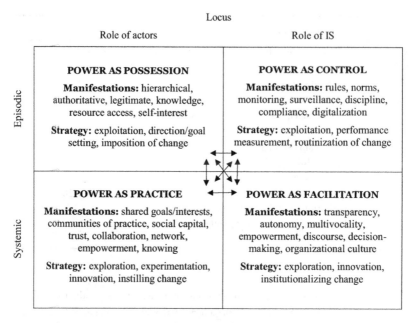

Locus

Figure 10.1 The Power Matrix

control, not just power as control as predominantly outlined in the literature. For example, strict hierarchy could be maneuvered through informal practices, networks and use of IS (Malaurent and Avison 2016; Simeonova 2014). Similarly, power as practice could lead to instances of power as possession, power as control, and power as facilitation. For example, an informal leader or community of practice could gain resources and legitimate power (Simeonova 2014). The role of IS predominantly depends on the role of actors and the strategy utilizing its facilitative or restrictive characteristics. However, implementation and use of IS could also challenge the status quo, current practices and redistributions of power. For example, the use of social media could enable multivocality and lead to empowerment (Huang et al. 2013). IS from a *power as control* could also limit the role of actors as outlined in an example of the use of Decision Support Systems and big data, where the system outputs have limited the power of the actors in strategic decision-making (Aversa et al. 2018). The increasing digitalization and the exploitation of digital technologies (*power and strategy as control*) could affect strategic decision-making (*power as facilitation*), collaboration, practice, exploration (*power and strategy as practice*) and also hierarchy and authority (*power as possession*). Digitalization and big data in organizations and society is pervasive, and accounting for the power dynamics are one (neglected) dimension in the evaluation of these technologies. Digital technologies are increasingly used for performance management and decision-making (Simeonova et al. 2018c). Using the Power Matrix we illustrate recursive links between power as possession, power as control, power as practice, and power as facilitation, explicating the interplay between different types of power, strategy, actors and IS.

Regarding strategy, the framework identifies links between power as possession and a type of IS strategy which is used by actors for *exploitation and imposition of change* but it also can help the *direction/goals setting and the triggering of change* (Lawrence et al. 2012; Marabelli and Galliers 2017). The strategic use of IS from the power as control perspective is manifested in *exploitation of technology, performance management and routinization of change*. Strategy from the power as practice and actors perspective is described as *exploration, experimentation, instilling change, and innovation*. It has been argued that crossing knowledge and political boundaries enables movement from knowledge re-use to creativity and innovation (Carlile 2004). In similar fashion, crossing the power and strategy boundaries may be an important avenue for research. Additionally, while research on the importance of achieving a balance of exploitation and exploration in ambidextrous organization is on-going (e.g., Cao et al. 2009; Lavie et al. 2010; March 1991; O'Reilly and Tushman 2013), links to power are lacking. Hence the framework could help consider different forms of power and issues in achieving ambidexterity.

Conclusion and Future Research

This chapter began by arguing that power dynamics are an important consideration for the study of strategic IS. Several dominant approaches to studying power were discussed, namely: the Foucauldian perspective, circuits of power, power and empowerment, episodic and systemic power. We argued that the episodic and systemic power perspective is a useful means of studying power because it helps to unpack the effects and interplay of different forms of power as well as integrating important considerations from the other approaches. An analytical framework has been proposed that accounts for the role of actors and IS as well as the episodic and systemic power dimensions. Future research could build on the ideas discussed and outlined in this chapter by (i) empirically demonstrating how power dynamics are infused within organizations, IS and strategy; (ii) considering different forms of power, their manifestations and their interplay as outlined in the Power Matrix framework; (iii) using the Power Matrix as a sensitizing lens for making sense of power issues, and (iv) continuing the discourse on power dynamics and raising such issues to the surface so that they can be better accounted for in strategic IS studies.

Notes

1   Refer to Jasperson et al. 2002; Bradshaw-Camball and Murray 1991 for variety of definitions of power.
2   For additional perspectives on power, e.g. philosophical foundations such as Lukes and Habermas, and such aspects as culture and discourse, refer to Clegg (1989), Clegg et al. (2006), Clegg and Haugaard (2009).

References

Alavi, M., and Leidner, D. E. (2001). Knowledge management and knowledge management systems: Conceptual foundations and research issues. *MIS Quarterly*, 25(1), 107–136.

Allen, D. K., Brown, A., Karanasios, S., and Norman, A. (2013). How should technologymediated organizational change be explained? A comparison of the contributions of critical realism and activity theory. *MIS Quarterly*, 37, 835–854.

Audzeyeva, A., and Hudson, R. (2016). How to get the most from a business intelligence application during the post implementation phase? Deep structure transformation at a UK retail bank. *European Journal of Information Systems*, 25(1), 29–46.

Aversa, P., Cabantous, L., and Haefliger, S. (2018). When decision support systems fail: Insights for strategic information systems from Formula 1. *The Journal of Strategic Information Systems*, 27, 221–236.

Avison, D. E., Cuthbertson, C. H., and Powell, P. (1999). The paradox of information systems: Strategic value and low status. *The Journal of Strategic Information Systems*, 8(4), 419445.

Azad, B., and Faraj, S. (2011). Social power and information technology implementation: A contentious framing lens. *Information Systems Journal*, 21(1), 33–61.

Backhouse, J., Hsu, C. W., and Silva, L. (2006). Circuits of power in creating de jure standards: Shaping an international information systems security standard. *MIS Quarterly*, 30(3), 413–438.

Blackler, F. (2011). Power, politics, and intervention theory: Lessons from organization studies. *Theory and Psychology*, 21, 724–734.

Bradley, R. V., Byrd, T. A., Pridmore, J. L., Thrasher, E., Pratt, R. M., and Mbarika, V. W. (2012). An empirical examination of antecedents and consequences of IT governance in US hospitals. *Journal of Information Technology*, 27(2), 156–177.

Bradshaw-Camball, P., and Murray, V. V. (1991). Illusions and other games: A trifocal view of organizational politics. *Organization Science*, 2(4), 379–398.

Bunderson, J. S., and Reagans, R. E. (2011). Power, status, and learning in organizations. *Organization Science*, 22, 1182–1194.

Busquets, J. (2010). Orchestrating smart business network dynamics for innovation. *European Journal of Information Systems*, 19(4), 481–493.

Cao, Q., Gedajlovic, E., and Zhan, H. (2009). Unpacking organizational ambidexterity: Dimensions, contingencies, and synergistic effects. *Organization Science*, 20(4), 781–796.

Carlile, P. R. (2002). A pragmatic view of knowledge and boundaries: Boundary objects in new product development. *Organization Science*, 13(4), 442–455.

Carlile, P. R. (2004). Transferring, translating, and transforming: An integrative framework for managing knowledge across boundaries. *Organization Science*, 15(5), 555–568.

Cendon, B. V., and Jarvenpaa, S. L. (2001). The development and exercise of power by leaders of support units in implementing information technology-based services. *The Journal of Strategic Information Systems*, 10(2), 121–158.

Chuang, C. H., Jackson, S. E., and Jiang, Y. (2016). Can knowledge-intensive teamwork be managed? Examining the roles of HRM systems, leadership, and tacit knowledge. *Journal of Management*, 42, 524–554.

Clegg, S. R. (1989). *Frameworks of Power*, London: Sage.

Clegg, S. R., Courpasson, D., and Phillips, N. (2006). *Power and Organizations*, London: Sage.

Clegg, S. R., and Haugaard, M. (Eds.). (2009). *The Sage Handbook of Power*. London: Sage.

Constantinides, P., and Barrett, M. (2006). Large-scale ICT innovation, power, and organizational change: The case of a regional health information network. *The Journal of Applied Behavioral Science*, 42(1), 76–90.

Contu, A. (2013). On boundaries and difference: Communities of practice and power relations in creative work. *Management Learning*, 45, 289–316.

Cook, S. D., and Brown, J. S. (1999). Bridging epistemologies: The generative dance between organizational knowledge and organizational knowing. *Organization Science*, 10, 381–400.

Deleuze, G. (1988). *Foucault*, Minnesota: University of Minnesota Press.

Dhillon, G. S., Caldeira, M., and Wenger, M. R. (2011). Intentionality and power interplay in IS implementation: The case of an asset management firm. *The Journal of Strategic Information Systems*, 20(4), 438–448.

Doolin, B. (2004). Power and resistance in the implementation of a medical management information system. *Information Systems Journal*, 14(4), 343–362.

Ezzamel, M., and Willmott, H. (2008). Strategy as discourse in a global retailer: A supplement to rationalist and interpretive accounts. *Organization Studies*, 29, 191–217.

Fairclough, N. (1992). *Discourse and Social Change*, Cambridge: Polity.

Fleming, P., and Spicer, A. (2014). Power in management and organization science. *The Academy of Management Annals*, 8(1), 237–298.

Foucault, M. (1977). *Discipline and Punish*, Peregrine: The Birth of the Prison, Vintage.

Foucault, M. (1979). *Discipline andPunish: The Birth of the Prison*, Harmondsworth: Penguin.

Foucault, M. (1980). *Power/Knowledge: Selected Interviews and Other writings, 1972–1977*, New York: Pantheon.

Galinsky, A. D., Magee, J. C., Gruenfeld, D. H., Whitson, J. A., and Liljenquist, K. A. (2008). Power reduces the press of the situation: Implications for creativity, conformity, and dissonance. *Journal of Personality and Social Psychology*, 95, 1450–1466.

Gohler, G. (2009). *Power to and Power Over*, In S. R. Clegg and M. Haugaard (Ed.), *The Sage Handbook of Power*, London: Sage.

Gray, P. H. (2001). The impact of knowledge repositories on power and control in the workplace. *Information Technology and People*, 14(4), 368–384.

Habermas, J. (1990). *Moral Consciousness and Communicative Action*, Cambridge, MA: MIT Press.

Hardy, C., and Leiba-O'Sullivan, S. (1998). The power behind empowerment: Implications for research and practice. *Human Relations*, 51(4), 451–483.

Hardy, C., and Thomas, R. (2014). Strategy, discourse and practice: The intensification of power. *Journal of Management Studies*, 51(2), 320–348.

Heizmann, H. (2011). Knowledge sharing in a dispersed network of HR practice: Zooming in on power/knowledge struggles. *Management Learning*, 42(4), 379–393.

Heizmann, H., and Olsson, M. R. (2015). Power matters: The importance of Foucault's power/knowledge as a conceptual lens in KM research and practice. *Journal of Knowledge Management*, 19(4), 756–769.

Hekkala, R., and Urquhart, C. (2013). Everyday power struggles: Living in an IOIS project. *European Journal of Information Systems*, 22(1), 76–94.

Huang, J., Baptista, J., and Galliers, R. D. (2013). Reconceptualising rhetorical practices in organisations: The impact of social media on internal communications. *Information and Management*, 50, 112–124.

Hussain, Z. I., and Cornelius, N. (2009). The use of domination and legitimation in information systems implementation. *Information Systems Journal*, 19(2), 197–224.

Introna, L. (2003). Disciplining information systems: Truth and its regimes. *European Journal of Information Systems*, 12, 235–240.

Jasperson, J. S., Carte, T. A., Saunders, C. S., Butler, B. S., Croes, H. J., and Zheng, W. (2002). Review: Power and information technology research: A metatriangulation review. *MIS Quarterly*, 26(4), 397–459.

Kärreman, D. (2010). The power of knowledge: Learning from "learning by knowledgeintensive firm". *Journal of Management Studies*, 47(7), 405–1416.

Knights, D., Murray, F., and Willmott, H. (1993). Networking as knowledge work: A study of strategic inter-organizational development in the financial services industry. *Journal of Management Studies*, 30(6), 975–995.

Lavie, D., Stettner, U., and Tushman, M. L. (2010). Exploration and exploitation within and across organizations. *Academy of Management Annals*, 4(1), 109–155.

Lawrence, T. B., Malhotra, N., and Morris, T. (2012). Episodic and systemic power in the transformation of professional service firms. *Journal of Management Studies*, 49(1), 102143.

Lawrence, T. B., Mauws, M. K., Dyck, B., and Kleysen, R. (2005). The politics of organizational learning: Integrating power into the 4I framework. *Academy of Management Review*, 30(1), 180–191.

Leonardi, P. M., Huysman, M., and Steinfield, C. (2013). Enterprise social media: Definition, history, and prospects for the study of social technologies in organizations. *Journal of Computer-Mediated Communication*, 19(1), 1–19.

Levina, N., and Vaast, E. (2008). Innovating or doing as told? Status differences and overlapping boundaries in offshore collaboration. *MIS Quarterly*, 32, 307–332.

Lyon, D. (1993). An electronic panopticon? A sociological critique of surveillance theory. *The Sociological Review*, 41(4), 653–678.

Malaurent, J., and Avison, D. (2016). Reconciling global and local needs: A canonical action research project to deal with workarounds. *Information Systems Journal*, 26, 227–257.

Marabelli, M., and Galliers, R. D. (2017). A reflection on information systems strategizing: The role of power and everyday practices. *Information Systems Journal*, 27, 347–366.

March, J. G. (1991). Exploration and exploitation in organizational learning. *Organization Science*, 2(1), 71–87.

Markus, M. L. (1983). Power, politics, and MIS implementation. *Communications of the ACM*, 26(6), 430–444.

Marshall, N., and Rollinson, J. (2004). Maybe Bacon had a point: The politics of interpretation in collective sensemaking. *British Journal of Management*, 15, 71–86.

McAfee, A. P. (2006). Enterprise 2.0. *The Dawn of Emergent collaboration, MIT Sloan Management Review*, 47, 21–28.

McBride, N. (2013). Power and the purpose of information systems: Lessons from lost civilisations, *UK Academy for Information Systems Conference Proceedings*.

McCabe, D. (2010). Strategy-as-power: Ambiguity, contradiction and the exercise of power in a UK building society. *Organization*, 17, 151–175.

Michailova, S., and Husted, K. (2003). Knowledge-sharing hostility in Russian firms. *California Management Review*, 45, 59–77.

Moe, C. E., Newman, M., and Sein, M. K. (2017). The public procurement of information systems: Dialectics in requirements specification. *European Journal of Information Systems*, 26(2), 143–163.

Muthusamy, S., and White, M. (2005). Learning and knowledge transfer in strategic alliances: A social exchange view. *Organization Studies*, 26, 415–441.

Ngwenyama, O., and Nielsen, P. A. (2014). Using organizational influence processes to overcome IS implementation barriers: Lessons from a longitudinal case study of SPI implementation. *European Journal of Information Systems*, 23(2), 205–222.

O'Reilly, C. A., and Tushman, M. L. (2013). Organizational ambidexterity: Past, present, and future. *Academy of Management Perspectives*, 27(4), 324–338.

Orlikowski, W. J. (1991). Integrated information environment or matrix of control? The contradictory implications of information technology. *accounting, Management and Information Technologies*, 1, 9–42.

Orlikowski, W. J. (2002). Knowing in practice: Enacting a collective capability in distributed organizing. *Organization Science*, 13, 249–273.

Power, D., and Gruner, R. L. (2017). Variable use of standards-based IOS enabling technologies in Australian SMEs: An examination of deliberate and emergent decision making processes. *European Journal of Information Systems*, 26(2), 164–184.

Pozzebon, M., and Pinsonneault, A. (2012). The dynamics of client-consultant relationships: Exploring the interplay of power and knowledge. *Journal of Information Technology*, 27(1), 35–56.

Raman, R., and Bharadwaj, A. (2012). Power differentials and performative deviation paths in practice transfer: The case of evidence-based medicine. *Organization Science*, 23(6), 1593–1621.

Ravishankar, M. N. (2015). The realignment of offshoring frame disputes (OFD): An ethnographic "cultural" analysis. *European Journal of Information Systems*, 24(3), 234246.

Ravishankar, M. N., Pan, S. L., and Myers, M. D. (2013). Information technology offshoring in India: A postcolonial perspective. *European Journal of Information Systems*, 22(4), 387402.

Sewell, G. (2005). Nice work? Rethinking managerial control in an era of knowledge work. *Organization*, 12(5), 685–704.

Silva, L. (2007). Epistemological and theoretical challenges for studying power and politics in information systems. *Information Systems Journal*, 17(2), 165–183.

Silva, L., and Backhouse, J. (2003). The circuits-of-power framework for studying power in institutionalization of information systems. *Journal of the Association for Information Systems*, 4(1), 294–336.

Silva, L., and Hirschheim, R. (2007). Fighting against windmills: Strategic information systems and organizational deep structures. *MIS Quarterly*, 31, 327–354.

Simeonova, B. (2014). *Knowledge Sharing and Knowledge Interaction Processes in Organizations*, London: University of London.

Simeonova, B. (2015). Power and knowledge within activity theory: Applying activity theory to knowledge sharing. *Proceedings of the 30th European Group for Organizational Studies*.

Simeonova, B. (2018). Transactive memory systems and Web 2.0 in knowledge sharing: A conceptual model based on activity theory and critical realism. *Information Systems Journal*, 28(4), 592–611.

Simeonova, B., Karanasios, S., Galliers, R. D., Kelly, P. R., and Mishra, J. (2018a). Where is power in information systems research? Towards a framework. *Proceedings of the 38th International Conference on Information Systems*.

Simeonova, B., Karanasios, S., Galliers, R. D., Kelly, P. R., and Mishra, J. (2018b). New ways of organising in collaborative knowledge sharing: Examining the effects of power. *Proceedings of the 34th European Group for Organizational Studies*.

Simeonova, B., Morton, J., Wilson, A., Marabelli, M., and Galliers, R. D. (2018c). Aligning practices in a pluralistic healthcare context using a performance improvement system. *Proceedings of the 38th International Conference on Information Systems*.

Smith, S., Winchester, D., Bunker, D., and Jamieson, R. (2010). Circuits of power: A study of mandated compliance to an information systems security "De Jure" standard in a government organization. *MIS Quarterly*, 34, 463–486.

Son, J. Y., Narasimhan, S., and Riggins, F. J. (2005). Effects of relational factors and channel climate on EDI usage in the customer-supplier relationship. *Journal of Management Information Systems*, 22(1), 321–353.

Wang, S., and Noe, R. A. (2010). Knowledge sharing: A review and directions for future research. *Human Resource Management Review*, 20(2), 115–131.

Webster, J. (1995). Networks of collaboration or conflict? Electronic data interchange and power in the supply chain. *The Journal of Strategic Information Systems*, 4(1), 31–42.

Willcocks, L. P. (2004). Foucault, power/knowledge and IS: Reconstructing the present, In J. Mingers and L. P. Willcocks (Eds.), *Social Theory and Philosophy for Information Systems*, Chichester: Wiley, 238–296.

Willcocks, L. P., and Lioliou, E. (2011). Everything is dangerous: Rethinking Michel Foucault and the social study of ICT, In R. D. Galliers and W. Currie (Eds.), *The Oxford Handbook of Management Information Systems: Critical Perspectives and New Directions*, Oxford: Oxford University Press, 174–198.

Willem, A., and Scarbrough, H. (2006). Social capital and political bias in knowledge sharing: An exploratory study. *Human Relations*, 59(10), 1343–1370.

Young, M. L., Kuo, F. Y., and Myers, M. D. (2012). To share or not to share: a critical research perspective on knowledge management systems. *European Journal of Information Systems*, 21(5), 496–511.

Zuboff, S. (1988). *In the Age of the Smart Machine: The Future of Work and Power*, New York: Basic Books.

Questions for Discussion

1   Why is it important to consider different forms of power along with the role of actors and IS?

2   Why are power dynamics under-researched and largely ignored in the field of IS? Do you consider power dynamics as an important aspect of organizations, IS and strategy?

3   What are the connections between the different power quadrants in the framework outlined in this chapter? How can power move from one quadrant to another through the implementation of IS and strategy?

4   Use the framework to evaluate the digital transformation examples and the roles of the Chief Digital Officers (CDOs) provided in chapters 6, 7, 8, and 9. How could the framework be used to explain the power of CDOs?

5   How might digital technology be described in terms of a power perspective? What are the interlinkages between the four forms of power in the framework and digital leadership, digital technology and digital transformation?

6   Given the growing importance of digital technology and the phenomenon of digital transformation, such theoretical tools as the framework presented in this chapter could enable greater understanding of power dynamics. Which aspects of the framework are most helpful in understanding power in digital transformations?

Further Reading

Marabelli, M., Galliers, R. D. (2017). A reflection on information systems strategizing: The role of power and everyday practices. *Information Systems Journal*, 27, 347–366.

Simeonova, B. (2018). Transactive memory systems and Web 2.0 in knowledge sharing: A conceptual model based on activity theory and critical realism. *Information Systems Journal*, 28(4), 592–611.

PART III

Organizing and Governing the IS Function

HAVING CONSIDERED FOUNDATIONS in IS strategy and strategizing, and new developments in the domain of digital strategy and organizational transformation, we now turn to the perennial issues of organizing and governing the IS function. Because decisions concerning investments in information technology occur regularly and because investments in technology need to be astutely managed to derive full value, organizations need sound principles for organizing and governing the IS function. The full contents of Part III are summarized in the second-from-top layer of Figure P3.1.

The first reading in this chapter is a highly cited *MIS Quarterly Executive* paper titled "Principles and Models for Organizing the IT Function" by Ritu Agarwal and V. Sambamurthy. The authors conducted a two-year study of how leading-edge firms organized their IT function with a view towards encouraging innovation and enabling superior business performance. The paper discusses three models of organizing: the Partner Model in which IT is an active partner in business innovation, the Platform Model in which IT provides the resources for business innovation, and the Scalable Model in which IT provides flexible and scalable resources for the business.

Given the cyclical nature of the economy, no CIO can expect to manage exclusively during periods of prosperity. The second reading examines different methods for managing the IT function during challenging economic times. The reading, titled "How CIOs Manage IT during Economic Decline: Surviving and Thriving amid Uncertainty" is authored by Dorothy Leidner, Robert Beatty, and Jane Mackay. Based on interviews with 20 CIOs of firms ranging in size from approximately $800 million to $10 billion, the authors identify four approaches to managing IT during economic decline: maintain the legacy, clean house, extend the lifecycle, and bulletproof the infrastructure. The four approaches vary depending on whether the CIO wishes to retain versus rethink the existing strategic plan and whether the CIO takes a short- or long-term perspective of IT. We believe the lessons learned in this paper extend across time

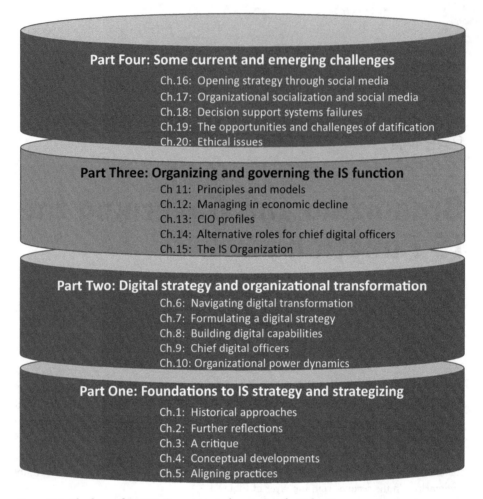

Figure P3.1 The focus of Part III: Organizing and governing the IS function

and place. Regardless of the trigger for economic decline, CIOs have choices to make when managing IT and this reading helps synthesize the options.

An objective of effective governance of IT is to improve organizational performance. IT is critical to helping organizations operate efficiently and helping organizations create value. The third reading considers the important role by the CIO in contributing to firm performance. Titled "CIO Leadership Profiles: Implications of Matching CIO Authority and Leadership Capability on IT Impact", this reading is authored by David Preston, Dorothy Leidner, and Daniel Chen. The authors develop a taxonomy of four CIO leadership profiles – the IT mechanic, the IT laggard, the IT advisor, and the IT orchestrator – that vary based on the dual dimensions of CIO leadership quality and CIO decision-making authority. The impact of IT on firm contribution is highest for the IT orchestrator CIO types and lowest for the IT mechanic CIO types. There may be times when an organization needs a good IT mechanic and times when it needs a skilled IT orchestrator. The reading offers guidelines for CIOs on actions to take to transition across the profiles.

In recent years, a new c-level position has been created in many organizations, that of the Chief Digital Officer (CDO). With digital innovation impacting virtually every industry, many organizations have been chosen to have a dedicated position to oversee digital innovation. Because of the close relationship between digital innovation and IT innovation, one might well wonder how this role differs from that of the CIO. The fourth reading in this chapter address this issue. Titled "Three Types of Chief Digital Officers and the Reasons Organizations Adopt the Role", this reading is authored by Sanja Tumbas, Nicholas Berente, and Jan vom Brocke. Based on interviews with 35 CDOs from various sectors, the authors describe three specific domains in which CDOs must be skilled in order to be highly effective as CDOs: digital innovation, data analytics, and customer engagement. In keeping with the previous readings that identify profiles of different approaches to the same role, the authors identify three types of CDOs and their accompanying characteristics.

The final reading in this chapter, "Rethinking the concept of the IS organization" by Joe Peppard, encourages managers to consider the option of not treating the IS organization as a sub-unit to be separately managed, but as a node in a social and knowledge network that is impacted by, and impacts, other nodes. Only then, argues the author, can IT generate sustained business value. Three organizing modes for generating value through IT: functional, partnership, and pervasive. The author suggests that there is no decidedly clear description as to what the IS organization should be. Less effort should be spent on attempting to optimize the IT unit per se (and the CIO's role per se) and more should be spent on coordinating and integrating relevant knowledge that is located organizational-wide. From this perspective, the business-IT "gap" or misalignment is much more of a knowledge gap manifested in relational issues.

Chapter 11

Ritu Agarwal and V. Sambamurthy

PRINCIPLES AND MODELS FOR ORGANIZING THE IT FUNCTION

HOW SHOULD FIRMS ORGANIZE THEIR IT FUNCTION?

HOW SHOULD CONTEMPORARY FIRMS organize their IT function? Despite more than 20 years of experience and insights, this question continues to dominate the attention and interest of CIOs and senior business executives. During the 1970s and 1980s, firms alternated between centralized models (where authority for the majority of IT decisions was located in the corporate IT group) and decentralized models (where the authority for most IT decisions was located in the divisional or functional IT units).

During the 1990s, many firms gravitated toward the federal organizational model, which dispersed control and authority for IT decisions. Corporate IS groups were vested with authority for IT infrastructure decisions while divisional units had the authority for decisions about strategic deployment of IT.[1] Researchers have concluded that this model of distributed governance and decision-authority is particularly appropriate for large, multidivisional firms because it balances enterprise priorities for scale and IT standardization with divisional priorities for IT innovation in their products, services, or customer relationships.[2]

However, the federal model and its distributed governance might not adequately address the strategic, organizational, and technological realities facing today's IT executives, for two reasons.

First, IT now plays a more prominent role in corporate agility, enabling rapid and continual business innovation in products, services, channels, and supply and demand chain management.[3] Hence, firms are investing heavily in enterprise digital platforms (such as enterprise resource planning, customer relationship management, supply chain management, and wireless technologies) to support innovations in their "ecosystems," that is, their business partnerships with customers, suppliers, and other specialist firms (such as contract manufacturers).[4] Decisions about business innovations require significant levels of collaboration and partnership between IT and business executives.

In their case study of Marshall Industries (now Avnet), El Sawy and his colleagues described how the IT function was organized for continuous IT-based innovation. Teams of IT and business executives responsible for innovation focused on drivers of business success, such as supply chain management and customer order capture.[5] Meanwhile, a small group managed the common IT infrastructure. This structure retains the fundamental characteristics of the federal model, but it emphasizes far greater collaboration between business and IT executives.

Second, today's accelerated rates of technological change and obsolescence in the IT market require organizational models that pay close attention to human capital and relationships with vendors and consultants.[6]

In their case study of Bell Atlantic (now Verizon), Clark and colleagues described an organizational model, called the Centers of Excellence, to develop and leverage human capital.[7] This model has three components:

1   Units called skillcenters focus on developing valued IT skills; IT professionals are assigned to these units to be trained and developed in those skills,
2   Account managers are IT professionals responsible for nurturing strategic ideas about IT use,
3   Temporary project teams are staffed with IT professionals from the skillcenters and are responsible for rapid applications delivery using the specifications created by the account managers.

While this centers of excellence model subscribes to the federal logic, it emphasizes greater centralization than the pure federal model, because most of the IT developers are centralized within the IT skillcenters.

Similarly, Cross and colleagues described British Petroleum's (now BP) IT organizational model that used multisourcing agreements to garner cost economy and flexibility.[8] In this model, the firm partnered with multiple external vendors and systems integrators to manage its IT infrastructure, utility services (e.g., helpdesk), and solutions delivery. Even though the model is consistent with the federal logic, it primarily aims to leverage external partners through a small corporate IS group; a limited number of IS professionals are located in divisions.

As these examples illustrate, novel IT organizational models are emerging. Yet, there has been no systematic effort to document them and examine where each might be appropriate. The field needs fresh thinking on the following questions:

•   What principles should be applied to organizing the IT function?
•   What IT organizational models are viable today?

In collaboration with the Advanced Practices Council of SIM International, we recently conducted a two-year study to discover answers to these two questions.[9] After interviewing CIOs and senior IT executives from nearly 30 firms, and conducting in-depth case studies of seven firms in different sectors of the economy, we identified new principles and organizational models for the IT function.

The principles explain how executives can think about organizing the IT function (see Table 11.1) to boost business innovation. When used to foster different roles for the IT function, they result in three different organizational models (see Table 11.2). Each model subscribes to the general principles, but combines them in distinct ways to support different value propositions and roles for IT.

Table 11.1 Organizing Principles for the IT Function

Guiding Principle	*Recommended Managerial Actions*
Organize IT to encourage co-evolution with the rest of the business. Organize IT to nurture relationship networks for visioning, innovation, and sourcing. Organize IT function to explicitly manage eight value-creating processes.	• Design reporting relationships for key IT executives that focus on strategic business drivers. • Engage IT executives in experimenting with new IT-enabled business models and business practices through appropriate incentives. • Nurture visioning, innovation, and sourcing networks through: 1. Internal coordination mechanisms, including executive councils, IT management councils, divisional steering councils, IT standing teams, account managers, divisional information officers, service level agreements, and informal relationship building. 2. External partnering tactics, such as multisourcing agreements, strategic alliances and joint ventures. • Adopt a modular approach to selecting optimal organizing options for individual value-creating IT processes.

Table 11.2 Features of the Three Organizational Models

	The Partner Model	*The Platform Model*	*The Scalable Model*
Strategic Positioning of IT	IT is an active partner in business innovation	IT provides the assets, services, and resources for business innovation across the enterprise	IT provides flexible and scalable resources for the business

Distinguishing Characteristics of the Model	• Business leadership in IT innovation through divisional information officers
	• Corporate IT catalyzes innovation through strategic consulting
	• Explicit focus on three types of costs
	  ○ Business applications costs
	  ○ Infrastructure costs
	  ○ Utility costs
	• Dual, matrixed reporting
		• Corporate IT as the factory: delivery of scaleable, seamless, and flexible infrastructure
		  ○ Enterprise-wide platform and capabilities
		• Business ownership of IT innovation
		  ○ Senior executives in business units
		  ○ Dotted line relationship with CIO
		• Account managers as liaisons between IT and business units
			• Centralized IT organization for leveragability
			  ○ Cross-unit asset utilization
			  ○ Centers of Excellence structures for human capital
			• Strong IT presence in business units
			• Multisourcing arrangements
			• Scaling for variable resource needs

(continued)

	The Partner Model	The Platform Model	The Scalable Model

Where does this Model Work?	• A need to promote business innovation through IT
	• Business executives lack a deep understanding of IT
	• Organizations with multiple related businesses
	• Strong IT leadership with a history of trust and credibility
		• Global businesses in multiple lines of business
		  ○ Unique IT needs across units
		• Strong level of IT knowledge among business managers
		  ○ High-tech sectors
			• Global businesses in related lines of business
			• Cyclical industries

First we describe the organizing principles, then the three organizational models. Our goal is to assist senior IT and business executives in assessing the appropriateness of their current IT organizational model and in perhaps determining a more appropriate model. Also, these descriptions respond to researchers' need for fresh insights about organizing the IT function.[10]

Principles for Organizing the IT Function

Three principles underlie new ways to organize the IT function (See Table 11.1):

Principle 1: Organize IT to Foster Co-evolution between the Business and the IT Function

The strategic role of IT is to enable innovative business strategies and processes. In the past, IT executives have focused on aligning their function with the business. But alignment can be too static for today's fast pace. A better goal is "co-evolution."

Co-evolution means that the capabilities of the IT function and the rest of the business develop iteratively and reciprocally over time. For example, firms that have developed business capabilities for "direct to the customer" order capture and fulfillment have invested in information technologies that allow customers to access their product databases through portals, configure their orders, and observe the progress on their order through the manufacturing and logistics processes. At the same time, newer technologies, such as personalization, enable companies to develop better business capabilities to customize their relationships with customers. For instance, they can capture and store customer profiles, differentiate customers' various levels of business with the firm, and offer customized pricing and services to individual or clusters of customers. Hence, the IT and business capabilities for customer relationship management intertwine, and develop iteratively over time.

The IT organizational structure must facilitate such natural occurrences of co-evolution. Although most firms have generally sought to align their IT capabilities with their business capabilities, the IT function's structure must also assist the firm in exploiting such IT-enabled opportunities as virtual integration, direct access to customers, and cross-divisional or business unit integration.[11]

For example, the executive management team at a large telecommunications firm in our study considered customer advocacy and customer relationships to be the strategic drivers of its business model. Therefore, management focused on facilitating co-evolution of IT and customer-centric capabilities by: (i) having the CIO report to the senior executive responsible for customer advocacy, and (ii) linking business and IT executives' compensation to customer-centric innovation utilizing IT.

Generally, emphasizing co-evolution extends a firm's existing emphasis on strategic alignment, where the IT function is already organized to support business strategies and capabilities. However, co-evolution requires going beyond the alignment model by emphasizing a two-way relationship between the development of business capabilities and IT capabilities. The alignment models have been criticized for placing IT management into a "lag" role which prevents IT investments and capabilities from potentially shaping business strategy.[12] Alignment thinking precludes our first principle: organizing to foster co-evolution of IT and the business.

Principle 2: Organize IT to Nurture Relationship Networks for Visioning, Innovation, and Sourcing

Generally, IT decision-making authority has been dispersed. This is not the most effective organizational structure, though, because it does not explicitly foster collaboration among the four stakeholders vital to successful management and use of IT: executive management, business management, IT management, and external vendors (Figure 11.1). IT's organizational structure must facilitate collaboration among these four to blend their knowledge and influence. We believe that three kinds of "relationship networks" are important for organizing IT activities to foster such collaboration: visioning networks, innovation networks, and sourcing networks.

Visioning networks are relationship networks among senior management and senior IT executives (e.g., the CIO and some of the CIO's direct reports). Their purpose is to foster collaboration among these executives for creating and articulating strategic vision about the role and value of IT in the firm. Visioning networks help top management teams describe their perspectives on the role of IT, their strategic priorities for IT use, and the links they see between IT and drivers of the business strategy.

The primary mechanism for establishing a visioning network is to have the CIO as a formal member of the top management team. Additionally, Rockart and colleagues have noted the trend toward using IT executive councils as a mechanism for visioning networks.[13] These councils include the CEO, COO, CIO, and other senior business executives as members. They devote time to developing, articulating, and maintaining the strategic vision of the use of IT in the firm.

Schein describes four perspectives of the strategic role of IT: automation, informating up to enhance command and control, informating down to promote decentralization and empowerment, and transformation, that is, using IT to reshape competition or the nature of the industry.[14] Visioning networks foster the sharing of such perspectives.

In our study, a large telecommunications firm considered customer relationships to be its strategic value-creating activity; therefore, the strategic role of IT is to enable and shape customer relationships. The visioning network mechanism they used was the CIO's formal membership in the top management team.

Table 11.1 shows a variety of mechanisms for all three relationship networks.

Innovation networks are relationship networks between business and IT executives. Their purpose is to foster collaboration between these executives when they are conceptualizing and implementing IT applications specifically applications that aim to enhance the firm's agility and innovation in customer relationships, manufacturing, product development or supply chain management. Innovation networks can utilize such coordination mechanisms as

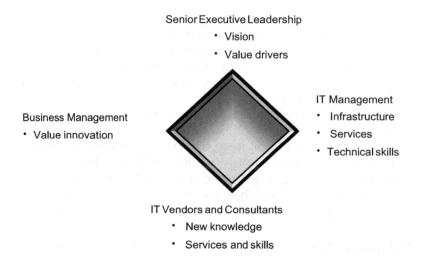

Figure 11.1 Key Stakeholders in The IT Relational Networks

executive councils, IT management councils, divisional steering councils, IT standing teams, account managers, and divisional information officers.

So whereas visioning networks engage top management to shape overall enterprise perspectives about the strategic role and value of IT, innovation networks focus on specific innovations and strategic IT applications.

In their study of about 40 firms, Brown and Sambamurthy found that innovation networks develop both through collaborations between business and IT executives and through collaborations among IT executives dispersed across the enterprise.[15] They also found that firms must use combinations of coordination mechanisms to nurture innovation.[16] Other IS researchers have found that the use of coordination mechanisms increases the likelihood of IT innovation occurring.[17]

Sourcing networks are relationship networks between IT executives and external partners. Their purpose is to foster collaboration between these internal and external parties when they are negotiating and managing efficient, cost-effective, and innovative uses of IT assets and services through multisourcing arrangements, joint ventures, or strategic alliances.

DiRomualdo and Gurbaxani demonstrate that sourcing networks can help companies not only lower their IT costs but also augment their IT capabilities and business thinking about innovative uses of IT.[18] Lacity and colleagues have also emphasized the importance of using specific organizational design mechanisms to leverage sourcing networks to achieve more effective management and use of IT.[19]

Principle 3: Organize IT to Explicitly Manage Eight Value-Creating Processes

In the past, the IT function had been viewed as a monolithic structure, and organizational design has focused primarily on finding the best options to manage infrastructure and deliver strategic IT applications. However, this approach proves to be limiting because IT functions in most modern firms perform a wider range of activities. As information technologies become a strategic differentiator, it is better to think of the IT function as a portfolio of eight value-creating processes each of which needs to be organized for its own best contribution and leverage. These eight form three sets of processes (See Figure 11.2 and Table 11.3), called foundation processes, primary processes, and secondary processes.

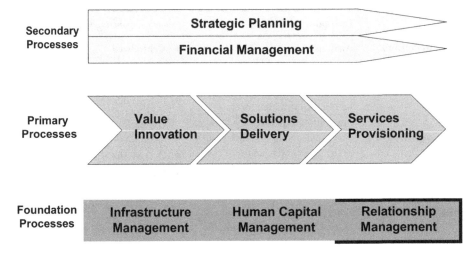

Figure 11.2 Organizational Building Blocks: Creating Value Processes

Table 11.3 Value-Creating Processes in the IT Function

Process	Description	Example Organizing Options
Infrastructure management	Building and managing the blueprint for investing in computing, networking, database, object-base, and other key infrastructure technologies. Includes establishment and management of IT infrastructure standards.	• Centralized • Outsourced • Leased
Human capital management	Identifying the know-how the IT function needs to possess, with respect to technology, business, and strategy. Acquiring, developing, and retaining IT talent.	• Centers of excellence
Relationship management	Partnering with internal clients, external vendors, and business peers to develop a shared understanding of IT's vision and role. Managing expectations across stakeholder groups.	• Formal councils and crossfunctional teams • Job rotation • Alliance management teams • Informal one-on-one relationships
Value-innovation	Strategic analysis of IT-based business opportunities and creative conceptualizations of ways in which IT can be used to strengthen business competencies, customer relationships, and business partner networks.	• Centralized, with account managers for individual units • Centralized, with mirror image units for individual businesses • Decentralized • Federal

(continued)

Process	Description	Example Organizing Options
Solutions delivery	Analysis of business needs for IT, conceptualizing of IT applications, and delivery of applications either through internal development, external contracting, or integration of packaged software.	• Centralized • Federal • Outsourced • Independent IT subsidiary
Services provisioning	The provisioning of utilities, such as the data center, and services, such as helpdesks and desktop management, for users across the corporation.	• Centralized • Decentralized • Outsourced
Strategic planning	Enterprise-wide activities aimed at establishing strategic business thrusts and determining how strategic IT thrusts will support the business.	• Centralized • Federal
Financial management	The structuring of service level agreements, tracking and benchmarking the costs of IT services, and developing the business case and ROI analyses of IT infrastructure investment proposals.	• Centralized

Foundation processes relate to creating and managing three fundamental IT capabilities: (1) IT infrastructure, (2) IT human capital, and (3) IT relationships (specifically, partnering with business executives and partnering with vendors and systems integrators). These IT capabilities are at the heart of how IT functions help their business partners differentiate their strategies and nurture continuous innovation through IT.[20]

Primary processes are those that must be managed in every IT function, to convert foundation IT capabilities into business applications and services. Three primary processes are (4) value-innovation (that is, conceptualizing strategic IT needs and opportunities in the form of applications), (5) solutions delivery (building IT applications), and (6) services provisioning (i.e., providing helpdesk, desktop configuration, and other support IT services). They are like the front office of IT or the touch points through which business clients perceive the quality, contributions, and effectiveness of the IT function.

Secondary processes are those important to the wellbeing of an IT function. Their contribution is exhibited by how well they support the foundation and primary processes. These two processes are (7) strategic planning and (8) financial management.

We recommend that IT management think modularly by selecting the best organizing option for each of the eight value-creating processes.[21] For example, in most firms, it is appropriate to manage the IT infrastructure through a centralized IT unit, to outsource specific infrastructure services (such as, web hosting), and to lease desktops for a faster technology refresh (for example, every two years). Such organization permits more rapid changes than decentralized IT or complete in-house sourcing of infrastructure services. Similarly, when it comes to organizing solutions delivery, possible choices include a corporate IT unit, divisional IT units, or strategic partnerships with third-party solutions developers.

Based on our research, Table 11.3 shows some of the appropriate choices for organizing each of the eight value-creating processes in today's firms. By thinking modularly, management chooses an option for each, and manages them all as a portfolio of activities within the IT function.

Modular thinking promotes flexibility in organizing the IT function. When changes in the business, technology, or the firm require attention to a specific value-creating process, IT functions that employ modular thinking can change the organizing option for just that process. For example, relying on packaged solutions rather than in-house coding can shift a firm's reliance from large internal applications development groups (either at corporate or in divisions) to sourcing relationships with systems integrators. If IT then needs to modify its solutions delivery process to adjust to, say, an organizational change, it can do so without significantly altering the IT function's overall structure. Similarly, companies can emphasize human capital management by recentralizing IT staff or creating centers of excellence, each focusing on specific systems. These structural shifts can be localized to human capital management only, and not require significant changes to other IT functions.

Taken together, these three principles represent fresh thinking about organizational design of the IT function, emphasizing co-evolution rather than alignment, emphasizing relationship networks that foster collaboration rather than dispersing IT decision-making authority, and emphasizing modularity in the IT function around value-creating processes rather than creating monolithic organizational architectures.

Three Organizational Models for the IT Function

In our research, we uncovered three viable IT organizational models. All draw upon the principles, yet have distinct goals.

The Partner Model, the first model, primarily aims to ensure that the IT function is an active and direct participant in collaborating with business executives to make business innovation through IT a reality.

The Platform Model, the second model, primarily aims to ensure that the IT function provides the assets, services, and resources for business innovation across the enterprise. Thus, the IT function acts as an enabler of innovation rather than as a direct catalyst for innovation, as in the Partner Model.

The Scalable Model, the third model, primarily aims for maximum flexibility in its people resources, so that the IT function can expand and contract in concert with business cycles. A salient aspect of this model, in contrast with the other two models, is that it makes extensive use of sourcing relationships with vendors and systems integrators to achieve flexibility in IT resources. This model seeks to facilitate IT-based business innovation without committing significant organizational investments to in-house IT resources.

The Partner Model: Being a Catalyst for Innovation

In this organizational model, IT is a proactive partner in the innovation process. It stimulates, catalyzes, and "seeds" thinking about strategic uses of IT. In particular, this model facilitates co-evolution through vigorous collaboration between business and IS executives, in both devising IT-enabled business capabilities and in setting the direction and timing of future IT capabilities.

The Partner Model focuses on innovation networks (from Principle 2) and emphasizes three value-creating processes in designing the IT function: value-innovation, relationship management, and financial management (in Principle 3).

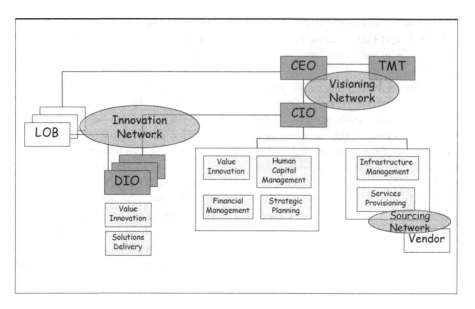

Figure 11.3 The Partner Model

A large hospitality firm. A primary example of the Partner Model in practice is at a large hospitality firm.

Principle 1: Co-evolution. When the current CIO arrived at this firm, IT was adequately aligned with the business strategy and adequately supported it. However, responding to the Internet, globalization, and competitive rivalry would require greater attention to business innovation and agility through IT. Corporate management expected IT to shape value-added services and relationships with customers and enhance brand equity. At the same time, to further develop customer relationships and heighten brand management, the firm became interested in using personalization, data mining, and wireless mobility technologies. In short, the firm realized it needed to transform IT from an alignment to a co-evolution mindset.

Furthermore, the CIO realized that the critical success factor for IT would be the effectiveness of the innovation network: how well IT and business executives would collaborate in generating a stream of innovative IT applications and in making IT investment choices. Finally, the CIO realized that success of his organizational model would hinge on the quality of the value-innovation process and how well this process blended IT and business capabilities and resources.

Principle 2: Relationship networks. Figure 11.3 shows the organizational model of the IT function at this hospitality firm. To sustain co-evolutionary thinking and strengthen the role of IT as a strategic differentiator, the CIO reported to the CEO and became a member of the senior executive leadership team. As illustrated in Figure 11.3, his membership in the top management team built the visioning network. The group recognized the transformative power of IT for their customer relationships, so they could provide the vision for directing IT innovation in customer-facing activities.

The firm's innovation network is promoted through interactions among Divisional Information Officers (DIOs) and their business peers in the lines of business. In addition, a limited set of partnerships with external vendors exists, providing sourcing networks, even though sourcing networks are not as salient at this firm as the other two types of relationship networks.

Three specific characteristics of this firm's organizational model warrant mention.

First, the divisional information officers are located in business units to strengthen the innovation networks.

They report both to the CIO and the president of their business unit. They collaborate with their business peers on two value-creating processes: value-innovation and solutions delivery. As members of their divisional executive team, they stimulate IT innovation in their division's business. They also belong to the IT management council (which comprises all senior IT executives and the CIO), so they share their division's IT needs, priorities, and issues with the rest of IT management. These interactions are important in shaping IT investments and priorities.

Second, to further strengthen value-innovation, a small strategic consulting group within corporate IS proactively seeds strategic thinking and innovation across the enterprise. This group of business and IT consultants works with the divisional information officers and executive teams in applying strategic thinking to IT-enabled opportunities and threats. The firm's business and IT executives attribute the success of their IT innovation activities to this strategic consulting group.

Third, the CIO and senior IT executives recognized that partnerships would be less effective if the business units did not fully understand IT costs. Therefore, the organizational model focuses on three types of IT costs: business applications costs, infrastructure and utility costs, and overhead costs. Management of costs can be seen as relating to the management of value-creating processes, Principle 3.

Principle 3: Value-creating processes. Business divisions own their own business applications costs because their executives develop the business cases for projects and provide the necessary funding. The division information officers assist the business executives in developing the business justification for projects and managing solutions delivery costs. Thus, applications costs are fully vested within the divisions.

Infrastructure and utility costs are managed as shared services and apportioned to divisions through chargebacks, which are negotiated annually with the divisions. The firm periodically benchmarks these utility and infrastructure costs to reassure division management of their low-cost competitiveness. IT management also uses the chargebacks as a partnership-building mechanism. Overall, their success is consistent with the observations of Ross and colleagues, who found that the biggest promise of chargebacks lies in fostering harmonious and trustful partnerships between IT and business units.[22]

Finally, overhead costs reflect the value-creating processes of strategic planning, financial management, and human capital management. The costs are incurred by the Office of the CIO and are managed as corporate headquarters costs.

Overall, by distinguishing among the costs of applications, infrastructure and utilities, and overhead, the hospitality firm's IT organizational model contributes significantly to creating enduring and amicable partner relationships.

Summary. This Partner Model is most appropriate for firms that want to promote business innovation through IT, but whose business executives lack a deep understanding of IT. The model provides pathways for business and IT executives to collaborate in innovation activities. This model is also appropriate for multidivisional firms that operate in related lines of business and seek to exploit cross-divisional synergies through IT-based innovations. Examples of such synergies include common customer relationship management, supplier management systems, and cross-business "bundled" offerings of products or services. Finally, this model works in firms that have strong IT leadership, and a history of trust and credibility between IT and the business. Harmonious and vibrant business-IT partnerships are likely to form and sustain IT innovation in these firms because the business managers are likely to be receptive to IT "seeding" ideas for IT innovation.

The Platform Model: Providing the Resources for Global Innovation

This model is appropriate for organizations where IT is primarily expected to provide infra-structure and tools to enable current and future business innovations in products, services, processes, or channels. The IT function excels in delivering a global infrastructure and ser-vices, and in rapidly delivering IT solutions. The IT function's primary goal is to "be a busi-ness within the business of the firm," delivering a scalable, seamless, and flexible infrastruc-ture, productivity tools for knowledge workers, and technologies and applications for global team collaboration.

In contrast with the Partner Model, IT is not expected to be an active collaborator in ini-tiating business innovations. Instead, it focuses on developing an enter-prise-wide platform and capabilities, which can be consistently and repeatedly leveraged in strategic IT applica-tions.

Within this model, the principle of co-evolution occurs through the actions of account managers, who act as liaisons between the IT function and the business units. They collabo-rate with business unit executives in directing IT capabilities toward developing and main-taining business unit capabilities. At the same time, they identify IT capabilities needed for future business opportunities or growth, and they sensitize corporate IT to future business needs for IT enablement.

The Platform Model utilizes both innovation and sourcing networks. Account managers facilitate the value-innovation process in the business units. At the same time, the manag-ers for the other value-creating processes particularly infrastructure management, solutions delivery, and services provisioning develop the needed IT capabilities in their areas so that they will be the preferred provider of choice to the business units.

A large high-tech firm. The IT function of a large, multidivisional high-tech firm, which is a market leader in semiconductors and telecommunications, illustrates this Platform Model (Figure 11.4). Its business executives are quite knowledgeable about IT and are there-fore willing to lead IT innovation. Even though IT provides "seed" ideas for innovation, the organizational philosophy and the IT savviness of the business executives make IT's primary

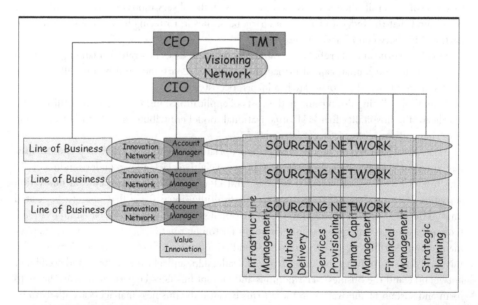

Figure 11.4 The Platform Model

role one of enabling and facilitating innovation through a world-class IT infrastructure and rapid applications delivery. In contrast with the hospitality firm, IT is not expected to be an active collaborator in innovation. However, it is expected to be world-class in managing IT: controlling interaction costs, providing IT infrastructure services and applications delivery, and being effective in anticipating and responding to the business unit IT needs.

Principle 1: Co-evolution. At this high-tech firm, account managers and line-of-business executives are responsible for co-evolution of business and IT capabilities (Figure 11.4). The line executives apply IT in developing business capabilities, collaborating with the account managers. The account managers also inform the rest of the IT function about needed future IT capabilities.

Principle 2: Partnership networks. The Platform Model focuses on innovation and sourcing networks, and less so on visioning networks. At this firm, innovation networks are nurtured through interactions between the account managers and the line executives.

Principle 3: Value-creating processes. While the account managers report to the CIO, they are viewed as advocating the value-innovation process in the business units. In addition, the IT function is organized around the value-creating processes of infrastructure management, solutions delivery, services provisioning, financial management, strategic planning, and human capital management. The CIO's direct reports manage each of these processes and are accountable for their excellence.

This firm draws on three significant characteristics of organizing via value-creating processes. First, account managers are viewed as facilitators of the value-innovation process, even though the business unit executives are in charge of the process.

In their role as facilitators, the account managers seek to understand their business clients' needs. They then plan product or service roadmaps to meet those IT needs. Where mandated, they must follow corporate IT infrastructure standards. Elsewhere, they can offer optional IT infrastructure services as either tiered or as pay-per-view services. They can also develop new IT products and services by collaborating with the IT executives responsible for the other value-creating processes. Finally, they coordinate delivery of IT services to the business units. Thus, they provide the "one-face window" into IT, they own the end-to-end client experience, and they are the ones responsible for assuring satisfaction with the IT services.

Second, the other value-creating processes are managed to enable innovation in the business units. The IT executives who manage infrastructure management, solutions delivery, and services provisioning, in particular, are accountable for world-class excellence and for being the provider of choice to the business units.

Account managers have the discretion to procure services from these internal sources or from external vendors. Therefore, the executives for IT's internal value-creating processes face outside competition and pressures to be efficient, economical, and effective service providers. Their revenue comes from the business units and is generated by the account managers. Generating revenue is part of the account managers' IT job. On the other hand, the other IT value-creating processes financial management, strategic planning, and human capital management "manage the business of IT."

Third, the account managers (because they are the IT executives responsible for the value-innovation process), along with the leaders of the other value-creating processes and the CIO collectively manage the IT function. They form the global IT management council and shape IT strategies, policies, and tactics. They meet semiannually to discuss client-related, strategic and operational, and short-term and long-term issues facing the IT business.

Summary. The Platform Model is most appropriate for global multidivisional firms that operate several distinct lines of business in which the business units have unique IT innovation needs. Following this model allows the IT function to respond in customized ways to the business units from a common base of IT assets, skills, and investments. Thus, the firms can reap IT economies of scale even though the individual units use IT in unique ways.

The model is also appropriate for firms with IT-savvy business executives because it positions the IT function as the partner of choice in delivering solutions to the business executives' innovation ideas. Thus, the Platform Model is particularly appropriate for high-tech firms those with a CEO or business executives with information technology backgrounds because these business executives are most likely to take responsibility for the value-innovation process.

The Scalable Model: Using Sourcing to Be Flexible

This organizational model is appropriate where IT is viewed as a strategic differentiator and an important element of business innovation, and corporate strategy is built around strategic flexibility that is, being able to quickly acquire resources when a market opportunity appears and, conversely, quickly shed resources when an opportunity becomes unprofitable. Firms that operate in a cyclical business environment also want the least fixed costs and committed resources, so they can expand and contract in response to their business environment. The Scalable Model is designed to enable flexible staffing and to enhance the IT function's ability to scale up and down along with business growth and contraction while continuing to nurture business innovation.

In this model, co-evolution relates to strategic flexibility: IT capabilities are used to build business capabilities that enable the firm to quickly seize new business opportunities or exit unprofitable ones. For example, the IT function can contribute to evolution by developing standardized IT-enabled processes and codified knowledge, which the business can then use to replicate itself in other parts of the world and more quickly enter new markets. The business can contribute to evolution by learning from current business activities and anticipating future business opportunities, thereby influencing development of new IT capabilities. Co-evolution occurs through collaboration of senior IT executives with managers of business units, processes, and geographical regions.

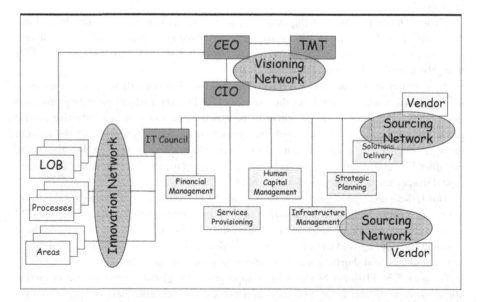

Figure 11.5 The Scalable Model

The Scalable Model emphasizes sourcing networks to leverage external partners, particularly for two IT value-creating processes, solutions delivery and services provisioning. Creative sourcing relationships permit the IT function to control IT costs while changing staff size in response to cyclical business conditions.

A large chemical firm. A large chemical firm that sells to businesses and aims to be the low-cost leader uses the Scalable Model (Figure 11.5) to leverage common business processes across its businesses and global markets. Given the vagaries of its cyclical industry, the firm values strategic flexibility so that it can contain costs in downturns and expand resources during growth times. IT has emerged as a strategic differentiator; its role is to facilitate low-cost leadership and strategic flexibility.

Principle 1: Co-evolution. Senior IT executives are located in processes, businesses, and geographic regions, and are responsible for the IT activities in their area. They have a dual reporting relationship to the CIO as well as their process owner, business unit head, or geographic region head. They belong to the CIO's global IT council and thereby provide links between the IT unit and the individual processes, businesses, or regions. This structure facilitates co-evolution by allowing the business capabilities to be shaped through IT capabilities, while ensuring that IT investments are influenced by business capability needs.

These senior IT executives are encouraged and rewarded for value-innovation, which requires them to understand what their business clients need. The firm uses a variety of formal methodologies to foster value-innovation including opportunity analysis, value assessment, and balanced scorecards.

Principle 2: Relationship networks. Solutions delivery is managed through relationships with external partners. In a cyclical industry, this chemical firm needed an innovative way to manage demand for IT applications. Periods of rapid growth would accelerate demand for skilled IT developers, while periods of business contraction led to IT staff reductions. To better manage demand for IT staff, the firm formed a consulting alliance to garner a "variable sourcing strategy for solutions delivery." The firm has a small in-house application development staff and obtains the rest from its consulting partner. It commits to pay for a minimum number of the consulting partners' people. When it needs more people, the consulting partner provides them at additional cost.

An alliance management office, with representatives from both parties, assigns the IT developers to individual projects. Another group, called the program management office, also with representatives from both sides, keeps track of the status of the various projects and the skills likely to be needed on future projects. These two bodies the alliance management office and the program management office are the firm's main sourcing-network mechanism, to manage their relationship with the external solutions delivery partner. Similarly, the firm utilizes external partners for infrastructure management, particularly desktop and telecommunications management.

Principle 3: Value-creating processes. Services provisioning is managed by a unit within corporate IT, even though its members are geographically dispersed and co-located with processes, businesses, and geographic regions. Human capital is nurtured through skill centers that focus on specific IT skills. These skill sets are identified by the program management office. Thus, the firm's value-creating processes are managed separately, sometimes utilizing external partners.

Summary. Global firms in related lines of business can benefit from the Scalable Model because its structure allows the IT organization to efficiently identify opportunities for value-innovation and exploit enterprise-wide synergies. Aligning IT executives with multiple horizontal views of the firm (i.e., processes and geographic areas) and vertical views of the firm (businesses) ensures that the IT function is tightly woven into the business. The IT

Management Council then brings these executives together to share ideas and insights, providing a business-based view of the enterprise as a whole.

When value is created through connectivity and standards, as is typically the case with global businesses with "similar" products, the Scalable Model explicitly directs managerial attention to these standards, through its emphasis on centralized procurement of services and centralized management of IT competencies.

In addition, the Scalable Model allows firms in cyclical industries to maintain flexibility. Through creative sourcing arrangements that permit speedy commitment to and divestiture of human capital, the model insulates the IT function from potential criticisms of being a cost drain on the business when the industry is in a recessionary cycle.

Conclusion

The purpose of creating principles and models for organizing IT is to facilitate executive thinking about positioning IT as a strategic differentiator. Our findings suggest that there is no single "best" IT organizational structure or governance arrangement because IT needs to respond to the unique environments within which it exists. We offer three models as benchmarks or archetypes for CIOs to consider in reassessing their organization's design. We further recommend a simple, four-step redesign process.

First, enumerate IT's value propositions. Using a visioning network, as described earlier, develop consensus with your business partners on IT's value propositions. These propositions need to embed senior management's views about the role of IT, articulate the ways in which IT delivers business value, and serve as the crucial foundation for organizing IT.

Second, determine which model comes closest to your situation. Juxtapose your IT value propositions, the nature of your business, your industry environment, and the IT sophistication and knowledge in your business units. This combination should point to one of the three models as the most appropriate, because, as noted, each model requires executives to focus on a different set of value-creating processes and relationship networks. Furthermore, each model highlights different strengths of coupling between IT and the rest of the business. Once these needs are understood, you can select the appropriate organizing options (i.e., governance and sourcing arrangements) for each value-creating process.

Third, manage the organizational transformation associated with the new design. This transition includes communicating the vision and rationale underlying the design, actually implementing the new organization, and initiating an assessment process.

Fourth, continue to reassess and adapt the organization design to ensure its continued relevance. Organizational designs will not be static. Fortunately, thinking modularly about value-creating processes (Principle 3) limits the potentially disruptive ripple effects that structural changes can cause.

Hopefully the organizing principles and models described here will stimulate CIOs and academic researchers to think about alternative approaches for organizing IT activities to meet today's business demands.

Notes

1   von Simson, E., "The 'Centrally' Decentralized IS Organization," *Harvard Business Review,* July-August 1990, pp. 158–162.
2   Brown, C.V. and Magill, S.L., "Alignment of the IS function with the Enterprise: Towards a Model of Antecedents," *MIS Quarterly* (18:4), December 1994, pp. 371–403; Sambamurthy, V. and Zmud,

R.W., "Factors Influencing Information Technology Management Architectures in Organizations: A Theory of Multiple Contingencies," *MIS Quarterly*, (23:2), June 1999, pp. 261–290.

3   Goldman, S.L., Nagel, R.N., and Preiss, K., *Agile Competitors and Virtual Organization: Strategies for Enriching the Customer,* New York, NY, Van Nostrand Reinhold, 1995; Sambamurthy, V., "Business Strategy in Hypercompetitive Environments: Re-thinking the Role of IT Differentiation," in R.W. Zmud (Ed.) *Framing the Domains of IT Management Research: Glimpsing the Future through the Past*, Pinnaflex Press, 2000; Venkatraman, N and Henderson, J., "Real Strategies for Virtual Organizing," *Sloan Management Review* (40:1), Fall 1998, pp. 33–48.

4   Barua, A., Konana, P., Whinston, A., Yin, F., "Driving E-Business Excellence," *Sloan Management Review* (43:1), Fall 2001, pp. 3644.

5   El Sawy, O., Malhotra, A., Gosain, S., and Young, K., "IT-intensive Value Innovation in the Electronic Economy: Insights from Marshall Industries," *MIS Quarterly* (23:3), September 1999, pp. 305–335.

6   Agarwal, R. and Ferratt, T.W., "Crafting an HR Strategy to Meet the Need for IT Workers," *Communications of the ACM* (44:7), 2001, pp. 59–64; DiRomualdo, A. and Gurbaxani, V., "Strategic Intent for IT Outsourcing," *Sloan Management Review* (39:4), Summer 1998, pp. 67–80.

7   Clark, C., Cavanaugh, N., Brown, C.V., and Sambamurthy, V., "Building Change Readiness Capabilities in the IS Organization: Insights from the Bell Atlantic Experience," *MIS Quarterly* (21:4), December, 1997, pp. 425–454.

8   Cross, J., Earl, M., and Sampler, J., "Transformation of the IT Function at British Petroleum," *MIS Quarterly* (21:4), December 1997, pp. 401–423.

9   Our study included in-depth telephone interviews with CIOs of 30 large firms in a variety of industries (manufacturing, financial services, high-tech, retail, and hospitality) and detailed case studies of seven firms. All of these firms are in leadership positions in their respective industries. Further, their peers and the trade press (*Fortune, CIO, Information Week,* etc.) regard them as being successful in business innovation through IT and in their ability to manage the IT challenges related to speedy delivery of projects, development and retention of IT human capital, and effective management of IT assets and external relationships.

10   Sambamurthy, V. and Zmud, R.W., "The Organizing Logic for an Enterprise's IT Activities in the Digital Era A Prognosis of Practice and a Call for Research," *Information Systems Research* (11:2) June 2000, pp. 105–111.

11   Venkatraman, N., "IT-Induced Business Reconfiguration," in M.S. Scott Morton (Ed.) *The Corporation of the 1990s: Information Technology and Organizational Transformation*, Oxford Press, 1991, pp. 122–158; Venkatraman and Henderson, ibid.

12   Henderson, J. and Venkatraman, N., "Strategic Alignment: A Framework for Strategic Information Technology Management," in T. Kochan and M. Useem (Eds.) *Transforming Organizations*, Oxford Press, New York, NY, 1992, pp. 97–117; Burn, J.M., "A Professional Balancing Act – Walking the Tightrope of Strategic Alignment," in C. Sauer and P. Yetton (Eds.), *Steps to the Future: Fresh Thinking on the Dynamics on IT-based Organizational Transformation*, Jossey-Bass, 1996, pp. 55–80.

13   Rockart, J.F., Earl, M.J., and Ross, J.W., "Eight Imperatives for the New IT Organization," *Sloan Management Review* (38:1), Fall 1996, pp. 43–56.

14   Schein, E.H., "The Role of the CEO in the Management of Change: The Case of Information Technology," In T.A. Kochan and M. Useem (Eds.), *Transforming Organizations,* Oxford University Press, 1992; Armstrong, C.P. and Sambamurthy, V., "Information Technology Assimilation in Firms: The Influence of Senior Leadership and IT Infrastructures," *Information Systems Research* (10:4), December 1999, pp. 304–327.

15   Brown, C.V. and Sambamurthy, V., "Coordination Theory in the Context of the IT Function: Linking the Logic of Governance and Coordination Mechanisms," University of Maryland Working Paper, 2002.

16   Brown and Sambamurthy, ibid.

17   Nambisan, S., Agarwal, R., and Tanniru, M., "Organizational Mechanisms for Enhancing User Innovation in Information Technology," *MIS Quarterly* (23:3), September 1999, pp. 365–395; Lind, M.R. and Zmud, R.W., "Improving Interorganizational Effectiveness Through Voice Mail Facilitation of Peer-to-peer Relationships," *Organization Science* (6:4), 1995, pp. 445–461.

18   DiRomualdo and Gurbaxani, ibid.

19   Lacity, M.C., and Willcocks, L.P, "An Empirical Investigation of Information Technology Sourcing Practices: Lessons from Experience," *MIS Quarterly* (22:3), 1998, pp. 363–408.

20   Ross, J.W., Beath, C.M., Goodhue, D.L., "Develop Long-term Competitiveness Through IT Assets," *Sloan Management Review* (38:1), 1996, pp. 31–45; Bharadwaj, A., "A Resource-Based Perspective on

Information Technology Capability and Firm Performance: An Empirical Investigation," *MIS Quarterly* (24:1), March 2000, pp. 169196; Bharadwaj, A., Sambamurthy, V., and Zmud, R. W., "Firmwide IT Capability: An Empirical Examination of the Construct and its Links to Performance," University of Maryland Working Paper, 2002; Feeny, D.F. and Wilcocks, L.P., "Core IS Capabilities for Exploiting Information Technology," *Sloan Management Review* (39:3), Spring 1998, pp. 9–21; and Marchand, D.A., Kettinger, W.J., and Rollins, J.D., "Information Orientation: People, Technology, and the Bottom Line," *Sloan Management Review* (41:4), Summer 2000, pp. 69–80.

21   Agarwal, R. and Sambamurthy, V., "Modus Operandi," *CIO Insight* (1:8), December, 2001, pp. 27–32.

22   Ross, J.W., Vitale, M.R., and Beath, C.M., "The Untapped Potential of IT Chargeback," *MIS Quarterly* (23:2), June 1999, pp. 215–237.

Questions for Discussion

1   Why does the current landscape demand the reexamination of organizing the IT function?

2   How can alignment and coevolution of the IT function and business be differentiated, and which is more important?

3   Can any or all of the relationship networks overlap, or exchange roles, to organize the IT function?

4   How can modular thinking help organize the IT function and associated value-creating processes?

5   Is outsourcing an efficient way to build a partner model?

6   How does the platform model support coevolution, partnership networks, and value creating processes?

7   What kind of value generation activities does the scalable model support?

Further Reading

Weill, P. (2004). Don't just lead, govern: how top-performing firms govern IT. *MIS Quarterly Executive*, 3(1), 1–17.

Wu, S.P., Straub, D., Liang, T. (2015). How information technology governance mechanisms and strategic alignment influence organizational performance: insights from a matched survey of business and IT managers. *MIS Quarterly*, 39(2), 497–518.

Chapter 12

Dorothy E. Leidner, Robert C. Beatty and Jane M. Mackay

HOW CIOS MANAGE IT DURING ECONOMIC DECLINE: SURVIVING AND THRIVING AMID UNCERTAINTY

The Economic Downturn Has Affected IT Budgets

PRIOR TO THE YEAR 2000, when the U.S. economy was strong and enterprise-wide systems were readily justifiable, many firms undertook large information technology (IT) initiatives. But in 2000, after almost a decade of high growth and low employment, the U.S. economy began to decline in most sectors. The e-commerce bubble burst and many high-flying IT and telecom companies began to decline rapidly. Some sought to contain or reduce costs through consolidation (see note 1). Concurrently, companies in many industries began questioning large IT initiatives, such as ERP (Enterprise Resource Planning) and CRM (Customer Relationship Management), because the reported failure rates were quite high.[1,2]

Since 2001, many IT budgets have inched up, at a declining rate. Overall, IT budgets increased about 8 percent in 2001,[3] but only .1 percent in 2002.[4] Even these essentially flat IT budgets in 2002, though, disguise how substantially some firms have cut back on IT spending. It is predicted that even if IT spending improves slightly in 2003, the increase will not clear out application backlogs.

The Research: Interviewing 20 CIOs

To uncover how CIOs manage during times of economic decline, we conducted interviews with 20 CIOs from across a range of industries—construction, financial retailing, general services, health services, insurance, IT consulting, manufacturing, retail, technology, and transportation. Thirteen of the organizations were headquartered in Dallas, Texas; five in Fort Worth, Texas; one in Houston, Texas; and one in California.

One retailer had revenue of $22B; the others had revenues between $818M and $9.8B. Company data was unavailable for five of the firms: four that were privately held and one that was a subsidiary.

Of the 20 CIOs, only five had occupied their current position for more than three years. Of the other 15, five had served between two and three years, six had served between one and two years, and four had served for less than one year.

Conducted between December 2001 and July 2002, most of the interviews were done in person over an hour and a half. A few of the interviews took place via conference calls. All the CIOs interviewed had a great deal of experience in the IT field and based on their experience both within their current organizations and at prior organizations, we have confidence that they were all highly competent, effective CIOs. Hence, we were in no position to compare or contrast the effectiveness of the CIOs. Rather, the interviews enabled us to discern four distinct approaches for IT management during economic decline.

In a December 2002 poll, 87 percent of Chief Information Officers (CIOs) stated that their application and project backlogs were putting their organizations' operability and competitive advantage at risk.[5] So while the economic downturn leads to pressures to reduce IT investments, demands for short-term profitability and long-term growth apply pressure to sustain IT investments.[6] As a result, CIOs have found themselves in the pressure-filled situation of facing, on the one hand, tightening budgets and skepticism about returns on large IT project investments, yet, on the other hand, the need to continue to convince top management of the importance of continuing to make substantial IT investments.

One piece of popular prescriptive advice to CIOs has been to outsource as much IT infrastructure as possible.[7] But many CIOs are reluctant to relinquish control, even though some outsourcers appear to be faring well in this downturn. For example, EDS recently signed a ten-year $4.5B agreement to re-engineer and manage Bank of America's voice and data networks.[8] Likewise, the City of Minneapolis selected Unisys to manage its IT infrastructure for $56M. The city expects to save $20M.[9]

When the economy changes as dramatically as it has over the past three years, CIOs face important decisions. Yet, there is little guidance on how they should best manage IT during such times. We know that the business environment influences organizational strategy and decision-making.[10] And we know that the environment can influence the value of information.[11] But we do not know how an economic decline influences the management of IT. Thus, we seek to answer the question: *How do CIOs manage IT during economic decline?*

Four Approaches to Managing IT During Economic Decline

We discerned four approaches for managing IT during economic decline, as shown in Figure 12.1. They vary along two dimensions: the perspective for determining IT's value (short-term vs. long-term) and the attitude toward the existing IT plan (retain vs. rethink). Each approach is characterized by a decision-making principle: Extend the Lifecycle, Bulletproof the Infrastructure, Clean House, or Maintain the Legacy.

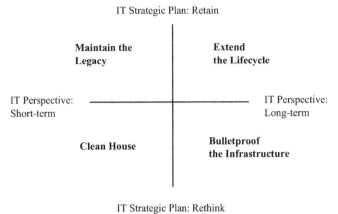

IT Strategic Plan: Retain

Maintain the Legacy

Extend the Lifecycle

IT Perspective: Short-term

IT Perspective: Long-term

Clean House

Bulletproof the Infrastructure

IT Strategic Plan: Rethink

Figure 12.1 Approaches to Managing IT During Economic Decline

In describing their management approach, the CIOs typically spoke of "we," meaning themselves and the firm's senior management team. The CIOs developed their IT plan for coping with the economic decline, then the senior management team discussed the plan and approved it.

Extend the Lifecycle Approach

CIOs using the Extend the Lifecycle approach take a long-term perspective on IT investments during an economic decline and choose to lengthen the timeframe of the current strategic IT plan, rather than cancel or re-evaluate it; see Table 12.1. As one CIO told us, "We have a strong commitment to our five-year plan, but we are not opposed to stretching it out." Showing confidence in the ultimate value of the IT plan, CIOs taking this approach aim to make steady, but slower, progress. Even when commitment to the plan is strong, though, the CIOs we interviewed believe it is wise to review the plan once or twice a year, and adjust project start dates when necessary. To conserve financial resources further, CIOs following this approach reduce or eliminate contractors on non-critical IT projects. At the same time, they make every effort to keep full-time staff and maintain the operational continuity of the department.

Senior managers who adopt this approach view IT investments as important to the firm's competitive success. Investments during prosperous times are conservative, following the dictum "we manage in the good times for the bad times." During downturns, the executives maintain confidence that previously funded IT projects continue to align with business plans, and thus are still appropriate.

The CIOs we interviewed believe it is important to avoid two extreme reactions during a decline: on the one end, "not cutting fast enough as revenues go away" and on the other, "abandoning IT initiatives so quickly that the future is mortgaged." The concern over these two extremes is that if an organization does not make budget cuts quickly enough, the firm's stock price will take a larger-than-necessary hit. However, if the organization makes budget cuts too quickly, then the future value of the firm will suffer.

Senior managers adopting the Extend the Lifecycle approach will spend resources on projects that have no immediate return, when these projects are strategic, not tactical or short-term. Hence, senior management commitment to IT is critical. As one CIO said, "You'd better communicate, you'd better leverage solutions, leverage resources, [and] leverage support or else you're not going to succeed in IT."

Table 12.1 Summary of the Extend the Lifecycle Approach

Approach	Extend the Lifecycle
Description	Senior managers maintain commitment to building systems in their strategic plan but stretch out the timeline for development and implementation
Objective	Reduce development costs while continuing to move forward with important applications
Strengths	Focuses on the future
	Keeps the organization at the forefront of technological development
Weaknesses	IT "Tunnel Vision"—The organization may be so focused on completing existing IT projects that it ignores opportunities that could provide a strong competitive advantage coming out of the downturn
CIO Challenges	Properly managing the cost-effective and timely completion of IT projects over an extended development period while continually initiating new projects that could give competitive advantage

The CIO at a manufacturing firm who takes the Extend the Lifecycle approach explains how his value is evaluated:

> The predominant piece of my rating is still around driving change, and the effectiveness and efficiency of the organization. [It is about] taking cost out and improving delivery at the same time. It is not just about running a great department; it is morphing and changing the business model [by] taking cost out of the process while improving delivery.

The strengths of this approach center around its commitment to future plans; the weakness centers around the potential loss of short-term competitive advantage.

Strength: There are no radical changes. This approach does not radically alter the composition of the IT department nor the existing project portfolio. Hence, when the economy begins to recover, the IT organization should have little difficulty increasing the speed of project delivery to pre-decline levels. However, IT does need to be perceived as adding value to the organization. Warns the CIO of a major manufacturing firm, "When you have turmoil and economic pressures, you'd sure better be able to show top management how you are generating revenue or saving costs."

Strength: Support for IT initiatives continues. Organizations that adopt this approach focus on adhering to the IT strategic plan and on the future value of IT projects. In fact, senior managers often view IT investments as less risky during a downturn than other investments, such as business acquisitions. Said the CIO of a major manufacturing company, "We [top management] really have to find investments that give us a good return, and in our case, these IT projects have fabulous returns…better than the bank and better than debt right now."

Weakness: Tunnel vision. While the Extend the Lifecycle approach aims to eventually complete the organization's most important strategic projects, it may lead to "tunnel vision" –i.e., it might limit the organization's ability to adapt to technological changes and obtain a short-term return or possibly a short-term competitive advantage. Moreover, if the organization is forced to adjust its strategic plan, its IT plan could lose relevance.

Bulletproof the Infrastructure Approach

CIOs using the Bulletproof the Infrastructure approach focus primarily on infrastructure projects; see Table 12.2. They take a long-term perspective believing that success in the next economic growth phase will come from having an infrastructure that permits the IT organization to plug-and-play both independent and integrated applications.

Table 12.2 Summary of the Bulletproof the Infrastructure Approach

Approach	Bulletproof the Infrastructure
Description	CIOs reconsider the existing IT plan and focus on projects designed to build the infrastructure
Objective	Prepare the IT infrastructure for the next growth phase so that applications can be quickly implemented and integrated
Strengths	Prepares for the future: paves the way for a breakaway
	Commits to an enterprise-wide IT infrastructure
Weaknesses	Assumes an extended infrastructure development time
CIO Challenges	Convincing top management that putting in place an excellent infrastructure will be key to rapid recovery and growth

The major aim of this approach is to create a foundation for integration. As one CIO notes, "I want to integrate these systems a little better so that I can run my systems cleaner and a lot more effectively." This approach involves rethinking the existing IT plan and reprioritizing projects. Hence, some approved projects are placed on indefinite hold during a downturn. "The wish list went away as we began to focus on the fundamental needs and requirements of the organization," says one CIO.

The Bulletproof the Infrastructure approach replaces customized homemade applications with "vanilla applications," notes one CIO (meaning standard off the shelf packages) or "off the shelf open system architecture programs," in the words of another. Due to the high cost and long development time of customized IT projects, firms following the Bulletproof the Infrastructure approach are willing to purchase reasonably priced packages that quickly address most of their users' requirements. For example, rather than invest significant time and money on a fully integrated, multi-module CRM system (that would require extensive tailoring and customization to meet all requirements), the CIO is more likely to recommend purchasing an inexpensive and standardized CRM module to address a distinct business need, such as partner relationship management. This approach trades lower system functionality for lower cost and faster implementation. But an added benefit is that standard IT applications are heavily discounted in a depressed IT market. Standard products also cost less to maintain. So this approach reduces the costs of maintaining the infrastructure in the future.

Organizations adopting the Bulletproof the Infrastructure approach have done so because they had embarked on a wide variety of systems when the economy was strong to remain competitive. Some systems were built in-house and some were externally developed, without a disciplined planning process. When the downturn hit, these IT departments had difficulty maintaining a consistent and reliable IT infrastructure because there were so many projects underway. As the CIO of a major technology company says,

During the period of rapid growth, we did not implement our applications with a good architectural view of how they were all going to work together. So we ended up with a lot of disjointed systems. [Even] databases outside a core area. have become so fragmented that it is now difficult to build new applications that require integrating all these apps we built the last several years.

When economic growth stagnated, management became concerned that not having a disciplined IT operating environment was leading to a state of disarray. Hence, when the economy begins to grow again, applications will be expensive and time-consuming to implement, placing the organization at a competitive disadvantage. In short, the absence of an enterprise-wide IT technology planning process during the economic growth of the 1990s has resulted in an IT infrastructure problem at these firms.

The challenge facing CIOs who adopt the Bulletproof the Infrastructure approach is to convince top management that the organization's future competitive success is directly tied to supporting business-critical IT projects—and these projects need a solid infrastructure. The importance of this reasoning is illustrated by the CIO at a transportation firm when he compares infrastructure planning to the shape of a pyramid, saying,

> [Let's] look at the pyramid [approach] again. If you have a weakness in your core base, that's where you should be spending your time in years of recession. Build the base so that when the economy recovers, you can quickly scale and recover. That's what we are doing here. We are building the base, getting a solid footing, and then we will be positioned to drive innovation. Driving innovation will be a lot easier if we are not doing a lot of retrofitting and patching with baling wire down to the base.

This same sentiment is articulated by the CIO of a retailing firm:

> I am going to kind of bulletproof my infrastructure and I am going to make it industrial strength because I know that this downturn is not going to last forever. When the economy does come back up.I am going to be a bit more prepared for the upswing. I was caught off guard the first time. So lesson learned. And I am prepared now.

Strengths and Weaknesses of the Bulletproof the Infrastructure Approach. The strengths of this approach center around its preparation for the future; the weakness, around the assumption that the decline will allow sufficient time to complete infrastructure changes.

Strength: There is commitment to an enterprise-wide IT infrastructure. This approach allows the CIO to justify infrastructure projects on the grounds that a stable and integrated IT infrastructure will be a competitive weapon, once the organization again experiences rapid growth. Given the pressures during high-growth periods to build projects that link important business processes among business units, infrastructure projects can get sidelined. Times of economic downturn, and the subsequent reduction in IT funding, provide an opportunity to re-focus IT spending on much needed projects that will stabilize the organization's IT infrastructure.

Strength: It paves the way for a breakaway. This approach also frees a firm to envision applications that support future growth. While funding is being allocated to infrastructure projects, planning attention can be directed toward applications that differentiate the company from its competitors, once the economy revives.

The CIO at a major technology company quotes his CEO as saying, "Let's invest more aggressively in systems that will differentiate us from our competition and help lead the breakaway [when the economic slowdown lessens]." Another CIO at a retailing firm states, "Our competition is not backing off one iota. What we better not do is really pull in and make serious cuts, and then come out of the cycle to find we are out of the ball game."

Weakness: It assumes a long period of decline. A major weakness of the Bulletproof the Infrastructure approach, though, is that it assumes the IT department will have a long time to create a stable, scalable, flexible, and fully integrated IT infrastructure anywhere from six months to two years.

If a firm launches into a number of long-term infrastructure projects assuming that it has a "two-year window" to complete these projects, and the economy "rebounds" in six months, then the firm is faced with deciding either to complete the existing infrastructure projects or divert IT resources to new projects that will provide competitive advantage. Management teams typically dislike spending scarce IT resources on projects that will not provide direct business benefits (such as, infrastructure projects), so they will likely apply immediate pressure on the IT department to work on new projects once the economy turns around. This pressure may result in infrastructure projects not being fully completed before new applications development begins.

The Clean House Approach

CIOs using the Clean House approach take a short-term view of IT, seeking applications with quick returns. They focus on re-assessing their IT plan, eliminating systems that do not support the organization's strategy, and developing a new, short-term-focused portfolio of systems for development; see Table 12.3. Convinced that proper IT investments are important to overall organizational success, these CIOs believe their current IT strategy must be overhauled to support the organization's current business plan.

Firms that have adopted the Clean House approach have done so to impose discipline. During the late 1990s, they had ready availability of money, so they rapidly implemented an unprecedented number of applications but lost discipline in making IT investment decisions. Senior managers recognized that the unbridled development of new IT systems was spiraling out of control, but they could do little to prevent well-financed business units from looking elsewhere for development whenever the IT department declined to undertake the project. The downturn has given the IT organization the opportunity to regain control.

Table 12.3 Summary of the Clean House Approach

Approach	Clean House
Description	The firm uses the downturn to re-evaluate existing and planned applications
Objective	To regain control over application development and implementation and ensure that systems being built are consistent with the firm's goals
Strengths	Eliminates projects the firm believes should not have been commenced in the first place
	Gives IT a greater role in determining what systems are necessary and on what platforms
Weaknesses	Heavy time consumption
	Might leave some business units frustrated with the IT group for not continuing to implement systems previously approved by the business unit
CIO Challenges	Building credibility in the IT group's decisions regarding which applications to build and which to scrap

One software company CIO says the downturn finally allows IT to "take an inventory on projects" and, with the support of senior management, require owners of planned-but-not-yet-developed systems to cost-justify those systems. "This is a healthy time for us," he says. "The growth and excessiveness of our budget in the 90s actually fueled us to do things that were not healthy for our business long-term." By re-evaluating the IT plan, the firm is eliminating many unnecessary projects and "trimming the budget so we can invest." A major challenge of this approach, though, is that CIOs must implement cost-saving measures as they develop a new strategy to use current IT resources better.

The Clean House approach thus allows CIOs to start over and develop an IT strategy for the organization's most important business needs. However, the CIOs must also convince top management that new IT planning policies are needed, so that business units spend their money on projects that meet enterprise-wide business objectives. Hence the enterprise-wide IT strategic model must closely align with the needs of the business units, by being based on their input. As one CIO notes, "What we have tried to do here is to map our IT investment back to [our] business strategies because IT is very much an enabler of those strategies."

To regain credibility with business unit managers, CIOs using the Clean House approach need to focus IT resources on short-term, highly visible projects that will provide tangible financial benefits to key operational business functions. By rapidly demonstrating the business value of IT, these CIOs can begin to re-establish the importance of the IT function to the organization. One CIO adopting this approach states that the best way he can re-establish the value of IT within the organization is to implement a new IT strategy that effectively mixes on-going infrastructure "foundation" work with IT projects that provide immediate financial returns or "quick wins" during the current business year.

Strengths and Weaknesses of the Clean House Approach. The strengths of the Clean House approach center around its reassessment of the alignment of IT projects to organizational strategy; the weaknesses center around the potential loss of credibility facing the IT organization.

Strength: IT strategy is customized. One advantage is that the organization takes the time to evaluate IT and scrutinize how well it is helping achieve short-term and long-term business objectives. From internal evaluation, the IT organization can better develop an enterprise-wide IT strategy that mirrors the business strategy, goals, and objectives.

One CIO describes his firm's old and new IT strategy development processes by analogy, saying,

> We used to drive down the freeway at midnight with no headlights. The way we saw where we were going was [by] shining a flashlight out the back window. But now we have turned on the headlights. We are learning to drive faster than a couple of miles an hour, but we still don't have a GPS system. We're working on getting that with some analytics.

Strength: Top management is committed to the IT strategy. To develop and implement a new IT strategy that meets the organization's needs, the top business managers must actively participate in the strategy development process. In so doing, their commitment to the final IT business model should be high, making implementation more likely.

Weakness: The process is time-consuming and expensive. The Clean House approach involves re-assessing the role of the IT function. Although this approach garners top management's commitment, it also consumes their limited time because they are expected to participate in strategy development. Given that the business units themselves likely face cost pressures from the downturn, the unit managers are unlikely to welcome additional time demands from the IT department. They have their own strategic re-evaluations to perform.

Weakness: Weakens organizational confidence in IT leadership. A primary CIO role is that of IT visionary. In eliminating some previously approved projects and requiring business units to justify other projects, CIOs might send the unintended message that the IT department is unable to manage growth. This perception might decrease unit leaders' confidence in the IT organization in the future.

Maintain the Legacy Approach

CIOs using the Maintain the Legacy approach (see Table 12.4) adopt the short-term perspective of just surviving the downturn by prolonging the life of the legacy to last through the decline. There is little or no future planning. Infrastructure improvements are shelved to be revisited when the economic decline ends. The application portfolio is not rethought or re-assessed; it is simply canceled until more prosperous times. Only investments that can demonstrate a quick return are considered. It is not uncommon to hear CIOs using this approach speak of a six-month or even three-month return on investment. Says one CIO, "In a good economy, an ROI of two to three years is okay. In a bad economy, less than one year is essential. In fact, if you can't get business value in six months, you should chuck the project."

Pressures to reduce IT expenditures force some CIOs to adopt this approach because they are only given enough financial resources to continue operating essential legacy systems. As one CIO states,

> A year ago, [we] focused very much on building an environment to integrate all the new systems we were going to need to support increased business. Now, the difference is, we are exploiting the same integration effort to extend the life of the legacy.

In adopting the Maintain the Legacy approach, CIOs need to develop standard ways of monitoring the legacy systems to receive "health alerts." Moreover, they need to find ways to improve business processes "without touching the legacy." One approach is to reduce technical personnel costs by converting to a people-less "dark" operations floor. The operations staff who maintain and manage the legacy systems are replaced by an integrated monitoring and alarm system. A "lights out" data center can save money and improve management of IT resources.

To "keep some of that back-room stuff going a long time," CIOs also must learn to "add things and change the business process by changing the interface to the system," rather than change the legacy system itself. For example, the IT department may convert the user interface of a mainframe-based decision support system from text-based to graphics-based. Says one CIO, "Instead of focusing on clever things, we just focus on what I would call traditional 'bread and butter' [projects]."

A significant challenge of the Maintain the Legacy Approach is how to handle layoffs. Because the old systems are running the business, these CIOs "can't get rid of the COBOL programmers" and are thus "forced to mortgage the future" by laying off the younger employees skilled in object-oriented programming, Java, and other current technologies. Therefore, it becomes important for the CIO to find ways to motivate the remaining older employees to develop new skills in current technologies. In one company, the average age of the IT workforce after layoffs was 47 years.

Table 12.4 Summary of the Maintain the Legacy Approach

Approach	Maintain the Legacy
Description	CIOs put a hold on the existing IT plan, assuming it can be continued when the economy starts recovering
	CIOs focus on continuing the life of legacy systems in the short term
Objective	Use the fewest resources possible to maintain current service levels until funding is available to move forward with planned applications
Strengths	Focus on ROI
	Focus on Cost Optimization (Cost Minimizer)
Weaknesses	Potential loss of most advanced designers and programmers whose skills are not needed on legacy systems
CIO Challenges	Maintaining internal morale as programmers are released
	Convincing senior management that outsourcing critical IT operations would be detrimental over the long term

Strengths and Weaknesses of the Maintain the Legacy Approach. Its strengths come from its "now" focus. Its weaknesses stem from its preservation of the past.

Strength: It focuses on IT return of investment. Most IT funding goes to maintain the legacy. Remaining funds are only invested in small projects that yield quick returns. So the approach forces a fast-return ROI discipline.

Strength: It focuses on optimizing current systems. The challenge facing CIOs who adopt this approach is to find new ways to provide business value from IT with equal or fewer financial resources than in the past. With limited resources, these CIOs focus almost exclusively on projects to refine and optimize the operation of existing business systems. For example, an organization may choose to analyze a critical business process to reduce its costs and improve its operation. The analysis may recommend replacing the sales department's manual "paper-based" order taking process with an on-line data entry system. Such a new interface would streamline this critical business process and would ultimately save the company money by eliminating unnecessary and time-consuming tasks.

Weakness: It jeopardizes the organization's competitive future. By focusing IT resources only on tactical (short-term) and operational (day-to-day) IT initiatives, an organization chooses to ignore emerging IT applications and technologies that may improve the firm's competitiveness in the future. Competitors that take a different approach may gain competitive advantage by implementing new technologies sooner—leaving the Maintain the Legacy CIOs to play technological "catch-up" to stay competitive

Weakness: It inhibits development of IT professionals. While short-term thinking might have a positive effect on identifying projects to develop, it is a weakness in IT staffing. The disadvantage of this approach is that the organization loses the IT employees needed to build future systems. One CIO confidently states that she will be able to rehire these people when the economy recovers, saying, "Let's face it, where are they going to get work right now?" Nevertheless, there is no guarantee that Maintain the Legacy organizations have the environment that will attract IT developers with the latest skills.

Movement Among the Approaches

Of the 20 firms in the study, nine use the Extend the Lifecycle approach; five, the Bulletproof the Infrastructure approach; three, the Clean House approach; and three, the Maintain the

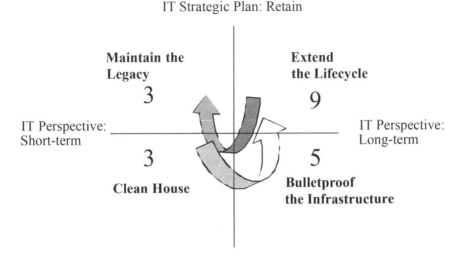

IT Strategic Plan: Retain

Maintain the Legacy
3

Extend the Lifecycle
9

IT Perspective: Short-term

IT Perspective: Long-term

3
Clean House

5
Bulletproof the Infrastructure

IT Strategic Plan: Rethink

Figure 12.2 Incidences and Patterns in the Approaches to Managing of IT During Decline

Legacy approach (see Figure 12.2). Although we conducted interviews at a single point in time, we could discern some movement among the four approaches. In fact, we found the approaches not necessarily binding. Some CIOs began with a less disruptive approach—such as the Extend the Lifecycle approach—and moved to progressively more disruptive approaches when more drastic cost-cutting measures became necessary.

Specifically, we saw firms moving from Extend the Lifecycle to Clean House to Maintain the Legacy. We also noted firms moving in the opposite direction, from Clean House, to Bulletproof the Infrastructure, to Extend the Lifecycle. These moves (depicted in Figure 12.2 as arrows), as well as the apparent preference for the Extend the Lifecycle approach, are discussed below.

Extend the Lifecycle Is the Most Popular Approach

As shown in Figure 12.2, nine of the 20 firms have adopted the Extend the Lifecycle approach to managing IT during the decline. There is no pattern discernible in terms of industry, organization size, or CIO tenure. What does seem common in these organizations, though, is their optimism that the decline will be ephemeral. If they can simply extend the current plan for a short while, they believe they can ride out the decline with few major changes to the application portfolio, development processes, or how IT decisions are made.

A second common aspect across these organizations is that they do not feel a large, immediate impact from the decline. Perhaps they are in a state of denial, or the effects have yet to ripple through the organization. In any case, if the economic decline continues through 2003, we believe several Extend the Lifecycle firms will be forced to take a more disruptive approach.

Moving from Extend the Lifecycle to Maintain the Legacy

None of the firms began as Maintain the Legacy, but some did progress to this approach after their other efforts to reduce IT expenditures did not suffice. When the economy began to decline the most common first step was to try to keep the current plan by stretching out the deadlines, and hence, expenditures (i.e., the Extend the Lifecycle approach). Following this, the next steps involved stopping initiatives and narrowing the horizon on expected benefits of new systems (i.e., the Clean House approach). The result is implementation of smaller-scale systems with shorter-term anticipated pay-off periods, as opposed to large systems with future benefits. The next step has been to look for ways to lower costs, such as outsourcing select parts of IT operations—for example, the desktop environment. It is only when the IT budget must be further cut that the CIOs adopt the Maintain the Legacy approach.

Whereas CIOs taking the Extend the Lifecycle approach appear to *assume* a short period of decline, those taking the Maintain the Legacy approach seem to *hope for* a short period of decline. In essence, if the decline continues and the organization is not able to cut sufficient costs by canceling new projects and maintaining the legacy, the only remaining option might be outsourcing. As one CIO from a major manufacturing firm states, "If sales continue to go down and you cannot afford the overhead of the business, you eventually have to consider outsourcing." However, none of the firms in our sample is currently considering a major outsourcing endeavor.

Moving from Clean House to Bulletproof the Infrastructure to Extend the Lifecycle

Although it might at first seem counter-intuitive, several firms did demonstrate a pattern of moving from the Clean House approach to Bulletproof the Infrastructure approach to Extend the Lifecycle approach. In fact, several of the firms currently in the Extend the Lifecycle quadrant had, prior to the decline, already undergone a major revision to the IS plan where they canceled many projects (i.e., Clean House approach) and a subsequent focus on building the infrastructure. The impetus was the arrival of a new CIO from the outside who faced an IT organization with a poor reputation for projects that had gone over budget and had failed to deliver the anticipated results.

All of the Clean House firms saw the economic decline as coming at a fortuitous time because they had lost control of their IT planning process and their application portfolio. It was high time to rethink the planning process and the content. None of these firms intend to remain in the Clean House state, though. Their goal is to use it to develop a new IT plan aligned with the organization's strategy, with a solid infrastructure that can support growth. Hence, we see evidence of firms aspiring to move from Clean House to Bulletproof the Infrastructure. But rather than simply initiate infrastructure projects, they believe it is impor-tant to first lay out a new long-term IT strategy that envisions the applications that will run on the new infrastructure. In effect, these firms are preparing themselves not only for growth but also positioning themselves to weather the next decline. During that decline, we would expect them to simply need to extend their lifecycle.

The Ups and Downs of Managing IT

Our research has addressed the question of how CIOs manage IT during economic decline. We have described four approaches to managing IT during periods of economic decline. Our interviews show a pattern of managing IT during periods of economic growth and decline (see Figure 12.3).

Specifically, all the organizations in our study faced common issues during the 1990s growth period. Rapid organizational growth fueled the need for new systems. Often, IT was unable, or perceived by business units to be unable, to sustain the rapid growth. So the

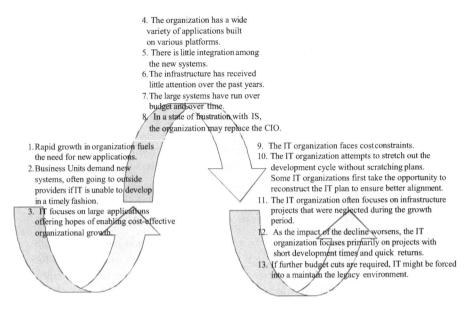

4. The organization has a wide variety of applications built on various platforms.
5. There is little integration among the new systems.
6. The infrastructure has received little attention over the past years.
7. The large systems have run over budget and over time.
8. In a state of frustration with IS, the organization may replace the CIO.

1. Rapid growth in organization fuels the need for new applications.
2. Business Units demand new systems, often going to outside providers if IT is unable to develop in a timely fashion.
3. IT focuses on large applications offering hopes of enabling cost-effective organizational growth.

9. The IT organization faces cost constraints.
10. The IT organization attempts to stretch out the development cycle without scratching plans. Some IT organizations first take the opportunity to reconstruct the IT plan to ensure better alignment.
11. The IT organization often focuses on infrastructure projects that were neglected during the growth period.
12. As the impact of the decline worsens, the IT organization focuses primarily on projects with short development times and quick returns.
13. If further budget cuts are required, IT might be forced into a maintain the legacy environment.

Figure 12.3 The Ups and Downs of Managing IT

business units went to third-party developers. Meanwhile, IT focused on large systems (often ERP) aimed at improving organizational efficiencies. With both inside and outside development taking place, the organization ended up with a complex array of systems built on various platforms and with little integration of data or systems. Moreover, the swift growth left little time to focus on infrastructure issues. More often than not, the large systems went well over budget and were late, leading to dissatisfaction with the IT department and, in some cases, replacement of the CIO.

At the start of the economic decline in 2000, most of the IT organizations in the study had a multitude of new systems, many on outdated infrastructure platforms. Some have chosen to maintain that platform until the good times return; others have decided to rebuild their infrastructure, anticipating good times ahead. On the applications side, some are using the downturn to scrap and reconstruct their strategic plan. Others are lengthening their plans.

Lessons from This Study

Given that economies move in cycles, can we draw lessons from the current cycle that CIOs can use to manage during future growth-decline cycles? We think three lessons are enduring.

Lesson 1: Disciplined IT Decision-Making Evens Out IT Ups and Downs

When organizations follow a structured, disciplined approach to IT decision-making, regardless of the current financial situation, they even out demands on the IT organization. Business demands and IT spending tend to move in concert with the economy. Employing a practical and responsible approach to IT spending during periods of prosperity more likely ensures that an organization's IT strategy will not be drastically affected during periods of economic decline.

In the 1990s, some IT organizations chose to hire contract consultants and offshore developers[12] to help keep pace with the high demand for new IT systems. Organizations that either ignored or abandoned their established IT project selection and approval practices during those fat 1990s then found themselves left with numerous projects in various phases of development when the economic growth began to decline and IT funding dwindled. Facing a declining or static IT budget, organizations once again "re-instated" or formalized procedures to ensure that funding only went to IT projects directly aligned with the organization's business strategy.

Many of the negative impacts from the economic downturn could have been moderated if organizations had adhered to a rigorous, structured IT planning and strategic decision-making process.

Lesson 2: Regular IT Strategic Reviews Build Business-Aligned Portfolios

Organizations that fail to perform a regular review of their projects compromise their systems development portfolio. It's during periods of economic growth when organizations are most likely to be so focused on staying competitive in their marketplace that they approve IT projects regardless of their alignment with the organization's business strategy. This laxity can decrease the performance of the organization, almost immediately, because these projects take resources away from projects that have strategic value.

This misappropriation of IT resources may artificially extend the time to complete key IT development projects. But it is not until the organization experiences a declining economy that it discovers it has been supporting IT projects that are not aligned with its strategic plan. That's when top management typically reviews the IT project portfolio and weeds out projects that do not support current and future strategic goals—either placing them on hold or canceling them.

Although it can be financially painful to absorb the costs of canceled IT projects, the exercise can renew top management's commitment to managing the alignment between business and IT strategies.[13] In truth, though, such reviews should take place no matter the economic environment.

Lesson 3: Balanced IT Spending Yields Business Agility

Organizations need to balance their IT spending among new systems development, maintenance, IT infrastructure, and integration projects. Unfortunately, very few management teams approve funding for IT infrastructure and integration when these projects conflict with new development, even though the executives know they need a flexible, scalable, and fully integrated enterprise-wide IT architecture. During periods of business prosperity, this unbalanced funding tendency is even more pronounced. The majority of IT funds are spent on new development, in hopes of improving competitive performance.

The result is new kinds of hardware and software being continually added to the IT infrastructure, with little consideration for how they will affect operating performance or whether they can share information across platforms.

Only when the economy slows down do organizations realize their unbalanced spending has led to an unstable IT infrastructure. To remedy this situation, management must allocate a significant portion of the IT budget to IT infrastructure projects. New development projects that might provide competitive advantage in a down economy must be delayed until a stable and fully integrated IT environment is in place.

Organizations that balance funding between new systems development and infrastructure are better placed to take advantage of business cycles. They are more agile.

Conclusion: CIOs Must Be Able to Facilitate Change as Their Environment Changes

In conclusion, our study found that some CIOs change their approach to managing IT as various economic and organizational changes occur. Such fluid movement through the four approaches demonstrates that CIOs must have the flexibility to modify IT strategy to meet changes in the business environment.

Continual change is now inherent in IT strategy development. Instead of developing an IT strategy and "selling" it to management, CIOs now need to facilitate solutions and assist business unit executives in locating the IT tools to integrate diverse solutions to form a cohesive working organization. Only then will IT strategy align with business goals during both the good times and the bad.

Notes

1   McCracken, B., "CRM – Failed Deployments … Frequent Autopsy Results," September 13, 2002, http://www.ecrmguide.com; and Hellweg, E., "CRM Success: Still the Exception, Not the Rule," *Business 2.0*, July 10, 2002.

2   For a discussion of the challenges of achieving benefits through CRM, see: Goodhue, D. L., Wixom, B. H., and Watson, H. J., "Realizing Benefits through CRM: Hitting the Right Target in the Right Way," *MISQ Executive*, June 2002, pp. 79–94; and Swift, R. S., "CRM is Changing Our Eras, the Information We Require, and Our Processes" *MISQ Executive*, June 2002, pp. 95–97.

3   Merian, L., "CIO Survey: 2001 Corporate IT Spending To Rise More Moderately Than in 2000," *Computerworld*, January 1, 2001.

4   "*CIO Magazine* Tech Poll," *CIO Magazine*, December, 2002, http://www.cio.com, January 16, 2003.

5   Ibid.

6   Ross, J.W. and Beath, C.M., "New Approaches to IT Investment," Sloan Management Review, 43:2, 2002, pp. 51–59.

7   Hagel III, J. and Brown, J.S., "Your Next IT Strategy," *Harvard Business Review*, 79:9, 2001, pp. 105–113.

8   "Bank of America and EDS Sign a 10-Year, $4.5 Billion Managed Network Outsourcing Agreement," *News Releases*, December 12, 2002. http://www.eds.com, January 17, 2003.

9   CIO.COM, Outsourcing Research Center, New Deals, December 2002, http://www.cio.com/research/outsourcing/newdeals.html.

10   Lawrence, P. and Lorsch, J., *Organization and Its Environment* (Boston: Harvard University Press), 1967.

11   Choudhury, V. and Sampler, J.L. "Information Specificity and Environmental Scanning: An Economic Perspective," *MIS Quarterly*, 21:1, 1997, pp. 25–53.

12   For a discussion on getting the most out of offshore development, see Carmen, E. and Agarwal, R.," The Maturation of Offshore Sourcing of Information Technology Work, *MISQ Executive*, June 2002, pp. 65–78.

13   For an excellent discussion on mastering strategic alignment, see Chan, Y., "Why Haven't We Mastered Alignment: the Importance of the Informal Organizational Structure," *MISQ Executive*, June 2002, pp. 97–112.

Questions for Discussion

1   Can commitment to an IT plan have negative consequences in the long run?

2   Why is having a strong IT infrastructure important to remain efficient and competitive in times of economic downturn?

3   Does the bulletproof approach restrict experimentation, and so innovation?

4   How can the clean house approach overcome challenges associated with adoption and adaptation of new routines/procedures?

5   How can organizations deal with disruptions in processes caused by stopping and restarting IT applications in maintaining the legacy approach?

6   Which of the four approaches, or a combination of the same, are ideal for organizations to adopt in order to remain competitive in times of economic downturn?

Further Reading

Xue, L., Ray, G., Bin, G. (2011). Environmental Uncertainty and IT Infrastructure Governance: A Curvilinear Relationship. *Information Systems Research*, 22(2), 389–399.

Xue, L., Ray, G., Sambamurthy, V. (2012). Efficiency or innovation: how do industry environments moderate the effects of firms' IT asset portfolios. *MIS Quarterly*, 36(2), 497–518.

Chapter 13

David S. Preston, Dorothy E. Leidner and Daniel Chen

CIO LEADERSHIP PROFILES: IMPLICATIONS OF MATCHING CIO AUTHORITY AND LEADERSHIP CAPABILITY ON IT IMPACT

The Importance of CIO Leadership to the Modern Organization

OVER THE PAST SEVERAL decades, information technology (IT) has become essential for organizations to increase operational efficiency and to obtain strategic success.[1] However, many organizations have experienced the "productivity paradox" – they have not been able to observe business value that is directly linked with their investments in IT. Savvy organizations have realized that they cannot derive business value by simply pouring vast sums of money into IT; rather, the strategic leadership of IT is the key to maximizing its potential benefits.

The chief information officer (CIO) plays a critical role in the ability of an organization to derive business value from IT. Organizations that view the CIO as a strategic asset are more likely to create business value through IT and thereby achieve superior business performance.[2]

However, not all firms need to include IT as an integral part of their business strategy. We argue that the impact of IT within an organization depends on the fit between the CIO and the strategic context of the organization. This article describes four distinct profiles of CIO leadership. We examine the influence of these four profiles on IT's contribution to a firm's performance and then assess the characteristics of each CIO leadership profile within organizations. The primary focus of our research is to enable organizations to understand how the fit between the CIO and the organizational context determines the benefits derived from IT. Given the potential importance of the CIO within the modern organization, as well as recent attention given to this topic, our findings provide criteria that enable an organization to examine its current CIO leadership profile and balance its return on IT investments.

Classifying CIO Leadership Profiles

We have classified CIO leadership on two dimensions:

- The CIO's strategic decision-making authority within the organization.
- The CIO's strategic leadership capability.

The Decision-Making Authority Dimension

CIO strategic decision-making authority is the degree to which the CIO has the authority to engage in strategic decision-making within the organization. Strategic decision-making is distinguished from tactical or operational decision-making in that it concerns decisions that will have a significant and lasting impact on organizational performance.

Given the pervasiveness of IT across functional groups and the intertwined nature of business and technology in modern organizations, the CIO should have the decision-making authority to lead strategic IT initiatives if IT is to contribute to the success of the organization. However, despite the strategic importance of IT, some CIOs are still not granted the same strategic decision-making authority as other business executives, and there are large differences in the strategic decision-making authority of CIOs across organizations. For instance, Kaarst-Brown[3] noted that "many IT executives are still not at the table because they are not viewed equal to their business peers." Other researchers have observed that, in many organizations, the CIO plays a critical role not only in IT strategic planning, but in business strategic planning as well.[4]

These disparities in the roles of CIOs across organizations are supported by the following statement from a CIO of a major Midwestern university, who was interviewed as part of our study. He said:

> In my years networking with various executives, I still find that many firms have completely different views on the strategic role of the CIO. In some organizations the purpose of the CIO is purely operational – he is there to essentially fix the pipes like a plumber. In other organizations, the CIO is considered to be a true strategic leader. In many organizations, the CIO may be stuck somewhere in the middle of this range.

The Leadership Capability Dimension

CIOs who have the authority to pursue strategic IT initiatives need to be capable leaders to successfully execute strategic projects; otherwise, the consequences for the organization could be problematic. Many CIOs are generally considered to be competent at managing the technical aspects of IT, such as keeping key systems operational; however, many CIOs fail as strategic leaders.[5]

This issue is of concern to organizations since it is through strategic leadership that CIOs can most significantly influence the impact of IT on organizational performance. CIOs who are effective strategic visionaries are well suited to select and champion strategic initiatives that are designed to increase organizational performance. On the other hand, CIOs who are not capable strategic leaders are likely to have a lower level of influence, or possibly even a detrimental influence, on the contribution that IT makes to organizational performance.

The CIO of a large private hospital in our study supported the importance of a capable IT leader to the organization. He said, "To truly make an impact, the CIO must have the ability to personally make strategic decisions. However, if the CIO does not have the background and experience to support the right decisions, the results can definitely be harmful."

The Four CIO Leadership Profiles

Using the two dimensions described above, we have constructed a 2x2 matrix that identifies four IT leadership profiles (see Figure 13.1):

- IT Orchestrator (high leadership capability, high decision-making authority).
- IT Mechanic (low leadership capability, low decision-making authority).
- IT Advisor (high leadership capability, low decision-making authority).
- IT Laggard (low leadership capability, high decision-making authority).

Overview of Research Methodology and Findings

Our research findings are derived from six semi-structured interviews with industry CIOs and pairs of survey responses (one from the CIO and at least one from a senior business executive) from 174 diverse organizations from a range of industries. (Fuller details of the research methodology and respondents are in the Appendix.[6])

We assigned each of the 174 CIOs to one of the four CIO leadership profiles.[7] The breakdown was as follows:

- IT Orchestrators: 55 (32%)
- IT Laggards: 32 (18%)
- IT Advisors: 31 (18%)
- IT Mechanics: 56 (32%)

Impact of CIO Leadership Profile on IT Contribution

For each of the profiles, we assessed the level of IT contribution to organizational performance by using various statistical techniques[8] to analyze the responses of the organizations' CEOs or other top business executives. We asked these business executives to assess the extent to which IT had contributed to the following seven areas of organizational performance: return on investment, sales revenue increase, market share increase, cost savings, operating efficiency, process improvement, and customer satisfaction. For each area, they rated the IT contribution level on a scale from 1 (IT contribution is minimal) to 5 (IT has contributed

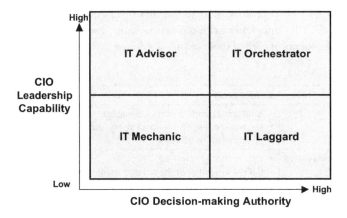

Figure 13.1 CIO Leadership Profiles

CIO Leadership Profile	IT Contribution Level (1 = Low; 5 = High)	
IT Orchestrator	3.54	
IT Advisor	3.26	
IT Laggard	2.81	
IT Mechanic	2.49	
Overall Average	*3.05*	

Figure 13.2 CIO Leadership Profiles and IT Contribution

to a very great extent). Based on these responses. we averaged the seven components of IT contribution for each CIO leadership profile. The results are shown in Figure 13.2.

The data in Figure 13.2 clearly illustrates how the CIO leadership profile impacts the level of contribution IT makes to organizational performance. We observed that the IT contribution level is higher than the overall average in firms where the CIO is classified as an IT Orchestrator or IT Advisor and lower than the average where the CIO is classified as an IT Laggard or IT Mechanic.[9] Firms with IT Orchestrators had the highest IT contribution level, while those with IT Mechanics had the lowest IT contribution level. Our analysis shows that the CIO's strategic decision-making authority and leadership capability collectively have a highly statistically significant impact on the contribution of IT to an organization's performance.

Other Factors Differentiating the Four CIO Leadership Profiles

Previous research has identified several factors that may help to further explain the differences between the IT contribution levels associated with each of the CIO leadership profiles. However, our study found that a CIO's age, gender, education level, business and IT experience, and length of service with the organization or as its CIO did not vary significantly across the four leadership profiles. But we did find significant differences in three factors – CIO attributes, CIO integration with top management, and organizational commitment to IT. The components of each of these factors are shown in Figure 13.3. Our

Factor	Components
CIO Attributes	• Strategic IT and business knowledge • Interpersonal skills (political savvy and communication ability)
CIO Integration with Top Management	• CIO reporting level • CIO is a member of the top management team
Organizational Commitment to IT	• Dedication of resources to IT • Strategic IT vision

Figure 13.3 Factors Differentiating CIO Leadership Profiles

study collected data on these six components so we could identify the distinguishing characteristics of CIOs in each leadership profile.

We describe the characteristics of each of the four CIO leadership profiles below in terms of "low," "average," or "high" ratings for each of these six components.[10] CIO knowledge (strategic knowledge and interpersonal skills) were rated by business executives on a scale of 1 (low) to 5 (high). CIOs used the same 1 to 5 scale to rate the level of IT resources. Business executives rated the organization's strategic IT vision (the degree to which IT is designed to transform the organization) on a scale of 1 to 3, where 1 equates to an "automative" vision, 2 equates to an "informative" vision, and 3 equates to a "transformative" vision.[11]

We found that four of these six components (the CIO's strategic knowledge, the CIO's interpersonal skills, the CIO's membership of the top management team, and the organization's strategic IT vision) directly influence the level of IT contribution within the organization.

Because of this, we pay particular attention to these four components in the following descriptions of each of the four CIO leadership profiles. For each profile, we also provide an illustrative example of a CIO we encountered in our research who fits into that classification.

Profile of the IT Orchestrator

In our study, 32% of CIOs were classified as IT Orchestrators. This type of CIO is an effective strategic leader who is granted a great deal of freedom in making strategic decisions. Such a CIO is empowered to influence organizational outcomes. We summarize the defining characteristics of IT Orchestrator CIOs in Figure 13.4.

The knowledge level and interpersonal attributes of IT Orchestrators are considerably higher than the overall average in our sample. Also, more of these CIOs report directly to the CEO and are formal members of the top management team. IT Orchestrators benefit from organizational support in the form of higher-than-average investments in IT. We posit that CIOs who are IT Orchestrators have the leadership skills that enable them to secure investments for IT. Alternatively an organization that invests highly in IT might actively seek a capable IT leader to handle such strategic responsibilities. Both explanations are plausible, and, in fact, some combination of the two may likely explain the higher-than-average investments in IT in these firms.

The CIO of a major electronics manufacturer provided insight into this phenomenon:

> I am not exactly sure of all the aspects that are required to make sure that IT delivers to the bottom line at the end of day. However, one thing I do know is

	CIO Attributes		CIO Integration with Top Management		IT Commitment	
	Strategic Knowledge (1-5)	Interpersonal Skills (1-5)	Percentage reporting to the CEO	Percentage a member of top management team	IT Resources (1-5)	Strategic IT Vision (1-3)
IT Orchestrator	High (4.10)	High (4.40)	High (60%)	High (89%)	High (3.90)	High (2.12)
Overall Average	3.53	3.87	47%	77%	3.54	1.93

Figure 13.4 IT Orchestrator – Summary of Characteristics

that I cannot perform – and as a result IT cannot deliver – if we [the IT department] are not provided with the proper funding and staff to get the job done.

We also found that not only do firms with IT Orchestrator CIOs make large investments in IT, they also generally espouse a vision that IT can strategically transform the organization. A transformative vision is consistent with high IT investment levels, and such firms may be ill-served without a CIO with the requisite strategic knowledge and interpersonal skills. However, it has been noted that CIOs with these attributes are in short supply. To maximize the impact on IT performance, such firms should employ a strategically capable CIO who is a formal member of the top management team and promote a transformative IT vision within the organization. Collectively, these practices can be taxing for the firm – but there are considerable benefits in terms of improved organizational performance. As our research has shown, organizations with an IT Orchestrator CIO obtain the greatest contribution from IT.

Illustrative Example of an IT Orchestrator CIO

"Midwestern General Hospital" (MGH) is a large general medical and surgical hospital with approximately 3,000 employees located in an urban center in the Midwestern United States. The contribution of IT to MGH's organizational performance was rated very high (4.43), well above the IT Orchestrator average of 3.54. MGH's CIO is considered a highly capable strategic leader (4.67) and is granted a high level of decision-making authority (4.60). All of these ratings are higher than the average ratings for IT Orchestrators, so MGH can be considered as a highly pronounced example of an organization with an IT Orchestrator CIO.

MGH's CIO is well suited for this leadership profile. He has a very high level of strategic knowledge and has developed complementary interpersonal skills. He is highly integrated within the business – he reports directly to the CEO and is a formal member of the top management team, which enables him to communicate ideas for strategic planning directly to other senior executives. He indicated that he has forged strong relationships with other members of the top management team. Such relationships are expected because a strategically capable and socially adept CIO with formal access to the top management team has the forum and ability to develop a partnership with the upper echelon of the organization.

We observed that MGH has a strong commitment toward IT since it dedicates a large amount of resources to IT and promotes a vision that the purpose of IT is to transform its current business processes. We therefore infer that MGH includes IT as a central part of its strategic mission and expects to yield commensurate benefits from its investments and organizational efforts to capitalize on IT.

The current CIO appears to be a good fit for MGH's organizational mission. This capable executive has been with MGH for 23 years and served as CIO for 18 years. However, MGH should consider grooming a replacement for this CIO since he is now in his mid-60s and may soon retire. MGH should ensure that the potential replacement is a strong leader who can meet the expectations for success set by MGH. However, IT leaders of this caliber are often in short supply.

Profile of the IT Mechanic

At the other end of the spectrum and in stark contrast to IT Orchestrators, IT Mechanic CIOs have a low level of both strategic effectiveness and strategic decision-making authority. We summarize the defining characteristics of IT Mechanic CIOs in Figure 13.5.

	CIO Attributes		CIO Integration with Top Management		IT Commitment	
	Strategic Knowledge (1-5)	Interpersonal Skills (1-5)	Percentage reporting to the CEO	Percentage a member of top management team	IT Resources (1-5)	Strategic IT Vision (1-3)
IT Mechanic	**Low (2.94)**	**Low (3.35)**	**Low (36%)**	**Average (73%)**	**Average (3.46)**	**Low (1.78)**
Overall Average	*3.53*	*3.87*	*47%*	*77%*	*3.54*	*1.93*

Figure 13.5 IT Mechanic – Summary of Characteristics

In our research, 32% of CIOs were classified as IT Mechanics. These CIOs generally had the lowest levels of strategic knowledge and weaker interpersonal skills. In addition, a lower percentage of these CIOs reported to the CEO than any of the other types of CIO. The CIO of a non-profit organization who was interviewed as part of this study noted:

> I can tell you first hand that the reporting level of the CIO is the indicator that you should look at if you want to examine if the organization considers IT to be strategically important. When I was a CIO in industry, I reported directly to the CEO, which enabled me to play a key role in the corporate strategy. In my current position, I report to an underling of the CEO, and I don't have the same influence to see that IT helps fuel the business.

Also, firms with an IT Mechanic CIO tend to have an IT vision that is more automation-oriented than transformative. Based on these collective findings, it is not surprising that the lowest contribution of IT to organizational performance was found in firms with IT Mechanic CIOs. The average IT contribution rating of 2.49 (on a scale of 1 to 5) in these firms indicates that IT does not contribute appreciably to the performance of the organization. However, it is important to note that this low level of IT impact may be consistent with the organizational goals of a firm. If a firm constrains its CIO's strategic decision-making authority and employs a CIO with only limited strategic leadership capability, it is a signal that IT is not viewed as a strategic enabler within the organization.

In fact, the high percentage of our sample that was classified as IT Mechanic CIOs may reflect an intentional decision on the part of top management teams to limit or neutralize the risk of investing in IT resources and in developing a strategic CIO. As expected, the contribution of IT to the performance of these organizations is not huge. At the same time, the risk of over-investing in IT with disappointing benefits is very low. We therefore consider employing an IT Mechanic CIO to be a risk-averse strategy aimed at minimizing potential IT investment risks while maintaining a functioning operational environment.

Illustrative Example of an IT Mechanic CIO

"Eastern General Hospital" (EGH) is a large general medical and surgical hospital with approximately 1,900 employees in a suburban setting in the eastern United States. The contribution of IT to organizational performance was rated as very low (1.81), well below the average of 2.49 for firms with IT Mechanic CIOs. EGH's CIO is not considered a capable strategic leader (2.33) and has a low level of decision-making authority (2.00).

EGH (unlike MGH – another general hospital) emphasizes neither the importance of the CIO position nor a strategic focus on IT. We observed that the CIO appears to be more characteristic of an operational manager than a true executive since he is not a formal member of the top management team and reports to the chief medical officer rather than to the CEO. EGH does not appear to have a strong strategic commitment to IT. Its vision is for IT to merely automate current operational processes and reduce costs. Therefore IT does not play a strategic role within EGH. However, it dedicates significant resources to IT, though they are geared toward operational rather than strategic goals.

The current CIO appears to be an appropriate fit for this managerial role (rather than an executive role) since he does not have strong strategic knowledge or interpersonal skills. Although he may have strong technical and managerial skills, he does not have the attributes needed by a transformational leader. However, the EGH's top executives appear to be satisfied with their CIO's current level of productivity and the status quo; the current CIO has been with EGH for 24 years and has served as CIO for 12 years despite his lack of leadership ability. His length of tenure in this position indicates that he may also be satisfied within his IT Mechanic role.

The EGH and MGH cases illustrate that organizations in the same business can successfully have CIOs with different leadership profiles. The important thing is to ensure a good level of fit between the CIO and the organizational context.

Profile of the IT Advisor

Organizations with an IT Advisor CIO (18% in our study) are of particular interest since they obtain a moderately high IT contribution but require fewer resources and less strategic commitment to IT than firms with an IT Orchestrator CIO. We use the label "IT Advisor" since this type of CIO has limited decision-making authority but is a highly capable leader with vast strategic knowledge who may be well suited to serve as a strategic advisor to the top management team on IT issues. Although the impact of IT in firms with IT Advisor CIOs is lower than in those with IT Orchestrator CIOs, it is higher than the overall average and higher than firms with IT Laggard or IT Mechanic CIOs. Thus even when the CIO's strategic decision-making authority is relatively low, as it is for firms with an IT Advisor CIO, having a capable leader in the CIO position helps IT contribute to organizational performance. This observation underscores the importance of strategic leadership skills for CIOs. We summarize the defining characteristics of this type of CIO in Figure 13.6.

	CIO Attributes		CIO Integration with Top Management		IT Commitment	
	Strategic Knowledge (1-5)	Interpersonal Skills (1-5)	Percentage reporting to the CEO	Percentage a member of top management team	IT Resources (1-5)	Strategic IT Vision (1-3)
IT Advisor	**High** **(4.04)**	**High** **(4.35)**	**Average** **(42%)**	**Average** **(77%)**	**Low** **(3.11)**	**Average** **(1.87)**
Overall Average	*3.53*	*3.87*	*47%*	*77%*	*3.54*	*1.93*

Figure 13.6 IT Advisor – Summary of Characteristics

Like IT Orchestrators, business executives consider IT Advisors to have strategic knowledge and strong interpersonal skills. However, there are several key factors that distinguish these two types of CIO. We observed that IT Advisor CIOs' integration with top management and their firms' IT visions are near the overall average. In addition, we observed that, even though firms with IT Advisor CIOs provide the lowest level of resources to the IT department, they still obtain a relatively high level of IT impact. Despite minimizing their IT investment and commitment. these firms are able to derive organizational benefits from IT by employing a capable CIO. In essence, their approach is a "low cost alternative" compared to firms with IT Orchestrator CIOs, which require substantial IT investments and dedication to a transformative IT vision.

Profile of the IT Laggard

Firms with an IT Laggard CIO have a level of IT contribution that is lower than average but higher than that of firms with IT Mechanic CIOs. IT Laggards are the inverse of IT Advisors since they are provided with a relatively high level of decision-making authority. but they do not have the requisite leadership skills to capitalize on the strategic authority provided to them. We summarize the defining characteristics of IT Laggard CIOs in Figure 13.7.

The strategic decision-making authority given to IT Laggard CIOs suggests that top management has high expectations for them to derive potential benefits from IT. However, it is possible that IT Laggards' leadership capability is hampered by a fairly conservative IT vision. Without a more aggressive IT vision, IT Laggards may be unable to capitalize on their decision-making authority and are consequently labeled as incapable leaders. We note that despite firms with IT laggard CIOs making higher-than-average investments in IT resources, they do not obtain the same level of impact as firms with more capable but underfunded IT Advisor CIOs.

Our analysis showed that the IT contribution in firms with IT Laggard CIOs was slightly higher than in those with IT Mechanic CIOs. This finding could indicate that IT Laggards are able to use some of their decision-making authority to lead initiatives that potentially have a moderate strategic impact and are within the scope of their abilities. It could also indicate that Laggards eschew potentially more risky initiatives that would have greater strategic impact but are outside of their "strategic comfort zone." Firms with IT Laggard CIOs might still target strategic IT initiatives but more likely under the guidance of the top management team than the CIO.

	CIO Attributes		CIO Integration with Top Management		IT Commitment	
	Strategic Knowledge (1-5)	Interpersonal Skills (1-5)	Percentage reporting to the CEO	Percentage a member of top management team	IT Resources (1-5)	Strategic IT Vision (1-3)
IT Laggard	**Low (3.11)**	**Low (3.36)**	**Average (47%)**	**Average (71%)**	**Average (3.47)**	**Average (1.97)**
Overall Average	*3.53*	*3.87*	*47%*	*77%*	*3.54*	*1.93*

Figure 13.7 IT Laggard – Summary of Characteristics

Illustrative Example of an IT Advisor CIO

"Wholesaler Inc." is a small to mid-sized wholesaler of recreational goods in the southeast of the United States, with approximately 200 employees. The contribution of IT to organizational performance was rated as moderately high (3.3), which is on par with the typical firm with an IT Advisor CIO. Wholesaler Inc.'s CIO is considered by business executives to be a capable strategic leader (4.33) but is not granted a high level of decision-making authority (2.60). Both of these ratings are close to the average for IT Advisor CIOs. This CIO is thus a quintessential IT Advisor – a CIO who is a strong strategic leader but does not have the authority to make strategic decisions independently.

The CIO's integration with the top ranks of Wholesaler Inc.'s management is typical of IT Advisors–he reports directly to the CEO but is not a formal member of the top management team. Wholesaler Inc.'s strategic IT vision is also typical of firms with IT Advisor CIOs. The most salient characteristic of Wholesaler Inc. is that it provides a low amount of resources to IT (2.33). This indicates that the firm wishes to minimize its direct IT investments even though it has a CIO who is a capable strategic leader. The combination of a minimalist approach from the business side and a strategic CIO means that Wholesaler Inc. is able to obtain a reasonably high level of IT contribution and a good "bang for the buck" from its IT investments and commitment to IT.

We note that IT investments do not directly influence the contribution of IT on organizational performance; however, investments in initiatives that are in accordance with organizational objectives may indirectly influence organizational success.

The CIO indicated that he has formed a very strong partnership with the top management team. This partnership may enable this knowledgeable and adept CIO to navigate the decision-making environment dominated by the top management team and act as an advisor for decisions on strategic IT initiatives.

Wholesaler Inc.'s CIO has been in this executive position for only three years. Therefore it is unclear whether he is content with an advisory role and will stay with the firm in the long run if he is not provided with the appropriate resources or decision-making authority to enable him to exploit his strategic leadership capabilities.

Three Key Lessons on IT Leadership

Given that the strategic management of IT continues to be a key issue for organizations, we summarize three key lessons based on our findings. We believe that these lessons provide insights for both IT executives and business executives about the role of IT leadership within the organization.

Illustrative Example of an IT Laggard CIO

"Parts Manufacturer Inc." (PMI) is a mid-sized U.S. parts manufacturer for several industry sectors, with approximately 600 employees. The contribution of IT to organizational performance is moderately low (2.71), which is on par with the IT Laggard average. Senior executives do not consider the CIO to be a capable strategic leader (2.67); however, this CIO is granted a high level of strategic decision-making authority (4.30).

This firm has a moderate level of IT commitment since its IT resources and strategic IT vision are on par with the average of firms with IT Laggard CIOs and with the overall average. In addition, the CIO's integration with top management is average since he is not a formal top management team member but does report directly to the CEO. We observed that PMI's CIO is in charge of a wide range of strategic decisions for IT; however, he does not have the strategic knowledge or interpersonal skills necessary for a strategic leader in this position. This accounts for PMI having a moderately low level of IT contribution, probably due to the relatively unprepared IT leader acting as the key decision maker within a firm that appears to seek only marginal gains from IT.

PMI's CIO indicated that he has a strong partnership with the top management team. Although he has the authority to make strategic decisions, he may choose to collaborate with top executives who can compensate for any deficits in his strategic knowledge base. However, the CIO's weak interpersonal skills may cast doubt on his assertion that he can foster such a relationship.

PMI provides its CIO with authority that, at present, he may not be equipped to handle. However, we note that he has been the firm's CIO for just two years. Perhaps he will acquire greater knowledge and interpersonal skills should he remain in this role for a longer period. To some degree, strategic knowledge, or the application of strategic knowledge, is company specific. The CIO's interpersonal skills may also further develop after he is able to understand the behavior and goals of PMI's top management.

Lesson 1: Know Thyself

CIOs will benefit from understanding their own leadership profile. Our findings clearly demonstrate that IT's contribution to organizational performance varies significantly across the four CIO leadership profiles. CIOs who want to increase the level of IT contribution to their organizations' performance can gain an understanding of how to achieve this by assessing their current profile.

Although organizations may not officially decree their CIOs' level of strategic decision-making authority, CIOs should assess their level of authority by evaluating their prior and current experiences in leading initiatives within their organizations.[12] However, CIOs must keep in mind that not all organizations expect a high level of contribution from IT. It is therefore also imperative for a CIO to understand the top management team's vision for IT. If that vision is transformative, the organization needs an IT Orchestrator CIO. If the vision is automative, a CIO that matches the IT Mechanic profile is appropriate. In firms where the vision is informative (i.e., the role of IT is to provide information to key decision-makers) an IT Advisor CIO will likely be needed.

By understanding his or her current profile, as well as the profile needed to support the top management team's vision for IT, the CIO can make adjustments to better serve the organization. Note, though, that the CIO's leadership ability is based on the top management team's perception. The CIO characteristics most readily changeable and within the CIO's control are strategic IT and business knowledge, and interpersonal skills (i.e., the CIO attributes listed in Figure 13.3). CIOs who want – or need – to adjust their own profile will need to begin with these attributes.

The other CIO characteristics (integration with top management and organizational commitment to IT) are generally not under the direct control of the CIO. However, the CIO can work to influence these characteristics by forging close relationships with the top management team, by ensuring that the IT function is a top performer on service-management metrics, by tracking the value of IT projects, and by identifying projects that have delivered on their business cases.

Lesson 2: The Global Digital Economy Will Need More IT Orchestrators

Two of the four CIO leadership profiles (IT Orchestrator and IT Mechanic) have a good match between the CIO's strategic decision-making authority and leadership capability, and two (IT Advisor and IT Laggard) have a mismatch. IT Orchestrator CIOs are well suited for organizations that want to be at the forefront of IT innovation. However, not all organizations currently believe that an IT Orchestrator is necessary; an IT Mechanic may be ideal for an organization that has only limited needs from IT and wishes to minimize IT costs. On the other hand, there is untapped potential from IT in organizations with IT Advisor or IT Laggard CIOs.

Although not all organizations see the need for an IT Orchestrator. the global digital environment in which many firms now operate increasingly demands that IT is used to help them achieve greater innovation and efficiency. Organizations operating in this environment will need IT to support their business strategies and will be best served by IT Orchestrator CIOs. IT Mechanics, IT Laggards, and IT Advisors may therefore have to evolve into IT Orchestrators.

Moreover, current IT Orchestrator CIOs who wish to continue maximizing the potential impact of IT will need to maintain a high level of decision-making authority and strategic leadership capability as the organizational structure and business priorities change with time. These CIOs need to ensure that they keep their strategic knowledge base current and their interpersonal skills polished. Since the top management team could be continually changing, the CIO must also consistently work to build and maintain strong partnerships with these top executives and develop a uniform agreement that IT is key to the firm's business strategy. Therefore IT Orchestrator CIOs must continually monitor their attributes and strive to improve them.

All CIOs, regardless of their current leadership profile, need to be aware that future trends will favor the appointment of IT Orchestrators. CIOs without the necessary attributes for the IT Orchestrator profile should be prepared to adapt (see Lesson 3); if they don't, they may find themselves out of a job. IT Advisors, IT Laggards, and IT Mechanics should therefore prepare to methodically reshape themselves as IT Orchestrators.

Lesson 3: IT Advisors, IT Laggards, and IT Mechanics Can Transition Across Profiles

Actions for IT Advisors. Our research has shown that an IT Advisor CIO can derive moderately high benefits from IT with minimal commitment of resources within an organization that generally has a moderate strategic IT vision. To transition to the IT Orchestrator profile, an IT Advisor needs to focus on obtaining additional funding and strive to instill a vision among top business executives that transformation through IT is fundamental to the firm's corporate strategy. To gain greater IT commitment from the organization, an IT Advisor CIO should demonstrate a track record for IT to the top management team by providing clear examples of how IT has delivered value to the business. An IT Advisor with strong interpersonal skills has the political savvy and communication skills to formulate and present business cases that show IT is critical to current and future operations and the business strategy. Such business cases will increase the firm's level of IT commitment and consequently increase the CIO's strategic decision-making authority.

Actions for IT Laggards. We found that IT Laggards' leadership capabilities generally fall short of what's needed to achieve the firm's strategic IT goals. IT Laggard CIOs should immediately address their shortcomings and should lobby the top management team to attend programs that will accelerate their personal development. These programs might be advanced business classes (e.g., graduate-level classes in strategy, finance, etc.) designed to improve their strategic knowledge, or executive development programs designed to enhance and refine IT Laggards' "soft" skills.

Actions for IT Mechanics. IT Mechanics who want to develop into IT Orchestrators must both improve their executive attributes and transform their organizations' view of IT. We recommend that IT Mechanic CIOs first focus on developing their leadership capabilities and then subsequently work to extend their decision-making authority. In essence, we are recommending that IT Mechanic CIOs first work to transition themselves into IT Advisors and subsequently work to transform themselves into IT Orchestrators.

Making Use of the CIO Leadership Profiles

The lessons learned from our study provide a lens through which CIOs and their senior business colleagues can understand their current CIO leadership profiles. An organization and its CIO can evaluate the current CIO leadership profile by focusing on the CIO's attributes, CIO integration within the firm, and the organization's IT commitment. The top management team can then assess if the profile meets the firm's plans to derive benefits from IT. The CIO can identify shortcomings in his or her own profile and take steps to remedy them so he or she can better serve the organization as the need for IT Orchestrators comes to the fore.

We believe that the profiles developed for this study and the quantified findings from our research will enable executives to directly influence the CIO leadership profile and the contribution made by IT within their organizations. We also believe that this study will provide a foundation for future research on the impact of CIOs on organizational practices and the bottom line of their firms.

Appendix: Research Methodology

To conduct this empirical study, we collected data in 2006/2007 from CIOs and their corresponding top business executives via a survey. The CIO is defined as the highest-ranking IT executive within the organization. Top business executives included the organization's CEO or business executives who are either formal members of the top management team or reported directly to the CEO. Business executives responded to questions on the quality of the CIO's leadership capabilities, attributes, the organization's strategic IT vision, and IT's contribution to organizational performance. CIOs responded to questions on their integration with top management and the resources provided to IT. Both the CIO and matched CEO or other top business executives responded to questions on the CIO's strategic decision-making authority, and the mean responses were used, after assessing the inter-rater reliability (the degree of agreement among respondents).

Matched-pair surveys from 174 diverse U.S.-based organizations within multiple industries were returned, providing responses from both the CIO and at least one corresponding top business executive. Among the 174 organizations, 78 (44.8%) were in the healthcare industry, 18 (10.4%) were in the manufacturing industry, 16 (9.2%) were in the finance industry, 15 (8.6%) were retailers or wholesalers, 15 (8.6%) were consulting firms, 8 (4.6%) were in the construction/real estate development industry, 8 (4.6%) were educational institutions, and the remaining 16 (9.2%) were from miscellaneous industries. All the organizations had annual revenue of more than $650,000, and the average number of employees was 7,643. The average age of the CIOs was 49.6 years, and average tenure as the firm's CIO was 8.8 years. Of the 174 CIOs, 35 (20.1%) were women and 139 (79.9%) were men.

Notes

1   For more on the critical role of IT in obtaining both efficiencies and strategic success, see Sambamurthy, V, Bharadwaj, A., and Grover, V. "Shaping agility through digital options: Reconceptualizing the role of information technology in contemporary firms," *MIS Quarterly* (27:2), 2003, pp. 237–263.

2   For a comprehensive analysis of the organizational views of CIOs and IT performance, see Chatterjee, D., Richardson, V. J., and Zmud, R. W. "Examining the shareholder wealth effects of announcements of newly created CIO positions," *MIS Quarterly* (25:1), 2001, pp. 43–70.

3   Insights into the variations in authority given to CIOs across organizations can be found in Kaarst-Brown, M. L. "Understanding an organization's view of the CIO: The role of assumptions about IT," *MIS Quarterly Executive* (4:2), 2005, p. 287.

4   Leidner and Mackay found that some CIOs were not only leading IT strategy, but were also initiating organizational strategy. See Leidner, D. E., and Mackay, J. M. "How Incoming CIOs Transition into Their New Jobs," *MIS Quarterly Executive* (6:1), 2007, pp. 17–28.

5   To obtain a valid and unbiased assessment of CIOs, it is necessary to get the viewpoint of business executives, rather than CIOs themselves. One of the few studies to have done this is Smaltz, D. H., Sambamurthy, V., and Agarwal, R. "The antecedents of CIO role effectiveness in organizations: An empirical study in the healthcare sector," *IEEE Transactions on Engineering Management* (53:2), 2006, pp. 207–222. For an in-depth look at CIOs and why they succeed, or fail, see Broadbent, M., and Kitzis, E. S. *The New CIO Leader*, Harvard Business School Press, 2006.

6   For further information about this study, please contact David Preston (d.preston@tcu.edu).

7   We assigned the 174 CIOs to the four leadership profiles based on high and low levels (with respect to the average value of the total sample) of decision-making authority and strategic leadership capability. We measured CIO decision-making authority as the degree to which the CIO has the authority to make strategic decisions to meet the organization's business needs, taking account of the following issues: strategic options, strategic actions, courses of action, IT initiatives, and IT investments. CIO strategic leadership capability was measured as the degree to which business executives rated the CIO as an effective strategic leader, a strategic business planner, and a visionary.

8   Statistical analyses included both hierarchical regression and one-way analysis of variance (ANOVA).

9   The results of our statistical analysis indicate that the IT contribution levels of each of the four CIO profiles are statistically different from the average. The IT contribution levels of Orchestrators and Mechanics were found, respectively, to be significantly higher and lower than the average (0.01 level of significance via a two-tailed t-test). Advisors were found to be significantly higher than average (0.10 level of significance via a one-tailed t-test). Laggards were found to be significantly lower than average (0.10 level of significance via a two-tailed t-test).

10   We tested the value of each component for each profile versus the average values across all CIOs via an ANOVA test. In our statistical analysis, profiles that had a component value significantly below or above the overall average were designated as "low" and "high," respectively. Profiles with characteristics that were not significantly different from the overall average were designated as "average."

11   At one extreme, some organizations espouse an automative vision where the role of IT focuses on replacing human labor and reducing operational costs. At the other extreme, some organizations espouse a transformative vision where the role of IT is to transform the organization through new products or business strategies. And some firms may have an informative vision, which can be considered as an intermediate level of transformation, where the role of IT is to provide information to key decision makers and employees. For more information, see Schein, E. H. "The role of the CEO in the management of change: The case of information technology" in Kochan, T. A., and Useem, M. (eds.) *Transforming Organizations*, Oxford University Press, 1992.

12   Our survey results found that CIOs and top management team members have a high degree of agreement on the CIO's perceived level of strategic decision-making authority. Therefore CIOs can generally accurately assess their level of decision-making authority in the organization.

Questions for Discussion

1   Why is it helpful to classify CIO leadership profiles?

2   Is strategy more suitable to a CIO role as compared to tactics? Discuss with respect to the four types of CIO profiles.

3   Is a large budget and investment in IT a prerequisite to having an effective IT Orchestrator CIO?

4   Is it better to have no CIO than to have an IT Mechanic CIO?

5   Which ones of the four CIO profiles do you believe can be most effective for IT impact? Is this dependent on the type of organization?

6   Can (and how can) CIO roles transition among the four CIO profiles?

Further Reading

Preston, D., Chen, D., Leidner, D. E. (2008). Examining the antecedents and consequences of CIO decision making authority. *Decision Sciences*, *39*(4), 605–642.

Karahanna, E., Preston, D. (2013). The effect of social capital of the relationship between the CIO and top management team on firm performance. *Journal of Management Information Systems*, *30*(1), 15–56.

Chapter 14

Sanja Tumbas, Nicholas Berente and Jan vom Brocke

THREE TYPES OF CHIEF DIGITAL OFFICERS AND THE REASONS ORGANIZATIONS ADOPT THE ROLE

The Rise of the Chief Digital Officer

THE CHIEF DIGITAL OFFICER (CDO) role has emerged in recent years and is attracting a great deal of attention.[1] Digital innovation impacts every industry, and as a response, many organizations have introduced this new leadership role in their C-suites.[2] However, since the CDO role is still in its nascent stages and not well defined, the role means different things to different organizations.

For example, some organizations leverage the role of the CDO to emphasize digital capabilities at a strategic level. CDOs are often key evangelists in organizations for a general entrepreneurial mindset and facilitators of enterprise-wide change associated with digital transformation.[3] In some organizations, CDO responsibilities are more tactical and involve leading a variety of specific initiatives and projects that digitally enable units across the organization and its customers. In other organizations, CDOs are charged with leading product and service innovation. Here, CDOs are often thought to exist at the intersection of different functions—most commonly IT and marketing, but also product development, technology strategy, communications, operations and others. Still other organizations address digital innovation through existing executive roles, such as CIOs.

Overall, there is little guidance on whether an organization should adopt a CDO role. To decide, organizations need answers to two particular questions: *What, specifically, do CDOs do? Why do different organizations establish the CDO role?* This article sets out to provide answers to these questions. We interviewed 35 CDOs across a wide variety of industry sectors to get insight into when adopting the CDO role makes sense (see Table 14.1 on next page).

Our research shows that the core reason organizations appoint a CDO is to drive business value from digital technologies. From our interviews (further information about the research

Table 14.1 Overview of Respondents

Company[6]	Industry Sector	Time in Position (years)	Country
FinancialServ 1	Banking and finance	0.25	U.S.
FinancialServ 2	Banking and finance	0.85	U.K.
InsuranceFirm	Insurance	0.85	U.S.
HealthRelated	Healthcare	1	Europe
RetailOrg	Retail	1.25	Australia
Manu&Retail	Retail and manufacturing	L	U.S.
RetailCommunication	Retail	3	Europe
Manufacturing 1	Custom part manufacturing	2	Europe
Manufacturing 2	Hard manufacturing	5.5	Canada
Manufacturing 3	Transportation vehicle	1.5	Europe
ArchitectureDesign	Architecture, engineering and construction	4	U.S.
SoftwareCom 1	Software	0.85	Europe
SoftwareCom 2	Software	L	U.S.
FinancialServ 3	Banking and finance	0.5	Europe
Media Publisher 1	News publishing	1.25	Europe
Media Publisher 2	News publishing	1.85	Europe
Media Publisher 3	Specialized publisher	2	Europe
Media Publisher 4	Specialized publisher	5.5	Europe
Media Publisher&TV 5	News publishing and broadcasting	0.5	Europe
Media Film 6	Film producer education/ non-profit	4	Canada
Media TV 7	TV broadcasting	3.5	U.S.
Media Advertising 8	Advertising	1	Europe
Media Advertising 9	Advertising	2	U.S.
Media Advertising 10	Advertising	1	South America
Media Advertising 11	Advertising	1	U.S.
GovInstitution	Governmental/non-profit	0.5	Europe
Labor Union	Association/non-profit	0.25	U.S.
EducationOrg 1	Education/non-profit	4	U.S.
CultureHouse 1	Culture/non-profit	1.5	U.S.
CultureHouse 2	Culture/non-profit	4	U.S.
DevelopSkill	Leadership education/ non-profit	L	Europe
EducationOrg 2	Education	2	U.S.
ConsumerGood 1	Consumer goods	1.5	U.S.
ConsumerGood 2	Consumer goods	L	U.S.
FinancialServ 4	Banking and finance	1	Europe

methodology is in the Appendix), we identified three focal domains where CDOs build digital capabilities to drive business value: digital innovation, data analytics and customer engagement. Furthermore, we suggest there is a distinct type of CDO associated with each of these digital capabilities—digital accelerator, digital marketer and digital harmonizer.

Based on these insights, we discuss the relationship between organizations' traditional IT functions and their emerging digital requirements, and describe how CDOs and CIOs can complement each other. We reflect on the role of the CDO in relation to the established role of the CIO—the executive most commonly charged with innovation with digital technologies.[4] Many CIOs are actively embracing new opportunities in digital innovation,[5] so the relationship between the CDO and CIO is an important one.

Characteristics of a Successful CDO

In our interviews with CDOs, we explored their roles by asking open-ended questions, including: Why did the organization create the CDO role? What are the tasks and responsibilities of the CDO? What kind of outcomes do CDOs drive?

In general, CDOs help their organizations to use digital technologies to create business value. They are engaged with developing digital capabilities in relevant domains and successfully using various classes of digital technologies to generate value. They need to continually focus on seizing new opportunities. An organization's CDO is responsible for questioning the existing business model and evaluating customer-centeredness, using a variety of data to gain insights. To cope with these business imperatives, the CDO must be well versed in experimenting with, and applying, a variety of digital technologies.

Successful CDOs need to actively sense the environment for emerging digital technologies and then work to build digital capabilities in their organizations. To attain goals associated with any digital capability, organizations must leverage various technologies, such as mobile apps, social media, the Internet of Things or other emerging domains. However, these emerging domains are ever-expanding. In our interviews, different CDOs emphasized distinct areas. For example, some emphasized mobility and the importance of mobile applications able to extend the digital experience to everyday interaction with mobile devices. The CDO of a museum explained how mobile apps extend the museum experience:

> That [mobile apps] was probably the most fundamental way that we changed the organization … digital is really integrated into the experience while you're in the institution, as well as [allowing you] to experience it offline if you can't come to the institution or [allowing you] to … have more experiences [when you get home]… The apps … we built [got] the museum outside the walls with the use of digital.
>
> CDO, CultureHouse 1

In addition to mobility, many CDOs emphasized the role of social media. Intense interaction with social media helps organizations to create a more precise profile of their customers and to engage with them through various channels. For example, the CDO of a manufacturing and retail organization described how his company had built capabilities around social media by emphasizing the value of "non-paid" customer acquisition:

> There is paid acquisition and non-paid. … Paid … includes channels such as Google AdWords, display affiliates, … paid social media, organic search and [so on]. … Then you'd have your unpaid channels within the acquisition bucket, ultimately driving traffic to your websites and mobile products.
>
> CDO, Manu&Retail

Overall, we found that all CDOs were very focused on building capabilities with a variety of digital technologies. There were, however, three specific domains on which different CDOs focused: digital innovation, data analytics and customer engagement. The relevant capabilities for each domain are summarized in Table 14.2, and we describe each domain below.

Table 14.2 Digital Capabilities of CDOs

CDO's Domain	Relevant Capability	Example Quotes
Digital Innovation	Building digital capabilities for intense experimentation; pursuing strategic changes to organizational processes, products, services and business models.	*"I think my largest problem is … how can you transform a business model from the print age… I think this is the hardest challenge: how do you do that step-wise in a certain amount of years [while] protecting the business you already have but also building a new model."* CDO, Media Publisher 1
Data Analytics	Building capabilities for data analysis to gain insights into both internal and external data sources.	*"With one of our design businesses—designing hotels, resorts and such—we were able to look at … Trip Advisor for … reviews of the facilities that we designed. … We're also looking at ways [of using] something from Trip Advisor. What is public data, what can we use from that and how do we do it? Likewise with design forums or discussion groups and [so on]. Those are the … non-structured data sets that we're interested in understanding: what's the general conversation, what's the general pulse?"* CDO, ArchitectureDesign
Customer Engagement	Establishing capabilities for providing intense focus on relationships with the organization's customers; delivering outstanding customer experience by also streamlining internal processes.	*"In healthcare, our customers [are] pharmaceutical companies, doctors and patients. Their expectations are changing from analog services to digital services. As a result, one of the things that I do is study my customers' customers' needs so that I can anticipate as a vendor what I should be supplying them with. In many ways, I'm studying patient needs and … doctor needs to figure out what pharmaceutical companies are going to need so that we become the … next generation supplier."* CDO, SoftwareCom 2

The Digital Innovation CDO Domain

CDOs need a strong focus on strategic changes to organizational processes, products, services and business models. For example, a bank's CDO described an intriguing way the bank is challenging its existing business model and creating a separate "pure digital experience":

> In my role as CDO … I'm trying to get people to do something non-conventional that normally happens in a conventional way: you go into a bank branch, you see somebody, you shake their hand, you get a bank account, you get a mortgage. These are things that are traditionally done in a more physical way.
>
> CDO, FinancialServ 1

However, this CDO is not sure how this experiment will turn out, but that is fine. To accomplish digital innovations, CDOs need to be comfortable with indeterminacy and with continually experimenting. According to our interviewees, strong CDOs take an agile approach to innovation and continually drive experimentation and iteration. The experimentation approach involves creating a minimal viable digital product and developing it further based on a pilot implementation and feedback. The CDO from a media company described this way of working:

> *[We] are able to set up small meetings where we can test our minimal viable products... just looking at the opportunities that digital brings to reach people in your target audience more times in the day, as well as to offer products to more people via other platforms. ... You build things very lightly, very agilely and very much focused on speed and getting something out into the market and into the hands of consumers as early as possible, and then start learning together with the consumer because of how they interact with your product. [You] ... look at that and then try and build ... capabilities from there.*
>
> CDO, Media Publisher 2

In all the interviews, a common theme for the foundation of a successful CDO was being comfortable with indeterminacy, experimentation, learning and adaptation.

The Data Analytics CDO Domain

In the age of "big data," our interviewees pointed out that strong CDOs develop or acquire capabilities for data analysis so they can gain insights from both internal and external data sources. Some CDOs explained how they had built up data analytics portfolios, which involved them using both openly available data from forums or similar websites (see Table 14.2), and also internal data, to improve performance:

> *Those are the more ... non-structured data sets that we're interested in understanding: what's the general conversation, what's the general pulse? [For example] in the hospitality world, our hotel and resort client is the operator [of flagship chains]—Hilton, Regent, etc. But to suddenly get feedback from the end user, the person or traveler checking into [the hotel or resort] ... gives us so much more information.*
>
> CDO, ArchitectureDesign

Not all CDOs need to be technical experts—they do not need to be able to analyze data directly—but they do need to understand what data can do for their organizations and lead the efforts to analyze data for new insights. It is important to note that it is not necessary for CDOs to fully understand data analytics. Again, though, they should take an experimentation-oriented approach to building analytics capabilities. Successful CDOs are comfortable with learning as they go—as the ArchitectureDesign CDO indicated: "In data analytics, we're still trying to figure out what we need to do." This was the case for virtually all the CDOs we interviewed.

The Customer Engagement CDO Domain

CDOs also focus intensely on relationships with their organizations' customers—understanding the customer experience and the role of digital technologies in this experience. The end customer was the center of attention across our sample of CDOs. For example, the CDO of a healthcare software vendor whose clients are pharmaceutical companies described how he studies the needs of patients and doctors (the pharmaceutical companies' customers). The insights he gains from studying patients and doctors enables him to learn what health-related companies will need in the future (see example in Table 14.2). Another organization, a training service provider, allows customers to access most of its offers before they subscribe to its service:

> As a university student or a company, you [used to] have to sign up on our website and pay before you saw any types of opportunities or talent. The difference [and the value] now is [you see all this right away]. ... it is very much like a social network.
>
> CDO, DevelopSkill

To be successful, it is becoming critical for CDOs to focus on their organizations' end customers:

> [We are] looking at what type of content people are responding to really well. Where is there room for opportunity? What posts are not working so well? ... Social media [is becoming more important] because a lot of our partners come to us for social media activation and campaigns.
>
> CDO, DevelopSkill

According to the CDOs we spoke with, focusing on end customers is not always the key priority for many functional units in an organization—particularly those units that service other areas of the organization. Without exception, the CDOs we spoke to have a laser-like focus on the end customer.

All three domains were relevant for all the CDOs we interviewed to a lesser or greater extent. CDOs are responsible for questioning existing business models, evaluating customer-centeredness and using a variety of data for gaining insights. To deal with these business imperatives, CDOs must be well versed in experimenting with, and applying, a variety of digital technologies. However, each of the CDOs we interviewed told us that one of the domains was their primary focus in their explanations of their work. Next, we present the three CDO types we identified and illustrate how the different types emphasized diverse domains during the interviews.

Three Types of CDOs

The three types of CDO we identified are digital accelerators, digital marketers and digital harmonizers.

Digital Accelerator CDOs

We classified 13 of the CDOs in our sample as digital accelerators. This type of CDO spanned various industries, including financial services, manufacturing and retail. As shown in Table 14.3, the common characteristic of digital accelerator CDOs is that they drive digital innovation—typically complementing existing IT leaders who are predominantly involved with supporting operational and mission-critical activities. The existing IT leadership in these organizations focused on maintaining and advancing the current IT infrastructure and architecture, with a strong emphasis on reliability, performance and security.

The 13 digital accelerator CDOs pointed out that their organizations needed a secondary IT-related function freed from responsibilities of maintaining the existing IT infrastructure. These CDOs have the freedom and flexibility to experiment intensely with a variety of digi-

Table 14.3 The Digital Accelerator CDO Approach

Dimension	Characteristics	Illustrative Quotes
Key Capability	Digital innovation	*"My primary KPI [key performance indicator] that I set for myself is to create a digital experience that includes other things as well. [We are] a mobile bank, we provision and sign up bank accounts, savings, lines of credit only via the mobile phone. We have a website as well, but there are no branches."* CDO, FinancialServ 1
Primary Objective	Experimentation and implementation	*"[The IT department] had a very traditional approach, wanting to buy very expensive analytics packages ... have a two-year roll-out. I was not willing to take that time. ... I'm very careful to say we don't do education or training ... we are not in the business of training people in Google analytics or training people very hands on."* CDO, EducationOrg 1
Reason for Establishing the Role	To adopt bimodal IT, allowing the IT function to focus on the underlying infrastructure	*"In the old-fashioned way, [the IT function] worked very [well]. I don't know how much you are familiar with this bimodal way of working [described by] Gartner ... I think we are very good in this mode, mode one I think is the lower one ... the [old IT] processes in this company are not made for fast failure and [trial] and error."* CDO, FinancialServ 3

tal technologies. According to many interviewees, the scope of the CDO is different from that of IT executives in their organizations—less focused on operational reliability and more focused on experimenting with new capabilities in novel areas:

> *You simply build something separate anew as if you were a start-up—[you] just build a completely parallel, new infrastructure. By doing that, you remove a lot of the tension between digital and IT and the need to transform the technology and the ways of working that exist in IT.*
>
> CDO, FinancialServ 2

The CDO of a financial service organization explained that her role is needed to focus on different forms of innovation because the CIO is taking care of the operations and maintenance of existing IT activities. The CDO of an insurance company shared similar thinking. He explained that "digital" cannot become the top priority of the traditional IT executive's agenda in every organization because there are so many other tasks involved in maintaining existing systems:

> *Traditional IT leaders... [face] tremendous pressures to deliver and execute and support the operational systems ... Digital was always ... going to be deprioritized because of those pressures to deliver and execute the operational system.*
>
> CDO, InsuranceFirm

Digital accelerator CDOs therefore complement more conservative IT organizations by focusing on rapid development and evaluation of digital technologies. This type of CDO is found in organizations with well-established structures where the IT functions operate according to principles that require long planning cycles and slower execution. The role of digital accelerator CDOs is to achieve fast results by facilitating continual experimentation with minimal viable products of digital innovations.

The focus on experimentation allows for more flexibility without needing to align with other ongoing IT-related activities. Continuous experimentation was a common characteristic of the digital innovation approach followed by digital accelerator CDOs. Although other types of CDOs also used experimental processes, experimentation was the defining characteristic of digital accelerator CDOs. In many ways, what they described was more like a "skunk works" rather than the cross-organizational scope of other types of CDOs. Digital accelerator CDOs reported being insulated from the demands of ongoing operations, which allowed them to freely evaluate, test and learn about different digital innovations.

A key principle for digital accelerator CDOs is that they reduce the cycle time required for different areas to consider and incorporate digital innovations (see Table 14.3). According to the CDO in a media organization, this requires a "we don't need to build and create everything" mindset and seeking out available options, including social media, crowd sourcing and other platforms.

Even though a digital accelerator CDO "owns" new digital innovation projects, it is still necessary to align with existing IT initiatives. As the CDO of a manufacturing company explained, it is important to learn to respect the existing IT landscape:

> We need to be sure that the 'second speed' IT respects the major infrastructure. ... We don't want to be cowboys ... not respecting what we [already] have security-wise, technology-wise and stuff like that. It's the right balance that we need to find. It wasn't evident [in] the last couple of years, but we're almost there now.
>
> CDO, Manufacturing 2

Digital accelerator CDOs are generalists—focusing on a variety of digital opportunities. Note, however, that not all CDOs complement the IT function; some complement different units such as marketing, as described below

Digital Marketer CDOs

This type of CDO guides the organization's digital marketing efforts with an emphasis on customer intimacy through technologies like social media and mobile computing, as well as intensive analysis of customer data. We classified eight of our interviewees as digital marketer CDOs whose roles had been established to streamline online and offline marketing channels for engaging with the customers. These CDOs complement marketing efforts by deploying digital technologies that can enhance products, customer relationships and competitive position. Table 14.4 summarizes the digital marketer CDO approach.

The CDO in a publishing organization described how IT people were moved out of the IT function to assist the marketing department and how this eventually evolved into the CDO role:

> I had to hire people [who] had to think about products. We had to create a support team ... and gradually my role evolved from being the old-school IT manager to somebody [who] was thinking along with the business. ... [I] was appointed to a role [where I was]

responsible for product development.... The people in my department were more technical, of course. In the last couple of years, [the] marketing [department] was more into doing digital developments. [This] is what we call e-marketing in terms of making sure that we have the correct profile of our customers ... so we also had to think how digital marketing could be [implemented].

CDO, Media Publisher 4

The CDO of a manufacturing company tasked with digitizing the customer-facing part of the organization told us that it may be better for traditional marketing to report to the CDO:

My role is actually ... unique in ... that I manage the brand as well. We've just [moved] to a completely new re-branding process... If I was ever to leave the company and move to a new CDO role, I would like those responsibilities as well, because I think ... the CMO, or senior marketing person, has to report into a CDO ... I mean marketing itself; I don't think marketers have kept up with digital technology.

CDO, Manufacturing 1

Although this CDO's view is not necessarily held by all CDOs, it does highlight the importance of digital innovation to current-practice marketing efforts. The digital marketer CDO role is integral to the role of customer-facing units and is thus concerned with establishing digital channels to the customer and mobile solutions, and with understanding user

Table 14.4 The Digital Marketer CDO Approach

Dimension	Characteristics	Illustrative Quotes
Key Capability	Data analytics	"Our clients are hotel chains like Hilton, the Regent, ... but [hotel users now participate in] online communities about design, about the spaces that are being built, etc. ... We track these ... sites looking for [information]. We also look at ... how [we] can learn from [things] like Trip Advisor, ... design forums or discussion groups and [so on]." CDO, ArchitectureDesign
Primary Objective	Customer intimacy	"He [the CMO] asked for some advice from someone like me to ... show him what was possible on a digital front. I gave him some comparables of companies who, in the consumer goods space, could demonstrate real power of the brand, real strategic advantages [from] ... digital ... and presented a new customer face that was more in keeping with the millennial market and the younger markets, which he wanted to attract." CDO, ConsumerGood 1
Reason for Establishing the Role	To create a consistent customer experience across digital and non-digital channels	"Marketing falls within my responsibility but also internal marketing, external communications and so on. Effectively, our customers or potential customers have multiple different touchpoints [from which] they can reach out to us. Effectively, I have to manage all of those." CDO Manufacturing 1

experiences in leveraging digital capabilities. As one CDO indicated, she was hired to bring digital competencies to her organization's marketing practices:

> Digital is very much about delivering, or having a direct-direct relationship with the end customer. I was hired ... to bring that skill level or experience to the company, where previously they were dealing with a business-to-business relationship. ... Yes, marketing falls within my responsibility, but also internal marketing, external communication and so on.
>
> CDO, Manufacturing 1

Some of the digital marketer CDOs in our study run the digital side of marketing quite independently and almost as a standalone unit. For example, the CDO of a consumer goods company described her unit as a standalone startup with very specific goals that involved a major project:

> There's a very clear goal to try and bring it all together. We started off in a very separate fashion with the digital store (like an Apple app store), where you could buy content, and an e-commerce store where you could buy the hard goods. Finally, last year, we managed to bring it together [in] one store so that customers could have one [purchasing] experience.
>
> CDO, ConsumerGood 2

In this company, the CDO's unit will likely persist in its current standalone mode for a limited period of time. At some point, the major project may well be subsumed by pre-existing functions, such as marketing and sales.

However, some digital marketer CDOs may take on responsibility for the marketing function (see CDO of Manufacturing 1 in Table 14.4). The digital marketer role is therefore often either temporary until the organization gets up to speed, when the role is subsumed by the broader marketing organization—or the CDO becomes responsible for all marketing activities.

Digital Harmonizer CDOs

In addition to complementing the IT or the marketing functions, some CDOs are brought in to take an aggregate view of all ongoing digital initiatives. These are what we term digital harmonizer CDOs. The 14 CDOs we classified as digital harmonizers were charged with linking together a wide variety of digital initiatives in many different areas of their organizations, a situation that was prevalent among media firms[7] in our sample. The digital harmonizer role is a way of bringing these initiatives under a single, typically more strategic, umbrella. Digital harmonizers aggregate the disparate digital efforts distributed across the organization into a single unit and coordinate them. They emphasize governance and the need for transparency in digital projects. Table 14.5 summarizes the digital harmonizer CDO approach.

The CDO of a pharmaceutical company vividly illustrated the digital harmonizer CDO role:

> The first thing I did was to establish a digital council, [which includes] our CIOs, [our] CMOs, our top leadership of the organization. As digital evolves in a company, you see a lot of things pop up in many places, but they [aren't aware of] each other... A lot of digital activity started before I was here. ... There was so much ... going on across

divisions, and teams and countries, that it really came bottom-up, and the top manage-
ment said, "Okay, we probably need to take all of this activity and put it into a strategic
approach."

CDO, HealthRelated

In her effort to elevate digital innovation activities to a more strategic level, the CDO of a museum explained how a lot of digital work had already been done in the organization, but it still needed direction, which she aimed to provide:

It was really more about changing the culture and the approach, the strategic approach,
to doing the work they were already doing, but doing it in a much more thoughtful way
[so] that the whole institution was working in the same direction, as opposed to children
in parallel play doing their own thing, which was how it was before.

CDO, CultureHouse 2

This CDO also often emphasized the need to catch up with digital trends at a strategic level, or to lead organization-wide digital transformation.

Table 14.5 The Digital Harmonizer CDO Approach

Dimension	Characteristics	Illustrative Quotes
Key Capability	Customer engagement	*"It's a complete shift in the way we deliver customer value because we understood that … other organizations like LinkedIn and other job postings [were] opening up their doors for anyone to look and see without having a payroll. We [asked ourselves] 'How do we make our organization more accessible to anyone?'"* CDO, DevelopSkill
Primary Objective	Enterprise integration	*"One of the things that I did was [to] build a digital strategy and a strategic plan for the next 10 years and … a road map. … [I] then worked with government, so that instead of everyone doing their own individual digital projects … there was a process in place where a group of people … at the working level [would] look at [digital ideas] and then … very senior [managers would] look at [the ideas] and set priorities and continue to evolve those priorities."* CDO, Culture House 2
Reason for Establishing the Role	When business silos are limiting the impact of digital innovation	*"When we set up new programs or projects, we create a team to work on [them].… We call [these teams] 'squads' in the same way that Spotify uses that term. [Thus] we create [a] central team of skills from [within] the organization. [For] example,… we put a couple of developers, a solution architect, a user researcher [together with] a data scientist and a designer [into a squad]… so [we] have the data side very much represented within the digital side as well. We make sure that we cover all relevant areas. These cross-functional teams [are] created from across … the different divisions, including digital, data and technology."* CDO, GovInstitution

Digital harmonizer CDOs both manage digital initiatives across the organization and elevate attention to these initiatives to a strategic level. Their organizations already have some level of digital capabilities, and one mechanism for raising attention to digital innovation to a strategic level is to add the CDO role to the C-suite. Digital harmonizers often described how they need to create connections between existing and new digital capabilities. The basic idea is to move digital innovation projects back to other functional groups after they have been implemented:

> Before having a digital [department], some organizations that were really innovation orientated had somebody in charge of R&D innovation. Marketing, [HR, finance, etc.] had their responsibilities, [but] digital changes [everything] because [its] scope ... is so vast, and it's so transversal. ... At [some] point, it's [maybe] important to have somebody covering all [the digital initiatives] and making the connections between everybody. ... But then every specialist has to take the responsibility for his or her own field, because at the end of the day, it's going to be innovation in marketing, or innovation in finance, etc.
>
> CDO, RetailCommunication

The role of the digital harmonizer CDO is to constantly act as an intermediary and, by doing so, achieve strategic visibility. However, this is not a pure top-down strategic role because the CDO needs to consider existing capabilities. The digital harmonizer creates links to the existing organization through a continuous flow of new ideas. Organizations with digital harmonizer CDOs emphasize visibility, prioritization and coordination of digital efforts (see Table 14.5).

In addition to their long-term and strategic focus, digital harmonizer CDOs indicated a concern for reconciling existing organizational values with digital innovations. Transitioning gradually toward a more digital organization is a long-term effort and can result in fundamental transformation.

Comparison of Three CDO Types

From our interviews, we saw that each CDO type focused mainly on one of the domains.[8] As shown in Table 14.6, each of the three CDO types focuses on building a distinct digital capability: the digital accelerator emphasizes shortening innovation cycles and experimentation; the digital marketer is highly focused on the data analytics domain; and the digital harmonizer aggregates existing digital initiatives to strategically engage with the customer and streamline existing and new digital initiatives.

Table 14.6 Overview of the Three Types of CDOs and Their Key Characteristics

Dimension	Digital Accelerator	Digital Marketer	Digital Harmonizer
Key Capability	Digital innovation	Data analytics	Customer engagement
Primary Objective	Experimentation and implementation	Customer intimacy	Enterprise integration
Reason for Establishing the Role	To adopt bimodal IT while allowing the IT unit to focus on the underlying infrastructure	To create a consistent customer experience across digital and non-digital channels	When enterprise business silos are limiting the impact of digital innovation

Bridging Traditional IT (CIO's Domain) and Digital Innovation (CDO's Domain)

Having looked at the three types of CDOs and their key capabilities, we now turn to the relationship between the CDO's and CIO's organizations. Over the years, the IT function in many organizations has evolved from being a supporting unit to become a critical strategic partner of other business units.[9,10] This strategic focus was often accompanied by greater attention to enterprise information systems (such as ERP and CRM) as critical enablers of business operations.

However, the evolution has pigeon-holed some CIOs, in terms both of the opinions of other business units and of the mindsets of CIOs themselves. Business units perceive CIOs as technical specialists who focus on enterprise systems and infrastructural investments, and are forced to conduct their processes through a standardized, centrally mandated architecture. Similarly, CIOs themselves often perceive their role as associated with enterprise systems and the IT infrastructure. As a consequence, experiments with digital innovations may not be high on a CIO's agenda because he or she is focused on maintaining large-scale mission-critical systems performance in a reliable and secure manner. Often, the CIO simply cannot add more responsibilities to her agenda, as illustrated by one of the CDOs we interviewed:

> The poor CIO is always worried about legacy systems, maintaining all of the right stuff for legal matters, compliance, regulation and so forth. [Given] that,... how can we [the organization] innovate [with IT]? Who [is thinking about]. what would we be doing [if we didn't have the boring email we've been using for 10 years]. How would we be tracking conversations? You ... need two positions. ... You have [huge] amounts of information that you need to maintain, and, suddenly, [the] person who's responsible for that ... no longer [has] any more time in their schedule. They [CDOs] [are not constrained by] worrying about existing hardware, and [it's not their responsibility] if there's an emergency ... or the power goes off or [a] cable is cut. They just keep focused on innovating.
>
> CDO, ArchitectureDesign

The increasing demand from the business for digital innovation means that there are notorious tensions in some organizations between business units and the IT function.[11] Even where there is no problem with alignment, IT departments often find themselves unable to keep up with the increasing demands from the organization.[12] As a result, user departments are increasingly running their own digital initiatives.[13] Doing this has become easier because of the availability of various social media platforms, cloud solutions, freeware or beta versions of software—technology that requires minimal up-front investment. Digital marketing strategies, in particular, often require little in the way of dedicated technology investments.[14] Similarly, modern HR units must now use digital recruitment.[15]

The challenges faced by large, preoccupied IT departments, the necessity of digital marketing, and other units like marketing and HR initiating their own digital innovation projects are all catalysts for adopting a CDO role.[16] In many ways the CDO acts as a buffer between the business and the IT unit. The CDO complements the IT unit, focusing on end customers and integrating existing and new digital initiatives. As one of our interviewees (the CDO of a media publisher) pointed out, the CDO role is vital for an organization's strategy:

> If you make it [the CDO role] a board-level function, there's usually a strategy shift which comes with it as well, and there's no such thing as a digital strategy. You just have

a [business] strategy ... if [in] 2015 ... you did not take into account that the world is changing because of digital, then [you had] a bad [business] strategy.

CDO, Media Publisher 2

All CDOs are concerned with digital innovation and getting closer to the customer in the digital space. They also need extensive knowledge of digital technologies and an awareness of data analytics capabilities. In addition to building up their organizations' digital capabilities, CDOs primarily lead the digital strategy. Such a strategy might be to partner with the "Googles and Watsons of this world," as the CDO of a pharmaceutical company explained:

We're really scientific chemistry nerds, and we don't have any ambition to be a technology company. In order to survive, we have to be very good at partnering with the top tech partners. [Without] ... advanced analytics and digital capabilities... it would be very difficult to stay competitive [and developing those capabilities in-house would not be possible]. [But] if we partner with the Googles ... or the Watson IBMs of this world, they have to be the best because [if they aren't] they'll lose ... customers.

CDO, HealthRelated

There are various reasons why an organization may decide to adopt a separate CDO role, including:

- The IT department is preoccupied with large-scale infrastructural projects or is in a weak political position
- The marketing department has a rigid focus on traditional marketing methods, and there is no trusted relationship between IT and marketing
- The organization has many local digital initiatives but lacks a strategic digital direction.

However, there are also many instances where the need for a CDO is not apparent—particularly in organizations where CIOs have found a way to "ambidextrously" drive rapid-paced digital innovation while simultaneously attending to the IT infrastructure.[17] For example, the CIO of Hilti, which manufactures premium power tools, points out how his IT function manages to balance continuous experimentation with new technologies while still maintaining its primary focus on enterprise-wide process management.[18] The IT function's experimentation has led to a focus on application software for Hilti's products, which has extended the reach of IT beyond the company's internal systems and processes.

There seems to be a similar shift occurring with other top-performing CIOs. A recent survey suggests that CIOs of highly successful organizations pay close attention to external customers and maintain a strong focus on innovation.[19] These practices are consistent with the activities of CDOs in our research.

It is also important to note that CIOs provide a solid foundation for CDOs to build digital capabilities. Over the years, CIOs have established stable robust infrastructures that provide the platform for what CDOs are able to accomplish. Without integrated processes, data transparency and information management policies in place, CDOs would not have a good basis for scaling their initiatives.

Thus, we conclude that a new executive role is needed to fill specific gaps in an organization's IT landscape. These gaps may be filled by existing executives (the CIO or the CMO) or by new digital executives (the CDO), but the key is to clearly delineate the space that the executive occupies. It is also important to define clear key performance indicators (KPIs) for all executives driving digital innovation. By clearly defining the roles of executives involved in digital innovations, it is possible to avoid situations where one person tries to navigate the whole digital transformation:

> Someone has hired someone to fill what they perceived to be a gap. That person [finds] ... it's hard to make things really happen because [they] don't have ... the [authority] to influence directly IT execution, operations, marketing or whatever. Put it this way, if somebody was to offer me a job as CDO where there's already a CIO, ... an operations person, ... marketing, and my job is to try to integrate all of these things, I would run for the hills.
>
> CDO, InsuranceFirm

Typically, IT-related skills and titles change rapidly. Even though CIOs have been around for decades, the role is still seen as ambiguous.[20] Thus, over time, the title "CDO" might evolve into other related roles, such as "chief innovation officer," "director of emerging platforms," "director of digital technologies" or "head of digital innovation."[21] In some organizations, the CDO role may re-merge with the existing CIO role or with the marketing unit. Nevertheless, all current evidence points to a future where "digital" will remain one of the top priorities in organizations, and executive leadership for digital innovation will be needed in one form or another.

Concluding Comments

We interviewed 35 CDOs from various industries. Our analysis is consistent with previous investigations that have found CDOs are central to innovative digital transformation efforts.[22] However, we have gone beyond previous work by reviewing a broader sample of organizations and identifying three distinct types of CDOs: digital accelerators, digital marketers and digital harmonizers. Digital accelerator CDOs mostly focus on establishing a digital innovation and experimentation capability; digital marketers emphasize data analytics; digital harmonizers focus on customer engagement. We categorized 13 of the 35 interviewed CDOs as digital accelerators, eight as digital marketers and 14 as digital harmonizers.

To provide a reference point for future studies, we have characterized these CDO types along three dimensions: key capabilities, objectives and reasons for establishing the role. The three CDO types differ along these dimensions and have distinct focal domains in which they build digital capabilities: digital innovation, data analytics and customer engagement. The distinction between CDO types and digital capabilities provides a framing for the role of future digital leaders, whatever their label might be. The CDO role is still emerging, and more and more organizations may decide to adopt the role. Alternatively, the CDO role may, in time, transform into other roles. At present, it is not possible to say which route will be most popular. In the meantime, organizations should consider appointing a CDO as a way to capitalize on the potential of digital innovation, and we believe this article can provide guidance on deciding whether to adopt this executive role.

Appendix: Research Methodology

We conducted a series of exploratory interviews with CDOs from a sample designed to include as wide a variety of industries as possible. To ensure we spoke with firms that were first movers worldwide, we approached the founder of CDO Club (http://cdoclub.com), the company that established the first CDO network. We joined CDO Club on LinkedIn and started approaching CDOs who were members of the group. The job titles of all informants in our sample explicitly stated "Chief Digital Officer."

As a result, we spoke with 35 CDOs from industries spanning automotive, financial services, healthcare, software, publishing, governmental and not-for-profit organizations in a variety of countries (see Table 14.1). The CDO role is fairly new, so most of our interviewees were in the first year or two in that position.

The data collection and analysis were iterative and emergent. After the first few interviews, we analyzed and coded the data, and used the initial codes in later interviews to contrast and compare further emerging themes. Since our study was exploratory, we aimed to find out what "digital" means; rather than providing definitions a priori our goal was to learn what digital meant from the CDO's perspective.

Notes

1 Rickards, T., Smaje, K. and Sohoni, V. "Transformer in chief: The new chief digital officer," McKinsey & Company, 2015.

2 Grossman, R. and Rich, J. *The Rise of the Chief Digital Officer*, Russell Reynolds Associates, 2016.

3 Singh, A. and Hess, T. "How Chief Digital Officers Promote the Digital Transformation of their Companies," *MIS Quarterly Executive* (16:1), March 2017, pp. 1–17.

4 Peppard, J., Edwards, C. and Lambert, R. "Clarifying the ambiguous role of the CIO," *MIS Quarterly Executive* (10:2), June 2011, pp. 115–117.

5 Weill, P. and Woerner, L. S. *Top-Performing CIOs in the Digital Era*, MIT Sloan CISR Research Breifing, Vol XVI, Number 5, May, 2016

6 Pseudonyms have been used for each of the companies.

7 Grossman, R. and Rich, J., "The Rise of the Chief Digital Officer," Russell Reynolds Associates, *Harvard Business School Publishing*, 2016.

8 Other researchers have recently identified additional CDO types, including entrepreneur, digital evangelist and coordinator (see Singh, A., and Hess, T., op. cit., March 2017). The digital accelerator encompasses the entrepreneurial spirit; the digital marketer has some characteristics of the digital evangelist but focuses primarily on developing digital marketing activities; the digital harmonizer to some extent is equivalent to the coordinator role but with a strong goal to streamline internal processes for achieving customer engagement

9 Agarwal, R. and Sambamurthy, V. "Principles and Models for Organizing the IT Function," *MIS Quarterly Executive* (1:1), March 2002, pp. 158–162.

10 Guillemette, M. and Pare, G. "Toward a New Theory of the Contribution of the IT Function in Organizations," *MIS Quarterly* (36:2), 2012, pp. 529–551.

11 Henderson, J. C. and Venkatraman, H. "Strategic Alignment: Leveraging Information Technology for Transforming Organizations," *IBM Systems Journal* (32:1), 1993, pp. 472–484.

12 "Surfing a digital wave, or drowning?" *The Economist*, December 13, 2013, available at http://www.economist.com/news/business/21591201-information-technology-everywhere-companies-it-departments-mixed.

13 Nylen, D., Holmstrom, J. and Lyytinen, K. "Oscillating Between Four Orders of Design: The Case of Digital Magazines," *Design Issues* (30:3), Summer 2014.

14 Deans, C. P. "The Impact of Social Media on C-level Roles," *MIS Quarterly Executive* (10:4), December 2011, pp. 187–200.

15 Purvis, J. "Human Resources Marketing and Recruiting: Essentials of Digital Recruiting," *Handbook of Human Resources Management*, August 31, 2015, pp. 53–71.

16 Hess, T., Matt, C., Benlian, A. and Wiesböck, F. "Options for Formulating a Digital Transformation Strategy," *MIS Quarterly Executive* (15:2), June 2016, pp. 123–139.

17 Gregory, R. W., Keil, M., Muntermann, J. and Mahring, M. "Paradoxes and the Nature of Ambidexterity in IT Transformation Programs," *Information Systems Research* (26:1), 2015, pp. 57–80.

18 vom Brocke, J. "Interview with Martin Petry on 'Digital Innovation for the Networked Society,'" *Business & Information Systems Engineering* (58:3), 2016, pp. 239–241.

19   Weill, P. and Woerner, L. S., op. cit., 2016.
20   Peppard, J., Edwards, C. and Lambert, R., op. cit., June 2011.
21   Bird, J. "Fierce competition for chief digital officers," *Financial Times*, September 29, 2015.
22   Singh, A. and Hess, T., op. cit., March 2017.

Questions for Discussion

1   Are CDO roles only relevant for companies with large R&D budgets?
2   How is the role of CDOs different from IT executives?
3   How can CDOs achieve a balance between experimentation and alignment with existing IT initiatives?
4   Should traditional marketing roles report to the CDO, or should it be the other way around? Is it better to have the CDO as a standalone unit?
5   Why is it important for organizations to consider having a CDO?
6   Is interviewing CDOs the best way to find if the role is needed in an organization?
7   What academic qualification, and/or professional experience do you think is required to acquire the CDO role?

Further Reading

Singh, A., Hess, T. (2017). How Chief Digital Officers Promote the Digital Transformation of their Companies. *MIS Quarterly Executive*, *16*(1), 1–17.
Sebastian, I., Ross, J., Beath, C., Mocker, M., Moloney, K., Fonstad, N. (2017). How big old companies navigate digital transformation. *MIS Quarterly Executive*, *13*(3), 197–212.

Chapter 15

Joe Peppard

RETHINKING THE CONCEPT OF THE IS ORGANIZATION

OVER THE LAST 50 years, scholars have used the information systems (IS) organization both as a dependent and as an independent variable in their research. Yet, do conceptualizations of the IS organization reflect findings from research studying requirements for successfully harnessing information, systems and technology to achieve operational and strategic objectives? Whilst this questions is of particular concern of this article, it also raise the wider issue as to the exact role, function and design of an IS unit in contemporary organizations and, indeed, whether the concept has outlived its usefulness. In particular, what actually is an IS organization in today's highly connected, 'always on', digital world.

Typically, researchers conceptualize abstract concepts in order to express them in ways that are accessible to direct study or to isolate them from the main phenomena of interest. In so doing, they create or fashion a mental structure of what can be an intangible notion. But any conceptualization must mirror reality if it is to be a legitimate representation. In the IS research literature, concepts such as technology acceptance (Davis, 1989; Venkatesh et al., 2003), IS service quality (Jiang et al., 2002; Pitt et al., 1995), end-user computer satisfaction (Doll & Torkzadeh, 1991), systems usage (Burton-Jones & Straub, 2006), information systems success (DeLone & McLean, 1992) and user involvement (Barki & Hartwick, 1989) are just some that have been conceptualized in studies. However, if a conceptualization does not accurately reflect the phenomena it purports to characterize, then any findings or conclusions will at best be compromised or at worse dangerous.

In this article, the notion of the IS organization, as defined and conceptualized in the research literature, is analyzed and assessed. In particular, the appropriateness of assumptions that lie behind these conceptualizations are surfaced and the implications of portrayals for theory development and practice are considered. As part of the analysis, findings from these studies are considered to determine whether they are actually contributing to the problems that many organizations are experiencing with their information technology (IT) investments, and their inability to achieve investment objectives (c.f. National Audit Office, 2006; Nelson, 2005; Shpilberg et al., 2007; The Royal Academy of Engineering, 2004).

This article first reviews the evolution of the concept of an IS organization, surfacing the different labels that have been attached to it over the years. It then moves on to develop a sensitizing lens to provide an overarching framework for the research. Having outlined the research method, we then present portrayals of the IS organization in research studies published in leading academic and practitioner journals. With the aid of the sensitizing lens, these are then critiqued and analyzed. The article concludes with the implications of this analysis for research, teaching and practice.

A Short History of the Evolution of the Information Systems Organization

What is today generally referred to as the *IS organization* in research studies represents a concept that has evolved over the last 60 years, not just in name, but in role, function and position in an organization. Words such as 'information', 'systems', 'services', 'processing', 'management', 'data', 'technology' and 'computer' have been combined in many permutations to refer to this organizational unit. Labels such as Computer Department, Electronic Data Processing (eDP) Department, Data Processing Department, IT Function, Management Information Systems (MIS) Department, Computer Services, Information Technology Department, Information Systems Department, IS Group, Information Systems and Technology Department, Information Services, Information Management Department, Digital Business Department and Business Technology are just some that have appeared over the decades and that can be found referred to in studies (e.g. Ahituv & Hadass, 1978; Jiang et al., 2003; Nelson & Cooprider, 1996; Olson & Chervany, 1980; Ranganathan & Kannabiran, 2004; Wang & Barron, 1995).

Moreover, these labels have also tended to change over time, with any modification in name usually reflecting a new role and focus for information, systems and technology. Early eDP Departments, for example, concentrated on just that, the processing of corporate data. The key role of such departments was essentially to keep the organization's computer system up and running. Data, in the form of punched cards, were brought to the computer room or bureau to be processed, usually in batch mode. At that time, technology investments were primarily made to automate clerical tasks, where cost reduction and improvements in efficiency were the key investment objectives. The subsequent focus on the provision of information for management decision-making saw many organizations rename this unit the MIS or Information Services Department. More recently, in some organizations, Digital Business Departments and Business Technology have appeared, replacing what may once have been called Data Processing Departments, reflecting the emergence of the internet, e-commerce, mobile, cloud computing and the increasing prevalence of IT in the conduct of business. One study has even introduced the label of the 'e-IT Department' (Earl & Khan, 2001).

Examining advances in technology and the corresponding shifts in the operational and strategic role reveal an evolution in how information, systems and technology is managed in an organization. Moreover, drawing on prescriptive and descriptive research studies (e.g. Agarwal & Beath, 2007; Broadbent & Kitzis, 2005; Chun & Mooney, 2009; Feeny & Ross, 2000; Li et al., 2006; Mack & Monnoyer, 2004; Peppard, 2010; Karahanna & Preston, 2013; Smaltz et al., 2006), we can also map the changing role of the most senior manager of the IS organization over time, which can be seen as a surrogate for the evolving requirements for the management of IS/IT, reflecting the shifting focus and emphasis of IT investments. In a similar fashion, labels attached to this leadership role have also evolved. Early incumbents were eDP managers evolving to IT managers/directors, chief information officer (CIO) and, more latterly, Chief Digital Officers (CDOs). What is without doubt, the management challenge is getting more complex as technology becomes more ubiquitous, applications become more sophisticated, IT deployment more pervasive, connectivity much easier and the role of IT becomes ever more strategic.

Sensitizing Lens

To establish a sensitizing lens through which to explore how the IS organization is conceptualized in studies, three related streams of research are examined and synthesized. The first is research that addresses the pertinent question of responsibility for IS and where it resides. The historical dominance of functional structures sees most organizations establish separate units based on roles, such as accounting, marketing, research and development, logistics and IS with clearly defined boundaries. These units are staffed by people with specialized knowledge, providing efficiency and productivity benefits to an organization as well as career paths and clarity of responsibilities (i.e. sales department for sales and manufacturing for production). Whilst this logic might work for some functions, all the evidence indicates that it proves problematic in the context of IS. A key reason for this relates to the ontological basis of IS – essentially what is being managed – the second theme that is explored. Building on the foundation established by these two research streams, the final stream is concerned with research that explores the challenge of coordinating and integrating knowledge, dispersed across multiple organizational units, to achieve IS value expectations.

Locus of Responsibility for Managing Information Systems

Over two decades ago, Boynton et al. (1992) posed the question 'whose responsibility is IT management?' advocating that line managers had a key role to play, a position that had been advocated by Rockart (1988) some years earlier where 'the line' was urged to take a strong leadership role in the management of IT.[1] Some years later, Rockart et al. (1996) noted that

> [u]nless IT is included in line managers' strategy and tactics, and unless line managers can effectively understand and implement a process view of the world, the best IT organizations are almost powerless. For the last decade, we and others have pointed out that line leadership is an absolute necessity.
>
> (p. 53)

In addition to line management, the crucial responsibilities of other non-IT employees in the success of IT projects (and consequently associated IT investments) is widely established (Kohli & Devaraj, 2003; Maklan et al., 2011; Peppard, 2007; Taylor-Cummings, 1998; Sauer & Cuthbertson, 2003) as is the call for strong partnerships between IS and non-IT staff (Peppard & Ward, 1999; Ross et al., 1996). This latter point acknowledging the disconnect that can exist between these two camps. Research exploring alignment between business and IS/IT strategies has identified the absence of a close relationship between 'the business' and IS organization – note reference to an explicit separation – and lack of support for IT from non-IT executives as key inhibitors (Fonstad & Subramani, 2009; Luftman & Brier, 1999). Studies have reported that addressing the social dimension is critical in achieving alignment between IS and business strategies (Schlosser et al., 2015), and that alignment is greatly facilitated when business and IS executives have shared domain knowledge as well as regular communication (Reich & Benbasat, 2000; Tan & Gallupe, 2006). The key role played by the chief executive officer in IT assimilation has also been highlighted in studies (Armstrong & Sambamurthy, 1999; Peppard, 2010).

The role of human agency, particularly 'users', is also widely acknowledged (Markus & Robey, 1988; Orlikowski & Baroudi, 1990; Orlikowski & Gash, 1994). Consequently, success with IS projects is less about technology deployment than it is about managing the organizational change that accompanies its deployment (Markus, 2004; Orlikowski & Hofman, 1997; Peppard & Ward, 2005; Peppard, 2007) with the payback from IT investments realized through the development and orchestrated interplay of complementary IT and business capabilities (Barua & Mukhopadhyay, 2000; Davenport et al., 2001; Hughes & Scott Morton, 2006; Peppard, 2007; Thorp, 1999). For analytical tools and other technology investments for tackling so called 'big data,' if employees cannot 'work with information' and give meaning to it, then it is unlikely that any insight will emerge no matter how successful the technology deployment is (Davenport, 1994; Davenport & Prusak, 1997; Kohli & Devaraj, 2003; Marchand & Peppard, 2013; Marchand et al., 2000).

Moreover, there is also growing consensus that authority and decision-making responsibility for the management of IS is no longer the monopoly of an IT management elite (Huang et al., 2010; Lohmeyer et al., 2002; Ross & Weill, 2002; Weill & Ross, 2004). Decisions, traditionally made within an IS organization (a legacy of an earlier era when the role of IT was less important in shaping performance), are being devolved into the remit of senior business executives, business line management and end users (Ross & Weill, 2002). The research work in IT governance, calling for the establishment of structures and instruments to frame behaviors regarding decision-making rights, attests to this (Agarwal & Sambamurthy, 2002; Weill & Ross, 2004). Governance mechanisms, such as steering committees and other cross unit forums, charge back and co-location focus on encouraging intra-organizational involvement and allocating responsibilities in considering IS issues and for IS decision-making. Crucially, and what is usually not made explicit, is that these mechanisms facilitate the bringing together of people with relevant knowledge to achieve particular outcomes. For example, charge back has been shown to foster communications between an IS function and business units with these conversations generating a shared understanding for both parties of the cost and benefits of alternative IS investments and service offerings (Ross & Feeny, 1999).

Ontological Assumptions of Information Systems Management

The prescriptions emanating from the previous discourse are premised on the assumption that they will improve how IS are managed in organizations. The phrases 'manage IS' and 'IS management' tend to be widely used, not only in the context of the IS organization, but also in the wider discourse within both the IS discipline and general management. But what does 'IS management' mean and, crucially, what is actually being managed? Is it concerned with the management of the IS organization? Or, is it about directly managing IS? These questions raise a more fundamental one, can IS *really* be managed?

Of course, any discourse around this latter question raises the wider issue as to what IS (both singular and plural) actually is/are (Alter, 2008; Beynon-Davis, 2010; Bryant, 2008; Lee et al., 2015; Paul, 2010a, b), its relationship to technology (Orlikowski, 2010; Orlikowski & Iacono, 2001; Orlikowski & Scott, 2008; Scott & Orlikowski, 2013) and, indeed, what constitutes the IS discipline (Banville & Landry, 1989; Benbasat & Zmud, 2003; March & Niederman, 2012; Somers, 2010). Moreover, addressing the question as to whether IS can be managed possibly gets to the nub of the issue of generating value from IS, and two contrasting perspectives can be gleaned from the discourse in the literature. The first is that IS can be managed; the second, that it can't.

In much of the IS literature, the dominant practice is to objectify IS (in fact, 'IS' and 'IT' are generally used interchangeably), portraying it as data, information (sometimes knowledge), systems, hardware, software (including licenses), contracts, staff and associated costs (e.g. development and maintenance). As such, it is depicted as something – essentially an artefact – that can be directly manipulated. Even with outsourcing, the decision is typically framed as deciding what should be resourced externally, and consequently, the outcome of any decision to outsource is considered as managing contracts, supply of services (e.g. service level agreements, service catalogues and change requests) and relationships. It may be this logic that sees organizations maintain an IS unit as a separate organizational construct, the assumption being that IS, as an objective construction, is manageable from within this structure. Importantly, what it suggests is that what is to be managed can be ring-fenced and contained within clear organizational boundaries, assigned a head (i.e. the CIO), given resources and a mandate that is often framed as optimizing or maximizing a return from any spend, all within an acceptable level risk. Indeed, it is in this context that different 'IT management profiles' frame Guillemette & Pare's (2012) typology of IS organizations.

As previously noted, the concept of 'IT management' dates back to an era when computers were large, complex and expensive, requiring specialist facilities and knowledge, where the key managerial challenge was to keep the computer functioning. The practice of IT management thus became associated with the management activities to keep the machine working, with requirements evolving over time to encompass the design and implementation of systems and the provision and presentation of information. And whilst the concept of *information systems* (as opposed to IT) management is now in common use, the tasks ascribed to IS management have expanded to include IS strategy formulation and execution, innovation, IT service management, IT implementation, project management, managing software development projects, protecting information assets, technology and service procurement, vendor management and, in many cases, the delivery of benefits from IT investments.

In fact, the notion of IS management is tautological, equating to the management of IS. It conjures up the notion that ontologically, IS the artefacts are something that can actually be managed. The focus of attention is thus on these artefacts and their management. Perhaps this is why management teams, who are disappointed with the perceived return from their IT investments, instigate programs to improve the performance of their IS organization; the assumption being that this is where the genesis of this problem lies. Indeed, studies reporting on such initiatives typically begin with this proposition (c.f. Cross et al., 1997; Vaast & Levina, 2006). For example Cross et al.'s (1997) presentation of the transformation of the IT function at British petroleum noted that '[i]n 1989, the *IT function* of the exploration and production division of British Petroleum Company set out to transform *itself* in response to a severe economic environment and poor internal perceptions of IT performance' (emphasis added).

If we take a contrasting perspective, where the focus is not to manage IT (or IS) *perse*, but to generate business value from IS note that we are not specifying what this value is other than have a positive impact on performance then a somewhat different agenda emerges. This viewpoint acknowledges IS in organizations as a situated and socially constructed phenomenon, enabling us to question the very nature of what is sought to be managed. Specifically, it proposes that IS is not a 'thing' or set of 'things' that can be managed or manipulated directly, but that generating value from IS is a multifaceted and complex challenge; it is clearly not about 'technical wizardry' (Dvorak et al., 1997). It necessitates understanding how IT impacts industry and competitive dynamics, identifying new strategic opportunities, assessing and assimilating technological innovations, deriving new technology-enabled business models and organizational blueprints, prioritizing investment opportunities, managing IT-enabled change, deploying appropriate technology, steering IT projects, managing risk, selecting and managing vendors, exploiting investments in technology, ensuring appropriate usage of information systems, creating the environment for staff to embrace the right behaviors and values to work with information and ensuring that the value delivered from any application of IT is captured by the organization. All related activities, practices and processes cannot happen within the confines of a separate organizational unit, labeled the IS organization, but are pervasive, organizational-wide concerns and endeavors.

Moreover, activities and practices are underpinned by the application of knowledge: knowledge that is distributed across the organization. For example, developing an IS strategy is a knowledge-based task, as is coding systems. Using information effectively is critically dependent on the application of knowledge to make sense of data and ascribe meaning to it. In fact, technical infrastructure is the embodiment of knowledge: knowledge that has been deployed by systems architects, developers, communications experts, etc. in its design and construction. Outsourcing arrangements can be similarly viewed as having a basis in knowledge; indeed, many organizations argue that they have outsourced their IT to an external service provider or vendor, as it will provide them with access to knowledge that they do not currently possess. The challenge in generating value from IS can therefore be framed as one concerned with coordinating and integrating this knowledge.

Generating Value from Information Systems: A Quest to Coordinate and Integrate Knowledge

What is being claimed in the previous discourse is that, the necessary responsibilities and knowledge to generate business value from IS are distributed throughout the organization, across departmental, functional, divisional and geographical boundaries; sometimes even organizational boundaries. Crucially, it is not located solely in an IS unit and under the jurisdiction of the CIO (Peppard et al., 2000; Sambamurthy & Zmud, 1997). For example, prescriptions around the IS strategy process demand the involvement of executive management if it is to be effective (Earl, 1989, 1993). This is because there is incomplete knowledge in a (separate) IS unit to successfully develop this strategy.[2] Similarly, IT project teams created to implement new information systems are typically composed of both IS specialists and managers and users from 'the business.' The reason is that the knowledge and skills to successfully implement a new IT system are not resident solely in the IT function. Studies have noted that '[a] project team, set up to design and implement a large-scope IT system, is essentially tasked with integrating distributed knowledge' (Newell et al., 2004) and that this integrative capability has important implications for its success (Mitchell, 2006; Orlikowski & Robey, 2004). Outsourcing research similarly highlights the challenge of knowledge coordination and integration in meeting expected outcomes (Espinosa et al., 2007; Faraj & Sproull, 2000; Gopal & Gosain, 2010; Mehta & Bharadwaj, 2015; Sabherwal, 2003).

In fact, much of the knowledge required to generate value for IS investments is under the control of other C-level executives and not the CIO (Peppard, 2007). This is why it has been stressed as being of crucial importance for the CIO to build relationships with these executives (Gerth & Peppard, 2014). Whilst not expressed in such terms, the rationale for this is, in effect, to ease access to knowledge resources under their influence. If not, gaining access to this knowledge will be difficult, if not impossible, to achieve. Through their IT governance initiatives organizations do seek to bring together those employees with relevant knowledge to make decisions concerning IS. Cross functional, departmental and divisional forums, such as steering committees, are established in recognition of the limitations of formal functional and hierarchical structures when diverse and dispersed knowledge is required.

Even with access, however, the organization must have a capability to integrate this knowledge (Grant, 1996; Kogut & Zander, 1996; Spender, 1996). Generating value from

IS thus becomes a task of coordinating and integrating relevant knowledge that is distributed organization-wide. This raises a conundrum for many CIOs: that they are held accountable for delivering value from IS investments without having access and authority over necessary knowledge resources (Peppard, 2007).

How distributed knowledge is coordinated and integrated is less developed in the literature. One perspective advocates the importance of networks of strong, personal relationships, developed over time, across groups, departments, functions and divisions that provide the basis for trust, cooperation and collection action (Adler & Kwon, 2002; Lin, 2001; Nahapiet & Ghoshal, 1998). Whilst this viewpoint suggests that this coordination and integration of knowledge is an attribute of relationships between people, not of the individuals themselves (Adler & Kwon, 2002), the cognitive challenge cannot be ignored as any integration will occur in the minds of managers.

Access to knowledge is thus dependent on an individual's network of ties as well as the nature and content of the relationship between parties (Adler & Kwon, 2002). With their IT governance mechanisms, such as cross department forums, organizations do attempt to facilitate the creation of these contacts and ties. However, to be effective they must be accompanied by recognition of the value of collaboration and shared knowledge that is based on a shared language and cognition to aid mutual understanding (Tsai & Ghoshal, 1998). The motivation to share and combine knowledge and collaborate is underpinned by trust as well as obligations that can be defined by the role and position that individuals have in the organization.

Summary of Sensitizing Lens

Table 15.1 summarizes the previous discussion, presenting a sensitizing lens with three contrasting perspectives (labeled Perspective P1, P2 and P3). These are distinguished by 'focus,' 'fundamental premise,' 'responsibility,' 'challenge' and 'assumptions.' P1 is essentially concerned with managing technology and built on the premise that its management can be contained within an organizational sub-unit. In contrast, P2 is premised on the shift to the broader IS construct but with responsibility for 'success' still residing within an IS unit. Whilst P2 and P3 acknowledge that necessary knowledge is distributed across the organization, they differ in how they address the challenge of harnessing it. P2 sees it as a relational challenge, gaining access to people and, implicitly, their knowledge; P3 frames it as a cognitive challenge to create shared understanding.

The not unreasonable assumption behind P3 is that organizations invest in IS to generate value, both operational and strategic. The argumentation developed in this section proposes that the achievement of this should therefore become the central focus rather than to merely 'manage IS'. The position drawn from the previous discourse proposes that this quest is an organizational-wide endeavor. Moreover, it has its roots in harnessing knowledge. A cornerstone of this perspective is that all this required knowledge is not located in one organizational unit labeled the IS organization. By viewing an organization as a distributed knowledge system, the coordination, integration, creation and application of knowledge becomes the key challenge.

Research Method and Data Analysis

To explore how the IS organization is portrayed in the literature, studies published in leading journals that report IS research were examined through the sensitizing lens developed previously. These journals, listed in Box 15.1, are those that typically appear in surveys as

Table 15.1 Sensitizing lens: contrasting perspectives from the literature

	Perspective 1 (P1)	*Perspective 2 (P2)*	*Perspective 3 (P3)*
Focus	Manage technology	Manage IS	Realization of value from IS
Fundamental premise	Necessary knowledge can be contained within an organizational unit with defined boundary	Necessary knowledge distributed across the organization	Necessary knowledge distributed across the organization
Responsibility for 'success'	IS unit	IS unit with input from outside the unit	Shared across the organization
Challenge	Intellectual: determining information requirements	Social: getting access to people	Cognitive: integrating knowledge
Assumption	• IT can be managed	• IS can be managed	• IS cannot be managed directly
	• Information needs can be translated into IT requirements	• Bringing relevant people together achieves knowledge integration	• Representing the knowledge of others will achieve shared understanding

foremost outlets for publishing scholarly research. It might be argued that other journals should be included, but the key objective was to ensure a spread of research outlets, reviewing processes and editorial policies in selecting articles for the research data base. To incorporate a practitioner perspective, we also added a number of journals with this bent.

To be included in the study, articles had to report research where the IS organization was either the dependent or dependent variable or being studied directly. We also sought to include articles studying activities that were positioned in the reported research as taking place within an IS organizations (e.g. relationship managers or competencies of IT professionals) as these would possibly provide a picture of what the researchers understood by the IS organization. Research conducted under the umbrella of IT governance was also included if the IS organization was a concept in the reported research (e.g. Schlosser et al., 2015) and a description or definition could be gleaned from the text.

In order to ensure completeness, we also identified published work frequently cited by a number of these articles but not published in the target journal list. These included some working papers (e.g. Feeny et al., 1987; Earl & Khan, 2001) and book chapters reporting

---

Box 15.1 List of journals included in study

Harvard Business Review	Journal of Strategic Information Systems
MIT Sloan Management Review	European Journal of Information Systems
MIS Quarterly Executive	International Journal of Information Management
Information Systems Management	Information & Management
MIS Quarterly	Information Technology & People
Information Systems Research	Journal of Information Technology
Communications of the ACM	Information and Organization
Journal of Management Information Systems	Organization Science

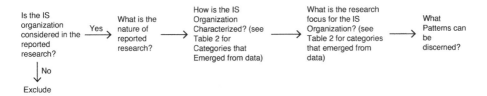

Figure 15.1 Summary of process to identify and analyze candidate articles.

research (e.g. Earl et al., 1996; Hodgkinson, 1996). Books were excluded from the study as they typically are not refereed.

Potential articles for inclusion in the study were identified first by keyword search in the target journals followed by a careful reading of their abstracts to narrow down the potential pool of articles to be reviewed (Figure 15.1). These candidate articles were read in detail and a final assessment made as to the appropriateness of each for inclusion in the study. From those finally selected, we determined whether the IS organization was the *dependent* or *independent* variable in the study or a descriptive account of an IS organization. Studies investigating the IS unit of a particular organization, if not made explicit in the article, were assumed to have the objective of improving either operational or strategic performance; they were therefore considered as an independent variable. Articles were also classified as to whether they were empirically based or conceptual treaties. To be considered as empirically based, information about data collection and analysis methods together with actual data, had to be presented in the article. An assessment was then made as to what the research understood by the concept of an IS organization, essentially how it was defined and conceptualized in the paper and used in the study. As shall be demonstrated in later discussions, this proved difficult as it was usually not made explicit in the majority of papers. Consequently, an assumption as to the nature of the IS organization was therefore gleaned from reading the text of the article and assessing how it is described and portrayed. The articles were also scrutinized to discern any patterns emerging over time with regard to changing conceptualizations of the IS organization; this included the role of its most senior executive. These patterns were coded and mapped against a chronological timeline.

The Information Systems Organization in Research Studies

Box 15.2 lists the 64 articles, dating back to 1978, included in the final analysis. Examining first the themes running through these studies over time, we can see that an early stream of research examined the location and position of the IS organization in the wider enterprise (e.g. Ein-Dor & Segev, 1980; Kroeber & Watson, 1979). A closely related research theme, and one that has persisted over time, is the design, configuration and optimal structure for the IS organization (e.g. Agarwal & Sambamurthy, 2002; Blanton et al., 1992; Boar, 1998; Earl et al., 1996; Gordon & Gordon, 2000; Ranganathan & Kannabiran, 2004; Vaast & Levina, 2006; Venkatraman & Loh, 1994; Zmud, 1984) where the debate has swung between centralization and decentralization (e.g. La Belle & Noyce, 1987; Zmud et al., 1986) with the middle-ground of a federal structure being proposed as a viable alternative (Hodgkinson, 1996; Rockart et al., 1996). The early centralization-decentralization debate related to the potential impact of IT on organizational structures, i.e. whether computerization would result in increased centralization or increased decentralization of decision-making authority (Burlingame, 1961; George & King, 1991; Leavitt & Whisler, 1958). Buchanan and Linowes (1980) consider the debate as concerned with the distribution of computing,

Box 15.2 Articles included in the final analysis

Reynolds & Yetton, 2015; Schlosser et al., 2015; Williams & Karahanna, 2013; Choudhary & Vithayathil, 2013; Guillemette & Pare, 2012; Sia et al., 2010; Huang et al., 2010; McDonald, 2007; Vaast & Levina, 2006; Porra et al., 2005; Bassellier & Benbasat, 2004; Ranganathan & Kannabiran, 2004; Weill, 2004; Jiang et al., 2003; Schwarz & Hirschheim, 2003; Brown & Ross, 2003; Ross & Weill, 2002; Chan, 2002; Agarwal & Sambamurthy, 2002; Gordon & Gordon, 2002; Benmati & Lederer, 2001; Earl & Khan, 2001; Sambamurthy & Zmud, 2000; Gordon & Gordon, 2000; Willcocks & Sykes, 2000; Purvis & McCray, 1999; Peppard & Ward, 1999; Brown, 1999; Mathiassen et al., 1999; El Sawy et al., 1999; Brown & Magill, 1998; Earl & Sampler, 1998; Fowler & Wilkinson, 1998; Feeny & Willcocks, 1998a (also 1998b); Boar, 1998; Clark et al., 1997; Agarwal et al., 1997; Cross et al., 1997; Brown, 1997; Prager, 1996; Earl et al., 1996; Nelson & Cooprider, 1996; Rockart et al., 1996; Hodgkinson, 1996; Moreton, 1995; Wang & Barron, 1995; Brown & Magill, 1994; Venkatraman & Loh, 1994; Blanton et al., 1992; Von Simson, 1990; Tavakolian, 1989; Swanson & Beath, 1989; Dearden, 1987; La Belle & Noyce, 1987; Zmud et al., 1986; Saunders & Scamell, 1986; Lucas, 1984; Zmud, 1984; Shore, 1983; Ein-Dor & Segev, 1980, 1982; Olson & Chervany, 1980; Kroeber & Watson, 1979; Ahituv & Hadass, 1978

particularly the question 'how can managers plan for the acquisition and use of minicomputers in their companies?' (p. 144). This discussion has been rekindled by Evaristo et al. (2005) who assess whether IT hardware architecture should be centralized or decentralized (see also Ahituv et al., 1989; Bacon, 1990).

There has also been a steady stream of research that has examined the relationship between organizational characteristics and the IS function (e.g. Olson & Chervany, 1980) with studies seeking to predict the design of the IS organization based on 'antecedent conditions' (Brown & Magill, 1994; Ein-Dor & Segev, 1980), a firm's competitive strategy (Tavakolian, 1989) or more recently cloud computing (Choudhary & Vithayathil, 2013). The role of the corporate IS function in the federal IS organization has also been studied (Hodgkinson, 1996) as well as perceptions of the power of the IS organization (Lucas, 1984; Saunders & Scamell, 1986). More recent research has focused on exploring IT governance structures (Brown, 1997, 1999; Sambamurthy & Zmud, 1999; Weill, 2004; Weill & Woodham, 2002).

Other research themes spotlight the IS organization itself and include the following: dealing with forces that maximize career path opportunities (Shore, 1983), identifying competencies for the IS function (Feeny & Willcocks, 1998a, 1998b), designing processes for the IS function (Brown & Ross, 2003), integrating 'core IT processes' (Purvis & McCray, 1999), management practices in the IS organization (Ranganathan & Kannabiran, 2004; Venkatraman & Loh, 1994), building change readiness capabilities in the IS organization (Clark et al., 1997), redesign (Vaast & Levina, 2006) and transforming the IS organization (Cross et al., 1997), infusing learning capabilities into the IS organization (Agarwal et al., 1997), management development initiatives in the IS organization (Mathiassen et al., 1999), how IS organizations deal with rapid change (Benmati & Lederer, 2001), power and the IS organization (Lucas, 1984) and options for resolving the tension between an IS organization and business units (Gordon & Gordon, 2002). This latter theme has also been explored in research that has studied the 'IT-business' relationship (Bassellier & Benbasat, 2004; Ward

& Peppard, 1996), 'the contribution of shared knowledge to IS group performance' (Nelson & Cooprider, 1996), and in studies that have explicitly sought to bridge the gap between the IS organization and other organizational sub-units (Peppard, 2001; Peppard & Ward, 1999; Taylor-Cummings, 1998). The role of the IS organization in organizational initiatives has also been researched, for example, in ERP implementations (Willcocks & Sykes, 2000), re-engineering projects (Moreton, 1995) and the formation and implementation of IS strategy (Fowler & Wilkinson, 1998).

Very few articles explicitly define what researchers understand by the IS organization in the study being reported. Whether as a dependent variable, or an independent variable, fewer even describe what an IS organization actually is. Indeed, in many articles, it is often designated as merely 'IS' or 'IT'; for example, '[s]hared roles and responsibility require trust and mutual respect between IT and clients' (Ross et al., 1996, p. 34); 'IT is a partner in the innovation process' (Agarwal & Sambamurthy, 2002); and '[o]ver the years, information technology (IT) has struggled with how to create an effective structure and processes' (Schwarz & Hirschheim, 2003, p. 129). Precisely what it does or its role is not explicitly stated, with descriptions couched in language projecting some vague notion that it is somehow involved with IT and sometimes information systems. Such descriptions lead only to the conclusion that it is a separate sub-unit in the organization led by, for example, the Vice President for IT, IT Director or CIO. This position is reinforced by research that has examined the 'location' of the IS organization in the enterprise – as if it can somehow be moved around like a piece on a chess board – and those studies that focus on its design and configuration.

A number of papers infer a distinction between the IS organization and 'the business' or other organizational units; the implication being that it is a separate part of the enterprise (c.f. Bassellier & Benbasat, 2004; Gordon & Gordon, 2002; Pawlowski & Robey, 2004; Ross et al., 1996; Schlosser et al., 2015; Ward & Peppard, 1996). What 'the business' represents is usually not defined, but the underlying discourse suggesting that it is essentially everything that exists outside the 'IS unit,' itself often not defined.

One striking finding from the articles analyzed is the lack of clarity in the writing and the inconsistency in usage of terminology in relation to both the description and conceptualization of the IS organization. We have already demonstrated that many articles present a vague notion of what the IS organization is, despite its central role in the reported inquiry. The use of language also hinders assessing what the reported research understands by the concept, causing confusion in making any assessment of the data, the analysis and the reported findings. In particular, usage of the word 'function' as in 'IS function' and in its plural form 'IS functions' can be subtle. The former typically refers to a sub-unit in an organization, whilst the latter seems to refer to a set of activities and tasks, but this is not always the case. For example, Grover et al. (1998) consider outsourcing as concerned with 'outsourcing IS functions to external service providers' (p. 80). They go on to define these functions as providing services such as application development and maintenance, systems operation, networks/telecommunications management and end-user computing support. La Belle and Noyce (1987) note '[f]our factors tend to drive the degree of centralization or decentralization of IT functions within an organization' (p. 78). Brown (1997) similarly uses the notion of IS functions in her study, writing that these functions include system development and maintenance, end-user computing support and applications planning. This is in contrast to portrayals of the IS function as an organizational entity, like marketing, finance or manufacturing functions, which dominate conceptualizations and contributes to the view of the IS organization as a separate sub-unit.

An analysis of the language used in describing the IS organization reveals that it is opaque, with little consistency in usage across studies. For example, is the concern of reported research with *activities*, as in Sambamurthy & Zmud's (2000) question '[h]ow should firms organize their IT activities?' (p. 106), also posed in Zmud's (1984) work 16 years earlier, or Brown's (1999) quest to 'increase our cumulative knowledge about what top-down mechanisms are being used to promote the coordination of IS activities across corporate/ division boundaries' (p. 421)? Blanton et al. (1992) seek to provide a 'better understanding of information technology organization' and set out the purpose of their study as 'to contribute towards a contingency theory of organizing IT activities into responsible IT groups (IT organization)' (p. 531).

Alternatively, is the focus on *resources* and the management of these resources, such as in Venkatraman (1997), Venkatraman and Loh (1994) and Sia et al. (2012). The debates around the merits and demerits of both centralization and decentralization have generally focused on where the control of these IT resources should reside, i.e. in a central IS organization or with local IS units. Gordon and Gordon (2002), for example, assert that 'most companies in order to grow will need to evolve, giving their business units more control over IT resources and functions' (p. 300). However, little indication is provided as to what these IT resources actually are, but inferences from the articles examined indicate that they primarily are people, technology, relationships and culture.

Moreover, is the concern of research with *IT assets* (assuming, of course, that these are different from resources)? IT assets have been defined as a highly competent IT human resource, a reusable technology base and a strong partnering relationship between IT and business management (Ross et al., 1996) somewhat analogous to the notion of resources referred to previously. Or is the issue being addressed the sourcing and provision of *IT services* to the business? This is typically where the debate around outsourcing often resides. More recent studies have focused on the locus and distribution of *decision-making* rights regarding IT (Sambamurthy & Zmud, 1999; Weill, 2004).

Notwithstanding the previous comments on the sometimes vague and imprecise language used in the analyzed articles, patterns that emerge suggest that reported studies fall into one of five clusters. These are illustrated in Table 15.2. In the table, we also show the three perspectives that make up the sensitizing lens and indicate the number of studies from each of the five clusters that subscribe to each perspective.

The first cluster is where the IS organization is the dependent variable in the study being reported (e.g. impact of organizational characteristics on the structure of the IS organization). In all papers in this cluster, it is conceptualized as a separate organizational sub-unit. A similar situation exists where the IS organization is the independent variable (e.g. its role in the success of ERP implementations) – the second cluster. Studies in both these clusters treat the IS organization as a 'black box', and none has attempted to describe or define it.

In contrast, the third cluster contains articles that focus directly on the IS organization, i.e. look within the 'black box'. Included articles study how it is designed, configured, structured or managed. Also included in this cluster is research examining specific aspects of an IS organization, such as the identification of competencies, building change readiness or infusing learning capabilities or studies exploring particular activities found in an IS organizations such as liaison roles, business competencies of IS professionals and how an IS organization can deal with rapid change. Most articles in this cluster contain empirical data, typically based on a case study methodology, with a small minority being conceptual treaties. Whilst often not identifying the scope of the IS organization, the inference from the research design and methodology underpinning these studies is that the IS organization is a separate sub-unit, with its own boundary that can be precisely defined. Indeed Chan (2002), in her study of alignment, notes an assumption in the design of the reported research that 'the boundaries of the IS function can be identified' (p. 97).

Table 15.2 Summary clustering of the 64 articles analyzed

Research focus for IS organization	Characterization of IS organization	Empirical articles	Conceptual articles	Total no. of articles	Lens perspective		
					P1	P2	P3
Dependent variable	Separate sub-unit	3	2	5	5		
Independent variable	Separate sub-unit	8	1	9	9		
Direct study of structures, processes and practices or studies of specic activities or aspects of an IS organization(s)	Separate sub-unit	29	2	31	31		
	Central/local IT units or 'Federated IS structure'	2		2		2	
	Distributed organization	3	1	4		4	
The IS organization required to accommodate future demands	Separate sub-unit		5	5		5	
	Acknowledgment that different arrangements for IS (organization) will be required in future with (some) activities and decisions occurring outside traditional functional boundaries		1	1		1	
While a concept in the reported research, no specic focus on IS organization but analysis of decision-making about IS in organization(s)	Separate sub-unit	2		2		2	
	Acknowledges the distributed nature of decision-making about IS and the need to promote responsibilities and accountabilities.	5		5		3	2
Total					45	17	2

IS, information systems; IT, information technology; P, perspective.

Whilst not directly studying an IS organization, articles grouped in the fourth cluster are conceptual and report what an IS organization of the future will possibly look like. Most articles here integrate literature at the time of publication with research findings from other organizational and management disciplines, particularly the organization sciences, proposing models, blueprints and frameworks and recommend best contemporary practice (e.g. Boar, 1998). Whilst using the concept of the IS organization to position the research, how it is portrayed is often not as an organizational sub-unit with defined boundaries, but as a distributed organization with interdependencies. However, the language used in these articles is opaque and conveys the impression that an explicit IS organization will still exist.

The final cluster contains studies that report on the distribution of decision-making authority and responsibility for IS in an organization. These papers typically address issues of (IT) governance and are of more recent interest to scholars. Often, they don't refer to the IS organization directly, *but*, in discussing the allocation of decision-making rights, most make a distinction between those that fall within the remit of an IS unit (i.e. CIO and IT management) and those that are best made by non-IT executives, usually referred to as 'in the business' or simply 'the business.' Studies explore mechanisms and processes to encourage consistency and coherence in decision-making behavior in respect of IS. These mechanisms tend to be for the purpose of allocating accountabilities and responsibilities and forums to being relevant people together, perhaps some form of IT steering committee for example. Only two of these articles, Reynolds and Yetton (2015) and Huang et al. (2010), would seem to adopt a P3 perspective.

We then analyzed the surveyed articles to determine if any patterns could be observed in the reported research that would enable us to discern different types of organizing modes. Our analysis enabled us to construct a typology distinguishing between three distinct types based on an underpinning dominant organizing logic. These three types are summarized in Figure 15.2. A perspective on the most senior person in the IS organization (which we refer to as the chief information officer, although the job title of the most senior responsible person has varied over the years) is also presented; however, this was not always discernable in all articles.

Type 1 represents the most widely subscribed view in the studies analyzed, driven by the logic of function and hierarchy. With this type, the IS organization itself is a component of the overall functional structure based on the organization of work by specialization. All necessary knowledge to achieve its functional objectives of keeping the IT systems working is contained

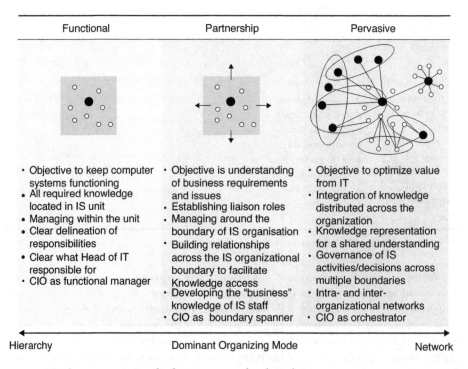

Functional	Partnership	Pervasive
• Objective to keep computer systems functioning • All required knowledge located in IS unit • Managing within the unit • Clear delineation of responsibilities • Clear what Head of IT responsible for • CIO as functional manager	• Objective is understanding of business requirements and issues • Establishing liaison roles • Managing around the boundary of IS organisation • Building relationships across the IS organizational boundary to facilitate Knowledge access • Developing the "business" knowledge of IS staff • CIO as boundary spanner	• Objective to optimize value from IT • Integration of knowledge distributed across the organization • Knowledge representation for a shared understanding • Governance of IS activities/decisions across multiple boundaries • Intra- and inter-organizational networks • CIO as orchestrator

Hierarchy   Dominant Organizing Mode   Network

Figure 15.2 Three organizing modes for generating value through IT.

within this unit. With this type, the CIO is a functional manager. *Type 2* is still ground in the IS organization being a separate unit, but it also seeks to manage around its boundary through the establishment of liaison roles to manage relationships with other areas of the organization. The focus of these relationships is to provide access to knowledge; in most cases, the reason for this is to determine requirements. With is type, the CIO performs the role of a boundary spanner. In contrast, *Type 3* takes a more pervasive perspective of an IS organization portraying it, not as an organizational unit *per se*, but concerned with the creation of intra-organizational and inter-organizational networks of connections for access to dispersed knowledge. The implicit assumption is that, this will lead to cognitive alignment. With an objective to optimize value generated from IT, it mirrors the contention of Sambamurthy and Zmud (2000) that any necessary competencies 'will be assembled, delivered, and then disassembled through a variety of intra and inter-organizational networks rather than through the IT function *acting quasi-independently* in a command and control manner' (pp. 112–113, emphasis added). In this type, the CIO plays an orchestrating role. We label these three types the *functional*, the *partnership* and the *pervasive* models, respectively.

Discussion

Our findings reveal that there is no clear and unambiguous definition or description as to what an IS organization actually is. This is remarkable, as it is not only a central concept in the IS discipline, but also the core focus of the majority of the articles analyzed; this is akin to studying 'technology acceptance' or 'IS service quality' without precisely defining what is understood by these concepts in reporting the research. Moreover, the assumption behind the overwhelming majority of studies, whether implicit or explicit, is that the IS organization is a separate and distinct sub-unit in the organization, and that it can be studied directly or isolated from the main phenomena of interest. Accordingly, the fundamental message that must be gleaned from this practice is that the 'management of IT' (which, apart from one study (Guillemette & Pare, 2012) is never defined in the included articles) can be contained within a separate organizational unit, with defined and identified boundaries (c.f. Chan, 2002). What this unit encompasses or its role and function is never revealed. Even Guillemette and Pare (2012) equate the management of IT, what they characterize by five different 'IT management models', as defining their proposed typology of IS organizations.

The implicit implication of this dominant portrayal of the IS organization is that the inability of an organization to *manage IT (or IS)*, and we are assuming by implication to optimize value from IS/IT, originates from within this unit. This perspective has consequently shaped research that focuses on addressing this failure with prescriptions from such studies recommending the tackling of the perceived inadequacies of this unit. These recommendations include calls for developing the 'hybrid manager' (Skyrme, 1992), 'reskilling the IS professionals' (Cross et al., 1997), introducing 'change agentry' as a skill for IS professionals (Markus & Benjamin, 1996), improving business competence of IT professionals (Bassellier & Benbasat, 2004), developing the credibility of IT specialists (Bashein & Markus, 1997) and building change readiness capabilities into the IT unit (Clark et al., 1997). Reports of such initiatives to improve 'the performance' of the IS organization, and again, we assume the contribution of IT are detailed in Cross et al. (1997); Vaast and Levina (2006) and Peppard (2001). These typically entail replacing the incumbent CIO, re-structuring the unit, sometimes even repositioning the unit in the organizational structure, re-engineering processes, reskilling IS unit staff, improving the quality of IT services and establishing relationships with appropriate stakeholders. Indeed, outsourcing might also be considered as a viable option.

However, if we, as suggested by Perspective 3 in our sensitizing lens, portray the generation of value from IS as requiring the coordination and integration of relevant knowledge, knowledge that is located organizational-wide, then conceptualizing the IS organization as a separate organization sub-unit is problematic. The challenge, therefore, is not to design an effective 'IS organization', but to somehow create the context to coordinate and integrate enterprise-wide knowledge. This is perhaps why strong relationships have long been recognized as essential in ensuring success with IT investments as these facilitate access to knowledge. However, access to knowledge is a necessary but not sufficient condition; the integration of this knowledge will invariably be required and this is a cognitive challenge. Moreover, this coordination and integration of knowledge needs to occur at all levels and not just at the most senior echelons of an organization. Knowledge, such as that required to work with and make sense of information (e.g. using analytical tools to support the generation of insight), is likely to be resident outside the traditional IS organization.

Consider that if all the knowledge required to manage IS can be contained within a separate organizational unit, then outsourcing would be the strategy of choice. Yet, the results of outsourcing have, by-and-large, been disappointing (Lacity et al., 2009, 2010). Even bounded tasks like outsourced software development demand the coordination and integration of knowledge if they are to achieve expected outcomes (Espinosa et al., 2003, 2007; Gopal & Gosain, 2010; Mehta & Bharadwaj, 2015).

Thus, the social context becomes a key aspect of generating value from IS. Whilst Chan (2002) highlighted the role of the 'informal organization' in achieving business/IT alignment, a plausible interpretation is that this is likely to be due to the inadequacies of formal organizational structures in supporting this coordination and integration of knowledge. Such integration requires the active participation of all key stakeholders as well as a shared understanding (Preston & Karahanna, 2009; Reich & Benbasat, 2000; Tan & Gallupe, 2006). If, for example, senior business management believe that IT is a cost to be minimized, this is going to greatly influence how they engage with IS issues and, in particular, their willingness to be involved in IS decision-making processes and assume responsibility for what they consider as falling within the remit of an IS organization. Similarly, if business managers are of the view that IT does not fall within their realm of responsibilities, and that it is the role of the IS organization – as a separate organizational sub-unit – to develop the IS strategy, prioritize IT spend, manage IT projects and deliver the expected business benefits from IT investments, and then, this is how they will behave towards IS issues and dictates their level of engagement and involvement. Research already reveals that the CIO role is an ambiguous role (Peppard et al., 2011) with senior business executives unsure as to what to expect of their most senior IS executive.

Therefore, the 'gap' between what is often referred to as 'the business' and 'IT' is perhaps more appropriately seen as a knowledge gap but one that manifests itself in relational issues. For example, the so called 'non-IT people' not appreciating their role in delivering expected benefits from IT investments and are then disappointed with project outcome. It may be a case that many business executives 'don't know what they don't know,' consequently do not give 'IT attention' (Huff et al., 2006) and therefore manage IS in a way that they believe will lead to success. If the managerial mind-set is shaped by an organizing logic that sees the IS organization as a separate unit this influences their behaviors, practices and response to any perceived problems with IT

To return to the research question as to whether conceptualizations of the IS organization reflect findings from research studying requirements for successfully harnessing information, systems and technology to achieve operational and strategic objectives, the evidence indicates that most don't. The majority conceptualize the IS organization as a separate unit, and whilst often not explicit, give the impression any perceived problems with IT can be addressed by either improved management, organization, skills or competencies within the boundaries of this unit (functional logic) or by better managing the interface with other parts of the organization (partnership logic). It is only a small number of studies that acknowledge the distributed nature of the so called IS organization in terms of responsibility and decision-making (pervasive logic). This can be seen with the more recent interest in IT governance. However, the assumption is that by implementing instruments of governance, shared understand will be achieved.

Treating the IS organization as a sub-unit capable of being separately managed may have been appropriate when computers (or machines, as they were often referred to) were first deployed, but this practice has become eroded with the passage of time, particularly as IS has assumed strategic importance. If, as strongly suggested by research, 'non-IT staff' (i.e. those employees who do not work directly in the IS organizational sub-unit or are not seen as having a formal IS role or designated as IS specialists), play such a crucial part in the generation of value from IT, do they not become part of the 'IS organization'? Perhaps this is what is being alluded to when it is said that IT is becoming embedded in the business. In a similar vein, Peppard and Ward (2004) noted that an organization's *IS capability*, what they defined as an ability to continuously deliver business value from IS, is rooted in 'the very fabric of the organization'. Where, then, are the boundaries of the IS organization? It becomes a pervasive structure akin to the pervasive organizing logic introduced in Figure 15.2, where activities, decisions and other resources are not located in a specific sub-unit.

However, in creating or describing a future state, we are often anchored and constrained in our thinking about the future by the past, and this can restrict and anchor our thinking and limit the sphere of possibility.[3] Thus, whilst a separate IS unit to maintain the running of the computer was appropriate when the operational and strategic role of IS was different than that of today, the evolution of future organizing models assume that there will be an IS unit in the organization. This may not be the case. For example, the emergence of end-user computing saw users undertake tasks that were previously performed by IT professionals which would have been unthinkable when 'computers' were first deployed. Today's practice of Bring Your Own Device would never have been entertained 50 years ago. Yet, it seems that many scholars continue to seek to build a better 'mouse trap.'

Implications for Research

The analysis presented in this article suggests that conceptualizing the IS organization as a precisely defined component of an organization, with its own boundary, processes, practices and management structures may represent research convenience rather than reflect the realities of generating business value from IS (as captured in Perspective 3 of the sensitizing lens). We have demonstrated that, whether as the dependent variable or independent variable in research or as a focus of study itself, it is predominantly portrayed as an organizational sub-unit, with its own boundary corralling all necessary knowledge to effectively manage IS. In contrast, research focused on understanding success with IS (in terms of generating business value) proposes that required knowledge is distributed across an organization. This suggests that there may be little utility in separating out a distinct IS organization with its own boundaries. If IS is indeed embedded 'in the business', what then is the IS organization in contemporary organizations?

A challenge for scholars therefore is to clearly define the IS organization — assuming, of course, that this is indeed possible or warranted. Perhaps, as we have suggested, the concept of an IS organization is a relic from the past. Do we now need a new 'scaffold' or concept to accommodate this conclusion? Is language, such as the universally accepted distinction between 'IT' and 'the business' a constraint? This raises the question as to what *should* and *should not* be included in any definition. In attempting to address this query, we encounter imprecision from the research literature. For example, are we considering decisions, resources, assets, activities, practices or all of these? What are the boundaries of the IS organization? If it has no boundaries, but the boundaries of the organization itself, then is it not impossible to treat it as a dependent or independent variable in studies? How then do you research a pervasive organization, where boundaries are at best blurred or, worse, unclear? To return to a question posed at the outset of this paper: how do you conceptualize such a construct?

One avenue of potential concern is whether the dominant conceptualization of the IS organization is leading to the development of theories and practices that are inappropriate to the realities of how value is generate by organizations from information technology? By treating the IS organization as a separate unit with defined boundaries might result in findings and recommendations that have the opposite intention. For example, the implication that an organization experiencing problems in generating business value from IS can address (i.e. solve) this problem by focusing attention on its IS organization.

Furthermore, with the exception of Guillemette and Pare (2012) there is surprisingly little theorizing around the concept of an IS organization in the literature. Moreover, despite being a central concept in the narrative within the academic writings, clear definitions are absent. At a fundamental level, the function and role of an IS organization in contemporary organizations is not evident from the research literature. Or more precisely, what is an IS organization? What does, or should, an IS organization do? Indeed, is the concept of an IS organization even relevant or useful today?

Implications for Practice

This analysis has some implications for practice. The fact is, most organizations today do have an IS organization: just look at any organization chart. We have already argued that treating the IS organization as a sub-unit capable of being separately managed is no longer appropriate today. Yet, most of the articles analyzed provide a perspective that equates improving the performance of the IS unit with positively impacting the value derived from IS investments. For example, many are implementing service improvement initiatives within their IS organizations in order to improve the quality of services delivered 'to the business'. Those attempting to increase service levels, decrease costs and improve security often look to the ITIL framework for guidance. ITIL is widely accepted as the world's leading compilation of IT best practice for IT Service Management. Establishing service level agreements (SLAs) is another popular strategy; in essence, SLAs define the penalty if service levels are not met. However, achieving specified service levels does not guarantee that that business value will be created. They may be a necessary, but are not a sufficient condition. Further, instituting SLAs also makes a fundamental distinction between 'provider' and 'customer' and does not recognize that value may in fact be co-created. There is a subtle but crucial distinction between improving *the performance of the IS organization* and improving the *performance of IS in the organization*.

The previous analysis questions the usefulness of prescriptions recommending treating the IS organization as a *profit center* or *running IT as a business* (c.f.. Kress, 2011; Lientz & Larssen, 2004; Lutchen, 2003). Many executive teams have gone down this route when seeking to push their IS organization to 'prove' that it is adding value to the business. It is consequently seen as a separate entity. Moreover, getting buy-in, involvement and the level of engagement from non-IT staff and other stakeholders, which research indicates is crucial for the generation of value from IS investments, may prove difficult with the establishment of the IT unit as a profit center. Psychologically, with a profit-orientation, it can be seen to be in conflict with the shared responsibility required, if value objectives are to be achieved. Consequently, the coordination and, particularly, the integration, of the knowledge to generate this value may be difficult to achieve.

The latter's cognitive challenge also plays a significant role in implementing IT governance structures. It cannot be assumed that the ability to represent each other's knowledge and a shared understanding will be automatically achieved by putting in place various instruments of governance.

The analysis presented in this paper also has implications for teaching. Popular text books addressing the management of IS and IT provide a contemporary view of the IS organization, what it is and its role in the organization. Yet, they too are opaque and vague. These text books are being used to educate future managers and thus play a key role in shaping their thinking. By portraying the IS organization as a separate unit in the organization, with its own leadership, administrative and management structures, processes and practices, they propagate a particular view which, as this paper has argued, contributes to the inability of organizations to deliver business value through IT. Students reading these studies are likely to be left with the impression of an IS organization that is removed from what is actually required to deliver business value.

Conclusion

At the beginning of the millennium, Sambamurthy and Zmud (2000) suggested that there were increasing signs that the accumulated wisdom regarding effective IS organizational architectures might be inadequate in shaping appropriate insights for contemporary practice. The research reported in this paper supports this position. We have examined studies where the IS organization is either the dependent or independent variable, studied directly or implicated by IT governance decisions. A key finding from the analysis is that the IS organization is generally not precisely defined, despite its pivotal role in the research being reported. In scrutinizing how the IS organization is portrayed, we found that the implicit assumption from the vast majority of studies is that it is a separate sub-unit in the organization. However, the evidence from studies that have examined how business value from IS is generated, presented in the sensitizing lens Perspective 3, paints a picture that is at odds with this dominant orthodoxy. Similarly, the socio-technical nature of IS also casts a shadow over this assumption. The perspective of the IS organization as a separate sub-unit may actually be contributing to problems that organizations have with their IT investments, particularly the inability to deliver business value.

If the value of technology is in its possession, then having a separate sub-unit in the organization responsible for its accumulation would be sufficient. With the IS organization concerned only with specifying, building, maintaining and running IT systems, delivering business value would only require making the right purchasing decisions, and the problems that many organizations face as a result of IT outsourcing would not exist. But this is not the case. If the ability to continuously generate value through IT is to be found in the very fabric of the organization, then isolating IT and designating it to be managed by an organizational sub-unit is likely to be a flawed practice.

In this article we have explored conceptualizations of the IS organization. Its objective has been to reflect on research practices and question the appropriateness of how we characterize the IS organization in our research. We hope that this article provokes a debate and that researchers will seek out new approaches that more accurately capture the realities of what is required to generate business value through IS.

In his poem *Among School Children*, Nobel prize-winner for literature, W.B. Yeats (1865–1939) wrote the line 'How do we know the dancer from the dance?', a line with strong resonance with the arguments presented in this paper. The *dancer–dance* also provides a metaphor to better understand the dichotomy that is alluded to in much of the research examined. Yeats was postulating that a dance is nothing without a dancer, and similarly, a dancer is insignificant without a dance to dance. How can we assess a dancer without seeing him/her actually dance? Similarly, how can we judge a dance without actually seeing it being performed? More profoundly, how do we then draw a distinction between the one who dances and what he/she is dancing? One cannot exist without the other. Between an organization and its IT systems, a similar interdependency is present. In today's information and technology-driven environment, an organization is unlikely to exist without IS; IS themselves cannot exist outside of their organizational context. In improving the contribution of IT to competitiveness, IS cannot be managed in isolation from the rest of the organization. It clearly cannot be managed solely from within a box on the organization chart.

Notes

1   The literature tends not to be precise in usage of the labels 'IT' and 'IS,' using them interchangeably. This goes to the heart of the second theme to be discussed in developing the sensitizing lens.
2   We can also argue that any involvement also gets stakeholder 'buy in' for any proposal and its successful implementation.
3   In a 1992 Editorial in *MIS Quarterly*, Blake Ives noted the limitations of drawing on the past for guidance about the future. He wrote: 'Industry understands that they must now re-engineer rather than just automate outdated methods. But within the information systems research community we continue to value an extensive trail of references that often reflect outdated assumptions and yesterday's economics. We are not necessarily paving the cow path, but rather extending it. It is a rare article that explores the implications of changing economics on the central research question or that challenges the dated assumptions upon which past works might have been based. If we are to re-engineer information systems research we must spend less time pouring over the archives and more time soaking in innovative organizations. It is there, rather than in the rear view mirror, that the realities of the transformation of information management will become apparent.'

References

Adler, P.S., Kwon, S.-W. (2002) Social capital: prospects for a new concept. *The Academy of Management Review*, 27, 17–40.

Agarwal, R., Beath, C. (2007) Grooming the 2010 CIO, A Report for the Society of Information Management, Advanced Practices Council.

Agarwal, R., Krudys, G., Tanniru, M. (1997) Infusing learning into the information systems organization. *European Journal of Information Systems*, 6, 25–40.

Agarwal, R., Sambamurthy, S. (2002) Principles and models for organizing the IT function. *MIS Quarterly Executive*, 1(1), 1–16.

Ahituv, N., Hadass, M. (1978) Organizational structure of a complex data processing department. *Information & Management*, 1(2), 53–57.

Ahituv, N., Neumann, S., Sviran, M. (1989) Factors affecting the policy for distributing computer resources. *MIS Quarterly*, 13(4), 389–401.

Alter, S. (2008) Defining information systems as work systems: implications for the IS field. *European Journal of Information Systems*, 17, 448–469.

Armstrong, C.P., Sambamurthy, V. (1999) Information technology assimilation in firms: the influence of senior leadership and IT infrastructures. *Information Systems Research*, 10(4), 304–327.

Bacon, C.J. (1990) Organizational principles of systems decentralization. *Journal of Information Technology*, 5(2), 84–93.

Banville, C., Landry, M. (1989) Can the field of MIS be disciplined? *Communications of the ACM*, 32(1), 48–60.

Barki, H., Hartwick, J. (1989) Rethinking the concept of user involvement. *MIS Quarterly*, 13(1), 53–63.

Barua, A., Mukhopadhyay, T. (2000) Information technology and firm performance: past, present, and future, In: *Framing the Domains of IT Management Research: projecting the Future through the Past*, Zmud, R.W. (ed). Pinnaflex Educational Resources, Cincinnati, Ohio.

Bashein, B.J., Markus, M.L. (1997) A credibility equation for IT specialists, *Sloan Management Review*, 38, 35–44.

Bassellier, G., Benbasat, I. (2004) Business competence information technology professional: conceptual development and influence on IT-business partnership. *MIS Quarterly*, 28(4), 673–694.

Benbasat, I., Zmud, R.W. (2003) The identity crisis within the IS discipline: defining and communicating the discipline's core properties. *MIS Quarterly*, 27(2), 183–194.

Benmati, J., Lederer, A.L. (2001) How IT organizations handle rapid IT change: five coping mechanisms. *Information Technology and Management*, 2, 95–112.

Beynon-Davis, P. (2010) The enactment of significance: a unified conception of information, systems and technology. *European Journal of Information Systems*, 19, 398–408.

Blanton, J.E., Watson, H.J., Moody, J. (1992) Toward a better understanding of information technology organization: a comparative case study. *MIS Quarterly*, 16, 531–555.

Boar, B.H. (1998) Redesigning the IT organization for the information age, *Information Systems Management*, Summer, 23–30.

Boynton, A.C., Jacobs, G.C., Zmud, R.W. (1992) Whose responsibility is IT management, *Sloan Management Review*, Summer, 32–38.

Broadbent, M., Kitzis, E.S. (2005) *The New CIO Leader: setting the Agenda and Delivering Results*. Harvard Business School Press, Boston.

Brown, C.V. (1997) Examining the emergence of hybrid IS governance solutions: evidence from a single case site. *Information Systems Research*, 8(1), 69–94.

Brown, C.V. (1999) Horizontal mechanisms under differing IS contexts. *MIS Quarterly*, 23(3), 421–454.

Brown, C.V., Magill, S.L. (1994) Alignment of the IS function with the enterprise: towards a model of antecedents. *MIS Quarterly*, 18(4), 371–404.

Brown, C.V., Magill, S.L. (1998) Reconceptualizing the context-design issue for the information systems function. *Organization Science*, 9(2), 176–194.

Brown, C.V., Ross, J.W. (2003) Designing a process-based IT organization. *Information Strategy: The Executive's Journal*, 19, 35–41.

Bryant, A. (2008) The future of information systems thinking informatically. *European Journal of Information Systems*, 17, 695–698.

Buchanan, J.R., Linowes, R.G. (1980) 'Making distributed data processing work', *Harvard Business Review*, 58, 143–161.

Burlingame, J.F. (1961) 'Information technology and decentralisation', *Harvard Business Review*, 40, 121–126.

Burton-Jones, A., Straub, D. (2006) Reconceptualizing system usage: an approach and empirical test. *Information Systems Research*, 17(3), 228–246.

Chan, Y.E. (2002) Why haven't we mastered alignment? The importance of the informal organization structure. *MIS Quarterly Executive*, 1(2), 97–112.

Choudhary, V., Vithayathil, J. (2013) The impact of cloud computing: should the IT department be organized as a cost center or a profit center? *Journal of Management Information System*, 30(2), 67–100.

Chun, M., Mooney, J. (2009) CIO roles and responsibilities: twenty five years of evolution and change. *Information & Management*, 45, 323–334.

Clark, C., Cavanagh, N., Brown, C.V., Sambamurthy, V. (1997) Building change readiness capabilities in the IS organization: insights from the Bell Atlantic experience. *MIS Quarterly*, 21(4), 425–454.

Cross, J., Earl, M.J., Sampler, J.L. (1997) Transformation of the IT function at British petroleum. *MIS Quarterly*, 21(4), 401–423.

Davenport, T.H. (1994) Saving IT's soul: human-centered information management, *Harvard Business Review*, 72, 119–131.

Davenport, T.H., Harris, J.G., Delong, D.W., Jacobson, A.L. (2001) Data to knowledge to results: building an analytical capability. *California Management Review*, 43(2), 117–138.

Davenport, T.H., Prusak, L. (1997) *Information Ecology: mastering the Information and Knowledge Environment*. Oxford University Press, New York.

Davis, F.D. (1989) Perceived usefulness, perceived ease of use, and user acceptance of information technology. *MIS Quarterly*, 13(3), 319–339.

Dearden, J. (1987) The withering away of the IS organization. *Sloan Management Review*, 28(4), 87–91.

DeLone, W.H., McLean, E.R. (1992) Information systems success: the quest for the dependent variable. *Information Systems Research*, 3(1), 60–95.

Doll, W.J., Torkzadeh, G. (1991) The measurement of end-user computing satisfaction: theoretical and methodological issues. *MIS Quarterly*, 15(1), 5–10.

Dvorak, R.E., Holen, E., Mark, D., Meehan, W.F. (1997) Six principles of high-performance IT. *The McKinsey Quarterly*, Number, 3, 164–177.

Earl, M.J. (1989) *Management Strategies for Information Technology*. Prentice-Hall, Inc., Upper Saddle River, NJ.

Earl, M.J. (1993) Experiences in strategic information systems planning. *MIS Quarterly*, 17, 1–24.

Earl, M.J., Edwards, B., Feeny, D.F. (1996) Configuring the IS function in complex organizations, In: *Information Management: the Organizational Dimension*, Earl, M.J. (ed), pp. 201–230. Oxford University Press, Oxford.

Earl, M.J., Khan, B. (2001) How IT departments are responding to the challenges of e-commerce, Centre for the Networked Economy, London Business School, CNE WP04/2001.

Earl, M.J., Sampler, J.L. (1998) Market management to transform the IT organization, *Sloan Management Review*, 40, 9–17.

Ein-Dor, P., Segev, E. (1980) Organizational arrangements for for MIS units. *Information & Management*, 3, 19–26.

Ein-Dor, P., Segev, E. (1982) Information systems: emergence of a new organization function. *Information & Management*, 5, 279–286.

El Sawy, O., Malhotra, A., Gosain, S., Young, K. (1999) IT-intensive value innovation in the electronic economy: insights from Marshall industries. *MIS Quarterly*, 23(3), 305–335.

Espinosa, J.A., Cummings, J.N., Wilson, J.M., Pearce, B.M. (2003) Team boundary issues across multiple global firms. *Journal of Management Information Systems*, 19(4), 157–190.

Espinosa, J.A., Slaughter, S.A., Kraut, R.E., Herbsleb, J.D. (2007) Team knowledge and coordination in geographically distributed software development. *Journal of Management Information Systems*, 24(1), 135–169.

Evaristo, J.R., Desouza, K.C., Hollister, K. (2005) Centralization momentum: the pendulum swings back again. *Communications of the ACM*, 48(2), 67–71.

Faraj, S., Sproull, L. (2000) Coordinating expertise in software development teams. *Management Science*, 46, 1554–1568.

Feeny, D., Ross, J.W. (2000) The evolving role of the CIO, Research and Discussion Paper, Oxford Institute of Information Management, Templeton College, Oxford.

Feeny, D.F., Earl, M.J., Edwards, B.R. (1987) Complex organizations and the information systems function: a research study, Oxford Institute of Information Management Research and Discussion Paper (RDP 87/7), Templeton College, Oxford.

Feeny, D.F., Willcocks, L. (1998a) Core IT capabilities for exploiting information technology. *Sloan Management Review*, 40, 9–21.

Feeny, D.F., Willcocks, L. (1998b) Redesigning the IS function around core capabilities. *Long Range Planning*, 31(3), 354–367.

Fonstad, N., Subramani, M. (2009) Building enterprise alignment: a case study. *MIS Quarterly Executive*, 8(1), 31–41.

Fowler, A., Wilkinson, T. (1998) An examination of the role of the information systems centre, *The Journal of Strategic Information Systems*, 7, 87–111.

George, J., King, J. (1991) Examining the computing and centralization debate. *Communications of the ACM*, 34(7), 63–72.

Gerth, A., Peppard, J. (2014) How newly appointed CIOs take charge. *MIS Quarterly Executive*, 13, 159–173.

Gopal, A., Gosain, S. (2010) The role of organizational controls and boundary spanning in software development outsourcing: implications for project performance. *Information Systems Research*, 21(4), 960–982.

Gordon, J.R., Gordon, S.R. (2000) Structuring the interaction between IT and business units: prototypes for service delivery, *Information Systems Management*, 17, 7–16.

Gordon, S.R., Gordon, J.R. (2002) Organizational options for resolving the tension between IT departments and business units in the delivery of IT services. *Information Technology & People*, 15(4), 286–305.

Grant, R.M. (1996) Prospering in dynamically competitive environments: organizational capability as knowledge integration. *Organization Science*, 7, 375–387.

Grover, V., Teng, J.T.C., Cheon, M.J. (1998) Towards a theoretically-based contingency model of information systems outsourcing. In: *Strategic Sourcing of Information Systems*, Willcocks, L.P., Lacity, M.C. (eds), pp. 79–101. John Wiley and Sons, Ltd., Chichester.

Guillemette, M.G., Pare, G. (2012) Toward a new theory of the contribution of the IT function in organization. *MIS Quarterly*, 36(2), 529–552.

Hodgkinson, S.L. (1996) The role of the corporate IT function in the federal IT organization, In: *Information Management: the Organizational Dimension*, Earl, M.J. (ed), pp. 247–269. Oxford University Press, New York.

Huang, R., Zmud, R.W., Price, R.L. (2010) Influence and the effectiveness of IT governance practices through steering committees and communication policies. *European Journal of Information Systems*, 19, 288–302.

Huff, S.L., Maher, P.M., Munro, M.C. (2006) IT and the board of directors: is there an IT attention deficit? *MIS Quarterly Executive*, 5(2), 2–14.

Hughes, A., Scott Morton, M.S. (2006) The transforming power of complementary assets, *MIT Sloan Management Review*, 48, 50–58.

Jiang, J.J., Klein, G., Carr, C.L. (2002) Measuring information systems service quality: SERVQUAL from the other side. *MIS Quarterly*, 26(2), 145–166.

Jiang, J.J., Klein, G., Pick, R.A. (2003) The impact of IS department organizational environments upon project team performances. *Information & Management*, 40, 213–220.

Karahanna, E., Preston, D.S. (2013) The effect of social capital of the relationship between the CIO and top management team on firm performance. *Journal of Management Information Systems*, 30(1), 15–55.

Kogut, B., Zander, U. (1996) What firms do? Coordination, identity, and learning. *Organization Science*, 7, 502–518.

Kohli, R., Devaraj, S. (2003) Realizing the business value of information technology investments: an organizational process. *MIS Quarterly Executive*, 3(1), 53–68.

Kress, R.E. (2011) *Running IT like a Business: accenture's Step-by-Step Guide*. IT Governance Publishing, Cambridge, UK, 1st November.

Kroeber, D.W., Watson, H.J. (1979) Is there a best MIS department location? *Information & Management*, 2, 165–173.

La Belle, A., Noyce, H.E. (1987) Whither the IT organization, *Sloan Management Review*, 28, 75–85.

Lacity, M., Khan, S., Yan, A., Willcocks, L. (2010) A review of the IT outsourcing empirical literature and future research directions. *Journal of Information Technology*, 24(4), 395–433.

Lacity, M., Shaji, A., Khan, A., Willcocks, L. (2009) A review of the IT outsourcing literature: insights for practice. *Journal of Strategic Information Systems*, 18(3), 130–146.

Leavitt, H., Whisler, T. (1958) 'Management in the 1980's', *Harvard Business Review*, 36, 41–48.

Lee, A.S., Thomas, M., Baskerville, R.L. (2015) Going back to basics in design science: from the information technology artefact to the information systems artefact. *Information Systems Journal*, 25, 5–21.

Li, Y., Tan, C.-H., Teo, -H.-H., Tan, B.C.Y. (2006) Innovative usage of information technology in Singapore: do CIO characteristics make a difference? *IEEE Transactions on Engineering Management*, 53(2), 177–190.

Lientz, B.P., Larssen, L. (2004) *Manage IT as a Business: how to Achieve Alignment and Add Value to the Company*. Elsevier Butterworth-Heinemann, Oxford.

Lin, N. (2001) *Social Capital: A Theory of Social Structure and Action*. Cambridge University Press, New York.

Lohmeyer, D., Pogreb, S., Robinson, S. (2002) 'Who's accountable for IT. The McKinsey quarterly, 2002 Special Edition: Technology.

Lucas, H.C., Jr. (1984) Organizational power and the information services department. *Communications of the ACM*, 27(1), 58–65.

Luftman, J., Brier, T. (1999) Achieving and sustaining business-IT alignment. *California Management Review*, 42(1), 109–122.

Lutchen, M. (2003) *Managing IT as A Business: A Survival Guide for CEOs*. Wileys, New York.

Mack, D., Monnoyer, E. (2004) Next generation CIOs, *McKinsey Quarterly*, 2, 2–8.

Maklan, S., Knox, S., Peppard, J. (2011) Why CRM fails and how to fix it. *MIT Sloan Management Review*, 52(4), 77–85.

March, S.T., Niederman, F. (2012) The future of the information systems discipline: a response to Walsham. *Journal of Information Technology*, 27, 96–99.

Marchand, D., Peppard, J. (2013) Why IT fumbles analytics, *Harvard Business Review*, 91, 104–112.

Marchand, D.A., Kettinger, W., Rollins, J.D. (2000) Information orientation: people, technology and bottom line, *Sloan Management Review*, 41, 69–80.

Markus, M.L. (2004) Technochange management: using IT to drive organizational change. *Journal of Information Technology*, 19, 3–19.

Markus, M.L., Benjamin, R.I. (1996) Change agentry the next IS frontier. *MIS Quarterly*, 20, 385–407.

Markus, M.L., Robey, D. (1988) Information technology and organizational change: casual structure in theory and research. *Management Science*, 34(5), 583–598.

Mathiassen, L., Borum, F., Pederson, J.S. (1999) Developing managerial skills in IT organizations – a case study based on action learning. *Journal of Strategic Information Systems*, 8, 209–225.

McDonald, M.P. (2007) The enterprise capability organization: a future for IT. *MIS QuarterlyExecutive*, 6(3), 179–192.

Mehta, N., Bharadwaj, A. (2015) Knowledge integration in outsourced software development: the role of sentry and *guard processes*. *Journal of Management Information Systems*, 32(1), 82–115.

Mitchell, V.L. (2006) Knowledge integration and information technology project performance, *MIS Quarterly*, 30, 919–939.

Moreton, R. (1995) Transforming the organization: the contribution of the information systems function. *Journal of Strategic Information Systems*, 4(2), 149–163.

Nahapiet, J., Ghoshal, S. (1998) Social capital, intellectual capital, and the organizational advantage. *Academy of Management Review*, 23, 242–266.

Nelson, K.M., Cooprider, J.G. (1996) The contribution of shared knowledge to IS group performance. *MIS Quarterly*, 20(4), 409–432.

Nelson, R.R. (2005) Project retrospectives: evaluating project success, failure, and everything in between, *MIS Quarterly Executive*, 4(3), 361–372.

Newell, S., Tansley, C., Huang, J. (2004) Social capital and knowledge integration in an ERP project team: the importance of bridging AND bonding. *British Journal of Management*, 15, S43–S57.

Office, N.A. (2006) Delivering Successful IT-enabled Business Change, Report by the Comptroller and Auditor General, HC 33–1, session 2006–2007, London, November.

Olson, M.H., Chervany, N.L. (1980) The relationship between organizational characteristics and the structure of the information services function. *MIS Quarterly*, 4(2), 57–68.

Orlikowski, S.D., Robey, D. (2004) Bridging user organizations: knowledge brokering and the work of IT professionals. *MIS Quarterly*, 28(4), 645–672.

Orlikowski, W. (2010) The sociomateriality of organizational life: considering technology in management research. *Cambridge Journal of Economics*, 34(1), 125–141.

Orlikowski, W., Gash, D. (1994) Technological frames: making sense of information technology in organisations. *ACM Transactions on Information Systems*, 12(2), 174–207.

Orlikowski, W., Hofman, D. (1997) An improvisational model for change management: the case of groupware technologies, *Sloan Management Review*, 38, 11–21.

Orlikowski, W., Scott, S.V. (2008) Sociomateriality: challenging the separation of technology, work and organization. *Annals of the Academy of Management*, 2(1), 433–474.

Orlikowski, W.J., Baroudi, J. (1990) Studying information technology in organisations: research approaches and assumptions. *Information Systems Research*, 2(1), 1–28.

Orlikowski, W.J., Iacono, C.S. (2001) Desperately seeking the 'IT' in IT research: a call to theorizing the IT artefact. *Information Systems Research*, 12(2), 121–134.

Paul, R.J. (2010a) Editorial: loose change. *European Journal of Information Systems*, 19, 379–381.

Paul, R.J. (2010b) What an information system is, and why it is important to know this. *Journal of Computing and Information Technology*, 18(2), 95–99.

Pawlowski, S.D., Robey, D. (2004) Bridging user organizations: knowledge brokering and the work of information technology professionals. *MIS Quarterly*, 28, 645–672.

Peppard, J.W. (2001) Bridging the gap between the IS organization and the rest of the business: plotting a route. *Information Systems Journal*, 11, 249–270.

Peppard, J.W. (2007) The conundrum of IT management. *European Journal of Information Systems*, 16, 336–345.

Peppard, J.W. (2010) Unlocking the performance of the chief information officer. *California Management Review*, 52(4), 73–99.

Peppard, J.W., Edwards, C., Lambert, R. (2011) Clarifying the ambiguous role of the chief information officer. *MIS Quarterly Executive*, 10, 197–201.

Peppard, J.W., Lambert, R.D., Edwards, C.E. (2000) Whose job is it anyway? Organizational information competencies for value creation. *Information Systems Journal*, 10(4), 291–323.

Peppard, J.W., Ward, J. (1999) Mind the gap': diagnosing the relationship between the IT organization and the rest of the business. *Journal of Strategic Information Systems*, 8, 29–60.

Peppard, J.W., Ward, J.M. (2004) Beyond strategic information systems: towards an IS capability. *Journal of Strategic Information Systems*, 13, 167–194.

Peppard, J.W., Ward, J.M. (2005) Unlocking sustained business value from IT investments. *California Management Review*, 48(1), 52–70.

Pitt, L.F., Watson, R.T., Kanvan, C.B. (1995) Service quality: a measure of information systems effectiveness. *MIS Quarterly*, 19(2), 173–185.

Porra, J., Hirschheim, R., Parks, M.S. (2005) Forty years of the corporate information technology function at Texaco Inc. a history. *Information and Organization*, 16(1), 82–107.

Prager, K. (1996) Managing for flexibility: the new role of the aligned IT organization. *Information Systems Management*, 13(4), 41–46,.

Preston, D., Karahanna, E. (2009) How to develop a shared vision: the key to strategic alignment. *MIS Quarterly Executive*, 8(1), 1–8.

Purvis, R.L., McCray, G.E. (1999) Integrating core IT processes: a case study. *Information Systems Management*, 16, 36–46.

Ranganathan, C., Kannabiran, G. (2004) Effective management of information systems function: an exploratory study of Indian organizations. *International Journal of Information Management*, 24, 247–266.

Reich, B.H., Benbasat, I. (2000) Factors that influence the social dimension of alignment between business and information technology objectives. *MIS Quarterly*, 24(1), 81–113.

Reynolds, P., Yetton, P. (2015) Aligning business and IT strategies in multi-business organizations. *Journal of Information Technology*, 30, 101–118.

Rockart, J. (1988) The line takes leadership IS management in a wired society. *Sloan Management Review*, 29, 57–64.

Rockart, J., Earl, M.J., Ross, J.W. (1996) Eight imperatives for the new IT organization, *Sloan Management Review*, 38, 43–55.

Ross, J., Weill, P. (2002) Six decisions your IT people shouldn't make, *Harvard Business Review*, 80, 85–91.

Ross, J.W., Beath, C.M., Goodhue, D. (1996) Develop long-term competitivesess through IT assets. *Sloan Management Review*, 38, 31–42.

Ross, J.W., Feeny, D.F. (1999) The Evolving Role of the CIO, Center for Information Systems Research, working paper 308, Sloan School of Management, Massachusetts Institute of Technology, Cambridge, MA.

The Royal Academy of Engineering (2004) *The Challenges of Complex IT Projects*. The Royal Academy of Engineering, London.

Sabherwal, R. (2003) The evolution of coordination in outsourced software development projects: A comparison of client and vendor perspectives. *Information and Organization*, 13(3), 153–202.

Sambamurthy, V., Zmud, R. (1999) Arrangements for information technology governance: a theory of multiple contingencies. *MIS Quarterly*, 23(2), 261–290.

Sambamurthy, V., Zmud, R. (2000) Research commentary: the organizing logic for an enterprise's IT activities in the digital era a prognosis of practice and a call for research. *Information Systems Research*, 11(2), 105–114.

Sambamurthy, V., Zmud, R.W. (1997) At the heart of success: organization wide management competencies, In: *Steps to the Future: fresh Thinking on the Management of IT-based Organizational Transformation*, Sauer, C., Yetton, P.W. & Associates (eds), pp. 143–163. Jossey Bass Publishers, San Francisco, CA.

Sauer, C., Cuthbertson, C. (2003) *The State of IT Project Management in the UK*. Templeton College, University of Oxford, Oxford, November.

Saunders, C.S., Scamell, R.W. (1986) Organizational power and the information services department: a reexamination. *Communications of the ACM*, 29(2), 142–147.

Schlosser, F., Beimborn, D., Weitzel, T., Wagner, H.-T. (2015) Achieving social alignment between business and IT an empirical evaluation of the efficacy of IT governance mechanisms. *Journal of Information Technology*, 30, 119–135.

Schwarz, A., Hirschheim, R. (2003) An extended platform logic perspective of IT governance: managing perceptions and activities of IT. *Journal of Strategic Information Systems*, 12, 129–166.

Scott, S.V., Orlikowski, W.J. (2013) Sociomateriality – taking the wrong turning? A response to Mutch. *Information and Organization*, 23, 77–80.

Shore, E.B. (1983) Reshaping the IS organization. *MIS Quarterly*, 7(4), 11–17.

Shpilberg, D., Berez, S., Puryear, R., Shah, S. (2007) Avoiding the alignment trap in information technology. *MIT Sloan Management Review*, 49(1), 51–58.

Sia, S.K., Soh, C., Weill, P. (2010) Global IT management: structuring for scale, responsiveness, and innovation. *Communications of the ACM*, 53(3), 59–64.

Skyrme, D. (1992) *From Hybrids to Bridge building, Research and Discussion papers, RDP92/1*. Oxford Institute of Information Management, Templeton College, Oxford.

Smaltz, D., Sambamurthy, V., Agarwal, R. (2006) The antecedents of CIO role effectiveness in organizations: an empirical study in the healthcare sector. *IEEE Transactions on Engineering Management*, 53(2), 207–222.

Somers, M.J. (2010) Using the theory of the professions to understand the IS identity crisis. *European Journal of Information Systems*, 19, 382–388.

Spender, J.C. (1996) Making knowledge the basis of a dynamic theory of the firm. *Strategic Management Journal*, 17, 45–62.

Swanson, E.B., Beath, C.M. (1989) Reconstructing the systems development organization. *MIS Quarterly*, 13(3), 293–305.

Tan, F., Gallupe, R.B. (2006) Aligning business and information systems thinking: a cognitive approach. *IEEE Transactions on Engineering Management*, 53(2), 223–237.

Tavakolian, H. (1989) Linking the information technology structure with organizational competitive strategy: a survey. *MIS Quarterly*, 13(3), 309–317.

Taylor-Cummings, A. (1998) Bridging the user-IS gap: a study of major information systems projects. *Journal of Information Technology*, 13, 29–54.

Thorp, J. (1999) *The Information Paradox: realizing the Business Benefits of Information Technology*. McGraw-Hill, Ryerson, Toronto.

Tsai, W., Ghoshal, S. (1998) Social capital and value creation: the role of intrafirm networks. *Academy of Management Journal*, 41(4), 464–476.

Vaast, E., Levina, N. (2006) Multiple faces of codification: organizational redesign in an IT organization. *Organization Science*, 17(2), 190–201.

Venkatesh, V., Morris, M.G., Davis, G.B., Davis, F.D. (2003) User acceptance of information technology: towards a unified view. *MIS Quarterly*, 27(3), 425–478.

Venkatraman, N. (1997) *Beyond Outsourcing: managing IT Resources as a Value Center*. Sloan Management Review, Spring, 51–64.

Venkatraman, N., Loh, L. (1994) The shifting logic of the IS organization: from technical portfolio to relationship portfolio'. *Information Strategy: The Executive's Journal*, Winter, 10, 5–11.

Von Simson, A.M. (1990) The "centrally" decentralized IS organization, *Harvard Business Review*, 68, 158–162.

Wang, E.T., Barron, T. (1995) Controlling information system departments in the presence of cost information asymmetry. *Information Systems Research*, 6(1), 24–50.

Ward, J., Peppard, J. (1996) Reconciling the IT/business relationship: a troubled marriage in need of guidance. *Journal of Strategic Information Systems*, 5(1), 37–65.

Weill, P. (2004) Don't just lead, govern: how top-performing firms govern IT. *MIS Quarterly Executive*, 3(1), 1–17.

Weill, P., Ross, J. (2004) *IT Governance: how Top Performers Manage IT Decision Rights for Superior Results*. Harvard Business School Press, Boston, MA.

Weill, P., Woodham, R. (2002) Don't just lead, govern: implementing effective IT governance, Center for Information Systems Research, Massachusetts Institute of Technology, CISR WP 326.

Willcocks, L.P., Sykes, R. (2000) The role of the CIO and IT function in ERP. *Communications of the ACM*, 43(4), 32–38.

Williams, C., Karahanna, E. (2013) Causal explanation in the coordinating process: a critical realist case study of federated IT governance structures. *MIS Quarterly*, 37, 933–964.

Zmud, R.W. (1984) Design alternatives for organizing information systems activities. *MIS Quarterly*, 8(2), 79–93.

Zmud, R.W., Boynton, A.C., Jacobs, G.C. (1986) The information economy: a new perspective for effective information systems management. *Database*, 18, 17–23.

Questions for Discussion

1   Why is it important to analyze and assess the conceptualization of a phenomenon?
2   What is meant by the sensitizing lens, and how was it used in for the study?
3   Discuss how 'human agency' is important in the management of information systems.
4   Discuss whether IS can be managed or not.
5   Why is knowledge important to generate value from information systems?
6   Is building networks the only way to coordinate and integrate knowledge for value generation from information systems?
7   Which among the three types of organizing logics is the most salient for generating value from information systems?
8   Why is the conceptualization and assessment of information systems important for practitioners?

Further Reading

Reynolds, P., Yetton, P. (2015). Aligning business and IT strategies in multi-business organizations. *Journal of Information Technology*, *30*, 101–118.
Peppard, J. W., Edwards, C., Lambert, R. (2011). Clarifying the ambiguous role of the chief information officer. *MIS Quarterly Executive*, *10*, 197–201.

PART IV

Some Current and Emerging Challenges

THUS FAR, WE HAVE DISCUSSED aspects of strategic information management by focusing, in Part I, on the process of information systems, planning, strategy and alignment; In Part II on digital transformation, key components of digital strategy, digital leadership, and power dynamics in organization, IS and strategy, and in Part III, on key principles for organizing the IT function, the role of CIO and CDO leadership, as well as reflecting on the very nature of the IS organizations. In Part IV, we present and discuss the *current and emerging challenges* that organizations face in the Digital Economy and the increasing use of digital technologies from which organizations attempt to gain benefit through their digital transformation. Such challenges include the use and management of social media, datification, algorithmic decision-making and the associated issues of "big data". The topics in Part IV are listed in the top layer of Figure P4.1.

Chapters 16 and 17 focus on the use of social media for strategizing (Chapter 16) and socialization (Chapter 17). The research on social media in the last decade has seen considerable increase in the areas of: knowledge sharing (Leonardi, 2014); strategy (Haefliger et al., 2011; Von Krogh, 2012); communication (Huang et al., 2013; Leonardi et al., 2013), enterprise social media and networks (Kane, 2015; Kane et al., 2014; Koch et al., 2013; Kuegler et al., 2015).

Chapters 18–20 consider another relevant, current issue in the Digital Economy that is linked to datification and the use of "big data". Issues associated with big data have recently been the focus of debate (e.g., Chen et al., 2012; Günther et al., 2017).

In Chapter 16, John Baptista, Alex Wilson, Bob Galliers and Steve Bynghall demonstrate how social media has the capability for open strategy through transparency, inclusiveness and the emergence of reflexivity. The chapter outlines different social media features and their effects on strategic activities given the shift from what can be seen as an analogue strategy process to that of a digital strategy process. Through seven case studies, the chapter outlines

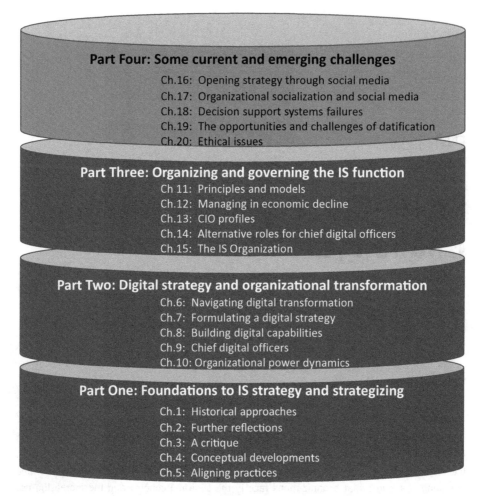

Figure P4.1 The focus of Part IV: Some Current and Emerging Challenges

four tensions in using social media in achieving transparent and inclusive strategic practices within organizations. To resolve these tensions the authors outline the need for organizations to develop a reflexive capability which enables them to integrate the feedback from social media and open strategy initiatives. The chapter describes three stages of gradual development of reflexiveness as an organizational capability arising from a dynamic process.

In Chapter 17, Dorothy Leidner, Ester Gonzalez and Hope Koch examine the introduction of enterprise social media (ESM) as a socialization tool for new IT hires within organizations. The chapter outlines the affordances of ESM, which are grouped around the areas of networking; organizational visibility; information gathering/sharing; and innovation. Through a qualitative case study, the interacting effects of these affordances are examined to demonstrate different levels of affordances. The chapter shows that different levels of affordances lead to different outcomes via five generative mechanisms: bureaucracy circumvention; the executive perspective; personal development; name recognition; and as a morale booster. The affordances of the ESM socialization program are actualized through the five generative mechanisms and result in eight outcomes. These are: productivity enhancement; additional work;

attractive job assignments; stress; social struggle a sense of social support; comfort around superiors; and cultural understanding.

In Chapter 18, Paolo Aversa, Laure Cabantous and Stefan Haefliger provide an example of a sophisticated decision support tool using big data to design and implement strategic decisions. The study demonstrates that overreliance on such systems could lead to strategic failure, as illustrated in the Formula 1 2010 championship. The case shows that, despite the significant investment in real-time decision support systems (DSS) with big data, the use of the strategic outputs led to Ferrari losing the Abu Dhabi race, and ultimately, the championship. The authors outline three interrelated sources of strategic failure with DSS and big data for strategic decision-making: (i) the situated nature and affordances of decision-making with big data; (ii) the distributed nature of cognition in decision-making; and (iii) the performativity of the DSS. They conclude that social and material practices need to be considered in strategic decision-making with DSS and big data, in order to account for the diversity of uses of these technologies, their affordance and interpretive flexibility, along with intangible aspects such as organizational culture.

In Chapter 19, Sue Newell and Marco Marabelli, discuss the strategic opportunities and challenges of algorithmic decision-making. Big data, which is captured through digitized services, is used and processed by algorithms to predict behaviors. The chapter outlines a number of discriminations which are associated with big data algorithmic decision-making either in products and services provided to groups ("big" data) or individuals ("little" data). The paper demonstrates how the use of big and little data in algorithmic decision-making can lead to discriminations and societal concerns. Thus, the chapter outlines tradeoffs and issues associated with the use of these data. These tradeoffs include: privacy versus security; freedom versus informed control; freedom versus uninformed control, and independence versus dependence. These tradeoffs are the basis for opportunistic strategic decision-making which can well lead to societal challenges. The authors conclude by arguing the increased responsibility and reflection in the use of big data and algorithms for decision-making. The chapter provides a useful segue to Chapter 20.

Thus, Chapter 20 by Kirsten Martin analyzes the ethical issues associated with big data as an industry. The author explains the beneficial uses of big data while also outlining some of the questionable uses of big data. The chapter outlines these ethical issues in four quadrants: issues with sources; issues with customers and use, and issues within a single supply chain, and within a system. The chapter concludes by developing guidelines for a sustainable big data industry, outlining the issues; the causes of current problems and potential solutions, and the roles of CIOs and CDOs in enacting these solutions. The chapter outlines additional questions and responsibilities regarding digital transformation, strategy and big data, and the roles of CIOs and CDOs in these contexts. Thus, the chapter brings the book to an appropriate conclusion given the emergent challenges they categorize.

References

Chen, H., Chiang, R.H., Storey, V.C. (2012). Business intelligence and analytics: From big data to big impact. *MIS Quarterly*, 36 (4), 1165–1188.

Günther, W.A., Mehrizi, M.H.R., Huysman, M., Feldberg, F. (2017). Debating big data: A literature review on realizing value from big data. *The Journal of Strategic Information Systems*, 26 (3), 191–209.

Haefliger, S., Monteiro, E., Foray, D., von Krogh, G. (2011). Social software and strategy. *Long Range Planning*, 44 (5–6), 297–316.

Huang, J., Baptista, J., Galliers, R.D. (2013). Reconceptualizing rhetorical practices in organizations: The impact of social media on internal communications. *Information and Management*, 50 (2–3), 112–124.

Kane, G.C. (2015). Enterprise social media: Current capabilities and future possibilities. *MIS Quarterly Executive*, 14 (1), 1–16.

Kane, G.C., Alavi, M., Labianca, G.J., Borgatti, S.P. (2014). What's different about social media networks? A framework and research agenda. *MIS Quarterly*, 38, 274–304.

Koch, H., Leidner, D.E., Gonzalez, E.S. (2013). Digitally enabling social networks: Resolving IT culture conflict. *Information Systems Journal*, 23, 501–523.

Kuegler, M., Smolnik, S., Kane, G.C. (2015). What's in IT for employees? Understanding the relationship between use and performance in enterprise social software. *The Journal of Strategic Information Systems*, 24, 90–112.

Leonardi, P.M. (2014). Social media, knowledge sharing, and innovation: Toward a theory of communication visibility. *Information Systems Research*, 25 (4), 796–816.

Leonardi, P.M., Huysman, M., Steinfield, C. (2013). Enterprise social media: Definition, history, and prospects for the study of social technologies in organizations. *Journal of Computer-Mediated Communication*, 19 (1), 1–19.

Von Krogh, G. (2012). How does social software change knowledge management? Toward a strategic research agenda. *The Journal of Strategic Information Systems*, 21 (2), 154–164.

Chapter 16

João Baptista, Alexander D. Wilson, Robert D. Galliers and Steve Bynghall

SOCIAL MEDIA AND THE EMERGENCE OF *REFLEXIVENESS* AS A NEW CAPABILITY FOR OPEN STRATEGY

S TRATEGY IS BOTH a statement of intent and a process by which that intent is formed and performed by members of organizations. The ownership of these two aspects of strategy has traditionally been with elite groups within organizations (Hambrick, 2007; Pettigrew, 1992). However, the rise of social media as a platform for open communication and wider engagement in organizational discourse has shifted attention to more collective views of strategy (Seidl and Whittington, 2014; Whittington, 2006).

Formalized strategy may still be managed from the top in many organizations but social media is adding pressure to make this process more porous and open to informal activity at the grassroots level and throughout (and even beyond) individual organizations. This is particularly relevant as the younger generation of "digital natives" (Helsper and Eynon, 2009) become more dominant given their aptitude to use social media to engage and interact with others (Tams et al., 2014; Vodanovich et al., 2010) and share knowledge (Morton et al., 2015).

The participative nature of social media changes the distribution of rhetorical resources and reshapes patterns of communication from univocal into multivocal organizational environments (Huang et al., 2015). Social media is intrinsic to knowledge management (Von Krogh, 2012), knowledge reuse (Majchrzak et al., 2013), distributed leadership (Sutanto et al., 2011), and in facilitating interaction and internal collaboration (Razmerita et al., 2014). However, it is the increased visibility of what others know through social media that creates conditions to leverage knowledge in new ways and promotes learning as a process that operates vicariously rather than through interpersonal experience (Leonardi, 2014). This is significant to strategy because of how social media accentuates the role and voice of every member of the organization by providing a platform for engagement and participation, as well as a more visible line of sight to strategy (Haefliger et al., 2011). Social media can have therefore the ability to extend reach and richness in the making and "doing" of strategy. In particular, social media has the potential to modify "how much" strategy is visible, and when and how individuals are able to participate in creating and shaping practices and content of strategic significance. It adds reach and volume of feedback ex-ante, but often also replaces traditional forms of communication of extant strategy.

It is therefore appropriate to broaden our view of strategy to include a wider set of activities with strategic impact within organizations, some of which have not been recognized as being sufficiently close to the practice of strategy (Bechky, 2011). This broader view of strategy reflects the growing number of modern work environments where strategy practice is shifting from being "exclusive and secretive" to becoming more "inclusive and transparent" (Whittington et al., 2011, p. 538). The issue is then how increasing *inclusiveness* (broader involvement of stakeholders) and *transparency* (wider access to content and information) interferes with established conventions around *who* should be involved in strategy and *how*, and the extent of *what* should be shared. For example, becoming more inclusive can challenge established hierarchical structures within organizations (Collier et al., 2004) and break with established conventions on strategy being the domain of a restricted group of top managers (Hambrick, 2007; Pettigrew, 1992) by opening up the potential involvement to other echelons in the organization, notably middle managers (Floyd and Wooldridge, 1994; Wooldridge and Floyd, 1990). Adding transparency can also be problematic because it creates conditions for equal voice and access to rhetorical resources by all members of the organization (Huang et al., 2013), challenging for example the status of middle management because they no longer moderate and intermediate knowledge exchanges. This echoes Bruhn and Ahlers (2013), who note the importance of integrating and embedding new communication channels in existing organizational and strategizing practices and processes.

This is causing significant changes to strategy as conventionally described; changes that go deep into the praxis of strategy, its norms and artefacts, as well as who is involved in formal and informal strategic activity in organizations (Whittington, 2006; Whittington et al., 2006, 2011). However, this leads to further ramifications to the democratization of strategy by establishing agile, responsive and capable organizations (Doz and Kosonen, 2008a, 2008b), crowdsourcing strategy dialogues (Stieger et al., 2012) and more democratized forms of strategy (Dobusch and Mueller-Seitz, 2012; Matzler et al., 2014; Stieger et al., 2012).

This paper focuses on social media as a platform for participation (Cotton et al., 1988) and considers its role in shaping and forming strategy within organizations (Mantere and Vaara, 2008). We pose the following guiding research question to deepen our understanding of this research puzzle: *How is the adoption of social media changing the nature of organizational strategizing?*

The paper is structured as follows. In this section we motivated the study by highlighting the role of social media in shaping strategic activity in organizations. Next we show how social media is changing the nature and dynamics of processes of strategizing in organizations and identify the research gap in our current understanding that we aim to address. The section that follows outlines our methodological approach to the empirical work by explaining the two stages undertaken to gather and analyze secondary and primary data. This two-pronged approach allowed us to intertwine a wide range of data from multiple sources with the concepts of open participation in organizational strategizing. We then report on our main findings, providing evidence of tensions and capability development in the organizations studied. In our analysis section we then review and conceptualize the dynamic nature of capability development by adding *reflexiveness* as a third dimension to Whittington et al.'s (2011) model of open strategy. Drawing on Gorli et al. (2015), we suggest that this capability embodies the process of integrating open and emergent feedback into the structural arrangements of organizations. Our conceptualization of the *reflexiveness* capability is a key contribution of our study. Lastly, we reflect on the potential for this capability to shift the governance of the organization towards *stewardship* as an overall organizational arrangement that is consistent with open strategizing practices in organizations.

Social Media Expansion into Processes of Strategizing

We commenced with a systematic and comprehensive review of case material publicly available such as blog posts, online magazines, news, industry reports, company reports, white papers, etc. This gave us a broad basis to understand the emerging use of social media in organizations. More particularly, the aim was to capture salient, current examples of the expansion of social media into processes of strategizing. This was achieved by analyzing the social media features used (column 1) and their specific strategic use (column 2) and to capture the effect on strategic activity (column 3). Table 16.1 shows a selection of representative examples of our initial analysis:

Table 16.1

Social media features	Examples: strategic use	Effects on strategic activity
Interaction with management Blogs, commenting, video casting, discussion forums, online communities, real-time online Q&As, social network updates, internal twitter	Dow Chemical, Lloyds Bank, ING, Nokia, Lloyd's Bank, Linden Labs, Alcatel-Lucent CEO at Dow Chemical was an early adopter of internal blog since 2007 called "Access Andrew". Received 24,000 visits per blog post and up to 50 comments. Employees are encouraged to leave comments, which are moderated but the CEO personally authors the blog and deals with hot topics himself. At Deutsche Bank some managers host "Ask Me Anything" sessions online where questions on any topic can be freely asked by any employee in the company.	Active use of social media to make the vision of senior management more transparent and gather support and feedback from employees. In some cases, this is used to define new strategic initiatives and support decision-making. It also provides a view on employee sentiment for senior management.
Extension of closed management meetings Real-time and post commenting on topics from management meetings, live updates on social networks, event blogs	Philips, Unilever, PwC, Dollar Financial, Grant Thornton Dollar Financial, the UK operations of US-based DFC Global Corp, a diversified financial services company, regularly film board meetings and post the videos on the intranet for employees to view. At Grant Thornton there is live blogging of senior management meetings.	Strategy meetings which were previously closed become more open, allowing more employees to engage and discuss strategic issues.

(continued)

Social media features	Examples: strategic use	Effects on strategic activity
Employee listening program Community groups, online portal for sharing feedback, custom-built forms for input of data, voting systems	HSBC, Virgin Media HSBC has a structured Employee Listening program for employees to talk about anything, these sessions are facilitated by managers. Managers then use a custom portal to record issues raised which is then analyzed to capture ideas and suggestions to improve the business.	Employees' concerns and issues are listened to and recorded, acting as a data input into strategic decision-making.
Ideation programs, managed input and consultation on specific initiatives Innovation Jam, ideation platforms, Wikis, voting systems, community groups, discussion forum, social network updates, microblogging and instant messaging	Avery Dennison, HCT Technologies, IBM, Grant Thornton, Red Hat, Luxottica Sano3 Aventis, ATOS, BNP Paribas, Virgin Media Within Sano3 Pasteur, Yammer was used as a community site for its "Women in Sano3 Pasteur" (WiSP) network. The network helps to promote gender balance in a company where women were originally only 20% of the workforce. Pressure from the group helped to change company policy and also meant the company won the Apec (French executive employment association) Gender Parity prize.	Specific initiatives which ask for input into a strategic level campaign or objective such as a values program. Gradual formation of incentives and measurement to recognize contributions from employee and management. Structured approaches to facilitate innovation. Recognition of issue-led communities leading to changes within company.
Open HR-related processes including peer recognition Badges and recognition, ratings, peer recognition systems, gami3cation	HCL Technologies, Xchanging At HCL Technologies the appraisal system is open so that management appraisal feedback is visible to all. Employees give feedback on managers. This helps to establish an open culture, which has resulted in further structured approaches to crowdsourcing strategy among employees.	Peer to peer recognition on employees and managers can identify issues, influence behaviors and also guide strategy as feedback cascades upwards.
Analysis of employee sentiment and social dynamics Polls and surveys; Analysis of community groups; Discussion groups; Social networks	HSBC, Nationwide Insurance, Philips Nationwide Insurance (USA) experimented with an app to identify employee sentiment on its Yammer social network, which was then used to help management make decisions. At Philips KPIs show strategic contribution of ESN to interaction between different groups.	Analysis of employee sentiment and relative identification of trends to inform and feed into strategy

Our analysis revealed various ways in which particular social media features are being used in strategizing. It also revealed that social media were used in combination or at times were replacing traditional approaches to strategy development that had often been based previously on paper communication and face-to-face meetings. This analysis showed a wide range of social media features being used within organizations such as blogging platforms, commenting, activity streaming, social networking, internal twitter, videocasting, online forums and chats, wiki editing, voting systems, ideation and collaborative platforms. It showed that these online services were increasingly used to engage employees in organizational activity and decision-making (Razmerita et al., 2014). In certain cases, social media were more deeply embedded, and effectively replaced traditional forms of organizational participation, and in this way social media became a significant influencing factor over the strategic outlook of these organizations (Haefliger et al., 2011).

In these organizations, strategic activity was shifting from "analogue" processes based on traditional tools, such as workshopping, stakeholder meetings, corporate events and sharing documents (Whittington, 2006; Whittington et al., 2006), towards new "digital" forms of strategic engagement and participation based on social media (Stieger et al., 2012). Figure 16.1 captures this finding by showing the increasing influence of social media over traditional approaches to managing strategy (Haefliger et al., 2011; Jarzabkowski and Kaplan, 2014; Whittington, 2006; Whittington et al., 2011). The concentric circles represent this gradual integration and often replacing in the use of social media in strategic activity in organizations. As per the examples shown in Table 16.1, the figure also highlights the way in which social media shifts attention from an approach to strategizing focused on tools and outcomes, towards an approach more based on strategy conversations, connectedness and engagement.

These findings motivated us to analyze the effects of participation through social media on organizational strategizing. In other words, to explore further this shift towards more participative forms of engagement and its potential to open up strategy content and modify strategy practices in organizations. This led us to explore how social media created new dynamics of interaction and placed pressure on organizations to manage emergent feedback from a much greater number stakeholders and media (Aral et al., 2013; Hienerth et al., 2011) with regard to strategic issues. In our study, we found different approaches to managing feedback. The emergence of new capabilities to manage new forms of participation and openness seemed to be a dominant theme across the case material.

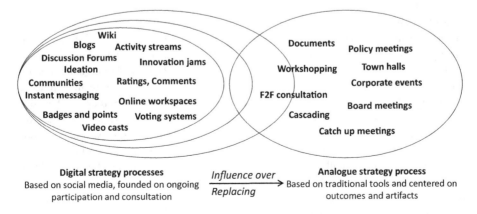

Figure 16.1 Digital and analogue strategy processes: social media expansion into processes of strategizing

Social Media and the Emergence of *Reflexiveness*

To understand this phenomenon it is essential to define and interpret the inherent characteristics of social media. Social media is not a singular technology. Rather, it is a broad category that includes various types of online services that add the ability for interactive and participative communication within social settings that form organizations. They are inherently contextual and become embedded in the practices and norms of these social groups. Social media are therefore better described as an emergent ensemble of features that forms context for social interactions (Spagnoletti et al., 2015), the shape of which is the result of the unique interplay with the context of use of each organization (Baptista, 2009). Other types of ICTs such as email are inherently more closed, transactional, and centered on individuals, whereas the essence of social media is based on providing high visibility and open participation. At the practical level, social media add features that enable for example the seamless sharing, commenting, responding, syndicating and interacting with content (text, voice and video) and connecting with others, and follow and interacting with their activity streams (Kaplan and Haenlein, 2010; Kietzmann et al., 2011) (see Table 16.1). Social media therefore provide a malleable platform, which is inherently organic, free-flowing and built to support dynamic and emergent feedback loops of communication within a social group.

Within organizations social media afford new types and patterns of communication and interactions, and have the potential to impact on its structure, governance and organizing principles (Leonardi et al., 2013; Treem and Leonardi, 2012; Vaast and Kaganer, 2013). The dynamic feedback loops that emerge through wider participation in strategic activity via social media can initially be in tension with extant formal structures and norms within organizations. However, organizations learn to manage and harness feedback as a useful resource. In so doing they become inherently more *reflexive* and able to move towards an organizational environment where there is wider participation and engagement in the shape of and direction of the strategy. Gorli et al. (2015, p. 3) suggest that the environment within an organization is reflexive when it gives "*managers and practitioners occasions to reflect on their systems of action, so that their imagination, inventiveness and enterprise can take wing.*" Social media stimulates this reflexivity as a new capability in organizations. The embedding of social media in the functioning of organizations means that feedback and participation is structurally part of the organization. Denyer et al. (2011, p. 393) reflect on the long term effects of social media adoption within organizations; they suggest that social media have the potential for "*reconfiguration and redesign of the whole socio-technical and managerial system*" with the potential to contribute for strategy practice to be inherently more reflexive (Wilson and Jarzabkowski, 2004, p. 15).

Reflexiveness—the ability to be reflexive—is a social concept that refers to the ability to integrate analysis of ourselves in thinking and action. At the individual level it means self-introspection and self-awareness but, in social settings, it involves interaction with others in the context of established norms within a social group. Thus, within organizations this capability requires feedback systems and refers to the ability of employees to apply practical reflexivity (Cunliffe, 2002) to give them structural conditions to be authors of their own workplace and play an active role in the daily "*production, reproduction and transformation of their work processes*" (Gorli et al., 2015, p. 3). Accordingly, organizations with low reflexivity only allow for low levels of agency in changing established social structure. In contrast, organizations with high reflexivity allow for high levels of agency and give individuals better ability to shape norms and structures of their own environment—which is what Gorli et al. (2015) say develops the ability for individual and collective authorship or in other words "*make sense of, and shape their organizational practices*". This then gives individuals an opportunity "*to perceive and pursue specific opportunities for influencing organizations and their contexts*" which is a shift from conventional approaches to strategy and organizing. It is this thread and link between social media use and the structural conditions for participation in organizational strategizing that is the focus of this study. We now review the research methods used to support this aim.

Research Approach and Methodology

To find evidence of social media use in organizational activity with strategic reach we started with a wide review of industry reports by systematically collecting any source of case material reported in the press as noted above. Our efforts were strengthened by one of the co-authors who is immersed in the social media field and is well informed of its practices. Our aim was to gain a rich insight into the possible practices across as many organizations as possible of social media used in strategic activity. Therefore, to address this recent and emerging phenomenon, our research adopted an exploratory design (Stebbins, 2001) combining two research methods to help gain breadth and depth. The study began with an extensive search and analysis of secondary data to build a broad understanding of how organizations use social media in open strategy initiatives. The second round of data collection gathered primary data and used semi-structured interviews. Informants were selected as they were responsible for, and embedded in, the running of social media driven open initiatives. Informants were drawn from seven organizations spanning different sectors.

In the first phase, the collection and analysis of secondary data focused on consultancy and management reports, company press releases, the business press and corporate blogs—all of which were deemed to be a rich source of data (Easterby-Smith et al., 2012) and give good coverage of organization's social media-led initiatives. Our initial search revealed data on 50 cases of organizations using social media in support of strategic initiatives. Following initial coding of these data, we identified 35 cases across 29 organizations which met the twofold criteria of social media use in our context: 1) being in-use (cases were rejected if they were using "primitive" technologies (Whittington et al., 2011)), and 2) were serving as the driver for open strategy (i.e. social media were aimed at increasing inclusion and transparency). These 35 cases were coded further to identify the social media tools and features employed, the intended effect on strategizing, the nature of emergent capabilities and the tensions encountered. This phase of the study provided the basis for our analysis of features of social media used to drive open strategy and enabled the synthesis of tensions between established ways of working user expectations and the configuration of openness achieved. These were written-up as vignettes to provide "systematically elaborated descriptions of concrete situations" (Schoenberg and Ravdal, 2000) which enabled us to collate and contrast different approaches to open strategy. The aim was to capture existing practices across the industry from secondary data using short vignettes (Friesl and Silberzahn, 2012) and then use this to conduct extended interviews with a smaller group of organizations for richer and deeper understanding of social media use in this context.

The second phase of data collection drew on interviews as a method to access rich, experiential accounts of social media technologies in-use and open strategy initiatives. Our aim was to gain first-hand, experiential accounts of how social media are deployed in support of open strategizing. We conducted extended, semi-structured interviews with ten respondents from seven different organizations (around 30 hours of audio recording were transcribed verbatim). The seven organizations were selected from the pool of cases gathered in the first phase of the empirical work. The transcripts were analyzed first independently and then jointly by the authors to capture the themes and experiences shared by our respondents. The themes were used as first order codes, which were subsequently used to recode interview data in order to capture quotations and evidence of how social media is being used in open strategy contexts. Table 16.2 summarizes the seven organizations studied and explains the selection criteria for each. Some of these organizations are also listed and featured in our preliminary findings in Table 16.1. However, in Table 16.2, we analyze new field work based on interviews, going beyond the public material covered earlier that led us to consider these organizations in greater depth.

Table 16.2 Details of semi-structured interviews, firm characteristics, and selection criteria

Organization	Characteristics	Salient insights of social media influence on strategic activity	Interviewee
Xchanging	9000 employees in 12 global locations, Technology services	Known to have recently implemented social media with significant impact on the practices and culture of the organization	Global Head of Internal Communications
Virgin Media	14,000 employees, UK-based Telecommunications	Reported as a case study for having an advanced online community-based customer service	Director of Technical Services, Head of eCustomer Care
HSBC	265,000 employees, Global with UK HQ, Financial services	Widely reported shift towards giving employees new ways to voice concerns and open up to senior management	Global Head of Insight, Culture and Group CEO communications
Grant Thornton	5000 employees, UK-based Accountancy. Partnership moving to shared ownership	Known case of a new CEO active on social media internally, with an open style of communication. Moving from partnership to shared ownership	Senior Manager for National Communications
IBM Studio	Several hubs in large cities, operates as subsidiary of IBM, Global IT and consulting services company	Set up to be the "agile" arm of larger IBM to allow employees to execute projects differently	Team Leader, Consultant, Senior Manager
Atos	93,000 employees, Global with headquarters in France, IT services	Very present in the press as a case of banning email internally. Very ambitious in social media	Group Chief Change Officer
Philips	105,000, Global with headquarters in Netherlands, Electronics	Known to have advanced metrics to capture social media collaboration and exchanges globally	Digital Communications Manager

The interviews revealed how social media are used, and how gradually they contribute to substantively opening approaches to strategic activity in each case. The experience of organizational actors tells us how particular tensions were played-out, what capabilities had developed, and whether the organization concerned had adapted its governance stance in response to, or in concert with, open strategy initiatives.

This dual method approach enabled us to gain insight into the variety of ways social media are used in open strategy as well as providing a window into the ways such ICT is shaping and challenging management practices. Our aim was to span meso-level patterns of ICT use in firms (cases drawn from secondary data) as well as granular examples anchored in strategic praxis (interviews). This approach enabled us to give situated accounts of organizational practices positioned in a broader context of social media usage. We investigated multiple cases, using complementary methods of data collection, seeking to identify common features of strategizing and strategic praxis supported by social media. The approach leads to the identification of common understandings, teleologies and rules driving the adoption of social media, each of which contributes to constellations of practices and material arrangements of open strategy (Schatzki, 2002; Seidl and Whittington, 2014).

Findings and Analysis: Becoming Structurally Open

We now present and discuss our findings. We first review key initiatives related to social media use with impact on strategic practice. We analyze how this stimulated the emergence of feedback loops, and their gradual embedding in significant aspects of organizations. We pay particular attention to the emergence of new ways of engaging employees in shaping the functioning of the environment that they belong to, which leads to tensions between new forms of participation and established structures and norms in the organization. Our findings suggest that organizations develop new capabilities in response to these tensions. We conceptualize these tensions and related capabilities and reflect on how they ultimately move strategic processes and thinking to become more distributed: seen as something shared, jointly achieved and enacted within organizations—a characteristic of organizations that have developed *reflexiveness* as a new capability.

Emergent Feedback Loops

The growing adoption of social media within the organizations studied created new and often unexpected forms of interaction and feedback. These new forms of managed and unmoderated communication underpinned changes across all organizations.

For example, the CEO and CFO or Xchanging held regular online chats with the employees. The questions posed by employees were unmoderated and responded to "on the spot" by them. This feedback feature was associated with a new culture of interaction between senior leaders and employees, and both the content and interaction were gradually more deeply embedded in the culture and processes of Xchanging as mentioned by the Global Head of Internal Communications:

> We had some live chats which we'd never been able to do before, so it was really interesting. We'd get the CEO and the CFO doing a live chat, so people could literally pile in and ask them questions. They were very open questions that they were expected to respond to on the spot, so a completely different culture, and really showing people that the C suite are accessible.

Feedback was also becoming part of the way of working among employees through the adoption of social networking, instant messaging and activity streaming. For example, the Digital Communications Manager at Philips highlighted how social media stimulated feedback and connected employees:

> *It's totally synchronized so every follower of me will see my intranet article. All my fol-*
> *lowers will be notified that I've been interactive with this article. This is really interesting*
> *because normally I would never go to the IT intranet but now I follow people from IT and*
> *they interact with IT intranet articles and then I go to the IT intranet as well to read those*
> *articles because they are of interest to me.*

Social media channels delivered wider and deeper use of feedback within the organizations studied and were a central theme in our analysis. In some organizations feedback from social media channels developed more naturally within the culture of the organizations, such as in the case of Philips where the culture was perceived to be open and relaxed. While in other organizations we noticed the need to follow a more formal approach to managing new feedback from social media. For example, HSBC created a structured program, called Exchange to stimulate feedback and engagement with employees and more specifically to *"put employees in a position where they have the freedom and the trust to talk about anything they want to talk about."* Feedback from employees under this program was initially pushed through the formal structures of the bank to ensure it was listened to by senior managers. However, expectations about using feedback became quickly accepted, as captured by the Global Head of Insight, Culture and Group CEO communications at HSBC:

> *In the early days I had to be really prescriptive and very, very strict actually with lead-*
> *ers. Because I think they had forgotten the art of listening and they'd forgotten the art of*
> *listening with intent.*

A more complex form of feedback was anonymous posting. Philips' social media channel called "Office World" allowed totally anonymous feedback. This feedback feature complemented other forms of social media feedback, but allowed employees to raise issues they otherwise would not without the safety of anonymous posting. The Digital Communication Manager at Philips described the use of this service:

> *everybody with a Philips email address can sign up for employee feedback anonymously,*
> *where your identity is protected … people share their feedback about certain things …*
> *you're free to say what you really think.*

The above highlights the emergence of new forms of social media feedback and novel forms of interaction, which were associated with new forms of participation increasingly structurally embedded in formal structures of organizations. Next we explore emergence of inherent tensions arising along the new emergent feedback loops.

Tensions from Integrating Open Feedback in Extant Structures and Norms

As identified previously, the adoption of social media can bring unprecedented levels of feedback and dialogue to organizational life. It also sets new expectations of participation and engagement in increasingly important and strategic aspects of the organization. Tensions emerge when the structures of organizations are then in opposition to these expectations of participation. We conceptualize four types of tensions experienced by organizations as they become more *transparent* and *inclusive* in their approach to strategizing (Whittington et al., 2011) using social media.

Tension 1 is characterized by frustration when organizations adopt social media but limit its reach *(inclusiveness)* and visibility of content *(transparency)*. User frustration ensues when they start to engage with social media and feedback features but realize that their contributions are moderated and/or restricted in terms of visibility. Imbalance and dissatisfaction emerge with the exclusion of certain groups or where the process and ability for employees to contribute is too rigidly controlled. This leads to inconsistencies between established norms and new expectations of open participation, as captured by the Global Head of Internal Communications at Xchanging:

> You know, you can't give people a voice and then tell them "well, actually, you can have a voice but only if you say what we want you to say". If you're going to give them a voice, then you have to listen. I think we've given them the voice and now we're learning to listen, but actively listen, and that's the difference.

She further reflected on the more structural implications of this tension. Employees were happy to engage with organizational discourse but expected in return their voice and contribution to be acknowledged and purposefully considered. This is illustrated in the following quote:

> As people get braver and start to ask questions of the senior leaders around their strategy, and they're being held accountable to it now, so people are saying, you know, "You said you'd deliver there. Where are we and what have you delivered and why haven't we delivered that?" The questions are really up front.

Typically, organizations react to this by taking strides towards increasing either *inclusiveness* and/or *transparency*. However, although this signifies that the effects of tension 1 are alleviated, it can produce different tensions.

Tension 2 is characterized by greater *inclusiveness* but still low *transparency* of strategy on social media. Typically, this means that greater inclusiveness provides conditions for all employees to contribute and participate in organizational discourse through social media tools. However, frustration emerges from this situation when management fails to allow the expression of conflicting views or are seen to not be engaging with employee views. Dissatisfaction emerges from limited ability to engage with strategy content and have meaningful conversations despite the wider access. We noticed this tension in Virgin Media for example with a significant emphasis on building a large and inclusive online community but where the focus was on specific topics and operational discussions.

Alternatively, organizations may focus on adding transparency via social media tools, rather than on widening reach. This is characterized as Tension 3 where content and information is open and visible but restricted to some closed groups. This inevitably causes division and instability. For example, knowledge workers may have more access to digital channels than their colleagues in factory or retail outlets. This type of tension was visible for example at IBM between the agile subunit based at the IBM Studio and the rest of IBM, the following quote by a Consultant illustrates how these tensions were felt by the IBM Studio team.

> They're trying to create this fast moving environment ... but based still around this very slow moving, large organization. So there's this little hub that's working to produce quickly, but still ... this huge process-orientated, monolithic organization behind it, that kind of fights with that ideal I think.

Organizations naturally respond to these tensions by rebalancing their internal structures to accommodate employee feedback. They may then reach a state where they have enabled wide reach (inclusiveness) and richness of content (transparency) so that all employees can openly interact with each other and content. However, our analysis suggests that this state is perhaps the most precarious of all because the expectations of participation are the highest but the organization has not yet developed appropriate structural conditions to incorporate the feedback created and use it meaningfully and strategically. We characterize this stage as tension 4.

Tension 4 therefore is also associated with tensions between the open nature of social media and established more closed and hierarchical structures. For example, where employees contribute openly to strategic discourse, but senior executives still retain discretion and control of what and how employees contribute to discourse around strategy content. Thus, a disconnect may arise between open feedback and the structures supporting the strategic development of the organization. Tension 4 is fostered by the existence of open communication, but without the associated redistribution of power and reward structures. Whittington et al. (2011, p. 535) allude to this when they say that:

> Inclusion and transparency do not extend to the transfer of decision rights with regard to strategy: openness refers to the sharing of views, information and knowledge, not a democracy of actual decision making.

Tension 4 is a corollary of this when organizations adopt social media to open strategizing but do not become more participative structurally in their strategy processes. The Director of Technical Services at Virgin Media reflected on how far they had gone to be both inclusive and transparent but were still under serious tensions to adjust more structurally to the new environment:

> We're still on that journey, that shift to really truly transform. It's almost a leap of faith to really move from [being] reactive, to be proactive … it's about relationships. It's quite a long lead time to get into that truly transformed space.

Figure 16.2 illustrates these tensions using a two dimensional diagram where each axis represents expansion of either inclusiveness or transparency. The four resulting quadrants capture the types of tensions described above.

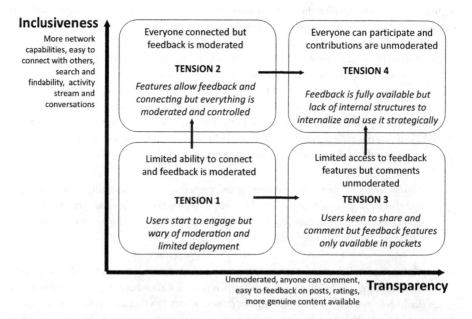

Figure 16.2 Tensions arising from increasing inclusiveness and transparency through social media

The effect of these tensions in the long-run was that organizations adjusted their internal structures to accommodate the new forms of interaction and feedback. Various adjustments were visible at various levels in the organizations studied but they had in common increased appreciation of the participative nature of social media. We now conceptualize these adjustments as the development of a new capability of *reflexiveness*.

Reflexiveness as a New Organizational Capability

Reflexiveness emerged as a new capability for managing the tensions described above. We suggest that the development of reflexiveness enabled organizations to successfully integrate emergent feedback from social media and harness advantages arising from engagement in open strategy initiatives. We characterize three stages in the progression towards gaining this new capability: 1) feedback accepted as valuable resource; 2) developing formalized structures to sustain open behaviors; and 3) strategic integration.

The **first stage** arises from structural adjustments in response to tension 1, specifically to the initial emergence of feedback features in organizations that social media provide. The main characteristic of this stage is the internal recognition that feedback from social media as a new resource that has value, needs attention and requires management. This recognition of feedback as useful for organizations was seen to develop gradually, for example the Global Head of Internal Communications at Xchanging said that they:

> had the platform for probably a year and a half, and I think we've grown more confident and trusting in the platform.

Another characteristic of increased reflexiveness is the stronger signals to encourage and stimulate open and unmoderated feedback from various areas of organizations. This type of feedback through social media is inherently emergent and unprompted, so it is outside the control of senior management. This often marks a departure from managed feedback through employee surveys for example, and so it requires new approaches. At HSBC the *Exchange* program was created to signal and create an environment for employees to provide unrestricted feedback.

As social media provide organizations with greater understanding and new methods for managing this type of feedback, new formalized structures emerge to monitor, measure and report feedback to executives, as captured in this quote from HSBC:

> "At one stage every business and every function head, including the head of communications for that area, got a report every quarter, and there was also a global HSBC one and that is the one that gets presented at the Board. We are reviewing this process to allow the full richness of the insights to be used rather than filtering all the insights to senior management through a single report," as reported by the Global Head of Insight, Culture and Group CEO communications.

Stage one encompasses the initial phases of the organization becoming aware of the new resource it has in terms of information and feedback, followed by structural adjustments where organizational members are made aware of the value of social media and the need to manage the new levels of feedback it provides.

Stage two in developing reflexiveness is a response to tensions 2 and 3 and is characterized by the greater level of formality in managing and using feedback internally. Often this was accompanied by formalized techniques to monitor the use of social media for sharing, collaborating and social networking for example. Some organizations then used this information as part of the reward structures for employees, so that they were directly incentivized to engage with feedback features with strategic significance in their organizations. One example from Philips was in identifying influential participants through advanced social network analysis as described by the Digital Communications Manager who said that they:

> Look at the influence, so how many group members and who are really influential, who have the highest response rate, the most active members. This is a really popular tool for the group admins.

Other organizations had also developed advanced systems to measure engagement with feedback features. At Atos for example the Group Chief Change Office referred to a new and sophisticated system of stars that helped management to manage content and contributions.

> We have a robust automated tool that captures the number of readers, the number of reactions, the number of posts, the number of people who subscribe and a few other parameters ... this gives you the number of stars. We believe that the value brought by this community is reflected by these stars.

However, some organizations moved further to establish a link between these metrics and the internal reward structures for employees. For example, at Philips they issued a regular report that assessed progress towards volume and quality of employee feedback and interaction, which was associated with internal bonus structures, the following quote.

> A lot of those functions have in their objectives to increase adoption of the social platform. if they meet their objectives they receive a bonus ...

These reward structures also worked to reward employee contributions through a system of badges which were seen as currency for influence. The Digital Communications Manager described the significance of the badges in profile development at Philips.

> Everybody can give it away. For example, if I go to my profile you will see my things. You see how many I received. I received one brand badge, three eager to win. I also received fifty-one great contributions and two very meaningful innovations. I have four inspire and one operational excellence. One I deliver results and twelve take ownership and thirty-one team up to excel. This says something about my personality of course.

However, there were organizations that demonstrated more advanced characteristics of *reflexiveness* where feedback was fully incorporated into the norms and ways of working in the organization, but also began to shape deeper aspects of the organization such as trusting attitudes and behavior, leadership styles and culture. These are the characteristics of stage three in the development of *reflexiveness* which emerge in response to tension 4. In these organizations feedback was not just integral to the normal functioning but was starting to shape and influence management styles, governance structures and strategy.

Linking feedback from social media with organizational strategy is a sign of a *reflexive* organization where strategy is more than a statement from senior management, to be instead seen to be a shared effort and co-created. This aspiration for the organization to develop the ability to use feedback from social media is captured by the following quote by the Global Head of Internal Communications at Xchanging.

hopefully slowly, bit by bit, we'll get to a point where, you know, we'll get people influenc-ing the strategy to come. Right now they [employees] are just reacting to what they're being told, but as their confidence builds and *as their leaders see that actually our employees aren't children and they do have some value to add, then it could influence things going forward … they [leadership team] would say okay, these people [employees] are asking questions for a good reason, and they have things I need to start thinking about a little bit more when I'm setting strategies. How I'll answer those, and if I can't answer them, then let's think about it and consider all the other options and maybe ask people's opinions.*

An integral part of this process towards becoming more reflexive at strategic level is a shift in leadership style and management approaches. Leaders that operate more consistently with the participative nature of the environment developed recognition and notoriety and become more influential, and ultimately rise in the organization. This shift to form management approaches more consistent with the participative nature of a reflexive organization is cap-tured by the following quote from HSBC stating how some leaders "got it" while others struggled with this new approach:

There was another cohort of leaders who just found this effortless. It was almost like a different breed of leader that had been quiet up until this point. Who would have thought you are now somebody who has followers rather than workers because you listened to them?

Further, we noted that this shift in leadership was reinforced as part of the Exchange program discussed previously, and other structural changes at HSBC. The following quote captures this link between leadership and a wider movement towards a more reflexive environment in the bank.

Antonio [CEO of HSBC Bank plc] runs a weekly column on a site called Connected. People have no problem speaking and posting their comments on the site. That's got nothing to do with social media though and I think this is where people get things confused. That is to do with Antonio. The one thing that he's made crystal clear as part of his leadership is that no one is ever going to be told to shut up. I think there has been something that has subliminally happened through Exchange. Like I have heard people say, "I'm part of a speak up culture, I'm going to voice this, and I'm not going to wait for Exchange". That's exactly what should be happening, people should feel that they can knock on people's doors and say things.

Similar evidence of progression was evident at Grant Thornton where the rise of a new CEO, Sacha Romanovitch, was linked to her growing profile and ability to engage and influence through social media. The Senior Manager for National Communications at Grant Thornton characterized her as *"the very definition of a social CEO"*. It is significant that as CEO she stated *"I don't want closed leadership conversations happening via email. I want them happening out in the big wide world"*. This was consistent with her view of the management of the organization which she said would like *"the vast majority of the management of the firm to be done in an open forum"*. All this marks a trajectory towards gaining capabilities to appropriate and engage with feedback at a strategic level.

In some organizations a deeper implication of this was the effect on governance. At Atos the adoption of social media and feedback was far-reaching and the organization was there-fore considering strategic implications of this. For them this had deep implications and repre-sented a transformation as reflected by the Group Chief Change Officer.

We are now at a step where we clearly see what the benefits will be when we move into a new model of organization. Not new tools, not a new hierarchy function supporting this way of work. When we really create a more agile organization, in which co-exists structurally a social organization and a classical hierarchical organization, and we make all these flow effortlessly, seamlessly. And of course now, we are speaking of a transformation, which starts with the senior managers and into all the organization.

Other organizations, recognizing the complexity of this transformation, took a different approach in reconciling the distinct nature of the two modes of working and organizing. For example, IBM created a separate unit called "IBM Studio" to operate according to the more "agile" and employee centered approach. By separating the Studio from the rest of the organization IBM expected to create an environment that gives:

> *individuals more free rein and autonomy on what they choose to work on, and how they're going to do it. The way that the team works, the tools that they use to operate on, and then even things that they do is very much open to them.*

The vision was "*that the rest of IBM catches up with us and operates in a model closer to the way we're working*" as stated by the Team Leader of IBM Studio. At the core of this new way of working was a view of individuals as active participants of the environment where they operate. It is significant that IBM created this as a separate entity because as stated "*If you try to change the ways of working and the culture to agile but at the same time keep on measuring and rewarding people, and using exactly the same metrics you have previously, that will fail.*"

The cross-organization analysis above highlights how the process of introducing social tools stimulates employee participation and feedback, but also leads to tensions and capability development, ultimately shifting deeper structures of organizations towards more participative environments where in some cases gives employees greater degree of influence over organizational strategy.

Conceptualizing *reflexiveness*

Across the cases analyzed we saw that the use of social media created conditions for individuals to contribute and engage in meaningful and significant aspects of their organizations' strategies. Social media provided a platform for appropriating strategic content, but also to shape that content by commenting and contributing to ongoing discourse in their organization. The feedback systems embedded in social media created structural conditions for individuals to become active participants of their own organizational settings. This is consistent with the view that strategic action involves individuals thinking and acting reflexively and is enabled by structural conditions in the organizational environment. A reflexive environment creates equal opportunities to all constituents for participation and engaging in feedback. Our analysis shows that the adoption of social media contributes to the creation of an environment and contextual conditions for reflexive behavior, which over time evolves to become a property of the organization as suggested by Gorli et al. (2015, p. 4):

> *Reflection thus becomes a collective ability to question the assumptions that underpin the organizing process. Although individual reflection is not eliminated, the attention paid to the organizational level stresses the impossibility of isolating reflection from the social and organizational micro-contexts in which courses of action are produced and reproduced.*

Although Gorli et al. (2015, p. 3) do not mention social media they indicate that these same properties or affordances of becoming more reflexive and open ultimately contribute to *"staff in an organization to become authors of their own work settings."* As strategy practice shifts from the realms of a privileged group to become recognized as a shared resource, it builds a capability that *"consists of a constant process of interrogation whereby we reconstruct shared meanings with others"* (Gorli et al., 2015, p. 5). Reflexiveness gives agency to employees to become actively *included* and derive meaning from more *transparent* information.

Thus, *reflexiveness* contributes a third dimension to Whittington et al.'s model of open strategizing as represented in Figure 16.3, thereby extending the open strategy literature. This added dimension captures the dynamic nature of the process of opening up strategic work within organizations.

This third dimension, as represented in Figure 16.3, injects the need for organizational capabilities to an otherwise static typology. In practical terms it represents the capability created by organizations to better manage feedback from individuals (as a result of a more transparent and inclusive environment) and use it positively to collectively shape the strategic direction of the organization. This is consistent with the view of strategy as a form of reflexive behavior that draws on learned *"institutionalised patterns and recipes for action"* but *"requires reflexivity in order to select the appropriate move at the appropriate time"* (Wilson and Jarzabkowski, 2004, p. 15). This situated and contextual view of strategy suggests that social media and its feedback features give individuals the ability to *"assume responsibility for, and constructively contribute to the goals of the organizations to which they belong"* (Gorli et al., 2015, p. 1), they call this *"practical reflexivity"*. As seen in the analysis of the case material the embedding of social media in the ways of working of the organization created conditions for the emergence of feedback, and in some cases the active participation in significant aspects of the organizations. In this respect their use creates the "reflexive" environment that Gorli et al. (2015) refers to in their study.

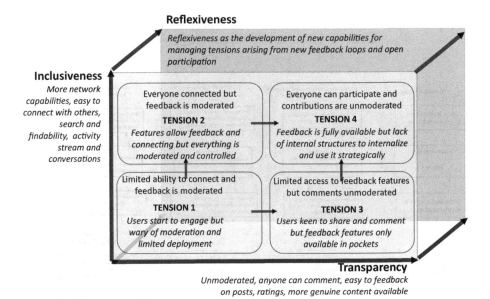

Figure 16.3 Tensions between open social media participation and extant structures as drivers for "reflexiveness" capabilities

We find that while social media create *inclusiveness* (by involving more individuals) and *transparency* (wider availability of information) through the embedding of social media features in organizations, *reflexiveness* is the ability to manage and appropriate this feedback structurally to shape the direction of the organization. We therefore suggest that increasing *inclusiveness* and *transparency* in strategy (Whittington et al., 2011) through social media in organizations stimulates the corresponding development of *reflexiveness.* These relationships are illustrated in Figure 16.3, where open strategy is a progression across the three dimensional axis.

Next, we take a more dynamic view of this process, to conceptualize the progression from tensions towards the development of new organizational capabilities, ultimately resulting in new but more consistent structural arrangements in the organizations.

Dynamic View of Tensions and Capabilities Development

We characterized the development of *reflexiveness* in three stages, as a gradual process of capability development as organizations adjust structurally to better manage emergent feedback from social media platforms. We noted how the normative structures shifted towards open communication and emergent feedback, gradually also shifting practices and behaviors. Figure 16.4 captures this process. It provides a dynamic and longitudinal representation of the process by which social media creates conditions to trigger tensions that encourage the development of new capabilities to better manage and integrate emergent feedback in the functioning of organizations. At the core of this process are the tensions characterized earlier in Figure 16.2. As discussed, these tensions trigger adjustments to the organization, rendering it more capable of managing and integrating emergent feedback within its work environment. Figure 16.4 shows two juxtaposing layers. The first layer shows the progression with the tensions identified. The second layer represents the new capabilities developed in response to the tensions.

This longitudinal conceptualization of the dynamics that push organizations towards more open practices in strategizing, and ultimately their organizing was for example seen at Atos, a process that was referred to as a "third revolution". But there were also instances of these deeper effects at the IBM Studio which operated under a distinct mandate from the rest of IBM to create conditions for a more collective and agile governance model. This mandate

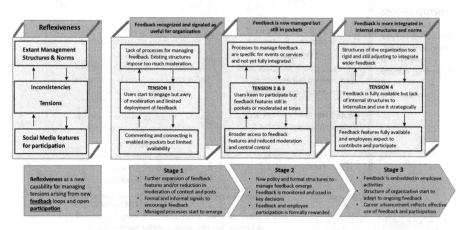

Figure 16.4 Dynamic and multi-level representation of the dynamic effects of tensions from social media use, and the emergence of reflexiveness *as a new organizational capability*

gave employees a higher degree of independence and ownership of their work, which made it much closer to a *"startup than other monolithic and sometime faceless organizations"*. This meant that individuals performed their work with limited supervision but still as part of an organized structure of ongoing peer evaluation, reinforcing collectively agreed contributions, while at the same time abandoning what is perceived by the group to be inferior or low priority. Also, at Grant Thornton deeper changes to reward structures and working arrangements were noticed, reflecting a move towards a governance model that is more centered on individuals as owners of their work, and better able to shape the direction of their organizations. Our study indicates that as organizations gain new capabilities to manage and integrate emergent feedback in their structures they become more reflexive, and consequently create conditions for *organizational authorship*, or in the words of Gorli et al. (2015, p. 5) they:

> encourage social actors to see themselves as *agents* and as *authors of the organizations and institutions in which they live. In other words, practical reflexivity is closely linked to the pursuit, enhancement and development of organizational authorship.*

It is the subtle but gradual shift in agency towards individuals as "stewards" of their own paths that cumulatively shift the structures of the organization towards what Hernandez (2012, p. 175) describes as "stewardship". She argues that individuals can *"collectively create feedback loop processes to systematically shift organizational governance from agency towards steward-ship"* (p. 172).

While Hernandez does not empirically explore these feedback loop processes, our study offers practical examples of how participative social media may offer such dynamics in the workplace, ultimately leading to what Hernandez suggests is a culture and normative envi-ronment where *"an affective sense of connection with others prompts individuals to feel compelled to positively influence the collective"* (p. 175). Moving towards a stewardship model reflects this progression towards giving individuals greater ability to participate in organizational life so that they increasingly feel owners of "strategy", as more broadly defined previously. It is this ability to shape the environment that employees operate in that we refer to as stewardship-based organizing, as conceptualized by Hernandez (2012).

These deeper changes represent what Hernandez (2012, p. 172) remark as *"feedback loop processes systematically shift organizational governance from agency towards stewardship"* and rep-resents the aggregated effect of new capability development. This reflects the progression from organizing strategic activity around processes that optimize employee activity around predetermined goals towards an approach that is more centered on individuals as active par-ticipants of their own work environments.

Concluding Remarks

This study has examined the role of social media as organizations embrace open strategy. We contend that social media have the potential to increase *inclusiveness* and *transparency* as two essential properties of open strategizing. However, these can initially create tensions and inconsistencies and so are not sufficient in themselves for openness. Our study suggests that organizations (including their leadership) respond to these tensions and learn to manage and integrate feedback from social media in their internal structures. We characterize this as a new capability of *reflexiveness* required for organizations to become more open.

The key engine for the development of *reflexiveness* arise from the tensions found between latent ways of undertaking strategy and the new levels of inclusive, transparent and participa-tive work enabled by social media. We argue that the use of social media within organizations generates emergent feedback loops that create new and higher expectations and norms of participation, ultimately moving organizations to become more centered on individuals' abilities to contribute to organizational life. We suggest that adopting participative practices and becoming more reflexive create conditions for organizational authorship, and a shift towards stewardship governance (Hernandez, 2012) where strategy is increasingly jointly owned by organizational actors who feel responsible for the collective, rather than disengaged employees operating by following norms and procedures. We suggest that the adoption of social media and the embedding of participative practices in the structure of organizations create conditions for strategy to become shared and collectively owned; one which positions many more organizational actors as strategy practitioners.

The interlinked nature of these areas reemphasizes the importance of forging a joint Information Systems – Strategy agenda for research and practice (Whittington, 2014). As discussed, there is much potential for social media to revolutionize strategizing as an open activity where stakeholders participate or take ownership of strategy content. Our study, thus, contributes to the literature on open strategy by advancing our understanding of emergent new arrangements in who is involved in strategy (practitioners) using what tools (artefacts) and how it is performed (praxis) ultimately detecting the emergence of new professional practices in this field (Whittington, 2006; Whittington et al., 2011, 2006). We also contribute to the Information Systems Strategy literature by reflecting on the role of and impact of ICTs such as social media in organizational strategizing (e.g., Chen et al., 2010; Galliers, 2011; Marabelli and Galliers, 2016), and their role in the development of new organizational capabilities (e.g., Peppard and Ward, 2004) but in particular to the growing literature that considers social media use in the workplace (e.g., Huang et al., 2013; Leonardi et al., 2013). We also contend that this study informs practice: the more we know of the tensions and capabilities arising from social media and participative platforms in the workplace, the better placed senior management will be in leveraging these new phenomena.

The study raises several important interrelated challenges for future research, including a reinvigoration of the role played by employees in defining strategy content. Further, and as we have argued, the features of social media, coupled with reflexive agents and modified governance structures, render both the practice and content of strategy contested and negotiable. A further strand of investigation could thus focus on the interrelationship between social media and governance—an important, yet underexplored, theme within open strategy. It is clear from our findings that participation played an important role in the emergence of feedback loops and engaging employees. However, an unresolved feature of our study concerns precisely how employees should participate in strategy using social media; participation from rendering strategy inclusive and visible may be perfunctory despite organizational actors appearing to take ownership of decision-making.

References

Aral, S., Dellarocas, C., Godes, D., 2013. Social Media and business transformation: A framework for research. *Information Systems Research* 24 (1), 3–13.

Baptista, J., 2009. Institutionalisation as a process of interplay between technology and its organizational context of use. *Journal ofInformation Technology* 24 (4), 305–319.

Bechky, B.A., 2011. Making organizational theory work: Institutions, occupations, and negotiated orders. *Organization Science* 22 (5), 1157–1167.

Bruhn, M., Ahlers, G.M., 2013. Integrated communication in the innovation process: An approach to integrated innovation communication. In: Pfeffermann, N., Minshall, T., & Mortara, L. (Eds.), *Strategy and Communication for Innovation*. Springer, Heidelberg, p. 139–160.

Chen, D.Q., Mocker, M., Preston, D.S., Teubner, A., 2010. Information systems strategy: Reconceptualization measurement, and implications. *MIS Quarterly* 34 (2), 233–238.

Collier, N., Fishwick, F., Floyd, S.W., 2004. Managerial involvement and perceptions of strategy process. *Long Range Planning* 37 (1), 67–83.

Cotton, J.L., Vollrath, D.A., Froggatt, K.L., Lengnickhall, M.L., Jennings, K.R., 1988. Employee participation—diverse forms and different outcomes. *Academy of Management Review* 13 (1), 8–22.

Cunliffe, A.L., 2002. Reflexive dialogical practice in management learning. *Management Learning* 33 (1), 35–61.

Denyer, D., Parry, E., Flowers, P., 2011. "Social", "Open" and "Participative"? Exploring personal experiences and organizational effects of enterprise 2.0 use. *Long Range Planning* 44 (5), 375–396.

Dobusch, L., Mueller-Seitz, G., 2012. Strategy as a practice of thousands. Academy of Management Best Paper Proceedings.

Doz, Y.L., Kosonen, M., 2008a. The dynamics of strategic agility: Nokia's rollercoaster experience. *California Management Review* 50 (3), 95–118.

Doz, Y.L., Kosonen, M., 2008b. *Fast Strategy: How Strategic Agility Will Help You Stay Ahead of the Game.* Pearson Education, Dorchester.

Easterby-Smith, M., Thorpe, R., Jackson, P.R., 2012. *Management Research.* Sage, London.

Floyd, S.W., Wooldridge, B., 1994. Dinosaurs or dynamos? Recognizing middle management's strategic role. *Academy of Management Executive* 8 (4), 47–57.

Friesl, M., Silberzahn, R., 2012. Challenges in establishing global collaboration: Temporal, strategic and operational decoupling. *Long Range Planning* 45, 160–181.

Galliers, R.D., 2011. Further developments in information systems strategizing: Unpacking the concept. In R. Galliers, W. Currie (Eds.), *The Oxford Handbook of Management Information Systems: Critical Perspectives and New Directions.* Oxford University Press, Oxford, p. 329–345.

Gorli, M., Nicolini, D., Scaratti, G., 2015. Reflexivity in practice: Tools and conditions for developing organizational authorship. *Human Relations* 68 (8), 1347–1375.

Haefliger, S., Monteiro, E., Foray, D., von Krogh, G., 2011. Social software and strategy. *Long Range Planning* 44 (5 – 6), 297–316.

Hambrick, D.C., 2007. Upper echelons theory: An update. *Academy of Management Review* 32 (2), 334–343.

Helsper, E.J., Eynon, R., 2009. Digital natives: Where is the evidence? *British Educational Research Journal* 36 (3), 503–520.

Hernandez, M., 2012. Toward an understanding of the psychology of stewardship. *Academy of Management Review* 37 (2), 172–193.

Hienerth, C., Keinz, P., Lettl, C., 2011. Exploring the nature and implementation process of user-centric business models. *Long Range Planning* 44 (5 – 6), 344–374.

Huang, J., Baptista, J., Newell, S., 2015. Communicational ambidexterity as a new capability to manage social media communication within organizations. *The Journal of Strategic Information Systems* 24 (2), 49–64.

Jarzabkowski, P., Kaplan, S., 2014. Strategy tools-in-use: A framework for understanding "technologies of rationality" in practice. *Strategic Management Journal* 36 (4), 537–558.

Kaplan, A., Haenlein, M., 2010. Users of the world, unite! The challenges and opportunities of social media. *Business Horizons* 53, 59–68.

Kietzmann, J.H., Hermkens, K., McCarthy, I.P., Silvestre, B.S., 2011. Social media? Get serious! Understanding the functional building blocks of social media. *Business Horizons* 54 (3), 241–251.

Leonardi, P.M., Huysman, M., Steinfield, C., 2013. Enterprise social media: Definition, history, and prospects for the study of social technologies in organizations. *Journal of Computer-Mediated Communication* 19 (1), 1–19.

Majchrzak, A., Wagner, C., Yates, D., 2013. The impact of shaping on knowledge for organizational improvement with wikis. *MIS Quarterly* 37 (2), 455–A412.

Mantere, S., Vaara, E., 2008. On the problem of participation in strategy: A critical discursive perspective. *Organization Science* 19 (2), 341–358.

Marabelli, M., Galliers, R., 2016. A reflection on information systems strategizing: The role of power and everyday practices. *Information Systems Journal.* 27 (3), 248–366.

Matzler, K., Fuller, J., Hutter, K., Hautz, J., Stieger, D., 2014. Open strategy—a new strategy paradigm? In K. Matzler, H. Pechlaner, B. Renzl (Eds.), *Strategie and Leadership.* Springer Fachmedien Wisbaden, 38–56.

Morton, J., Wilson, A., Cooke, L., 2015. Collaboration and knowledge sharing in open strategy initiatives. In iFutures 2015. Sheffield iSchool Conferences.

Peppard, J., Ward, J., 2004. Beyond strategic information systems: Towards an IS capability. *The Journal of Strategic Information Systems* 13, 167–194.

Pettigrew, A.M., 1992. On studying managerial elites. *Strategic Management Journal* 13 (S2), 163–182.

Razmerita, L., Kirchner, K., Nabeth, T., 2014. Social media in organizations: Leveraging personal and collective knowledge processes. *Journal of Organizational Computing and Electronic Commerce* 24 (1), 74–93.

Schatzki, T.R., 2002. *The Site of the Social: A Philosophical Account of the Constitution of Social Life and Change.* Pennsylvania State University Press, University Park, Pennsylvania.

Schoenberg, N.E., Ravdal, H., 2000. Using vignettes in awareness and attitudinal research. *International Journal of Social Research Methodology* 3 (1), 63–74.

Seidl, D., Whittington, R., 2014. Enlarging the strategy-as-practice research agenda: Towards taller and flatter ontologies. *Organization Studies* 35 (10), 1407–1421.

Spagnoletti, P., Resca, A., Sæbø, Ø., 2015. Design for social media engagement: Insights from elderly care assistance. *The Journal of Strategic Information Systems* 24 (2), 128–145.

Stebbins, R.A., 2001. *Exploratory Research in the Social Sciences.* Sage, London.

Stieger, D., Matzler, K., Chatterjee, S., Ladstaetter-Fussenegger, F., 2012. Democratizing strategy: How crowdsourcing can be used for strategy dialogues. *California Management Review* 54 (4), 44–68.

Sutanto, J., Tan, C.-H., Battistini, B., Phang, C.W., 2011. Emergent leadership in virtual collaboration settings: A social network analysis approach. *Long Range Planning* 44 (5), 421–439.

Tams, S., Grover, V., Thatcher, J., 2014. Modern information technology in an old workforce: Toward a strategic research agenda. *The Journal of Strategic Information Systems* 23 (4), 284–304.

Treem, J., Leonardi, P., 2012. Social media use in organizations: Exploring the affordances of visibility, editability, persistence, and association. *Communication Yearbook* 36, 143–189.

Vaast, E., Kaganer, E., 2013. Social media affordances and governance in the workplace: An examination of organizational policies. *Journal of Computer-Mediated Communication* 19 (1), 78–101.

Vodanovich, S., Sundaram, D., Myers, M., 2010. Research commentary-digital natives and ubiquitous information systems. *Information Systems Research* 21 (4), 711–723.

Von Krogh, G., 2012. How does social software change knowledge management? Toward a strategic research agenda. *The Journal of Strategic Information Systems* 21 (2), 154–164.

Whittington, R., 2006. Completing the practice turn in strategy research. *Organization Studies* 27 (5), 613–634.

Whittington, R., 2014. Information systems strategy and strategy-as-practice: A joint agenda. *The Journal of Strategic Information Systems* 23 (1), 87–91.

Whittington, R., Molloy, E., Mayer, M., Smith, A., 2006. Practices of strategising/organising: Broadening strategy work and skills. *Long Range Planning* 39 (6), 615–629.

Whittington, R., Cailluet, L., Yakis-Douglas, B., 2011. Opening strategy: Evolution of a precarious profession. *British Journal of Management* 22 (3), 531–544.

Wilson, D.C., Jarzabkowski, P., 2004. Thinking and acting strategically: New challenges for interrogating strategy. *European Management Review* 1 (1), 14–20.

Wooldridge, B., Floyd, S.W., 1990. The strategy process, middle management involvement, and organizational performance. *Strategic Management Journal* 11 (3), 231–241.

Questions for Discussion

1   How does social media alter the communication and strategizing in organizations?

2   Is the process of strategizing shifting to inclusive and transparent? What is the role of social media in such a shift? How does such shift affect power redistribution in organizations?

3   Using the Power Matrix (chapter 10), analyze what is the role of actors (strategists and social media users) and IS (social media) and how do these affect strategizing?

4   Could resistance be observed in the shift from analogue strategy process to a digital strategy process? Where and how would such resistance get observed?

5   How would the tensions between feedback from social media and formal structures and norms within organizations get resolved? How can organizations develop a reflexive organizational capability? Who would manage the development of such capability and help resolve any emerging tensions?

6   Why the use of social media does not guarantee achieving transparency and inclusivity in organizations?

Further Reading

Huang, J., Baptista, J., Galliers, R.D. (2013). Reconceptualizing rhetorical practices in organizations: The impact of social media on internal communications. *Information and Management*, *50*, 112–124.

Tavakoli, A., Schlagwein, D., Schoder, D. (2017). Open strategy: Literature review, re-analysis of cases and conceptualisation as a practice. *The Journal of Strategic Information Systems*, 26 (3), 163–184.

Chapter 17

Dorothy E. Leidner, Ester Gonzalez, and Hope Koch

AN AFFORDANCE PERSPECTIVE OF ENTERPRISE SOCIAL MEDIA AND ORGANIZATIONAL SOCIALIZATION

T**HE CHALLENGE OF SOCIALIZING** newcomers has become an ever more pressing issue for organizations as the nature of work has increasingly shifted from long-term employment within a single employer marked by slow but steady upward progression to more short-term positions and lateral movements across a variety of different organizations (Wright, 2013). With organizational affiliation waning, occupational affiliation has been on the rise. Whereas in the 1970s, workers were more likely to change their occupation than their employer, by the early 1990s, changing employers had become more common than changing occupations (Rose, 1995). Information technology (henceforth, IT) workers are among those who demonstrate greater occupational than organizational loyalty (O'Mahony and Bechky, 2006). The problem of employee flight is substantial: the cost of losing an employee is up to three times the employee's salary (Farren, 2007; Insala, 2010). According to an IT staffing company, the direct and indirect costs incurred by organizations in replacing a single employee who makes $60,000 per year reach approximately $150,000 (Del Monte, 2018). The lack of organizational loyalty is important not just in terms of the costs an organization faces in hiring and training replacements, but also in the productivity losses incurred when well-trained IT workers leave a project before completion and the team must either redistribute the work or integrate a new member. So significant is the problem of IT talent and retention, that the issue has been rated by CIOs as the 2nd or 3rd most important issue facing IT leaders for five consecutive years in the SIM survey on IT issues and Trends (Kappelman et al., 2018).

One way that organizations may increase employee loyalty to the organization is through socialization programs (Reichers, 1987). Facing large numbers of new IT workers entering the workforce (US Bureau of Statistics, 2015) as well as the challenge of integrating experienced workers, IT departments are showing increased interest in socialization programs designed not just to train new employees in task-related skills, but also to instill a sense of loyalty to the organization in hopes of increasing the organizational affiliation of its IT workforce. Given the costs associated with hiring and training new IT employees as well as the loss in productivity incurred when valuable employees leave, the issue of effectively socializing new IT employees is of strategic importance to IT departments. Socialization is the process whereby newly hired employees learn the beliefs, values, orientations, behaviors, social knowledge, and work place skills necessary to successfully fulfill their new organizational roles and responsibilities (Fisher, 1986; Louis, 1980; Schein, 1968; Van Maanen and Schein, 1979). Socialization leads to positive outcomes such as better job performance, less stress, higher job satisfaction, and reduction in intent to leave (Ashford and Black, 1996; Fisher, 1985; Kammeyer-Mueller and Wanberg, 2003). While the benefits of socialization are clear, the means of achieving effective socialization are complex with many tools and techniques available. Historically, socialization programs have relied upon formal onsite orientation sessions, offsite training sessions, buddy systems, mentoring programs, and business trips with co-workers (Louis et al., 1983).

Recently, organizations have begun implementing enterprise social media (ESM) as an informal organizational socialization tool. Social media allows users to create, edit and exchange web-based content (Kaplan and Haenlein, 2010), thereby enabling organizations and employees to foster relationships, share knowledge and collaborate (Boyd and Ellison, 2007). ESM have a role to play in organizational innovation, operations, and human relations (Kane, 2015). Considering the potential role of ESM in an organization's IS strategy is important for organizations that wish to realize business value from ESM (Kane, 2015). Academic and practitioner research has encouraged IS managers to develop a social media strategy based on the capabilities of social media platforms to manage interpersonal networks and share content. These capabilities are well-suited for socialization programs (Kane, 2015; Kane et al., 2014). Organizations have begun using ESM systems to help new employees learn about their jobs, their colleagues, and the organization (Bennett et al., 2010). ESM enables fast and extensive knowledge sharing and facilitates open conversations (Thomas and Silverstone, 2015) both of which can foster new hire socialization. Moreover, ESM provide various opportunities such as self-marketing and relationship building that extend beyond the embedded functions and features of the technology and that may hold important ramifications for new hire socialization and, in essence, make the socialization process an "open" one. Much as ESM has been shown to enable open strategizing with a resultant sense of community and stronger organizational commitment (Hutter et al., 2017), ESM may enable open socialization wherein active participation may result in a strong sense of community and commitment.

However, the multivocality enabled through ESM in which more voices are heard and more messages are generated (Huang et al., 2013, 2015) may shift the control of organizational communication away from central, largely senior, sources to employees who have access to, and choose to engage with, the ESM. While such participation changes the rhetorical practice of organizations, in a sense democratizing the practice (Huang et al., 2013), it may also create conflicts and tensions (Huang et al., 2015). For example, in the context of open strategy, ESM has been shown to create tensions between the participatory practices of the technology and the existing managerial practices (Baptista et al., 2017). Such tensions might also be created in the application of ESM to organizational socialization practices. Formal socialization programs have been carefully scripted by senior management to convey a desired organizational message, culture, and mission. The introduction of ESM as informal socialization tools has the potential to threaten this careful scripting and disrupt the cultural norms of the organization. ESM thus have both the potential to foster a greater sense of community and organizational commitment, but also the potential to create tensions. Given the strategic importance of socialization in the current organizational context of decreasing organizational commitment marked by frequent job changes, ESM for socialization are strategically important systems and must be mindfully implemented in order to produce effective results.

Despite the strategic importance of ESM systems in organizations (Gartner Inc, 2014; Kane, 2015) and the strategic importance of attracting, training and retaining a skilled IT workforce (Kappelman et al., 2018), few studies to date have investigated the use of ESM for employee socialization (VanOsch and Coursaris, 2014). In order to contribute to our understanding of how ESM affects employee socialization, this paper invokes a case study of an organization that had recently incorporated ESM into its IT new hire program. Drawing upon technology affordance theory as our lens, we address the following research question: how do ESM affordances influence the socialization of IT new hires? This paper is organized as follows. We first provide the theoretical foundation. We then present the method, a case description and the analysis followed by the implications, limitations, and conclusion.

Theoretical Foundation

Our investigation draws from organizational socialization research (Kammeyer-Mueller and Wanberg, 2003; Van Maanen and Schein, 1979) and from the technology affordance perspective of information systems (Majchrzak et al., 2013). The research on organizational socialization informs our understanding of the socialization process. We then apply the technology affordance perspective as the theoretical foundation for understanding how and why ESM may alter socialization processes and outcomes.

Organizational Socialization

Organizational socialization is a learning process wherein newly hired employees acquire the requisite knowledge, skills, values, and norms to enable them to perform their roles in their organization (Bauer and Erdogan, 2011; Berger and Luckmann, 1967; Fisher, 1986; Van Maanen and Schein, 1979). Four elements comprise the socialization process: task mastery (learning how to perform one's job), role clarification (gaining an understanding of one's job), acculturation (adjusting to the organization's culture), and social integration (developing relationships with others in the organization, especially peers and superiors) (Morrison, 1993). Effective socialization practices are those that enable newly hired individuals (henceforth, new hires) to achieve proximal outcomes of self-efficacy, role clarity, knowledge of organizational culture, and a sense of belongingness (Bauer and Erdogan, 2011; Kammeyer-Mueller and Wanberg, 2003).

The socialization process can take place formally via institutionalized socialization and training programs as well as informally through interactions among employees and observation. Indeed, how one is socialized is as important as the content of socialization (Ashforth et al., 2007) and the initial socialization experience has implications for perceptions, behaviors and attitudes that remain throughout an individual's employment in the organization (Fisher, 1986; Wesson and Gogus, 2005). As the importance of informal socialization practices became recognized and as the organizations into which individuals were being socialized became increasingly characterized by distributed teams and virtual communities, the potential importance of information technology in socialization processes began to receive research attention.

IT has been shown to play an important role in not only the initial socialization into a group, but also in the ongoing socialization that is particularly important in distributed and/or virtual settings (Oshri et al., 2007). According to Oshri et al. (2007), difficulties in sharing norms, attitudes, and behaviors can be alleviated by the use of electronic communication and collaboration tools before, during and after face-to-face meetings. For example, video-conferences can be used to introduce new team members to each other, which may serve as an important socialization tool prior to a face-to-face meeting of the team whereas email may be used to clarify key points both before and after face-to-face encounters. Some research indicates that the formation of virtual communities can assist in the socialization of employees. In this case, the role of IT is to enable communication and knowledge sharing which facilitate learning, identity formation, and relationship development (Allee, 2000; Brown and Duguid, 2000; Chang et al., 2009; Wasko and Faraj, 2005; Wenger et al., 2002), all of which are considered essential components of socialization. To date, the research on IT in socialization has largely focused on traditional communication and collaboration tools (e.g., email, video conferencing, intranets, online chats) (Oshri et al., 2007) and on knowledge sharing platforms (Brown and Duguid, 2000; Chang et al., 2009). IT use in these studies has focused on individuals' behaviors (e.g., information seeking vs. contribution) and the content of information exchange (such as questions, internal documents, and clarifications). To further advance our understanding of the role of IT in socialization, we investigate a new technology being used for socialization (ESM). Our research seeks to uncover the mechanisms through which ESM influences the socialization processes and socialization outcomes of organizational new hires. In order to delve deeply into the question of how ESM influences organizational socialization, we draw from the theory of technology affordance.

Technology Affordances Perspective

In the IS literature (e.g., Kane et al., 2011; Leonardi, 2011; Markus and Silver, 2008), affordances refer to possibilities for action offered to an individual by an object (Volkoff and Strong, 2013). An affordance is a property of the relationship between an actor and an object (Volkoff and Strong, 2013) and thus, represents an opportunity for action (Hutchby, 2001; Stoffregen, 2003). One affordance arising from the relation between a user and a technology can provide multiple affordances and produce multiple outcomes (Treem and Leonardi, 2012; Volkoff and Strong, 2013). In the same manner, the interaction between the user and the technology can afford actions that create hindrances.

In spite of its growing prevalence in IS studies, IS researchers have yet to agree on how to distinguish technology affordance from technology use. The term affordances has been described in manifold ways such as: "what is offered, provided, or furnished to someone or something by an object," "a property of the relationship between an object and an actor which is defined as an opportunity for action," "the potential for behaviors associated with achieving an immediate concrete outcome," (all the above from Volkoff and Strong, 2013, pp. 822–823), "the action potential that can be taken given a technology" (Majchrzak, et al. 2013, p. 39), "a relational construct linking the capabilities afforded by technology artifacts to the actors' purposes" (Faraj and Azad, 2012, p. 26), "the possibilities of using select features or combinations of features in a way meaningful to the user's goals, abilities, and line of action" (Faraj and Azad, 2012, p. 26), and as something "constituted in relationships between people and the materiality of the things with which they come in contact" (Treem and Leonardi, 2012, p. 146). These views of affordance emphasize that affordance is an action (or potential for action until it has been actualized) and that it is a fundamentally different perspective than merely looking at technology use or technology feature use.

However, in spite of this conceptual separation of use and affordances in word, in practice, much of the IS affordance research does not sufficiently distinguish between features, use, and action. Treem and Leonardi (2012), for example, describe four affordances of social media: persistence, visibility, editability, and association. However, these are not actions. Rather, these are attributes of the technology. Other affordances research mingles the concepts of feature use and affordance. For example, Majchrzak and Markus (2013) assign the affordance label "metavoicing" to the action of "reacting online to others' presence, profiles, content and activities." Yet reacting online via voting or commenting or other social media features is a direct use of the features of social media. Similarly, when describing electronic health record (EHR) affordances, Strong et al. (2014) label as an affordance the "capturing and archiving digital data about patients", yet capturing and archiving data are using EHR features to capture and record data. Likewise, they label "accessing and using patient information anytime from anywhere" as an affordance whereas these are again direct uses of system features, as is "monitoring organizational operations." Moreover, the literature on affordance has been inconsistent in carefully distinguishing the outcome of affordance actualization from the affordance itself. For example, Strong et al. (2014) identify "capturing and archiving digital data" and "standardizing data, processes, and roles" as EHR affordances. They then identify as outcomes the fact that "digital data about patients are captured and archived" and that "data, processes, or roles are standardized." The outcomes are the same as the affordances. Because of the failure to meticulously distinguish use from affordances and affordances from outcomes, the result is that the distinction between use, affordances, and outcomes becomes muddled.

To clarify our position on these conceptual distinctions, we provide an example of commuting to work. One might choose to ride a train to commute to work. Riding the train is the equivalent of using the technology. In this case, the technology in question (e.g., the train) is an object that moves. By definition, to "ride" is to be carried by an object that moves. As one uses the technology (e.g., rides the train), one might engage in various affordances, such as working, sleeping, meditating, or conversing with another passenger. These affordances are possible by virtue of the fact that the individual chose to ride the train (e.g., use the technology). One could achieve these same affordances via other means, such as if one took a bus or a taxi to work and one could also achieve these affordances without going to work at all. However, if the goal is to get to work and one takes advantage of a moving object to get to work (e.g., one rides the moving train), then as one uses the object to achieve a particular goal (getting to work), one may benefit from other affordances along the way. Riding the train is the direct use of the object whereas working, sleeping, meditating, or conversing are not uses of the train itself, but affordances made possible by the train ride. One might be tempted to say that the outcome is that the individual arrives at work, but this is the outcome of riding the train, not the outcome of the affordances produced by riding the train. An outcome of affording the ride on the train to work, for example, may be that the individual completes more work in a given day than he would if he drove to work. Or perhaps the outcome of the individual who afforded the ride to meditate is that this individual arrives at work in a relaxed state of mind. The affordance lens is a powerful tool for helping IS researchers understand the choices made regarding a technology and the consequences of these choices.

We suggest that to move forward in affordance research, it is important to carefully and intentionally separate technology use from technology affordance, and technology affordance from outcomes of the affordance, in order to understand how the use of technology features provide affordances to individuals and how these affordances produce outcomes. The affordance perspective has both theoretical and methodological implications. Theoretically, it helps provide an explanation of how and why technology produces affordances and outcomes. Methodologically, it requires researchers to carefully distinguish between use, affordance, and outcomes in their analysis. Applying this to our context of ESM and new hire socialization, an affordance perspective will allow us to investigate the interactions between new hires and the ESM in ways that go beyond the use of the ESM's features in order to explain how the affordances actualized by new hires affects their socialization into the organization.

Method

Because studies of ESM within organizational socialization programs are scarce, we chose to study one case in depth. In Dube and Pare's (2003) study of IS positivist case research, 60% of all studies they found were of a single case with 40% being multi-case studies. Since Dube and Pare's analysis, single case studies continue to be well represented in top IS journals (e.g., Bygstad et al., 2016; Chua et al., 2012; Gregory et al., 2013, 2015; Sarker et al., 2012; Seidel et al., 2013 to name but a few) because of their potential to discover new insights through unique, extreme, or revelatory cases. According to Yin (1989), a single case study is appropriate in three situations when the case: (1) represents the critical situation in testing a well-formulated theory, (2) represents an extreme or unique instance, or (3) is a revelatory inquiry. In this latter case, a researcher has an opportunity to observe and analyze a phenomenon previously inaccessible to scientific investigation. Our case fits the second and third situations. At the time we began collecting data, the case was very unique. Organizations were just beginning to adopt ESM and IT departments were not widely using ESM and certainly not as part of a new hire program. Moreover, it was not previously possible to study how social media influences the socialization of new hires, because as a phenomenon, it had only begun to exist.

Data Collection

We refer to our case organization as Financial Services Plus (FSP), a pseudonym. Our data collection spanned the course of eight years. Our continuous involvement over a long period of time allowed us to acquire a deep contextual understanding of the IT department and its new hire program and rich insights into the interactions of new hires with the ESM.

Data collection consisted of face-to-face interviews with new hires, middle managers and executives. We collected additional data by attending events, meeting with employees during off-time (i.e., dinner and or breaks), observations, and reading weekly journals maintained by new hire interns. Since 2007, we have conducted over 100 interviews and 8 focus groups with 50 of FSP's professional IT and human resource employees.

Table 17.1 lists the demographics of the employees who participated in our interviews. Table 17.6 in the Appendix details the focus groups conducted. During the focus groups, we had round-table discussions with multiple participants. These discussions were very important to our understanding of the ESM and the organizational context. We recognize the possibility that focus group settings might constrain a participant's answers. We therefore rely on the focus group observations as helpful in understanding the context surrounding the introduction and use of the ESM, but base our detailed analysis on the interview data.

Culturally, our new hire interviewees were similar. Most participants were United States citizens who had recently graduated from a four-year degree program in management information systems or computer science. Employees in a variety of roles (i.e., new hires, managers, and human resource professionals) took part in our interviews and focus groups.

The interviews were semi-structured. Questions centered around what the ESM allowed the new hires to do, what ESM activities they participated in, what happened once they started using the ESM system, and challenges the system created. The interviews lasted between 30 and 60 minutes. Most interviews were recorded and transcribed. In

Table 17.1 Interviewee demographics.

Role	No. interviewed	No. of Interviews	Gender	Experience at FSP	Level of seniority
IT Interns	6	8	4 males/2 females	< 3months	Low
IT New Hires	25	40	22 males/3 females	< 3years	Low
IT Managers	11	33	6 males/5 females	15–20 years	Medium/high
IT Professionals	1	2	1 male	5 years	Medium
HR Professional	2	9	1 male/1 female	> 5years	Medium
IT Executives	5	13	3 males/2 females	2–25 years	Medium/high
Totals	50	105			

cases where it was not possible to record (for example, a few interviews with managers took place over lunch and background noise interfered with recording), detailed notes were taken.

Data Analysis

Because our aim was to understand how the affordances actualized from the ESM created outcomes for new hires, we adopted a critical realist data analysis approach focused on uncovering the generative mechanisms that explain empirical outcomes. As explained by Volkoff and Strong (2013), the identification of affordances helps researchers specify mechanisms that explain the outcomes of the introduction of new technology in organizations. Generative mechanisms are the causal structures that explain empirical outcomes (Bygstad et al., 2016). Here, we do not expound on the principles of critical realism because these are well addressed in the IS literature (see, for example, Mingers et al., 2013; Williams and Karahanna, 2013; Wynn and Williams, 2012). Less well explained are the specific data analysis procedures one should follow in seeking to identify generative mechanisms. Authors describe various procedures. Williams and Karahanna (2013) describe four steps: identifying the critical events; explicating the structure and context from the event analysis; identifying generative mechanisms through retroduction; and confirming the generative mechanisms through empirical corroboration. Henfridsson and Bygstad (2013) describe a four step process of using open coding to identify key events: identifying the objects of the case, identifying key mechanisms through retroduction, and analyzing contextual conditions and outcomes of the mechanisms. Mingers et al. (2013) also describe four steps in the DREI methodology: describe the events, retroduce explanatory mechanisms, eliminate false hypotheses, and identify correct mechanism. Bygstad et al. (2016) provide a six step framework: description of events and issues; identification of key entities; theoretical re-description; retroduction (identification of immediate concrete outcomes, analysis of the interplay of human and technical entities, identification of candidate affordances, and identification of stimulating and releasing conditions); analysis of the set of affordances and associated mechanisms; and assessment of explanatory power.

Taking inspiration from these various suggestions on how to analyze data from a critical realist perspective, we undertook a five step process. The first step was an open coding of the transcripts and notes with a view towards identifying key events in the new hire program leading to and following the introduction of the ESM and identifying the features and functionalities of the ESM. The second step involved an analysis of the perceived outcomes of the ESM. This step entailed another round of data coding wherein we looked specifically for references to the impact of the ESM on the new hires. This process was iterative in that we began with a long list of stated outcomes, but then developed general categories within which to group similar outcomes. The third step entailed coding for affordances. This step involved carefully reading the interview transcripts and field notes to look for statements about how the ESM was used. It was critical in this stage to separate direct use of system features from the affordances such use provided. For example, creating user profiles is a use whereas building relationships with peers is an affordance. This step was very iterative with the three researchers working independently to identify candidate affordances, discuss them, refine them, and return to the data to corroborate them with examples. As previously mentioned, prior research discussing social media affordances has tended to confound use of features with affordances. We therefore began our analysis of affordances with a clean slate, allowing the affordances to emerge from the data. The fourth step was our retroduction in which we linked affordances into strands of affordances and associated these affordance strands with particular outcomes. Through this process of linking affordances into strands (or patterns of actualized affordances) and affordance strands to outcomes, we were able to abstract the generative mechanisms. Our final step was to establish the context of the affordances, outcomes, and mechanisms. In this step, we looked for insights into why some new hires experienced socialization and others did not. This analysis revealed three types of users who actualized different affordance strands and experienced different socialization outcomes.

The FSP Case Description

FSP is one of the largest providers of financial planning, investments, insurance, and banking in the United States. FSP's IT department houses 2500 employees among which roughly 10% are new hires. FSP's IT department has historically suffered from a 60–70% new hire turnover rate, reflecting the IT department's struggle to acclimate and socialize new hires into its IT workforce.

To improve the organizational socialization of new hires, FSP charged an IT director with revamping FSP's new hire program. The IT director leveraged social media technologies and implemented an ESM tool, called OnBoard, a pseudonym. OnBoard is a Web 2.0 technology that consists of features inclusive of, but not restricted to, social networks, discussion forums, micro blogs, and profile pages. OnBoard consists of a technical and social system. The social system consists of face-to-face events and meetings. The technical system consists of the social media platform. OnBoard complemented the standard 6-week orientation period by providing a platform for new hires to get to know one another and stay in touch during their three-year new hire program.

Leadership of the ESM comes from a core team of six IT new hires responsible for creating and maintaining the OnBoard technical and social system. The IT new hire program director chooses these leaders from a pool of new hires who have been identified by existing core team members and who have expressed interest in leading OnBoard. Core team members can serve a maximum of two years, but most serve one year.

Within the second year of OnBoard's implementation, the human resources (HR) director recognized IT new hires' involvement with OnBoard's socializing activities and officially integrated OnBoard as part of the HR's organizational recruiting and onboarding efforts. HR gives new hires access to OnBoard as soon as they accept a position so that they can start connecting with other new hires. Then, after going through FSP's new employee training program, new hires use OnBoard to continue their socialization into the organization.

To date, executives credit OnBoard with reducing turnover, increasing employee engagement, and improving morale. Middle managers who had previously been involved in mentoring new hires report spending less time as a mentor, something they viewed as a personal benefit of OnBoard. In addition, executives began using OnBoard to solicit input from new hires on new products and services FSP was considering.

Whereas the organizational perspective of OnBoard's outcome was overwhelmingly positive, the new hires' perspectives of OnBoard were more nuanced. New hires reported a wide range of outcomes from OnBoard, including such positive outcomes as productivity enhancement, attractive job assignments, comfort around superiors, and a sense of support as well as negative outcomes such as additional work, stress, and social struggle. Table 17.7 in the Appendix lists the outcomes with supporting quotes and examples.

Case Analysis

We begin our analysis by describing the three types of users that emerged from our analysis (Table 17.2). We label the three types as go-getters, work-players, and just-doers (Table 17.2). The go-getters were the most active OnBoard users. They used many features on a daily basis and viewed their engagement with OnBoard as an opportunity to grow professionally. The work-players were active OnBoard users and engaged in both social and work-related uses of OnBoard, but tended to not take leadership roles that demanded time and energy. The just-doers were the least active users of OnBoard, consuming, but not contributing, information and avoiding activities that were not directly work-related. Of the 31 new hires and interns interviewed, 12 were go-getters, 11 were work-players, and eight were just-doers. Following Table 17.2, we will highlight the differences across these three groups as we describe the affordances, generative mechanisms and outcomes.

Table 17.2 The three emergent user groups.

Type of user	Frequency of use	Description	Type of usage:
The go-getters	High	Go-getters use many of the features of the system on a daily basis and integrate it into their work day activities. They view their involvement with the system as a way to grow professionally, build their social network, and demonstrate leadership. Most go-getters are members of the core team responsible for the OnBoard social and technical system	Activities include: Create, manage, and read content Develop features of the system Spearhead, organize, promote, find volunteers and acquire executive sponsorship for events Share ideas, insights about topics, and information
The work-players	Low-medium	The work-players view the system as fun and find enjoyment in helping others. They have less home and family responsibility than the just-doers. Specifically, the work-players enjoy the social aspects of the system while getting their work done and participate in such activities without regard to time or location	Activities include: Participate in social events both during and after work Initiate meet-up events Chat online with co-workers Provide others with information or guidance as needed

Type of user	Frequency of use	Description	Type of usage:
The just-doers	None to low	The just-doers prioritize their other responsibilities such as work, family and outside interests above investing in the OnBoard community. Therefore, they avoid using the system and play a limited role in creating and contributing to OnBoard. They view the system as a poor use of time	Activities include: Ask for help on solving an issue Search for information on a specific work topic (e.g., "how to do")

Table 17.3 shows the system features, use of the features, and the associated affordances. As noted, we carefully distinguish between use of the features and the affordances provided by such use. Because we are using affordances to identify the generative mechanisms connecting the OnBoard system to outcomes, we will only briefly describe the affordances.

Affordances

Networking Affordances

OnBoard affords users the ability to build relationships, interact with peers, socialize both during and after working hours and take a break during the workday. New hires' first OnBoard exposure precedes their first workday, when they use OnBoard to connect with FSP new hires that graduated from their university (Affordance 1, Table 17.3). A new hire described his pre-first day experience using OnBoard as "the best type of networking you can do because it allows you to have a connection with someone prior to your first day at work." During orientation, OnBoard provides a way for new hires to get to know one another by facilitating open communication (Affordance 2, Table 17.3). When formal orientation concludes and new hires enter their various work groups, OnBoard allows them to maintain connections from their hiring class.

By promoting interactions, informal online communication, and socializing, OnBoard helps new hires become friends with co-workers. New hires can plan informal meet-up events that occur outside of work hours (Affordance 3, Table 17.3). Meet-up events may include playing sports, picnicking or other forms of entertainment. OnBoard's search feature enables new hires to find others with similar interests. Then new hires reach out to those with similar interests to chat online and take a break (Affordance 4, Table 17.3). As a result of regular interactions, new hires meet after working hours to socialize and decompress from the rigor of the workday. It is through this type of interaction that new hires establish relationships that reach beyond their departmental boundaries.

Although go-getters, just-doers, and work-players all actualize the affordance of establishing relationships and interacting with peers to some extent, the just-doers did not actualize the affordances of socializing or taking a break. Their tendency is to only actualize affordances that directly apply to their work responsibility. Consequently, just-doers develop a smaller and work-focused network in comparison to the go-getters and work-players.

Organizational Visibility Affordances

OnBoard affords organizational visibility to IT new hires by providing opportunities for them to participate in OnBoard sponsored events, build peer relationships, develop and

Table 17.3 FSP's OnBoard Features, Uses and Affordances.

OnBoard features	OnBoard uses	Affordances	Go-getters	Work-players	Just-doers
User profile, sports page, entertainment	• Create personal profiles • Connect to others • List friends • Market skills and abilities • Post status updates • Social searching: Read about others, look up people from their university and hometown • Set up meet-ups for sport matches • Track sport match winners • Highlight hotspots in the area • Set up socializing outings for after work	*Networking* 1. Building Relationships with Peers 2. Interacting with Peers 3. Socializing 4. Taking a Break	✓ ✓ ✓ ✓	✓ ✓ ✓ ✓	✓ ✓
Event planning	• Use crowd-sourcing features (e.g., commenting and voting) to determine what type of event to plan, to choose event leaders and volunteers, and to gauge input on event planning such as time, location and food • Use posting feature to market events and rsvp for events • Use sharing feature to post comments and pictures from the event	*Organizational visibility* 5. Participating in OnBoard Events 6. Building Relationships with Peers 7. Demonstrating Leadership 8. Interacting with Superiors	✓ ✓ ✓ ✓	✓ ✓ ✓	

OnBoard features	OnBoard uses	Affordances	Go-getters	Work-players	Just-doers
Pulse, discussion boards, relocation page, maps	• Make brief comments about what's going on at work—e.g., the pulse of the place • Discuss and arrange opportunities for training, education, certification and study group sessions • Lists and search for housing, roommates, carpools, and ride sharing arrangements • List local area places that provide employee discounts and where employees frequent	*Information gathering / sharing* 9. Finding resources 10. Helping peers	✓ ✓	✓ ✓	✓
Discussion boards and house calls	• Search departments where IT employees can work • Arrange to work in a new area for a day	*Innovation* 11. Broadening perspective 12. Acquiring new technology skills 13. Acquiring insight on new processes, products and services for management	✓ ✓ *[a]	✓ ✓	✓ ✓

[a] The "acquiring insight on new products and services" was an affordance actualized by senior management.

demonstrate leadership skills, and interact with superiors. All new hires who attend an OnBoard event have the possibility to interact with executives. Events have included executive luncheons, casino nights, coding competitions, and cross-fit workouts. All events must have an executive who has agreed to sponsor and attend the event. This rule serves as an important enabler of the visibility affordances. However, those new hires who lead events, (e.g., the go-getters) work much more closely with executives than do the work-players and just-doers who, at most, attend the event and briefly meet the executives. A go-getter comments: "OnBoard has helped me develop some leadership at an early stage in my career; it made me aware of how to get things done." Another go-getter discussed how OnBoard allowed leaders to "promote the event, seek volunteers, connect with the next lead, and give event updates." This type of exposure gives new hires a chance to make a name for themselves in front of management and peers. In the words of one go-getter, "I know so many more executives outside of my department than most of my teammates do. There's no telling ten years down the road what promotional opportunities I'll have and what these connections will do for me."

As the go-getters actualize the affordance of demonstrating leadership skills (Affordance 7, Table 17.3), they create an affordance of interacting with superiors (Affordance 8, Table 17.3) for the just-doers and the work-players. While the work-players will take advantage of such of an opportunity, the just-doers are less likely to participate in such events and pass on this affordance. By participating in OnBoard events (Affordance 5, Table 17.3), the work-players informally meet senior management and executives. Informal interaction with executives through participation in OnBoard events (e.g., Wounded Warrior, paintball, American Idol, and others) made new hires feel comfortable around superiors. Benefits of this include helping new hires approach superiors with less hesitation, relieving pressure in formal meetings, making new hires feel that management is interested in their well-being, and that they matter.

Information gathering/sharing Affordances

OnBoard affords new hires the ability to find resources and help peers as they settle into their new community. OnBoard provides various web pages (e.g., apartment lists, roommate lists, carpools, and recommended restaurants) with information to aid the new hires in their search for housing, transportation and shopping. All new hires who use OnBoard have the possibility to actualize the affordance that helps them gain or share information. A go-getter who is "not from this area" discussed how OnBoard made her aware of local businesses that give discounts to FSP employees and helped her find housing and a roommate. The information gathering affordance was especially helpful early on when new hires were embarrassed to admit what they did not know. As explained by a work-player:

> So you come to work your first day and you've just got hundreds of questions.
> You can bug your point of contact to death with all of those questions, but you
> don't really want to. So that's another thing that OnBoard kind of helps with.

This information gathering/sharing affordance was particularly helpful when new hires were struggling with assignments in that it linked them to information that they needed to complete their tasks more efficiently. For example, a work-player talked about how OnBoard introduced him to a tool that would automatically tell him everything about the databases his programming affected, including the owners. This tool automated the slow, time consuming process he was following.

All three groups of users actualized the finding resources affordance. By contrast, the helping peers affordance was only actualized by the work-players and go-getters. The information gathering/sharing affordance in OnBoard requires action from new hires to contribute the resources that helps others. In one example, a go-getter created a "Navigating FSP: The Series" where he wrote a weekly report addressing the things he wished he would have known when he started. This included all the acronyms employees use and how to find one's car in the parking lot. OnBoard users who provide such information are actualizing the affordance of helping peers (Affordance 10, Table 17.3) that allows other new hires to actualize the finding resources affordance (Affordance 9, Table 17.3). Work-players and go-getters derived satisfaction from helping peers. In the words of a work-player, "OnBoard allows me to mentor other new hires because I can relate to the kind of things they are going through; helping makes me feel good."

Innovation Affordances

Innovation affordances include two affordances for new hires broadening perspective and acquiring new technology skills and one for senior management acquiring insight on new products and services. The latter was not an originally envisioned function of OnBoard, but as executives began to see the variety of ways in which new hires used OnBoard, they realized OnBoard's potential for igniting organizational innovation. The new hire affordance of acquiring new technology skills (Affordance 12, Table 17.3) first emerged after a technology vice president expressed displeasure about OnBoard's social events during the workday. A concerned go-getter took this to heart and decided to organize an event with work, rather than social, purposes in mind. The go-getter initiated a coding competition. The competition challenged new hires to develop an application of their choice on a mobile platform with which FSP was experimenting. All participants, go-getters, work-players and just-doers expanded their technical skills by working nights and weekends to learn the mobile development language and build the application. In this way, the go-getters affording OnBoard to create a work-related outcome of benefit to FSP resulted in work-players as well as just-doers acquiring new technical skills. In another example, a go-getter discussed how OnBoard facilitates what were referred to as house calls. Through house calls, new hires can visit other work areas that interest them. This allows the new hires who wish to transition to another area to learn about the work area (Affordance 11, Table 17.3) before formally committing. A go-getter described this broadening perspective affordance as one that helps him with his career development. "I never feel trapped, because I know I can always transfer to a new area." He further explained that visiting areas lets him know how his work impacts other areas and vice versa.

Thus far, our analysis has focused on the primary users the new hires for whom FSP developed the OnBoard system. However, senior executives, who were not engaged with OnBoard outside of sponsoring and attending events organized by the go-getters, soon recognized that the platform itself could be of value to them as well and began to request feedback from new hires on new product offerings and software development (Affordance 13, Table 17.3). An executive stated:

> OnBoard is a good sounding board for us as management to bounce ideas off of the young people. Let's face it, they are highly educated and tech savvy. If we want to know something, we can start a discussion on OnBoard and see what they say.

Executives began tasking go-getters with identifying groups of new hires with 0–5 years of work experience to provide feedback and future perspective on various tools. One such effort resulted in the creation of an app that allowed "customers who are being deployed to hit a button on their mobile phone and initiate a flow of events they want to happen." As further explained by the executive:

> Lots of times people only have 24 h notice before being deployed and they need to make some financial changes as part of the deployment – like increase life insurance and reduce car insurance since they are storing the car. This way they can spend time with their family and not spend their last hours working with their financial institution.

So pleased were executives with the newfound innovation potential of OnBoard that they further extended OnBoard to reach other users. One such extension of OnBoard is iInnovate, a SharePoint site that serves as an innovation lab where anyone with an idea to improve organizational processes, products or services can submit their suggestion. Another extension of OnBoard is Dev.Ask, an internal website that allows developers to post questions for the entire development community about coding or processes. In this way, the initial affordances of OnBoard that were actualized by the new hires, namely the networking and visibility affordances, triggered an interest in senior executives to enable other affordances through OnBoard that led to outcomes that were far removed from the initial desire to socialize new hires with OnBoard.

The Interacting Effects of Affordances

Identifying the single affordances of OnBoard serves as the first step in understanding how the actualization of affordances in OnBoard affects new hires' socialization into the organization. Considering that multiple affordances are present at the same time, it is important to understand the nature of their relationships (Strong et al., 2014). Consistent with Strong et al. (2014), certain affordances, later termed "higher-level" by Bygstad et al. (2016), can only be actualized after basic affordances. We refer to these as first-order and second-order affordances to highlight that the second-order affordances cannot be actualized until the first-order affordances have been actualized and to avoid implying that "basic" affordances are somehow easier or simpler to actualize than "higher-order" ones because in our case, this is not found to be true. The first-order affordances were no easier or simpler to activate than the second-order nor did the second-order affordances demand any higher level of thinking or perception to activate. In our case, the interacting with peers, demonstrating leadership, and participating in OnBoard events acted as first-order affordances. The actualization of these first-order affordances then allowed new hires to actualize second-order affordances, which collectively resulted in outcomes. As described in Table 17.4 (and Table 17.7 in the Appendix) and explained in the following section, strands of first and second-order affordances abstract into generative mechanisms that explain how the affordances lead to the outcomes (see Table 17.5 for a summary of the outcomes).

We next explain these strands of interacting affordances and the generative mechanisms they form as well as the outcomes that the generative mechanisms explain.

Generative Mechanisms

Bureaucracy Circumvention

Interacting with peers is a first-order affordance that makes several other affordances possible, including building relationships, finding resources, and helping peers. Together, these affordances explain the outcome of productivity enhancement through the generative mechanism we refer to as "bureaucracy circumvention" (see Table 17.4). Many large

Table 17.4 Generative Mechanisms, Affordances, and Outcomes.

Generative mechanisms	First-order affordances	Second-order affordances	Outcomes	User type
Bureaucracy Circumvention	* Interacting with Peers	* Building Relationships with Peers * Finding Resources * Helping Peers	• Productivity Enhancement	All 3
Executive Perspective	* Interacting with Peers * Participating in OnBoard Events	* Building Relationships with Peers * Building Relationships with Superiors * Helping Peers	• Cultural Understanding	GGs and WPs
Personal Development	* Demonstrating Leadership * Participating in OnBoard Events	* Building Relationships with Peers * Building Relationships with Superiors * Finding Resources * Helping Peers * Acquiring Insights on New Products/Services	• Productivity Enhancement • Attractive Job Assignments • Comfort around Superiors	All 3 GGs, WPs GGs, WPs
Name Recognition	* Demonstrating Leadership * Participating in OnBoard Events	* Building Relationships with Peers * Building Relationships with Superiors * Socializing * Helping Peers * Acquiring New Job Skills	• Comfort around Superiors • Additional Work • Stress • Social Struggle	GGs, WPs GGs GGs GGs, JDs
Morale Booster	* Demonstrating Leadership * Interacting with Peers * Participating in OnBoard Events	* Building Relationships with Peers * Building Relationships with Superiors * Finding Resources * Helping Peers * Socializing * Taking a Social Break	• Cultural Understanding • Sense of Social Support	GGs, WPs All 3

Key: GG: Go-Getters WP: Work-Players JD: Just-Doers.

Table 17.5 Outcomes.

Outcome	Quote / example	User type
1. Productivity enhancement	A work-player working on a recruitment video could not use video or camera equipment in the building without permission, which "often took weeks because security is thorough." The new hire was able to reach out to a peer he met through OnBoard and within days his video request was approved.	All 3
2. Additional work	A go-getter had to work on all of the images on the OnBoard site. This led to the creation of a Geocaching site, where she spent time creating rollover graphics. She stated: "this is all done outside of my regular working hours."	GGs
3. Attractive job assignments	A go-getter described his experience of meeting an executive at an OnBoard event, who then asked him to run the United Way campaign because of his experience with OnBoard. A work-player got transferred to the coveted mobile development group after winning an OnBoard coding competition.	GGs, WPs
4. Stress	A go-getter discussed his stress of balancing OnBoard with work: our managers support OnBoard, but we understand that our job is #1 and OnBoard is #2; OnBoard is volunteer work so OnBoard can get a little stressful for us because it takes a lot of time when an event comes up. A go-getter discussed his supervisor finding out he was doing extra graphics work for a senior executive he met through OnBoard. His boss explained, "I didn't know you were doing that."	GGs
5. Social struggle	A go-getter described his frustration by stating: "it is hard to satisfy everyone; they [new hire peers] complain about events or voice how we could have done something better. I am like if you want to complain put on an event yourself."	GGs, JDs
6. Sense of social support	A go-getter relied on OnBoard people to support her and listen to what she is going through and commented: I was stressed about when a server was going to be ready for my job. We were working long hours to complete the project. Rather than going through the whole internal process, I was able to instant message my contact. He put me at ease and then I stopped stressing.	All 3
7. Comfort around superiors	A work-player stated: "I get to know executives on a personal level that makes it easier to present in front of them during formal meetings; I learn how to better communicate with them."	GGs, WPs
8. Cultural understanding	A work-player described that his experience volunteering side by side with executives at Wounded Warriors helped him understand OnBoard's mission and its customers. He stated, "now more than ever I understand why I need to build the video system that will allow our customers to interact with loan officers from conveniently located branches."	GGs, WPs

companies face a similar bureaucratic structure with rigid policies, procedures and hierarchies to follow. The bureaucracy circumvention mechanism is not about violating policies, but rather accelerating the response time by knowing who in the company is able to help. In the examples below, we explain how the four affordances comprising this strand of affordances leads to the outcome of productivity enhancement via the bureaucracy circumvention mechanism.

New hires gave several examples of productivity enhancement made possible through their affordance of OnBoard. On one occasion, a go-getter who was trying to meet a deadline for a database modification (e.g., table structure, permissions, and other) circumvented the standard process by reaching out to someone he knew personally through OnBoard This simplified the process because "they are more likely to take you seriously when they know who you are instead of just some random person coming with a problem." This then enabled him to check the status of his needed database change. This information, from his fellow new hire, assured him that the database group was working on the needed modification and that he'd be able to deliver the project on time. The new hire was able to get the necessary information because he had a close relationship with someone in the database group that he had formed through his affording of OnBoard to establish relationships with peers. In another example, management charged a work-player new hire with producing a recruitment video. Said the new hire, FSP is "bureaucratic with a strong chain of command and complex processes and procedures." To accomplish their work, new hires were frequently left waiting on access, permission or someone to do something. This new hire in charge of the recruitment video was met head on with FSP's bureaucracy. He could not use video or camera equipment in the building without permission from security, which "often took weeks because security is thorough." By contacting a peer whom the new hire had met through OnBoard and who had connections to the security group, the new hire was able to bypass the waiting process and accelerate the approval of his video request. The peer knew exactly with whom he needed to speak and within days his video request was approved.

In general, new hires report that the relationships they form through OnBoard and their ability to find resources through the peers they meet enable them to get things done more efficiently, as summarized by one new hire:

> The more people I know during a project, the better I can get things done that I need done. When I meet somebody in a network or at any social activity that OnBoard sponsors, later on in a project when I need help on a certain thing like testing, I can be like, oh I know this person. I can ask him to see if I can get a resource.

An executive described the complexity of FSP as one that makes it difficult to

> learn who to go to with different issues and the OnBoard alumni group does worlds of good in shortcutting some of that and helping these kids (i.e., IT new hires inclusive of go-getters, work-players, and just-doers) get up to speed in learning who, what, when, where, why, and how.

The new hires who had developed the most extensive networks and had the strongest ties with their superiors the go-getters were not surprisingly the ones able to achieve this outcome.

The bureaucracy circumvention mechanism involves not just the actors themselves availing themselves of an affordance, but other actors (e.g. peers) must also actualize the affordance of helping peers. An important goal of socialization programs is to equip new hires with a level of confidence in the skills they need to do their jobs and fulfill their responsibilities. This is referred to as "self-efficacy" (Bauer and Erdogan, 2011). Experiencing productivity and being able to circumvent bureaucracy in order to get a job done arguably facilitates new hires' confidence in their ability to perform their job tasks (e.g. self-efficacy).

Executive Perspective

Interacting with peers and participating in OnBoard events are first-order affordances that make possible the affordances of building relationships with peers and superiors and helping peers. Jointly, these affordances explain the outcome of organizational culture understanding via the generative mechanism that we label "executive perspective" (see Table 17.4) by which we mean the new hires' ability to see things through the perspective of executives.

Learning about organizational culture and learning how to fit into the organizational culture is an important part of socialization (Bauer and Erdogan, 2011). New hires provided various examples of how their assimilation into the culture of FSP was an outcome of their OnBoard involvement. As explained by a just-doer:

> What helped about OnBoard is that I was thrown into FSP. I didn't know anything about FSP. All I know is that this building is a mile long and people lose their cars on the first day. I have no idea how to get anywhere, but with this OnBoard they have helped me understand the company culture, help me understand what I need to do to be successful, and even give me opportunities to talk to the people I need to further my career and things that matter most to me.

New hires claimed to be "learning about FSP through superiors' eyes." In another example, a work-player explained how volunteering side by side with executives at events like Wounded Warriors helped him understand FSP's mission and its customers. Reflecting on his Wounded Warrior volunteer experience, a work-player said, "now more than ever I understand why I need to build the video system that will allow our customers to interact with loan officers from conveniently located branches." Though invisible and intangible, the executives' perspective is much different than "what you get down in the weeds." This executive perspective mechanism of executive perspective explains how the affordance strand of interacting with peers, participating with OnBoard events, building relationships with peers and superiors, and helping peers lead to the outcome of cultural understanding. Gaining knowledge about the organizational culture allows new hires to develop a sense of belonging, which makes them feel accepted by their peers and superiors and helps new hires understand how to complete their work tasks within the organization standards. This is referred to as social acceptance and role clarity respectively (Bauer and Erdogan, 2011).

Personal Development

Demonstrating leadership is a unique first-order affordance because the outcomes of this affordance also depend on other actors being willing to participate in the events that were developed by the actor taking a leadership role. Therefore, the first-order affordance of participating in OnBoard events becomes available for other new hires. These two first-order affordances are actualized by different groups of actors and make several other affordances possible, including building relationships with peers and superiors, finding resources, helping peers, and acquiring insights on new products/services. These first-order and second-order affordances explain the outcomes of productivity enhancement, attractive job assignments, and comfort around superiors via the generative mechanism we label as "personal development" (see Table 17.4). The personal development mechanism is about new hires experiencing professional growth.

While go-getters organize most events, and in so doing demonstrate leadership, work-players and just-doers attend these events. As a go-getter comments: "OnBoard has helped me develop some leadership at an early stage in my career; it made me aware of how to handle myself more professionally." One just-doer described his participation in OnBoard planning meetings. As an example of how OnBoard helped him achieve productivity enhancement, the just-doer stated:

> I was in one of the OnBoard meetings and at this meeting I met one guy who was more on the financial side and he knew a lot about the financial system I was working on. I was able to ask him a bunch of questions to help me understand the system and what I was supposed to be doing.

In another example, the following quote from a work-player illustrates how OnBoard helped him enhance his productivity:

> OnBoard serves as a way to get to know other parts of the business. I work as a business analyst that develops software that logs all incidents (e.g., problems) for management. OnBoard has served me as a resource. There have been cases where I met this one guy then I needed his help a couple of days later. In the long-term, I have an advantage over others because I have gotten to know a lot more people throughout the business than those that I met during my new employee orientation, who I have never seen at an OnBoard event; so I'll have more resources as far as contacts than new hires that do not participate.

An important outcome of this strand of affordances was attractive job assignments. For example, the winners of the coding competition described earlier received new job assignments in FSP's prestigious mobile development division.

Establishing relationships with superiors facilitated a sense of new hire comfort around superiors. The following quote illustrates how a go-getter was able to interact with the Chief Information Officer (CIO) in an informal setting: "I met the CIO at a casino night event organized by OnBoard and I was able to chat with the CIO and get to know him on a personal basis." Another go-getter described OnBoard usage as one that has helped him "make connections with executives" and mentioned that "executives came out to our paint ball event, which shows that they are part of the team and our interactions at such events gives a new meaning into the open door policy" at FSP. In addition, work-players became comfortable sharing opportunities, problems and insights with management. In another example, a work-player talked to an executive about a defect he had found in FSP's infrastructure. A manager explains:

> So we have a person who has been here less than a year. He showed a defect to a full vice president, who immediately realized that the young individual was

correct. The vice president went into an immediate, rapid response to fix it. And it wasn't that the guy [new hire] is so much smarter than everyone else … it was just that a fresh set of eyes saw something, raised a question, and he was right.

While all three types of users benefited from some level of personal development, the go-getters and the work-players were the ones to achieve the most benefit because of their involvement in planning and organizing OnBoard events and higher participation in attending such events.

Name Recognition

Demonstrating leadership and participating in OnBoard events are two first-order affordances that make possible the affordances of building relationships with peers and superiors, socializing, helping peers, and acquiring new job skills. Collectively, these affordances lead to a beneficial outcome of the new hires feeling comfortable around superiors (as opposed to intimidated or nervous), but also to several negative outcomes, including additional work, stress, and social struggle. The mechanism that links the affordances of demonstrating leadership, participating in OnBoard events, building relationships with peers and superiors, socializing, helping peers, and acquiring new job skills to the outcomes of productivity enhancement, comfort around superiors, additional work, stress, and social struggle is what we refer to as "name recognition" (see Table 17.4). The name recognition mechanism is about establishing a reputation within the organization.

Many large organizations tend to have hierarchal structures that make it difficult to meet executives. Yet, OnBoard affords new hires the opportunities to establish relationships with peers and superiors while socializing. For example, when participating in the executive luncheons, new hires experience an intimate setting that allows them to build trust and personal relationships with executives. A go-getter stated: "having lunch with executives has helped us with our career growth because we get to know them personally." And as stated by a work-player: "I get to know executives on a personal level that makes it easier to present in front of them during formal meetings; I learn how to better communicate with them." The following quote from an executive reinforces the sentiment: "the COO of FSP knows 12 members of OnBoard because he works with OnBoard on a regular basis; he is on a first name basis with them."

Since go-getters lead events and manage the OnBoard ESM system, go-getters tap into the affordance that helps them expand their skills beyond their current job assignment. The skills include leadership, communication, marketing, salesmanship, project management, budget management, creativity, and SharePoint administration. These new skills often led to additional work. On one occasion, a go-getter with experience in website development was assigned the task of working on all the images displayed in OnBoard. This led to the creation of a Geocaching site, where she spent time creating rollover graphics. She stated: "this is all done outside of my regular working hours." A top manager stated that he "has now given OnBoard members (e.g., go-getters) new tasks, which includes creating videos that help the new hires know things they need to do at the organization as part of an employee development plan." In another example, a go-getter described his experience of meeting an executive at an OnBoard event as one that not only provided him with "getting to know the executive on a personal level," but one that led to the executive asking him to run the United Way campaign. These additional opportunities were extra tasks that superiors asked the recognized new hires to execute in addition to their assigned job responsibilities. A go-getter comments about how assuming additional responsibilities created additional stress and led him to transition away from OnBoard:

> I was so ready to relieve the stress from that part of my life. Possibly because of being on the core team, my job responsibilities started picking up more and more. So, after a year of being on the core team, I had so much work going on that I just didn't have any time for that anymore.

Even though the go-getters followed management's mandate, superiors viewed OnBoard participation as discretionary and time for which they could not charge FSP. Superiors recognized OnBoard's benefits, even asking OnBoard go-getters to promote OnBoard to college recruitees, and yet new hires still had to confine their OnBoard use to non-working hours such as breaks, lunches, and evenings. This created a sense of inequity among new hires and made it difficult at times for OnBoard's leaders to recruit their replacements. For example, the less active new hires experienced some resentment and alienation, as the quote from a just-doer below illustrates:

> I am married; I can't play intramurals from 6 to 9. There are some definite disadvantages to not participating completely. Around here, just because it is such a big company, it is who you know. A lot of the times job postings are filled before they are even posted internally. If you play on a sports team with someone, they are more likely to say, "hey we have this position opening," before the job is even posted internally.

Given the link between networking and promotion, new hires that did not participate in OnBoard events resented the opportunities afforded to those who did (i.e., go-getters and work-players). Yet, just-doers prioritized family, work tasks, and off-time over committing to OnBoard events or increasing their involvement. They viewed OnBoard as simply "more work to be done" or "a waste of time" and limited their level of usage. This perception blinded just-doers to the value in OnBoard's outcomes. A work-player who later agreed to lead OnBoard explains how OnBoard's core team initially alienated the new hire community:

> People [fellow new hires] didn't really appreciate that they were the core team. They had their own shirts. They distinguished themselves on the website. OnBoard is supposed to make everyone equal. It is a community.

The quote alludes to the social struggle that some new hires perceived as a result of the go-getters' relationships with superiors. Recognizing that superiors provided OnBoard's leaders additional opportunities and at times favorable work assignments, some work-players, just-doers, and even middle management experienced jealousy. The new hires resented that they were seemingly penalized for not fully participating in something that was outside their job scope and that superiors wanted them to relegate to after hours. In addition, middle managers resented that they didn't get the same opportunity to build their name by participating in social events that exposed them to top management. One middle manager comments:

> I started in 1991. Back then there was a training program and they put you to work. It was up to you to stay up with the people you went through the training program with. Now new hires have OnBoard that makes it easier for them to stay connected with others and meet new people. I never got to meet the CEO like the new hires do. The only opportunity I had for promotion was if someone passed away or retired. Now promotion is more merit based and new hires can push themselves up through the five levels at FSP. And with new hires interacting with executives and promotion by committee, they have a definite advantage.

Since go-getters knew that their reputation depended on OnBoard's success, they had a personal stake in making OnBoard prosper. Go-getters depended on their fellow new hires to participate in OnBoard, attend events, add content, and volunteer, but they had no control over the level of participation of their peers. Rather, go-getters involved in this process felt pressured to cajole their peers into participation in order for OnBoard events to succeed. A go-getter comments:

> The most stressful thing is that you're organizing events where you're the one whose neck is on the line, but you are almost never the one actually doing the work. You are heavily dependent on people in the community to help you out.

As the quote above illustrates, go-getters recognized that a bad event reflects negatively on their leadership and may create a negative reputation with peers and management. The following quote eludes to a go-getter's frustration: "it is hard to satisfy everyone; they complain about events or voice how we could have done something better." Therefore, go-getters experienced a social struggle in that their reputation depended on the participation of work-players and just-doers both of which felt that the go-getters benefited more from their participation than they did.

Morale Booster

Interacting with peers, demonstrating leadership, and participating in OnBoard events are first-order affordances that makes possible the affordances of building relationships with peers and superiors, finding resources, helping peers, socializing, and taking a social break. Together, these affordances explain the outcomes of cultural understanding and sense of social support via the generative mechanism we label "morale booster" (see Table 17.4). As the examples below illustrate, the morale booster mechanism raises the spirits of the new hires and provides them positive energy.

New hires provided several examples of the outcomes of cultural understanding and sense of social support. The following quote from a go-getter illustrates how OnBoard helps new hires learn about the organizational culture:

> OnBoard puts on events just for interns right when they get here, then puts together the end of the year OnBoard trip, which was a scavenger hunt at Schlitterbahn. Many of these interns when hired seem generally excited when they come on board. It seems to help them not to be shy or feel lost because they are not really sure of what their place is, so I think that OnBoard events make people feel a lot more comfortable when they start by having a role in OnBoard right away and feel important, which helps them learn about the organization as they are establishing their work role.

In another example, a just-doer explains:

> OnBoard has a welcoming party just for new hires, so right off the bat we had a get together of all the brand new hires explaining to us what OnBoard was, why it was important to you to know the culture here and what it could help us with.

He continued to describe this experience as one where he felt that OnBoard provided him a "support system that would help guide him and help him instead of just being thrown into the workplace." The following quote from a just-doer illustrates how OnBoard provides a sense of social support:

> I knew I would have a support system here to kind of guide me and help me instead of just being thrown into the workplace. OnBoard helps in having those friendships and those bonds with people outside of your area and I think for me knowing what other people are doing, what is acceptable, and asking them questions that you are afraid to ask your manager makes it easier.

Most new hires want to feel welcomed and important when entering an organization. When new hires are treated special and given opportunities to get to know others, socialize, and take breaks from their work tasks to build and reinforce relationships, they experience a boost in their emotion and confidence. At times, the peer and superior relationships and interactions turned into mentoring. As the quote below shows, go-getters experience a sense of satisfaction from helping their peers:

> Mike (a just-doer) is going through all the same stuff I went through – being overwhelmed in the Java training, feeling you're not worth your paycheck. It's a nice feeling to help him through this stuff because it's kind of overwhelming at first.

Thus, mentoring peers and being the go-to-person for other new hires gives go-getters a certain feeling of satisfaction in providing social support to others. Both the morale of those helping and the morale of those receiving help is boosted and through this boosting, important outcomes from the OnBoard affordances result.

Summary

Our findings illustrate how OnBoard's affordances led to various outcomes for different actor groups via the five generative mechanisms of bureaucracy circumvention, executive perspective, personal development, name recognition, and morale booster. The outcomes experienced were both positive and negative, consistent with the power of social media to unleash forces for both (Huang et al., 2015). We next discuss the important theoretical and managerial implications.

Implications

To date, ESM research has examined such issues as managing employee relations, balancing social and work life, managing knowledge, changing organizational culture and promoting innovation (Bradley and McDonald, 2011; Koch et al., 2013; Louis et al., 1983; Mullaney, 2012). Our research extends the work on ESM to the important domain of organizational socialization. The objective of this study was to understand how ESM influences the organizational socialization of new hires. Our study has implications for research in the areas of organizational socialization and technology affordances.

Socialization Research

Our research offers three implications for socialization research. First, given that social media is an important tool in the development of social capital (Kane et al., 2014) and that social capital can be helpful as well as burdensome (Oldroyd and Morris, 2012), one might expect both positive and negative socialization consequences for employees that use the ESM. Our research helps shed light on these consequences of ESM use. Individuals who are more inclined to participate in a social media system, or who have more time to do so, reap higher rewards. Yet they are not being rewarded for job performance so much as for system participation. This raises two issues. First, their use might very well distract them from their work, or, as experienced by several of our informants, lead to additional work outside of their primary responsibility. This can lead to role confusion and lower productivity. Second, because the system use is divorced from the actual work tasks facing the new hires, it is not yet known whether the new hires who are gaining visibility and reaping the visibility benefits that provide them with more attractive job assignments are actually the new hires with the greatest aptitude for the work tasks and roles. Instead, it is possible that those who have the highest ESM performance (e.g., organize the most and best events and provide the most information) are not actually those who have the highest job acumen. Research into top performers in organizations has found that top performers are many times more valuable in generating business value than lower performing peers (Ernst et al., 2000; Narin and Breitzman, 1995). Star employees those who demonstrate superior performance and who are highly visible in the labor market (Groysberg et al., 2008) experience a "cumulative advantage" whereby their productive resources increase at a considerably greater rate than their less visible and valuable peers (Oldroyd and Morris, 2012) . Because of their importance, star employees are well rewarded and highly influential. For new hires, the relevant labor market is the internal one wherein they vie for attractive job assignments after they have become fully entrenched in the organization. The go-getter users of the ESM at FSP display the characteristics of "stars" they demonstrate superior performance in the ESM and they become highly visible in the internal labor market of their organization. Yet because ESM performance is not necessarily predictive of work task performance, the organization runs the risk that the use of ESM as a socialization mechanism inadvertently creates stars who will not be able to shine outside of the ESM. Future research is needed to understand the ways in which ESM performance is, and is not, tied to actual work performance so that organizations can design incentive mechanisms to encourage those uses that improve work performance and discourage those uses that do not.

A second important implication of our study for organizational socialization research is that even as social bonding may emerge through ESM use for socialization, so too do social struggles. Management may intend for social media to serve as an inclusive mechanism whereby all new hires may establish relationships, but because relationships help develop social capital (Coleman, 1988; Nahapiet and Ghoshal, 1998) and social capital results in social power (Bourdieu, 1986; Burt, 1995), the implications extend well beyond a new hire socialization program. Recent research emphasizes that the socialization process of "becoming" includes "becoming unequal" meaning that occupational socialization creates inequality (Anteby et al., 2016). Although the work emphasizes segregation across occupations within an industry (for example, women tend to be more represented as nurses and men, as doctors), our research suggests that this process of becoming unequal through socialization may also occur within an occupational group (in this case, a group of IT new hires). In our case, the go-getters accrued greater connections to people and resources than the work-players and just-doers and, consequently, greater power. In such a situation, power struggles will ensue; in this case, social power struggles and inequalities form. This then results in divisiveness from a very system intended to promote inclusiveness. A stream of research is developing in the area of individual and group marginality and how marginality is tied to innovative behavior and performance. Marginality is a condition of disadvantage facing individuals or groups resulting from vulnerabilities that arise from unfavorable environmental, cultural, social, political and economic factors (Billson, 1996). Some of the negative consequences of marginality include limited career choices, poor performance, isolation, and exclusion (McLaughlin, 2000). Through socialization, segregation of members in an occupational group becomes naturalized. Given the potential of ESM to both promote belongingness and yet create marginality, future research should probe more deeply into how to avoid marginalization as a side effect of ESM use.

Our study offers a third important implication for organizational socialization research, shedding light on how changes to the organization itself occur via the socialization process. Socialization research focuses on how new employees can learn about the organization and how to do their jobs (Jones, 1986; Saks and Ashforth, 1997). It largely assumes a static, and single, organizational culture into which successive groups of new hires are socialized and views new hires as the target of socialization programs (Ashforth and Saks, 1996; Taormina, 1994). Our findings challenge these assumptions. First, our study suggests that even as new hires were learning the norms and culture of FSP, they were simultaneously altering the culture and norms through their engagement with the OnBoard system. What was before an 8–5 highly hierarchical environment where work-private boundaries were strong is becoming a much more organic, less hierarchical environment where boundaries between work and private life are more porous. Consequently, future new hires will learn norms that are quite different from the norms that the previous new hires were learning. By virtue of the previous new hires using the system to learn FSP's norms, they were actually simultaneously changing the norms. Hence, introducing a change to the socialization practices resulted in a change to the organization's culture into which socialization takes place. This resulted in a dual culture facing the new hires. Some new hires embraced an emerging flexible culture built around OnBoard and based on the reputation economy with blurred work-life boundaries whereas others new hires maintained the traditional bureaucratic culture allowing for work-life separation and valuing hourly productivity. It may be that, in the future, an important work skill will be the ability to cope with seemingly inconsistent cultural norms embedded in various technology-based work practices. Second, our study suggests that the new hires shifted from a state of being socialized into the organization into a state of socializing each other into the organization. The very role of the new hire socialization process changed as the HR department began to observe the direct benefits of the ESM on new hire socialization. As HR began to incorporate the system into its own human resources' processes, new hires experienced a shift in perspective from being the target of socialization efforts to being the means of socialization efforts. Future research is needed to investigate how role flipping making new hires both the leaders of and recipients of socialization initiatives facilitates or impedes assimilation into the organization as well as group and organizational cohesiveness and identity.

Technology Affordance Research

In terms of technology affordance, our study also offers important implications. The affordance lens compels scholars to contemplate the relationship between the potential action to be taken and technology capabilities (Faraj and Azad, 2012; Lee, 2010; Majchrzak et al., 2007) as well as the relationship between affordances and outcomes (Faraj and Azad, 2012; Volkoff and Strong, 2013) . Volkoff and Strong (2013) suggest that it is important to study the affordances themselves in order to gain a deeper understanding of how change occurs following the introduction of a new IT. The technology affordance research suggests that affordances when actualized by different actors even for similar objectives have differing outcomes for themselves and for others (Bygstad et al., 2016). Our findings extend this research by demonstrating (1) how affordances of different groups of actors intertwine to produce outcomes not just for the actors themselves but also for non-actors and (2) how outcomes for one group of actors produces affordances for another group of actors.

Concerning the first, our findings provide insights into a phenomenon that we will refer to as the second-hand effects of technology. With their use of the OnBoard system, the new hires impacted middle managers, non-users of the OnBoard system. In the case of middle managers, the second-hand effects were the reduced time they had to invest in mentoring new hires, a positive effect, but also the feeling of resentment at new hires getting to meet senior managers that they had not even met. This feeling of resentment underscored a deeper concern that they might be disadvantaged by the visibility accruing to some of the new hires. IS research has long focused on use and users as important components in an information system. Our findings suggest that non-users are also affected by an IS in important ways. Future research should delve more deeply into this issue of the second-hand effects of technology.

In terms of the second, our research shows that outcomes do not just reinforce the actualization of affordances, as prior research has demonstrated (Volkoff and Strong, 2013), but that outcomes create new affordances for different sets of actors. In our case, new hires meeting senior managers as a result of their participation in OnBoard events not only made the new hires more comfortable around their superiors, but also led to new affordances for senior managers, who recognized the potential insights new hires could provide into new product and service ideas and who therefore began soliciting feedback from new hires. This eventually led to entirely new outcomes the Dev.Ask and iInnovate solutions. Thus, affordances, actors, and outcomes intertwine with each other and create new affordances and outcomes for new sets of actors. Moreover, our findings suggest that outcomes stemming from the actualization of an affordance depend not only on how one user group uses the affordance, but are also contingent on how another group does, or does not, make use of the same or new affordance. In our case, this is vividly illustrated by the go-getters receiving benefits that were contingent upon how the other two groups actualized affordances. Without the work-players and just-doers actualizing the affordances of participating in OnBoard, the go-getters group would not have obtained the advantageous socialization benefits like superior recognition and positioning themselves for promotion. Future research can pay closer attention to the co-dependency of non-actualization of affordances by one group of actors with the actualization of affordances by another group of actors.

Limitations and Conclusions

This study's implications need to be considered in light of the limitations. First, the results relied on data collection from a single organization. Given that organizations use various socialization programs, our study raises questions of generalizability. It is possible that new hires may experience different outcomes in other organizations. While our study does achieve within-case generalizability (Lee, 1989; Pan and Tan, 2011), our insights may be seen as untested hypotheses (Lee and Baskerville, 2003). Future research might empirically test the relationship between the various mechanisms and outcomes. For example, researchers could compare the relative effectiveness of productivity enhancements to new hires via the two mechanisms of bureaucracy circumvention and personal development or researchers could examine other technology that create affordances that enable these same mechanisms. In like fashion, researchers could examine the relationship of the executive perspective mechanism and cultural understanding, comparing the effectiveness of this mechanism toward the achievement of shared cultural understanding to other mechanisms used to engender cultural understanding, such as company policy manuals and online courses. One might go even further to consider how these mechanisms might be useful in other contexts, such as how the executive perspective mechanism might be useful in achieving social alignment. Second, we rely on the new hires' perception of ESM use, not a quantitative measure of use time or frequency. New hires might have over or under-estimated their interaction with the system. Nevertheless, this does not undermine the importance of the relationships uncovered. The new hires perceived the affordances we uncovered and based upon their self-reported level of engagement with the system, three distinct categories of users were identifiable. Future research might extend this by examining how users manage their usage level, increasing or decreasing their usage to fit what they feel is the "right" or "ideal" usage level. Furthermore, future research might examine whether users, once they have positioned their usage level relative to others, feel capable of becoming more engaged or feel trapped in a certain pattern of usage.

In spite of the above limitations, our study offers an important extension to ESM research. Previous research on social media in organizations has focused on such important issues as how organizations can use social media to manage public perception (Benthaus et al., 2016), how organizations must learn communicational ambidexterity to fully manage social media as a strategic capability (Huang et al., 2015), how internal social media systems form a symbolic capital that employees seek to govern (Karoui et al., 2015), and how ESM influences employee performance (Kuegler et al., 2015). Our research examines a previously unaddressed phenomenon of how ESM influences the socialization of new hires. Given the importance of new hire socialization in ensuring a productive and committed workforce, the incorporation of ESM into the organizational socialization process is of strategic importance to organizations and the IS organization responsible for designing such systems. Our study uncovers five important mechanisms through which ESM influences organizational socialization: bureaucracy circumvention, executive perspective, personal development, name recognition, and morale booster. That ESM are capable of producing such important mechanisms is noteworthy in itself. That these mechanisms enable IT new hires to be more productive and more comfortable in their new organization is of keen importance to organizations challenged with recruiting, training, and maintaining a skilled IT workforce. While our study indicates that ESM usage facilitates the acclimation of new hires into a large organization and facilitates their productivity, it also shows that ESM can create social struggle, isolation, and resentment among new hires. For this reason, managers should think carefully about their ESM strategy and consider how to encourage uses that create positive socialization benefits as well as positive productivity benefits without inadvertently fostering social divisiveness.

Acknowledgment

A previous version of this paper appeared in the proceedings of HICSS 2015 as Gonzalez, E., D. Leidner, and H. Koch, "The Influence of Social Media on Organizational Socialization," Proceedings of the 48th Annual Hawaii International Conference on System Sciences, 2015. Publication was made possible, in part, by support from the Open Access Fund sponsored by the Baylor University Libraries.

Appendix A

(See Tables 17.6 and 17.7).

Table 17.6 Focus group conducted.

Focus group and focus	Date/length	Focus group attributes
Core Team, Generation 2 Learn about OnBoard	6/27/ 2009, 1 h	6 IT new college hires (5 males/1 female) Each had < 3 years tenure at FSP Members of the core team
FSP employees from a local university. Participated in an OnBoard lunch aimed at helping new hires connect with people who graduated from their University.	6/27/09, 1 h	10 new college hires and interns, 2 IT manager, lead University recruiter, executive sponsor 13 male/1 female
Learn how they use OnBoard and their acclimation to FSP College recruits and FSP's recruiting staff. Learn about FSP's culture, new hire program and OnBoard initiative	4/22/10, 2.5h	7 college recruits; Human Resources Advisor, College Recruiting; Talent Supply and Programs, Staffing Advisor; Program Manager, College Relations Supply and Programs; 3 human resource managers; 1 human resource recruiter, 1 IT middle manager, 1 executive, eight males, 7 females
Employees involved with OnBoard Discuss OnBoard and FSP's new hire program	7/14/10, 1 h	3 IT new hires, 1 IT new hire core team members, 2 managers that oversee the IT new hire program, 3 executives, 7 males/2 females
Core Team, Generation 3 Discuss OnBoard's evolution	7/14/10, 1 h	5 new hire core team members 3 males/2 females
FSP's managers Learn about FSP's college new hire program	9/29/11, 3h	4 FSP managers, 2 new hires 4 male/2 female
FSP managers and new hires Learn what FSP's new hires are doing and necessary skills Tour FSP's new corporate office in Plano, TX. Meet with FSP's lead recruiter and recent MIS graduates to learn what they are doing at FSP and how to improve the MIS curriculum	11/12/14, 4h	2 IT managers, 3 IT new hires 4 male/2 female
Discuss IT new hire and intern program and job roles	9/28/ 2016, 1 h	2 IT managers, 2 new hires 2 female/2 male

Table 17.7 Generative Mechanisms, Affordances, Outcomes, and Examples.

Generative mechanisms	First-order affordances	Second-order affordances	Outcomes	Example
Bureaucracy circumvention	• Interacting with Peers	• Building Relationships with Peers • Finding Resources • Helping Peers	Productivity enhancement	**Go-Getter:** In an effort to meet a deadline used OnBoard to circumvent FSP's standard processes and check the status of his needed database change. This information, from his fellow new hire, assured him that the database group was working on the needed modification and that he'd be able to deliver the project on time. Compared to his peers, this new hire was able to get the necessary information because he had a close relationship with someone in the database group that he had formed by affording OnBoards to establish peer relationships. He states: FSP is "bureaucratic with a strong chain of command and complex processes and procedures." **All New Hires:** To accomplish their work, new hires were frequently left waiting on access, permission or someone to do something. As an example, when FSP's new hire director charged a new hire with making a recruitment video, the new hire was met head on with FSP's bureaucracy: he could not use video or camera equipment in the building without permission from security, which "often took weeks because security is thorough." The new hire was able to reach out to a peer he met through OnBoard. The peer knew exactly with whom he needed to speak and within days his video request was approved. The quote below further illustrates OnBoard's self-efficacy benefits. "The more people I know during a project, the better I can get things done that I need done. When I meet somebody in a network or at any social activity that OnBoard sponsors, later on in a project when I need help on a certain thing like testing, I can be like, oh I know this person. I can ask him to see if I can get a resource. An executive describes how FSP's complexity makes it difficult to learn who to go to with different issues and the OnBoard alumni group does worlds of good in shortcutting some of that and helping these kids (IT new hires inclusive of go-getters, work-players, and just-doers) get up to speed in learning who, what, when, where, why, and how; knowing how to be comfortable in saying that they don't know anything about this and who to go to."

(continued)

Generative mechanisms	First-order affordances	Second-order affordances	Outcomes	Example
Executive perspective	• Interacting with Peers • Participating in OnBoard Events	• Building Relationships with Peers • Building Relationships with Superiors • Helping Peers	• Cultural understanding	**Go-Getter:** Explains OnBoard's role communicating with new hires. Many of these communications invite new hires to social events like Air Force graduation. The new hires that attend build relationships with peers and superiors and help their peers—especially since most events require that the new hires put on the event. Through the process of peers and superiors reviewing the communication, everyone develops a better idea of FSP's culture. 'I am one of the Communications people. I write the emails, we do a lot of the meeting invites. We also have a little newsletter, so we keep that on OnBoard and we also email it out, so that's a big part of Communications. It's important because we're kind of the face of OnBoard as far as communication out to the members of the social networking system. When I first started, it was kind of scary to click send on the email because it was going to like 300 people and copied to some executives and so forth and I'd think, "I hope this looks good …". We have everyone review everything and have it run by other members of the Core Team, so it's kind of scary.' **Work-Player:** New hires get to "learn about FSP through their superiors' eyes." The executives' perspective is so much different than "what you get down in the weeds." Volunteering side by side with executives at events like Wounded Warriors helped him understand FSP's mission and its customers. Reflecting on his Wounded Warrior volunteer experience, he comments: "now more than ever I understand why I need to build the video system that will allow our customers to interact with loan officers from conveniently located branches."

Generative mechanisms	First-order affordances	Second-order affordances	Outcomes	Example
Personal development	• Demonstrating Leadership • Participating in OnBoard Events	• Building Relationships with Peers • Building Relationships with Superiors • Finding Resources • Helping Peers • Acquiring Insights on New Products/Services	• Productivity Enhancement • Attractive Job Assignments • Comfort around Superiors	**Work-Player:** explains how OnBoard helped him enhance his productivity. "OnBoard serves as a way to get to know other parts of the business. I work as a business analyst that develops software that logs all incidents (e.g., problems) for management. OnBoard has served me as a resource. There have been cases where I met this one guy then I needed his help a couple of days later. In the long-term, I think I am at an advantage from others because I have gotten to know a lot more people throughout the business than those that I met during my new employee orientation, who I have never seen at an OnBoard event; so, I'll have more resources as far as contacts than new hires that do not participate." **Just-Doer:** mentions that he did not participate much in OnBoard social events; however, he did participate in OnBoard planning meetings. The just-doer states: I was in one of the OnBoard meetings. One guy was more on the financial side and he knew a log about the financial system I was working on. I was able to ask him a bunch of questions to help me understand the system and what I was supposed to be doing. **Go-Getters:** Recounted a technology vice president chastising them about too many OnBoard social events during the workday and sharing with them management's vision for OnBoard. This resulted in a coding competition that the go-getters orchestrated with FSP's technology fellows. The competition challenged new hires to develop an application of their choice on a mobile platform with which FSP was experimenting. All participants (e.g., go-getters and work-players) expanded their technical skills. The winners received new job assignments in FSP's mobile development division and their application launched FSP's development for the Android. **Go-Getter:** describes his personal relationship with a superior: "I met the CIO at a casino night event organized by OnBoard." This experience allowed the new hire to chat with the CIO in an informal setting that made it easy for him to present in front of superiors in formal meetings.

(continued)

Generative mechanisms	First-order affordances	Second-order affordances	Outcomes	Example
				Work-Player: Talked to an executive about a defect he'd found in FSP's infrastructure. A manager explains: So we have a person who has been here less than a year. He showed a defect to a full vice president, who immediately realized that the young individual was correct. The vice president went into an immediate, rapid response to fix it. And it wasn't that the guy [new hire] is so much smarter than everyone else … it was just that fresh set of eyes saw something, raised a question, and he was right.
Name recognition	• Demonstrating Leadership • Participating in OnBoard Events	• Building Relationships with Peers • Building Relationships with Superiors • Socializing • Helping Peers • Acquiring New Job Skills	• Comfort around Superiors • Additional Work Stress • Social Struggle	**Go-Getter:** states: "I get to know executives on a personal level that makes it easier to present in front of them during formal meetings; I learn how to better communicate with them." "The COO of FSP knows twelve members of OnBoard because he works with the on OnBoard on a regular basis; he is on a first name basis with them." **Go-Getters:** "I had to work on all of the images on the OnBoard site. This led to the creation of a Geocaching site, where I spent time creating rollover graphics. This is all done outside of my regular working hours." A go-getter described his experience of meeting an executive at an OnBoard event, who then asked him to run the United Way campaign because of his experience with OnBoard. A top manager stated that "he has now given OnBoard members (e.g., go-getters) new tasks, which includes creating videos that help the new hires know things they need to do at the organization as part of an employee development plan." Go-Getter: comments about how the additional responsibilities in his team led him to additional stress and to transition away from OnBoard. I was so ready to relieve the stress from that part of my life. Possibly because of being on the core team, my job responsibilities started picking up more and more. So, after a year of being on the core team, I had so much work going on that I just didn't have any time for that anymore.

Generative mechanisms	First-order affordances	Second-order affordances	Outcomes	Example
				Go-Getter: describes his frustration: "it is hard to satisfy everyone; they [other new hires and superiors] complain about events or voice how we could have done something better." Complaints included OnBoard initiatives that didn't go well, ideas for other events or how the go-getters could do better. As a go-getter user put it: "The frustrating thing about being a leader is people saying how come you guys aren't doing this or I want this, and I was looking at them, saying like if you want it, you do it. And it was really funny that we got tons of complaints saying you guys aren't doing enough of this and enough of that."
				Work-Players and Just-Doers: For example, participating less frequently created some negative social struggles including resentment and alienation.
				Work-Player: who later agreed to lead OnBoard and thus transitioned to a Go-Getter explains how OnBoard's core team initially alienated the new hire community, "People [fellow new hires] didn't really appreciate that they were the core team. They had their own shirts. They distinguished themselves on the website. OnBoard is supposed to make everyone equal. It is a community." **Just-Doer:** states, "I am married; I can't play intramurals from 6 to 9. There are some definite disadvantages to not participating completely. Around here, just because it is such a big company, it is who you know. A lot of the times job postings are filled before they are even posted internally. If you play on a sports team with someone they are more likely to say, "hey we have this position opening," before the job is even posted internally."

(continued)

Generative mechanisms	First-order affordances	Second-order affordances	Outcomes	Example
Morale booster	• Demonstrating Leadership • Interacting with Peers • Participating in OnBoard Events	• Building Relationships with Peers • Building Relationships with Superiors • Finding Resources • Helping Peers • Socializing • Taking a Break	• Cultural Understanding • Sense of Social Support	**Go-Getter referring to all users:** explains how OnBoard helps new hires learn about the organizational culture and feel supported, OnBoard puts on events just for interns right when they get here. It then puts together the end of the year OnBoard trip, which was a scavenger hunt at Schlitterbahn. Many of these interns when hired seem genuinely excited when they come on board. It seems to help them not to be shy or feel lost because they are not really sure of what their place is, so I think that OnBoard events make people feel a lot more comfortable when they start by having a role in OnBoard right away and feel important, which helps them learn about the organization as they are establishing their work role. **Go-Getter:** relied on OnBoard people to support her and listen to what she was going through, "I was stressed about when a server was going to be ready for my job. Rather than going through the whole internal process, I was able to IM my contact. He put me at ease and then I stopped stressing." **Just-Doer:** explains how OnBoard provides a sense of social support, I knew I would have a support system here to kind of guide me and help me instead of just being thrown into the workplace. OnBoard helps in having those friendships and those bonds with people outside of your area and I think for me knowing what other people are doing, what is acceptable, and asking them questions that you are afraid to ask your manager makes it easier.

References

Allee, V., 2000. Knowledge networks and communities of practice. *OD Pract.* 32, 1–15.

Anteby, M., Chan, C. K., and DiBenigno, J., 2016. Three lenses on occupations and professions in organizations: Becoming, doing and relating. *Acad. Manage. Ann.* 10, 183244. doi:10.1080/1941 6520.2016.1120962.

Ashford, S. J., and Black, J. S., 1996. Proactivity during organizational entry: The role of desire for control. *J. Appl. Psychol.* 81, 199–214. doi:10.1037/0021-9010.81.2.199.

Ashforth, B. E., and Saks, A. M., 1996. Socialization tactics: Longitudinal effects on newcomer adjustment. *Acad. Manage. J.* 39, 149–178.

Ashforth, B. E., Sluss, D. M., and Saks, A. M., 2007. Socialization tactics, proactive behavior, and newcomer learning: Integrating socialization models. *J. Vocat. Behav.* 70, 447–462.

Baptista, J., Wilson, A., Galliers, R. D., and Bynghall, S., 2017. Social media and the emergence of reflexiveness as a new capability for open strategy. *Long Range Plann.* 322–336.

Bauer, T. N., and Erdogan, B., 2011. Organizational socialization: The effective onboarding of new employees. In: Zedeck, E. (Ed.) *APA Handbook of Industrial and Organizational Psychology*. American Psychological Association, APA, pp. 51–64.

Bennett, J., Owers, M., Pitt, M., and Tucker, M., 2010. Workplace impact of social networking. *Prop. Manage.* 138–148.

Benthaus, J., Risius, M. R., and Beck, R., 2016. Social media management strategies for organizational impression management and their effect on public perception. *J. Strateg. Inf. Syst.* 25, 127–139.

Berger, P. L., and Luckmann, T., 1967. *The Social Construction of Reality: A Treatise in the Sociology of Knowledge*. Anchor Books, Doubleday, New York.

Billson, J. M., 1996. No owner of soil: The concept of marginality revisited on its sixtieth birthday. In: D. Routledge (Ed.) *Marginality: Theoretical Perspectives*. Sage, Thousand Oaks, CA, pp. 1–14.

Bourdieu, P., 1986. The forms of capital. In: J. G. Richardson (Ed.), *Handbook of Theory and Research for the Sociology of Education*. Greenwood Publishing Group Inc, Westport, CT, pp. 241–258.

Boyd, D. M., and Ellison, N. B., 2007. Social network sites: Definition, history, and scholarship. *J. Comput. Mediat. Commun.* 13, 210–230.

Bradley, A., and McDonald, M., 2011. *The Social Organization: How to Use Social Media to Tap the Collective Genius of Your Customers and Employees*. Harvard Business Review Press, Boston, MA.

Brown, J. S., and Duguid, P., 2000. *The Social Life of information, First Ed*. Harvard Business Review Press, Boston, MA.

Burt, R. S., 1995. *Structural Holes: The Social Structure of competition, First Ed*. Harvard University Press, Boston, MA.

Bygstad, B., Munkvold, B. E., and Volkoff, O., 2016. Identifying generative mechanisms through affordances: A framework for critical realist data analysis. *J. Inf. Technol.* 31, 83–96.

Chang, J., Chang, W., and Jacobs, R., 2009. Relationships between participation in communities of practice and organizational socialization in the early careers of South Korean IT employees. *Hum. Resour. Dev. Int.* 12, 407–427.

Chua, C. E. H., Lim, W. K., Soh, C., and Sia, S. K., 2012. Enacting clan control in complex IT projects: A social capital perspective. *Mis Q.* 36, 577–600.

Coleman, J., 1988. Social capital in the creation of human capital. *Am. J. Sociol. Suppl.* 94, S95–S120.

Del Monte, J., 2018. IT Empoyer Information Cost of Hiring/Retention (COH). Retrieved March 12, 2018 from www.jdapsi.com/Client/articles/coh.

Dube, L., and Pare, G., 2003. Rigor in information systems positivist case research: Current practices, trends, and recommendations. *Mis Q.* 27, 597–635.

Ernst, H., Leptein, C., and Vitt, J., 2000. Inventors are not alike: The distribution of patenting output among industrial R&D personnel. *IEEE Trans. Eng. Manage.* 47, 184199.

Faraj, S., and Azad, B., 2012. The Materiality of Technology: An Affordance Perspective. In: P. M. Leonardi, B. A. Nardi & J. Kallinikos (Eds.), *Social Interaction in a Technology World*. Oxford University Press, Oxford, pp. 237–258.

Farren, C., 2007. Help new hires succeed: Beat the statistics. Retrieved May 28, 2012 from www.masteryworks.com.

Fisher, C. D., 1985. Social support and adjustment to work: A longitudinal study. *J. Manag.* 11, 39–53.

Fisher, C. D., 1986. Organizational socialization: An integrative view. *Res. Pers. Hum. Resour. Manage.* 4, 101–145.

Gregory, R. W., Beck, R., and Keil, M., 2013. Control balancing in information systems development offshoring projects. *Mis Q.* 37, 1211–1231.

Gregory, R. W., Keil, M., Muntermann, J., and Mahring, M., 2015. Paradoxes and the nature of ambidexterity in IT transformation programs. *Inf. Syst. Res.* 26, 57–80.

Groysberg, B., Lee, L. E., and Nanda, A., 2008. Can they take it with them? the portability of star knowledge workers' performance. *Manage. Sci.* 54, 1213–1230.

Henfridsson, O., and Bygstad, B., 2013. The generative mechanisms of digital infrastructure evolution. *Mis Q.* 37, 907–931.

Huang, J., Baptista, J., and Galliers, R. D., 2013. Reconceptualizing rhetorical practices in organizations: The impact of social media on internal communications. *Inf. Manage.* 50, 112–124.

Huang, J., Baptista, J., and Newell, S., 2015. Communication ambidexterity as a new capability to manage social media communication within organizations. *J. Strateg. Inf. Syst.* 24, 49–64.

Hutchby, I., 2001. Technologies, texts and affordances. *Sociology* 35, 441–456.

Hutter, K., Nketia, B. A., and Fuller, J., 2017. Falling short with participation different effects of ideation, commenting, and evaluating behavior on open strategizing. *Long Range Plann.* 50, 335–370.

Inc, G., 2014. Social media best practices for SMBS can make success a reality. [WWW Document]. URL www.gartner.com (accessed 3.1.15).

Insala, 2010. Mentoring for onboarding: Increase new hire retention and maximize hiring investment. Retrieved May 24, 2012 from www.insala.com.

Jones, G. R., 1986. Socialization tactics, self-efficacy, and newcomers' adjustments to organizations. *Acad. Manage. J.* 29, 262–279.

Kammeyer-Mueller, J. D., and Wanberg, C. R., 2003. Unwrapping the organizational entry process: Disentangling multiple antecedents and their pathways to adjustment. *J. Appl. Psychol.* 88, 779.

Kane, G. C., 2015. Enterprise social media: Current capabilities and future possibilities. *MIS Quart. Executive* 14 (1), 1–16.

Kane, G. C., Alavi, M., Labianca, G. J., and Borgatti, S. P., 2014. What's different about social media networks? a framework and research agenda. *Mis Q.* 38, 274–304.

Kane, G. C., Bijan, A., Majchrzak, A., and Faraj, S., 2011. The paradoxical influence of social media affordances on intellectual capital creation. *Proc. of Acad. of Manag.*, San Antonio, TX.

Kaplan, A. M., and Haenlein, M., 2010. Users of the World, Unite! The challenges and opportunities of social media. *Bus. Horiz.* 53, 59–68.

Kappelman, L., Johnson, V., Maurer, C., McLean, E., Torres, R., David, A., and Nguyen, Q., 2018. The 2017 SIM IT issues and trends study. *MIS Quart. Executive* 17 (1), 53–88.

Karoui, M., Dudezert, A., and Leidner, D., 2015. Strategies and symbolism in the adoption of organizational social networking systems. *J. Strateg. Inf. Syst.* 24, 14–32.

Koch, H., Leidner, D. E., and Gonzalez, E. S., 2013. Digitally enabling social networks: Resolving IT culture conflict. *Inf. Syst. J.* 23, 501–523.

Kuegler, M., Smolnik, S., and Kane, G., 2015. What's in IT for employees? Understanding the relationship between use and performance in enterprise social software. *J. Strateg. Inf. Syst.* 24, 90–112.

Lee, A. S., 1989. A scientific methodology for MIS case studies. *Mis Q.* 13, 33–50.

Lee, A. S., and Baskerville, R. L., 2003. Generalizing generalizability in information systems research. *Inf. Syst. Res.* 14 (3), 221–243.

Lee, C. S., 2010. Managing perceived communication failures with affordances of ICTs. *Comput. Hum. Behav.* 26, 572–580.

Leonardi, P. M., 2011. When flexible routines meet flexible technologies: Affordance, constraint, and the imbrication of human and material agencies. *Mis Q.* 35, 147–167.

Louis, M. R., 1980. Surprise and sense making: What newcomers experience in entering unfamiliar organizational settings. *Adm. Sci. Q.* 26, 226–251.

Louis, M. R., Posner, B. Z., and Powell, G. N., 1983. The availability and help-fullness of socialization practices. *Pers. Psychol.* 857–866.

Majchrzak, A., Faraj, S., Kane, G. C., and Azad, B., 2013. The contradictory influence of social media affordances on online communal knowledge sharing. *J. Comput.-Mediat. Commun.* 19, 38–55. doi:10.1111/jcc4.12030.

Majchrzak, A., Jarvenpaa, S., and Hollingshead, A., 2007. Coordinating expertise among emergent groups responding to disasters. *Organ. Sci.* 18, 147–161.

Majchrzak, A., and Markus, L., 2013. Technology affordances and constraints in Management Information Systems (MIS). In: Kessler, E. (Ed.) *Encyclopedia of Management Theory.* Sage Publications Inc, Thousand Oaks, CA, pp. 832–836.

Markus, M. L., and Silver, M. S., 2008. A Foundation for the study of IT effects: A new look at DeSanctis and poole's concepts of structural features and spirit. *J. Assoc. Inf. Syst.* 9, 609–632.

McLaughlin, N., 2000. The sociology of philosophies: A global theory of intellectual change. *J. Hist. Behav. Sci.* 36, 171–174.

Mingers, J., Mutch, A., and Willcocks, L., 2013. Critical realism in information systems research. *Mis Q.* 37, 795–802.

Morrison, E. W., 1993. longitudinal study of the effects of information seeking on newcomer socialization. *J. Appl. Psychol.* 78, 173–183.

Mullaney, T., 2012. "Social business" launched this burger. [WWW Document]. URL www.usatoday.com/(accessed 5.24.12).

Nahapiet, J., and Ghoshal, S., 1998. Social capital, intellectual capital, and the organizational advantage. *Acad. Manage. Rev.* 23, 242–266.

Narin, F., and Breitzman, A., 1995. Inventive productivity. *Res. Policy* 24, 507–519.

O'Mahony, S., and Bechky, B. A., 2006. Stretchwork: Managing the career progression paradox in external labor markets. *Acad. Manage. J.* 49, 918–941.

Oldroyd, J., and Morris, S., 2012. Catching falling stars: A human resource response to social capital's detrimental effect of information overload on star employees. *Acad. Manage. Rev.* 37, 396–418.

Oshri, I., Kotlarsky, J., and Willcocks, L. P., 2007. Global software development: Exploring socialization and face-to-face meetings in distributed strategic projects. J. Strateg. Inf. Syst. 16, 25–49.

Pan, S. L., and Tan, B., 2011. Demystifying case research: A Structured-Pragmatic-Situationasl (SPS) approach to conducting case studies. *Inf. Organ.* 21, 161–176.

Reichers, A. E., 1987. An interactionist perspective on newcomer socialization rates. *Acad. Manage. Rev.* 12, 278–287. doi:10.2307/258535.

Rose, S. J., 1995. Declining job security and the professionalization of opportunity. (No. 95-04). National Commission for Employment Policy Research.

Saks, A. M., and Ashforth, B. E., 1997. Organizational socialization: Making sense of the past and present as a prologue for the future. *J. Vocat. Behav.* 51, 234–279.

Sarker, S., Sarker, S., Sahaym, A., and Bjorn-Anderson, N., 2012. Exploring value co-creation in relationships between an ERP vendor and its partners: A revelatory case study. *Mis Q.* 36, 317–338.

Schein, E. H., 1968. Organizational socialization and the profession of management. *Ind. Manage. Rev.* 9, 1–14.

Seidel, S., Recker, J., and Vom Brocke, J., 2013. Sensemaking and sustainable practicing: Functional affordances of information systems in green transformation. *Mis Q.* 37, 1275–1299.

Stoffregen, T. A., 2003. Affordances as properties of the animal-environment system. *Ecol. Psychol.* 15, 115–134.

Strong, D. M., Volkoff, O., Johnson, S. A., Pelletler, L. T., Tulu, B., Bar-On, I., Trudel, J., and Garber, L., 2014. A theory of organizational EHR affordances actualization. *J. Assoc. Inf. Syst.* 15, 53–85.

Taormina, R. J., 1994. The organizational socialization inventory. *Int. J. Sel. Assess.* 2, 133–145.

Thomas, R. J., and Silverstone, Y., 2015. How smart ceos use social tools to their advantage. *[WWW Document]. URL* www.hbr.org/(accessed 3.1.15).

Treem, J. W., and Leonardi, P. M., 2012. Social media use in organizations: Exploring the affordances of visibility, editability, persistence, and association. *Commun. Yearb.* 36, 143–189.

US Bureau of Statistics, 2015. Economic News Release [WWW Document]. URL www.bls.gov/bls/newsrels.htm (accessed 6. 3.16).

Van Maanen, J., and Schein, E. H., 1979. Toward a theory of organizational socialization. *Res. Organ. Behav.* 1, 209–264.

VanOsch, W., and Coursaris, C. K., 2014. Social media research: An assessment of the domain's productivity and intellectual evolution. *Commun. Monogr.* 81, 285–309.

Volkoff, O., and Strong, D. M., 2013. Critical realism and affordances: Theorizing IT-associated organizational change processes. *Mis Q.* 37, 819–834.

Wasko, M. M., and Faraj, S., 2005. Social capital and knowledge contribution. *Mis Q.* 29, 35–57.

Wenger, E., McDermott, R., and Snyder, W. M., 2002. *Cultivating Communities of Practice: A Guide to Managing knowledge, First Ed.* Harvard Business Review Press, Boston, MA.

Wesson, M. J., and Gogus, C. I., 2005. Shaking hands with a computer: An examination of two methods of organizational newcomer orientation. *J. Appl. Psychol.* 90, 1018–1026.

Williams, C., and Karahanna, E., 2013. Causal explanation in the coordinating process: A critical realist case study of federated IT governance structures. *Mis Q.* 37, 933–964.

Wright, A., 2013. 5 Trends changing the nature of work. *Society for Human Resource Management*. [WWW Document]. URL www.shrm.org/hr-today/news/hr-news/pages/5-trends-changing-the-nature-of-work.aspx (accessed 3. 1.15).

Wynn, D., and Williams, C. K., 2012. Principles for conducting critical realist case study research in information systems. *Mis Q.* 36, 787–810.

Yin, R. K., 1989. *Case Study Research: Design and Methods*. Sage Publications, Newbury Park, California.

Questions for Discussion

1   How can organizations achieve affiliation and commitment of the workforce? How can workforce get retained? What is the role of socialization programs? How can these get achieved through using enterprise social media?

2   How can ESM be used to convey the organizational culture and mission? Discuss the interlinkage between organizational culture and new hires. How are these affected through the use of ESM?

3   What power dynamics and redistribution are observed when using ESM?

4   Why the same affordances have different effects on various users and non-users? Could these effects get achieved using different affordances and mechanisms?

5   Would such socialization programs have different effects in different organizations? What are the contingent conditions for their success? How should such programs get implemented and managed?

6   What should the management involvement in these programs entail to ensure these are successful and sustainable?

Further Reading

Du, W. D., Pan, S. L., Leidner, D. E., Ying, W. (2019). Affordances, experimentation and actualization of FinTech: A blockchain implementation study. *The Journal of Strategic Information Systems*, 28 (1), 50–65.

Karahanna, E., Xu, S. X., Xu, Y., Zhang, N. A. (2018). The affordances–features perspective for the use of social media. *Management Review*, 42, 1–24.

Chapter 18

Paolo Aversa, Laure Cabantous and Stefan Haefliger

WHEN DECISION SUPPORT SYSTEMS FAIL: INSIGHTS FOR STRATEGIC INFORMATION SYSTEMS FROM FORMULA 1

DECISION SUPPORT SYSTEMS (DSS), which often process big data using models and output results through multiple interfaces, increasingly pervade knowledge-intensive professions from traffic control, health, to security, and finance (George et al., 2014, Constantiou and Kallinikos, 2015, Galliers et al., 2017). Data support strategic decision-making in various ways by feeding models and technologies of visualization and control (Brynjolfsson and McAfee, 2012, McAfee et al., 2012, Baesens et al., 2014, Loebbecke and Picot, 2015). Recently, scholars and practitioners have agreed on the bourgeoning importance of DSS and big data for strategic decisions, which—if properly leveraged—can positively contribute to firm performance, profit, growth, and competitive advantage (Davenport and Harris, 2007, LaValle et al., 2011, McAfee et al., 2012). Information System (hereafter IS) research on big data and decision support systems has primarily focused on the technological aspects and design challenges of big data (Chen et al., 2012, 2014) and only recently started considering the organizational dimensions of strategic decision-making with big data (Constantiou and Kallinikos, 2015, Poleto et al., 2015, Gunther et al., 2017). We argue that the design and use of tools in context deserve more attention given the well-known challenges of modern DSS, particularly when big data further complicate their functioning. This organizational dimension of decision-making builds on the managerial definition of big data and associated challenges (McAfee et al., 2012): (1) Sources of data become increasingly diverse, multiple, and dynamic; (2) More stakeholders in decision-making generate and analyze data using more and more devices; (3) Feedback speed and volume of data favors the non-human actors (e.g., Artificial Intelligence and similar solutions).

In this paper, our aim is to contribute to strategic IS research on DSS by showing the value for top management of considering the organizational dimension of decision-making with big data, in situations that are strategic to a firm's competitive advantage. To do so, we analyze in detail an extreme case of decision-making with DSS with big data leading to failure of strategic dimensions in Formula 1 (F1): the 2010 Abu Dhabi grand prix where the Ferrari team lost the F1 world championship due to what was considered by many a judgment error in retrospect (Allen, 2010, Collantine, 2010). We choose this event for three main reasons. First, given the clear relation between DSS and performance in F1 and the fact that, in this field, performance and competitive advantage are unmistakably measurable (Gino and Pisano, 2011, Marino et al., 2015, Aversa and Berinato, 2017), F1 has been mentioned as an ideal setting for studying the use of big data (George et al., 2014: 321), and it is particularly suitable to observe DSS-aided decision-making under pressure. Second, this decision failure case epitomizes business situations where time is critical and information systems cannot be separated from their context of use, neither in space nor in time. It is therefore an ideal case to shed light on the strategic implications of the design and use of DSS for organizations—which ultimately determine organizations' success or failure. Third, and importantly, this case exemplifies the three challenges of big data and creates inroads into a research agenda in strategic IS with the development of decision-making tools in mind. The development of tools and information technology artifacts is the domain of design science (March and Smith, 1995, Hevner et al., 2004) that includes the organizational domain by taking into account the user (Markus and Silver, 2008) as well as the openness of a system that remains incomplete (Garud et al., 2008, von Krogh and Haefliger, 2010).

In order to analyze this iconic case of DSS with big data under time pressure, we adopt a practice-based perspective (Nicolini, 2011, Gherardi, 2012). This perspective has gained increasing interest both in the IS (Arnott and Pervan, 2014, Peppard et al., 2014, Cecez-Kecmanovic et al., 2014a, 2014b) and strategic management (Wagner et al., 2010, Cabantous and Gond, 2011, Vaara and Whittington, 2012, George et al., 2014, Whittington, 2014, Jarzabkowski and Kaplan, 2015) communities over the recent years. As applied to strategic decision-making with DSS, a practice-based approach invites IS scholars to consider not just the individuals who make the decisions (together with their cognition) but instead to study the "practice of deciding." In other words, this perspective suggests approaching decision-making as a situated, social and material practice involving the decision makers, the technologies, and the specificities of the decision contingencies, in order to study how the relations between all these elements constitute decisions and ultimately to evaluate their outcomes (Cabantous et al., 2010, Cabantous and Gond, 2011).

Our practice-based interpretation of the case leads us to question the public interpretations of the "heroic" individual user of a DSS who succeeds or fails and we reveal three groups of insights: the first is about the closely connected sets of biases at the intersection of the human and the machine. IT and DSS with big data are not simply at the service of a boundedly rational human decision maker, even if that is the sole public interpretation of the events. A more nuanced analysis of this strategic decision failure reveals the importance of considering decision-making with big data as a socially situated practice, and hence to consider the affordances of IT artifacts and the organizational context. It also shows that strategic decision-making with big data must be understood within a distributed cognition approach; and finally shows the importance of considering the performative power of the models that aggregate and structure the data entering the DSS. Ultimately, our analysis shows the importance of considering decision-making with DSS and big data as a social and material practice given the diversity of uses of decision-making technologies and artifacts in time and space, while paying careful attention to their interpretive flexibility or affordance (Zigurs et al., 1988, DeSanctis and Poole, 1994, Markus and Silver, 2008, Junglas et al., 2013, Bernhard et al., 2014) as well as other intangible aspects such as organizational culture (Schein, 1985, Barney, 1986, McDermott and O'Dell, 2001, Suppiah and Singh Sandhu, 2011).

Overall, our analysis leads to more questions than answers because it invites a reading of the failure case that goes beyond what the press and observers took as a first conclusion in order to stimulate research in strategic IS and systems design. Our analysis also enables us to develop a compelling research agenda for strategic IS scholars, which, in line with recent key contributions (Arnott and Pervan, 2014, Peppard et al., 2014), pays particular attention to the role of recent DSS for strategic purposes, including the interactions between the technical and organizational dimensions of decision-making as a response to the challenges laid out by authors who recently addressed the business promise of big data (Davenport and Harris, 2007, Jacobs, 2009, Baesens et al., 2014, Lazer et al., 2014, Loebbecke and Picot, 2015, Poleto et al., 2015). We conclude our paper by discussing implications for design science and the management of strategic information systems.

Theoretical Background

The strategic use of IS in practice can lead to individual and organizational failure, and it is one of the foremost challenges of scholarship to help decision makers and support their potential to make successful decisions (McAfee et al., 2012, Gunther et al., 2017). Several key strategic domains in organizations e.g., those related to business models, innovation, and operations are strongly influenced by decisions taken with the help of DSS and big data. Advances in technology as well as in the theoretical understanding of the role that material artifacts such as IS play in collaboration and decision-making (Orlikowski, 2000, Leonardi, 2011, Nicolini et al., 2012) have led strategy and IS scholars to increasingly study practice as a sight of research (Mazmanian et al., 2014, Jarzabkowski and Kaplan, 2015, Scarbrough et al., 2015). Fundamentally, this is because the strategic outcome of decisions partly depends on the actual use, *in situ,* of the tools available to the decision makers. The input and models that constitute a DSS are as important as the decision makers who employ them towards a desired outcome, which is why "decision-making 'disasters' may stem from the oversimplification or misrepresentation encoded in tools" (Jarzabkowski and Kaplan, 2015: 538, March, 2006). The affordances of the tools (e.g., DSS, models, screens with visual representations etc.) represent our first point of departure when studying a case of strategic decision failure.

DSS have a long history of taking into account groups of decision makers and the types of tasks they face (DeSanctis and Gallupe, 1987) as well as the processes and approaches of implementing systems in practice (Earl, 1993). Only more recently have scholars called for closer attention to the doing and thinking of individuals and their artifacts (Cecez-Kecmanovic et al., 2014b). In this view on strategic IS, the missing elements include a holistic, integrated perspective rather than different approaches (Earl, 1993): a practice-based approach "prefers concrete micro actions rather than abstract macro analysis" (Peppard et al., 2014: 1). Such a practice approach to decision-making may bring to the fore how and why different uses of tools such as DSS lead to various outcomes and help IS scholars relax some of the prevalent dualities between human and computer, or between thought and action (Feldman and Orlikowski, 2011). Yet, this approach is still not fully developed in strategic IS. This brings us to our second starting point, which considers that cognition is not simply located in the (head of the) decision maker but is distributed across a variety of entities (Boland et al., 1994). We shift the locus of decision-making for strategic purposes from the mind of the individual(s) making the decisions, to the network of artifacts and human beings involved in the practice of deciding. Approaching cognition and decision-making as a distributed phenomenon (Hutchins, 1995a, 1995b) can help strategic IS scholars to better understand how the specificities of the decision situations, as well as the relations and entanglements between human (e.g., decision makers) and non-human (e.g., models, screens, software, remote partners) entities shape decisions with DSS and big data. It also brings into the picture the importance of organizational culture as background contingency affecting ex-ante the decision process design, and ex-post the interpretation of the outcome (Schein, 1985, Barney, 1986).

A third point of departure is equally rooted in long-standing thinking about strategic IS, namely the status of belief in policy and the role of "semi-confusing information" (Hedberg and Jonsson, 1978). According to Hedberg and Jonsson (1978), the embedded rules and models within an IS can stabilize or destabilize organizational action and, therefore, its outcomes, and competitive advantage. The appropriate triggers for change can be located in the use of semi-confusing information feeding into the models that organizational actors trust or follow. Thus, in response to the increasingly prominent role played by models and artificial intelligence today, a practice approach is well suited to reveal the performative dimension of strategic IS. Performativity studies focus on the transformative power of models, seen as intermediary devices between theory and reality (or myth and environment, in Hedberg and Jonsson, 1978), in shaping practice, and document the feedback loops between reality and the models embedded in these tools (Callon, 1986, MacKenzie and Millo, 2003). Models—like those embedded in DSS—are (imperfect) "representations" of the real world, and actors use them to model and change the reality (Morgan, 2012), so that their nature and enactment shape reality itself in a recursive way. Approaching decision-making from a practice perspective could help IS scholar better understand how advanced DSS, which are "models" that integrate both expert knowledge of IS engineers and the knowledge of the users, are used and manipulated and, ultimately, how the models embedded in the tools play an active role in decision-making.

In summary, we approach strategic decision-making supported by IS from a practice perspective that borrows from pivotal work combining strategy-as-practice with IS research (Arnott and Pervan, 2014, Peppard et al., 2014, Whittington, 2014). Specifically, we probe a critical case of strategy failure because, theoretically, such a case may reveal the challenges for the design of IS in high resolution due to the collapse of a routine event: multiple actors interpret, ex-post, what went wrong and reflect intensely upon the sources of failure, not least because of the dramatic costs for the organization (in our case, Ferrari's underperformance). Given the proposed focus on the use of tools in context (Jarzabkowski and Kaplan, 2015) and on episodes of strategizing (Whittington, 2014), we analyze the causes of failure in detail starting from three salient issues that appear in traditional research on DSS and dominate a practice perspective today: affordances, distributed cognition, and performativity. Our effort aims to synergistically continue the route clearly identified by recent contributions (Arnott and Pervan, 2014, Peppard et al., 2014) towards an integrated perspective that foster an holistic view of the critical use of DSS, particularly when the combined effect of big data and pressuring conditions favor erroneous use and highlight systematic pitfalls related to strategy design and implementation.

Method

Empirical Setting

Our contribution is grounded in events happening in a competitive setting that is ideal to observe causes and effects of decision-making with big data: the last race of 2010 Formula 1 World Championship, taking place in the UEA, Abu Dhabi Grand Prix (Yas Marina racetrack). Former works have already leveraged the Formula 1 setting to advance strategy-related contributions (e.g., Castellucci and Ertug, 2010, Jenkins, 2010, Aversa et al., 2015, Piezunka et al., 2018). In this occasion Ferrari's driver Fernando Alonso unexpectedly lost the F1 Driver World Championship due to what media and field experts unanimously have defined as its team's mistaken "race strategy." Such strategy was driven by a modern DSS system that heavily relied on big data (Collantine, 2010).

A F1 team's most evident strategic objective is winning car races of the F1 World Championship, thus obtaining the best performance within the season and maximizing the income derived from superior race performance (mostly through monetary prizes, increasing sponsorship, and enhanced global visibility). Every year, the *Federation Internationale de l'Automobile* (i.e., FIA), which is the governing body that rules the sport and the industry, allocates the revenues with the F1 teams on a proportion of their race results. Accordingly, most of the teams' efforts and investments are aimed at improving the technological performance of their cars on the racetrack, and thus their sport achievements—which are fundamentally correlated (Sylt and Reid, 2010, Aversa et al., 2015).

F1 cars are incredibly complex vehicles whose architecture reaches its performance peak only when the combination of its parts is perfectly balanced (Marino et al., 2015). During the race, this architectural balance is obtained through an ad-hoc set-up conducted by the engineers in the pits before the race and by the drivers based on the instruments available in the car cockpit during the race. Each driver can adjust several parameters such as movable wings, suspensions, engine mapping, weight ballast, and breaking distribution to optimize the functioning of their car. All F1 cars use special high-performing tire sets that are available in different compounds and designed to better perform under different weather conditions (e.g., dry, semi-wet, wet race etc.). As tire sets deteriorate rapidly through the race, F1 teams can call their cars to the pit-lane in order to change the worn tire set with a set of fresh ones. Today, a tire change called in technical jargon "pit-stop" (Leslie, 2015), involves 20 people performing 34 actions in around 2.3 s, but overall each car spends between 20 and 30 s in driving through the pit-lane, changing tires, and getting back into the action of the racetrack (i.e., in technical jargon this is referred as "pitting" the car). Teams can perform several pit-stops per race (usually between one and four depending on the specific race and tire characteristics).

Defining the number and timing of pit-stops are two of the most critical decisions for a team during a F1 race. Teams' decisions vary massively on both aspects and they determine success and failure in races. To monitor, analyze, and deploy the best strategy during a race (vis-a-vis current conditions and competitors' strategy), each F1 vehicle combines advanced telemetry systems with a complex modeling simulation (Bi, 2014). Telemetry in F1 is the transmitting of streams of live data sourced by racing car sensors—there are between 160 and 300 on each car—generating between 1 and 20 gigabyte of data in each race. The output is sent (often through a proprietary wireless protocol based on around 800 channels) to each team's data elaboration center in the racetrack pits and simultaneously rebounded to the "remote garage" back in the company headquarters in Europe. There, a team made of up to 30 engineers and IT specialists runs simulations that forecast the possible race outcome given the current car's data (i.e., race performance, activity of the subparts, and drivers' biophysical data etc.), the relative position of the other cars on the track and their most likely race strategy as well as a variety of other factors. The models that are used to run these simulations are based on assumptions that derive from the team strategists' experience, as well as historical data from previous races—about 60% of the data generated by the car is used in that race, while the remaining 40% is stored for later applications. The outcome of this modeling is a selected portfolio of strategic options that is sent back to the "race pitwall" (i.e., the data analysis center at the racetrack), where the chief race strategist has only a few minutes to cross check the selected strategic options with the data in his control displays, consult with

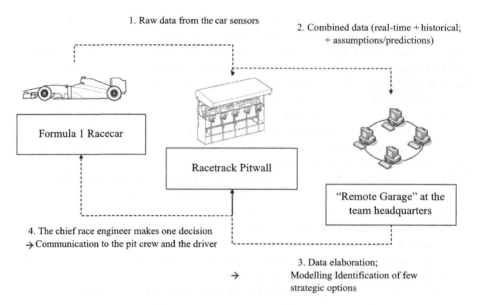

1. Raw data from the car sensors

2. Combined data (real-time + historical; + assumptions/predictions)

Formula 1 Racecar

Racetrack Pitwall

"Remote Garage" at the team headquarters

4. The chief race engineer makes one decision
→ Communication to the pit crew and the driver

3. Data elaboration;
Modelling Identification of few
strategic options

→

Figure 18.1 DSS with real-time big data in Formula 1 racing.

the race engineer in charge of the team's cars, and make a decision—such as "to pit" the car, wait until a later lap, or not pitting at all (see Figure 18.1).

The complexity of this process and the incredible (time) pressure during the racing competition push most of the companies to hire entire teams of IT specialists for data telemetry and data analysis and to spend around 5% of their yearly budget—which is between $150 and $500 million per year—in developing a high-performing and reliable real-time DSS with big data. F1 championships are won or lost partly because of this process and the events and practices in racing represent a promising arena for research in strategic IS both due to the fast-paced decision practices and due to the ongoing development of tools that support strategic decisions under high pressure.

Data Collection

The secrecy of the F1 world, the risk of retrospective call biases, and the limited number of acknowledgeable informants to report on such iconic events represent a major challenge for information collection in this setting. Despite this challenge, we nonetheless managed to conduct a series of exclusive semi-structured interviews with some of the (very few) people directly involved with this strategic decision, namely F1 executives Chris Dyer (Chief Race Strategist at Ferrari—in charge of calling the final pit-stop strategy), Piergiorgio Grossi (Chief Information Officer at Ferrari—who supervised the design and implementation of the DSS), and Otello Valenti (Head of HR at Ferrari—in charge on inquiring on the team's responsibilities after the race). These interviews aimed at gaining details and granularity of the decision-making context, including information on the sequence of events, the nature of the DSS, the support technologies, and the types of data used, as well as the interaction between human and technological agents. We also inquired about Ferrari's organizational and decision-making culture. In order to complement out "off-the-record" account of the race, we also interviewed three F1 journalists who oversaw the race from the media box above the pit-lane. In our interviews with journalists, we covered similar topics as with the executives, but we also inquired about the rumors, "paddock talks" and the actions not reported by the media. All in all, the interaction with our six expert informants accounted for an average of 2.5 h each, for total of 18 h of engagement. The interviews were recorded, transcribed, and analyzed in conjunction with the archival sources. As we were concerned for the small number of informants, we asked F1 professionals whether other people should have been considered as acknowledgeable informants, but were told that the few people we had met were those who had made the decision, and no-one could have provided a more fine-grained report of what exactly happened.

We complemented this unique set of interviews with publicly available real-time information about the race. As per usual F1 rules, all communication during the race happens via radio and the communication with the driver are recorded and available for research purposes, while the communications between the team members is owned by Ferrari, and are not accessible. We therefore collected the official Ferrari driver Fernando Alonso communication with the Chief Race Strategist at the pitwall (Chris Dyer).

Finally, in order to have the most comprehensive interpretation of the sequence of events and attribution of responsibilities for the (failing) decision at Ferrari, we searched the media database Factiva for all sources (e.g., newspapers, blogs, etc.) in English language published about the focal event (Siggelkow, 2007) two weeks before and up to one year later. Keywords like "Abu Dhabi," "UAE," "Grand Prix," "Yas Marina," "F1," "Formula 1," "Ferrari," "Alonso," where combined in multiple forms to retrieve the documents. We ultimately retained 52 documents (around 120 pages) out of the 356 documents that the search returned.[1] These documents include interviews taken close before, during, or right after the event—which partially reduces concerns for retrospective call biases, and contain detailed opinions and interpretations from key stakeholders such as Ferrari's President, Ferrari F1 team CEO, Ferrari's Technical Director, FIA's president, other drivers, engineers, mechanics, technicians, Formula 1 journalists, and fans.

Data Analysis

Our analysis was aimed to identify the factors that played a significant role in determining Ferrari's race strategy and its unsuccessful turnout. Following standard practices in grounded theory (Strauss and Corbin, 1990), two scholars intimately familiar with F1 (both from an industry as well as academic perspective) discussed the materials and reconstructed the sequence of events and decisions using tables and schemes. We leveraged a set of the most significant quotes from the event protagonists to enhance our descriptive narrative of the events. Then, we adopted a systematic approach to concept development and grounded theory articulation, by focusing on aggregating the available evidence to identify a set of explanatory constructs (Gioia et al., 2012a). Moving from *first-order concepts* (i.e., evidence from the field such as individual "Overconfidence biases", "Attention bases issues") we identified *second-order themes* at a higher level of abstraction (e.g., "Cognitive biases"; "Factors enhancing cognitive biases") and ultimately *aggregate dimensions* that point to specific theoretical perspectives (e.g., "Individual bounded cognition"). In this process, a third scholar (less familiar with the setting) acted as devil's advocate (Gioia et al., 2012b: 19, Van Maanen, 1979) and challenged the interpretation and aggregation results. Questionable interpretations were discarded. Finally, following commons visualization practice (Corley and Gioia, 2004), we built a table reporting the data structure (see Table 18.2). As we analyzed the data, we carefully searched for explanations and justification of the decision, and tried to disentangle the chain of causes that determined the final outcome, particularly when this was grounded in the contingencies that affected the decision. We also aimed at separating the opinions from the media and the public, while comparing them to the evidence we collected from the field and from the interviews with the protagonists.

Decision Support System Failure: Observations from Formula 1

Chronicle of the Race: F1 Abu Dhabi Grand Prix 2010

On Sunday November 14th 2010, the German driver Sebastian Vettel crossed the finish line of the Grand Prix of Abu Dhabi as first, and gained the Formula 1 World Championship on a Red Bull Racing car. This moment became a memorable event in the history of F1 as it represented an unprecedented case on many aspects. It was the first time Red Bull Racing won the F1 World Constructor's Championship; the first time Sebastian Vettel won the F1 Driver's Championship; and the first time that Formula 1 raced in Abu Dhabi, UAE. In addition, the results of the race came rather unexpected: Before the Abu Dhabi's showdown the Driver's Championship ranking had been dominated by Fernando Alonso of the Ferrari team (246 points) followed by Mark Webber of Red Bull Racing team (238 points), while Sebastian Vettel followed in third position (232 points). Vettel had performed very well throughout the weekend, obtaining the best lap during Saturday's qualifying session, and thus the pole position in the starting grid for the Sunday's race.

However, the media and the public opinion unanimously agreed that him winning the world championship would have not been possible without a key strategic mistake made by the Ferrari team, which unequivocally compromised not only Alonso's race but also his possibility to win the F1 Driver's World Championship title (see among others interpretations by Allen, 2010, Collantine, 2010). Even in the case of Vettel's victory of the Abu Dhabi grand prix, Alonso would have been able to maintain the top spot of the championship tally—and thus graduating F1 world champion—by finishing in 4th place; and yet the team's decision in an early pit-stop timing "contrived to lose him positions so he ended up seventh" (Allen, 2010). Table 18.1 shows the participants and the final ranking at the end of the 2010 Abu Dhabi race.

At the 2010 Abu Dhabi race, Ferrari's strategy was in the experienced hands of the Australian Chief Race Strategist, Chris Dyer. Despite being the first time ever that a F1 grand prix was taking place at Yas Marina Circuit in Abu Dhabi (UEA), Chris Dyer could count on his long experience in F1 that started in 1997 with Arrows and continued since 2001 at Ferrari where he had significantly contributed to winning five World Championships with Michael Schumacher (one of the most successful drivers in F1 history) and one championship with the Finnish driver Kimi Raikkonen. The DSS used by the Ferrari team at the 2010 Abu Dhabi race was one of the finest and most advanced in the entire F1 circus: a Monte Carlo simulation model with deterministic parameters designed by the Ferrari IT department under the coordination and supervision of Piergiorgio Grossi, at the time Ferrari's Chief Information Officer.

At the very first lap the driver Michael Schumacher (Mercedes team) had an accident that stopped his car and forced him to retire. As often in these cases, to help officers safely clear the tarmac from the broken car and its debris, the "safety car" was called out to the track and all F1 cars slowly proceeded in line behind it until works were completed and the track was restored. During this time, some mid-field cars pitted. Alonso had started the race in third position and was quickly overtaken by McLaren's driver Jenson Button in the first lap, while Mark Webber (2nd in the championship) maintained his 5th position from qualifying. With Sebastian Vettel leading, it was imperative for Alonso to keep his 4th position, or the difference in points gained would make Vettel win the championship. In this context, it was Mark Webber (5th position) who represented the biggest threat for Alonso. Ferrari head strategist, Chris Dyer, thus mainly based Alonso's strategy on Webber's moves. Relatively early in the race, at lap 11 of 55, Webber's car experienced rapid tire degradation and was called to the pits to substitute his worn tire set with a fresh one. In order to maintain the gap

Table 18.1 2010 Abu Dhabi grand prix statistics.

Rank	Driver	Constructor	Laps	Time/retired	Start grid	Pts	Pit-stop at lap
1	Sebastian Vettel	Red Bull-Renault	55	39:36.8	1	25	24
2	Lewis Hamilton	McLaren-Mercedes	55	10.162	2	18	23
3	Jenson Button	McLaren-Mercedes	55	11.047	4	15	39
4	Nico Rosberg	Mercedes	55	30.747	9	12	1
5	Robert Kubica	Renault	55	39.026	11	10	46
6	Vitaly Petrov	Renault	55	43.52	10	8	1
7	Fernando Alonso	Ferrari	55	43.797	3	6	15
8	Mark Webber	Red Bull-Renault	55	44.243	5	4	11
9	Jaime Alguersuari	Toro Rosso-Ferrari	55	50.201	17	2	1
10	Felipe Massa	Ferrari	55	50.868	6	1	13
11	Nick Heidfeld	BMW Sauber-Ferrari	55	51.551	14		15
12	Rubens Barrichello	Williams-Cosworth	55	57.686	7		18
13	Adrian Sutil	Force India-Mercedes	55	58.325	13		47
14	Kamui Kobayashi	BMW Sauber-Ferrari	55	59.558	12		33
15	Sebastien Buemi	Toro Rosso-Ferrari	55	+ 1:03.178	18		37
16	Nico Hulkenberg	Williams-Cosworth	55	+ 1:04.763	15		46
17	Heikki Kovalainen	Lotus-Cosworth	54	+ 1 Lap	20		41
18	Lucas di Grassi	Virgin-Cosworth	53	+ 2 Laps	22		1
19	Bruno Senna	HRT-Cosworth	53	+ 2 Laps	23		1
20	Christian Klien	HRT-Cosworth	53	+ 2 Laps	24		1
21	Jarno Trulli	Lotus-Cosworth	51	Rear wing	19		28
Retired	Timo Glock	Virgin-Cosworth	43	Gearbox	21		40
Retired	Michael Schumacher	Mercedes	0	Collision	8		–
Retired	Vitantonio Liuzzi	Force India-Mercedes	0	Collision	16		–

with Webber, Ferrari Chief Strategist "pitted" Alonso soon after Webber (lap 15 or 55). The outcome of this pit-stop decision was aimed to make Alonso come out of the pit-lane in front of Webber, but in 12th position, behind drivers who had not pitted yet.

To make Alonso end up in the desired 4th position, Ferrari's team was assuming Alonso to be able to overtake the cars racing in front of him. Alonso had in fact a competitive driving style, with particular skill in overtaking, and his Ferrari had a much quicker pace than the cars ahead. However, the Abu Dhabi racetrack characteristics were making overtaking very difficult for all cars, and indeed very few overtakes had happened until that moment. Alonso surprisingly got stuck behind other less performing cars such as the Renault driven by Vitaly

Petrov. To win the championship, Alonso could afford to leave only Vettel and other three competitors in front of him but his early pit had laid another four cars ahead of him—two of which (Vitaly Petrov's Renault and Nico Rosberg's Mercedes) had already pitted opting for a single pit strategy, and thus would not be stopping again; while others more ahead were able to pit and still rejoin the race in front of Alonso. As a result, Alonso finished his race in 7th position, thus concluding the F1 Driver's World Championship in 2nd place with only 1-point difference from Sebastian Vettel.

Post-race analysis highlighted how this outcome could have been reverted, had Chris Dyer decided not to pit Alonso right after Webber. All other things equal, had Ferrari left Alonso out and called him to pit around 20 laps later than when he pitted, the situation would have allowed Alonso to rejoin the race in 4th position and win the world title (Allen, 2010).

Media and Public Interpretation

All the secondary sources and expert opinions we retrieved converged in attributing to the *individual bounded cognition* of the decision maker (Ferrari's Chief Strategist Chris Dyer) the main responsibility for the negative result (see the 1st aggregate dimension in Table 18.2). Heads at Ferrari identified the decision to pit Alonso at lap 15 as the critical error, and ultimately blamed Chris Dyer who made that strategic call.

> *"We made a wrong decision in terms of strategy ... we were unduly concerned about the wear rate of the soft tires and we did not take into consideration the difficulty of getting past other cars on the track." Stefano Domenicali, Ferrari F1 Team Principal*

External experts also agreed in identifying this a key strategic mistake by Chris Dyer:

> *"Ferrari snatched defeat from the jaws of victory in Abu Dhabi. Fernando Alonso's race hinged on a critical strategic decision to pit early, which left him stuck behind Vitaly Petrov." Keith Collantine, Editor at F1Fanatic.com*

(Allen, 2010)

Media mentioned, directly or indirectly, several cognitive biases, including Chris Dyer's switch of attention from achieving the actual goal (ending the race in 4th position) to out-racing the closest competitor (Mark Webber, which in the end represented a minor threat compared to Sebastian Vettel). For example, an expert informer wrote:

> *"The reason they made the mistake was because they were too concerned with what Mark Webber was doing and failed to see the bigger picture." James Allen, F1 Editor at Financial Times*

(Allen, 2010)

Media also blamed Dyer's overconfidence, and his overly optimistic belief that his driver (Alonso) could successfully overtake the cars in front. This is probably motivated by the fact that Fernando Alonso was one of the best drivers in overtaking, held the highest number of points at the beginning of the race, and was racing with a very quick car. Also, Ferrari was aware of its proficiency in DSS with big data development, compared to the other competitors in F1. Other key factors were pointed out as to enhancing the negative effects of such cognitive biases: For example, time pressure during the decision—there were only few

Table 18.2 Data source and data structure.

Data source	First-order concepts	Second-order themes	Aggregate dimensions
Media and external informants	Switch of attention from achieving the actual goal (ending the race in 4th position) to out-racing the closest competitor (Mark Webber, which in the end represented a minor threat compared to Sebastian Vettel). Fernando Alonso was one of the best drivers in overtaking, held the highest number of points at the beginning of the race, and was racing with a very quick car (Ferrari)	Cognitive biases	0 – Individual bounded cognition
	Time pressure during the decision (there are only few minutes and laps to ultimately decide whether to pit or not)		
	Task overload (many different technical tasks must be performed during the racing weekend) Novelty of the situation (first race ever in Abu Dhabi)	Factors enhancing cognitive biases	1 – Situated nature of the decision-making process/Affordance
Direct observation, primary evidence and interviews with the main actors	Possible causes of distractions in the decision place (e.g., cars passing next to the pitwall)		
	Visual separation/distance between the decision makers and the actual race		
	Unique responsibility of the Chief strategist in the decision	Ergonomics of the decision-making situation	
	Organizational culture favoring blaming and "scapegoats."	Organizational culture	
	Hierarchical structure (chain of command in decision-making)		
	Under-specialization of the professional role		
	Impossibility to "ignore/disregard" the output of the DSS		

(continued)

Data source	First-order concepts	Second-order themes	Aggregate dimensions
Direct observation, primary evidence and interviews with the main actors	Several people involved in the analysis of the data (but a single decision maker)	Social distribution of the cognitive task (DM) Material distribution of the cognitive task (DM)	2 – Distributed cognition
	Reliance on DSS to compute the best strategy		
	Radio-mediated communication (possible noise, no visual contact)		
	Impossibility to modify or adapt the DSS during the decision process	Temporal distribution of the cognitive task (DM)	
	The parameters for the underlying assumptions in the model are set before the race		
	Assumptions based on complex algorithms, and the DSS which provide inputs in the decision-making process.	Technical specificities of DSS and assumptions embedded in DSS	3 – Performativity
	No possibility to include intuitive judgment in the decision process or the DSS.		
	The model does not provide probability estimates on the different options (e.g., the decision makers is only informed about which are the best options, but there is no indication on their probability of leading to a positive outcome, nor what is the probability difference between these options and the other alternatives)		
	The model does not have a learning function (it cannot include some changing conditions emerged during the race such as the general difficulty to overtake)		
	Firm-based DSS system (i.e., the instruments tend to focus on data of the team's car, while developing limited insights on competitors)	Information, data	
	No historical data on relevant parameters (i.e., likelihood of overtaking in this specific circuit)		

minutes and laps to ultimately decide whether to pit or not—and task overload, as there were many different technical tasks that Dyer had to perform during the racing weekend and his Chief Strategist role was not seen as a "full-time" activity. Experts claim that Dyer made a decision

> "[that] was wrong not because of a bug (in the DSS), but because of the settings and the probabilities and so on. What I think is that with a different pressure, with more people looking at it, or focused mindset, probably it was not so difficult to understand that the software was wrong and there was something else to do. I am sure that Chris at home, without any data would have not called the driver in. He was kind of distracted." Piergiorgio Grossi, Head of IT at Ferrari.
>
> interview, 2015

Finally, field evidence suggested that the novelty of the race (it was the first F1 race ever in Abu Dhabi), and Dyer's limited personal experience in that specific track might have biased his decision and underemphasized the challenges in adopting a race strategy mostly based on overtaking.

After debriefing on the race result, Ferrari executives decided to fire Chris Dyer, which terminated his involvement in F1 for 6 years (as in 2016 he came back to F1 with team Renault).

> The Australian Chris Dyer—that everyone pointed as the main cause of the decision in Abu Dhabi that costed Fernando Alonso the world title—had been late to come back ... Last December, he was fired from his role as head strategist because of his decision on November 14, for that mistake, for that moment when Alonso entered the box too early, at lap 16, to copy Webber, and lost any opportunity to win the world title ...
>
> (Sanz, 2011)

Today, after more than 7 years from that historical moment, and despite the many technological and organizational upgrades undergone to prevent such mistakes and improve several aspects of its their DSS, Ferrari has still not won the F1 Driver's World Championship.

Towards a More Holistic Interpretation of the Case

While media and expert explain decision-making solely through an individual bounded cognition lens, our analysis of the case sheds light on three additional challenges beyond individual cognitive biases. The data we collected about the case, together with the practice perspective that guided our analysis of this data, first suggest that the material and social context of the decision-making situation needs to be included in the analysis in order to derive useful lessons from this failure (see aggregate dimension 1 in Table 18.2). We found for instance that the ergonomics of the situation played a role: the pitwall location as a decision place can create possible causes of distractions (e.g., loud cars passing by the pit-lane and thus next to the pitwall; television broadcasting and photographers shooting the decision-making process; weather conditions such as hot temperature). Also, despite being placed right next to the starting grid, the pitwall crew is facing a wall of flat screens that create a visual separation/distance between the decision makers and the actual race. In addition, our case suggests that the broader organizational context in which the decision is made is of crucial importance to understand decision failures. Ferrari's strong chain of command and hierarchical structure—with little possibility of bottom up interventions and unilateral responsibility attribution to the Chief Strategist—as well as a specific organizational culture that favors blaming and "scapegoats"—and which in recent years brought the team to substitute three acclaimed senior technical executives (Chris Dyer, Aldo Costa, and James Allison) and two sporting directors (Stefano Domenicali, and Marco Mattiacci) as a response to disappointing racing results—impacted on the decision maker. Other elements can help understand the decision failure, including the under-specialization of the professional role of the Chief Strategist at Ferrari that at the time was a part-time task for engineering directors; and a clear rule that prevented from disregarding the output of the DSS. This latter element seems crucial in our case, as reported by our interviewees. Yet, the DSS was programmed to feedback only two options and Dyer, who was required by team procedures to pick the best option out of those offered by the DSS, correctly picked the best of the two. Unfortunately, this was not good enough to keep the 4th position and win the championship:

> "We were deciding between A and B, and we chose A. What we miss in the end was option C, which at that time still looked a much better option. Option C was quite different from A and B. A and B were stop-now or stop in 5 laps time, option C was stopping in 15 laps time or something ... Option B was kind of local maximum, it was better than one lap before, better than one lap after B, better the two laps after B, but it actually it was not better than 10 laps after B. So, fundamentally, we missed option C. The option C would have put us in the position to finish fifth or perhaps fourth at the end of the race" Chris Dyer, Head of Strategy at Ferrari.
>
> interview, 2015

This "third option" (that had reasonably higher chances of winning) was not included among the DSS options, and following it would have meant for Dyer disregarding the team rule. This would have not been a problem, in case this option brought Ferrari and Alonso to winning the championship; but as F1 is a turbulent environment where anything can happen and results can be reverted by random happenings like a tire puncture, in case of failure (with a unique decision maker, and a blame culture) this decision would have put Chris Dyer in hard-to-justify position with his superiors. This point shows the importance of deeply understanding the organizational culture where the decision takes place, since this culture shapes decision makers' perception of what the DSS affords them to do, and their final actions.

A second important insight that emerges from our analysis as key to understand the several causes of the decision failure is *distributed cognition* (see aggregate dimension 2 in Table 18.2). This notion refers to the sharing the cognitive tasks between people, and with artifacts across time. In our case, the interplay of Ferrari team members in charge of the race strategy, such as Chris Dyer (Head of Race Strategy), Andrea Stella (Fernando Alonso's Race Engineer), and Robert Smedley (Felipe Massa's Race Engineer), their mutual communication practices and their interaction with the DSS to define the pit-stop strategy also partly explains the decision that was taken. For example, it is reasonable to suggest that the location of the remote garage of analysts in Ferrari's headquarters (Maranello, Italy) far away from the race track, influenced the decision-making process. Importantly, recognizing the distributed nature of cognition leads to a closer analysis of the interactions between the human agents involved in the decision-making practice and the technology. In fact, the material aspect of distributed cognition reveals as the decision maker relied on an advanced DSS under the assumption this would compute the best possible strategy. The decision was communicated via radio to the other team members—which could reveal challenges due to noise and/or lack of visual contact; and ultimately the DSS suffered from a temporal distortion because its basic assumptions and underlying parameters could not be significantly updated during the race (for example there was no way to input a lower likelihood of successful overtaking, as it emerged during the race).

Third and finally, our case suggests that greater attention should be paid to the *performative* aspects of the DSS (see aggregate dimension 3 in Table 18.2). Evidence from the field revealed that complex algorithms in the simulation system and the DSS provided hard-to-manage inputs in the decision-making process. There was however hardly any possibility to integrate the emerging decision maker's intuition in the decision process or in the DSS. Further, the model did not provide probability estimates on the different options (e.g., there was no indication on their probability of leading to a positive outcome, nor what was the probability difference between these options and the other alternatives) nor it included a learning function that could have refined its outcome based on the difficult overtaking that every driver was experiencing during the race. In simple words, the system could not update some key changing conditions that emerged during the race such as the general difficulty to overtake. Information and data held a performative function as well. In general, DSS appeared to be relatively "firm-based"—that means that the instruments tended to focus on data of the team's car (e.g., focus on Ferrari), while developing more limited insights on competitors. Further, there were no historical data on relevant parameters of the Yas Marina circuit (i.e., likelihood of overtaking in this specific circuit) as this was the first time F1 was racing in UEA.

In summary, Chris Dyer himself publicly acknowledged his mistake but nonetheless emphasized how this was the best possible solution (and the only allowed) given the two options that the DSS had suggested and given the overall constraints. A perspective mainly focused on individual cognitive bias fails to provide a more comprehensive understanding of the broader challenges in the decision. Simply put, Chris Dyer's mistake was influenced by a complex and intricate combination of factors that included not only his personal judgment, but also a miscalculation of the DSS that was embedded in a system of practices that did not allow the decision maker to disregard it and a set of contextual features that exacerbated the situation: such as time and psychological pressure; the impossibility of directly observing the race; and mediated communication with other key agents (among others). Evidence we collected from the field by adopting an integrated practice-based perspective suggests that to reach a deeper and more systemic understanding the interpretation of the facts includes, in addition to *Individual bounded cognition,* three other key aspects *(1) Situated nature of the decision-making process/Affordance; (2) Distributed cognition;* and *(3) Performativity.*

The fact that even iconic and visible events involving performance and technology-driven companies such as Ferrari receive a narrow and individualistic interpretation of failure and success drives home a sound and compelling case for a more holistic approach in future research on decision-making. The case from Formula 1 should support such an agenda as it represents a world that has traditionally pioneered the most advanced decision support systems (including big data) and is famous for meticulously analyzing every decision in order to optimize any outcome down to a fraction of a second—as this could separate the winners from the losers. Every detail counts. Thus, in the following section, we leverage reflections from this case to discuss implications for strategic IS and suggest a practice-based agenda.

Discussion: Towards a Research Agenda

As a direct consequence from our insights into the case, we discuss and derive an agenda for research for IS scholars around three lines of inquiry: (1) The material and social features of the decision situation, including the specificities of the organizational culture that impact on decision-making (e.g., blame culture) and the interpretive flexibility (or affordances) of DSS; (2) The distributed nature of cognition along three dimensions, namely temporal (i.e. cognition is distributed across time), social (i.e. the division of cognitive labor between individuals), and material (i.e., human beings interact with non-human entities in decision-making with big data); and; (3) The performative dimension of the models incorporated in big data decision tools. Along these lines, we generalize to the field of strategic IS and advance a set of theoretical reflections that deserve attention before including the specific view of design science and tools that follows from these reflections. The agenda stems from the perspectives outlined in Table 18.3.

Table 18.3 The three facets of the phenomenon and research questions.

Facets of the phenomenon		Research questions
Situated nature of decision-making with big data	Features of decision-making situation, including the elements of the organizational culture that play an important role in the way organizational actors make sense of the decision situation (e.g., blame vs. just culture, accountability), the ergonomics of the decision situation (e.g., visual and audio environment). These characteristics of the decision situation shape how actors interpret what the DSS allows them to do	What are the characteristics of the decision situation in which actors use the DSS features and how these characteristics shape actors' perception of the DSS affordances?
Distributed cognition in bigdata decision-making	Fine-grained account of the collectives of human entities, and non-human entities (e.g., technologies, algorithms) making the decision	How does the socio technical "agencement" of the human and non-human actors lead to decisions?
	Description of the cognitive division of labor between team members (social distribution), and of the ways in which the cognitive decision task is distributed across time (pre-computation), and with the artifacts (e.g. DSS) used by actors to make the decision (material distribution)	
Performative dimension of decision-making tools	Assumptions embedded in the Ferrari DSS have been enacted through the decision-making process. How were unexpected events modeled (e.g., safety car, competitor's change of strategy; possible accidents) and how does the responsibility of the decision maker vary? What is (not) included in the model?	How do the theories and assumptions encapsulated into DSS actively participate in decision-making?

The Situated Nature of Decision-Making

Decision-making with DSS and big data is a situated activity, that is an activity that takes place in a social, physical, and technical environment. Recognizing the situated nature of decision-making with DSS and big data allows conceiving it as social practice, and thus directs our attention to the features of the decision-making situation that might influence decision makers' perceptions of what the technologies they use afford them to do (Gibson, 1979). This line of inquiry thus suggests studying how some elements of the organizational culture influence the way organizational actors make sense of the decision situation (e.g., blame vs. just culture, accountability) as well as the ergonomics of the decision situation such as the visual and audio environment (e.g., Schein, 1985, Weick, 1987, Suppiah and Singh Sandhu, 2011). Ultimately, it directs our attention to decision makers' perception of the interpretive and material affordance for action provided by DSS with big data decision-making technologies. Table 18.4 lists some of the research questions associated to a situated approach to DSS with big data decision-making practice.

First, a practice-based approach to decision-making with DSS and big data shows the importance of considering seriously the social and material context of deciding with such technologies, and the features of the situation within which decisions are made. It could lead strategic IS scholars to explore the practices of decision-making with big data (e.g., how do organizational actors use big data DSS?) and to identify the features of the decision situation (e.g., spatial layout of the work environment) as well as the organization's decision culture that impact on decision makers' perceptions of the affordances of DSS. The notion of "affordance" (Gibson, 1979, Hutchby, 2001) refers to the idea that the objects and artifacts that actors use are subject to "numerous interpretation and uses and [do] not allow, or 'afford', any interpretation or use: [their] constituent properties have specific effects on actions" (Giraudeau, 2008: 294). The literature on affordances in management (e.g., Giraudeau, 2008, Orlikowski and Scott, 2008, Jarzabkowski and Kaplan, 2015) shows that the intentions of the tool's designers and the material properties of the tools are not the sole determinants of the ways management tools or technologies are used. These two elements matter, but the context of use also matters since it influences how users interpret what the

Table 18.4 Studying the situated nature of decision-making with big data.

Research questions	Research designs for Strategic IS
1. How do the systems interact with the use and design of the spatial layout of the work environment when decision-making is based on big data?	Study the social decision context of DSS by exploring the micro-practices of decision-making with big data taking into account the perceptions of affordances of DSS
2. What are the cultures of uses of big data DSS, and how do they best enhance decision quality and performance?	Compare social decision contexts of DSS, decision-making cultures with DSS (including affordances) across organizations
3. How do the uses of big data DSS change an organization's decision-making culture (e.g., effects on organizational reconfiguration; governance)	Compare practices and systems use over time and across space and the use of similar DSS across organizations in comparable contexts
	Given complex causal effects, explore cases where management designs strategy processes and governance in coordination with strategic information systems and big data use

tools allow them to do, and therefore how they use it—that means their affordances. It is important to note that, while this approach considers that "the materiality of an object favors, shapes or invites" a set of specific uses, it also recognizes that the materiality of an object "at the same time, constrains, a set of specific uses" (Zammuto et al., 2007: 752). In-depth qualitative studies focusing on the affordances of DSS with big data could help address these questions and reveal the usage flexibility of such tools.

Second, strategic IS researchers could study the effectiveness of distinct cultures of DSS use in order understand if some cultures of use of DSS with big data lead to greater decision quality than others. Strategy researchers have long studied the relationship between decision quality and decision processes (Fredrickson, 1984, Dean and Sharfman, 1996, Elbanna and Child, 2007). Yet, this research has yielded mixed results (see Forbes, 2007 for an overview) and it is not clear whether such decision processes always pay in terms of decision quality. Strategic IS scholars could contribute to this debate by bringing in the notion of affordances. It would be important to consider how analytical decision tools (such as big data decision systems) are used in practice, and how different cultures of use of these tools are related to decision quality. Having decision tools that enable extensive data collection and comprehensive data analysis is important, but might not be enough to improve decision quality. Ultimately, what matters is the way these tools are used. In-depth qualitative studies recognizing the flexibility of use of DSS with big data could help better understand how decision systems improve decision quality: How are big data decision tools used in practice to make decisions? What organizational capabilities are needed to use big data effectively? And what cultures of uses of big data DSS best enhance decision quality and performance?

Third, strategic IS scholars could also study how the introduction of big data DSS change an organization's decision-making culture. The causal links between the cultures of DSS use and the organization design and routines are likely to be complex. Cases are needed to establish the effects of the use of DSS with big data on how members of the organization make decisions, collaborate, communicate, and jointly make use of the systems in place. Conversely, the IS assumes a strategic role and their design is likely to affect the way decision-making integrates into management functions and controls. Further, the microstructures of a DSS and the access it provides to data, scenarios, levers for action and so forth, may impact on the way decisions are taken and the ultimate performance of the decision-making process. Ditto, the role of the pitwall in F1 represents a stark example for the critical role of a DSS layout in physical space and its use in time.

The Distributed Nature of Cognition in Decision-Making

Decision-making with big data involves the use of DSS if only to make the volume and speed of available information manageable for the decision makers. While one set of research questions relates to the system itself and its use in a specific cultural and organizational context, there is a second set of questions that points to how cognition—understood as a temporally, socially and materially distributed phenomenon—operates when deciding with big data DSS. We need more understanding of the cognitive roles played by big data DSS and how such systems interact with the information processing activities of their users (Norman, 1991). In his seminal work, Hutchins refers to cognitive systems that function inside individuals, between individuals and their use of tools, in a group of individuals in interaction, or between a group and their use of tools (Hutchins, 1995a: 373) and points to the possibility that cognition is distributed across time, with the notion of pre-computation. Recognizing that cognition is diffused beyond the mind of a single individual has important consequences for an analysis of decision-making with big data DSS, because the decision makers rely on support systems as well as on each other as a group.

As the F1 case shows, despite recent technological advances, the DSS are still far from being fail-safe, and their limitations are exacerbated under pressure and time constraints. In retrospect, decision makers tend to blame each other rather than understanding the implications of the distributed agents involved in the decision: for developers of strategic IS a more precise understanding of decision-making role distributions among human and non-human agents is fundamental to attribute improvements and innovate.

In Table 18.5, we identify three illustrative research questions to help understand the distributed nature of cognition when strategic IS plays a key role. First, recognizing the distributed nature of decision-making with big data DSS directs our attention towards the interactions between human (e.g., the decision makers) and non-human (e.g., big data decision tools) actors involved in the decision-making situation. This calls for fine-grained studies of the interactions between decision makers and DSS during the decision-making process. For example, during a F1 race: Which systems and individuals are involved in which part of the analysis that leads to a decision to stop the car? Who is reflecting on the impending decision with which analysis and data?

A second set of questions that IS scholars could investigate relates to the distribution of decision-making tasks across team members and through time. They could, for instance, test the interactions between the multiple decision makers and the DSS and ultimately study the implications of pre-computation on the way decision makers perceive what the tools' affordances are. In doing so, they could also explore regularities for consistency with interpretations and organizational routines. Third and finally, in-depth investigations of the distributed nature of decision-making with big data DSS can help understand the ways in which such tools extend human cognitive capabilities, by limiting some well-known decision biases. Recent studies in the field of cognitive psychology show that decision biases (Kahneman and Tversky, 1982; Manktelow, 2012) can be limited by an effective use of material artifacts (e.g., Villejoubert and Vallee-Tourangeau, 2011, Vallee-Tourangeau et al., 2015). We still

Table 18.5 Studying how cognition is distributed in decision-making with big data.

Research questions	Research designs for strategic IS
1. What cognitive roles do strategic information systems and decision tools play in decision-making?	Trace the interactions between decision makers and DSS systems during the decision-making process, for example during a F1 race. Which systems and individuals are involved in which part of the analysis that leads to a decision? Who is reflecting a decision with what?
2. How is the cognitive task distributed across team members and through time?	Test the interactions between the multiple decision makers and the DSS
	Study the implications of pre-computation on the affordances
	Explore regularities for consistency with interpretations and organizational routines
3. How do big data decision tools extend human cognition and/or generate new decision biases?	Explore the extent to which big data decision tools improve human cognitive abilities and/or generate (new) biases in decision processes. Study how these decision tools reconfigure the decision task performed by human beings and if they change the balance between intuition and analysis

do not know, however, the extent to which the use of artifacts, such as big data DSS, limit some of these biases (and if so, which ones?) and therefore play the role of cognitive artifacts extending human cognitive capabilities; or, if decision-making practices associated with the use of big data DSS lead to new types of decision biases. Strategic IS scholars could address these questions by using a distributed cognitive perspective that study the effects of material artifacts on decision-making.

Decision-Making in Practice: The Performativity of Models

The concept of performativity, as developed in economic sociology (Callon, 1998, MacKenzie et al., 2007), directs our attention to the role of expert bodies of knowledge (e.g., theories, formulae, models) in the functioning of the economy and organizational life. An expert body of knowledge such as economics does not simply describe an existing external economy but actively participates in the economy and can even "perform" (or bring into being) that economy that it is meant to describe (Callon, 2007). Building on this concept, and strategy-as-practice research, Cabantous and Gond (2011) have argued that rational decision-making is something that organizational actors make possible by mobilizing, in their daily practice, decision-making tools rooted in rational choice theory. In using these tools, they bring into being a specific theory of choice, namely rational choice theory (Cabantous et al., 2010, Cabantous and Gond, 2011).

Generally, approaching decision-making as a performative practice recognizes the social activities that produce decisions, and, importantly, directs our attention to the theories (and assumptions) embedded in the tools used to support the decision-making. This notion helps capture the ways in which a model (or a "representation of reality") interplays with the world it describes, and reveals how the models and the contexts of application wherein they function are mutually generative and selective. As applied to decision-making with big data DSS, such an approach questions the relationship between big data DSS and the "reality" they are supposed to describe by revealing the co-creation and the potential feedback loops between the properties of the models and the effects of action based on the models. For instance, MacKenzie and Millo (2003) show how the Black-Scholes-Merton formula for option pricing progressively acquired a performative power. A central element in their story is the incorporation of the formula into portable programmable calculators used by traders at the Chicago Board Exchange. The more traders used these devices to calculate the price of options, the more the formula became predictive of option prices. In other words, the formula, which initially did not well represent the reality of option pricing, eventually provided an accurate description of reality as traders relied on devices that incorporated the formula.

Cabantous and Gond's idea that rational decision-making, in practice, is performative can serve as a foil to a deeper exploration of the kind of performative processes and outcomes associated to the practice of deciding with big data. Table 18.6 summarizes the three sets of research questions associated to our enquiry into the performative nature of the practice of deciding with big data.

A focus on the performativity of decision practices first foregrounds the analysis of the models (e.g., optimization models, multicriteria decision models) that are encapsulated into decision tools. Such an approach to decision-making seems especially promising in the case of big data DSS, since these systems include complex "models," materialized into software and hardware. These systems are, like any models, intermediary devices between theory and data; they embody a simplified way of representing reality (Morgan, 2012). As a result, when decision makers use big data DSS, they rely on these "models" to act, and hence enable the model to impact on social reality. In this perspective, the relationship between users and system forms agencies of assessment capable of enacting different realities (Cecez-Kecmanovic

Table 18.6 Studying the performativity of big data decision support systems.

Research questions	Research designs for strategic IS
1. What is the source and nature of the assumptions and information that enter big data DSS?	Establish a base-line for rational decision-making in terms of time, space, communication, power relations, cultural contexts etc.
2. What type of performativity can emerge from the use of big data DSS?	Compare devices and models with practice and outcome in terms of effectiveness and convergence or divergence
3. What are the implications of using big data DSS given their potential performativity?	Investigate the learning effects and mimetic behavior among competitors' use of big data DSS

et al., 2014b). In other words, models inside DSS are not only representations of reality but also actors (generators of actions) that impact the reality that the model is supposed to represent. Yet, we are only at the beginning of research about the models (as representations of reality and as actors themselves) encapsulated in and enacted in the use of DSS. The specific inclusions and exclusions of data create relations between the DSS and their users that perform reality and can be considered acting in multiple rounds: design, use, reuse, and so forth.

Approaching decision-making with big data DSS as performative practice also raises a question as to the type of performativity that can emerge from such tools. MacKenzie (2008) distinguished between three types of performativity. "Barnesian" performativity happens when the use of a model or formula alters decision-making processes and makes them more similar to their depiction by the decision model (as in the case of the Black-Scholes-Merton formula). This type of performativity is rare. Two other more common types of performativity are "generic" performativity—i.e., when actors use decision model in their practice —and "effective" performativity—i.e., when the use of a decision model has an impact on decision-making processes. With which type of performativity—generic, effective, or Barnesian—are big data DSS models associated?

Third, our case showed that in some contexts, DSS using big data play a key role in strategy and that some ways of using DSS can have devastating effects. Understanding their performative potential becomes particularly critical in cases when decision makers need to act under time pressure and limited information. If big data DSS allow actors to be potentially more performant by making better decisions—partly thanks to the performativity of the system—then research is compelled to investigate the feedback loops associated with the use of big data DSS (e.g., their learning effects). How do observers and market participants understand the performativity of the DSS they use? What are the elements that drive performance and how is the impact attributed to the systems in use, the availability and analysis of big data, and the practice of systems use?

It is here that the three elements of our research agenda converge because decision makers act with and through DSS. For example, race engineers closely observe competitors' behaviors and make decisions based on how they believe others strategize including the recursive loops implied. This affects the practice of decision-making with the DSS, the distributed cognition of the decision makers and their organizational environment, and the performativity of the support systems. Big data, as well as increasing pressure and turbulence in the environment exacerbate the underlying effects. Only a comprehensive, integrated agenda can link these seemingly separate questions. Appropriate research designs include the information technology explicitly in the analysis (Orlikowski and Iacono, 2001) and theorize within a complex web of practices, events, and results. We turn to more specific issues for strategic IS next.

Conclusion

Starting with a closer look at the Abu Dhabi F1 race in 2010 we ground our observations of strategic decision-making with big data DSS in an empirical analysis of the case and identify three understudied areas of research for IS scholars interested in improving decision-making practice and understand such phenomena from a systemic perspective. To have a comprehensive understanding, all three domains need to be carefully considered through an integrated perspective. First, the affordances of the DSS require attention: organizations specify systems according to their needs and build special and temporal structures that influence the decision-making practice, and ultimately contribute to the firm's strategy. Research could benefit from attending to a number of questions pertinent when taking a practice-based view on strategic decision-making. Further, decision-making is a collective task and thinking in organizations occurs collectively. A practice-based approach to decision-making with big data DSS invites IS scholars to fully recognize the distributed nature of cognition, not least because deciding with big data DSS enhances the volume and speed of information and requires interpretation via multiple decision makers. Lastly, we have argued that a practice-based approach to decision-making with big data DSS points to the overlooked performativity of DSS and invites strategic IS scholars to build on insights from recent research on model use and performativity. DSS make extensive use of models with their necessary simplifications and assumptions. Understanding the working of the assumptions in practice, the feedback loops, and the performative effects is important in identifying biases and potential failures ahead of time.

Finally, because our findings challenge the design of the tools themselves, we derive two implications of our research for research designs in strategic IS. The development of artifacts in information technology is the domain of design science (March and Smith, 1995, Hevner et al., 2004, Gregor and Hevner, 2013). As data stems from multiple sources within and beyond the organization, a first implication of our research is that the development of any DSS system needs to take into account the dynamic technical environment of a context that is being developed by multiple stakeholders. This could result in the need to design for incompleteness (Garud et al., 2008) and close consideration of the relationship between the technological artifacts and the users (DeSanctis and Poole, 1994, Markus and Silver, 2008). In particular, affordance and the potential openness of the design to other organizations and individuals in the environment (von Krogh and Haefliger, 2010) point to implications for design science. In a competitive arena such as F1, where rules and standards dictate a framework for innovation of the automotive and support technologies (Aversa et al., 2015), the focal organization is not alone and the decision maker does not act in isolation. Taking the team-level knowledge, dynamics and the competitive dynamics into account creates additional complexity for the design of the system (Erden et al., 2008).

Second, the design of IS follows feedback cycles in as far as the competent building of artifacts draws on knowledge in rigorous implementation and on problems in relevant implementation (Hevner, 2007). In this respect, design science influences and is influenced by the practice of use (DeSanctis and Poole, 1994, Markus and Silver, 2008, von Krogh and Haefliger, 2010) and new research designs should focus on how the perception, treatment, and interpretation of data systematically influence decision-making, if they do. This is part of the DSS yet more subtle than the programming itself. Following the example of F1, the sensory data from the car on the racetrack may receive a certain weight in the decision-making process relative to the communication data. This relative weight of data sources, the time delays, and other factors are programmed and modeled into the DSS and may favor specific outcomes. Such outcomes, if systematic, may in turn reinforce requirements to be programmed into the system and support the models chosen, hence an effective performativity of the DSS. A hypothesis at this point, we suggest research design in strategic IS to carefully appreciate the potential performativity in the design through the models used and the assumptions made.

Scholars have highlighted how understanding the implications of DSS and big data is (and will increasingly be) at the core of firms' performance and competitive advantage. Such technologies underpin the creation, development and performance of strategic decisions related to business models, work-practices, stakeholder interests, organizational models (Gunther et al., 2017). Failing to appreciate the nuanced implications of such contemporary phenomena can lead to severe costs and organizational failure. Hence, we posit that fully understanding (in an integrated fashion) the effects of decision-making with DSS in practice, represents a paramount aspect that deserves scholarly and professional investigation.

The race to lead the "big data revolution" (Mayer-Schonberger and Cukier, 2013) keeps going within and beyond the racetrack but challenges remain compelling. Formula 1, again, exemplifies this situation. Particularly after Ferrari's fiasco in 2010, teams have significantly increased their investments in trying to optimize these critical decision-making processes. Yet, the challenge is far from being fully resolved. For example at the 2015 Monte Carlo Grand Prix Mercedes failed to transform the information of its DSS and, by making a wrong pit-stop call, jeopardized their driver's, Lewis Hamilton's, victory (Johnson, 2015). The software as well as inter-team communication were blamed for the mistake, which is particularly noteworthy given the fact that Mercedes was recently awarded for developing the best DSS visualization tool in F1 (Caskill, 2015). All in all, this confirms that even in fields that pioneer the most advanced DSS with big data, unveiling the perils and pitfalls of technology-based decision-making still represents a timely and compelling task with major strategic implications. We hope that our agenda will stimulate scholars and executives' inquiring and ultimately contribute valuable insights for theory and practice.

Note

1   All materials are available upon request, including videos of the race and audio commentaries.

References

Allen, J., 2010. How did Ferrari make that strategy mistake with Alonso. *James Allen on F1*, <www.jamesallenonf1.com/2010/11/how-did-ferrari-make-that-strategy-mistake-with-alonso/>.

Arnott, D., Pervan, G., 2014. A critical analysis of decision support systems research revisited: the rise of design science. *J. Inform. Technol.* 29 (4), 269–293.

Aversa, P., Berinato, S., 2017. Sometimes, less innovation is better. *Harvard Bus. Rev.* 6, 38–39.

Aversa, P., Furnari, S., Haefliger, S., 2015. Business model configurations and performance: a qualitative comparative analysis in Formula One racing, 2005-2013. *Indust. Corpor. Change* 24 (3), 655–676.

Baesens, B., Bapna, R., Marsden, J.R., Vanthienen, J., Zhao, J.L., 2014. Transformational issues of big data and analytics in networked business. *MIS Quart.* 38 (2), 629–631.

Barney, J.B., 1986. Types of competition and the theory of strategy: toward an integrative framework. *Acad. Manag. Rev.* 11 (4), 791–800.

Bernhard, E., Recker, J.C., Burton-Jones, A., 2014. Affordances in information systems: theory development and open challenges. *J. Assoc. Inform. Syst.* 15, 54–86.

Bi, F., 2014. How Formula One teams are using big data to get the inside edge. Forbes.com, <www.forbes.com/sites/frankbi/2014/11/13/how-formula-one-teams-are-using-big-data-to-get-the-inside-edge/>.

Boland R.J. Jr., Tenkasi, R.V., Te'eni, D., 1994. Designing information technology to support distributed cognition. *Organ. Sci.* 5 (3), 456–475.

Brynjolfsson, E., McAfee, A., 2012. *Race against the Machine: How the Digital Revolution Is Accelerating innovation, Driving productivity, and Irreversibly Transforming Employment and the Economy*. Digital Frontier Press.

Cabantous, L., Gond, J.-P., 2011. Rational decision making as performative praxis: explaining rationality's eternel retour. *Organ. Sci.* 22 (3), 573–586.

Cabantous, L., Gond, J.-P., Johnson-Cramer, M., 2010. Decision theory as practice: crafting rationality in organizations. *Org. Stud.* 31 (11), 1531–1566.

Callon, M., 1986. Some elements of a sociology of translation: domestication of the scallops and the fishermen of St. Brieuc Bay. Power, Action, Belief: new Sociol. *Knowledge* 32, 196–223.

Callon, M., 1998. Introduction: the embeddedness of economic markets in economics. *Sociol. Rev.* 46 (S1), 1–57.

Callon, M., 2007. What does it mean to say that economics is performative? In MacKenzie, D., Muniesa, F., Siu, L. (Eds.), *Performing Economics*. Princeton University Press, Princeton.

Caskill, S., 2015. Data visualisation projects win first F1 Connectivity Prize. *TechWeekEurope.co.uk*, <www.techweekeurope.co.uk/networks/broadband/f1-connectivity-prize-tata-173914#Cg6XL7LgUSsm723C.99>.

Castellucci, F., Ertug, G., 2010. What's in it for them? advantages of higher-status partners in exchange relationships. *Acad. Manag. J.* 53 (1), 149–166.

Cecez-Kecmanovic, D., Galliers, R.D., Henfridsson, O., Newell, S., Vidgen, R., 2014a. The sociomateriality of information systems: current status, future directions. *MIS Quart.* 38 (3), 809–830.

Cecez-Kecmanovic, D., Kautz, K., Abrahall, R., 2014b. Reframing success and failure of information systems: a performative perspective. *MIS Quart.* 38 (2), 561–588.

Chen, H., Chiang, R.H., Storey, V.C., 2012. Business intelligence and analytics: from big data to big impact. *MIS Quart.* 36 (4), 1165–1188.

Chen, M., Mao, S., Zhang, Y., Leung, V.C., 2014. *Big Data: Related technologies, Challenges and Future Prospects*. Springer, Heidelberg.

Collantine, K., 2010. How Alonso lost the championship in Abu Dhabi. *F1Fanatic.co.uk*, <www.f1fanatic.co.uk/2010/11/14/how-alonso-lost-the-championship-in-abu-dhabi/>.

Constantiou, I.D., Kallinikos, J., 2015. New games, new rules: big data and the changing context of strategy. *J. Inform. Technol.* 30 (1), 44–57.

Corley, K.G., Gioia, D.A., 2004. Identity ambiguity and change in the wake of a corporate spin-off. *Adm. Sci. Quart.* 49 (2), 173–208.

Davenport, T.H., Harris, J.G., 2007. *Competing on Analytics: The New Science of Winning*. Harvard Business Press, Harvard.

Dean, J.W., Sharfman, M.P., 1996. Does decision process matter? A study of strategic decision-making effectiveness. *Acad. Manag. J.* 39 (2), 368–392.

DeSanctis, G., Gallupe, R.B., 1987. A foundation for the study of group decision support systems. *Manage. Sci.* 33 (5), 589–609.

DeSanctis, G., Poole, M.S., 1994. Capturing the complexity in advanced technology use: adaptive structuration theory. *Org. Sci.* 5 (2), 121–147.

Earl, M.J., 1993. Experiences in strategic information systems planning. *MIS Quart.* 17 (1), 1–24.

Elbanna, S., Child, J., 2007. Influences on strategic decision effectiveness: development and test of an integrative model. *Strateg. Manag. J.* 28 (4), 431–453.

Erden, Z., Von Krogh, G., Nonaka, I., 2008. The quality of group tacit knowledge. *J. Strateg. Inf. Syst.* 17 (1), 4–18.

Feldman, M.S., Orlikowski, W.J., 2011. Theorizing practice and practicing theory. *Organ. Sci.* 22 (5), 1240–1253.

Forbes, D.P., 2007. Reconsidering the strategic implications of decision comprehensiveness. *Acad. Manag. Rev.* 32 (2), 361–376.

Fredrickson, J.W., 1984. The comprehensiveness of strategic decision processes: extension, observations, future directions. *Acad. Manag. J.* 27 (3), 445–466.

Galliers, R.D., Newell, S., Shanks, G., Topi, H., 2017. Datification and its human, organizational and societal effects: the strategic opportunities and challenges of algorithmic decision-making. *J. Strateg. Inf. Syst.* 26, 185–190.

Garud, R., Jain, S., Tuertscher, P., 2008. Incomplete by design and designing for incompleteness. *Org. Stud.* 29 (3), 351–371.

George, G., Haas, M.R., Pentland, A., 2014. Big data and management. *Acad. Manag. J.* 57 (2), 321–326.

Gherardi, S., 2012. *How to Conduct a Practice-based Study: Problems and Methods*. Edward Elgar Publishing, Cheltenham.

Gibson, J., 1979. *The Ecological Approach to Visual Perception*. Houghton-Mifflin, Boston, MA.

Gino, F., Pisano, G.P., 2011. Why leaders don't learn from success. *Harvard Bus. Rev.* 89 (4), 68–74.

Gioia, D.A., Corley, K.G., Hamilton, A.L., 2012a. Seeking qualitative rigor in inductive research: notes on the Gioia methodology. *Org. Res. Methods* 16 (1), 15–31.

Gioia, D.A., Corley, K.G., Hamilton, A.L., 2012b. Seeking qualitative rigor in inductive research: notes on the gioia methodology. *Org. Res. Methods* 16 (1), 16–31.

Giraudeau, M., 2008. The drafts of strategy: opening up plans and their uses. *Long Range Plan* 41 (3), 291–308.

Gregor, S., Hevner, A.R., 2013. Positioning and presenting design science research for maximum impact. *MIS Quart.* 37 (2), 337–356.

Gunther, W.A., Mehrizi, M.H.R., Huysman, M., Feldberg, F., 2017. Debating big data: a literature review on realizing value from big data. *J. Strateg. Inf. Syst.* 26 (3), 191–209.

Hedberg, B., Jonsson, S., 1978. Designing semi-confusing information systems for organizations in changing environments. *Acc. Organ. Soc.* 3 (1), 47–64.

Hevner, A., March, S.T., Park, J., Ram, S., 2004. Design science in information systems research. *MIS Quart.* 28 (1), 75–105.

Hevner, A.R., 2007. A three cycle view of design science research. *Scandinavian J. Inform. Syst.* 19 (2), 87–92.

Hutchby, I., 2001. Technologies, texts and affordances. *Sociology* 35 (2), 441–456.

Hutchins, E., 1995a. How a cockpit remembers its speeds. *Cognit. Sci.* 19 (3), 265–288.

Hutchins, E., 1995b. *Cognition in the Wild*. MIT Press.

Jacobs, A., 2009. The pathologies of big data. *Commun. ACM* 52 (8), 36–44.

Jarzabkowski, P., Kaplan, S., 2015. Strategy tools-in-use: a framework for understanding "technologies of rationality" in practice. *Strateg. Manag. J.* 36 (4), 537–558.

Jenkins, M., 2010. Technological discontinuities and competitive advantage: a historical perspective on Formula 1 motor racing 1950–2006. *J. Manage. Stud.* 47 (5), 884–910.

Johnson, D., 2015. Lewis Hamilton Monaco farce blamed on 'gremlin' as Mercedes F1's Toto Wolff faces the fans. *Telegraph.co.uk*, <www.telegraph.co.uk/sport/motorsport/formulaone/11631579/Lewis-Hamilton-Monaco-farce-blamed-on-gremlin-as-Mercedes-F1s-Toto-Wolff-faces-the-fans.html>.

Junglas, I., Goel, L., Abraham, C., Ives, B., 2013. The Social component of information systems—how sociability contributes to technology acceptance. *J. Assoc. Inform. Syst.* 14 (10), 585–616.

Kahneman, D., Tversky, A., 1982. The psychology of preferences. *Sci. Am.* 246 (1), 160–173.

LaValle, S., Lesser, E., Shockley, R., Hopkins, M.S., Kruschwitz, N., 2011. Big data, analytics and the path from insights to value. *MIT Sloan Manage. Rev.* 52 (2), 21.

Lazer, D., Kennedy, R., King, G., Vespignani, A., 2014. The parable of Google Flu: traps in big data analysis. *Science* 343, 1204–1206.

Leonardi, P.M., 2011. When flexible routines meet flexible technologies: affordance, constraint, and the imbrication of human and material agencies. *MIS Quart.* 37 (1), 147–167.

Leslie, J., 2015. All you need to know about a Formula 1 pit stop. < www.carthrottle.com/post/all-you-need-to-know-about-a-formula-1-pit-stop/>.

Loebbecke, C., Picot, A., 2015. Reflections on societal and business model transformation arising from digitization and big data analytics: a research agenda. *J. Strateg. Inf. Syst.* 24 (3), 149–157.

MacKenzie, D., Millo, Y., 2003. Constructing a market, performing a theory: the historical sociology of a financial derivatives exchange. *Am. J. Sociol.* 109 (1), 107–145.

MacKenzie, D.A., 2008. *An engine, Not a Camera: How Financial Models Shape Markets*. MIT Press, Cambridge, MA and London.

MacKenzie, D.A., Muniesa, F., Siu, L., 2007. *Do Economists Make Markets? on the Performativity of Economics*. Princeton University Press, Princeton.

Manktelow, K. (2012). *Thinking and Reasoning: An Introduction to the Psychology of Reason. Judgment and Decision Making*. Psychology Press. Hove, UK.

March, J.G., 2006. Rationality, foolishness, and adaptive intelligence. *Strateg. Manag. J.* 27 (3), 201–214.

March, S.T., Smith, G.F., 1995. Design and natural science research on information technology. *Decis. Support Syst.* 15 (4), 251–266.

Marino, A., Aversa, P., Mesquita, L., Anand, J., 2015. Driving performance via exploration in changing environments: evidence from Formula One racing. *Organ. Sci.* 26 (4), 1079–1100.

Markus, M.L., Silver, M.S., 2008. A foundation for the study of IT effects: a new look at DeSanctis and Poole's concepts of structural features and spirit. *J. Assoc. Inform. Syst.* 9 (10), 609–632.

Mayer-Schonberger, V., Cukier, K., 2013. *Big Data: A Revolution that Will Transform How We live, work, and Think.* Houghton-Mifflin Harcourt, New York.

Mazmanian, M., Cohn, M.L., Dourish, P., 2014. Dynamic reconfiguration in planetary exploration: a sociomaterial ethnography. *MIS Quart.* 38 (3), 831–848.

McAfee, A., Brynjolfsson, E., Davenport, T.H., Patil, D., Barton, D., 2012. Big data: the management revolution. *Harvard Bus. Rev.* 90 (10), 61–67.

McDermott, R., O'Dell, C., 2001. Overcoming cultural barriers to sharing knowledge. *J. Knowledge Manage.* 5 (1), 76–85.

Morgan, M.S., 2012. *The World in the Model: How Economists Work and Think.* Cambridge University Press, Cambridge.

Nicolini, D., 2011. Practice as the site of knowing: insights from the field of telemedicine. *Org. Sci.* 22, 602–620. doi:10.1287/orsc.1100.0556.

Nicolini, D., Mengis, J., Swan, J., 2012. Understanding the role of objects in cross-disciplinary collaboration. *Organ. Sci.* 23 (3), 612–629.

Norman, D. A. (1991). Cognitive artifacts. *Designing interaction: Psychology at the human-computer interface,* 1(1), 17–38.

Orlikowski, W.J., 2000. Using technology and constituting structures: a practice lens for studying technology in organizations. *Organ. Sci.* 11 (4), 404–428.

Orlikowski, W.J., Iacono, C.S., 2001. Research commentary: desperately seeking the "IT" in IT research—a call to theorizing the IT artifact. *Inform. Syst. Res.* 12 (2), 121–134.

Orlikowski, W.J., Scott, S.V., 2008. Sociomateriality: challenging the separation of technology, work and organization. *Acad. Manage. Ann.* 2 (1), 433–474.

Peppard, J., Galliers, R.D., Thorogood, A., 2014. Information systems strategy as practice: micro strategy and strategizing for IS. *J. Strategic Inform. Syst.* 23 (1), 1–10.

Piezunka, H., Lee, W., Haynes, R., Bothner, M.S., 2018. Escalation of competition into conflict in competitive networks of Formula One drivers. In: Proceedings of the National Academy of Sciences. (forthcoming).

Poleto, T., de Carvalho, V.D.H., Costa, A.P.C.S., 2015. The roles of big data in the decision-support process: an empirical investigation. *Decision Support Systems V-Big Data Analytics for Decision Making,* pp. 10–21: Springer.

Sanz, M., 2011. Yo fui el responsable de lo de Abu Dabi (I was the responsible for Abu Dhabi). Marca. com, <www.marca.com/2011/09/09/motor/formula1/1315594760.html>.

Scarbrough, H., Panourgias, N.S., Nandhakumar, J., 2015. Developing a relational view of the organizing role of objects: a study of the innovation process in computer games. *Org. Stud.* 36 (2), 197–220.

Schein, E.H., 1985. *Organisational Culture and Leadership: A Dynamic View.* Jossey-Bass Pub, San Francisco, CA.

Siggelkow, N., 2007. Persuasion with case studies. *Acad. Manag. J.* 50 (1), 20–24.

Strauss, A., Corbin, J.M., 1990. *Basics of Qualitative Research: Grounded Theory Procedures and Techniques.* Sage Publications Inc, London.

Suppiah, V., Singh Sandhu, M., 2011. Organisational culture's influence on tacit knowledge-sharing behaviour. *J. Knowled. Manage.* 15 (3), 462–477.

Sylt, C., Reid, C., 2010. Formula money: money Sport Media limited.

Vaara, E., Whittington, R., 2012. Strategy-as-practice: taking social practices seriously. *Acad. Manage. Ann.* 6 (1), 285–336.

Vallee-Tourangeau, G., Abadie, M., Vallee-Tourangeau, F., 2015. Interactivity fosters Bayesian reasoning without instruction. *J. Exp. Psychol. Gen.* 144 (3), 581–603.

Van Maanen, J., 1979. The fact of fiction in organizational ethnography. *Adm. Sci. Quart.* 24 (4), 539–550.

Villejoubert, G., Vallee-Tourangeau, F., 2011. Constructing preferences in the physical world: a distributed-cognition perspective on preferences and risky choices. *Front. Psychol.* 2, 1–4.

von Krogh, G., Haefliger, S., 2010. Opening up design science: the challenge of designing for reuse and joint development. *J. Strateg. Inf. Syst.* 19 (4), 232–241.

Wagner, E.L., Newell, S., Piccoli, G., 2010. Understanding project survival in an ES environment: a sociomaterial practice perspective. *J. Assoc. Inform. Syst.* 11 (5), 1.

Weick, K.E., 1987. Organizational culture as a source of high reliability. *California Manage. Rev.* 29 (2), 112–127.

Whittington, R., 2014. Information systems strategy and strategy-as-practice: a joint agenda. *J. Strateg. Inf. Syst.* 23 (1), 87–91.

Zammuto, R.F., Griffith, T.L., Majchrzak, A., Dougherty, D.J., Faraj, S., 2007. Information technology and the changing fabric of organization. *Org. Sci.* 18 (5), 749–762.

Zigurs, I., Poole, M.S., DeSanctis, G.L., 1988. A study of influence in computer-mediated group decision making. *MIS Quart.* 12 (4), 625–644.

Questions for Discussion

1   What do you think the role of AI will entail in the future? Would AI and big data be useful in high pressure, uncertainty and turbulent environment/conditions?

2   How are knowledge-intensive professions changing because of increased digitalization, use of decision support systems and big data?

3   Utilize the Power Matrix (chapter 10) to evaluate the role of the Chief Strategist and the Decision Support System in strategic decision-making. How is power redistributed?

4   What is the role of organizational culture, distributed cognition, social material practice, affordances, technology and judgement in strategic decision-making? How does organizational culture affect knowledge sharing and strategic decision-making?

5   How should decision-makers use algorithms and big data to inform decisions?

6   How could technology and big data be used to avoid errors and for prospective decision-making, rather than retrospective as outlined in the chapter?

Further Reading

Dremel, C., Wulf, J., Herterich, M. M., Waizmann, J. C., Brenner, W. (2017). How AUDI AG Established Big Data Analytics in Its Digital Transformation. *MIS Quarterly Executive*, 16(2).

Ebrahimi, S., Hassanein, K. (2018). Data analytics competency for improving firm decision making performance. *The Journal of Strategic Information Systems*, 27(1), 101–113.

Chapter 19

Sue Newell and Marco Marabelli

STRATEGIC OPPORTUNITIES (AND CHALLENGES) OF ALGORITHMIC DECISION-MAKING: A CALL FOR ACTION ON THE LONG-TERM SOCIETAL EFFECTS OF 'DATIFICATION'

T HE LAST DECADE has witnessed the widespread diffusion of digitized devices that have the ability to monitor the minutiae of our everyday lives (Hedman et al., 2013). Nolan (2012, p. 91) argues that 'Global IT has enabled information on most everything to flow most everywhere at stealth speed'. The data trail we leave is increasingly used by companies to manage employees and target and personalize products and services for clients and customers, based on developing algorithms that can make predictions about individuals by recognizing complex patterns in huge data sets compiled from multiple sources. In this article we consider some of the observed and potential consequences of this new type of data-driven, algorithmic decision-making, illustrating that while it can offer strategic opportunities for business and sometimes benefits for individuals, there are also costs, hence raising societal issues: as Galliers et al. (2012) indicate, there can be a difference between how *business* is benefiting and how *society* is benefiting – or otherwise.

The IS literature has already raised social and ethical concerns associated with IT (Smith, 2002; Smith and Hasnas, 1999), and in particular those concerns are often associated with privacy issues (e.g., see Belanger and Crossler, 2011; Chan et al., 2005; Coll, 2014; Greenaway and Chan, 2005). However, few IS studies have linked these concerns with the digitization of our everyday life (exceptions include Abbas et al., 2014; Boyd and Crawford, 2014; Lyon, 2014; Slade and Prinsloo, 2013), and fewer still have discussed this phenomenon in relation to algorithmic decision-making (one exception being Schroeder and Cowls, 2014). Here, we focus on the consequences of 'algorithmic decision-making', which occurs when data are collected through digitized devices carried by individuals such as smartphones and technologies with in-built sensors – and subsequently processed by algorithms, which are then used to make (data-driven) decisions. That is, decisions are based on relationships identified in the data, and the decision maker often ignores why such relationships may be present (Mayer-Schonberger and Cukier, 2013). While these data-driven decisions made by businesses lead to personalized offerings to individuals, they also result in the narrowing of their choices (Newell and Marabelli, 2014).

Given the above, we argue that algorithmic decision-making has societal consequences that may not always be positive and, in this Viewpoint article, we aim to articulate such concerns. In so doing, we bring to the fore the issues related to algorithmic decision-making and highlight the interdisciplinary nature of this topic (Chen et al., 2012; Smith et al., 2011). As we have indicated, some work has been done to shed light on the social implications of the widespread diffusion of digital devices in the IS community, but also in other disciplines such as sociology – as in the work of Lyon (2001, 2003, 2014), Doyle et al. (2013), and Ball (2002, 2005) on impacts of monitoring and surveillance on society, and of Castells et al. (2009) and Campbell and Park (2008) on societal changes determined by the diffusion of digital devices. Here, we call for IS research that examines (and challenges) corporations (and governments) in terms of the strategic decisions that are being made based on data that we are now constantly providing them (see also MacCrory et al., 2014), whether we realize it or not. Next, we define some key concepts and set the boundaries of our analysis.

Big Data, Little Data, and Algorithmic Decision-making

Data-driven or 'algorithmic' decision-making is based on collecting and analyzing large quantities of data that are then used to make strategic decisions. Algorithmic decision-making incorporates two main characteristics: firstly, decision-makers rely on information provided by algorithms that process huge amounts of data (often big data, as we will explain next); secondly, the reasons behind the 'suggestions' made by the algorithms are often ignored by decision-makers (Mayer-Schonberger and Cukier, 2013). We expand on both characteristics below.

Digitized Technologies and Data Analytics

Data that originate from digitized devices are increasingly permeating our everyday lives. These digitized devices have the ability to keep track of and record what we do. As a result, somebody else may eventually be able to use the data thus produced – often with purposes different from those originally intended. Thus, we focus on 'digital traces' – all data provided by individuals (1) during 'IT-related' activities, captured from social networks, online shopping, blogs, but also ATM withdrawals, and other activities that will leave a 'trace' (Hedman et al., 2013; Wu and Brynjolfsson, 2009) and (2) that are captured through technologies that we use that have in-built sensors. These technologies include LBS (Location-Based Technologies) that are IT artifacts equipped with GPS systems and so have the ability to collect a user's location such as a smartphone with GPS – see Abbas et al. (2014) and Michael and Michael (2011) for social implications – and other surveillance and monitoring devices – see the previously cited work of Lyon (2001, 2003, 2014) for privacy implications.

It is clear that the huge amount of digital trace data that are collected through the many digitized devices that we now use to support our daily activities fall into the 'big data' umbrella.

The big data (analytics) concept is very similar to the more familiar (and less sexy) business intelligence that has been studied for the past decade or so (e.g., Negash, 2004; Power, 2002; Rouibah and Ould-ali, 2002; Thomsen, 2003). McAfee and Brynjolfsson (2012). Following Gartner (2001) definition, it is the three Vs of big data[1] on which we focus: Volume (the amount of data determines value); Variety (data arise from different sources/databases and are cross-matched to find relationships), and Velocity (data are generated quickly). Big data encompasses much more than this individually generated data trail (see Chen et al., 2012 for a broad discussion of big data analytics) but here we focus just on this everyday digital trail that we each leave. That is, we focus on *those* big data that are generated by individuals during their everyday lives (and are captured as digital traces). In other words, we focus on data that arise as a consequence of each of us now being a 'walking data generator' (McAfee and Brynjolfsson, 2012, p. 5). This attention to the digitization of our everyday life allows us to narrow the focus of our inquiry and to expand on concerns regarding the use (and abuse) of one aspect of big data analytics that concerns algorithm-driven decision-making and associated personalization – to which we now turn.

Algorithmic Decision-making

(Big) data captured through digitized devices are processed by algorithms aimed at predicting what a person will do, think and like on the basis of their current (or past) behaviors. These algorithms can predict particular outcomes, as with the numbers of 'friends' on Facebook being used to predict a person's credit risk (www.google.com/patents/US8560436) or an individual's Facebook 'likes' on a college Facebook page, used to predict her/his willingness to become a donor (www.nytimes.com/2015/01/25/technology/your-college-may-be-banking-on-your-facebook-likes.html7_r=0). Interestingly, these predictions often represent a black-box: while humans must decide what to measure and produce the algorithms to analyze the data being collected, these decisions do not necessarily involve understanding the causes and consequences of particular patterns of behavior that are identified (Mayer-Schonberger and Cukier, 2013). Rather, it is deemed sufficient that connections are discovered. Traditionally, making decisions has been a human-centered, knowledge-based activity with humans discriminating on the basis of an understanding of theory or context (Tsoukas and Vladimirou, 2001). By contrast, algorithmic decision-making means that discriminations are increasingly being made by an algorithm, with few individuals actually understanding what is included in the algorithm or even why. In other words, it is seen as being sufficient that an algorithm is successfully predictive, never mind if the reasons for the associations found in the data from different sources are unknown. We argue that this is likely to create problems when no one in a corporation really understands why some decisions are made. For example, one could argue that the last financial crisis was at least partially a product of this problem, with the algorithms that predicted the pricing for mortgage-backed securities clearly not taking into account all the risks while at the same time not being subject to question because the basis of the algorithm was neither clear nor easily accessible, either to the senior managers in the financial institutions where the algorithms were being used or to the credit rating agencies who were evaluating these products (Clark and Newell, 2013).

In sum, here we focus on data collected through digitized devices that we increasingly use to support our everyday activities. This is 'big data', because the three (or more) Vs of Gartner's (2001, 2012) definition apply. In fact, data coming from digitized technologies are high in volume because of the widespread diffusion of digital devices that allow access to social networks at any time, as well as all other types of technologies that record what we do even if we do not 'own' them (e.g., surveillance cameras, or an ATM card machine, where the usage information goes into our bank's database). Thus, data come from different sources (variety). For instance, data used for making 'algorithmic decisions' may come from a combination of contributions on social networks and LBS systems (e.g., a 'check in'), or spending capacity of consumers associated with personal facts of individuals (e.g., the partner's birthday). Data velocity is clearly another characteristic of the digitization of our everyday life, because we are 'walking data generators' 24/7 and 'More data cross the Internet every second than were stored in the entire Internet just 20 years ago' (McAfee and Brynjolfsson, 2012, p. 4). On this point, it is worth noting that most of the digitized devices that collect such individual level activity data fall under the Internet of Things (IoT) umbrella (Miorandi et al., 2012; Xi et al., 2012). However, we do not restrict our analysis to those digitized devices that are connected to the Internet because some devices remain (for now) independent of the Internet (e.g., some OBD devices). One such example is provided by Progressive Insurance in the USA (www.progressive.com), which provides a memory stick that is plugged into a car's onboard computer and the data must be uploaded to the insurance company rather than automatically sent via the Internet.

Potential discriminations associated with the (ab)use of algorithmic decision-making: big and little data

The use of algorithmic decision-making associated with data coming from the digitization of our everyday lives improves the capacity of a business to make discriminations. Thus, businesses have always discriminated in terms of to whom they offer products and services, because products and services are targeted to different audiences (we cannot, unfortunately all afford to buy a Bentley car). With algorithmic decision-making they are simply taking this a step further. For example, they can now much more precisely target and personalize offerings to customers and potential customers – those predicted to buy particular products or services. As a more specific example, a car's computer that monitors speed, usage of brakes, horn, lights, etc. (such as Progressive Insurance's OnStar OBD technologies mentioned above) has the ability capture all these details that are then sent to data centers. Computers then analyze the (big) data and insurance companies are able to use the results to discriminate (e.g., by charging young men higher premiums because the data indicate that they – generally – drive less safely than other categories of drivers). Such data-driven decision-making has been questioned because it can go against the ethical principle of equal or fair treatment. This is exemplified in the recent case in the EU, where insurers are required to no longer use statistical evidence about gender differences to set premiums. Thus, despite the fact that gender differences are clear from the data (e.g., young male drivers are ten times more likely to be killed or injured than those – of both sexes – over the age of 35; women live, on average, longer than men), it is considered to be discriminatory (following an EU ruling that came into effect in December 2012) to use this trend evidence to differentiate between premiums (e.g., car insurance or actuarial rates) for men and women. The point about this change in the law is that it was considered to be discriminatory because, for example, while young men in general may drive more recklessly and so be more prone to accidents, an individual young man may not and would therefore be discriminated against when insurers set premiums based on group trends observable in collective data.

While using big data and algorithmic decision-making to observe trends and so discriminate between groups of individuals can have social consequences that are potentially unfair, this targeting can now be taken further when data are used not to predict group trends but to predict the behavior of a specific individual. This is sometimes described as 'little' data – although it should be noted that little data are actually based on big data but are simply used in a more targeted way. Thus, little data focuses on the everyday minutiae of specific individuals, using computing capacity to collect extremely granular data (Munford, 2014). Drawing on the previous example of a car's OBD, little data can now allow us to concentrate on a specific driver, and we can decide whether an individual is a good or bad driver based on the sensor data from his/her car. Sensors have the ability to capture individual's behaviors and are widespread. As an illustration, consider that approximately 85% of handsets now have a GPS system chipset installed (Abbas et al., 2014). By using sensor data, the insurer would not be setting premiums based on the general trends in accident rates between groups, but instead would base their calculations on the actual driving habits of an individual. However, if little data are more 'objective' in terms of discriminations made by corporations, it probably poses more issues for societies given the observed or potential social consequences; for instance, in terms of an individual's privacy (Lyon, 2014) or in terms of the exploitation of the vulnerable – an issue that IS scholars seem not to have fully addressed as yet.

It is then clear that algorithmic decision-making poses two main concerns in terms of big and little data: first, (in terms of big data) this data trail provides the opportunity for organizations to move to algorithmic decision-making, which McAfee and Brynjolfsson (2012) argue, is superior to traditional 'HiPPO' (highest-paid person's opinion) decision-making. Algorithmic decision-making is, they argue, *superior* to human judgment-based decisions because of all the inherent biases in human judgment (Hodgkinson et al., 2002). However, we question this assumption because making decisions on the basis of big data (and algorithms) might create unfair discriminations. Second, we argue that monitoring an individual's behavior poses societal concerns since 'the digital artifacts will be able to remember where they [individuals] were, who used them, the outcomes of interactions, etc.' (Yoo, 2010, p. 226) and this often happens without individuals even being aware that they are being monitored. Thus, we posit that undertaking research to assess these societal harms, so that corporations can be held responsible and citizens become more aware, can potentially be very useful.

Below we identify three tradeoffs that involve issues associated with the use by corporations (and governments) of data from digitized devices that support our daily activities, and in particular with the strategy of using data analytics. The first of these considers the privacy of individuals versus security for society – an issue that is preeminent in people's minds following the recent terrorist attacks, particularly in Paris, in January 2015.

Tradeoffs and Societal Issues Associated with Big (and Little) Data

Privacy versus Security

Digitized devices can improve security, and examples include the security-tracking systems adopted for prison populations, when prisoners are released but are required to wear a tracking ankle-bracelet. These systems are aimed at improving the overall security of our society, with the sensor acting as a deterrent for prisoners to escape or commit a crime when they are on parole. Other instances where security is enhanced by everyday digitized devices is in the capacity of sensors to trace a stolen device, or a kidnapped child, as in the case that occurred in September 2013 in Texas, where the Houston police were able to trace the whereabouts of a kidnapper by tracing the iPad that he had with him in his car (http://abc13. com/archive/9242256/). A similar example relates to police authorities being able to detect a crime because it is all 'caught on tape', for example with sensor-activated security cameras and, potentially, Google Glass or other camera-based devices that are now routinely carried by many.

All these examples of companies, government agencies and private individuals using digitized technologies to increase security come at some costs in terms of individuals' privacy. In terms of locating a lost smartphone, it has to be the user who, deliberately, accepts giving up her/his (right of) privacy by activating the 'find my phone' option (https://itunes.apple.com/us/app/find-my-iphone/id376101648?mt=8). The example of Google Glass or digital cameras worn, for example, by cyclists or skiers to record their journey, is more complex since the privacy that a user gives up affects others' privacy, thus representing a shift from the individual to the societal level. In some circumstances one's use of social software applications affects others' privacy, as for example, for people who are tagged in somebody's Facebook profile without them knowing. Perhaps not surprisingly, privacy advocates have argued that in these types of exchanges consumers are justified in expecting that the data they collect and share should remain private among those to whom it was originally disclosed – dependent on users' risk perceptions, as noted by Gerlach et al. (2015) – rather than being shared with third parties who may subsequently behave opportunistically (Beldad et al., 2011; Petronio, 2002).

Thus, it is clear that improving security across society, based on digital devices, can impact on individual's privacy. Some companies are doing something about this. For instance, Facebook no longer allows a user's 'wild tagging' and, instead, an automatic email is sent to a user who is tagged, for approval (or at least this is a configurable option under privacy settings). Yet, the exponential diffusion of tracking software embedded in social networks such as Facebook and the sensors and cameras in many other digital devices lead us to think that it will be hard for organizations (or governments) to regulate how individuals use responsibly technologies that enable tracking (i.e., in a way that balances security and privacy). The societal issue is raised because the move towards using devices and applications to gain increased security comes at the expense of reduced privacy. This points to a question about whether users (and more broadly society) want to give up some security potential to ensure more privacy (Culnan and Williams, 2009; Velasquez, 2006). This is a decision that citizens need to debate with their politicians (Dinev et al., 2008) and that governments in turn need to debate with businesses, since it is businesses that collect and analyze digital traces. This is exemplified by the Lee Rigby case (the British soldier killed on a street in London), where Facebook was accused of not helping to protect security because it did not use its analytical capability to detect and report the fact that the killer was posting that he was intending to commit just such a murder (www.theguardian.com/uk-news/live/2014/nov/25/lee-rigby-woolwich-inquiry-report-published-live-coverage).

Other privacy/security tensions are reflected in the current debate on whether US police officers should wear cameras following recent cases involving police officers' improper use of force (see for instance the developments over the Michael Brown case www.cnn.com/2014/12/04/us/eric-garner-ferguson-body-cameras-debate/). Here, a sensor technology would be employed but would not actually generate data that will be processed by algorithms, since the camera records would be reviewed only in particular circumstances. However, this and other types of sensor are pervasive (Lyytinen and Yoo, 2002) (and invasive), and the data (e.g., the camera records) would be stored. In such circumstances, we do not know whether in the future somebody will develop an algorithmic-based decision system to analyze the data (e.g., to assess the performance of police officers). It is thus clear that the widespread diffusion of digitized technologies can be harmful to individuals' privacy while justified by corporations and governments in the name of public security – a tradeoff widely discussed by Lyon (2003, p. 79) in terms of ID cards that are supposed to improve national security in that he raises the issue of whether as citizens we are willing to 'pay the price in liberty for security'. This tradeoff, then, raises complex social issues because of the ready availability of these data and because of the capacity of algorithms to discriminate almost in real time – for instance, to determine that particular categories of people (based on race, income, job, etc.) are more likely to commit a crime, and could, therefore, be subjected to higher levels of policing and potentially also face discrimination in other areas (Lyon, ibid).

This, therefore, pits an individual's privacy against the security of society, but also suggests broader social issues in terms of freedom versus control, as we articulate next.

Freedom versus Control

The 'datification' of everything means that we can use devices to constantly track every decision made and place that a person visits (be they an employee, a citizen, or our child), and use these data to monitor and control (some now prefer to use the term 'nudge') behavior (Whitman, 2011). This second tradeoff between freedom and control is more complex than the previous one because, here, individuals can be aware that they are being controlled. This is informed control (e.g., because they are required to carry RFID badges at the work place or maybe even have chips implanted under their skin, another example of invasive technology – www.bbc.co.uk/news/technology-31042477 – or because they decide to use an electronic collection system in their car to drive through tolled roads and bridges). However, they can also be controlled without knowing that they are being monitored. This is uninformed control. Uninformed control happens, for instance, when tracking cookies monitor someone's online activity, or, more generally, when 'second hand' use of data originating from digitized technologies are used.

Freedom versus Informed Control

Surveillance based on parents tracking their children's every move (e.g., using an application on the child's smartphone) is clearly informed control and would allow parents to feel that they are in control of their children's movements. However, the loss of freedom (and privacy, as we have already pointed out) of those subjected to this surveillance might have far-reaching effects, for instance in terms of children's feelings of personal responsibility. After all, we know that punishment is not always an effective deterrent because, once the punishment is removed, the individual often resorts to the prior (undesirable) behavior; so, if individuals conform only because they know they are being monitored, will their behavior change once the monitoring ceases? With constant surveillance, like punishment, while we may change behavior, the beliefs about what is appropriate or inappropriate may remain (Podsakoff et al., 1982; Staples, 2013). This tension, then, is between improved control (by business but also government or private citizens) at the expense of individuals feeling that they have some freedom and autonomy – a feeling that we know has a significant influence on motivation in the long-term (Hasan and Subhani, 2011). One such example is Hitachi's new digital identification badge that collects data on individual employees' exact location within an office, records who the person has spoken to, for how long and how energetically (www.cnn.com/2014/02/02/opinion/greene-corporate-surveillance). Adopting this kind of technology as a strategy for constant monitoring may, however, affect employees' motivation and perhaps also their capacity to produce disruptive innovation. Indeed, productivity might benefit (at least in the short term) from such an aggressive approach to control in the workplace. However, the longer-term consequences of such constant surveillance may be more problematic. For instance, Lyon (2003, p. 20) points out that a 'surveillance system obtains personal and group data in order to classify people and populations according to varying criteria, to determine who should be targeted for special treatment, suspicion, eligibility, inclusion, access, and so on', arguing that such 'social sorting' leads to long-term discriminations. He states that 'data about transactions is used both to target persons for further advertising and to dismiss consumers who are of little value to companies' (ibid,; 1), leading to long-term social differences. Moreover, breakthrough innovation, which is more risky and leads to more frequent 'failures' (O'Reilly and Tushman, 2004), might be jeopardized because individuals who are constantly monitored are less likely to expose themselves to failure in front of their peers and superiors. This suggests that those making strategic decisions about how to use this new tracking technology (whether business, government or private individual) might want to think about reducing the amount of surveillance on employees, customers, family members or citizens since this would be the price they might want to pay for allowing people to feel in control of the decisions they make – in other words, being informed and not automated to use the language of Zuboff (1984). This supports our argument that a tradeoff emerges between control and freedom in the context of the digitization of our everyday lives.

Freedom versus Uninformed Control

The feeling of being controlled, as we have discussed, might lead to some unwanted consequences (e.g., loss of a sense of responsibility or lower productivity in the work place). However, probably a more relevant societal issue emerges when control (over an individual's freedom) is made without the individual even knowing that she/he is being controlled (when this is not made explicit or is not requested). To this end, here we provide an example involving individuals' online activities, where the 'free' access to information is increasingly controlled as Internet companies (social networks, news, etc.) now determine (based on algorithms) what we see. For instance, we may see many posts about the newest iPhone (6, at the time of our writing) and assume that many of our Facebook friends are posting articles about this new technology. However, the frequency with which we see these posts may be partially due to us having clicked on an advertisement related to the iPhone 6: Facebook's algorithm decides that we are interested in such products and then shows us others' posts that are related to the iPhone 6. A consequence of such use of algorithms by corporations to decide – for the consumer – the posts, news or advertising that they are exposed to, is that it may lead to a slow and often subtle manipulation of consumers' worldviews as well as to new forms of discrimination. Simply put, what is presented to the reader is decided by an algorithm – tapping into prior searches – and is not based on an explicit personal choice. An example of uninformed control by a corporation that produces worrisome societal issues is found in the account presented by Eli Pariser, who showed that 'Facebook was looking at which links I clicked on, and it was noticing that I was clicking more on my liberal friends' links than on my conservative friends' links. And without consulting me about it, it had edited them out. They disappeared' (Pariser, 2011). In the longer term, this manipulation by corporations of what the consuming public is exposed to – exposing us only to things that we like (or the things that an algorithm assumes we like) – may produce societal changes. For instance, our exposure to online diversity will be reduced, as in the example of Eli Pariser. More recently, Greg Marra, a Facebook engineer argued that, 'We think that of all the stuff you've connected yourself to, this is the stuff you'd be most interested in reading', explaining further that an algorithm monitors 'thousands and thousands' of metrics to decide what we should see on our Facebook page. These metrics include what device we use, how many comments or 'Likes' a story has received and how long readers spend on each article/post. The assumed goal, as a New York Times article suggests, is that companies are using algorithmic decision-making 'to identify what users most enjoy' (www.nytimes.com/2014/10/27/business/media/how-facebook-is-changing-the-way-its-users-consume-journalism.html?_r=0). However, this also indicates that this practice of showing us only things that 'fit' with our (little) data profile, limits our possibility to choose, and might inhibit our capacity to make informed decisions (on what we buy and even what we think).

These strategies, then, that are adopted by organizations to allow them to tailor results and personalize offerings to individual consumers are leading to citizens (i.e., all us of who 'surf the web') being exposed to less and less diversity online. A potential consequence is that we may become less tolerant to diversity, meaning that we may as a result become less able to listen to someone who thinks differently (e.g., a Republican, in Pariser's example). Moreover, there may be other, more worrying consequences in the long-term that are associated with race-diversity intolerance and the increased exploitation of the vulnerable. For example, in relation to the latter issue, if algorithms work out who is less capable of making good financial decisions, personalized advertisements can then be sent persuading these people to take out risky loans, or high-rate instant credit options, thereby exploiting their vulnerability. The strategic use of our own data by corporations to personalize our Internet, in other words, is just another and potentially more pernicious way of allowing discrimination; pernicious because the only person who has access to the outcomes of the discrimination is the individual being discriminated against (who is often not aware of the fact that they are exposed to discriminatory information – uninformed control), making it easy for unscrupulous businesses to use personalization in a way that harms the vulnerable.

Another way to illustrate how societal concerns emerge as a consequence of businesses (and governments) using data from the digitization of our everyday life is by articulating the tradeoff between independence and dependence, to which we now turn.

Independence versus Dependence

Citizens in many countries increasingly depend on digital devices for many activities. However, here, a tradeoff originates from the tension between the willingness to depend on IT devices and being able to live without them (i.e., to be independent), should the need arise. Think of our decreasing sense of direction due to our dependency on GPS systems or, were we to consider safety issues, think of those sensor-based systems that are able to park our car – or even drive it! These driving systems use onboard cameras and laser rangefinders to identify obstacles (or hazards, if the onboard computer controls the car while it is 'in motion'); then an algorithm is able to scan the surrounding environment and to identify safe zones, avoiding for example other cars (see for instance a 2012 MIT study on these algorithms – http://newsoffice.mit.edu/2012/mechanical-engineers-develop-intelligent-car-co-pilot-0713). In the case of car autopilots, algorithmic decision-making has a twofold role: first, data on 'real drivers' are collected and analyzed so that the algorithm can make the appropriate decisions (e.g., reacting as a driver would, but with the difference that the algorithm is never tired or inattentive, thus carrying a safety advantage with respect to humans). Second, sensors embedded in cars (laser rangefinders, in this example) collect environmental data that are analyzed in real time, so the algorithm has the ability to either assist the driver by supporting his/her decisions (with warnings to the driver) or to make decision on its own – when the car is in full autopilot mode. Drivers, thus, are somewhat 'tempted' to benefit from the comforts companies now design into their products using digital technology, but this necessarily takes place at the expense of our future independence. In fact, if our car computer emits a warning signal while we drive on a highway, suggesting that we should slow down, we might argue that it is because the GPS embedded in the car computer has just received a 'traffic warning' or, because the weather channel is broadcasting heavy rain in minutes, or because we are about to drive through a road work area, but we do not really know the actual reason of the warning, yet we slow down – this (again) illustrating that algorithmic decision-making incorporates advantages (in this context, for users) but at the same time precludes a full understanding of why some decisions are being made. This limits learning through practice (Brown and Duguid, 1991) that in the long term might modify an individual's ability to learn new tasks and, more generally, adapt to the workplace or to society more generally (Dall'Alba and Sandberg, 2010; Nicolini et al., 2003).

While it is certain that there are good reasons for companies designing and for users adopting these automated systems, as we saw, this might also lead to a change in our ability to undertake particular activities without sensors, and learn. In the example of the autopilot, once our car parks itself, will we forget how to park on our own? IT-assisted systems have been around for a while in commercial planes, but pilots are constantly trained on how to pilot a plane in case the autopilot stops working. However, would individuals be trained on how to drive a car once such 'autopilot' systems become common in private motor vehicles? This example brings to the fore the point that digital technologies and devices (and the associated algorithmic decision-making) are increasingly influencing and even managing our lives, leaving unanswered the question on whether these algorithms are just supporting our activities, or whether they are actually in charge (e.g., controlling what we do) – and if they are taking over, does this excess of control occur at the expense of our ability to improvise and respond to emergencies? Thus, in the car example, it is clear that issues associated with safety emerge. In fact, as car drivers who now rely on sensors, we do not have the luxury that airline pilots have, of simulators to ensure that we maintain our skills so that we are prepared for an emergency. Nevertheless, even pilots (who, unlike private citizens, are trained on how to operate aircrafts) are not free of the consequences from technology that 'takes over', as the US NTSB (National Transportation Safety Board) reports in relation to some major plane accidents (see for instance the case of Air France Flight 447 in 2009, http://spectrum.ieee.org/riskfactor/aerospace/aviation/air-france-flight-447-crash-caused-by-a-combination-of-factors).

The negative consequences of an excess of IT dependence are associated with the risks we are exposed to when we forget how to do certain things. Progress necessarily involves automation (and the loss of certain manual capacities), and many innovations developed by corporations positively contribute to our quality of life (and to our safety). However, it is digital devices and the associated algorithmic decision-making that pose issues, especially when supervising or undertaking human activities that might involve life-threatening outcomes were the technology to stop working. Moreover, because of the connectivity between sensor devices, there is also the potential of chaos occurring if everything stops working for everyone simultaneously. In particular, we argue, it is the diffusion of such IT automations among common citizens that creates threats were we to become fully dependent on the technology and unable to operate without it. However, the adoption of some of these automations is (or will become) virtually mandatory for many – creating discriminations against those who do not conform. One simple example relates to US residents who, if desiring to use cars equipped with a standard stick shift (instead of an automatic), will have to pay more, just because 'standard' is not a standard in the US. On the other hand, those who can only drive automatic cars will have to pay more if they want to rent a car when they travel overseas, because most cars will have a standard shift and there will be a premium for an automatic car. This point raises the issue of the role of business in promoting such (automated) digitized technologies: does business have a responsibility for thinking about such consequences and building in opportunities for learning to reduce our overdependence?

In sum, we argue that this tradeoff is affected by the willingness of users to give up some of the comforts that come from dependence on IT, in the interests of preserving their ability to cope when the IT does not work as expected. Yet, digital technologies are extremely tempting, and now widely adopted. For instance past research on mobile technologies has already shed light on users' needs to be 'always on', with the consequence that a feeling of 'dependency' arises (Jarvenpaa and Lang, 2005). However, here we go beyond the psychological feeling of dependency and point to the users' need to be somewhat assisted (if not led or managed) by digital technology (that involves algorithmic decision-making) – with discrimination being the consequence of not conforming to this dependence. Companies too need to include sensor-based technologies in their products and services to remain competitive. For example, a logistics company that does not use GPS-equipment to determine best routing opportunities would experience difficulties in finding partners to develop a supply chain being thus discriminated against (again, for not conforming). However, we suggest that companies might also usefully start to think about how they can and should, in some circumstances at least, support the development of the ability to cope with situations of technology failure, with the consequence that algorithms assist decision-makers but do not entirely take over from human judgment. In our view, a balance must be struck, which to date seems to favor increasing dependence on IT over being able to cope in the face of IT failure.

We have thus far identified three key tradeoffs: between privacy and security, control and freedom, and dependence and independence, which are obviously inter-related. We do not claim that these are the only tensions that are relevant; however, they do allow us to provide concrete examples of strategic opportunities for businesses as well as societal issues emerging from corporations' (and governments') exploitation of data coming from the widespread use of digital technologies that support – and impact – our everyday lives. In the next section we discuss the more general social issues arising from these tensions.

Social Consequences of Digital Technology and Algorithmic Decision-making

While in the past knowledge and learning have been recognized as path-dependent (Cohen and Levinthal, 1990; Zahra and George, 2002), in this era of widespread diffusion of digital technologies that capture our everyday activities, our awareness about things appears to be not so much path-dependent as *determined* by our past actions and algorithmic rules. For example, the algorithm EdgeRank is used by Facebook to weight 'likes' and modify an individual's Facebook page as a result, therefore manipulating the 'wisdom of the crowd' (Kittur et al., 2007). While this may make sense from a marketing perspective for businesses (e.g., it is helpful to identify a customer's interests), it poses concerns for society because of the potential broader and longer-term social impacts. More specifically, our examples for each tension suggest that businesses (and at times governments and private individuals) are generally in favor of a more secure society over an individual's privacy, of a more controlled population (employees, customers and citizens) over individual freedom – leaving more and more people increasingly dependent upon technology, at the expense of personal independence.

To consider these issues, we start from the premise that digital trace data *is here to stay;* companies will increasingly include tracking software and sensors in the products and the services they offer, and so collect masses of data on our everyday habits with a view to using these data to develop algorithms that drive decision-making. In fact, whether data are gathered from social networks, an ATM transaction, or from a sensor-based device, there are many aspects associated with companies using such data that many users want, hence it is unlikely to 'go away'. As a result, businesses will keep exploiting big and little data potentials to profile customers, please social network users, and grant (commercial) opportunities to those who, at best, accept being controlled, reducing their need to learn while giving up some privacy. On the one hand, individuals benefit from corporations' use of big/little data analytics – one can save some money on an insurance policy, access a free show if willing to watch commercials, or just be pleased to see that everybody thinks her/his way (see the Facebook experiment by Pariser, above). On the other hand, businesses are aware that improving their knowledge about employees and customers will lead to more control of employees and more (addressed and effective) sales, and therefore more profits. And it is this enticement by the business world that leads people to assume that they have to give up some privacy/freedom/ independence, whether this is because it is a way to access a line of credit to buy a house or because they want to use social networks to fulfill their social needs (Kane, 2014).

As we previously pointed out when we provided our definition of algorithmic decision-making, this might lead to very superficial understandings of why things happen, and this will definitely not help managers, as well as 'end users' build cumulative knowledge on phenomena. Since decisions are made following an algorithm, how the algorithm came up with a particular result is unknown; as a result, there will be very little opportunity to learn from mistakes. Ironically, therefore, decision-makers might be losing the capacity to make decisions on their own, thereby making them a good example of (over) dependence on digital technology and algorithmic decision-making (cf. our third tradeoff). However, perhaps more important (from a societal perspective) than the lack of lessons learned, is the need to discuss the creation of new forms of discrimination as a result of algorithmic decision-making and the associated personalization of information. Think again of when algorithms determine that particular categories of people (e.g., based on race, income, job) are more likely to commit a crime and, as a result, those concerned find difficulty in obtaining a loan or changing job, never mind being subjected to tighter police scrutiny. This clearly violates basic privacy rights, but is justified based on the idea that it will increase security in society. Or, think again of the control exercised by algorithms in sensor-equipped cars on teenagers: these data are used by insurance companies to decide whether a driver is good or bad, again on the basis of an algorithm (the tradeoff between control and freedom). Similarly, when we give new technologies the possibility to take over our learning and let our car park and drive for us (or let our car 'suggest' what we should do in order to perform a perfect parallel park), our decision-making is being driven by algorithms (the tradeoff between independence and dependence).

These tradeoffs operate together rather than independently. For instance, if we use an app. that 'knows' what music we like so that, when we start driving, we do not need to search for a particular song, this is because we have enabled functionality on our radio/phone that is able to 'see' our favorite playlists, or that looks into our past purchases. For instance, iTunes Genius works with a 'secret algorithm' created by Apple that compares our library of tracks to all other Genius users' libraries and considers complex 'weight factors' to then come up with the appropriate playlist for a specific user (Mims, 2010). Here, we do not aim to go into technical details on how these algorithms work – as Apple engineer Erik Goldman said, the algorithm is 'secret', jokingly noting that 'if he told you how Genius works, he'd have to kill you' (Mims, ibid.) – to highlight the relevance and commercial value of these algorithms. However, this example reflects how, in some circumstance we are literally at the mercy of an algorithm, which makes a decision for us. What if we look for vegetarian food just because we go out for dinner with friends who happen to be vegetarian? Does this mean that, due to the connections between databases of large companies (or because of tracking cookies), we will be denied the opportunity of seeing advertisements for steakhouses on our Facebook webpage? Or will we be classified as good drivers because a sensor detects that most of the time we obey speed limits (even if the reason is that we know that where we drive the speed limits are strictly enforced)? Or will our preferences in terms of the music that we listen to be so reinforced by the automatic selections based on the algorithm that we reduce our exposure to alternative genres?

It is clear that the three tradeoffs showcase interests and needs of individuals on the one hand, and the somewhat opportunistic strategic moves of businesses (and governments) on the other. Moreover, our discussion illustrates the relevant role of algorithms in making decisions about an individual's characteristics/preferences based on trends, and therefore about what individuals should see and are likely to buy. Eric Schmidt (Google)

Digital technology

Digital Traces: all data provided by individuals during 'IT-related' activities, that leave a 'trace'	Sensors: LBS (location Based Tehnologies) and other surveillance and monitoring devices

Tradeoffs

Tradeoff: Privacy vs. security	Tradeoff: Control vs. freedom	Tradeoff: Dependence vs. independence

Algorithmic decision-making and discriminations (examples)

Violation privacy to increase security might have the result that an algorithm *determines* that particular categories of people are more likely to commit a crime	An algorithm assumes that we like some products more than others, but the same algorithm hides what we might not like, originating discriminations	Algorithmic decision-making support (or take over on) our lives; however, there are penalties for those who do not conform

Main tension

Individuals: willing to give up their privacy, freedom, and independence, to explore new opportunities of the digitization of everyday life	Businesses: keen on exploiting new opportunities deriving from the digitization of everyday life, but sometimes with costs to some individuals

Figure 19.1 A summary framework of the consequences of an algorithm-based world.

said in 2010 that, 'It will be very hard for people to watch or consume something that has not in some sense been tailored for them'. This statement involves privacy issues (businesses will know almost everything about consumers), control issues (consumers are literally monitored and then controlled with choices made for them), and dependence issues (loss of independence in making informed decisions, since the information provided about a specific choice will be driven by online feeds – created by algorithms). We posit that IS research is needed to examine the social issues that are emerging in relation to the strategic uses made by corporations of data from the digitization of our everyday lives. With the intention to provide an overall picture of the ethical issues and challenges created by this increasing trend, above we present a framework (Figure 19.1) that illustrates how digital technology (first layer) generates tradeoffs (second layer), when this technology is combined with algorithmic decision-making (third layer), leading to tensions (fourth layer). This summary framework has the purpose of showcasing strategic opportunities as well as societal challenges in an era of widespread diffusion of digital technology, and of supporting further interdisciplinary research on this topic, along with our suggested new avenues of research and potential research questions (in the last section that follows).

Research Agenda and Concluding Remarks

We do not know for sure the extent to which digital technology and the associated big/ little data analytics are going to impact society in the long term. However, we suggest that individuals seem to be likely to accept the 'dark side' of datification through digital traces (always there), and constant monitoring through sensors because they are persuaded that the benefits outweigh the costs. Thus, businesses (and governments) try to send to citizens the message that security is more important than privacy (to fight terrorism, for instance). And the same businesses make us believe that if we want to quickly find what we are looking for (whether it is a movie that we like, through Netflix, or a specific piece of information, through Google) we need the support of algorithms, that 'know' us and what we want – precluding our exposure to diversity. And finally, businesses develop digital technologies that 'help' us do new things more quickly, but simultaneously make us more reliant on (and so more vulnerable to) these same technologies as well as reducing our ability to learn.

Therefore we suggest that research should be carried out that considers broad social issues associated with businesses' (and government's) strategic use of data, especially so because we currently have very little understanding of what the consequences of corporations' non-responsible use of these data will be for society (Tene and Polonetsky, 2013), albeit we have suggested some negative impacts above. One way of looking at these social issues may be using an ethical dilemma lens, where we consider individuals' right to maintain their privacy, freedom and independence, against businesses' right to discriminate to promote sales – using cutting-edge technology such as big data analytics. We suggest that such dilemmas can be addressed using the teleological or deontological approaches to ethics (or both). The deontological approach (utilitarianism) is the best-known consequentialist theory (Bentham, 1776; Mill, 1863), and suggests that ethical behavior is one that maximizes societal welfare while minimizing social harm (Berente et al., 2011; Vallentyne, 1987). According to this approach, insurance companies may be right in being algorithm driven – thus applying higher premiums to those who, according to the data analytics, are more at risk of having car accidents. However, the (contrasting) deontological approach bases ethical decisions on broad, universal ethical principles and moral values such as honesty, promise keeping, fairness, loyalty and rights (e.g. to safety, privacy) so that the process or means by which an individual does something, rather than the outcome, is the focus of decision-making (e.g. lying is dishonest as it is one's duty to be honest regardless of whether this might lead to some ultimate good), therefore the end never justifies the means (Mingers and Walsham, 2010). According to this latter approach, discriminations should not take place if a minority is adversely and unfairly treated – never mind if following an algorithm maximizes positive consequences for society. More specifically, here we want to identify research questions that examine the social issues related to each of our tradeoffs, as described next.

Firstly, in terms of the tradeoff between privacy and security, one aspect that deserves attention relates to how far different countries (and regulators) will balance this tradeoff. From an ethical perspective, for instance, they might choose to privilege the maximization of societal welfare (so taking a teleological approach) or to pay attention to 'minorities', who are penalized by the discriminations of algorithmic decision-making (deontological approach). Information privacy laws and regulations – how citizens perceive (the value of) privacy – are country-specific and are related to cultural and historical issues (Milberg et al., 1995). One example is the recent debate about the 'right to be forgotten' (http://ec.europa.eu/justice/data-protection/files/factsheets/factsheet_data_protection_en.pdf), which forced Google to delete some information (and to implement processes to do so in the future, should people ask) from the results of its search engine in Europe, while this issue is not perceived currently as a relevant one in other countries such as in the US. To this end, it would be interesting to dig deeper into research questions such as: 'How far do institutions and governments influence the balance between privacy and security associated with digital technologies that collect data on our everyday lives?' 'What are the historical, cultural and social reasons behind the variety of approaches to digital privacy adopted by different countries?' 'Do these different approaches reflect differences in citizens' ethical and moral values?' 'Do (or will) social networks have the ability, in the long term, to modify ethical and moral values about privacy in different countries?' 'Will the diffusion of digital technology (and the IoT) lead to the standardization of ethical and moral values across countries, in the long-term?'

In terms of the tradeoff between freedom and control, we know very little about how far users are aware that they are being controlled by large Internet companies (especially if we think of 'second hand' data), and if they are, it would be interesting to learn about whether individuals' needs to enact social networks (Kane, 2014) prevail over the potentially uncomfortable feeling of being profiled (little data). Moreover, we do not have specific quantitative data that illustrates the effectiveness of algorithmic decision-making in identifying people's needs – for instance we know that little data has the ability to 'know' (or assume) what people want to purchase on the basis of a number of digital traces, but little is know about the actual revenues that derive from this – and whether the costs of implementing 'smart' algorithms and maintaining expensive hardware that can process big data is covered by the increased sales. We should assume that businesses achieve positive bottom lines from big data, since datification and algorithmic decision-making is widely adopted and is expensive (www.forbes.com/sites/ciocentral/2012/04/16/the-big-cost-of-big-data/), but we do not know, in concrete terms, the extent to which this has improved sales, customer satisfaction, inventory management or other financial, operational and organizational parameters. Knowing this would perhaps indicate a price for a loss of individuals' privacy and freedom. After all, one of the commonly cited examples of the usefulness of algorithmic decision-making was of Google being able to predict the location of a US flu epidemic, based on searches for flu remedies, faster than the Center for Disease Control (CDC). Yet, the story often remains untold, that they have been unable to repeat this success (www.theguardian.com/technology/2014/mar/27/google-flu-trends-predicting-flu). Thus, it is important that we conduct research that looks at the benefits for citizens of having a 'tailored' Internet, as against the costs of the benefits of living in an 'Internet bubble'. And finally there is a question about, 'what ethical guidelines might businesses usefully adopt to manage big/little data and produce the algorithms from these data'? For instance, Facebook has indicated that they have developed ethical policies for those who design algorithms, but such policies are not disclosed to the public. It is important that we research these issues so that we understand the ways in which businesses are using algorithms for discriminating so that we can enter a debate with business about associated ethical concerns (much as, for example, was the case in relation to the use of child labor in the past). Consider, for example, a monitoring system that profiles utility customers and sets different prices for gas and electricity, based on geographical areas and demand (another example of uninformed control). In this instance, maximizing societal welfare (cheap electricity for the majority) at the expense of minorities may well be unacceptable from an ethical standpoint (since those who end up paying more, are likely ironically also to be the very people who may be the most vulnerable and least able to pay). As a start in this process, we need research that sheds better light on the overall awareness of individuals in terms of how their data are being used by businesses and whether people are happy with this, especially as this exploits the more vulnerable in society. Thus, while big data analytics has the potential to shed light on important human and societal issues (Markus, 2015), this should not happen at the expense of the vulnerable.

In terms of the tradeoff between independency and dependency, we think that major societal issues are associated with the lack of opportunities for individuals to learn – and this poses issues from a knowledge creation and sharing perspective. As we pointed out earlier in this article, knowledge develops cumulatively and, according to the practice perspective (Feldman and Orlikowski, 2011; Sandberg and Tsoukas, 2011; Schatzki et al., 2001; Whittington, 2014) knowledge equates with practice. However, in the context of this tradeoff, it is the algorithm that gains knowledge about the minutiae of individuals – for instance, analyzing how humans drive a car, so that it can then operate as such, while humans may not gain a better understanding from this process. This poses relevant issues that involve both the private and work life of individuals. For example, 'will individuals lose their capacity to learn (even from mistakes)?' 'Will IT-assisted systems reach a point that they will impair an individual's problem solving skills and abilities in her/his everyday life?' This issue can be taken further if we refer to the potential decreased ability of managers to make decisions on their own, due to the few opportunities to 'practice' decision-making processes. For instance, 'Will an individual's capacity to adapt to a new organization and a new job be compromised by increased control (made by algorithms, and that leads to living in a "bubble", see our previous discussion of Pariser's "experiment"), which makes people less likely to be flexible and accepting towards diversity?' Also, there is the issue of the legitimacy of decisions that are based on algorithms and whether they will be accepted by those affected by the decision when the reasons for the decision are not actually known, even by those developing the algorithms. Thus, 'will businesses face more claims of unfair discrimination in the future when people identify that they have been treated differently to others but when the justification for this is not understood and cannot be clearly articulated by anyone?' 'The computer says "no"' (e.g., www.youtube.com/watch?v=AJQ3TM-p2QI), may come to be an unacceptable justification for being discriminated against as we are increasingly confronted by this 'rationale'.

The examination of the above social issues demands a multi-disciplinary approach that considers economic, legal, organizational, ethical, cultural and psychological consequences of the digitization of our everyday lives for different populations. In examining these issues, we would do well to remember that the ways new computing technologies (and the associated data) are used is not neutral in terms of the consequences for the human actors who leave digital traces that are then collected and analyzed. Corporations (and governments) have choices about how and what digital traces they collect and measure, and about the algorithms that they develop to make decisions based on this measurement, even if these decisions are increasingly distributed throughout a corporation rather than in the hands of the CIO (Nolan, 2012). These choices raise fundamental social questions as we have seen. As researchers we have an opportunity – and a responsibility (cf. Desouza et al., 2006, 2007) – to expose this empirically and theoretically and so promote an agenda of 'responsible analytics' that attempts to reduce the long-term negative social consequences of this new era concerned with the digitization of society.

In conclusion, this paper is an explicit call for action. We argue that researchers as well as practitioners should take these issues into serious consideration and articulate an interdisciplinary debate on how the datification of our everyday lives and the associated algorithmic decision-making (and the IoT) will affect society. This consequent research agenda requires a multi-disciplinary perspective. The issues are extremely relevant, strategic research topics. Whether we are interested in finding ways to increase business value or we are concerned with broader social issues of equality and democracy, they require immediate action. Strategic IS scholars are interested in 'the way IT "delivers the goods" by providing business AND social benefits' (Galliers et al., 2012, emphasis added). We would argue that minimizing social harm, even if to a minority, should be added to this agenda.

Note

1   The definition of big data was updated by Gartner in 2012 as they now describe the concept as 'high volume, high velocity, and/or high variety information assets that require new forms of processing to enable enhanced decision-making, insight discovery and process optimization (Gartner, 2012). Moreover, others have added 'new Vs' – e.g., veracity, variability, visualization, and value, viewing big data in terms of 5 or even 7 Vs. Here, where we stick with the original definition (Gartner, 2001) as this reflects the essence of big data for the purposes of this article.

References

Abbas, R., Katina, M., Michael, M. G., 2014. The regulatory considerations and ethical dilemmas of location-based services (LBS): a literature review. *Inf. Technol. People* 27 (1), 2–20.

Ball, K., 2002. Elements of surveillance: a new framework and future directions. *Inf. Commun. Soc.* 5 (4), 573–590.

Ball, K., 2005. Organization, surveillance, and the body: towards a politics of resistance. *Organization* 12 (1), 89–108.

Belanger, F., Crossler, R. E., 2011. Privacy in the digital age: a review of information privacy research in information systems. *MIS Q.* 35 (4), 1017–1041.

Beldad, A., de Jong, M., Steehouder, M., 2011. I trust not therefore it must be risky: determinants of the perceived risk of disclosing personal data for e-government transactions. *Comp. Hum. Behav.* 27 (6), 2233–2242.

Bentham, J., 1776. *A Fragment of Government*. London (Preface, 2nd para).

Berente, N., Gal, U., Hansen, S., 2011. Ethical implications of social stratification in information systems research. *Inf. Syst. J.* 21 (4), 357–382.

Boyd, D., Crawford, K., 2014. Critical questions for big data: provocations for a cultural, technological, scholarly phenomenon. *Inf. Commun. Soc.* 15 (5), 662–679.

Brown, J. S., Duguid, P., 1991. Organizational learning and communities of practice: towards a unified view of working, learning, and innovation. *Organ. Sci.* 2 (1), 40–57.

Campbell, S. W., Park, Y. J., 2008. Social implications of mobile telephony: the rise of personal communication society. *Sociol. Compass* 2 (2), 371–387.

Castells, M., Fernandez-Ardevol, M., Linchuan Qiu, J., Sey, A. (2009). *Mobile Communication and Society: A Global Perspective*. The MIT Press, Cambridge, MA.

Chan, Y. E., Culnan, M. J., Greenaway, K., Laden, G., Levin, T., 2005. Information privacy: management, marketplace, and legal challenges. *Commun. AIS* 16, 270–298.

Chen, H., Chiang, R. H. L., Storey, V. C., 2012. Business intelligence and analytics: from big data to big impact. *MIS Q.* 36 (4), 1165–1188.

Clark, C., Newell, S., 2013. Institutional work and complicit decoupling across the U.S. capital markets: the case of rating agencies. *Bus. Ethics Q.* 23(1),1–30.

Cohen, W. M., Levinthal, D. A., 1990. Absorptive capacity: a new perspective of learning and innovation. *Adm. Sci. Q.* 35 (1), 128–152.

Coll, S., 2014. Power, knowledge, and the subjects of privacy: understanding privacy as the ally of surveillance 17(10), 1250–1263.

Culnan, M. J., Clark-Williams, C., 2009. How ethics can enhance organizational privacy: lessons from the choicepoint and TJX data breaches. *MIS Q.* 33 (4), 673–687.

Dall'Alba, G., Sandberg, J., 2010. Learning through practice: professional and practice-based learning, 1, 104–119.

Desouza, K. C., Ein-Dor, P., McCubbrey, D. J., Galliers, R. D., Myers, M. D., Watson, R. T., 2007. Social activism in information systems research: making the world a better place. *Commun. Assoc. Inf. Syst.* 19, 261–277.

Desouza, K. C., El Sawy, O. A., Galliers, R. D., Loebbecke, C., Watson, R. T., 2006. Beyond rigor and relevance towards responsibility and reverberation: information systems research that really matters. *Commun. Assoc. Inf. Syst.* 17 (16).

Dinev, T., Hart, P., Mullen, M., 2008. Internet privacy concerns and beliefs about government surveillance an empirical investigation. *J. Strateg. Inf. Syst.* 17 (3), 214–233.

Doyle, A., Rippert, R., Lyon, D., 2013. *The Global Growth of Camera Surveillance*. Routledge Publisher.

Feldman, M. S., Orlikowski, W., 2011. Theorizing practice and practicing theory. *Organ. Sci.* 22 (4), 1240–1253.

Galliers, R. D., Jarvenpaa, S. L., Chan, Y. E., Lyytinen, K. L., 2012. Strategic information systems: reflections and prospectives. *J. Strateg. Inf. Syst.* 21 (2), 85–90.

Gartner, 2001. 3D data management: controlling data volume, velocity, and variety, by D. Laney <http://blogs.gartner.com/doug-laney/files/2012/01/ad949-3D-Data-Management-Controlling-Data-Volume-Velocity-and-Variety.pdf> (accessed 06.02.15).

Gartner, 2012. The importance of 'big data': a definition, by Beyer M.A., Laney D. <www.gartner.com/document/2057415>.

Gerlach, J., Widjaja, T., Buxmann, P., 2015. Handle with care: how online social network providers' privacy policies impact users' information sharing behavior. *J. Strat. Inf. Syst.* 24 (1), 33–43.

Greenaway, K., Chan, Y. E., 2005. Theoretical explanations for firms' information privacy behaviors. *J. Ais* 6 (6), 171–198.

Hasan, S., Subhani, M., 2011. Top management's snooping: is sneaking over employees' productivity and job commitment a wise approach. *Afr. J. Bus. Manage.* 6 (14), 5034–5043.

Hedman, J., Srinivasan, N., Lindgren, R., 2013. Digital traces or information systems: sociomateriality made researchable. In: Proceedings of the 34th ICIS. Milan, Italy.

Hodgkinson, G. P., Maule, A. J., Brown, N. J., Pearman, A. D., Glaister, K. W., 2002. Further reflections on the elimination of framing bias in strategic decision-making. *Strateg. Manag. J.* 23 (11), 1069–1073.

Jarvenpaa, S. L., Lang, K. R., 2005. Managing the paradoxes of mobile technology. *Inf. Syst. Manage.* 22 (4), 7–23.

Kane, G. C., 2014. Psychological stages of symbolic action in social media. In: Proceedings of the 35th ICIS December 14-17. Auckland, NZ.

Kittur, A., Chi, E., Pendleton, B. A., Suh, B., Mytkowicz, T., 2007. Power of the few vs. wisdom of the crowd: Wikipedia and the rise of the bourgeoises. WWW: World Wide Web 1 (2), 19–28.

Lyon, D., 2001. *Surveillance and Society: Monitoring Everyday Life*. McGraw-Hill International Publisher, Philadelphia.

Lyon, D., 2003. *Surveillance as Social Sorting: Privacy, Risk, and Digital Discrimination*. Routledge, London.

Lyon, D., 2014. Surveillance, snowden, and big data: capacities, consequences, critique. *Big Data Soc.* 1 (2). doi:10.1177/2053951714541861.

Lyytinen, K., Yoo, Y., 2002. Issues and challenges in ubiquitous computing. *Commun. ACM* 45 (12), 62–96.

MacCrory, F., Westerman, G., Alhammadi, Y., Brynjolfsson, E., 2014. Racing with and against the machine: changes in occupational skill composition in an era of rapid technological advance. In: Proceedings of the International Conference of Information Systems (ICIS). Auckland, NZ.

Markus, M. L., 2015. New games, new rules, new scoreboards: the potential consequences of big data. *J. Inf. Technol.* doi:10.1057/jit.2014.28 (available online 20.01.15).

Mayer-Schonberger, V., Cukier, K., 2013. *Big Data: A Revolution that Will Transform How We Live, Work, and Think*. Houghton Mifflin Harcourt Publishing Company, New York.

McAfee, A., Brynjolfsson, E., 2012. Big data: the management revolution. *Harv. Bus. Rev.* 90 (10), 60–68.

Michael, K., Michael, M. G., 2011. The social and behavioral implications of location-based services. *J. Loc. Based Serv.* 5 (3-4), 121–137.

Milberg, S. J., Burke, S. J., Smith, H. J., Kallman, E. A., 1995. Values, personal information, privacy, and regulatory approaches. *Commun. ACM* 38 (12), 65–74.

Mill, J. S., 1863. Utilitarianism, reprinted in 1906 in Chicago by the University of Chicago Press (first appearance in Fraser's Magazine, in 1861, then collected and reprinted as a single book in 1863).

Mims, C., 2010. How iTunes genius really works, *MIT Technology Review* <www.technologyreview.com/view/419198/how-itunes-genius-really-works/> (accessed February 02.02.15).

Mingers, J., Walsham, G., 2010. Toward ethical information systems: the contribution of discourse ethics. *MIS Q.* 34 (4), 833–854.

Miorandi, D., Sicari, S., De Pellegrini, F., Chlamatac, I., 2012. Internet of things: vision, applications, and research challenges. *Ad Hoc Netw.* 10, 1497–1516.

Munford, M., 2014. Rule changes and big data revolutionise Caterham F1 chances. *The Telegraph*, Technology Section, 23 February 2014 <www.telegraph.co.uk/technology/technology-topics/10654658/Rule-changes-and-big-data-revolutionise-Caterham-F1-chances.html> (accessed 15.11.14).

Negash, S., 2004. Business intelligence, communication of the association for information systems, *13* (article 15) <http://aisel.aisnet.org/cais/vol13/iss1/15>.

Newell, S., Marabelli, M., 2014. The crowd and sensors era: opportunities and challenges for individuals, organizations, society, and researchers. In: Proceedings of 35th ICIS, December 14-17. Auckland, NZ.

Nicolini, D., Gherardi, S., Yanow, D., 2003. Introduction: toward a practice-based view of knowing and learning in organizations. In: Nicolini, D., Gherardi, S., Yanow, D. (Eds.), *Knowing in Organizations: A Practice-based Approach*. Barnes & Noble, New York.

Nolan, R., 2012. Ubiquitous IT: the case of the Boeing 787 and implications for strategy research. *J. Strateg. Inf. Syst.* 21 (2), 91–102.

O'Reilly, C. A., Tushman, M. L., 2004. The ambidextrous organizations. *Harv. Bus. Rev.*, April, 1-10, 38.

Pariser, E., 2011. Beware online 'filter bubbles' TED-2011 <www.ted.com/talks/eli_pariser_beware_online_filter_bubbles> (accessed 01.10.14).

Petronio, S., 2002. *Boundaries of Privacy: Dialectics of Disclosure*. State University of New York Press, Albany, NY.

Podsakoff, P., Todor, W., Skov, R., 1982. Effects of leader contingent and noncontingent reward and punishment behaviors on subordinate performance and satisfaction. *Acad. Manag. J.* 25 (4), 810–821.

Power, D. J., 2002. *Decisions Support Systems: Concepts and Resources for Managers*. Quorum Books, Westport, CT.

Rouibah, K., Ould-ali, S., 2002. Puzzle: A concept and prototype for linking business intelligence to business strategy. *J. Strateg. Inf. Syst.* 11 (2), 133–152.

Sandberg, J., Tsoukas, H., 2011. Grasping the logic of practice: Theorizing through practical rationality. *Acad. Manag. Rev.* 36 (2), 338–360.

Schatzki, T. R., Knorr-Cetina, K., von Savigny, E., 2001. *The Practice Turn in Contemporary Theory*. Routledge, London.

Schroeder, R., Cowls, J., 2014. Big data, ethics, and the social implications of knowledge production. GeoJournal <https://dataethics.github.io/proceedings/BigDataEthicsandtheSocialImplicationsof KnowledgeProduction.pdf> (accessed 24.01.15).

Slade, S., Prinsloo, P., 2013. Learning analytics: Ethical issues and dilemmas. *Am. Behav. Scient.* 57 (10), 1510–1529.

Smith, H. J., 2002. Ethics and information systems: Resolving the quandaries. *ACM SIGMIS Datab.* 33 (3), 8–22.

Smith, H. J., Dinev, T., Xu, H., 2011. Information privacy research: An interdisciplinary review. *MIS Q.* 35 (4), 989–1016.

Smith, H. J., Hasnas, J., 1999. Ethics and information systems: The corporate domain. *MIS Q.* 23 (1), 109–127.

Staples, W. G., 2013. *Everyday Surveillance: Vigilance and Visibility in the Postmodern Life*. Rowman & Littlefield, Lanham.

Tene, O., Polonetsky, J., 2013. Big data for all: Privacy and user control in the age of analytics, 11 Nw. *J. Technol. Intellect. Prop.* 239 <http://scholarlycommons.law.northwestern.edu/njtip/vol11/iss5/1> (accessed 02.11.14).

Thomsen, E., 2003. BI's promised land. *Intell. Enterp.* 6 (4), 21–25.

Tsoukas, H., Vladimirou, E., 2001. What is organizational knowledge? *J. Manage. Stud.* 38 (7), 973–993.

Vallentyne, P., 1987. The teleological/deontological distinction. *J. Value Inq.* 21, 21–32.

Velasquez, M., 2006. *Business Ethics: Concepts and Cases*. Upper Saddle River, NJ, Pearson.

Whitman, G., 2011. The new paternalism: Unraveling 'nudge'. *Econ. Affairs* 31, 4–5.

Whittington, R., 2014. Information systems strategy and strategy-as-practice: A joint agenda. *J. Strateg. Inf. Syst.* 23 (1), 87–91.

Wu, L., Brynjolfsson, E., 2009. The future of prediction: How google searches foreshadow housing prices and quantities. In: Proceedings of 31st ICIS, December 15-18. Pheonix, AZ, paper 147.

Xi, F., Yang, L. T., Wang, L., Vinel, A. 2012. Internet of things. *Int. J. Commun. Syst.* 25, 1101–1102.

Yoo, Y., 2010. Computing in everyday life: A call for research on experiential computing. *MIS Q.* 34 (2), 213–231.

Zahra, S. A., George, G., 2002. Absorptive capacity: A review, reconceptualization, and extension. *Acad. Manage. Rev.* 27 (2), 185–203.

Zuboff, S., 1984. *In the Age of Smart Machine: The Future of Work and Power*. Basic Books, New York.

Questions for Discussion

1   What are the benefits for individuals, organizations, governments, society of the increasing use of digital technology and big data?

2   Can algorithms understand and interpret patterns of activities to predict behavior and preferences?

3   What are the implications of the use of algorithmic decision-making on innovation, e.g. automated systems?

4   How to tackle increasing dependence on IT devices for products and services?

5   Would algorithms hamper learning. How could organizations support learning and innovation?

6   What are the economic, legal, organizational, ethical, cultural, and psychological consequences of digitalization? How are these different for different cultures and populations?

Further Reading

https://journals.sagepub.com/toc/jina/30/1

Chapter 20

Kirsten E. Martin

ETHICAL ISSUES IN THE BIG DATA INDUSTRY

The Big Data Industry

BIG DATA RECEIVES a lot of press and attention—and rightly so. Big Data, the combination of greater size and complexity of data with advanced analytics,[1] has been effective in improving national security, making marketing more effective, reducing credit risk, improving medical research and facilitating urban planning. In leveraging easily observable characteristics and events, Big Data combines information from diverse sources in new ways to create knowledge, make better predictions or tailor services. Governments serve their citizens better, hospitals are safer, firms extend credit to those previously excluded from the market, law enforcers catch more criminals and nations are safer.

Yet Big Data (also known in academic circles as "data analytics") has also been criticized as a breach of privacy, as potentially discriminatory, as distorting the power relationship and as just "creepy."[2] In generating large, complex data sets and using new predictions and generalizations, firms making use of Big Data have targeted individuals for products they did not know they needed, ignored citizens when repairing streets, informed friends and family that someone is pregnant or engaged, and charged consumers more based on their computer type. Table 20.1 summarizes examples of the beneficial and questionable uses of Big Data and illustrates the potential confusion on how Big Data fits in a community—if at all.

Part of the ambiguity in researching Big Data is choosing what to study. Big Data has been framed as: (1) the *ability* to process huge "treasure troves" of data and predict future outcomes, (2) a *process* that "leverages massive data sets and algorithmic analysis" to extract new information and meaning, (3) an *asset*, (4) a *moment* where the data volume, acquisition or velocity limits the use of traditional tools and (5) a *tactic* to operate at a large scale not possible at a smaller scale.[3]

Framing Big Data as an asset, ability or technique sterilizes an important ethical discussion. Big Data is mistakenly framed as morally neutral or having benefits that outweigh any costs. Grand statements such as "Big Data itself, like all technology, is ethically neutral"[4] are

Table 20.1 Examples of Beneficial and Questionable Uses of Big Data

	Beneficial Uses	Questionable Uses
By Technology		
License Plate Readers	Reading passing cars for tolls on highway; police locating stolen car	Used by private detectives; placed on trucks to gather license plate data broadly
Facial Recognition	Finding potential terrorists at large sporting events	Used by social networking sites to identify members in pictures
GPS	Location-based coupons; traffic predictions; directions on map	Location-based stalking; iPhone as a homing beacon
By Context		
Healthcare	Treatment of cancer; health of pregnancy; Google Flu Trends	Discrimination in healthcare and insurance; app knows how fit you are
	Insights into interaction between medications from search terms; insights into hospital spread of infections	Development of a health score from purchase habits and from search terms
	Identifying veterans' potential suicidal thoughts	
Education	Personalizing student instruction Accountability for performance by school	Using data for possible admissions discrimination
	Identifying students at risk of dropping out	
Electricity	Turning on/off home electricity	Allowing criminals to know if you are home; smart homes hacked
LawEnforcement	Machine learning to identify burglar; accessing phone records to identify potential suspects in a mugging	Accessing smartphone without a warrant; identifying suspects by web browsing habits
	New York Fire Department using data mining to predict problems	Individuals under scrutiny for not participating in tracking
Retail	Improving layout of store based on typical movements of customers	Tracking movements/shopping habits of spectators at a stadium using Verizon's Precision Marketing Insight program
	Better coupons, suggested items	
	WalMart's use of RetailLink to integrate suppliers with onsite supplier inventory	Price discrimination (e.g., Amazon, Orbitz)
		Target sending notice of pregnancy to unsuspecting teen's parents
Urban Planning	Traffic management; smart grid technology	Identifying who is listening to which radio station; EZ Pass responder tracked everywhere
	Use of popular app by competitive cyclists and runners for road planning	Possibility of hackers changing traffic lights and creating traffic jams
	Identifying areas for road improvement	Identifying areas for road improvement but focusing only on those with mobile apps

implicit in reports that focus on the strategic and operational challenges of Big Data, but which largely ignore the ethical and social implications.[5] The growing field of data analytics excludes ethical analysis in both practice and academia. Yet creating, aggregating and selling data can change relationships and business models and requires rethinking information governance strategies—including issues concerning ethics and privacy.[6]

I suggest Big Data should be analyzed as the Big Data Industry (BDI) in order to identify the systemic risks in current Big Data practices. Such an approach situates Big Data within a larger system of firms, organizations, processes and norms for analysis. The volume, variety and velocity[7] of the data, plus the novel analytics required to produce actionable information, renders Big Data a difference in kind rather than degree. To create and use these large data sets to maximum effect, many firms aggregate data to create a new "whole" and sell access to this new data set.

The separate and distinct firms in the Big Data Industry work through agreements to produce a product (Big Data) for customers—similar to any other industry.[8] In response, CIOs and CDOs (Chief Data Officers) are shifting to an outward, strategic focus in leveraging Big Data rather than the inward, service focus used for traditional data. At present, however, there are not yet any industry norms or supply chain best practices that can guide them.[9]

This article examines the ethical issues in the nascent Big Data Industry. Industries are the aggregate of firms involved in the production and distribution of a product—e.g., the software industry, the ERP industry, the automobile industry, etc. Importantly, if a market exists for a product, then a corresponding industry exists to meet that demand. And, as the market for Big Data continues to grow and be measured, the corresponding Big Data Industry, comprised of those firms involved in the production, analysis and use of Big Data, begins to coalesce around standard industry practices. (Note that this article focuses on privacy issues in the U.S. Big Data Industry; as described in the panel below, the privacy regulatory environments in the U.S. and Europe differ significantly.)

Privacy: U.S. Versus EU

The use of Big Data in Europe faces a distinct set of regulatory constraints governed by the EU's Data Protection Directive (95/46/EC) and, for example, the United Kingdom's Data Protection Act 1998. Regulations require those using "personal data" to abide by the directive's requirements to being fair, to be clear as to the purpose of gathered information and, problematic for Big Data, to strive for minimization. See also the Bureau of National Affairs' World Data protection Report 14(9) as well as the U.K.'s Information Commissioner's Office Big Data and Data Protection (2014).

For example, Facebook recently was unable to comply with the stricter EU regulations because of a lack of adequate consent and control for users: Facebook users have no true opt-out mechanism, no valid consent for the transfer of data to third parties and a general lack of control over their data. In other words, Facebook's "take it or leave it" approach to choice is not sufficient for European law.[10] Generally, privacy is taken more seriously by regulators in the EU (and by U.S. companies doing business in Europe), with "data subjects" having a right to be forgotten, authentic user consent and a general leaning toward "opt-in" as the default.[11]

The article first examines the information supply chain within the Big Data Industry, including upstream sources of data and downstream uses of data. Next, it examines two crucial consumer-related ethical issues created by systemic norms and practices of the Big Data Industry: (1) the negative externality of surveillance and (2) destructive demand. Remedies for these potential issues are proposed, with the goal of fostering a sustainable Big Data Industry.

An industry-level analysis extends the examination of Big Data in three ways. First, framing Big Data as an industry highlights the participants, power relationships and systemic issues that arise within the production and use of Big Data, insights that are not available when Big Data is isolated as a technology. Second, an industry-level analysis captures pervasive industry practices that are missed when considering single uses of Big Data. These systemic issues can be resolved with the industry-specific measures described in the analysis. Finally, an industry-level analysis broadens the number of interested parties to all who have a stake in creating a sustainable Big Data Industry. All companies in controversial industries have their legitimacy questioned and have a vested interest in creating sustainable industry norms. In other words, the recognition that bad behavior may delegitimize the entire industry provides an incentive for industry leaders to curb such practices.[12] A brief overview of the leading firms in the Big Data Industry is given in the left panel on the next page.

The Big Data Industry's Supply Chain

Within the Big Data Industry, data, such as online consumer data or location data from an application, is passed from one firm to the next within an information supply chain, comparable to supply chains in traditional industries (see text panel on the next page). Within this supply chain, consumers provide information to firms, which then pass it to tracking companies, which may also pass it to data aggregators. Data aggregators act as distributors by holding consolidated information of many users across many contexts.

Supply Chains

In a traditional business model, supply chains comprise a series of firms working together to deliver value by transforming raw material into a finished product. Trees are harvested in the forest, traded to the pulp manufacturer and eventually become the paper used to print an article; tomatoes are picked, packed, shipped and crushed into sauce to be used on a delivered pizza. The figure below illustrates a generic supply chain: each firm adds value to the product or service to transform the raw materials in one location and deliver a finished product to the end customer through value creation and trade.

All supply chains carry ethical issues both downstream and upstream. Software companies must ensure that their products are not eventually sold in Syria through a distribution center in Dubai; Apple is held accountable for the working conditions of its upstream suppliers, such as Foxconn. Supply chain researchers examine upstream sourcing issues, looking at how supplier selection takes account of, for example, the way forests are harvested in the paper industry or how apparel is manufactured overseas, as well as following products downstream through logistics and eventual sale and use (Figure 20.1).

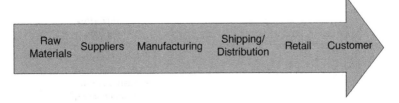

Figure 20.1 Supply chains

Data aggregators or data brokers may sell the information to researchers, government agencies or polling companies, or an ad network may use the information from an aggregator or broker to place an advertisement on a website when a user returns to browse or shop online. Survey firms, academic research teams, government agencies or private firms may also contract with a data broker directly to use data to supplement survey research, make employment decisions and investigate possible criminal activity. An information supply chain is thus created with multiple firms exchanging information and adding value to the data.

As with traditional supply chains, the information supply chain can be analyzed both by the downstream distribution and use of Big Data as well as by the upstream sourcing (see Figure 20.2).

The issues arising from the downstream use of Big Data and upstream sourcing of information are summarized in Figure 20.3 and described in detail below.

Issues with Downstream Customers and Uses of Big Data

As shown in Table 20.1, downstream uses of Big Data can be perceived as producing beneficial and questionable (often unethical and harmful) outcomes. However, the potential harm that can result from using Big Data should not detract from the benefits—from curing diseases to identifying fraud. Nonetheless, selling information increases the risk of secondary misuse of the data, with eventual harmful impacts on users. While the potential harm from *incorrect* information or false conclusions merits attention, harm downstream in the supply chain includes harm from the *correct* conclusions. For instance, Target famously correctly identified a pregnant teenager based on her purchase history and sent a congratulatory letter to her house, which was seen by her parents who were unaware that their daughter was pregnant.[13]

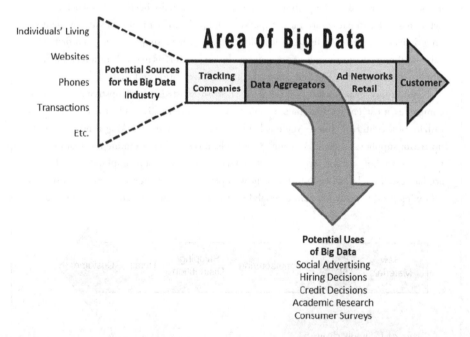

Figure 20.2 Example of Information Supply Chain Within the Big Data Industry

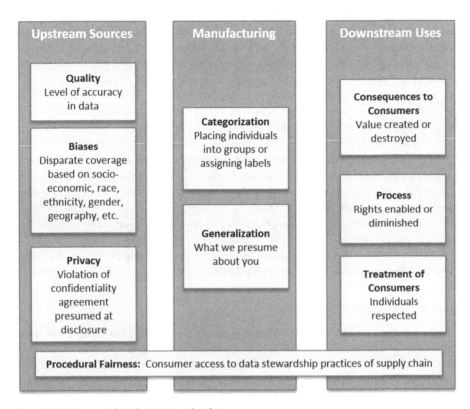

| Upstream Sources | Manufacturing | Downstream Uses |

Quality
Level of accuracy in data

Biases
Disparate coverage based on socio-economic, race, ethnicity, gender, geography, etc.

Privacy
Violation of confidentiality agreement presumed at disclosure

Categorization
Placing individuals into groups or assigning labels

Generalization
What we presume about you

Consequences to Consumers
Value created or destroyed

Process
Rights enabled or diminished

Treatment of Consumers
Individuals respected

Procedural Fairness: Consumer access to data stewardship practices of supply chain

Figure 20.3 Issues within the BDI Supply Chain

The harmful effects of using Big Data can be extended to include:

- *Value destruction* (rather than creation) for stakeholders
- *Diminished rights* (rather than realized) for stakeholders
- *Disrespectful* to someone involved in the process (rather than supporting them).

Such effects are not possible without information provided upstream, thereby linking all supply chain members to the eventual uses of information.[14]

First, data uses can be analyzed based on the *consequences* to the individual. More obvious adverse consequences include being denied credit, losing a job, having secrets outed to your family, paying more for insurance, etc. For example, information may be used downstream to modify insurance premiums or mortgage rates. However, there can also be positive consequences, as when downstream use identifies trends in demographics such as flu outbreaks, or prioritizes search results for a travel site.[15] Table 20.1 focuses on the consequences (both good and bad) from the use of Big Data.

A more egregious yet subtle consequence is what law scholar Ryan Calo conceptualizes as digital market manipulation. When firms know more information about consumers with an ever better ability to fine-tune the consumer experience, they are able to influence consumers at a personal level and to trigger vulnerability in consumers in their marketing.[16] Calo's argument suggests that Target, for example, would not only identify a consumer who is pregnant, but could also engineer food cravings in her through subtle triggers. As summarized by Calo, firms will increasingly be in the position to create "suckers" rather than waiting for one to be born every minute.

The harm resulting from the use of Big Data can also be identified by asking not only how value is created or destroyed for individuals, but also whether individuals' *rights are being realized* in the process of using the data. Barocos and Selbst nicely illustrate the harm that can arise not only from the information supply chain, but also from the process followed in using Big Data. Big Data may develop learned prejudice algorithms based on pre-existing information. By basing predictive algorithms on previous data patterns, learned prejudice builds on previously institutionalized prejudice—for example, in areas such as college admissions or when a Google search on black-sounding names brings up arrest records. Such algorithms can produce objectionable outcomes, as with accidental or intentional discrimination.[17]

Finally, categorizing individuals under certain headings can be disrespectful to them— for example, the categorization of individuals based on their personal history, such as rape victim status, becomes an exercise in objectifying individuals as a mere category. Big Data aggregators have been known to list individuals by classifications such as alcoholics, erectile dysfunction sufferers and even as "daughter killed in car crash."[18] Even without value being destroyed, individuals can be disrespected through objectifying them as a mere category— particularly a category that overwhelms in significance, such as being the victim of a crime, struggling with an addiction or coping with a death.

Issues with Upstream Sources

In addition to the possible downstream harmful effects of using Big Data, firms in the information supply chain must also contend with issues concerned with upstream suppliers of data, in particular the possibility of partnering with bad suppliers. The ability to develop an ever-greater volume, velocity and variety of data requires large, complex and distributed data sets from many sources. Sources of data within the Big Data Industry include consumers, products, location, machines and transactions (and all combinations of these). In fact, the variety of combined data differentiates Big Data from traditional data analysis: many data sources combine data types or use data in novel ways. This pooling of diverse, sometimes innocuous, pieces of data contributes to a greater potential for statistical significance or to making sense of new knowledge.[19]

Within the Big Data Industry, upstream sources may be undesirable because of the quality of information, biases in the data and privacy issues in the collection and sharing of information. Data quality may be an issue due to inaccuracies in the data or a lack of coverage.[20] Inaccuracies may arise from the manner in which the data was collected, the degree of imputed[21] data within the data source or from deliberate obfuscation by users.[2224] Assessing the quality of upstream data is similar to assessing the quality of upstream sources in a manufacturing supply chain, where firms are free to specify the quality they desire for their products. However, firms using upstream information further down the information supply chain will be held accountable for the quality of that information.

Data may also have biases that skew it toward specific types of users, such as a particular race, ethnicity, gender, socioeconomic status or location. Using upstream data further down the supply chain requires an understanding of the level of bias in the data—skewed data will skew the results and limit the generalization of the findings. For example, location tracking can be beneficial to the community when used for transit scheduling; however, if one group is systematically ignored in the source data (e.g., groups with less access to mobile devices used to track location data), that group will not benefit from the improved transit system or may have traffic flow inaccurately predicted.[23]

Finally, and importantly for the ethical implications of the Big Data Industry, the firm supplying data should be assessed on how it respects privacy in the collection of information. Consumers disclose information within a set of privacy rules, and sharing that information with other firms in the supply chain may breach their privacy expectations. In other words, information always has "terms of use" or norms governing when, how, why and where it can be used.[24] For example, information shared with Orbitz, a travel website, has a distinct set of privacy expectations based on the individual's relationship with the website and the context of the interaction. Individuals may expect location information to be used to offer hotel or restaurant discounts for their destination, but they do not expect that information be passed to data aggregators and used a year later to make pricing decisions. Users disclose information with a purpose in mind and within an implicit confidentiality agreement.

Privacy law scholar Woodrow Hartzog suggests that this confidentiality agreement should be honored by firms that subsequently receive or gather the information within a concept of "chain link confidentiality."[25] The expectations present at initial disclosure—who should receive information, how it can be used, how long it will be stored—should persist throughout the online information supply chain.

Role of Firms in the Information Supply Chain

In conventional supply chains, upstream suppliers may have quality problems or unethical business practices that taint the final product. In the 1990s, for example, Wal-Mart and Nike infamously relied on overseas manufacturers that used child labor and unsafe working conditions. More recently, Apple has grappled with the reputational problems arising from using Foxconn, a supplier with harsh working conditions. Firms that willingly enter a supply chain have an obligation to ensure that the practices of other firms in the chain match their own. Similarly, organizations within the information supply chain are held responsible for the data stewardship practices of both upstream and downstream partners.

An organization's responsibility within a supply chain is derived from the benefits it receives from the practices of the supply chain. In accepting those benefits, the firm implicitly signs up to the practices of the supply chain—including potentially questionable practices of upstream sources. Nike benefits from the practices of its suppliers even though the working conditions of those suppliers leave a lot to be desired.

Each firm in the Big Data Industry contributes to, and benefits from, an information supply chain and willingly takes on part of the responsibility for actions and practices within that chain. For example, when Facebook seeks to use information from upstream data brokers such as Acxiom, Epsilon, Datalogix and BlueKai,[26] it must not only worry about its own collection methods, but also the upstream sources' data collection methods. Choosing and creating supply chains means that firms are responsible for the conduct and treatment of users throughout the chain. Thus Nike is held responsible for how its products are sourced, and coffee retailers are held responsible for how their coffee is farmed.

Systemic Issues in the Big Data Industry

As described above, the role of firms within their information supply chain should be analyzed, but the Big Data Industry includes firms that are developing generalized norms and practices. In effect, the *systemic* participation in the Big Data Industry gives rise to "everyone does it" ethical issues—where norms of practice are beginning to form across many firms and supply chains, as illustrated in Figure 20.4. Quadrants A and B capture the ethical issues within a single supply chain, as described above.

This section examines the ethical issues captured by Quadrants C and D, and links them to parallel, more traditional industries. The first issue is creating negative externalities (or surveillance as pollution), where surveillance is a byproduct of the systematic collection,

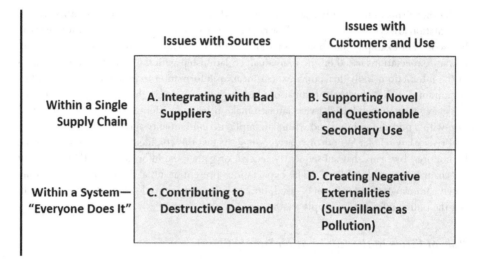

	Issues with Sources	Issues with Customers and Use
Within a Single Supply Chain	A. Integrating with Bad Suppliers	B. Supporting Novel and Questionable Secondary Use
Within a System— "Everyone Does It"	C. Contributing to Destructive Demand	D. Creating Negative Externalities (Surveillance as Pollution)

Figure 20.4 Current Ethical Issues within the Big Data Industry

aggregation and use of individual data (Quadrant D). The second is the growing problem of destructive demand within the Big Data Industry (Quadrant C), where the need for consumer data is pressuring consumer-facing firms to collect and sell increasing amounts of information with lower standards. Both sets of ethical issues stem from the *systemic* norms and practices within the industry. In addition, both are more consumer or individual-focused and may apply to a particular subset of firms within the Big Data Industry.

The ethical issues that have to be faced at both the supply chain level and the industry level are summarized in Table 20.2 (For comparison, the table provides corresponding examples from traditional industries; it also describes how CIOs and CDOs will have to deal with the issues.)

Creating Negative Externalities (Or Surveillance as Pollution)

In all markets, costs regularly accrue to parties not directly involved in an immediate decision or exchange. For example, a firm making steel can create harm to the community in the form of the pollution it produces. The steel company may contract with a customer—which does not feel the effects of pollution—without including the "cost" of pollution. This is an example of a *negative externality*, which exists when the harm done to others is not taken into account in the immediate transaction.[27]

There are also negative externalities in the Big Data Industry arising from the aggressive focus on collecting consumer data. The danger is that disclosing personal data can become the default, and individuals who choose *not* to disclose can be harmed. For example, individuals who attempt to opt out of aggressive data collection by using TOR[28] or other obfuscation technologies may be targeted by the National Security Agency as suspicious.[29] The harm to individuals who do not share their data is a result of the decisions of the majority who do share.

More complicated is when the harmful effect is compounded by many parties in an industry acting in a similar way. For example, a manufacturing firm may not take account of the harmful effects on the local community of the pollution it produces. However, the *aggregated* harm of pollution from manufacturers worldwide becomes a problem for society in general through global warming. Aggregated negative externalities are a consequence of "everyone

Table 20.2 Ethical Issues in the Big Data Industry

Ethical Issues	Big Data Industry Examples	Traditional Industry Examples	As Faced by CIOs and CDOs
Supply Chain Level			
Unfair or objectionable harms from using Big Data	Harms from downstream use, such as using Big Data to discriminate in consumer credit decisions or college admissions	Sale of computer systems in Iran or Syria; use of product in crime	How do downstream users of your data protect the consumer data or impact consumers?
Gathering of data as an intrusion or violation of privacy	Questionable upstream sourcing, such as purchasing location data surreptitiously gathered from mobile applications or using data from invisible web beacons unknown to user	Apple and Foxconn; Nike and sweatshops	What questions do you ask about using data from unknown or questionable sources?
Industry Level			
Harm to those not involved in the immediate decision or transaction caused by broad tracking of consumers and collection of information	Negative externality of surveillance, such as the hidden and systematic aggregation of data about individuals	Steel industry and pollution	How is your company pollution possibly contributing to surveillance by participating in broad user tracking—or partnering with someone who does?
Focus on resale of consumer data; treating consumers simply as a means to supply the secondary market of information traders	Destructive demand, such as creating a flashlight application just to gather user contact or location data	Demand for residential mortgages created by the mortgage-backed securities industry; websites and applications used as bait	How is your company creating destructive demand by using data of questionable quality or that was collected by breaching privacy expectations?

does it"— the harm results from the fact that the practice is pervasive in an industry. The harm from aggregated actions across an industry is more than the sum of the harms caused by individual firms.

Firms within the Big Data Industry create an aggregated negative externality because they contribute to a larger system of surveillance through the breadth of information gathered and because firms that collect and aggregate data are invisible to users. In general, surveillance conflicts with the need of individuals to be unobserved as well as their need for uniqueness and a sense of self. An individual's personal space permits "unconstrained, unobserved physical and intellectual movement" to develop as an individual and to cultivate relationships.[30] Surveillance can cause harm by violating the personal space—both physical and metaphorical—that is important to develop as an individual and within relationships.

Importantly, the fear of being watched and judged by others causes "spaces exposed by surveillance [to] function differently than spaces that are not so exposed" by changing how individuals behave and think.[31]

Surveillance works by affecting not only those who are being watched, but also those who are *not actually* being watched. In fact, the mere belief that someone is being watched is enough for individuals to act as though they are under surveillance. Prisons are designed so that only some of the prisoners are watched, but the prisoners do not know specifically who is being watched at any one time. Individuals do not need to know they are under surveillance to act as though they are under surveillance. Importantly for the Big Data Industry, the negative externality of surveillance means the industry can rely on those individuals not currently being watched to believe and act as though they are under surveillance.

Surveillance is particularly effective in changing behavior and thoughts when individuals (1) cannot avoid the gaze of the watcher and (2) cannot identify the watchers.[32] By aggregating data across disparate contexts online, the Big Data Industry contributes to the perception that surveillance is impossible to avoid yet also creates a data record that tells a richer, more personalized story than individual data points.[33] Broad data aggregators summarize highly diverse data (the "variety" in Big Data) so they can analyze individualized behavior. In addition, most data aggregators are invisible to the user and thereby aggravate the surveillance problem by being not only unknown, but also unreachable. Unknown and invisible firms that gather and store data contribute to the perception of omnipresent and omniscient surveillance and exacerbate the power imbalance between the watched and the watcher.[34]

Currently, the Big Data Industry does not consider or take account of the negative externality of surveillance. Firms that capture, aggregate or use Big Data create a cost to the larger community in the form of surveillance.

Contributing to Destructive Demand

In addition to the aggregate harm of surveillance, the Big Data Industry has the potential to foster *destructive demand* for consumer data when firms exert pressure on consumer-facing organizations to collect more information. As described below, consumers unknowingly can become suppliers to a secondary Big Data market.

The main source of information for the Big Data Industry is a byproduct of legitimate transactions with consumer-facing firms. Data is collected from a transaction in the primary market—e.g., checking the weather, buying groceries, using a phone, paying bills, etc.—and is then aggregated and merged to create a large robust data set. In effect, that data is seen as sitting inventory when a firm in the secondary Big Data market—such as a data broker or tracking company—creates value through the secondary use of the data. The consumer data from the initial transaction, such as buying books on Amazon or reading news on *The New York Times*, can be sold or repurposed in a secondary market without losing value. Examples of destructive demand created by secondary markets are described in the panel on the following page.

A tipping point exists where the product— whether residential mortgages as described in the panel or consumer information—is no longer *pushed* into the secondary market, but rather the secondary market becomes a *pull* for the product of the primary, consumer-targeted market. In this situation, the secondary market creates a destructive demand by exerting pressure on suppliers to adopt questionable or unethical practices to meet the demands of the secondary market. Primary market firms (e.g., residential mortgage originators) then treat customers as a mere means[35] to the secondary market (for mortgage-backed securities). The demand becomes particularly destructive when the service in the primary market serves as a lure (or bait) for the supply of the secondary market—as when mortgage originators became a lure to produce mortgages for the mortgage-backed securities market.

Within the Big Data Industry, websites and applications with trusted relationships with consumers can become the bait for Big Data, such as when a flashlight application tracks your location or when a website with numerous tracking beacons[36] stores consumer information. The primary market promises a customer-focused relationship (first-market relationship) when it is actually attempting to sell customers' information to a secondary market.

The attributes of the mortgage-backed securities market, and the destructive demand it created, provide a warning for the secondary market for consumer information in the Big Data Industry. The demand for the primary market becomes destructive:

1   *Where the secondary market becomes as or more lucrative than the primary market.* For example, the fee charged to consumers for mortgages was dwarfed by the profits from the sale of mortgages into the secondary market. Mortgage originators could lose money on a mortgage but still make a profit by selling the mortgage in the secondary market. Within the Big Data Industry, problems will arise when the sale of consumer information is more lucrative or, at minimum, equals the profits from the primary market activities, such as selling an application or providing a service.

2   *When the quality in the secondary market is less than in the primary market*—i.e., when the quality requirements of data brokers or data aggregators do not match the expectations of consumers who disclose information. For example, the mortgage-backed securities market was not concerned about the quality of the residential mortgages they purchased from originators.

Examples of Destructive Demand from Secondary Markets

Secondary markets can be beneficial. A secondary market for bicycles and cars can increase the life of the product. In fact, customers may be more willing to invest in a car in the primary "new car" market knowing that the robust secondary market for used cars exists to sell the car when necessary. Other secondary markets create value from items that would otherwise be thrown away—e.g., the byproduct from cattle ranching (wax) or from steel-making (scrap metal). The secondary market allows firms to capture value from seemingly waste products, such as ranchers selling the byproduct of cow fat used for candles.

However, secondary markets can apply perverse pressures to distort the demand, quality or price in the primary market. An example is the market for carbon credits. Firms who create HFC-23, a super greenhouse gas, as a byproduct of their manufacturing are paid to destroy it to prevent the gas causing environmental damage. However, the secondary market for HFC23 became too lucrative: some firms had an incentive to create HFC-23 so they would be paid to destroy it. In fact, the World Bank paid $1 billion to two chemical factories in China to destroy HFC-23, and later evidence suggested these firms may have deliberately overproduced the gas so they could be paid to destroy it in the secondary market.

More problematic is when the secondary market begins to systematically distort the primary market, as in the well-known case of mortgage-backed securities and the residential mortgage market. The primary market for mortgages is between a lender and home-buyer. Financial institutions lend money to qualified individuals to buy a home at a rate that takes into account the potential risk of the individual defaulting on the loan.

A secondary market for residential mortgages uses consumer mortgages as the inventory for a new financial instrument: mortgage-backed securities (MBS). The MBS market increased dramatically between 2000 and 2008, and the associated demand for consumer mortgages to feed the MBS market led to lax sourcing in the primary mortgage market.

Interestingly, the price did not change in the primary market; rates and interest rate spreads remained steady throughout the growth in the MBS market. However, the quality standards for consumer mortgages required in the primary market dropped to match the (lower) requirements in the secondary market. More mortgage originations and fewer denials led to a greater number of high-risk borrowers through lax sourcing for the MBS market.

This mismatch between the quality required in the secondary and primary markets proved particularly hazardous. The interests of firms in the secondary market did not align with those of consumers, and without a relationship with consumers there were higher default rates for the mortgages included in their MBS. However, when incentives of the secondary market were aligned with the primary market of the consumer, as in the case of affiliated investors, economists found no change in the mortgage default rates. The increase in private securitization by non-commercial bank financial firms, with lower requirements for quality, created a destructive demand for lower quality mortgages in the primary market.

3. *When firms in the primary market have limited accountability to consumers for their transactions in the secondary market.* Primary market firms can hide their bad behavior when they sell into the secondary market because their activity in the secondary market is not visible or incorporated in the primary market. The term "moral hazard" refers to when individuals or institutions do not bear the full consequences of their actions, as in the case of mortgage originators selling bad loans into the MBS secondary market. In the Big Data Industry, consumer-facing organizations are currently not held accountable for selling access to consumer data even by market forces, and their activities in the secondary market are invisible to the primary consumer market.

Guidelines for a Sustainable Big Data Industry

The Big Data Industry is currently in a unique, yet vulnerable, position, with identified systemic risks but without clear industry leaders to develop cooperative strategies. Moreover, the power of Big Data is generated by non-consumer-focused firms that aggregate and distribute the data, and regulating such firms has met with questionable success in the other industries.[37] However, all firms are tainted by the bad behavior and questionable practices of others in their industry and have a stake in a sustainable resolution. Three types of firms in the Big Data Industry are of particular importance in creating sustainable industry practices:

1   Possible leaders in the industry, which could emerge from their unique position as gatekeepers, such as consumer-facing companies, website operators and application providers. These companies control how information is initially gathered and how it is subsequently shared.
2   Organizations with unique influence and knowledge in the area of Big Data analytics, such as the American Statistical Association and the Census Bureau, as well as HHS and the National Research Council (which govern academics' Institutional Review Boards). These organizations have the stature and deep knowledge of research, data sets, analytics and confidentiality to begin to set standards of practice.
3   Providers of key products within the Big Data Industry, such as Palantir, Microsoft, SAP, IBM, etc. These companies have few competitors and unique knowledge of analytic products and services, and can offer advice to firms at a critical point to analyze and use Big Data.

As this article has shown, the ethical issues and problems facing the Big Data Industry are similar to those faced by other industries. Practical solutions to creating mutually beneficial and sustainable relationships within the industry include visible data stewardship practices, greater data due process internally and using the services of a data integrity professional. These solutions, which are summarized in Table 20.3 and Figure 20.5, directly address the issues identified in this article. (Table 20.3 also describes how CIOs and CDOs can address the problems.) Despite the potential to create harm, the Big Data Industry has the potential to be a force for good and the focus therefore should be on implementing the solutions described below to create value for all stakeholders.[38]

Table 20.3 Possible Solutions to the Big Data Industry's Ethical Issues

Type of Issue	Cause of Problem	Potential Solution	As Faced by CIOs and CDOs
Data Stewardship			
Supply Chain Sourcing and Use Issues	Firms not accountable for conduct of upstream sources and downstream customers	Illustrate role of firm in larger supply chain Make machine-readable notification of supply chain information available to policy makers, reports and privacy advocates	Identify and take ownership of upstream sources and downstream customers/uses of data Ensure information about data stewardship practices is available to experts and novices
	Supply chain not visible	Make data stewardship practices of supply chain visible	Do not enter into confidentiality agreements that preclude explaining your data partners, either upstream sources or downstream users
Data Due Process			
Surveillance as Negative Externality	Harm to others not captured by firms collecting, storing or using personally identifiable information(PII)	Minimize surveillance Internalize cost of surveillance with increased data due process	Make tracking visible to consumer (Industry) Require additional data due process for firms acquiring and retaining PII
Data Integrity			
Destructive Demand for Consumer Information	Secondary market of data trading has lower quality requirements than primary consumer-focused market	Use a data integrity professional when handling or selling PII	(Industry) Institute data integrity professional or board for projects partnering with Big Data sources and customers
	Secondary market is not visible to primary market (consumers)	Make activity in secondary market visible to regulators and consumers	Account for and communicate additional risk from partnering in secondary market for Big Data through disclosure

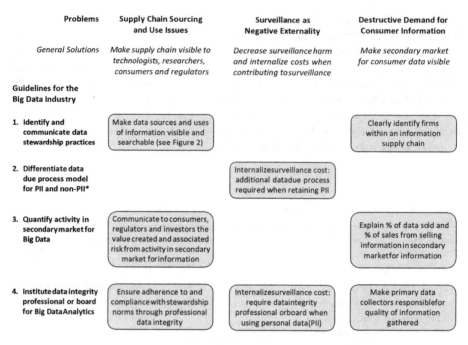

Problems	Supply Chain Sourcing and Use Issues	Surveillance as Negative Externality	Destructive Demand for Consumer Information
General Solutions	*Make supply chain visible to technologists, researchers, consumers and regulators*	*Decrease surveillance harm and internalize costs when contributing to surveillance*	*Make secondary market for consumer data visible*
Guidelines for the Big Data Industry			
1. Identify and communicate data stewardship practices	Make data sources and uses of information visible and searchable (see Figure 2)		Clearly identify firms within an information supply chain
2. Differentiate data due process model for PII and non-PII*		Internalize surveillance cost: additional data due process required when retaining PII	
3. Quantify activity in secondary market for Big Data	Communicate to consumers, regulators and investors the value created and associated risk from activity in secondary market for information		Explain % of data sold and % of sales from selling information in secondary market for information
4. Institute data integrity professional or board for Big Data Analytics	Ensure adherence to and compliance with stewardship norms through professional data integrity	Internalize surveillance cost: require data integrity professional or board when using personal data (PII)	Make primary data collectors responsible for quality of information gathered

Figure 20.5 Guidelines for a Sustainable Big Data Industry
*The ability to fully differentiate between personally identifiable information (PII) and non-PII is debatable, as argued by Narayanan, A. and Shmatikov, V. "Myths and Fallacies of Personally Identifiable Information," **Communications of the ACM** (53:6), (2010), pp. 24–26.

Identify and Communicate Data Stewardship Practices

Current information supply chains are not visible, putting consumers at a disadvantage in choosing preferred supply chains or holding a firm responsible for its decision to join a particular supply chain. Such information asymmetries could be minimized by clearly illustrating the upstream sourcing information and downstream use in order to report the data stewardship practices. Data stewardship includes the rules about internal treatment and external sharing of information for different types of data. Industry groups can develop data stewardship best practices for firms and, more importantly, coalesce around a format for communicating data stewardship practices.

Making the supply chain visible will clearly identify a firm's position in the chain and enable the firm to take responsibility for the upstream and downstream practices of others. A firm's different upstream sources of information, the type of information collected, its internal uses and storage, and the firm's possible downstream customers and recipients are all important for understanding the entirety of the supply chain and the firm's data stewardship practices. An illustrative example is shown in Figure 20.6. The data sources, type of data and level of identifiability are important for understanding the upstream sourcing practices; the firm's primary use, secondary use and storage explains the purpose and vulnerability of the data; and the types of data, recipients and level of trust in the recipients explains the downstream uses of the data collected.

While the information supply chain may look complicated, a similar problem has been resolved in areas such as free-trade coffee, organic food and sustainable fishing: trusted supply chains are identified, certified and valued by customers and customer groups. The information supply chain of a particular firm should be similarly available to industry groups, customer groups and regulators that have the knowledge necessary to certify a level of

Upstream Information Flow   **Downstream Information Flow**

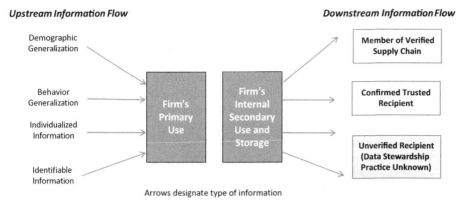

Arrows designate type of information

Figure 20.6 Example of a Firm's Information Supply Chain Diagram

data stewardship within the supply chain. Making information supply chains available in a machine-readable form would support the illustration in Figure 20.6, as has been developed and effectively called for by Cranor.[39] Users would then be able to identify and choose trusted and certified supply chains.

Providing information about a firm's larger supply chain and data stewardship practices in a uniform way is critical not only for helping users directly, but also for allowing researchers, reporters, technologists and academics to easily diagram and analyze the many different supply chains and provide an audit trail for the data.

Differentiate Data Due Process Requirements for Personal Data

Two approaches can be used to manage surveillance as a negative externality: (1) individual firms can reduce their role in contributing to surveillance and (2) the industry can implement policies to internalize the cost of surveillance for firms. First, surveillance is most effective (and therefore most harmful) when the watcher is hidden yet omnipresent.[40] Firms can reduce their role in consumer surveillance by becoming more visible to the consumers and by limiting data collection. The negative externality of surveillance suggests that firms that are invisible to users, such as data aggregators and data brokers, have a special role in the online surveillance system. Both data aggregators and data brokers are invisible to users while aggregating data across diverse sources. Making the tracking of individuals obvious at the time of data collection can diminish the harm of surveillance.

In addition to decreasing the effectiveness and related harm of surveillance, internalizing the cost of surveillance for firms is an effective tool to diminish this negative externality. For example, data brokers and aggregators that store and distribute information within the Big Data Industry could have additional data due process requirements imposed on them for collecting, retaining and distributing personally identifiable information (PII). While some have claimed that PII is not clearly distinguishable,[41] firms that retain information that can be linked back to an individual so it can be fused with other information about the same individual should have an additional obligation of data due process.

Citron and Pasquale outline three areas of data due process requirements, which are instructive moving forward: (1) identifying audit trails, (2) offering interactive modeling and (3) supporting user objections.[42] In addition to firms being required to provide an audit trail for how information is sourced, used and distributed similar to that shown in Figure 20.6, they could also be required to offer interactive modeling of the use of information and a process to enable individuals to examine and object to the information stored. These additional requirements would impose a cost on those that opt to retain personally identifiable information. The additional obligations would increase the cost of retaining the information, internalize the previously externalized harm (surveillance) and possibly dissuade some firms from using and retaining PII.

Requiring better internal oversight of the data stewardship practices and additional data due process procedures would increase the cost of holding individualized yet comprehensive data and internalize the cost of contributing to surveillance. Many negative externalities are beyond the scope of a single firm to rectify; the cost of reigning in surveillance is too much for one firm to bear and the effect of a single firm changing its data practices would be minimal. For those that wish to use large samples of personally identifiable information, better data governance together with the services of a data integrity professional—who is certified and held accountable for the data practices of the firm—would ensure that data stewardship practices and data due process are followed. Similarly, an internal consumer review board, as advocated by Calo and cited in the draft White House Consumer Privacy Bill of Rights Act of 2015, would similarly internalize the cost of storing and using personally identifiable data.[43]

Quantify Activity in the Secondary Market for Big Data

Destructive demand flourishes when the interests of the secondary market for consumer information are not aligned with the primary market and when the secondary market is not visible to the primary market. By linking all relevant firms through an information supply chain, firms in the secondary market have "skin in the game" and thus an incentive to align interests.[44] In other words, by framing themselves as members of a larger supply chain, firms have a vested interest in ensuring others in the chain uphold data stewardship and data due process practices. Otherwise, their reputation would be at risk.

In addition, by making the secondary market more visible to the primary market, the primary market can take into consideration secondary market firms' actions. Consumers may be more (or less) willing to divulge information to a firm in the primary market depending on its type of involvement in the secondary market for selling information. Importantly, the current approach, where the secondary market for Big Data is invisible to the primary consumer-facing market, does not allow for such feedback.

Aligning interests not only benefits the primary market; it can also benefit quality and trusted firms in the secondary market. For example, within the mortgage-backed securities market, unaffiliated financial companies, which did not have interests aligned with the primary market, were not able to sell their securities at the same rate as those companies that were affiliated. In other words, this secondary market recognized the inherent risk of trading with companies whose quality criteria did not align with the consumer market. For the Big Data Industry, history suggests there would be a market for quality data practices in the secondary market for Big Data.

Institute Data Integrity Professional or Board for Big Data Analytics

The practical implications of these guidelines call for renewed attention to the training and development of data integrity professionals. The focus of their training should be on incorporating an ethical analysis, which is consistent with FTC Commissioner Julie Brill's focus on the role of technologists in protecting privacy in the age of Big Data, as well as Mayer and Narayanan's call for engineers to develop privacy substitutes within their design.[45]

First, professional data scientists are needed to implement the solutions outlined above to curtail surveillance and destructive demand, as well as to ensure data stewardship practices. Currently, advice for Big Data professionals, including data scientists, data analytics specialists, and business intelligence and analytics specialists, focuses on the challenges in using Big Data, such as leadership, talent management, technology, decision making and company culture. There is little advice on ensuring data integrity.[46]

Second, consumer review boards, made up partly of professional data scientists, would oversee and authorize research on human beings within the commercial space. As Calo notes, academics are required to receive clearance to conduct research from their Institutional Review Board and undertake associated training, even when the research is for societal benefit. Yet private companies conduct research without oversight, even when at the expense of the consumer.[47] Revelations that OKCupid and Facebook[48] had conducted experiments on users without their knowledge only show how prescient Calo was in the call for consumer review boards; and effective consumer review boards would require data integrity professionals.

Finally, academic institutions continue to develop degree courses in business analytics, business intelligence and data analytics to train Big Data professionals—but they do not require students to take a course in ethics. A survey of the top 15 such programs shows the intense focus on technique, with little regard given to privacy, ethics or corporate and professional responsibility.[49] Accreditation for such programs should require them both to train data integrity professionals who graduate with a degree in data science, data analytics or business intelligence, and to support the solutions proposed in these guidelines.

Concluding Comments

This article has examined Big Data within the context of the Big Data Industry and identified persistent issues and points of weakness in current market practices. In doing so, it has examined the industry's information supply chain of upstream suppliers and downstream uses of data, the ethical issues arising from the negative externality of surveillance caused by persistent tracking, aggregation and the use of consumer-level data, and the potential destructive demand driven by the secondary market for consumer information. Importantly, the article has identified the Big Data Industry as having both economic and ethical issues at the individual firm, supply chain and general industry level and has suggested associated solutions to preserve sustainable industry practices.

Notes

1   Both the size of the data set, due to the volume, variety and velocity of the data, as well as the advanced analytics, combine to create Big Data. Key to definitions of Big Data are that the amount of data and the software used to analyze it have changed and combine to support new insights and new uses. See also Ohm, P. "Fourth Amendment in a World without Privacy," *Mississippi. Law Journal* (81), 2011, pp. 1309–1356; Boyd, D. and Crawford, K. "Critical Questions for Big Data: Provocations for a Cultural, Technological, and Scholarly Phenomenon," *Information, Communication & Society* (15:5), 2012, pp. 662–679; Rubinstein, I. S. "Big Data: The End of Privacy or a New Beginning?," *International Data Privacy Law* (3:2), 2012, pp. 74–87; and Hartzog, W. and Selinger, E. "Big Data in Small Hands," *Stanford Law Review Online* (66), 2013, pp. 81–87.

2   Ur, B. et al. "Smart, Useful, Scary, Creepy: Perceptions of Online Behavioral Advertising," presented at the Symposium On Usable Privacy and Security, July 11–13, 2012, Washington, D.C. See also Barocas, S. and Selbst, A. D. "Big Data's Disparate Impact," 2015, draft available at SSRN 2477899; and Richards, N. M. and King, J. H. "Three Paradoxes of Big Data," *Stanford Law Review Online* (66), 2013, pp. 41–46.

3   In order of reference: Barocas, S. and Selbst, A. D., op. cit., 2014; Hartzog, W. and Selinger, E., op. cit., 2013; *Big Data Management & Analytics*, Gartner, 2014, available at http://www.gartner.com/

technology/topics/big-data.jsp; Mayer-Schonberger, V. and Cukier, K. *Big Data: A Revolution That Will Transform How We Live, Work, and Think*, Houghton Mifflin Harcourt, 2013; Richards, N. M. and King, J. H., op. cit., 2013.

4   Wen, H. "Big ethics for big data," *O'Reilly Radar*, June 11, 2012, available at http://radar.oreilly.com/2012/06/ethics-big-data-business-decisions.html.

5   For example, Gartner notes that there are three strategic and operational challenges: information strategy, data analytics and enterprise information management, but makes no mention of ethical challenges. See also *Big Data and Privacy: A Technological Perspective*, Report to the President, 2014, available at https://www.whitehouse.gov/sites/default/files/microsites/ostp/PCAST/pcast_big_data_and_privacy_-_may_2014.pdf; *Big Data Platform Bringing Big Data to the Enterprise*, IBM; and Manyika, J. et al. *Big Data: The next Frontier for Innovation, Competition, and Productivity*, McKinsey & Company, 2011, available at http://www.mckinsey.com/insights/business_technology/big_data_the_next_frontier_for_ innovation.

6   The shift to creating value through monetizing data impacts relationships with stakeholders as well as policies internal to the organization—see Tallon, P. P, Short, J. E and Harkins, M. W. "The Evolution of Information Governance at Intel," *MIS Quarterly Executive* (12:4), 2013, pp. 189–198; Najjar, M. S. and Kettinger, W. J., "Data Monetization: Lessons from a Retailer's Journey," *MIS Quarterly Executive* (12:4), 2013, pp. 213–225.

7   The 3Vs of Big Data—volume, variety and velocity—were originally defined in a META/Gartner report but have subsequently been expanded with veracity, value, validity, variability and even visualization, leading to the term "V confusion"—see Grimes, S. "Big Data: Avoid 'Wanna V' Confusion," *InformationWeek*, August 7, 2013, available at http://www.informationweek.com/big-data/big-data-analytics/big-data-avoid-wanna-v-confusion/d/d-id/1111077?.

8   Firms monetizing the value of data require new tactics and strategies as well as, perhaps, accounting rules to capture the value (and risk) created in new transactions. See Monga, V. "The Big Mystery: What's Big Data Really Worth?," *Wall Street Journal*, October 13, 2014, available at http://blogs.wsj.com/cfo/2014/10/13/the-big-mystery-whats-big-data-really-worth/.

9   Lee, Y. et al., "A Cubic Framework for the Chief Data Officer: Succeeding in a World of Big Data," *MIS Quarterly Executive* (13:1), 2014, pp. 1–13.

10   See also Lomas, N. "Facebook's Data Protection Practices Under Fresh Fire In Europe," *TechCrunch*, available at http://social.techcrunch.com/2015/02/23/facebook-ad-network/.

11   Scott, M. "Where Tech Giants Protect Privacy," *The New York Times*, December 13, 2014, available at http://www.nytimes.com/2014/12/14/sunday-review/where-tech-giants-protect-privacy.html.

12   The BDI requires not only information brokers to aggregate data, but also hardware, software and professional services firms to support the collection, storage and use of the data. Leaders include firms focused on analytics solutions (e.g., SAS, IBM, SAP) as well as industry specialists (e.g., Amazon Web Services) and service providers (Accenture). For more information, see Robb, D. "Top 20 Big Data Companies," Datamation, November 20, 2014, available at http://www.datamation.com/applications/top-20-big-data-compa-nies-1.html. Importantly, many firms combine products and services that support the BDI—e.g., IBM (hardware, software and services), HP (cloud and storage), Dell (storage), SAP (analytics), Teradata and Oracle (hardware, software, services), SAS and Palantir (analytics and software) and Accenture (software and services). See Leopold, G. "Big Data Rankings: Leaders Generated $6B in Revenues," Datanami, December 4, 2014, available at http://www.datanami.com/2014/12/04/big-data-rankings-leaders-generated-6b-revenues/. While hardware, software, analytics and even technology consulting firms make most of the industry leader lists, missing are the data brokers and data aggregators that make up the information supply chain discussed in the next section.

13   Duhigg, C. "How Companies Learn Your Secrets," *The New York Times*, February 16, 2012, available at http://www.nytimes.com/2012/02/19/magazine/shopping-habits.html.

14   As stated by Bambauer, "estimating harm is a wearisome task"—see Bambauer, J. "Other People's Papers," draft paper, 2014, p. 15, available at http://masonlec.org/site/rte_uploads/files/Bambauer_Other_Peoples_Papers_GMU.pdf. Bambauer categorizes privacy harms as arising from collection, risk of misuse, aggregation, obstruction and hassle; Richards lists sorting, discrimination, persuasion and blackmail as potential harms—Richards, N. M. "The Dangers of Surveillance," *Harvard Law Review*, 2013, available at http://harvardlawreview.org/2013/05/the-dangers-of-surveillance/; Calo focuses more broadly on objective and subjective harms—Calo, M. R. "Boundaries of Privacy Harm," *Indiana Law Journal* (86), 2011, pp. 1131–1162.

15   For example, car insurance companies are moving toward usage-based premiums based on driving data collected in real time—see Boulton, C. "Auto Insurers Bank on Big Data to Drive New Business,"

Wall Street Journal, February 20, 2013, available at http://blogs.wsj.com/cio/2013/02/20/auto-insurers-bank-on-big-data-to-drive-new-business/. Similarly, health insurance companies can deny services and increase premiums through accessing data online—see Gittelson, K. "How Big Data Is Changing Insurance," *BBC News*, November 15, 2013, available at http://www.bbc.com/news/business-24941415.

16   Calo, M. R. "Digital Market Manipulation," *The George Washington Law Review* (82:4), 2013, pp. 995–1051.

17   For the concept of objectionable classification and biases, see Barocas, S. and Selbst, A. D., op. cit., 2015; Sweeney, L. "Discrimination in Online Ad Delivery," *acmqueue* (11:3), 2013, available at http://queue.acm.org/detail.cfm?id=2460278; and Cohen, J. E. "What Privacy Is for," *Harvard Law Review* (126), 2013, pp. 1904–1933.

18   For examples of objectionable categorizations, see Hill, K. "Data Broker Was Selling Lists Of Rape Victims, Alcoholics, and 'Erectile Dysfunction Sufferers'," *Forbes*, September 19, 2013, available at http://www.forbes.com/sites/kashmirhill/2013/12/19/data-broker-was-selling-lists-of-rape-alcoholism-and-erectiledysfunction-sufferers/.

19   Groves has previously categorized data sources as organic vs. designed—Groves, R. M. "Three Eras of Survey Research," *Public Opinion Quarterly* (75:5), 2011, pp. 861–871. Sources have also been categorized as analog vs. digital in *Big Data and Privacy: A Technological Perspective*, Report to the President, 2014. However, the differences in these categories are not always clear or meaningful in determining the appropriateness of the supplier.

20   For an analysis of quality and bias issues in Big Data sources, see Boyd, D. and Crawford, K. *Critical Questions for Big Data: Provocations for a Cultural, Technological, and Scholarly Phenomenon*, Microsoft Research, 2012; Lerman, J. "Big Data and Its Exclusions," *Stanford Law Review Online* (66), 2013, pp. 5563; and Crawford, K. "The Hidden Biases in Big Data," *Harvard Business Review*, April 1, 2013.

21   Imputation is the process of replacing missing data with substituted values.

22   The role of obfuscation in protecting privacy is examined in Brunton, F. and Nissenbaum, H. "Vernacular resistance to data collection and analysis: A political theory of obfuscation," *First Monday* (16:5), 2011.

23   O'Leary, D. E. "Exploiting Big Data from Mobile Device Sensor-Based Apps: Challenges and Benefits," *MIS Quarterly Executive* (12:4), 2013, pp. 179–187.

24   Nissenbaum, H. *Privacy in Context: Technology, Policy, and the Integrity of Social Life*, Stanford University Press, 2009; Martin, K. "Understanding Privacy Online: Development of a Social Contract Approach to Privacy," *Journal of Business Ethics*, 2015, pp. 1–19; and Richards, N. M. and King, J. H. "Big Data Ethics," *Wake Forest Law Review* (23), 2014.

25   Hartzog, W. "Chain-Link Confidentiality," *Georgia Law Review* (46), 2011, pp. 657–704.

26   Hill, K. "Facebook Joins Forces With Data Brokers To Gather More Intel About Users For Ads," *Forbes*, February 27, 2013, available at http://www.forbes.com/sites/kashmirhill/2013/02/27/facebook-joins-forces-with-data-brokers-to-gather-more-intel-aboutusers-for-ads/.

27   Coase illustrated negative externalities with the example of a spark from a train that causes harm to farmers along the tracks—Coase, R. H. "Problem of Social Cost," *Journal of Law and Economics* (3), 1960, pp. 1–44. Importantly for Coase, negative externalities do not necessarily require government intervention, which carries its own cost, but may be resolved through private ordering between parties.

28   TOR—The Onion Router—is a service to make accessing websites anonymous. Users' requests are routed among many other TOR users' requests and are bounced throughout the TOR network of client computers to remain hidden to outsiders. For more information, see https://www.torproject.org.

29   Zetter, K. "The NSA Is Targeting Users of Privacy Services, Leaked Code Shows," *WIRED*, July 3, 2014.

30   Fried, F. *An Anatomy of Values: Problems of Personal and Social Choice*, Harvard University Press, 1970; and Rachels, J. "Why Privacy Is Important," *Philosophy & Public Affairs*, 1975, pp. 323–333.

31   Cohen, J. E. "Privacy, Visibility, Transparency, and Exposure," *The University of Chicago Law Review* (75:1), 2008, pp. 181–201. The inability to escape online surveillance is illustrated in Brunton, F. and Nissenbaum, H., op. cit., 2011, and Strandburg, K. J. "Home, Home on the Web and Other Fourth Amendment Implications of Technosocial Change," *Maryland Law Review*, (70:3), 2011. In the words of Cohen, "Pervasive monitoring of every first move or false start will, at the margin, incline choices toward the bland and mainstream" thereby causing "a blunting and blurring of rough edges

and sharp lines."—Cohen, J. E. "Examined lives: Informational privacy and the subject as object," *Stanford Law Review*, (52), 2000, pp. 1373–1438.

32   Cohen, J. E., op. cit., 2008.

33   The Mosaic Theory of privacy explains why privacy scholars are concerned with all elements of tracking, including transaction surveillance and purchasing behavior. This theory suggests that the whole of one's movements reveal far more than the individual movements—where the aggregation of small movements across contexts is a difference in kind and not in degree. See Kerr, O.S. "The Mosaic Theory of the Fourth Amendment," *Michigan Law Review* (111:3), 2012; and *United States v. Jones*, Supreme Court of United States, January 23, 2012, available at http://www.supremecourt.gov/opinions/11pdf/10-1259.pdf.

34   Richards, N. M., op. cit., 2013.

35   The Mere Means Principle is an ethical principle that posits that you should never treat people merely as a means to your own ends.

36   A tracking is an often-transparent graphic image, usually no larger than 1 pixel x 1 pixel, that is placed on a website that is used to monitor the behavior of the user visiting the site.

37   For a comparison of regulating the credit reporting industry with regulating Big Data, see Hoofnagle, C. J. *How the Fair Credit Reporting Act Regulates Big Data*, paper presented at Future of Privacy Forum Workshop on Big Data and Privacy: Making Ends Meet, September 10, 2013, available at http://papers.ssrn.com/sol3/papers.cfm?abstract_id=2432955.

38   For a balanced view on solutions that both optimize the use of technology and respect privacy and ethics, see Mayer, J. and Narayanan, A. "Privacy Substitutes," *Stanford Law Review Online* (66), 2013, pp. 89–96; and Bambauer, J., op. cit., 2014.

39   Cranor, L. F. "Necessary but Not Sufficient: Standardized Mechanisms for Privacy Notice and Choice," *Journal on Telecommunications and High Technology Law* (10), 2012, pp. 273307. Rather than focus on the type of information, the firm's storage, information use or third-party access to data would be highlighted if such tactics diverge from commonly accepted practices. Research demonstrates that users care most about the possible secondary use or third-party access to information both online and with mobile devices, as noted by Martin, K., op. cit., 2015; Shilton, K. and Martin, K. E. "Mobile Privacy Expectations in Context," *Telecommunications Policy Research Conference* (41), 2013; and Martin, K. E. "Privacy Notices as Tabula Rasa: An Empirical Investigation into How Complying with a Privacy Notice Is Related to Meeting Privacy Expectations Online," *Journal of Public Policy and Marketing*, 2015.

40   Cohen, J. E., op. cit., 2008.

41   Ohm, P. "Broken Promises of Privacy: Responding to the Surprising Failure of Anonymization," *UCLA Law Review* (57), 2009, pp. 1701–1777; and Narayanan, A. and Shmatikov, V. "Myths and Fallacies of Personally Identifiable Information," *Communications of the ACM* (53:6), 2010, pp. 24–26.

42   Citron, D. K. and Pasquale, F. "The Scored Society: Due Process for Automated Predictions," *Washington Law Review* (89), 2014, pp. 1–33; see also Crawford, K. and Schultz, J. "Big Data and Due Process: Toward a Framework to Redress Predictive Privacy

43   Calo, R. "Consumer Subject Review Boards: A Thought Experiment," *Stanford Law Review Online* (66), 2013, pp. 97–102.

44   For the mortgage-backed securities market, skin in the game— and aligning interests—was effective to avoid losses—James, C.M. "Mortgage-Backed Securities: How Important Is 'Skin in the Game'?," *FRBSF Economic Letter*, December 13, 2010.

45   Brill, J. *A Call to Arms: The Role of Technologists in Protecting Privacy in the Age of Big Data*, Sloan Cyber Security Lecture by Commissioner Julie Brill, Polytechnic Institute of NYU, October 23, 2013; Mayer, J. and Narayanan, A., op. cit., 2013.

46   Chen, H., Chiang, R. H. L. and Storey, V. C. "Business Intelligence and Analytics: From Big Data to Big Impact," *MIS Quarterly* (36:4), 2012, pp. 1165–1188.

47   McAfee, A. and Brynjolfsson, E. "Big Data: The Management Revolution," *Harvard Business Review*, October 2012.

48   Stampler, L. "Facebook Isn't the Only Website Running Experiments on Human Beings," *Time*, July 28, 2014, available at http://time.com/3047603/okcupid-oktrends-experiments/.

49   The survey includes both bachelor's and master's programs from across schools/programs such as business and engineering. See http://www.informationweek.com/big-data/big-data-analytics/big-data-analytics-masters-degrees-20-top-programs/d/did/1108042?page_number=3 and http://analytics.ncsu.edu/?page_id=4184. Programs reviewed include Bentley, Columbia, LSU, NYU, GWSB, Northwestern, Rutgers, CMU, Harvard, MIT, NCSU, Stanford, UT Austin and UC Berkeley. Both *InformationWeek*'s and NCSU's lists focus on U.S. universities.

Questions for Discussion

1   What are the benefits and challenges of the use of big data? How can the benefits get maximized and the challenges reduced?
2   How are the roles of the CIO and CDO changing in the big data industry? How should the CIO/CDO manage big data?
3   How can industries and governments mitigate the negative effects of big data in the supply chain?
4   How would the framework presented help organizations and governments mitigate the issues identified? What policies and standard should get introduced to that effect?
5   What are the differences between the different countries regarding the use of big data and consequent ethical issues?
6   How can practices improve and the economic and ethical issues reduce?

Further Reading

Bhimani, A., Willcocks, L. (2014). Digitisation, 'Big Data' and the transformation of accounting information. *Accounting and Business Research*, *44*(4), 469–490.
Günther, W. A., Mehrizi, M. H. R., Huysman, M., Feldberg, F. (2017). Debating big data: A literature review on realizing value from big data. *The Journal of Strategic Information Systems*, *26*(3), 191–209.

Index

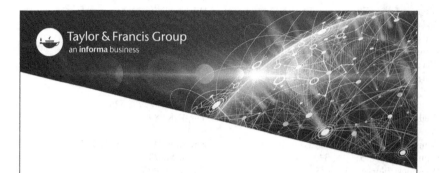